THE GORBACHEV BIBLIOGRAPHY

THE GORBACHEV BIBLIOGRAPHY

1985-1991

A Listing of Books and Articles in English
On Perestroika in the USSR

Compiled and Edited by
Joseph L. Wieczynski

Norman Ross Publishing Inc.
New York, New York

Also edited by Joseph L. Wieczynski:

The Gorbachev Encyclopedia: Gorbachev, The Man and His Times (1993)
The Gorbachev Reader (1993)
Operation Barbarossa (1993)

The above books are available through Norman Ross Publishing Inc.

Library of Congress Cataloging-in-Publication Data

Wieczynski, Joseph L., 1934-
　　　The Gorbachev bibliography : 1985-1991 -- books and articles in English on perestroika in the USSR / compiled and edited by Joseph L. Wieczynski.
　　　　x + 275　p.　　cm.
　　　Includes bibliographical references and index.
　　　ISBN 0-88354-275-7 (alk. paper)
　　　1. Perestroika--Soviet Union--Bibliography. 2. Soviet Union--History--1985-1991--Bibliography.
I. Title.
Z2510.3.W54　1995
[DK286]
　　　　　　　　　　　　　　　　　　　　　　　　　　　　　　　　95-45265
　　　　　　　　　　　　　　　　　　　　　　　　　　　　　　　　CIP

Norman Ross Publishing Inc.
330 West 58th Street, New York, NY 10019
Manufactured in the United States of America

Dedicated to my ancestors
the families
Baranowski
and
Wieczynski

and for
Kim and Daniel

PREFACE

In the history of scholarship, perhaps no body of literature has had a more controversial reception than the surveys and analyses of Mikhail S. Gorbachev's years in power (1985-91). Because specialists in Kremlinology and related fields of study had failed to anticipate the outcome of Gorbachev's policies of *perestroika* and *glasnost'*, few Western scholars were prepared for the dramatic events that led to the liberation of the Eastern European countries, the emergence of separatist movements in the Soviet Union, the collapse of the Soviet system of government and the final dissolution of the USSR. In the United States, government agencies, community groups, school faculties, clubs and other associations scrambled to find specialists in Russian and Soviet studies able to explain to them the radical events unfolding in the former Soviet bloc. Many of us who had devoted our professional lives to earlier periods of Russian and Slavic history found ourselves pressed into service, delivering talks to excited audiences, speaking on educational and public television and radio, working with high school and community college faculty in devising ways to convey to students the meaning of the events that saturated the media and dominated their attention each day.

The scholarly products of those years were often produced in the same frenzy. Since earlier analyses of the Soviet world had never anticipated that the demise of the USSR could be so sudden and thorough, entirely new approaches to the field of study seemed appropriate. At the same time, journalists working in and around the Soviet bloc became the main interpreters of the events they reported. The reflection and detachment so essential to scholarly work were luxuries no one could afford. Consequently, the body of writings on Gorbachev's regime was rushed into print, at times with excessive haste, to satisfy the public thirst for immediate knowledge and the pressing demands of instructors in classrooms at all levels of education. Small wonder that standards of scholarly work and review frequently were applied sparingly or not at all. Scholarly writings also were impaired by the ongoing collapse of the Soviet world. Journalists' attempts at analysis, their conclusions and their perception of events, were made obsolete in a matter of days by new twists and turns taken by Gorbachev's government as it sought to stave off disaster.

Yet for all that, the writings cited in this bibliography have a vigor, excitement and appeal unmatched by any similar corpus of intellectual endeavor. Imagine the delight of the ancient historians who chronicled the downfall of classical civilizations, had they had use of the systems of communication and technology enjoyed by those of us who recorded and explained the final days of the Soviet order. The grand scholarly interpretations of the Gorbachev years will not be written by our generation, nor should they be. But future analysts will benefit from the body of primary and secondary source materials that we have left them, impressive in its volume and scope, if not always in its depth and perception. This bibliography is a first step in organizing part of that legacy for those who will build upon our work in years to come.

* * * * * * * * * * *

In compiling this bibliography, I have attempted to include all English-language books and articles produced by the major publishing houses and the leading academic and popular journals, as well as more obscure sources. I have not cited articles from popular periodicals and newspapers, unless they contain noteworthy interpretation or vital information beyond the simple reporting of news. Similarly, I thought it fruitless to cite the numerous pieces published in the *Current Digest of the Soviet Press*, since its purpose was to report current affairs and editorial opinion on most recent events in the USSR and its satellites. But it did seem reasonable to mention a few atlases, city guides and other practical handbooks that might be unknown to some users of this work. I did not include material on the administration of President Boris Yeltsin, unless those sources contain references to or interpretations of Gorbachev's years in office. Many of the citations in this bibliography were drawn from the standard academic electronic databases, as well as from several more obscure databases ("Medline" and "Agricola," for instance). I ended my search in July 1994.

Dividing this material into subsections was no simple task. Quite frequently titles could be introduced under several headings. I have attempted to classify citations in ways likely to be most useful for scholars and other researchers. General users of this volume probably will easily discover my method of classification and undoubtedly can pursue material through the index of authors at the end of this work.

The first two sections of this work contain listings of publications that offer immediate sources of reference (textbooks, bibliographies, atlases and similar material) or are compilations of writings by several authors devoted to a common theme. The sections that follow attempt to facilitate consultation of this volume by grouping titles within common categories, some of which are peculiar to the Soviet experience in Gorbachev's day ("democratization," for example, and "defense conversion").

I am indebted to many colleagues who contributed eagerly to this project and improved it in ways too numerous to specify. Anne Fitzpatrick, Burt Kaufman, Barbara Reeves, Bill Ochsenwald and Kathy Jones, my colleagues at Virginia Tech, made many suggestions concerning relevant works in their respective fields of study or assisted me in other ways. Mary F. Zirin shared with me information from her vast bibliography of works on women in the USSR and Eastern Europe. Stephen K. Wegren, Eugene Huskey, William A. Clark, Norma Noonan, Walter C. Clemens, Jr. and other noted scholars were kind enough to review the sections dealing with their fields of expertise. My wife Jo was extremely helpful in preparing the manuscript for publication. Errors and omissions should be attributed to me alone.

I also wish to thank the College of Arts and Sciences of Virginia Tech for providing funds in support of this and similar projects.

Joseph L. Wieczynski
Department of History
Virginia Polytechnic Institute and State University
Blacksburg, Virginia
August 1994

CONTENTS

THE GORBACHEV BIBLIOGRAPHY

I. Textbooks, Bibliographies and Other Works of Reference

BOOKS

1. *ABSEES: The American Bibliography of Slavic and East European Studies* (Stanford: American Association for the Advancement of Slavic Studies, produced at the Library of Congress, annually).

2. Armstrong, John A., *Ideology, Politics and Government in the Soviet Union*, 3rd ed. (Lanham, MD: University Press of America, 1986).

3. Barry, Donald D., and Carol Barner-Barry, *Contemporary Soviet Politics: An Introduction*, 4th ed. (Englewood Cliffs, NJ: Prentice Hall, 1991).

4. Batalden, Stephen K., and Sandra L. Batalden, *The Newly Independent States of Eurasia: A Handbook of the Former Soviet Republics* (Phoenix: Oryx, 1993).

5. -----, ed., *Russia & Eurasia Documents Annual* (Gulf Breeze, FL: Academic International Press, 1987-92 and continuing).

6. Battle, John M., and Thomas D. Sherlock, *Gorbachev's Reforms: An Annotated Bibliography of Soviet Writings*, Part I: 1985-June 1987 (Gulf Breeze, FL: Academic International Press, 1988).

7. Black, J. L., ed., *"Into the Dustbin of History"! The USSR from August Coup to Commonwealth, 1991: A Documentary Narrative* (Gulf Breeze, FL: Academic International Press, 1993).

8. -----, ed., *USSR Documents Annual* (Gulf Breeze, FL: Academic International Press, annually since 1987).

9. Bradshaw, Michael J., ed., *The Soviet Union: A New Regional Geography?* (New York: Halsted Press, 1991).

10. Brown, Archie, *The Soviet Union: A Biographical Dictionary* (New York: Macmillan Publishing Co., 1991).

11. Center for Democracy in the USSR, *Glasnost Information Bulletin* (New York, 1987-90).

12. *Country Reports*: Baltic Republics; Commonwealth of Independent States; Georgia, Armenia, Azerbaijan, Kazakhstan, Central Asian Republics; Russia; Ukraine, Belarus, Moldova (London: Economist Intelligence Unit, 1992 and continuing quarterly); replaces *Country Report: USSR*, published through 1991; also produces annual *Country Profile* for each nation reported.

13. Cracraft, James, ed., *The Soviet Union Today: An Interpretative Guide*, 2nd ed. (Chicago: University of Chicago Press, 1988).

14. Croucher, Murlin, comp., *Slavic Studies: A Guide to Bibliographies, Encyclopedias, and Handbooks*, 2 vols. (Wilmington, DE: Scholarly Resources, Inc., 1992).

15. Crowley, Joan Frances, and Dan Vaillancourt, *Lenin to Gorbachev: Three Generations of Soviet Communists*, updated ed. (Arlington Heights, IL: Harlan Davidson, 1993).

16. *Current Digest of the Soviet Press* (now renamed *Current Digest of the Post-Soviet Press*), translations of major reports, commentary and features from the Soviet and post-Soviet media.

17. Dagne, Theodore S., *Soviet Glasnost and Perestroyka: A Summary of Major Issues and Chronology, November 1989-February 1990* (Washington, DC: Library of Congress, Congressional Research Service, 1990).

18. Daniels, Robert V., ed. and trans., *A Documentary History of Communism and the World: From Revolution to Collapse* (Hanover, NH: University Press of New England, 1993).

19. -----, ed. and trans., *A Documentary History of Communism in Russia: From Lenin to Gorbachev* (Hanover, NH: University Press of New England, 1993).

20. Davies, R. W., *The Soviet Union*, 2nd ed. (Boston: Unwin Hyman, 1989).

21. Dawisha, Karen, and Bruce Parrott, eds., *The International Politics of Eurasia: Newly Independent States Enter the Twenty-First Century*, 3 vols. and continuing (Armonk, NY: M. E. Sharpe, 1994).

22. Diller, Daniel C., *Russia and the Independent States* (Washington, DC: Congressional Quarterly, Inc., 1993).

23. *Directory of Scholars in Slavic Studies in Institutes of the Russian Academy of Sciences* (Stanford: American Association for the Advancement of Slavic Studies, 1993).

24. Dukes, Paul, *A History of Russia: Medieval, Modern, Contemporary*, 2nd ed. (Durham, NC: Duke University Press, 1990).

25. Dunlop, John B., *The Rise of Russia and the Fall of the Soviet Empire* (Princeton: Princeton University Press, 1993).

26. Dziewanowski, M. K., *A History of Soviet Russia*, 3rd ed. (Englewood Cliffs, NJ: Prentice Hall, 1989).

27. Gaddis, John Lewis, *Russia, the Soviet Union, and the United States: An Interpretive History*, 2nd ed. (New York: McGraw-Hill, 1990).

28. Geron, Leonard, and Alex Pravda, comp. and eds., *Who's Who in Russia and the New States* (New York: I. B. Tauris, distributed by St. Martin's Press, 1993).

29. Getty, J. Arch, and V. A. Kozlov, eds., *Research Guide to the Russian Center for the Preservation and Study of Documents of Contemporary History* (Pittsburgh: Center for Russian and East European Studies, University of Pittsburgh, 1993).

30. Gilbert, Martin, *Atlas of Russian History*, 2nd ed. (New York: Oxford University Press, 1993).

31. Goldman, Minton, ed., *Russia, Eurasia, and Central/Eastern Europe*, 5th ed. (Guilford, CT: Dushkin Publishing Group, Inc., 1994).

32. Grant, Steven A., *A Scholar's Guide to Russian, Central Eurasian, and Baltic Studies*, 3rd ed. (Baltimore: Johns Hopkins University Press, 1994).

33. Green, Barbara B., *The Dynamics of Russian Politics: A Short History* (New York: Praeger, 1994).

34. Hecht, Leo, *The USSR Today: Facts and Interpretations*, 3rd rev. ed. (Springfield, VA: Scholasticus Publishers, 1987).

35. Held, Joseph, ed., *The Columbia History of Eastern Europe in the Twentieth Century* (New York: Columbia University Press, 1992).

36. Henige, David P., comp., *Serial Bibliographies and Abstracts in History: An Annotated Guide* (Westport, CT: Greenwood Press, 1986).

37. Hintzman, Bonnie, *A Bibliography on Glasnost' and Perestroika: Gorbachev's Policies of Reform and Openness* (Monticello, IL: Vance Bibliographies, 1989).

38. Hosking, Geoffrey A., *The First Socialist Society: A History of the Soviet Union from Within*, enlarged ed. (Cambridge, MA: Harvard University Press, 1990).

39. Johnson, Eric, *Central Asia: A Survey of Libraries and Publishing in the Region* (Washington, DC: IREX Research Services, 1993).

40. Jones, Anthony, and David E. Powell, eds., *Soviet Update, 1989-1990* (Boulder, CO: Westview Press, 1991).

41. Karasik, Theodore W., ed., *Russia & Eurasia Facts & Figures Annual* (Gulf Breeze, FL: Academic International Press, annually).

42. Kea, Charlotte, *Glasnost' and Perestroika under Gorbachev: A Chronology, July 1987-December 1988* (Washington, DC: Library of Congress, Congressional Research Service, 1989).

43. Kirk, Robert S., *U.S.-Soviet Relations in the Age of Perestroika: Selected References, 1985-1990* (Washington, DC: Library of Congress, Congressional Research Service, 1990).

44. Kort, Michael, *The Soviet Colossus: The Rise and Fall of the USSR*, 3rd ed. (Armonk, NY: M. E. Sharpe, 1993).

45. Louis, Victor, and Jennifer Louis, *The Complete Guide to the Soviet Union* (New York: St. Martin's Press, 1991).

46. MacKenzie, David, and Michael W. Curran, *A History of Russia, the Soviet Union and Beyond*, 4th ed. (Belmont, CA: Wadsworth Publishing Company, 1993).

47. Magnusson, Magnus, and Rosemary Goring, eds., *Chambers Biographical Dictionary* (Edinburgh: W & R Chambers Ltd., 1990).

48. Magocsi, Paul Robert, *Historical Atlas of East Central Europe* (Seattle: University of Washington Press, 1993).

49. Malia, Martin, *The Soviet Tragedy: A History of Socialism in Russia, 1917-1991* (New York: Free Press, 1994).

50. Mann, Dawn, Robert Monyak and Elizabeth Teague, *The Supreme Soviet: A Biographical Directory* (Washington, DC: Center for Strategic and International Studies, 1989).

51. Mastro, Joseph P., comp., *USSR Calendar of Events* (Gulf Breeze, FL: Academic International Press, annually since 1987).

52. McCauley, Martin, *The Soviet Union, 1917-1991*, 2nd ed. (White Plains, NY: Longman Publishing Group, 1993).

53. -----, ed., *Russia and the Successor States Briefing Service* (London: Longman, 1994 and continuing).

54. McClellan, Woodford, *Russia: The Soviet Period and After*, 3rd ed. (Englewood Cliffs, NJ: Prentice Hall, 1994).

55. Medish, Vadim, *The Soviet Union*, rev. 4th ed. (Englewood Cliffs, NJ: Prentice Hall, 1991).

56. Michta, Andrew A., *The Government and Politics of Post-communist Europe* (New York: Praeger, 1994).

57. Miles, F. Mike, *Soviet "Restructuring" under Gorbachev: A Chronology, January 1985-June 1987* (Washington, DC: Library of Congress, Congressional Research Service, 1987).

58. Murarka, Dev, *Gorbachov: The Limits of Power* (London: Hutchinson, Ltd., 1988).

59. Neubert, Michael, *Library Assessment Project: Siberia* (Washington, DC: IREX Research Services, 1993).

60. *The New Moscow: City Map and Guide*, 2nd ed. (Montpelier, VT: Russian Information Services, 1994).

61. *1989 USSR Census* (Minneapolis: East View Publications, 1992).

62. Nordquist, Joan, comp., *Glasnost': The Soviet Union Today: A Bibliography* (Santa Cruz, CA: Reference and Research Services, 1989).

63. Parker, John W., *Kremlin in Transition*, vol. 1: *From Brezhnev to Chernenko, 1978-1985*; vol. 2: *Gorbachev, 1985-1989* (Boston: Unwin Hyman, 1991).

64. Pozin, Mikhail A., comp., *Russian-English/English-Russian Dictionary of Free Market Economics* (Jefferson, NC, and London: McFarland, 1993).

65. *Public Papers of the Presidents of the United States: George Bush (1989-1993)* (Washington, DC: US Government Printing Office, 1989-94).

66. *Public Papers of the Presidents of the United States: Ronald Reagan (1985-1989)* (Washington, DC: US Government Printing Office, 1985-90).

67. Rahr, Alexander, *A Biographical Dictionary of 100 Leading Soviet Officials* (Boulder, CO: Westview Press, 1990).

68. *Register of Field Research on Eastern Europe, Mongolia and the USSR* (Princeton: International Research and Exchange Board, Inc., annually).

69. Reshetar, John S., Jr., *The Soviet Polity: Government and Politics in the USSR*, 3rd ed. (New York: Harper & Row, 1989).

70. Riasanovsky, Nicholas V., *A History of Russia*, 5th ed. (New York: Oxford University Press, 1993).

71. *Russia Survival Guide: Business and Travel*, 5th ed. (Montpelier, VT: Russian Information Service, 1994).

72. Rywkin, Michael, *Moscow's Lost Empire* (Armonk, NY: M. E. Sharpe, 1994).

73. *A Scholars' Guide to the Humanities and Social Sciences in the Soviet Successor States: The Academies of Sciences of Russia, Armenia, Azerbaidzhan, Belarus, Estonia, Georgia, Kazakhstan, Kyrgyzstyan, Latvia, Lithuania, Moldova, Tadzhikistan, Turkmenistan, Ukraine and Uzbekistan*, 2nd ed. (Armonk, NY: M. E. Sharpe, 1993).

74. Shaw, Warren, *The World Almanac of the Soviet Union: From 1905 to the Present* (New York: World Almanac, 1990).

75. Shlapentokh, Vladimir, with Neil F. O'Donnell, *The Last Years of the Soviet Empire: Snapshots from 1985-1991* (Westport, CT: Praeger, 1993).

76. *The Soviet World, 1948-1989* (Leiden: IDC Microform Publishers, 1989).

77. Staar, Richard F., and Margit N. Grigory, eds., *Yearbook on International Communist Affairs* (Stanford: Hoover Institution Press, annually).

78. Stern, Geoffrey, ed., *Atlas of Communism* (New York: Macmillan, 1991).

79. Stroynowski, Juliusz, *Who's Who in the Socialist Countries of Europe: A Biographical Encyclopedia of More Than 12,600 Leading Personalities in Albania, Bulgaria, Czechoslovakia, German Democratic Republic, Hungary, Poland, Romania, Yugoslavia*, 3 vols. (Munich-New York: Saur, 1989).

80. Taras, Raymond C., ed., *Handbook of Political Science Research on the USSR and Eastern Europe* (Westport, CT: Greenwood Press, 1992).

81. *The Tauris Soviet Directory: The Elite of the USSR Today* (London: I. B. Tauris & Co., Ltd., 1989).

82. Tolz, Vera, comp., *The USSR in 1989: A Record of Events*, ed. by Melanie Newton (Boulder, CO: Westview Press, 1990).

83. Treadgold, Donald W., *Twentieth Century Russia*, 7th ed. (Boulder, CO: Westview Press, 1989).

84. Twining, David T., *The New Eurasia: Guide to the Republics of the Former Soviet Union* (New York: Praeger, 1993).

85. US Central Intelligence Agency. Directorate of Intelligence. *Directory of Soviet Officials. Science and Education* (Springfield, VA: US Department of Commerce, National Technical Information Service, 1989).

86. US Information Agency, *Directory of Resources for International Cultural and Educational Exchanges* (Washington, DC: USIA, 1987).

87. US Library of Congress, Federal Research Division, *Soviet Union: A Country Study*, 2nd ed. (Washington, DC: Government Printing Office, 1991).

88. *USSR: The Decisive Years* (Toronto: Key Porter Books, distributor for Novosti, 1991).

89. Von Laue, Theodore, *Why Lenin? Why Stalin? Why Gorbachev?* 3rd ed. (New York: Harper Collins, 1993).

90. Walker, Martin, *The Cold War: A History* (New York: Henry Holt, 1994).

91. Weeks, Albert L., comp., *The Soviet Nomenklatura: A Comprehensive Roster of Soviet Civilian and Military Officials* (Washington, DC: Washington Institute Press, 1987).

92. Westwood, J. N., *Endurance and Endeavour: Russian History, 1812-1992*, 4th ed. (New York: Oxford University Press, 1993).

93. *Where in Moscow*, 4th ed. (Montpelier, VT: Russian Information Service, 1994).

94. *Where in St. Petersburg*, 2nd ed. (Montpelier, VT: Russian Information Service, 1994).

95. White, Stephen, ed., *Handbook of Reconstruction in Eastern Europe and the Soviet Union* (Detroit: Gale Research, 1991).

96. Wieczynski, Joseph L., ed., *The Gorbachev Encyclopedia: Mikhail Gorbachev, The Man and His Times, March 11, 1985-December 25, 1991* (Salt Lake City: Charles Schlacks Jr., Publisher, 1993).

97. -----, ed., *The Gorbachev Reader* (Salt Lake City: Charles Schlacks Jr., Publisher, 1993).

98. -----, ed., *The Modern Encyclopedia of Russian and Soviet History*, 54 vols. (Gulf Breeze, FL: Academic International Press, 1976-90).

99. Wixman, Ronald, *The Peoples of the USSR; An Ethnographic Handbook* (Armonk, NY: M. E. Sharpe, 1988).

100. Woronitzin, Sergej, *A Directory of Prominent Soviet Economists, Sociologists, and Demographers by Institutional Affiliation*, ed. by Robert Farrell (Munich: Radio Liberty, 1987).

101. Wren, Melvin C., *The Course of Russian History*, 5th ed. (Prospect Heights, IL: Waveland Press, 1994).

102. Young, Stephen W. *et al.*, *One Nation Becomes Many: The ACCESS Guide to the Former Soviet Union* (Washington, DC: ACCESS, 1993).

103. Zemtsov, Ilya, *Encyclopedia of Soviet Life* (New Brunswick, NJ: Transaction, 1991).

104. Zickel, Raymond E., ed., *Soviet Union: A Country Study* (Washington, DC: Library of Congress, 1991).

ARTICLES

105. American Association for the Advancement of Slavic

Studies, "Russian, Eurasian, and East European Research in Progress," *AAASS Newsletter* (updated annually).

106. "A Chronology of *Perestroika*," *Perestroika Annual*, 1 (1988), 329-32.

107. "Gorbachev: Meet His Team," *Economist*, 194 (16 Mar. 1985), 27.

108. "Gorby Fever and the Publishing Body Politic," *Publishers Weekly*, 236 (27 Oct. 1989), 42.

109. Hartgrove, J. Dane, "Soviet Union," *American Historical Association Recently Published Articles*, 12, no. 2 (Summer 1987), 93-100.

110. Heleniak, Timothy, "Glasnost and the Publication of Soviet Census Results," *Journal of Soviet Nationalities*, 2, no. 1 (Spring 1991), 139-60.

111. Kraus, Herwig, "Heads of the Governments and Leading State and Legislative Officials of the USSR Union Republics and the Baltic States," *Report on the USSR*, 3, no. 7 (15 Feb. 1991), 15-16.

112. McIntosh, Jack, "Canadian Publications on the Soviet Union and Eastern Europe," *Canadian Slavonic Papers*, published annually in issue no. 4.

113. Nelson, Susan H., "Title VIII and *Perestroika*," *AAASS Newsletter*, 29, no. 5 (Nov. 1989), 7-8.

114. Reddaway, Peter, "The End of the Empire" (Review Article), *New York Review of Books*, 38 (7 Nov. 1991), 53-59.

115. Remnick, Richard, "Dead Souls" (Review Article), *New York Review of Books*, 38 (19 Dec. 1991), 72-81.

116. Rubinstein, Alvin Z., "Documentation: The USSR in Turmoil; Views from the Right, Center, and Left," *Orbis*, 35, no. 2 (Spring 1991), 267-86.

117. Sagers, Matthew J., "News Notes," *Soviet Geography*, a regular feature; contents cataloged by subject in "Twenty Years of News Notes: A Listing from *Soviet Geography*, 1970-1990," *Soviet Geography*, 32, no. 7 (Sept. 1991), 474-509.

II. Collections of Documents, Essays and Research Materials
BOOKS

118. Aganbegyan, Abel, *Perestroika 1989* (New York: Charles Scribner's Sons, 1988).

119. American Bar Association, National Institute, *The Soviet Union and Eastern Europe: Recent Developments in Trade, Investment and Finance* (Chicago: American Bar Association, 1988).

120. *The Arctic—Choices for Peace and Security: Proceedings of a Public Inquiry* (Seattle: Gordon Soules Book Publishers, 1989).

121. Aurbach, Laurence J., ed., *Beyond Perestroika: Options for a New Soviet Union* (Chicago: American Bar Association, 1991).

122. Balzer, Harley D., ed., *Five Years That Shook the World: Gorbachev's Unfinished Revolution* (Boulder, CO: Westview Press, 1991).

123. Bernards, Neal, *et al.*, *The Soviet Union: Opposing Viewpoints* (St. Paul: Greenhaven Press, 1988).

124. Bialer, Seweryn, ed., *Politics, Society and Nationalism in Gorbachev's Russia* (Boulder, CO: Westview Press, 1989).

125. Black, J. L., ed., *The Gorbachev Reforms* (Gulf Breeze, FL; Academic International Press, 1988).

126. Bloomfield, Jon, ed., *The Soviet Revolution: Perestroika and the Remaking of Socialism* (London: Lawrence and Wishart, 1989).

127. Bochkarev, Andrei G., and Don L. Mansfield, eds., *The United States and the USSR in a Changing World: Soviet and American Perspectives* (Boulder, CO: Westview Press, 1992).

128. Bouma, Erin L., ed., *Big Ships Turn Slowly: The Soviet Union in Transition* (Washington, DC: World Media Association, 1989).

129. Bradley, Bill, Hans-Dietrich Genscher, Harry Ott and John C. Whitehead, *Implications of Soviet New Thinking: Summary Report of International Conference, St. Paul, Minn., October 9-11, 1987* (New York: Institute for East-West Security Studies, 1987).

130. Bremmer, Ian, and Raymond Taras, eds., *Nations and Politics in the Soviet Successor States* (Cambridge, MA: Cambridge University Press, 1992).

131. Breslauer, George W., ed., *Analyzing the Gorbachev Era* (Berkeley: University of California, 1989).

132. -----, *Can Gorbachev's Reforms Succeed?* (Berkeley: California Center for Slavic and East European Studies, University of California, 1990).

133. -----, ed., *Dilemmas of Transition in the Soviet Union and Eastern Europe* (Berkeley: University of California at Berkeley, International and Area Studies, 1991).

134. Brigham, Lawson W., ed. *The Soviet Maritime Arctic* (Annapolis, MD: Naval Institute Press, 1991).

135. Brumberg, Abraham, ed., *Chronicle of a Revolution: A Western-Soviet Inquiry into Perestroika* (New York: Pantheon, 1990).

136. Centre for Policy Studies, *A Year in the Life of Glasnost: Collection of Essays* (London: Centre for Policy Studies, 1988).

137. Clark, Susan L., ed., *Gorbachev's Agenda: Changes in Soviet Domestic and Foreign Policy* (Boulder, CO: Westview Press, 1989).

138. Colton, Timothy J., and Robert Legvold, eds., *After the Soviet Union: From Empire to Nations* (New York: W. W. Norton, 1992).

139. Crummey, Robert O., ed., *Reform in Russia and the U.S.S.R.: Past and Prospects* (Urbana, IL: University of Illinois

Press, 1989).

140. Dallin, Alexander, ed., *The Gorbachev Era* (New York: Garland Publishers, 1992).

141. -----, and Condoleezza Rice, eds., *The Gorbachev Era* (Stanford: Stanford Alumni Association, 1986).

142. -----, and Gail W. Lapidus, eds., *The Soviet System in Crisis: A Reader of Western and Soviet Views, Reprinted with a New Conclusion* (Boulder, CO: Westview Press, 1991).

143. Dyker, David A., ed., *The Soviet Union under Gorbachev: Prospects for Reform* (New York: Croom Helm, 1987).

144. Eberstadt, Nick, *The Poverty of Communism* (New Brunswick, NJ: Transaction Books, 1988).

145. Eisen, Jonathan, comp. and ed., *The Glasnost Reader* (New York: New American Library, 1990).

146. Evans, Alfred B., Jr., and Sylvia Woodby, eds., *Restructuring Soviet Ideology: Gorbachev's New Thinking* (Boulder, CO: Westview Press, 1990).

147. Frost, Gerald, ed., *Europe in Turmoil: The Struggle for Pluralism* (New York: Praeger, 1991).

148. Gorbachev, Mikhail S., *Selected Speeches and Articles* (Moscow: Progress Publishers, 1987).

149. -----, *Speeches and Writings* (Oxford and New York: Pergamon, 1986).

150. -----, *Socialism, Peace and Democracy: Writings, Speeches and Reports by Mikhail Gorbachev* (London: Zwan Publications, 1987).

151. -----, *Toward a Better World* (New York: Richardson and Steirman, 1986).

152. Graubard, Stephen R., ed., *Eastern Europe-Central Europe-Europe* (Boulder, CO: Westview Press, 1991).

153. -----, *Exit from Communism* (New Brunswick, NJ: Transaction Publishers, 1993).

154. Gurtov, Mel, ed., *The Transformation of Socialism: Perestroika and Reform in the Soviet Union and China* (Boulder, CO: Westview Press, 1990).

155. Harle, Vilho, and Jyrki Iivonen, eds., *Gorbachev and Europe* (New York: St. Martin's Press, 1990).

156. Hasegawa, Tsuyoshi, and Alex Pravda, eds., *Perestroika: Soviet Domestic and Foreign Policies* (Newbury Park: Sage, 1990).

157. Hawkes, N., ed., *Tearing Down the Curtain* (London: Hodder and Stoughton, 1990).

158. Hewett, Ed A., and Victor Winston, eds., *Milestones in Glasnost and Perestroyka*, vol. 1: *Politics and People*; vol 2: *The Economy* (Washington, DC: Brookings Institution, 1991).

159. Holman, Paul, *et al.*, *The Soviet Union after Perestroika: Change and Continuity* (Washington, DC: Brassey's, 1991).

160. Ieda, Osamu, ed., *New Order in Post-Communist Eurasia* (Sapporo, Japan: Slavic Research Center, Hokkaido University, 1993).

161. Iivonen, Jyrki, ed., *The Changing Soviet Union in the New Europe* (Brookfield, VT: E. Elgar, 1991).

162. Kukathas, C., D. Lovell and W. Maley, eds., *The Transition from Socialism* (Melbourne: Longman Cheshire, 1991).

163. Lane, David, ed., *Elites and Political Power in the USSR* (Aldershot: Edward Elgar, 1988).

164. -----, *Russia in Flux: The Political and Social Consequences of Reform* (Brookfield, VT: Edward Elgar, 1992).

165. Lapidus, Gail W., ed., *The New Russia* (Boulder, CO: Westview Press, 1994).

166. -----, and Guy E. Swanson, eds., *State and Welfare USA/USSR: Contemporary Practice and Policy* (Berkeley: Institute of International Studies, University of California, 1988).

167. -----, and Jonathan Haslam, eds., *The Chinese and Soviet Experiences: A Conference Report* (Berkeley: Berkeley-Stanford Program on Soviet International Behavior, 1987).

168. Laqueur, Walter, John Erickson *et al.*, *Soviet Union 2000: Reform or Revolution?* (New York: St. Martin's Press, 1990).

169. Lefever, Ernest W., and Robert D. Vander Lugt, eds., *Perestroika: How New Is Gorbachev's New Thinking?* (Washington, DC: Ethics and Public Policy Center, 1989).

170. Lerner, L., and D. Treadgold, eds., *Gorbachev and the Soviet Future* (Boulder, CO: Westview Press, 1988).

171. Mastny, Vojtech, ed., *Soviet/East European Survey, 1985-86: Selected Research and Analysis from Radio Free Europe/Radio Liberty* (Durham, NC: Duke University Press, 1987).

172. McCauley, Martin, ed., *Gorbachev and Perestroika* (New York: St. Martin's Press, 1990).

173. Melville, Andrei, and Gail W. Lapidus, eds., *The Glasnost Papers: Voices on Reform from Moscow* (Boulder, CO: Westview Press, 1990).

174. Mezhenkov, Vladimir, ed., *Soviet Scene 1987: A Collection of Press Articles and Interviews* (London: Collet, 1987).

175. -----, and Eva Skelley, eds., *Perestroika in Action: A Collection of Press Articles and Interviews* (London: Collets, 1988).

176. -----, eds., *One Way Ticket to Democracy: A Collection of Press Articles and Interviews* (London: Collets, 1989).

177. Miller, R. F., J. H. Miller and T. H. Rigby, eds., *Gorbachev at the Helm* (London: Croom Helm, 1987).

178. Minagawa, Shugo, ed., *Thorny Path to the Post-Perestroika World: Problems of Institutionalization* (Sapporo, Japan: Slavic Research Center, Hokkaido University, 1992).

179. Moser, Charles, ed., *Combat on Communist Territory* (Lake Bluff, IL: Regnery Gateway, 1985).

180. Mount, Ferdinand, ed., *Communism: A TLS Companion* (Chicago: University of Chicago Press, 1993).

181. Nelson, Daniel, and Rajan Menon, eds., *The Limits to Soviet Power* (Lexington, MA: Lexington Press, 1989).

182. Niiseki, Kinya, ed., *The Soviet Union in Transition* (Boulder, CO: Westview Press, 1987).

183. Nogee, Joseph L., ed., *Soviet Politics: Russia after Brezhnev* (New York: Praeger, 1985).

184. O'Loughlin, John, and Herman van der Wusten, eds., *The New Political Geography of Eastern Europe* (London: Belhaven Press, 1993).

185. Paul, Ellen Frankel, ed., *Totalitarianism at the Crossroads* (New Brunswick, NJ: Transaction, 1990).

186. Poznanski, Kazimierz Z., ed., *Constructing Capitalism: The Reemergence of Civil Society and Liberal Economy in the Post-Communist World* (Boulder, CO: Westview Press, 1992).

187. Pugh, Michael, and Phil Williams, eds., *Superpower Politics: Change in the United States and the Soviet Union* (New York: St. Martin's Press, 1990).

188. Ralston, Richard E., ed., *Communism-Its Rise and Fall in the Twentieth Century: From the Pages of the Christian Science Monitor* (Boston: Christian Science Publishing Society, 1991).

189. Rieber, Alfred J., and Alvin Z. Rubinstein, eds., *Perestroika at the Crossroads* (New York: M. E. Sharpe, 1991).

190. Rogers, Allan, ed., *The Soviet Far East: Geographical Perspectives on Development* (New York: Routledge, 1990).

191. Ross, Clark G., ed., *The Proceedings of the Dean Rusk Conference on Gorbachev's Soviet Union: Reform or Revolution?* (Davidson, NC: Davidson College, 1991).

192. Rowen, Henry S., and Charles Wolf Jr., eds., *The Future of the Soviet Empire* (New York: St. Martin's Press, 1987).

193. Rozman, Gilbert, ed., *Dismantling Communism: Common Causes and Regional Variations* (Washington, DC: The Woodrow Wilson Center Press, 1992).

194. Schulze, Fred, comp. and ed., *The USSR Today: Perspectives from the Soviet Press*, 8th ed. (Columbus, OH: Current Digest of the Soviet Press, 1991).

195. Schweitzer, Carl-Christoph, ed., *The Changing Western Analysis of the Soviet Threat* (New York: St. Martin's Press, 1990).

196. Solomon, Susan Gross, *Beyond Sovietology: Essays in Politics and History* (Armonk, NY: M. E. Sharpe, 1993).

197. Sonnenfeldt, Helmut, ed., *Soviet Politics in the 1980s* (Boulder, CO: Westview Press, 1985).

198. *Soviet Union, 1988-1989: Perestroika in Crisis?* (Boulder, CO: Westview Press, 1990).

199. Spring, D. W., ed., *The Impact of Gorbachev: The First Phase, 1985-1990* (New York: Pinter, 1991).

200. Staar, Richard F., and Margit N. Grigory, eds., *Yearbook on International Communist Affairs: Parties and Revolutionary Movements* (Stanford: Hoover Institution Press, annually).

201. Timofeyev, Lev, ed., *The Anti-Communist Manifesto: Whom to Help in Russia* (Bellevue, WA: Free Enterprise Press, 1990).

202. Urban, G. R., ed., *Can the Soviet System Reform? Seven Colloquies About the State of Soviet Socialism Seven Decades after the Bolshevik Revolution* (New York: Pinter Publishers, 1990).

203. Urban, Joan Barth, ed., *Moscow and the Global Left in the Gorbachev Era* (Ithaca: Cornell University Press, 1992).

204. Urban, Michael E., ed., *Ideology and System Change in the USSR and Eastern Europe* (New York: St. Martin's Press, 1992).

205. Veen, Hans-Joachim, ed., *From Brezhnev to Gorbachev: Domestic Affairs and Foreign Policy* (New York: St. Martin's Press, 1987).

206. Walker, Martin, *The Waking Giant: Gorbachev's Russia* (New York: Pantheon Books, 1986).

207. Wood, Alan, and R. A. French, eds., *The Development of Siberia: People and Resources* (New York: St. Martin's Press, 1989).

208. Worster, Donald, ed., *The Ends of the Earth* (Cambridge: Cambridge University Press, 1989).

ARTICLES

209. Elliott, J., ed., "Gorbachev and Glasnost: A Symposium," *Survey*, 30 (Oct. 1988), 1-123.

210. "Exit from Communism" (Special Issue), *Daedalus*, 121, no. 2 (Spring 1992), 1-263.

211. "Glasnost, Perestroika, and Novoye Myshleniye: Reform in the Soviet Union and Eastern Europe-Symposium," *PS*, 21 (June 1989), 208-14.

212. "Gorbachev's Era of New Thinking," *Journal of International Affairs*, 42 (Spring 1989), 267-486.

213. Holt, R. R., and B. Silverstein, eds., "The Image of the Enemy: U.S. Views of the Soviet Union," *Journal of Social Issues*, 45, no. 2 (Summer 1989), 1-175.

214. "Man of the Decade: Gorbachev," *Time*, 135 (1 Jan. 1990), 42-45.

215. "The Molotov-Ribbentrop Pact: The Documents," *Lituanus*, 35, no. 1 (Spring 1989), 47-74.

216. "Reform in Russia: A Symposium," *Wilson Quarterly*, 13 (Spring 1989), 36-61.

217. Shabad, Theodore, "Panel on the Soviet Union in the Year 2000," *Soviet Geography*, 28, no. 6 (June 1987), 388-433.

218. "Symposium on U.S.-Soviet Military and Economic Relations," *New York University Journal of International Law and Politics*, 22, no. 3 (Spring 1990), 373-595.

219. Wieczynski, Joseph L., ed., "Mikhail S. Gorbachev: A Scholarly Symposium on His Years in Power," *Soviet and Post-Soviet Review*, 19, nos. 1-3 (1992), 185-288; 20, no. 1 (1993), 1-10.

220. -----, ed., "M. S. Gorbachev and His Reform of the Soviet System: A Scholarly Symposium," *Soviet Union/Union Sovietique*, 16, nos. 2-3 (1989), 163-255.

III. Afghanistan, Soviet War in

BOOKS

221. Alexiev, Alexander R., *The United States and the War in Afghanistan* (Santa Monica, CA: RAND, 1988).

222. Amstutz, J. Bruce, *Afghanistan: The First Five Years of Soviet Occupation* (Washington, DC: National Defense University Press, Government Printing Office, 1986).

223. Anwar, Raja, *The Tragedy of Afghanistan: A First-Hand Account* (New York: Verso, 1988).

224. Armstrong, G. P., *Afghanistan: The Soviet Strategic Dilemma* (Ottawa, Canada: Dept. of National Defence, Directorate of Strategic Analysis, 1987).

225. Arnold, Anthony, *The Fateful Pebble: Afghanistan's Role in the Fall of the Soviet Empire* (Novato: Presidio Press, 1993).

226. Bocharov, Gennady, *Russian Roulette: Afghanistan through Russian Eyes* (New York: HarperCollins, 1990).

227. Bonner, Arthur, *Among the Afghans* (Durham, NC: Duke University Press, 1987).

228. Borovik, Artyom, *The Hidden War: A Russian Journalist's Account of the Soviet War in Afghanistan* (New York: Atlantic Monthly Press, 1990).

229. Daley, C., *Afghanistan and Gorbachev's Global Foreign Policy* (Santa Monica, CA: RAND, 1989).

230. Eliot, Theodore L., *Gorbachev's Afghan Gambit*, National Security Paper, 9 (Cambridge, MA: Institute for Foreign Policy Analysis, 1988).

231. Emadi, Haffizullah, *State, Revolution and Superpowers in Afghanistan* (New York: Praeger, 1990).

232. Farr, Grant M., and John C. Merriam, eds., *Afghan Resistance: The Politics of Survival* (Boulder, CO: Westview Press, 1987).

233. Ghaus, Abdul S., *The Fall of Afghanistan: An Insider's Account* (Washington, DC: Pergamon-Brassey's International Defense Publications, 1989).

234. Girardet, Edward, *Afghanistan: The Soviet War* (New York: St. Martin's Press, 1986).

235. Hauner, Milan, *The Soviet War in Afghanistan: Patterns of Russian Imperialism* (Lanham, MD: University Press of America, with the Foreign Policy Research Institute, 1991).

236. -----, and Robert Canfield, eds., *Afghanistan and the Soviet Union: Collision and Transformation* (Boulder, CO: Westview Press, 1989).

237. Huldt, Bo, and Erland Jansson, eds., *The Tragedy of Afghanistan: The Social, Cultural, and Political Impact of the Soviet Invasion* (New York: Croom Helm, 1988).

238. Khalilzad, Zalmay, *Prospects for Afghanistan* (Washington, DC: Woodrow Wilson International Center for Scholars, Kennan Institute, 1986).

239. Khan, Riaz M., *Untying the Afghan Knot: Negotiating the Soviet Withdrawal* (Durham, NC: Duke University Press, 1991).

240. Klass, Roseann, ed., *Afghanistan: The Great Game Revisited* (New York: Freedom House, 1987).

242. Lessing, Doris M., *The Wind Blows Away Our Words-And Other Documents Relating to the Afghan Resistance* (New York: Vintage Books, 1987).

243. Pilon, Juliana G., *The Report That the U. N. Wants to Suppress: Soviet Atrocities in Afghanistan* (Washington, DC: Heritage Foundation, 1987).

244. Rogers, Tom, *The Soviet Withdrawal from Afghanistan: Analysis and Chronology* (Westport, CT: Greenwood Press, 1993).

245. Roy, Olivier, *Islam and Resistance in Afghanistan* (New York: Cambridge University Press, 1986).

246. Saikal, Amin, and William Maley, eds., *The Soviet Withdrawal from Afghanistan* (Cambridge: Cambridge University Press, 1989).

247. Sen Gupta, Bhabani, *Afghanistan: Politics, Economics, and Society: Revolution, Resistance, Intervention* (Boulder, CO: L. Rienner Publications, 1987).

248. Shansab, Nasir, *Soviet Expansion in the Third World: Afghanistan, a Case Study* (Silver Spring, MD: Bartleby Press, 1986).

249. Tabibi, Abd al-Hakim, *The Legal Status of the Afghan Resistance Movement* (Cedar Rapids, Iowa: Igram Press, 1986).

250. Trottier, Paul, *Soviet Influence on Afghan Youth* (Washington, DC: US Department of State, 1986).

251. Urban, Mark, *War in Afghanistan*, 2nd ed. (New York: St. Martin's Press, 1990).

252. US Congress. Commission on Security and Cooperation in Europe. *Implementation of the Helsinki Accords: Soviet Involvement in Afghanistan, 3 May 1990*. 101st Congress, 2nd Session (Washington, DC: Government Printing Office, 1990).

253. US Congress. Commission on Security and Cooperation in Europe. *Implementation of the Helsinki Accords: Soviet Violations of the Helsinki Accords in Afghanistan: Hearing*. 99th Congress, 4 Dec. 1985 (Washington, DC: Government Printing Office, 1986).

254. US Congress. House. Committee on Foreign Affairs. Subcommittee on Asian and Pacific Affairs. *Developments in*

Afghanistan, February 1988, 100th Congress, 2nd Session (Washington, DC: Government Printing Office, 1989).

255. US Congress. House. Committee on Foreign Affairs. Subcommittee on Asian and Pacific Affairs. *The Geneva Accords on Afghanistan*. 100th Congress, 2nd Session (Washington, DC: Government Printing Office, 1989).

256. Weinbaum, Marvin G., *Pakistan and Afghanistan: Resistance and Reconstruction* (Boulder, CO: Westview Press, 1994).

257. White, Anthony G., *A Military Look at the Afghanistan Invasion: A Selected Bibliography* (Monticello, IL: Vance Bibliographies, 1986).

258. Witherell, Julian W., *Afghanistan: An American Perspective. A Guide to U.S. Official Documents and Government-Sponsored Publications* (Washington, DC: Library of Congress, 1986).

ARTICLES

259. Alexiev, Alex, "U.S. Policy and the War in Afghanistan," *Global Affairs*, 3, no. 1 (Winter 1989), 81-93.

260. Allen, Thomas B., with Ken Strafer, "The USSR's `Hidden War' Goes On," *Sea Power*, 28, no. 9 (Aug. 1985), 37ff.

261. Arnold, Anthony, "Perspectives on Afghanistan" (Review Article), *Problems of Communism*, 36, no. 5 (Sept-Oct. 1987), 69-76.

262. Barnes, Fred, "Victory in Afghanistan: The Inside Story," *Reader's Digest*, 133, no. 800 (Dec. 1988), 77-83.

263. Bennigsen, Alexandre, "Winning the War for Afghanistan," *National Review*, 39 (8 May 1987), 36-38.

264. Bokhari, Imtiaz H., "Evolution of a Dual Negotiation Process: Afghanistan," *Annals of the American Academy of Political and Social Science*, no. 518 (Nov. 1991), 58-68.

265. Bradsher, Henry S., "Stagnation and Change in Afghanistan," *Journal of South Asian and Middle Eastern Studies*, 10, no. 1 (Fall 1986), 3-35.

266. Chanda, Nayan, "The Afghan Connection," *Far Eastern Economic Review*, 130 (5 Dec. 1985), 30-31.

267. -----, "No More Evil Empire," *Far Eastern Economic Review*, 129 (18 July 1985), 46.

268. -----, "Time to Go Home," *Far Eastern Economic Review*, 138 (24 Dec. 1987), 30-31.

269. Cogan, Charles G., "Shawl of Lead: From Holy War to Civil War in Afghanistan," *Conflict*, 10, no. 3 (1990), 189-204.

270. Collins, George W., "The War in Afghanistan," *Air University Review*, 37, no. 3 (Mar-Apr. 1986), 42-49.

271. Collins, Joseph J., "The Soviet Military Experience in Afghanistan," *Military Review*, 65, no. 5 (May 1985), 16-28.

272. Daley, T., "Afghanistan and Gorbachev's Global Policy," *Asian Survey*, 29, no. 5 (May 1989), 496-513.

273. Davison, Kenneth L., Jr., "The Geopolitics of Soviet Withdrawal from Afghanistan," *Strategic Review*, 18, no. 1 (Winter 1990), 39-48.

274. Derleth, J. W., "The Soviets in Afghanistan: Can the Soviets Fight a Counterinsurgency War?" *Armed Forces and Society*, 15, no. 1 (Fall 1988), 33-54.

275. "Documentation: Afghanistan," *Survival*, 30, no. 4 (July-Aug. 1988), 291-309.

276. Dupree, Louis, "The Soviet Union and Afghanistan in 1987," *Current History*, 86, no. 522 (Oct. 1987), 333ff.

277. Eliot, Theodore L., "Afghanistan in 1989: Stalemate," *Asian Survey*, 30, no. 2 (Feb. 1990), 158-66.

278. -----, "Afghanistan in 1990: Groping Toward Peace," *Asian Survey*, 31, no. 2 (Feb. 1991), 125-33.

279. Fane, Daria, "After Afghanistan: The Decline of Soviet Military Prestige," *Washington Quarterly*, 13, no. 2 (Spring 1990), 5-16.

280. Ford, Christopher A., "Afghanistan: A Political Settlement?" *Harvard International Review*, 9, no. 5 (May-June 1987), 26-28.

281. Galster, Steven R., "Waiting in Afghanistan: What Will Follow the Pullout?" *Nation* (2 Jan. 1989), 9-12.

282. Galuszka, Philip, *et al.*, "As Kabul Teeters, Gorbachev Lands on His Feet," *Business Week* (20 Feb. 1989), 51.

283. Ghausuddin, "An Artist in Afghanistan," *New York Review of Books*, 33 (12 June 1986), 38-39.

284. Gibbs, D., "Does the USSR Have a `Grand Strategy'? Reinterpreting the Invasion of Afghanistan," *Journal of Peace Research*, 24 (Dec. 1987), 365-79.

285. Goldman, Minton F., "The USSR and Afghanistan: Obstacles to Disengagement," *Asian Thought and Society: An International Review*, 16, no. 47 (May-Sept. 1991), 139-46.

286. Grosscup, Beau, "The Middle View: Confronting the Reality of Terrorism," in *The Explosion of Terrorism* (Far Hills, NJ: New Horizon Press, 1987).

287. Holstein, W. J., *et al.*, "Gorbachev Raises the Ante in Afghanistan," *Business Week* (20 May 1985), 83.

288. Hyman, Anthony, "Afghanistan's Uncertain Future," *Report on the USSR*, 2, no. 12 (23 Mar. 1990), 15-16.

289. -----, "Soviet Advisers and Help for Afghanistan," *Report on the USSR*, 2, no. 9 (2 Mar. 1990), 305.

290. Johns, Michael, "The Lessons of Afghanistan: Bipartisan Support for Freedom Fighters Pays Off," *Policy Review*, no. 40 (Spring 1987), 32-35.

291. Kamrany, Nake M., "The Continuing War in Afghanistan," *Current History*, 85, no. 513 (Oct. 1986), 333-36.

292. Kaplan, Robert D., "Afghanistan: Postmortem," *Atlantic Monthly*, 263, no. 4 (Apr. 1989), 26ff.

293. Karp, Craig M., "The War in Afghanistan," *Foreign Affairs*,

64, no. 5 (Summer 1986), 1026-47.

294. Keegan, John, "The Ordeal of Afghanistan," *Atlantic Monthly*, 159, no. 5 (Nov. 1985), 94-105.

295. Khalilzad, Zalmay, "Moscow's Afghan War," *Problems of Communism*, 35, no. 1 (Jan-Feb. 1986), 1-20.

296. -----, "The Soviet Dilemma in Afghanistan," *Current History*, 84, no. 504 (Oct. 1985), 334-37.

297. -----, "The War in Afghanistan," *International Journal*, 41, no. 2 (Spring 1986), 271-99.

298. Klass, Roseann, "Toward Understanding Afghanistan, Present and Future" (Review Article), *Soviet Union/Union Sovietique*, 15, no. 1 (1988), 75-79.

299. Kornienko, G. M., "The Afghan Endeavor: Perplexities of the Military Incursion and Withdrawal," *Journal of South Asian and Middle Eastern Studies*, 7, no. 2 (Winter 1994), 2-17.

300. Laber, Jeri, "Afghanistan's Other War," *New York Review of Books*, 33 (18 Dec. 1986), 3ff.

301. Laffin, John, "Afghanistan War," in his *The World in Conflict 1990: Contemporary Warfare Described and Analysed* (Washington, DC: Brassey's, 1990), 1-17.

302. "Last Exit from Kabul," *Economist*, 310 (4 Feb. 1989), 31-32.

303. Leslie, D. S., and R. G. Helms, "United Nations Good Offices Mission in Afghanistan and Pakistan: Lessons from a Peacekeeping Experience," *Canadian Defence Quarterly*, 19, no. 1 (Summer 1989), 51-54.

304. Lifschultz, Lawrence, "Afghan Negotiations: Can the Pieces Fit into Place?" *Nation* (31 May 1986), 751-56.

305. "The Little Missile That Could," *Army*, 39, no. 5 (May 1989), 30-33.

306. Maley, William, "Soviet-Afghan Relations After the Coup," *Report on the USSR*, 3, no. 38 (20 Sept. 1991), 11-15.

307. McCain, Morris, "On Moscow's Southern Flank: Iran, Afghanistan, and Pakistan," *Journal of South Asian and Middle Eastern Studies*, 11, no. 1-2 (Fall-Winter 1987), 5-20.

308. McCormick, Kip, "Perspectives on Afghanistan: The Evolution of Soviet Military Doctrine," *Military Review*, 67, no. 7 (July 1987), 61-72.

309. Mecham, Michael, "U. S. Credits Afghan Resistance with Thwarting Soviet Air Power," *Aviation Week & Space Technology* (13 July 1987), 26-27.

310. Mendelson, Sarah E., "Internal Battles and External Wars: Politics, Learning and the Soviet Withdrawal from Afghanistan," *World Politics*, 45, no. 3 (Apr. 1993), 327-60.

311. Naumov, Vladislav, "Soviet Tactics in Afghanistan," *Freedom at Issue*, no. 90 (May-June 1986), 25-27.

312. Noorzoy, M. Siddieq, "Soviet Economic Interests in Afghanistan," *Problems of Communism*, 36, no. 3 (May-June 1987), 43-54.

313. Perkovich, George, "The Afghanistan War: Bear in a Briar Patch: Prospects for a Soviet Pullout," *Commonweal* (18 Dec. 1987), 725-26.

314. Person, Lawrence, "The Way to Afghan Peace," *World & I* (Jan. 1992), 214-21.

315. Ping, Ai, "Fighting Intensifies as Soviet Troops Withdraw," *Beijing Review*, 31 (5 Sept. 1988), 16.

316. Prokhanov, Aleksandr, "Afghan Questions: A Writer's Opinion," *Soviet Law and Government*, 27, no. 3 (Winter 1988-89), 50-54.

317. Quinn-Judge, Sophie, "A Costly Adventure," *Far Eastern Economic Review*, 139 (21 Jan. 1988), 15-16.

318. -----, "Diplomacy of Defeat: Soviets Re-examine Policies after Failed Intervention," *Far Eastern Economic Review*, 143 (2 Mar. 1989), 34.

319. Rais, Rasul Bakhsh, "Afghanistan after the Soviet Withdrawal," *Current History*, 91, no. 563 (Mar. 1992), 123-27.

320. Rashid, Abdul, "The Afghan Resistance and the Problem of Unity," *Strategic Review*, 14, no. 3 (Summer 1986), 58-66.

321. Rashid, Ahmed, "Scramble for Influence: Iran, Saudi Arabia Vie to Shape Afghan Peace," *Far Eastern Economic Review*, 147 (18 Jan. 1990), 19-20.

322. -----, "A State of Siege: Soviets Fail to Persuade Pakistan to Compromise," *Far Eastern Economic Review*, 143 (16 Feb. 1989), 12-13.

323. -----, "Unwilling Allies: Pakistanis Want an Afghan Peace," *Nation* (31 Jan. 1987), 110ff.

324. Rezun, Miron, "Afghanistan's Agony," *International Perspectives*, 18, no. 2 (1989), 17-20.

325. -----, "The Great Game Revisited," *International Journal*, 41, no. 2 (Spring 1986), 324-41.

326. Rubin, Barnett R., "Afghanistan: `Back to Feudalism'," *Current History*, 88, no. 542 (Dec. 1989), 421ff.

327. -----, "Afghanistan: The Next Round," *Orbis*, 33, no. 1 (Winter 1989), 57-72.

328. -----, "Cantering Down a Dark Defile: Afghanistan's Uncertain Fate," *Nation* (27 Feb. 1989), 264-70.

329. Rubinstein, Alvin Z., "Afghanistan and the USSR: Speculations on a National Tragedy," *Orbis*, 30, no. 4 (Winter 1987), 589-608.

330. -----, "Afghanistan at War," *Current History*, 85, no. 509 (Mar. 1986), 117ff.

331. Saikal, Amin, "The USSR in Afghanistan: Regional Implications," in *The Indian Ocean as a Zone of Peace* (New York: International Peace Academy, 1986), 61-78.

332. Sardar, Riffat, "The Afghan Crisis: Seven Years Later," *Journal of South Asian and Middle Eastern Studies*, 9, no. 2

(Winter 1985), 67-81.

333. Sawhny, Karan, "The New Afghan Military Balance," *Contemporary Review*, 253, no. 1474 (Nov. 1988), 232-36.

334. Schultheis, Rob, "In Afghanistan, Peace Must Wait," *New York Times Magazine* (29 Dec. 1991), 14ff.

335. Sheikh, Ali T., "The New Political Thinking: Gorbachev's Policy toward Afghanistan and Pakistan," *Asian Survey*, 28, no. 11 (Nov. 1988), 1170-87.

336. Shipler, David K., "Out of Afghanistan" (Review Article), *Journal of International Affairs*, 42 (Spring 1989), 477-86.

337. Simpson, Colin, "The Afghan Resistance Picture," *Contemporary Review*, 251, no. 1459 (Aug. 1987), 81-83.

338. Sliwinski, Mark, "Afghanistan: The Decimation of a People," *Orbis*, 33, no. 1 (Winter 1989), 39-56.

339. "Soviets Completing Afghan Pullout," *Congressional Quarterly Weekly Report*, 47 (11 Feb. 1989), 274.

340. "Statement by General Secretary of the CPSU Central Committee Mikhail Gorbachev on Afghanistan," *Soviet Military Review*, no. 3 (Mar. 1988), 2-4.

341. Strmecki, Marin, "Can the Afghan Rebels Win?" *National Review*, 38 (4 July 1986), 32ff.

342. -----, "Gorbachev's New Strategy in Afghanistan," *Strategic Review*, 15, no. 3 (Summer 1987), 31-42.

343. -----, "Operation Avalanche and the Soviet Capitulation," *American Spectator*, 21, no. 4 (Apr. 1988), 15-17.

344. Tripathi, Deepak, "Afghanistan: The Last Episode?" *World Today*, 48, no. 1 (Jan. 1992), 1-2.

345. Tsagolov, Kim, and Artem Borovik, "Afghanistan: A Preliminary Review," *Soviet Law and Government*, 29, no. 2 (Fall 1990), 64ff.

346. Weisman, Steven R., "The Great Game: The Afghan War as Seen from Kabul," *New Republic* (10-17 Aug. 1987), 20-23.

347. Wheeler, Charles G., "Perspectives on Afghanistan: The Forces in Conflict," *Military Review*, 67, no. 7 (July 1987), 54-60.

348. Willey, Fay, "Gorbachev's Afghan Gambit: A New Troop-Pullout Plan Has Pakistan Worried," *Newsweek*, 111 (22 Feb. 1988), 35.

349. Williams, Lynna, "Afghanistan," *Atlantic*, 265 (Mar. 1990), 75-79.

350. Wirsing, Robert G., "Pakistan and the War in Afghanistan," *Asian Affairs: An American Review*, 14, no. 2 (Summer 1987), 57-75.

351. Wood, William B., "Long Time Coming: The Repatriation of Afghan Refugees," *Association of American Geographers Annals*, 79, no. 3 (Sept. 1989), 345-69.

352. Yetiv, S. A., "How the Soviet Military Intervention in Afghanistan Improved the U.S. Strategic Position in the Persian Gulf," *Asian Affairs: An American Review*, 17, no. 2 (Summer 1990), 62-81.

IV. Agriculture

BOOKS

353. *Agricultural Reform in Developing Countries: Reflections for Eastern Europe*, Agriculture and Rural Development Working Paper no. 538 (Washington, DC: The World Bank, 1990).

354. Boyd, Michael L., *Organization, Performance and System Choice: East European Agricultural Development* (Boulder, CO: Westview Press, 1991).

355. Brada, Josef C., and Karl-Eugen Wadekin, eds., *Socialist Agriculture in Transition: Organizational Response to Falling Performance* (Boulder, CO: Westview Press, 1988).

356. Braverman, Avishay, and J. Luis Guasch, *Agricultural Reform in Developing Countries: Reflections for Eastern Europe* (Washington, DC: The World Bank, 1990).

357. Brooks, Karen McConnell, *Agriculture and Five Years of Perestroika* (St. Paul: Institute of Agriculture, Forestry and Home Economics: University of Minnesota, 1990).

358. Claudon, Michael P., and Tamar L. Gutner, eds., *Putting Food on What Was the Soviet Table* (New York: New York University Press, 1992).

359. Cochrane, Nancy J., and Miles J. Lambert, *Agricultural Performance in Eastern Europe, 1987* (Washington, DC: US Department of Agriculture, Economic Research Service, Agriculture and Trade Analysis Division, 1988).

360. Deutsch, Robert, *The Food Revolution in the Soviet Union and Eastern Europe* (Boulder, CO: Westview Press, 1986).

361. *Food and Agricultural Policy Reforms in the Former USSR: An Agenda for the Transition* (Washington, DC: World Bank, 1992).

362. Gorbachev, Mikhail Sergeevich, *On the Agrarian Policy of the CPSU in the Present Conditions: Report and Closing Remarks by the General Secretary of the CPSU Central Committee at the Plenary Meeting of the CPSU Central Committee, March 15-16, 1989* (Moscow: Novosti Press Agency Pub. House, 1989).

363. Gray, Kenneth R., *Selected Bibliography of Sources on Soviet Agriculture* (Washington, DC: Woodrow Wilson International Center for Scholars, Kennan Institute, 1986).

364. -----, ed., *Soviet Agriculture: Comparative Perspectives* (Ames: Iowa State University Press, 1990).

365. Hedlund, Stefan, *Private Agriculture in the Soviet Union* (New York: Routledge and Kegan Paul, 1989).

366. *International Agriculture and Trade Reports. Situation and Outlook Series: Former USSR* (Washington, DC: USDA, Economic Research Service, 1993).

367. Jones, James R., ed., *East-West Agricultural Trade* (Boulder, CO: Westview Press, 1986).

368. Kaplan, Cynthia S., *The Party and Agricultural Crisis Management in the USSR* (Ithaca: Cornell University Press, 1987).

369. Koopman, Robert B., *Efficiency and Growth in Agriculture: A Comparative Study of the Soviet Union, United States, Canada and Finland* (Washington, DC: Department of Agriculture, Economic Research Service, 1989).

370. Litvin, Valentin, *The Soviet Agro-Industrial Complex: Structure and Performance* (Boulder, CO: Westview Press, 1987).

371. Medvedev, Zhores A., *Soviet Agriculture* (New York: W. W. Norton, 1987).

372. Moskoff, William, ed., *Perestroika in the Countryside: Agricultural Reform in the Gorbachev Era* (Armonk, NY: M. E. Sharpe, 1990).

373. Nove, Alec, *Soviet Agriculture: The Brezhnev Legacy and Gorbachev's Cure* (Santa Monica, CA: RAND/UCLA Center for the Study of Soviet Behavior, 1988).

374. Organization for Economic Cooperation and Development, *The Soviet Agro-Food System and Agricultural Trade: Prospects for Reform* (Paris: OECD, 1991).

375. Prosterman, Roy L., and Timothy Hanstad, *The Prospects for Individual Peasant Farming in the USSR*, RDI Monographs on Foreign Aid and Development, no. 6 (Seattle: Rural Development Institute, 1991).

376. -----, *An Update on Individual Peasant Farming in the U.S.S.R.*, RDI Monographs on Foreign Aid and Development, no. 8 (Seattle: Rural Development Institute, 1991).

377. Pryor, Frederic L., *The Red and the Green: The Rise and Fall of Collectivized Agriculture in Marxist Regimes* (Princeton: Princeton University Press, 1992).

378. Shanin, Teodor, *Defining Peasants: Essays Concerning Rural Societies, Expolary Economics and Learning From Them in the Contemporary World* (Cambridge: Basil Blackwell, 1990).

379. Shend, Jaclyn Y., *Agricultural Statistics of the Former USSR Republics and the Baltic States*, Statistical Bulletin no. 863 (Washington, DC: USDA, Economic Research Service, 1993).

380. *Soviet Agriculture and Trade Under Perestroika* (Tunbridge Wells: Agra Europe, 1990).

381. US Congress. House. Committee on Agriculture. *Current Agricultural Situation in Russia: Hearings*, 103rd Congress, 1st Session (Washington, DC: Government Printing Office, 1993).

382. US Congress. House. Committee on Agriculture. Subcommittee on Wheat, Soybeans and Feed Grains. *Review of the United States Sale of Wheat, Soybeans, and Feed Grains to the Soviet Union: Hearing...*, 102nd Congress, 1st Session (Washington, DC: Government Printing Office, 1991).

383. US Congress. House. Committee on Agriculture. Subcommittee on Wheat, Soybeans, and Feed Grains. *Soviet Agriculture and Outlook for Soviet Purchases of Grain and Oilseeds: Hearings...*, 101st Congress, 2nd Session (Washington, DC: Government Printing Office, 1991).

384. US Congress. House. Committee on Ways and Means. *Extension of Nondiscriminatory Treatment to the Products of the Soviet Union: Report*, 102nd Congress, 1st Session (Washington, DC: Government Printing Office, 1991).

385. US Congress. House. Select Committee on Hunger. International Task Force. *Hunger in the Soviet Union: Fact or Fantasy? Hearing...*, 102nd Congress, 1st Session (Washington, DC: Government Printing Office, 1991).

386. US Congress. Joint Economic Committee. *Agricultural Reform in the Soviet Union and China*. 101st Congress, 1st Session (Washington, DC: Government Printing Office, 1989).

387. US Congress. Joint Economic Committee. *Gorbachev's Economic Plans*, vol. 2 (100th Congress, 1st Session (Washington, DC: Government Printing Office, 1987), section VI.

388. US Congress. Joint Economic Committee. *The Former Soviet Union in Transition*, vol. 2, 103rd Congress, 1st Session (Washington, DC: Government Printing Office, 1993), section IIIB.

389. US Congress. Senate. Committee on Agriculture, Nutrition and Forestry. *International Trade: Soviet Agricultural Reform and the US Government Reponse: Report* (Gaithersburg, MD: General Accounting Office, 1991).

390. US Congress. Senate. Committee on Agriculture, Nutrition and Forestry. *Possible Impact on Agriculture of the Explosion of the Soviet Nuclear Plant at Chernobyl. Hearings*. 99th Congress, 15 May 1986 (Washington, DC: Government Printing Office, 1986).

391. US Department of Agriculture. *Former USSR Agriculture and Trade Report: Situation and Outlook Series*, RS-92-1 (Washington, DC: USDA, Economic Research Service, 1992).

392. Van Atta, Don, ed., *The "Farmer Threat": The Political Economy of Agrarian Reform in Post-Soviet Russia* (Boulder, CO: Westview Press, 1993).

393. Wadekin, Karl-Eugen, ed., *Communist Agriculture: Farming in the Soviet Union and Eastern Europe* (London: Routledge, 1990).

394. -----, and F. Kuba, eds., *The Soviet Agro-Food System and Agricultural Trade: Prospects for Reform* (Washington, DC: Organization for Economic Co-operation and Development Publications and Information Centre, 1991).

395. Yin, John, *Infrastructure of the Soviet Agriculture* (Sudbury, Ontario: Northernmost View Press, 1991).

396. Zeimetz, Kathryn A., *USSR Agricultural Trade* (Washington, DC: US Department of Agriculture, Economic Research Service, 1991).

ARTICLES

397. Ash, Tim, Keith Howe and Robert Lewis, "An Example of the Crisis in Specialized Agriculture: The Decline in Egg Production," *Report on the USSR*, 3, no. 7 (15 Feb. 1991), 8-10.

398. -----, "Private versus Public Agriculture," *Report on the USSR*, 2, no. 47 (23 Nov. 1990), 6-8.

399. -----, "USSR Harvest: Bleak Future for Food Supplies," *Report on the USSR*, 3, no. 45 (8 Nov. 1991), 7-10.

400. -----, "USSR Harvest Failure Forecast," *Report on the USSR*, 3, no. 34 (23 Aug. 1991), 1-3.

401. Axelrod, Saul, "Perestroika and Contingency Management: Soviet Agricultural Reform," *Journal of Applied Behavior Analysis*, 24 (Spring 1991), 175.

402. Birkenes, Robert M., "Grain Crisis in the Soviet Union," *Report on the USSR*, 2, no. 32 (10 Aug. 1990), 9-10.

403. Bromley, Daniel, "Revitalizing the Russian Food System: Markets in Theory and Practice," *Choices*, 8, no. 4 (4th Quarter 1993), 4-8.

404. Brooks, Karen, "Gorbachev Tries the Family Farm," *Bulletin of the Atomic Scientists*, 44, no. 10 (Dec. 1988), 26-29.

405. -----, "Lease Contracting in Soviet Agriculture in 1989," *Comparative Economic Studies*, 32, no. 2 (Summer 1990), 85-108.

406. -----, "Soviet Agriculture's Halting Reform," *Problems of Communism*, 39, no. 2 (Mar-Apr. 1990), 29-41.

407. -----, "Soviet Agriculture under Perestroika," *Current History*, 89, no. 549 (Oct. 1990), 329ff.

408. -----, *et al.*, "Agriculture and the Transition to the Market," *Journal of Economic Perspectives*, 5, no. 4 (Fall 1991), 149-61.

409. Bush, George, "Presidential Mission to Assess Soviet Food Situation," *US Department of State Dispatch*, 2 (7 Oct. 1991), 735.

410. Butterfield, Jim, "Devolution in Decision-Making and Organizational Change in Soviet Agriculture," *Comparative Economic Studies*, 32, no. 2 (Summer 1990), 29-64.

411. Channon, John, "The Fall and Rise of the Soviet Peasantry: Some Observations on Gorbachev's Recent Agricultural Reforms," *Slovo: A Journal of Contemporary Soviet and East European Affairs*, 2, no. 1 (May 1989), 14-32.

412. Chotiner, Barbara Ann, "On Communist Agriculture" (Review Article), *Problems of Communism*, 39, no. 2 (Mar-Apr. 1990), 120-24.

413. Christopher, M., "Boosting Farm Output," *Scholastic Update*, 118 (7 Mar. 1986), 8.

414. Claudon, Michael, "Fix What's Broken: Rethinking Soviet Reforms," *Newsletter for Research on Soviet and East European Agriculture*, 14, no. 1 (Mar. 1992), 1ff.

415. "The Cloud Over Russia's Crops and Energy," *Economist*, 299 (10 May 1986), 69-70.

416. Coffman, Richard W., "Legal Aspects of Soviet Agricultural Reform: The Collective Contract," *Columbia Journal of Transnational Law*, 24, no. 2 (1986), 339-63.

417. Cook, Edward C., "Reforming Soviet Agriculture: Problems with Farm Finances and Equity Considerations," *Comparative Economic Studies*, 32, no. 2 (Summer 1990), 65-84.

418. Danilov, Viktor P., "October and the Party's Agrarian Policy," *Soviet Law and Government*, 27, no. 4 (Spring 1989), 35-51.

419. Despres, Laure, and Ksenya Khinchuk, "The Hidden Sector in Soviet Agriculture: A Study of the Military Sovkhozy and Auxiliary Farms," *Soviet Studies*, 42, no. 2 (Apr. 1990), 269-94.

420. Dima, Nicholas, "Can the `Former' Soviet Union Feed Itself? (An Appraisal of the Natural and Human Environment)," *Journal of Social, Political and Economic Studies*, 16, no. 4 (Winter 1991), 423-40.

421. Dovring, Folke, "New Directions in Soviet Agriculture," *Current History*, 86, no. 522 (Oct. 1987), 329ff.

422. Durgin, Frank, "Private Farms in the USSR," *Newsletter for Research on Soviet and East European Agriculture*, 13, no. 2 (June 1991), 24-31.

423. Emel'ianov, A., "Agrarian Reform and Socioeconomic Structures of the Modern Countryside," *Problems of Economics*, 33, no. 10 (Feb. 1991), 70-82.

424. Floroff, O., and S. W. Tiefenbrun, "New Soviet Fundamentals of Law on Land Ownership," *New York International Law Review*, 4 (Summer 1991), 92-106.

425. Franklin, Daniel, "Land of Milk and Cabbage," *Economist*, 307 (9 Apr. 1988), 9-11.

426. -----, "Perestroika on the Farms," *World Today*, 45, no. 5 (May 1989), 73-74.

427. Galuszka, Philip, "An Apple a Day Keeps *Perestroika* Rolling Along," *Business Week* (31 Aug. 1987), 41-42.

428. Gorbachev, Mikhail, "The CPSU's Agrarian Policy at the Stage of Developed Socialism," *World Marxist Review*, 25 (Oct. 1982), 1-8.

429. "Gorby's Farm Reform: A Hard Row to Hoe," *U.S. News & World Report*, 106 (27 Mar. 1989), 9-10.

430. Hanson, Philip, "Soviet Food Shortages: Chaos Rather Than Famine," *Report on the USSR*, 2, no. 51 (21 Dec. 1990), 6-7.

431. Haupt, R., "Soviet Farmers Reap Frustration," *World Press Review*, 38 (Dec. 1991), 48.

432. Johnson, D. Gale, "Agricultural Productivity in the Soviet Union," *Current History*, 84, no. 504 (Oct. 1985), 321ff.

433. -----, "Possible Impacts of Agricultural Trade Liberalization in the USSR," *Comparative Economic Studies*, 32, no. 2 (Summer 1990), 144-54.

434. -----, "Trade Effects of Dismantling the Socialized Agriculture of the Former Soviet Union," *Comparative Economic Studies*, 35, no. 4 (Winter 1993), 21-32.

435. Kramer, M., "Can Gorbachev Feed Russia?" *New York Times Magazine* (9 Apr. 1989), 42ff.

436. Kruse, L., "Revolution in Russia," *Successful Farming*, 89 (Oct. 1991), 12-13.

437. Kuba, Ferdinand, "Agricultural Reform in the USSR," *OECD Observer* (Apr-May 1988), 8-10.

438. -----, "Restructuring Soviet Agriculture," *OECD Observer*, no. 174 (Feb-Mar. 1992), 23-26.

439. -----, "Soviet Agriculture under the Restructuring Policies," *Outlook on Agriculture*, 18, no. 1 (1989), 7-11.

440. Laird, Roy D., "Perestroyka and Soviet Agriculture," *Problems of Communism*, 36, no. 6 (Nov-Dec. 1987), 81-86.

441. -----, and Betty A. Laird, "*Glasnost, Perestroika,* and Gorbachev's Policies: The Built-in Contradictions of Soviet Socialism," *Studies in Comparative Communism*, 23, no. 2 (Summer 1990), 115-24.

442. "Legal Aspects of Soviet Agrarian Reform: The Collective Contract," *Columbia Journal of Transnational Law*, 24 (1986), 339-63.

443. Liefert, William M., Robert B. Kooperman and Edward C. Cook, "Agricultural Reform in the Former Soviet Union," *Comparative Economic Studies*, 35, no. 4 (Winter 1993), 49-68.

444. Macey, David A. J., "Gorbachev and Stolypin: Soviet Agrarian Reform in Historical Perspective," *Comparative Economic Studies*, 32, no. 2 (Summer 1990), 7-28.

445. Markish, Yuri, and Edward Cook, "Investment in Agriculture and Food Sectors," *USSR Agriculture and Trade Report: Situation and Outlook Series* (Washington, DC: USDA, Economic Research Service, 1991).

446. Marrese, Michael, "Hungarian Agriculture: Lessons for the Soviet Union," *Comparative Economic Studies*, 32, no. 2 (Summer 1990), 155-69.

447. McIntyre, Robert J., "Eastern European Success with Socialized Agriculture: Developmental and Sovietological Lessons," *Review of Radical Political Economics*, 23, no. 1-2 (Spring-Summer 1991), 177-86.

448. -----, "The Phantom of the Transition: Privatization of Agriculture in the Former Soviet Union and Eastern Europe," *Comparative Economic Studies*, 34, no. 3-4 (Fall-Winter 1992), 81-95.

449. "A Night on the Fruited Plain," *Business Week* (5 June 1989), 57ff.

450. Nikiforov, L., "The Agrarian Crisis and Agrarian Reform," *Problems of Economics*, 34, no. 6 (Oct. 1991), 24-47.

451. Nikonov, A., "Agro-Industrial Science on the Road to Restructuring," *Soviet Law and Government*, 26, no. 2 (Fall 1987), 24-36.

452. Pallot, Judith, "Rural Depopulation and the Restoration of the Russian Village under Gorbachev," *Soviet Studies*, 42, no. 4 (Oct. 1990), 655-74.

453. -----, "Update on Russian Federation Land Reform," *Post-Soviet Geography*, 34, no. 3 (Mar. 1993), 211-17.

454. Pryor, Frederic L., "When Is Collectivization Reversible?" *Studies in Comparative Communism*, 24, no. 1 (Mar. 1991), 3-24.

455. Rabinovich, B., "Landed Property and Payment for Land During the Transition to a Market," *Problems of Economics*, 34, no. 6 (Oct. 1991), 61-69.

456. Reynolds, Sarah, "RSFSR Congress Puts Private Land Ownership on Hold," *SEEL: Soviet and East European Law*, 2, no. 2 (Mar. 1991), 8ff.

457. Rhodes, Mark, "Food Supply in the USSR," *Report on the USSR*, 3, no. 41 (11 Oct. 1991), 11-16.

458. Rodale, R., "A Land Without Farms," *Organic Gardening*, 35 (Nov. 1988), 21-23.

459. -----, "Soviet Gardening," *Organic Gardening*, 35 (Oct. 1988), 23-24.

460. Rose, Richard, and Yevgeniy Tikhomirov, "Who Grows Food in Russia and Eastern Europe?" *Post-Soviet Geography*, 34, no. 2 (Feb. 1993), 111-26.

461. Sallnow, John, "Perestroika and Farming Privatization," *Geographical Magazine*, 62 (Jan. 1990), 14-15.

462. Satter, David, "Why Russia Can't Feed Itself," *Reader's Digest*, 135 (Oct. 1989), 61-66.

463. Schmitt, Gunther, "The Rediscovery of Alexander Chayanov," *History of Political Economy*, 24, no. 4 (Winter 1992), 925ff.

464. Seim, D., "When Chrystal Speaks, Gorbachev Listens," *Farm Journal*, 111, no. 11 (Sept. 1987), 19-21.

465. Severin, Barbara S., "The 1992 Grain Harvest in Russia and the Republics," *Post-Soviet Geography*, 33, no. 9 (Sept. 1992), 557-68.

466. Shaposhnikov, A. N., "The Problem of Developing Independent Peasant Initiative in Russia," *International Social Science Journal*, 42, no. 2 (May 1990), 193-207.

467. Shmelev, G., "Property in Land: The Historical Aspect," *Problems of Economics*, 34, no. 6 (Oct. 1991), 48-60.

468. Stankievich, Walter, and Kathleen Mihalisko, "Private versus Collective Farms: The View from Belorussia," *Report on the USSR*, 2, no. 3 (19 Jan. 1990), 25-27.

469. Stebelsky, Ihor, "Restructuring Soviet Agriculture: Towards a Spatial Dimension," *Soviet Geography*, 31, no. 7 (Sept. 1990), 500-08.

470. Teague, Elizabeth, "New Incentives Lure Townspeople into the Fields," *Report on the USSR*, 2, no. 42 (19 Oct. 1990), 17-19.

471. Trimble, J., "Moscow's Bumper Crop of Troubles," *U.S. News & World Report*, 109 (27 Aug-3 Sept. 1990), 31-33.

472. US Department of Commerce, "Trade Watch: Agriculture Exports," *Business America*, 111, no. 22 (19 Nov. 1990), ii.

473. -----, "Trade Watch: U.S.-Soviet Grains Agreement," *Business America*, 111, no. 12 (18 June 1990), ii.

474. Van Atta, Don, "Back to the Future in the Soviet Countryside?" (Review Article), *Problems of Communism*, 40, no. 1-2 (Jan-Apr. 1991), 155-64.

475. -----, "Farms Declare `Grain Strikes'," *Report on the USSR*, 2, no. 8 (28 Feb. 1990), 9-11.

476. -----, "First Results of the `Stolypin' Land Reform in the RSFSR," *Report on the USSR*, 3, no. 29 (19 July 1991), 20-23.

477. -----, "'Full Scale, Like Collectivization, but Without Collectivization's Excesses': The Campaign to Introduce the Family and Lease Contract in Soviet Agriculture," *Comparative Economic Studies*, 32, no. 2 (Summer 1990), 109-43.

478. -----, "Ligachev Rallies Opposition to Land Reform," *Report on the USSR*, 2, no. 47 (23 Nov. 1990), 10-12.

479. -----, "Theorists of Agrarian *Perestroika*," *Soviet Economy*, 5, no. 1 (Jan-Mar. 1989), 70-99.

480. -----, "The USSR as a `Weak State': Agrarian Origins of Resistance to *Perestroika*" (Review Article), *World Politics*, 42, no. 1 (Oct. 1989), 129-49.

481. Vincent, G., "Kremlin Shuffle Brightens Ag Sales Prospects," *Successful Farming*, 86 (Dec. 1988), 12ff.

482. -----, "Soviet Farm Manager Goes for Profit," *Successful Farming*, 87 (Jan. 1989), 50.

483. Wadekin, Karl-Eugen, "Seasonal Fluctuations in Livestock Numbers and Meat Procurement," *Report on the USSR*, 3, no. 22 (31 May 1991), 4-6.

484. -----, "Soviet Agriculture in 1989: A Third Year of Near Stagnation," *Report on the USSR*, 2, no.7 (16 Feb. 1990), 5-8.

485. "A Wave of Change in Soviet Agriculture," *Successful Farming*, 88 (Feb. 1990), H4.

486. Wegren, Stephen K., "Agricultural Reform in the Non-chernozem Zone: The Case of Kostroma Oblast," *Post-Soviet Geography*, 33, no. 10 (Dec. 1992), 645-85.

487. -----, "Dilemmas of Agrarian Reform in the Soviet Union," *Soviet Studies*, 44, no. 1 (Jan. 1992), 3-36.

488. -----, "Food Prices in the USSR," *Report on the USSR*, 2, no. 12 (23 Mar. 1990), 13-15.

489. -----, "From Stalin to Gorbachev: The Role of the Soviet Communist Party in the Implementation of Agricultural Policy," *Studies in Comparative Communism*, 23, no. 2 (Summer 1990), 177-90.

490. -----, "Market Reform and Public Opinion," *Report on the USSR*, 2, no. 48 (30 Nov. 1990), 4-8.

491. -----, "Peasant Farming and Agrarian Reform in Russia," *Problems of Communism*, 41, no. 3 (May-June 1992), 107-21.

492. -----, "Private Agriculture in the Soviet Union under Gorbachev," *Soviet Union/Union Sovietique*, 16, no. 2-3 (1989), 105-43.

493. -----, "Private Agriculture in the USSR," *Report on the USSR*, 3, no. 12 (22 Mar. 1991), 10-12.

494. -----, "Regional Differences in Private Plot Production and Marketing: Central Asia and the Baltics," *Journal of Soviet Nationalities*, 2, no. 1 (Spring 1991), 118-38.

495. -----, "Rural Reform and Political Culture in Russia," *Europe-Asia Studies*, 46, no. 2 (1994), 215-42.

496. -----, "The Social Contract Reconsidered: Peasant-State Relations in the USSR," *Soviet Geography*, 32, no. 10 (Dec. 1991), 653-82.

497. -----, "Two Steps Forward, One Step Back: The Politics of an Emerging New Rural Social Policy in Russia," *Soviet and Post-Soviet Review*, 19, no. 1-3 (1992), 1-53.

498. Weickhardt, George G., "Gorbachev's Record on Economic Reform," *Soviet Union/ Union Sovietique*, 12, no. 3 (1985), 251-76.

499. Wiens, Thomas B., "Agriculture in the Soviet Union and China: Implications for Trade-Discussion," *American Journal of Agricultural Economics*, 67, no. 5 (Dec. 1985), 1063-66.

500. Zaslow, David, "Modernization of Soviet Agricultural Machine Building: The Example of Tractor Production," *Soviet Geography*, 30, no. 7 (Sept. 1989), 559-75.

V. Arts and Culture; Cinema; Theater; Music

BOOKS

501. Brown, Matthew Cullerne, and Brandon Taylor, eds., *Art of the Soviets: Painting, Sculpture and Architecture in a One-Party State, 1917-1992* (Manchester: Manchester University Press, distributed by St. Martin's Press, 1993).

502. Bushnell, John, *Moscow Graffiti: Language and Subculture* (Boston: Unwin Hyman, 1990).

503. Choldin, Marianna Tax, and Maurice Friedberg, eds., *The Red Pencil: Artists, Scholars and Censors in the USSR* (Boston: Unwin Hyman, 1989).

504. Dugin, Evgeni, comp., *Perestroika and Development of Culture: Literature, Theatre and Cinema* (New Delhi: Sterling, 1989).

505. Galichenko, Nicholas, and Robert Arlington, eds., *Glasnost-Soviet Cinema Responds* (Austin: University of Texas Press, 1991).

506. Goldfarb, Jeffrey C., *Beyond Glasnost': The Post-Totalitarian Mind* (Chicago: University of Chicago Press, 1989).

507. Horton, Andrew, and Michael Brashinsky, *The Zero Hour: Glasnost and Soviet Cinema in Transition* (Princeton: Princeton

University Press, 1992).

508. Kostrzewa, Robert, ed., *Between East and West: Writings from "Kultura"* (New York: Hill & Wang, 1990).

509. Lahusen, Thomas, with Gene Kuperman, eds., *Late Soviet Culture: From Perestroika to Novostroika* (Durham, NC: Duke University Press, 1993).

510. Laqueur, Walter, *Soviet Realities: Culture and Politics from Stalin to Gorbachev* (New Brunswick, NJ: Transaction, 1990).

511. Lauridsen, Inger Thorup, and Per Dalgard, eds., *The Beat Generation and the Russian New Wave* (Ann Arbor: Ardis, 1990).

512. Lawton, Anna, *Kinoglasnost: Soviet Cinema in Our Time* (New York: Cambridge University Press, 1993).

513. Likhachev, Dmitrii S., *Reflections on Russia* (Boulder, CO: Westview Press, 1991).

514. Litvinov, Victor, *The Posters of Glasnost' and Perestroika* (New York: Penguin Books, 1989).

515. Matejka, Ladislav, ed., *Cross Currents 11: A Yearbook of Central European Culture* (New Haven: Yale University Press, 1992).

516. Mukhametshin, Boris, *Gorbyshow: Anti-Posters for Our Time* (Riverside, CA: Xenos Books, 1991, distributed by Borgo Press).

517. Nove, Alec, *Glasnost' in Action: Cultural Renaissance in Russia* (Boston: Unwin Hyman, 1989).

518. Petrie, Graham, and Ruth Dwyer, eds., *Before the Wall Came Down: Soviet and East European Filmmakers Working in the West* (Lanham, MD: University Press of America, 1990).

519. *The Quest for Self-Expression: Painting in Moscow and Leningrad, 1965-1990* (Columbus, OH: Columbus Museum of Art, distributed by the University of Washington Press, 1990).

520. Ramet, Sabrina Petra, *Rocking the State: Rock Music and Politics in Eastern Europe and Russia* (Boulder, CO: Westview Press, 1994).

521. Ross, David A., ed., *Between Spring and Summer: Soviet Conceptual Art in the Era of Late Communism* (Cambridge, MA: MIT Press, 1990).

522. Ryback, Timothy W., *Rock Around the Bloc: A History of Rock Music in Eastern Europe and the Soviet Union* (New York: Oxford University Press, 1990).

523. Siefert, Marsha, ed., *Mass Culture and Perestroika in the Soviet Union* (New York: Oxford University Press, 1991).

524. Solomon, Andrew, *The Irony Tower: Soviet Artists in a Time of Glasnost* (New York: Knopf, 1991).

525. Stites, Richard, *Russian Popular Culture: Entertainment and Society since 1900* (Cambridge: Cambridge University Press, 1992).

526. US Congress. Commission on Security and Cooperation in Europe. *Implementation of the Helsinki Accords: Restrictions on Artistic Freedom in the Soviet Union; and the Budapest Cultural Forum: Hearings.* 99th Congress, 29 Oct.-11 Dec. 1985 (Washington, DC: Government Printing Office, 1986).

527. *Voices of Freedom: Polish Women Artists and the Avant-Garde* (Catalog) (Washington, DC: National Museum of Women in the Arts, 1991).

528. White, Anne, *De-Stalinization and the House of Culture: Declining State Control over Leisure in the USSR, Poland and Hungary, 1953-89* (New York: Routledge, 1990).

ARTICLES

529. "After the Revolution: Art in Eastern Europe," *ARTnews*, 89, no. 5 (May 1990), 151.

530. Akinsha, Konstantin, "After the Coup: Art for Art's Sake?" *ARTnews*, 91 (Jan. 1992), 108-13.

531. -----, "A Soviet-German Exchange of War Treasures?" *ARTnews*, 90, no. 5 (May 1991), 134-39.

532. -----, "The Turmoil over Soviet War Treasures," *ARTnews*, 90, no. 10 (Dec. 1991), 110-15.

533. -----, "Two Million Rubles in Three Days," *ARTnews*, 90, no. 10 (Dec. 1991), 29.

534. -----, "Who Owns the Hermitage?" *ARTnews*, 90, no. 9 (Nov. 1991), 56ff.

535. -----, and Grigorii Kozlov, "The Soviet War Treasures: A Growing Controversy," *ARTnews*, 90, no. 7 (Sept. 1991), 112-19.

536. Antic, Oxana, "Museums versus the Church," *Report on the USSR*, 3, no. 33 (16 Aug. 1991), 18-20.

537. Bahry, Romana, and Alexander Rudiachenko, "Rock and Roll Always Lives: The Rise of Rock and Roll in Soviet Ukraine," *Compass: A Jesuit Journal*, 9, no. 1 (1991), 45-49.

538. Barnett, A., "Perestroika against Pessimism," *New Statesman*, 115 (6 May 1988), 16-18.

539. Barol, B., "Bourgeois Blues," *Newsweek*, 105 (25 Mar. 1985), 46.

540. Beck, Ernest, "Hungary: After the Soft Revolution," *ARTnews*, 90, no. 2 (Feb. 1991), 96-98.

541. Berger, Maurice, "Of Cold Wars and Curators," *Artforum*, 27, no. 6 (Feb. 1989), 86-92.

542. Bogemskaya, Ksenila, "The Open-Air Market for Art: The Commercial Expression of Creativity," *Journal of Communication*, 41, no. 2 (Spring 1991), 19-30.

543. Bogomolov, Yuri, "The Revitalization of the Soviet Film Industry," *Journal of Communication*, 41, no. 2 (Spring 1991), 39-45.

544. "Bold Signal: A Film Confronts Stalin's Legacy," *Newsweek*, 109 (5 Jan. 1987), 20-21.

545. Bonet, Pilar, "Soviet Art for Export," *World Press Review*,

34 (Dec. 1987), 60.

546. Bowlt, John E., "Perspective: How *Glasnost'* Is It?" *ARTnews*, 87, no. 9 (Nov. 1988), 216.

547. ----, "Rehabilitating the Russian Avant-Garde," *ARTnews*, 88 (Feb. 1989), 116-19.

548. Boyes, Roger, "Poland: Getting Closer to the Customer," *ARTnews*, 90, no. 2 (Feb. 1991), 94-96.

549. Brashinsky, Michael, "The Ant Hill in the Year of the Dragon," *New Orleans Review*, 17, no. 1 (Spring 1990), 74-78.

550. Braun, Kazimierz, "The Underground Theater in Poland under Martial Law During the Last Years of Communism," *Polish Review*, 38, no. 2 (1993), 159-86.

551. Breazeale, H., "Trailblazers of the US/USSR Dance Exchange," *Dance Magazine*, 61 (Apr. 1987), 70-72.

552. Budiak, Ludmilla M., "'We Cannot Live This Way': Reflections on the State of Contemporary Soviet Film," *Film Quarterly*, 44, no. 2 (Winter 1990-91), 28-33.

553. Bushnell, John, "An Introduction to the Soviet *Sistema*: The Advent of Counterculture and Subculture" (Review Article), *Slavic Review*, 49, no. 2 (Summer 1990), 272-77.

554. Chetverikov, Nikolai N., "Samizdat without the Halo: A Commentary on the Role of Culture in *Perestroika*," *Perestroika Annual*, 1 (1988), 237-51.

555. Christensen, Peter G. , "Tengiz Abuladze's *Repentance*: Despair in the Age of Perestroika," *Soviet and East European Drama, Theatre and Film* (8 Dec. 1988), 2ff.

556. Chtiguel, Olga F., "Czechoslovak Theatre During the Velvet Revolution," *Soviet and East European Performance*, 10, no. 2 (Summer 1990), 21-26.

557. ----, "Without Theatre, the Czechoslovak Revolution Could Not Have Been Won," *TDR: The Drama Review*, 34, no. 3 (Fall 1990), 88-96.

558. Clark, Andrew, "Coping with Freedom," *World & I* (Dec. 1990), 164-69.

559. Colton, Timothy J., "The Cultural Factor and the Soviet Future," *Studies in Comparative Communism*, 20 (Autumn-Winter 1987), 287-90.

560. "Communist Party Central Committee Discusses Ways to Prevent Commercialization of Culture," *Contemporary Review*, 258, no. 1500 (Jan. 1991), 8-11.

561. Condee, Nancy, and Vladimir Padunov, "The Cultural Combat Zone: Where Is the DMZ?" *Soviet Union/Union Sovietique*, 15, no. 2-3 (1989), 167-85.

562. ----, "The Frontiers of Soviet Culture: Reaching the Limits?" *Harriman Institute Forum*, 1, no. 5 (May 1988), 1-8.

563. ----, "Reforming Soviet Culture/Retrieving Soviet History," *Nation*, 244 (13 June 1987), 815-20.

564. Daly, Conor, "An Interview with Tenghiz Abuladze," *Center for Slavic and East European Studies Newsletter* (Oct. 1987), 1ff.

565. Domberg, John, "East Germany: After the Wall," *ARTnews*, 89, no. 5 (May 1990), 160-63.

566. ----, "Ludwig Looks East," *ARTnews*, 87 (Dec. 1988), 40.

567. Dunlop, John B., "Soviet Cultural Politics," *Problems of Communism*, 36, no. 6 (Nov-Dec. 1987), 34-56.

568. Ebon, M., "The Rise and Fall of a Literary Commissar," *Far Eastern Economic Review*, 140 (7 Apr. 1988), 46.

569. Elsom, John, "Coping with Glasnost," *World & I* (Jan. 1990), 258-61.

570. ----, "Theater: Glasnost Comes to Bulgaria," *World & I* (Mar. 1990), 156-61.

571. ----, "Together Again," *World & I* (Dec. 1990), 154-59.

572. Emerson, Caryl, "Glasnost' in Russian Music: The Musorgsky Jubilee During a Time of Trouble," *Slavic Review*, 51, no. 3 (Fall 1992), 544-56.

573. Esterow, Milton, "Can a Socialist Win in a Free Market? Pavel Khoroshilov as Leo Castelli," *ARTnews*, 88, no. 7 (Sept. 1989), 51ff.

574. Fairbanks, C. H., Jr., "Gorbachev's Cultural Revolution," *Commentary*, 88 (Aug. 1989), 23-27.

575. Ferris, Byron, "Soviet Graphic Design," *Communication Arts*, 33, no. 1 (Mar-Apr. 1991), 34-43.

576. Flatow, Sheryl, "Ananiashvili and Liepa at the New York City Ballet: *Glasnost'* in Action," *Dance Magazine*, 62, no. 6 (June 1988), 48-50.

577. Forest, J., "Christ Meets Stalin in Soviet-Made Film," *Christian Century*, 104 (12-19 Aug. 1987), 676-77.

578. Fraser, Hugh, "No Shortages at USSR Film Mart," *Variety*, 345, no. 8 (2 Dec. 1991), 65-66.

579. ----, "Soviet Breakup Cuts Film Industry Loose," *Variety*, 345, no. 13 (13 Jan. 1992), 65-66.

580. Friedberg, Maurice, "The Cultural Scene in the USSR: Winter, 1991," *Studies in Comparative Communism*, 24, no. 2 (June 1991), 225ff.

581. Friedrich, Otto, "Can the Bolshoi Adapt to the Times?" *Time*, 138 (8 July 1991), 64-65.

582. Gambrell, J., "*Perestroika* Shock," *Art in America*, 77 (Feb. 1989), 124ff.

583. ----, "The Perils of *Perestroika*," *Art in America*, 78 (Mar. 1990), 46ff.

584. Garafola, Lynn, "Vladimir Vasiliev: Champion of Perestroika," *Dance Magazine*, 64 (Nov. 1990), 50-53.

585. Gardner, Colin, "Brave New World," *Artforum*, 29, no. 6 (Feb. 1991), 109-14.

586. Garside, A., "Jazz Me Those Soviet Blues," *Down Beat*, 55

(Apr. 1988), 12.

587. "*Glasnost* Rock," *Rolling Stone* (14-28 Dec. 1989), 58-59.

588. Goodman, Walter, "Communism at the Movies," *New Leader* (11-15 Jan. 1988), 15-16.

589. Gray, L. V., "Americans Dance in Uzbekistan," *Dance Magazine*, 62 (Sept. 1988), 10.

590. Grenier, Richard, "Russia's *Cerceau*: The Loneliness of the Long-Distance Humanist," *World & I*, 6, no. 1 (Jan. 1991), 152-55.

591. Hammond, Pamela, "Czech Graphics: Creativity in the Shadow of Political Oppression," *ARTnews*, 90, no. 8 (Oct. 1991), 144.

592. Hardison, Londre Felicia, "Impressions of Theatre in a Changing Political Climate: Warsaw, Berlin and Budapest," *Soviet and East European Performance*, 10, no. 1 (Spring 1990), 20-26.

593. Hejma, Ondrej, "Czechoslovakia: Tom Velvet," *ARTnews*, 90, no. 2 (Feb. 1990), 98-100.

594. Hochfield, Sylvia, "Soviet Art: New Freedom, New Directions," *ARTnews*, 86, no. 8 (Oct. 1987), 102-07.

595. -----, "Soviet Union: Reinventing an Art World," *ARTnews*, 90, no. 2 (Feb. 1991), 90-93.

596. Horn, M., and J. Trimble, "Moscow's Cultural Revolution," *U.S. News and World Report*, 101 (15 Dec. 1986), 68-70.

597. "How Can You Create While Standing at Attention?" *Soviet Law and Government*, 28, no. 1 (Summer 1989), 24-36.

598. Hughes, L., "The West Comes to Russian Architecture," *History Today*, 36 (Sept. 1986), 27-34.

599. Hunt, M., "Whither Glasnost?" *Dance Magazine*, 62 (May 1988), 34.

600. Huyssen, Andreas, "After the Wall: The Failure of German Intellectuals," *New German Critique*, no. 52 (Winter 1991), 109-43.

601. Ilyashov, Anatoli, "Perestroika from Below, Written and Directed by Daniel J. Walkowitz," *American Historical Review*, 96, no. 4 (Oct. 1991), 1138-40.

602. Johnson, B. D., "*Glasnost* on Screen," *Maclean's*, 101 (26 Sept. 1988), 62.

603. Johnson, Robert, "Reporter's Notebook: Glasnost Glitch," *Dance Magazine*, 66 (Mar. 1992), 44-50.

604. Kamoouh, Claude, "The End of National Culture in Eastern Europe," *Telos*, no. 89 (Fall 1991), 132-37.

605. Kavolis, Vytautas, "The Second Lithuanian Revival: Culture as Performance," *Lituanus*, 37, no. 2 (Summer 1991), 52-64.

606. Kenez, Peter, "The Cultural Revolution in Cinema," *Slavic Review*, 47, no. 3 (Fall 1988), 414-33.

607. -----, "Now Playing in Moscow: `Gorbashow' and the Flicks," *New Leader* (6 Apr. 1987), 10-12.

608. Khaniutin, Alexei, "Teenage Samizdat: Song-Album Scrapbooks as Mass Communication," *Journal of Communication*, 41, no. 2 (Spring 1991), 55-85.

609. Kniazeva, Marina L., "Theater on the Market," *Journal of Communication*, 41, no. 2 (Spring 1991), 31-38.

610. Kolesnik, Svetlana, "Advertising and Cultural Politics," *Journal of Communication*, 41, no. 2 (Spring 1991), 46-54.

611. Kouymjian, Dickran, "The Status of Artists and Intellectuals in Soviet Armenia," *Armenian Review*, 42, no. 3 (Autumn 1989), 53-62.

612. Kroll, J., "The Pas de *Perestroika*," *Newsweek*, 110 (14 Dec. 1987), 42-43.

613. Krukones, James, "The Glasnost Film Festival" (Review Article), *American Historical Review*, 96, no. 4 (Oct. 1991), 1134-38.

614. -----, "Glasnost on the Cuyahoga: The First Cleveland Film Conference," *Soviet and East European Performance*, 11, no. 1 (Spring 1991), 61-65.

615. Kurti, Laszlo, "Rocking the State: Youth and Rock Music Culture in Hungary," *East European Politics and Societies*, 5, no. 3 (Fall 1991), 483-513.

616. Laber, Jeri, "The Moscow Book Fair: Glasnost Has Its Limits" *New York Times Book Review* (11 Oct. 1987), 13-14.

617. Law, Alma, "Revolution in the Soviet Theater," *Harriman Institute Forum*, 2, no. 7 (July 1989), 1-8.

618. Lawton, Anna, "Soviet Cinema Four Years Later," *Wide Angle*, 12, no. 4 (Oct. 1990), 8-25.

619. London, John, and Joanna Harris, "New Battlegrounds or Peace in Our Time: The Theatre and Literature under Ceausescu," *Soviet and East European Performance*, 10, no. 3 (Winter 1990), 19-20.

620. I. Lukshin, "Mass Culture and Soviet Fine Arts," *Soviet Education*, 33, no. 5 (May 1991), 35-41.

621. Mandel, H., "The State of Jazz in the Soviet Union," *Down Beat*, 55 (Sept. 1988), 25-28.

622. Marcus, Naomi, "Glasnost's First Gold Record," *Mother Jones*, 13, no. 8 (Oct. 1988), 30-31.

623. -----, "Let Freedom Rock," *Scholastic Update*, 122 (18 May 1990), 14-15.

624. Marranca, Bonnie, and Gautam Dasgupta, "The Culture of Perestroika," *Performing Arts Magazine*, 11, no. 3; 12, no. 1 (1988-89), 205-10.

625. "Mass Culture and Perestroika in the Soviet Union," *Journal of Communications*, 41, no. 2 (Spring 1991), 7-200.

626. Medvedev, Roy, "Meetings and Conversations with Aleksandr Tvardovskii," *Michigan Quarterly Review*, 28, no. 4 (Fall 1989), 604-38.

627. ----, Richard Lourie "Bits of Light in a Gray World: Cultural Life in the Soviet Union," *Dissent*, 34, no. 1 (Winter 1987), 46-51.

628. ----, "Cultural Revival in the Soviet Union: Report from Moscow," *Dissent*, 35, no. 1 (Winter 1988), 15-20.

629. Meisler, S. "Casting a *Glasnost* Glow on Once-obscured Artists," *Smithsonian*, 20 (Dec. 1989), 130ff.

630. Menashe, Louis, "Festivals: Documentary Films in St. Petersburg," *Soviet and Post-Soviet Review*, 20, no. 2-3 (1993), 241-44.

631. ----, "Glasnost in the Soviet Cinema," *Cineaste*, 16, no. 1-2 (1987-88), 28-33.

632. Messener, Azary, "Linguistic Relativity and Perestroika," *Etc.*, 46 (Winter 1989), 299-305.

633. Milova, Maya, "Soviet Art Market," *International Affairs* (Moscow), no. 5 (May 1991), 72-76.

634. Misiano, Victor, and Jane Bobko, "Spiritual Materialism, Material Spiritualism: The New Russian Art Market," *Arts Magazine*, 66, no. 5 (Jan. 1992), 50-53.

635. "Moscow Digs `Cats': Scalpers Get Busy," *Variety*, 331, no. 5 (25 May 1988), 1-2.

636. "Mother Russia's New Red Carpet," *U.S. News & World Report*, 102 (2 Feb. 1987), 10.

637. Mulligan, Tom, "Romania: The Standards of Change," *ARTnews*, 90, no. 2 (Feb. 1991), 100-01.

638. Muratov, Sergei Aleksandrovich, "An Alternative View," *Journal of Communication*, 41, no. 2 (Spring 1991), 16-17.

639. Murrell, G. D., "When the Desert Blooms: Cultural Developments under Gorbachev," *Survey*, 30 (Oct. 1988), 59-78.

640. Nepomnyashchy, Catharine Theimer, "Perestroika and the Soviet Creative Unions," in John O. Norman, ed., *New Perspectives on Russian and Soviet Artistic Culture* (New York: St. Martin's Press, 1994), 131-51.

641. Olcott, Anthony, "Readers and Writers in the USSR," *Soviet Union/ Union Sovietique*, 15, no. 2-3 (1988), 201-18.

642. Olson, Alan M., "Glasnost and Enlightenment," *Philosophy Today*, 34 (Summer 1990), 99-110.

643. Orlova, Irina, "Notes from the Underground: The Emergence of Rock Music Culture," *Journal of Communication*, 41, no. 2 (Spring 1991), 66-71.

644. Oseka, Andrzej, "The Free Market and Cultural Freedom," *Uncaptive Minds*, 32, no. 3 (May-July 1990), 28-30.

645. Oslzly, Petr, "On Stage with the Velvet Revolution," *TDR: The Drama Review*, 34, no. 3 (Fall 1990), 97-108.

646. O'Steen, Kathleen, "Glasnost So Far a Thin Wedge, But Soviet Theater Loosening," *Variety*, 330, no. 11 (6 Apr. 1988), 70.

647. Pehe, Jiri, "Culture Under New Economic Conditions," *Report on Eastern Europe*, 1, no. 36 (7 Sept. 1990), 11-14.

648. Pellicani, Luciano, "The Cultural War Between East and West," *Telos*, no. 89 (Fall 1991), 127-31.

649. Perlmutter, Archie, and Ruth Perlmutter, "Czech Cinema After the Revolution," *Ukrainian Quarterly*, 47, no. 1 (Spring 1991), 34-42.

650. Perlmutter, Ruth, and Archie Perlmutter, "East European Films after *Glasnost*," *East European Quarterly*, 24, no. 1 (Spring 1990), 101-12.

651. Pintos, V., "Rocking the Musical Boat," *World Press Review*, 37 (Feb. 1990), 40.

652. Protsman, Ferdinand, "East Berlin: Beginning Anew," *ARTnews*, 89, no. 2 (Feb. 1990), 67.

653. Ramet, Pedro, and Sergei Zamascikov, "The Soviet Rock Scene," *Journal of Popular Culture*, 24, no. 1 (Summer 1990), 146-74.

654. Raskin, Victor, "Casualty of Glasnost: Soviet Jokes and Political Humor," *World & I*, 6, no. 4 (Apr. 1991), 646-57.

655. Reed, S. K., "Stas Namin and Ludmila Senchina Reign Over the Pop Scene, While Rock's Underground Rumbles," *People Weekly*, 27 (6 Apr. 1987), 46ff.

656. "A Return to Reason: Selling the Russian Heritage," *ARTnews*, 90, no. 1 (Jan. 1991), 39-40.

657. Rhodes, M., "Cultural Exchange within the Global Village," *Horizon*, 30 (Dec. 1987), 9.

658. Rinehart, D., "Rebels with a Balance: Soviet Artists and Athletes Want to Keep More of the Dollars They Earn Abroad," *Maclean's*, 102 (3 July 1989), 20-21.

659. Robinson, Harlow, "Facing the Music: *Perestroika* and the High Arts," *Soviet Union/Union Sovietique*, 15, no. 2-3 (1988), 151-66.

660. Romanenko, Alla, "Perestroika, Glasnost and Theatre," *Soviet Literature*, no. 9 (1988), 184-89.

661. Ryback, Timothy W., "Raisa Gorbachev Is An Elvis Fan, and Other Reasons Why Scholars Should Study the Role of Rock in Eastern Europe," *Chronicle of Higher Education*, 36, no. 38 (6 June 1990), B1ff.

662. ----, "Red Suede Shoes: Gorbo, Get on Down," *New Republic* (9-16 Jan. 1989), 13-14.

663. Rudall, Nicholas, "Restructuring Lithuanian Theater," *World & I*, 6, no. 8 (Aug. 1991), 202-07.

664. Rzhevsky, Nicholas, "Soviet Film," *Soviet and East European Performance*, 11, no. 1 (Spring 1991), 58-60.

665. Sanders, Ivan, "The Quest for Central Europe," *Wilson Quarterly*, 14, no. 2 (Spring 1990), 26-36.

666. Schechter, Joel, *et al.*, eds., "Soviet Theater under Glasnost," *Theater*, New Haven, 20, no. 3 (Fall 1988), 1-96.

667. Schindehette, S., "*Glasnost* Glitters as Ballerina Natalia Makarova Dances Again with Russia's Kirov Ballet," *People Weekly*, 30 (22 Aug. 1988), 42-44.

668. Schlechner, Richard, "After the Fall of the Wall," *TDR: The Drama Review*, 34, no. 3 (Fall 1990), 7-9.

669. Schmemann, Serge, "Glasnost: Between Hope and History," *New York Times Book Review*, 92 (26 Apr. 1987), 12-13.

670. Schmidt-Hauer, C., "New Cultural Freedom," *World Press Review*, 33 (Dec. 1986), 15-16.

671. Self, Gloria, "Mission to Moscow," *San Diego*, 41, no. 11 (Sept. 1989), 108ff.

672. Shchepotinnik, Peter, "With Perestroika, without Tarkovsky," *New Orleans Review*, 17, no. 1 (Spring 1990), 79-83.

673. Shvidkoi, Mikhail, "The Effect of Glasnost: Soviet Theater from 1985 to 1989," *Theater, New Haven*, 20, no. 3 (Fall 1989), 7-12.

674. Smelyansky, Anatoly, "`Glasnost' Produces a Cultural Revolution: `Our Country and Theater Live in Anticipation'," *World Press Review*, 37 (Feb. 1990), 32-34.

675. Smith, Valerie, "The Czech Point: Finding a Third Way," *Artforum*, 29, no. 5 (Jan. 1991), 82-88.

676. Solomon, Andrew, "The Art of *Perestroika*," Part 2, *Artforum*, 27, no. 9 (May 1989), 16-17.

677. -----, "Vanguard Artists," *World Press Review*, 37 (Feb. 1990), 38.

678. -----, "What in the World: The Art of *Perestroika*," *Artforum*, 27, no. 3 (Nov. 1988), 9-11.

679. "The Soul Appears," *Economist*, 316 (21 July 1990), 91-92.

680. "Soviet Film, Music Industries Embrace Perestroika," *Variety*, 337, no. 2 (Oct. 1989), 286ff.

681. Sperling, Valerie, "Peeking Behind the Celluloid Curtain: Glasnost and Explicit Sex in the Soviet Union," *Journal of Popular Film and Television*, 18 (Winter 1991), 154-63.

682. Steinmetz, L., "The Four Soviet Cultures," *National Review*, 39 (23 Oct. 1987), 32ff.

683. Stites, Richard, "Soviet Popular Culture in the Gorbachev Era," *Harriman Institute Forum*, 2, no. 3 (Mar. 1989), 1-8.

684. Taylor, Markland, "Soviet Union Spearheads Reform as Control Passes to Artists," *Variety*, 334, no. 12 (12 Apr. 1989), 105-06.

685. Thoron, Elise, and Afanasy Sablinsky, eds., "Soviet Theater under Glasnost," *Theater, New Haven*, 20, no. 3 (Fall 1989), 1-96.

686. Thorson, Alice, "The Art of Diplomacy," *ARTnews*, 87 (Mar. 1988), 32.

687. -----, "The Soviet Art World Cuts Loose," *World & I* (Dec. 1990), 206-17.

688. Ulyanov, Mikhail A., "Theatre and *Perestroika*," *Perestroika Annual*, 1 (1988), 167-84.

689. "Underground," *New Yorker* (10 Dec. 1990), 44-45.

690. Vamos, Miklos, "Hungary for American Pop," *Nation*, 252 (25 Mar. 1991), 374-76.

691. Vaucher, Andrea, "Hollywood on the Volga," *American Film*, 16, no. 4 (Apr. 1991), 34-37.

692. Walker, Richard W., "Gavel *Glasnost'*," *ARTnews*, 87, no. 6 (Summer 1988), 15-16.

693. -----, "The Making of a Market," *ARTnews*, 88, no. 3 (Mar. 1989), 138-43.

694. -----, "Profit Sharing Soviet Style," *ARTnews*, 88, no. 3 (Mar. 1989), 41.

695. Wallach, A., "Marketing *Perestroika*," *Art in America*, 77 (Apr. 1989), 53ff.

696. "Western Art in Moscow," *Economist*, 309 (1 Oct. 1988), 102-03.

697. White, Ann, "Optimists and Oblomovs in Gorbachev's House of Culture," *Soviet Union/Union Sovietique*, 14, no. 2 (1987), no. 2, 181-96.

698. Willis, M. E., "Kiroviana: The Glasnost Difference," *Dance Magazine*, 63 (July 1989), 36-41.

699. Wishnevsky, Julia, "The Arts: Crisis or Renewal?" *Report on the USSR*, 3, no. 1 (4 Jan. 1991), 1-3.

700. -----, "Cultural Politics in 1991," *Report on the USSR*, 3, no. 51-52 (20 Dec. 1991), 7-11.

701. Woll, Josephine, "Glasnost' and Soviet Culture," *Problems of Communism*, 38, no. 6 (Nov-Dec. 1989), 40-50.

702. -----, "Soviet Cinema: A Day of Repentance," *Dissent*, 35, no. 2 (Spring 1988), 167-69.

703. Woolgar, Claudia, "The Rise and Fall of Gorbachev" (Play), *World & I* (Dec. 1990), 160-63.

704. Yevtushenko, Yevgeny, "A Rebirth of Soviet Arts," *World Press Review*, 34 (Feb. 1987), 26-28.

705. Young, Cathy, "Black Beauty," *World & I*, 6, no. 10 (Oct. 1991), 222-27.

706. Young, Deborah, "Brave New World Means New Deals for Studios," *Variety*, 343, no. 13 (8 July 1991), 40-41.

707. -----, "New Soviet Film Companies Flock to Croissette," *Variety*, 343, no. 6 (20 May 1991), 6.

708. -----, "Soviet Showbiz Future Looks Rosy," *Variety*, 344, no. 8 (2 Sept. 1991), 1-2.

709. Young, Pamela, "Culture and *Glasnost*," *Maclean's*, 102 (31 July 1989), 42-43.

710. -----, "A Dance for Detente," *Maclean's*, 100 (Feb. 1987) 74.

711. Yurieff, Michael, "Soviet and American Scholars Gather at

Harvard Theatre Collection," *Soviet and East European Performance*, 11, no. 2 (Summer 1991), 19-21.

712. Zakharov, Mark A., "Nostalgia for Meyerhold," *Perestroika Annual*, 2 (1989), 233-49.

713. Zassoursky, Yassen N., "Mass Culture as Market Culture," *Journal of Communication*, 41, no. 2 (Spring 1991), 13-18.

714. Zinn, L., "*Glasnost* in the Galleries: The Surge in Soviet Art," *Business Week* (15 May 1989), 157.

715. Zvereva, Mariya, "The Burden of Freedom," *World & I*, 6, no. 5 (May 1991), 176-81.

VI. Autobiographies, Biographies and Memoirs
BOOKS

716. Arbatov, Georgy, *The System: An Insider's Life in Soviet Politics* (New York: Time Books, 1992).

717. Boldin, Valery, *Ten Years That Shook the World: The Gorbachev Era as Witnessed by His Chief of Staff* (New York: Basic Books, 1994).

718. Bonner, Yelena, *Alone Together* (New York: Alfred A. Knopf, 1986).

719. -----, *Mothers and Daughters* (New York: Knopf, 1992).

720. Bourne, Peter G., *Fidel: A Biography of Fidel Castro* (New York: Dodd, Mead, 1986).

721. Butson, Thomas G., *Gorbachev: A Biography* (New York: Stein & Day, 1985).

722. Daniloff, Nicholas, *Two Lives, One Russia* (Boston: Houghton Mifflin, 1988).

723. Doder, Dusko, and Louise Branson, *Gorbachev: Heretic in the Kremlin* (New York: Viking, 1990).

724. Drell, Sidney D., and Sergei P. Kapitza, eds., *Sakharov Remembered: A Tribute by Friends and Colleagues* (New York: American Institute of Physics, 1991).

725. Fischer, Mary Ellen, *Nicolae Ceausescu: A Study in Political Leadership* (Boulder, CO: Lynne Rienner, 1989).

726. Gilbert, Martin, *Shcharansky: Hero of Our Time* (New York: Viking, 1986).

727. Gorbachev, Raisa, *I Hope* (New York: Harper Collins, 1991).

728. Gromyko, Andrei, *Memoirs*, trans. by Harold Shukman (New York: Doubleday, 1990).

729. Havel, Vaclav, *Letters to Olga* (New York: Knopf, 1989).

730. -----, *Open Letters: Selected Writings, 1965-90* (New York: Vintage, 1992).

731. -----, *Summer Meditations* (New York: Vintage 1993).

732. -----, and Karel Hvizdala, *Disturbing the Peace: A Conversation with Karel Hvizdala*, trans. by Paul Wilson (New York: Knopf, 1990).

733. Jurgens, Urda, *Raisa: The 1st Lady of the Soviet Union*, trans. by Sylvia Clayton (New York: Summit Books, 1990).

734. Kapuscinski, Ryszard, *Imperium* (New York: Knopf, 1993).

735. Khrushchev, Nikita S., *Khrushchev Remembers: The Glasnost Tapes* (Boston: Little, Brown & Co., 1990).

736. Kurski, Jaroslaw, *Lech Walesa: Democrat or Dictator?* (Boulder, CO: Westview Press, 1993).

737. Ligachev, Yegor, *Inside Gorbachev's Kremlin: The Memoirs of Yegor Ligachev* (New York: Pantheon Books, 1993).

738. Medvedev, Zhores A., new ed. *Gorbachev* (New York: W. W. Norton, 1991).

739. Morrison, John, *Mikhail S. Gorbachev: An Intimate Biography* (New York: Time Books, 1988).

740. -----, *Boris Yeltsin: From Bolshevik to Democrat* (New York: Dutton, 1991).

741. Narkiewicz, Olga A., *Soviet Leaders: From the Cult of Personality to Collective Rule* (New York: St. Martin's Press, 1986).

742. Nitze, Paul H., with Ann M. Smith and Steven L. Rearden, *From Hiroshima to Glasnost': At the Center of Decision: A Memoir* (New York: G. Weidenfeld, 1989).

743. Pozner, Vladimir, *Parting with Illusions* (New York: Atlantic Monthly Press, 1990).

744. Quayle, Dan, *Standing Firm: A Vice-Presidential Memoir* (New York: HarperCollins, 1994).

745. Reagan, Nancy, *My Turn* (New York: Random House, 1989).

746. Reagan, Ronald, *An American Life* (New York: Simon and Schuster, 1990).

747. Sakharov, Andrei, *Memoirs* (New York: Knopf, 1990).

748. -----, *Moscow and Beyond, 1986-1989* (New York: Knopf, 1991).

749. Sheehy, Gail, *Gorbachev: The Making of the Man Who Shook the World* (London: Heinemann, 1991).

750. Shevardnadze, Eduard, *The Future Belongs to Freedom* (London: Sinclair-Stevenson, 1991).

751. Shultz, George P., *Turmoil and Triumph: My Years as Secretary of State* (New York: Scribner's, 1993).

752. Sobchak, Anatoly, *For a New Russia: The Mayor of St. Petersburg's Own Story of the Struggle for Justice and Democracy* (New York: Free Press, 1991).

753. Solovyov, Vladimir, and Elena Klepikova, *Boris Yeltsin: A Political Biography* (New York: G. P. Putnam's Sons, 1992).

754. Sudoplatov, Pavel, and Anatoli Sudoplatov, *Special Tasks: The Memoirs of an Unwanted Witness-A Soviet Spymaster*

(Boston: Little, Brown and Co., 1994).

755. Talbott, Strobe, *The Master of the Game: Paul Nitze and the Nuclear Peace* (New York: Vintage Books, 1989).

756. Thatcher, Margaret, *The Downing Street Years* (New York: HarperCollins, 1993), esp. 450-85 and chapter 26: "The World Turned Right Side Up," 768-815.

757. Walesa, Lech, *A Way of Hope* (New York: Henry Holt & Co., 1987).

758. Weinberger, Caspar W., *Fighting for Peace: Seven Critical Years in the Pentagon* (New York: Warner Books, 1990).

759. Yanowitch, Murray, ed., *A Voice of Reform: Tatiana I. Zaslavskaia* (Armonk, NY: M. E. Sharpe, 1989).

760. Yeltsin, Boris, *Against the Grain: An Autobiography* (New York: Summit Books, 1990).

761. -----, *The Struggle for Russia* (New York: Times Books, 1994).

762. Zemtsov, Ilya, *Chernenko, the Last Bolshevik: The Soviet Union on the Eve of Perestroika* (New Brunswick, NJ: Transaction Publishers, 1989).

763. -----, and John Farrar, *Gorbachev: The Man and the System* (New Brunswick, NJ: Transaction Publishers, 1989).

ARTICLES

764. Balina, Marian, "The Autobiographies of Glasnost: The Question of Genre in Russian Autobiographical Memoirs of the 1980s," *Auto-Biography Studies*, 7, no. 1 (Spring 1992), 13-26.

765. "The Black Woman Russian Expert [Condoleezza Rice] Who Advised President Bush at Washington Summit," *Jet*, 78 (18 June 1990), 4-7.

766. Blyth, M., "A New Style First Lady," *Ladies Home Journal*, 104 (Sept. 1987), 98ff.

767. Bonner, Yelena, "On Gorbachev," *New York Review of Books*, 37, no. 8 (17 May 1990), 3-5.

768. -----, "On Sakharov's Memoirs," *New York Review of Books*, 38 (10 Oct. 1991), 7-8.

769. "Boris Yeltsin: Crown Commissar?" *Glasnost*, 3, no. 2 (Oct-Dec. 1990), 4-13.

770. Brown, Bess, "Nursultan Nazarbaev of Kazakhstan: A Profile," *Report on the USSR*, 3, no. 22 (31 May 1991), 10-13.

771. Buckley, William F., "Breakfast with Gorbachev," *National Review*, 44 (8 June 1992), 62.

772. Bukovsky, Vladimir, "Glasnost," *Vital Speeches of the Day*, 53 (15 July 1987), 596-600.

773. Bush, George, "Gorbachev's Contributions Remembered," *US Department of State Dispatch*, 2 (30 Dec. 1991), 911.

774. "Changing the Guard," *Newsweek*, 105 (24 Mar. 1985), 22ff.

775. Chua-Eoan, H. G., "My Wife Is a Very Independent Lady,"

Time, 131 (6 June 1988), 38ff.

776. Crozier, Brian, "Gorbachev, Foundation Man," *National Review*, 45 (19 July 1993), 25-26.

777. Darrach, B., "Ronald Reagan and Mikhail Gorbachev," *People Weekly*, 32 (Fall 1989), 44-46.

778. "The Dissident as President: Exclusive Interview with Vaclav Havel," *World & I* (March 1990), 44-49.

779. Distelheim, L., "Czechoslovakia 1968: Dubcek 1988," *Life*, 11 (July 1988), 40ff.

780. Frye, Timothy, "A Portrait of Anatolii Sobchak," *Report on the USSR*, 2, no. 33 (17 Aug. 1990), 8-11.

781. -----, "Ruslan Khasbulatov, El'tsin's Deputy," *Report on the USSR*, 2, no. 38 (21 Sept. 1990), 26-27.

782. Fuller, Elizabeth, and Mark Deich, "Interview with Gary Kasparov," *Report on the USSR*, 2, no. 5 (2 Feb. 1990), 18-20.

783. "Gorbachev," *World Press Review*, 32 (May 1985), 35-40.

784. Gorbachev, Raisa, "My Story," *Good Housekeeping*, 213 (Nov. 1991), 144ff.

785. Green, M., "Revolutionary Raisa," *People Weekly*, 24 (2 Dec. 1985), 58-63.

786. Gustafson, Kerstin, "Raisa Gorbachev: The First Soviet First Lady," *Soviet Life* (June 1990).

787. Havel, Vaclav, "History of a Public Enemy," *New York Review of Books*, 37 (31 May 1990), 36-44.

788. -----, "On Home," *New York Review of Books*, 38 (5 Dec. 1991), 49.

789. -----, "Reflections on a Paradoxical Life," *New York Review of Books*, 37 (14 June 1990), 38.

790. -----, Dana Emingerova and Lubos Beniak, "'Uncertain Strength': An Interview with Vaclav Havel," *New York Review of Books*, 38 (15 Aug. 1991), 6ff.

791. Kaufman, B., and T. B. Feldman, "Keeping Up with Mrs. Gorbachev," *McCall's*, 115 (Mar. 1988), 140-43.

792. Keller, Bill, "Sakharov's List," *New York Times Magazine* (15 Feb. 1987), 34ff.

793. Ketchian, Sonia, "Meeting with Yelena Bonner," *Ararat*, 27, no. 2 (Spring 1986), 2-5.

794. Kline, Edward, "Andrei Sakharov: Gorbachev's Loyal Opposition," *Freedom at Issue*, no. 97 (July-Aug. 1987), 28-30.

795. Lourie, Richard, "The Smuggled Manuscript: Translating Sakharov's *Memoirs*," *New York Times Book Review* (3 June 1990), 3ff.

796. Mann, Dawn, "Valentin Fedorov: An Economist Becomes a Politician," *Report on the USSR*, 2, no.25 (22 June 1990), 6-7.

797. Martin, L., "Thoroughly Modern Raisa," *World Press Review*, 35 (Jan. 1988), 19.

798. Meier, Andrew, "Shaky Foundation: Gorbachev's Afterlife," *New Republic* (7 Sept. 1992), 23-24.

799. Methvin, Eugene H., "Yeltsin Rising," *National Review*, 43 (23 Sept. 1991), 41-43.

800. "Mikhail Gorbachev," *People Weekly*, 32 (25 Dec. 1989-1 Jan. 1990), 58-59.

801. "Mikhail Gorbachev: Private Citizen," *Time*, 139 (9 Mar. 1992), 34-35.

802. Nelan, B. W., "A Chat with the Gorbachevs," *Time*, 139 (25 May 1992), 51.

803. "On Gorbachev: A Talk with Andrei Sakharov," *New York Review of Books*, 35 (22 Dec. 1988), 28-29.

804. "Perestroika Personified" [Abel Aganbegian], *Economist*, 305 (28 Nov. 1987), 51.

805. Petro, Nicolai N., "The Rising Star of Russia's Vice-President" [Rutskoi], *Orbis*, 37, no. 1 (Winter 1993), 107-22.

806. Rahim, Azra Kureishy, "George Frost Kennan: From Cold Warrior to Cold War Iconoclast, 1940-1950," *Pakistan Horizon*, 43, no. 3 (July 1990), 73-96.

807. Sakharov, Andrei, "Moscow and Beyond," trans. by Antonina Bouis, *Harriman Institute Forum*, 3, no. 11 (Nov. 1990), 1-30.

808. Sanders, J., "Young, Gifted and Red: Mikhail Gorbachev Injects New Blood into the Kremlin Gerontocracy," *People Weekly*, 23 (25 Mar. 1985), 38ff.

809. Semel, G., interviewer, "Whatever Mikhail Gorbachev's Other Worries, the Birthmark on His Head Isn't One of Them," *People Weekly*, 24 (18 Nov. 1985), 61-62.

810. Sharansky, Natan, "The Legacy of Andrei Sakharov," *Journal of Democracy*, 1, no. 2 (Spring 1990), 35-40.

811. Stang, A., "Party Hack Under Her Silk Babushka," *Conservative Digest*, 14 (Mar. 1988), 61ff.

812. Sulla, Alexander, "Ruslan Khasbulatov: A Rising Power in Russia?" *World & I*, 7, no. 4 (Apr. 1992), 82-83.

813. Taubman, Philip, "Key Men in the Kremlin," *New York Times Magazine* (6 Dec. 1987), 98.

814. Trillin, Calvin, "Uncivil Liberties," *Nation*, 250 (5 Mar. 1990), 298.

815. "A Who's Who of *Perestroika*," *Perestroika Annual*, 1 (1988), 12-29; 2 (1989), 7-17.

816. Wierzbicki, Piotr, "Lech Walesa: The Sphinx from Gdansk," *Uncaptive Minds*, 3, no. 5 (Nov-Dec. 1990), 27-31.

817. Winn, Marie, "Vaclav Havel: The Czechs' Defiant Playwright," *New York Times Magazine* (25 Oct. 1987), 78ff.

818. "Yeltsin" [Man of the Year], *Time*, 137 (7 Jan. 1991), 37.

VII. Business and Foreign Investment; Joint Ventures
BOOKS

819. American Management Association, *Doing Business with the Soviet Union* (New York: AMA Membership Publications Division, 1988).

820. Artisien, Patrick, Matija Rojec and Marjan Svetlicic, eds., *Foreign Investment in Central and Eastern Europe* (Basingstoke and London: St. Martin's Press, 1993).

821. Aulin, Lisen, *Establishing Joint Ventures in the USSR* (Boston: Kluwer Law and Taxation Publishers, 1990).

822. Brada, Joseph C., and Michael P. Claudon, eds., *Reforming the Ruble: Monetary Aspects of Perestroika* (New York: New York University Press, 1990).

823. Braginsky, Mikhail, *Joint Ventures: Benefit for All* (Moscow: Novosti Press Agency, 1988).

824. Britt, Lawrence, *Rethinking Business with the U.S.S.R.* (Washington, DC: Johns Hopkins University Foreign Policy Institute, 1988).

825. Carey, Sarah, ed., *Legal Regulations on Joint Ventures in the USSR*, 2 vols. (Washington, DC: USSR Chamber of Commerce and Industry and Steptoe & Johnson, 1989).

826. Carvounis, Chris C., and Brinda C. Carvounis, *U.S. Commercial Opportunities in the Soviet Union: Marketing, Production and Strategic Planning Perspectives* (New York: Quorum Books, 1989).

827. Claudon, Michael P., and Tamar L. Gutner, eds., *Investing in Reform: Doing Business in a Changing Soviet Union* (New York: New York University Press, 1991).

828. Daniels, John D., and Lee H. Radebaugh, *International Business: Environments and Operations* (Reading, MA: Addison-Wesley, 1993).

829. Danton de Rouffignac, Peter, *Doing Business in Eastern Europe* (East Brunswick, NJ: Nichols/GP, 1991).

830. Dhanji, Farid, and Branko Milanovic, *Privatization in Eastern and Central Europe: Objectives, Constraints, and Models of Divestiture* (Washington, DC: World Bank, Country Economics Department, 1991).

831. *The Economist Business Traveller's Guide: USSR* (New York: Prentice Hall, 1989).

832. Gelb, Alan H., and Cheryl W. Gray, *The Transformation of Economies in Central and Eastern Europe: Issues, Progress and Prospects* (Washington, DC: World Bank, 1991).

833. Hecht, James L., ed., *Rubles and Dollars: Strategies for Doing Business in the Soviet Union* (New York: HarperBusiness, 1991).

834. Hewett, Ed A., *Open for Business: Russia's Return to the Global Economy* (Washington, DC: Brookings Institution, 1992).

835. Hupp, John P., ed., *Business and Commercial Laws of Russia: Translations with Expert Commentary* (New York: McGraw-Hill, 1993).

836. Isbell, P., and J. Daniel, *Major Business Organisations of Eastern Europe and the Soviet Union, 1991: Albania, Bulgaria, Czechoslovakia, Hungary, Poland, Romania, USSR, Yugoslavia* (New York: Graham & Trotman, 1991).

837. Kirk, Robert S., *U.S.-Soviet Commercial Relations in the Age of Perestroika: Selected References, 1985-1989* (Washington, DC: Library of Congress, Congressional Research Service, 1989).

838. Knight, Misha G., *How to Do Business with Russians: A Handbook and Guide for Western Business People* (New York: Quorum Books, 1987).

839. *The Legal Status of Joint Ventures in the USSR* (Moscow: Nauka Publishers, 1989).

840. Liebowitz, Ronald D., ed., *Gorbachev's New Thinking: Prospects for Joint Ventures* (Cambridge, MA: Ballinger Publishers, 1988).

841. Minakir, Pavel A., and Olga M. Prokapalo, *Russian Pacific Rim: Investment and Business Opportunities 1992-1993* (Los Gatos, CA: Soviet and European Research Institute, 1993).

842. Osakwe, Christopher, *Soviet Business Law: Institutions, Principles, and Processes* (Salem, NH: Butterworth Legal Publishers, 1991).
16.5

843. -----, *The Soviet Joint Venture Process: Law and Practice* (Stoneham, MA: Butterworth Legal Publishers, 1990).

844. Pilon, Juliana G., *A Yellow Light on U.S. Joint Ventures with the Soviets* (Washington, DC: Heritage Foundation, 1988).

845. Practising Law Institute, *Legal and Practical Aspects of Doing Business with the Soviet Union* (New York: Practising Law Institute, 1988).

846. *Price Waterhouse Information Guide: Doing Business with the Soviet Union* (New York: Price Waterhouse, 1989).

847. Razvigorova, E., and G. Wolf Laudon, eds., *East-West Joint Ventures: The New Business Environment* (Cambridge, MA: B. Blackwell, 1991).

848. Reid, Elspeth, ed., *Foreign Investment and the Law in the Russian Federation* (Edinburgh: The David Hume Institute, 1992).

849. Shelton, Judy, *The Coming Soviet Crash: Gorbachev's Desperate Pursuit of Credit in Western Financial Markets* (New York: Free Press, 1989).

850. Sherr, Alan B., *et al.*, *International Joint Ventures: Soviet and Western Perspectives* (New York: Quorum Books, 1991).

851. Starr, Robert, and Sally March, *Joint Ventures in the USSR* (New York: Worldwide Information, 1989).

852. Theroux, Eugene, *The Harper Collins Business Guide to Moscow* (New York: Perennial Library, 1990).

853. -----, director, *A New Look at Doing Business with the Soviet Union* (New York: Practising Law Institute, 1989).

854. Thomas, Bill, and Charles Sutherland, *Red Tape: Adventure Capitalism in the New Russia* (New York: Dutton, 1993).

855. United Nations Centre on Transnational Corporations, *Joint Ventures as a Form of International Economic Cooperation* (New York: Taylor & Francis, 1988).

856. US Congress. House. Committee on Energy and Commerce. Subcommittee on Telecommunications and Finance. *Telecommunications Opportunities in Eastern Europe.* 101st Congress, 2nd Session, 17 May 1990 (Washington, DC: Government Printing Office, 1990).

857. US Congress. House. Committee on Ways and Means. *U.S. Trade Relationship with the Soviet Union and Eastern Europe, the Implications of "Europe 1992" on American Direct Investment, and Foreign Investment in the United States.* 101st Congress, 2nd Session, 24 Jan.-18 Apr. 1990 (Washington, DC: Government Printing Office, 1990).

858. US Congress. Senate. Committee on Small Business. *To Examine Small Business Trade Opportunities with the Soviet Union and Eastern Europe.* 101st Congress, 2nd Session, 23 Mar. 1990 (Washington, DC: Government Printing Office, 1990).

859. US Department of Commerce, *Obstacles to Trade and Investment in the New Republics of the Former Soviet Union* (Springfield, VA: US Department of Commerce, National Technical Information Service, 1992).

860. Westbrook, Christine, and Alan B. Sherr, *U.S.-Soviet Joint Ventures and Export Control Policy* (Providence, RI: Center for Foreign Policy Development, Brown University, 1990).

861. Wetzler, Monte E., director, *Joint Ventures and Privatization in Eastern Europe* (New York: Practising Law Institute, 1991).

862. Winter, David, ed., *Eastern Bloc Joint Ventures: Papers Delivered at the Conference in Warsaw, Poland 22-24 April 1990* (London: International Bar Association, 1990).

863. Xueref, Carol, ed., *Guide to Joint Ventures in the USSR* (Paris: International Chamber of Commerce, 1988).

ARTICLES

864. Afanasyeva, Larisa, "Insurance and Risk Management of Joint Ventures in the USSR," *New York University Journal of International Law and Politics*, 22, no. 3 (Spring 1990), 447-59.

865. -----, and Alexey Klishin, "Wholly-Owned Subsidiaries in the U.S.S.R.?" *CTC Reporter* (Spring 1989), 57-61.

866. Albin, Adam J., "Joint Venture Law in the Soviet Union: The 1920s and the 1980s," *Northwestern Journal of International Law and Business*, 9 (1989), 633-57.

867. Allen, Robert E., *et al.*, "What Is Your Greatest Concern About Expanding into Eastern Europe?" *Columbia Journal of*

World Business, 26, no. 1 (Spring 1991), 18-19.

868. Arbess, Daniel J., "A Few Things U.S. Businesspeople Should Know About Joint Ventures in the Soviet Union: A Lawyer's View," *New York University Journal of International Law and Politics*, 22, no. 3 (Spring 1990), 411-34.

869. Aronson, Tracey E., "The New Soviet Joint Venture Law: Analysis, Issues and Approaches for the American Investor," *Law and Policy in International Business*, 19, no. 4 (1987), 851-92.

870. Baker, Mark, "Growing Economic Problems Place New Strains on JVs" [Joint Ventures], *Business in Eastern Europe*, 19, nos. 51-52 (17 Dec. 1990), 409-10.

871. Beliaeva, Marina, "USSR Law Aims to Broaden Foreign and Domestic Investors' Rights," *SEEL: Soviet and East European Law*, 1, no. 10 (Jan. 1991), 8ff.

872. Berman, P., "The Five-Percenters: Moscow's Pet Capitalists," *Forbes*, 143 (6 Feb. 1989), 93-97.

873. Block, Kevin P., "The Disciplining and Dismissal of Employees by Joint Ventures in the USSR," *George Washington Journal of International Law and Economics*, 232, no. 3 (1990), 619-67.

874. Bost, David M., "The 1987 Soviet Joint Venture Law: New Possibilities for Cooperation and Growth in East-West Relations," *Denver Journal of International Law and Policy*, 17, no. 3 (Spring 1989), 581-99.

875. Boukaouris, G. N., "Joint Ventures in the Soviet Union, Czechoslovakia and Poland," *Case Western Reserve Journal of International Law*, 21 (Winter 1989), 1-53.

876. Bradshaw, Michael J., "Joint Ventures for Perestroika," *Geographical Magazine*, 62 (Oct. 1990), 10-14.

877. Brady, Rose, "Fast Food Is Coming, Fast Food Is Coming," *Business Week* (1 Dec. 1986), 50.

878. -----, and D. Greising, "They Know How to Capitalize on Chaos," *Business Week* (27 Apr. 1992), 106ff.

879. -----, and Peter Galuszka, "Let's Make a Deal-But a Smaller One," *Business Week* (20 Jan. 1992), 44-45.

880. Brank, Laurie M., "*Perestroika* in Eastern Europe: Four Joint Venture Laws in 1989," *Law and Policy in International Business*, 21, no. 1 (1989), 1-32.

881. Brougher, Jack, "U.S.S.R. Trade Climate Is Improving after January Trade Talks," *Business America* (4 Mar. 1985), 23.

882. Brown, Leslie, "Tomsk Is Open for Business," *Business America*, 112, no. 11 (3 June 1991), 2-5.

883. Browning, Graeme, "The Soviet Far East," *National Journal*, 23, no. 46 (16 Nov. 1991), 2795-99.

884. Buckley, William F., "Pepsi at the Summit," *National Review*, 40 (24 June 1988), 57.

885. -----, "The `Pepski' Crusade," *National Review*, 37 (20 Sept. 1985), 55.

886. Bugromenko, V. N., "Regional Development, Economic Accountability, and Social Justice," *Soviet Geography*, 32, no. 8 (Oct. 1991), 538-41.

887. "Building a Presence in the USSR: Some Basics," *Business International*, 37, no. 16 (23 Apr. 1990), 125-26.

888. Burt, Jeffrey A., "Joint Venture Experience: Observations on the Business and Legal Challenges," *New York University Journal of International Law and Politics*, 22, no. 3 (Spring 1990), 435-45.

889. Bush, Keith, "Credit Rating of the Soviet Union Slips," *Report on the USSR*, 2, no. 11 (16 Mar. 1990), 8-11.

890. "Business Opportunities in Ukraine," *Forum*, no. 79 (Fall 1989), 25-27.

891. Caccavo, K. R., "The Pizza Diplomats," *Nation's Business*, 76 (Sept. 1988), 59.

892. Carey, Sarah, "A New Era for Foreign Investment in the USSR," *SEEL: Soviet and East European Law*, 1, no. 9 (Nov. 1990), 1ff.

893. -----, "Foreign Investment in the USSR," *Harriman Institute Forum*, 3, no. 2 (Feb. 1990), 1-7.

894. -----, "Joint Ventures in the Soviet Economy," *Harvard International Review*, 13, no. 2 (Winter 1990-91), 38-39.

895. Carpenter, Russell H., Jr., and Bradford L. Smith, "U.S.-Soviet Joint Ventures: A New Opening in the East," *Business Lawyer*, 43 (Nov. 1987), 79-91.

896. Castro, J., "*Perestroika* to Pizza," *Time*, 131 (2 May 1988), 52-53.

897. Clarke, Christopher F., "The Soviet Joint Venture Decree and Soviet Labor Law," *Virginia Journal of International Law*, 30, no. 3 (Spring 1990), 761-94.

898. Copetas, A. Craig, "An American in *Perestroika*," *Regardie's*, 9, no. 4 (Apr. 1989), 96ff.

899. Corcoran, Dan, "Try and Become a Businessman (Private Business through the Prism of American Experience)," *International Affairs* (Moscow), no. 8 (Aug. 1991), 58-74.

900. Cutler, Blayne, "Measuring Glasnost In and Out of the USSR," *Consumer Markets Abroad* (Feb. 1988), 2-11.

901. Dean, R. N., "Considering Business Opportunities in the Soviet Union in the 1990s," *Private Investors Abroad* (1991), 11.1-.24.

902. Denber, Rachel, "Soviet Decree on Forced Sale of Foreign Currency Does Not Affect Foreign Capital," *SEEL: Soviet and East European Law*, 1, no. 9 (Nov. 1990), 6.

903. "Doing Business with the USSR: In Conversation with Leonid Shalagin," *Freedom at Issue*, no. 115 (July-Aug. 1990), 20-24.

904. Dunn, Keith M., "The New Soviet Joint Venture Regulations," *North Carolina Journal of International Law and Com-*

mercial Regulation, 12 (Spring 1987), 171-86.

905. Eberstadt, Nicholas N., "How Not to Aid Eastern Europe," *Commentary*, 92 (Nov. 1991), 24-30.

906. Engelhart, Michael A., and Thomas J. Presby, "Report from Eastern Europe: An Investor's Guide to Eastern Europe," *International Economic Insights*, 2, no. 1 (Jan-Feb. 1991), 41-43.

907. English, Richard D., "Privatization by General Fund: Economic Empowerment for Central and Eastern Europe," *George Washington Journal of International Law and Economics*, 24, no. 3 (1991), 527-86.

908. Ericson, Richard, "USSR Law on Entrepreneurial Activity," *SEEL: Soviet and East European Law*, 2, no. 4 (June 1991), 5ff.

909. "Exclusive Interview [with Gorbachev]: What Gorbachev Wants from Business," *Fortune*, 122 (31 Dec. 1990), 62-64.

910. Farrell, John P., "Monitoring the Great Transition," *Comparative Economic Studies*, 33, no. 2 (Summer 1991), 9-28.

911. Farren, Michael, "Opportunities and Challenges in the New European Market," *Business America*, 112, no. 4 (11 Feb. 1991), 6-7.

912. Felker, T. L., "Perestroyka and Western Direct Investment: The Task of Integrating a Western Company into the Changing Soviet Economy," *University of Pennsylvania Journal of International Business Law*, 12 (1991), 219-44.

913. "Foreign Investment in the Soviet Union, Eastern Europe and Yugoslavia" (Bibliography), *Texas International Law Journal*, 25 (Winter 1990), 99-117.

914. "Foreign Investment: New Soviet Joint Venture Law-Edict on the Procedures for the Creation in the USSR of Joint Enterprises, in Which Soviet Organizations and Firms from Capitalist and Developing Countries Are Partners...," *Harvard International Law Journal*, 28 (Spring 1987), 473-81.

915. Frenkel, William G., "Soviet Cooperatives: New Private Enterprises as Trade and Foreign Investment Partners in the U.S.S.R.," *ICSID Review: Foreign Investment Law Journal*, 4 (1989), 63-89.

916. -----, and Michael Y. Sukhman, "New Foreign Investment Regimes of Russia and the Other Republics of the Former U.S.S.R.: A Legislative Analysis and Historical Perspective," *Boston College International and Comparative Law Review*, 16, no. 2 (Summer 1993), 321ff.

917. Freund, William, "Economic Trends and Opportunities in the 1990s," *World & I* (Nov. 1990), 117-23.

918. Galuszka, Philip, *et al.*, "Letting Western Business In," *Business Week* (20 Apr. 1987), 40.

919. -----, and R. Brady, "The Chill Is Gone, and U.S. Companies Are Moscow-Bound," *Business Week* (5 June 1989), 64.

920. -----, *et al.*, "Western Business May Get a Piece of Perestroika," *Business Week* (28 Dec. 1987), 70.

921. Geoffrey, Oliver D., and Erwin P. Eichmann, "European Community Restrictions on Imports from Central and Eastern Europe: The Impact on Western Investors," *Law and Policy in International Business*, 22, no. 4 (1991), 721-86.

922. Giddings, Jane, and Vladimir Belykh, "Economic Sanctions in the Soviet Economy: Securing the Due Performance of the Contract of Delivery," *International and Comparative Law Quarterly*, 36 (1987), 383-89.

923. Giges, N., "Colgate, P&G Pack for Road to Russia," *Advertsing Age* (12 Mar. 1990), 56.

924. "Glasnost: Joint Ventures Now Permitted in the Soviet Union," *Florida International Law Journal*, 3 (Fall 1987), 125-49.

925. Goldman, A., "Dollars and Sickles," *National Review*, 40 (25 Nov. 1988), 39ff.

926. Golia, Marlene, "Researching the Soviet Consumer," *International Executive*, 32, no. 3 (Nov-Dec. 1990), 7-8.

927. Grant, Wyn, "Business Associations in Eastern Europe and Russia," *Journal of Communist Studies*, 9, no. 2 (June 1993), 86ff.

928. Griffin, Andrew T., and Larry D. Soderquist, "Private Companies in the Soviet Union: Cooperatives in the Era of Perestroika," *Harvard International Law Journal*, 32, no. 1 (Winter 1991), 201-25.

929. Hanson, Philip, "Joint Ventures Still Expanding Despite Everything," *Report on the USSR*, 3, no. 32 (9 Aug. 1991), 6-7.

930. "The Harriman Manganese Concession in the Soviet Union: Lessons for Today," *International Tax and Business Lawyer*, 9 (Summer 1991), 209-71.

931. Hawkins, Robert, and Dan Penn, "RSFSR Proposes Drafts on Foreign Investment," *SEEL: Soviet and East European Law*, 1, no. 8 (Oct. 1990), 8-9.

932. Hazard, John N., "Opportunities and Problems for Joint Ventures in Soviet Law," *New York University Journal of International Law and Politics*, 22, no. 3 (Spring 1990), 407-10.

933. Hertzfeld, Jeffrey M., "Applicable Law and Dispute Settlement in Soviet Joint Ventures," *ICSID Review: Foreign Investment Law Journal*, 3 (1988), 249-62.

934. -----, "Joint Ventures: Saving the Soviets from Perestroika," *Harvard Business Review*, 69, no. 1 (Jan-Feb. 1991), 80-91.

935. Hines, Jonathan, and Juliette Passer, "Decree of the President of the USSR on Foreign Investments in the USSR," *SEEL: Soviet and East European Law*, 1, no. 8 (Oct. 1990), 3.

936. Hober, Kaj, "Joint Stock Companies a la Russe," *SEEL: Soviet and East European Law*, 1, no. 6 (Aug. 1990), 2ff.

937. Holden, Constance, "What *Perestroika* Means for American Business," *Science*, 239 (4 Mar. 1988), 1088-89.

938. "Home Court Advantage? Are U.S. Sports Franchises Negotiating with Soviet Athletes at Their Own Risk?" *Suffolk Transnational Law Journal*, 13 (Fall 1989), 201-28.

939. "International Joint Enterprises in the Soviet Union," *UCLA Pacific Basin Law Journal*, 6 (Fall 1989), 121-33.

940. "International Law Symposium `89," *Whittier Law Review*, 11 (1989), 323-478.

941. "Joint Venture Law in the Soviet Union: The 1920s and the 1980s," *Northwestern Journal of International Law and Business*, 9 (Winter 1989), 633-57.

942. "Joint Ventures Add to Russian Oil Production," *Oil and Gas Journal*, 92, no. 11 (14 Mar. 1994), 34-35.

943. "Joint Ventures in the Soviet Union: Problems Emerge," *University of Puget Sound Law Review*, 13 (Fall 1989), 165-96.

944. Kavass, Igor I., "Aspects of Soviet Law on Joint Ventures, Foreign Trade, and Investment: A Bibliographic Guide of Current Literature in English," *Vanderbilt Journal of Transnational Law*, 24, no. 2 (1991), 415-48.

945. Kelly, Peter M., and Dale A. Kimball, Jr., "Foreign Investment in the Soviet Union, Eastern Europe and Yugoslavia," *Texas International Law Journal*, 25, no. 1 (Winter 1990), 99-118.

946. King, R. W., and Philip Galuszka, "The Twain Are Meeting-And Cutting Deals," *Business Week* (7 Dec. 1987), 88.

947. Koch, June Q., "Glasnost' and Soviet Construction: New Opportunities for American Business," *Columbia Journal of World Business*, 23, no. 2 (Summer 1988), 85-89.

948. Kolb, Joseph I., "The Psychological Shock of Soviet Perestroika," *International Affairs* (Moscow), no. 9 (Sept. 1991), 33-38.

949. Korovikov, Igor, "Business in the USSR: A Play without Rules and Trumps," *International Affairs* (Moscow), no. 11 (Nov. 1991), 68-79.

950. Kovalyov, Alexander, "Law and Joint Ventures," *International Affairs* (Moscow), no. 1 (Jan. 1992), 80-89.

951. Kraus, James R., "U.S. Leaders Take Cautious Tack in Dealings with Soviet Union," *American Banker*, 152 (20 Dec. 1987), 1-2.

952. Kroncher, Allan, "State Control and Private Enterprise," *Soviet Analyst*, I: 17, no. 3 (10 Feb. 1988), 7-8; II: 17, no. 5 (9 Mar. 1988), 5-6.

953. Kuhlman, James A., "Perestroika as a Western Marketplace," *Business and Economic Review*, 36 (Apr-June 1990), 24-34.

954. Laurita, Tom, and Michael McGloin, "US-Soviet Joint Ventures: Current Status and Prospects," *Columbia Journal of World Business*, 23, no. 2 (Summer 1988), 43-51.

955. "Leasing Law Gives Foreigners Right to Lease Soviet Property," *SEEL: Soviet and East European Law*, 1, no. 1 (Feb. 1990), 1ff.

956. Lenorovitz, Jeffrey M., "Selenia and Soviets Complete Pact for Air Traffic Control Joint Venture," *Aviation Week & Space Technology*, 133, no. 15 (8 Oct. 1990), 46.

957. -----, "Soviets Open Engine Industry, Seek Business Ties with West," *Aviation Week & Space Technology*, 132, no. 16 (16 Apr. 1990), 16.

958. Lewald, R., "Ivan Starts Learning the Capitalist Ropes," *Business Week* (2 Nov. 1987), 154.

959. Lewenz, Susan M. H., "Soviet Plans to Improve Quality Should Expand U.S. Opportunities," *Business America*, 28 (Sept. 1987), 14.

960. Lieberman, Edward H., *et al.*, "Investment in the Soviet Union and Hungary: A Comparison of the New Soviet and Hungarian Investment and Tax Laws," *George Washington Journal of International Law and Economics*, 23, no. 1 (1989), 1-57.

961. Litman, George L., "U.S.-U.S.S.R. Cooperate in Construction Field," *Business America*, 111, no. 16 (27 Aug. 1990), 14-15.

962. Lottman, Herbert R., "Soviet Official Reports 30 Joint Ventures with Other Nations," *Publishers Weekly*, 237, no. 11 (16 Mar. 1990), 11.

963. Marlatt, Alyse, "Opportunities in the Soviet Food Industry Market," *Business America*, 111, no. 13 (2 July 1990), 10-11.

964. Matthews, Chris, "GE Finds Encouraging Signs in Gorbachev's Perestroika," *Business International*, 36, no. 11 (20 Mar. 1989), 81-82.

965. McCarthy, Daniel J., Sheila M. Puffer and Peter J. Simmonds, "Riding the Russian Roller Coaster: U.S. Firms' Recent Experience and Future Plans in the Former USSR," *California Management Review*, 36, no. 1 (Fall 1993), 99-115.

966. McDaniel, Donna, "The Bolshoi Mac," *World & I*, 6, no. 1 (Jan. 1991), 234-41.

967. McManus, J., and M. Loeb, "What Gorbachev Wants from Business," *Fortune*, 122 (31 Dec. 1990), 62-64.

968. McMillan, Carl H., "Eastward Ho? The Pros and Cons of Tackling What May Be the Last Frontier of International Business," *Canadian Business Review*, 17, no. 2 (1990), 17-21.

969. -----, "Joint Ventures in Arctic Resource Development," *Northern Perspectives*, 16, no. 4 (1988), 17-19.

970. Meadows, James E., and Christopher Evans, "Software Protection in Transactions with the Soviet Union," *Computers and Law*, (1987), 24-28.

971. Mecham, Michael, "Collapse of Eastern Bloc Boosts Well-Positioned Charter Operators," *Aviation Week & Space Technology*, 135, no. 17 (28 Oct. 1991), 43-47.

972. Mirabito, Richard, "Prospects for Western Investment: A Comparison of Joint Venture Laws in the Soviet Union, Yugoslavia and China," *Boston College International and Comparative Law Journal*, 12 (1989), 103-49.

973. Moore, W. John, "Perestroika on the Potomac," *National Journal*, 22, no. 6 (10 Feb. 1990), 318-22.

974. Mueller, William, "Soviet Ventures: A Capital Idea,"

Nation's Business, 78 (Oct. 1990), 42-44.

975. Murrell, Peter, "Symposium on Economic Transition in the Soviet Union and Eastern Europe," *Journal of Economic Perspectives*, 5, no. 2 (June 1991), 203-10.

976. -----, and Mancur Olson, "The Devolution of Centrally Planned Economies," *Journal of Comparative Economics*, 15, no. 2 (June 1991), 239-65.

977. Nail, Jim, "New USSR Tax Law May Damage Western Interests," *Business in Eastern Europe*, 19, no. 35 (27 Aug. 1991), 281-83.

978. Naylor, Thomas H., "The Reeducation of Soviet Management," *Across the Board*, 25 (Feb. 1988), 28-37.

979. Nemec, Linda E., "Soviet Economic Reform Program Creates Opportunities and Risks for Foreign Firms," *Business America*, 111, no. 23 (3 Dec. 1990), 22-24.

980. Neubecker, R., "Big Deals Run into Big Trouble in the Soviet Union," *Business Week* (19 Mar. 1990), 58-60.

981. Newcity, Michael, "Joint Ventures in the USSR Must Pay Turnover and Import-Export Taxes," *SEEL: Soviet and East European Law*, 1, no. 10 (Jan. 1991), 10.

982. -----, "Tax Issues in Soviet Joint Ventures," *Texas International Law Journal*, 25, no. 2 (Spring 1990), 163-208.

983. Newman, P. C., "Cohon's Hamburger Diplomacy," *Maclean's*, 101 (30 May 1988), 44.

984. "New Soviet Air Service Rights Awarded to Alaska Airlines, Federal Express," *Aviation Week & Space Technology*, 133, no. 11 (10 Sept. 1990), 66.

985. "New Soviet Export Licensing Requirements," *SEEL: Soviet and East European Law*, 1, no. 3 (Apr. 1990), 7.

986. "The New Soviet Joint Venture Law: Analysis, Issues and Approaches for the American Investor," *Law and Policy in International Business*, 19 (1987), 851-92.

987. Nicandros, Constantine S., "Russian Oil, Western Investment: Putting the Puzzle Together," *World Today*, 49, no. 10 (Oct. 1993), 186-88.

988. Nigh, Douglas, and Karen D. Smith, "The New US Joint Ventures in the USSR: Assessment and Management of Political Risk," *Columbia Journal of World Business*, 24, no. 2 (Summer 1989), 39-44.

989. Nigh, Douglas, Peter Walters and James A. Kuhlman, "US-USSR Joint Ventures: An Examination of the Early Entrants," *Columbia Journal of World Business*, 25, no. 4 (Winter 1990), 20-27.

990. Nofelt, Ulf, "Are There Still Opportunities in the U.S.S.R. for Western Companies?" *International Executive*, 31, no. 6 (May-June 1991), 40-43.

991. -----, "An Update on Venturing in the Soviet Union," *International Executive*, 32, no. 4 (Jan-Feb. 1991), 24-26.

992. Osakwe, Christopher, "The Death of Ideology in Soviet Foreign Investment Policy: A Clinical Examination of the Soviet Joint Venture Law of 1987," *Vanderbilt Journal of Transnational Law*, 22 (1989), 1-125.

993. Ottley, Bruce L., and Younghee Jin, "Liability for Defective Products in the Soviet Union: Socialist Law Versus Soviet Reality," *Northwestern Journal of International Law and Business*, 8 (1988), 640-65.

994. Ovchinnikov, Konstantin, "Third World Markets: Mirages and Prospects," *International Affairs* (Moscow), no. 5 (May 1991), 54-58.

995. Pallay, Stephen, "French Consortium Success: Political Support Vital," *Business in Eastern Europe*, 19, no. 38 (17 Sept. 1990), 307.

996. Passer, Juliette, and Robert Hines, trans., "Gorbachev Decree Allows Direct Foreign Investment in the USSR," *SEEL: Soviet and East European Law*, 1, no. 8 (Oct. 1990), 3.

997. Pavluk, Jonathan, "Flexibility Sought in Soviet Foreign Investment Legislation," *SEEL: Soviet and East European Law*, 1, no. 5 (June-July 1990), 3.

998. -----, "Foreign Firms Allowed to Open Ruble Accounts in Soviet Banks," *SEEL: Soviet and East European Law*, 2, no. 2 (Mar. 1991), 7.

999. -----, "Soviet Leasing Principles May Engender New Types of Commercial Venture," *SEEL: Soviet and East European Law*, 1, no. 2 (Mar. 1990), 8-9.

1000. Pettibone, Peter J., "Negotiating a Business Venture in the Soviet Union," *Journal of Business Strategy*, 12, no. 1 (Jan-Feb. 1991), 18-23.

1001. Pollath, Reinhard, and Thomas Toeben, "Foreign Investment in Eastern Europe," *Journal of International Taxation*, 2, no. 2 (July-Aug. 1991), 104-11.

1002. "Practicing Law and Doing Business in the Soviet Union: Third Annual Ernst C. Stiefel Symposium," *New York Law School Journal of International and Comparative Law*, 11 (1990), 433-518.

1003. "Procter and Gamble: Perestroika in Soapland," *Economist*, 311 (10 June 1989), 69-71.

1004. "Prospects for Western Investment: A Comparison of Joint Venture Laws in the Soviet Union, Yugoslavia, and China," *Boston College International and Comparative Law Review*, 12 (Winter 1989), 103-49.

1005. Rabinovich, Pyotr S., "The Procedure for Signing Transactions with Soviet Foreign Trade Organizations," *International Lawyer*, 22 (Spring 1988), 143-65.

1006. Rahman, M. Zubaidur, "New Joint Venture Accounting Regulations in the USSR: A Step Toward the Introduction of International Accounting Standards," *SEEL: Soviet and East European Law*, 1, no. 10 (Jan. 1991), 9ff.

1007. "Reinventing a Law on Inventions: International Aspects of the New Russian Patent Law," *George Washington Journal of International Law and Economics*, 25 (1991), 171-226.

1008. Richardson, David W., "*Glasnost*: Joint Ventures Now Permitted in the Soviet Union," *Florida International Law Journal*, 3 (1987), 125-49.

1009. Ross, Kelly, "Recent Developments: Foreign Investment: New Soviet Joint Venture Law-Edict on the Procedures for the Creation in the USSR of Joint Enterprises...," *Harvard International Law Journal*, 28, no. 2 (Spring 1987), 473-81.

1010. Rosten, K. A., "Soviet-U.S. Joint Ventures: Pioneers on a New Frontier," *California Management Review*, 33, no. 2 (Winter 1990), 88-108.

1011. Rumer, Boris Z., "Helping Russians Go into Business," *World Monitor*, 4, no. 2 (Feb. 1991), 48-53.

1012. "Russian Soviet Federated Socialist Republic: Law on Foreign Investments in the RSFSR," *International Legal Materials*, 31, no. 2 (Mar. 1992), 397-423.

1013. Ruth, Stephen, "International Joint Enterprises in the Soviet Union," *UCLA Pacific Basin Law Journal*, 6 (1989), 121-33.

1014. Saliman, S. Gerald, "An Analysis of the Changing Legal Environment in the USSR for Foreign Investment," *Law and Policy in International Business*, 22 (1991), 1-36.

1015. Schares, Gail, *et al.*, "When the Kremlin Calls, Capitalists Lend More Than Their Ear," *Business Week* (15 Aug. 1988), 56-57.

1016. Schwartz, E. J., "Recent Developments in the Copyright Regimes of the Soviet Union and Eastern Europe," *Journal of the Copyright Society of the U.S.A.*, 38 (Spring 1991), 123-226.

1017. Shadbolt, R. A., "Contracting for Construction Projects with the USSR," *International Construction Law Review*, 7 (Oct. 1990), 379-85.

1018. Shaw, Denis J. B., and Michael J. Bradshaw, "Geography of Joint Ventures," *Soviet Geography*, 32, no. 3 (Mar. 1991), 199-202.

1019. Sheedy, John F., and Richard N. Dean, "Gaining a Foothold in the Soviet Market: How to Establish a Representative Office," *International Law*, 25 (Spring 1991), 103-25.

1020. Sheets, K. R., "Comrade Capitalists, Come Make Money in the Soviet Union," *U.S. News & World Report*, 102 (19 Jan. 1987), 39.

1021. Sherr, A. B., and M. Hayes, "Joint Venture Partners Speak Out: Interviews and Surveys of Participants," *East European/Soviet Union Executive Guide* (3 June 1991), 18-21.

1022. Shpil'ko, S., "Attitude of the Population toward Joint and Foreign Entrepreneurship in the USSR," *Problems of Economics*, 33, no. 11 (Mar. 1991), 79-85.

1023. "The Slepak Principles Act and Soviet Union-United States Joint Ventures: Profits or People?" *Loyola of Los Angeles International and Comparative Law Journal*, 13 (Dec. 1990),

365-92.

1024. Slider, Darrell, "Embattled Entrepreneurs: Soviet Cooperatives in an Unreformed Economy," *Soviet Studies*, 43, no. 5 (1991), 797-821.

1025. Smucker, Conrad J., "Soviet Taxation of United States Businesses: State of the Law and Recommendations," *Tax Lawyer*, 42 (1989), 801-20.

1026. "Software Protection in Transactions with the Soviet Union," *Rutgers Computer and Technology Law Journal*, 12 (1986), 133-67.

1027. "The Soviet Joint Venture Decree and Soviet Labor Law," *Virginia Journal of International Law*, 30 (Spring 1990), 761-94.

1028. "Soviet Joint Ventures: Providing for Appropriate Dispute Resolution," *Cornell University International Law Journal*, 23 (Winter 1990), 107-31.

1029. "Soviet JV [Joint Venture] Strikes; How to Keep Employees Happy," *Business in Eastern Europe*, 19, no. 20 (14 May 1990), 163.

1030. "Soviet JVs [Joint Ventures] May Soon Face Trade Union Challenge," *Business International*, 36, no. 40 (9 Oct. 1989), 307.

1031. "Soviet Union on the Road to the World Market," *International Affairs* (Moscow), no. 7 (July 1991), 69-80.

1032. Spaeth, S. M., "The Deregulation of Transportation and Natural Gas Production in the United States and Its Relevance to the Soviet Union and Eastern Europe in the 1990s," *University of Bridgeport Law Review*, 12 (1991), 43-95.

1033. Stephan, Paul B., III, "The Restructuring of Soviet Commercial Law and Its Impact on International Business Transactions," *George Washington Journal of International Law and Economics*, 24 (1990), 89-102.

1034. -----, "Soviet Law and Foreign Investment: Perestroyka's Gordian Knot," *International Lawyer*, 25 (Fall 1991), 741-54.

1035. Stokes, Bruce, "East Bloc Pot of Gold?" *National Journal*, 22, no. 6 (10 Feb. 1990), 312-17.

1036. -----, "Moscow's Out Shopping for Western Cash," *National Journal*, 23, no. 22 (1 June 1991), 1292-93.

1037. Surrey, W. H., and V. Lechtman, "The New Soviet Joint Venture Law: A Political Curiosity or a Real Investment Opportunity?" *Private Investors Abroad* (1988), 6.1-.38.

1038. Swindler, Geoffrey D., "Joint Ventures in the Soviet Union: Problems Emerge," *University of Puget Sound Law Review*, 13 (1989), 165-96.

1039. "Taxing Joint Ventures in the Eastern Bloc," *International Executive*, 32, no. 2 (Sept-Oct. 1990), 27-28.

1040. Thayer, Ann M., "Soviet Loosening of Regulations Paves Way to U.S. Ventures There," *Chemical and Engineering News*, 67 (3 Apr. 1989), 15-18.

1041. Tiefenbrun, S. W., "Joint Ventures in the USSR, Eastern

Europe and the People's Republic of China as of December 1989," *New York University Journal of International Law and Policy*, 21, 4 (Summer 1989), 667-794.

1042. Tomarchio, Jack Thomas, "Joint Venture Law in Eastern Europe," *Journal of European Business*, 2, no. 5 (May-June 1991), 12-18.

1043. "To Russia With Cash," *Maclean's*, 102 (13 Nov. 1989), 42ff.

1044. "Trade and Foreign Investment in Eastern Europe and the Soviet Union: Special Symposium Issue," *Vanderbilt Journal of Transnational Law*, 24 (1991), 205-448.

1045. "Union of Soviet Socialist Republics: Decree of the USSR Supreme Soviet Putting into Effect the Fundamentals of Legislation on Investment Activity in the USSR, and Text of the Fundamentals; Edict of the President on Foreign Investments in the USSR; Edict of the President on the Introduction of a Commercial Rate of Exchange of the Ruble," *International Legal Materials*, 30, no. 4 (July 1991), 913-66.

1046. US Department of Commerce, "Agribusiness Council Is Following Up on Recent Initiatives in Eastern Europe," *Business America*, 111, no. 16 (27 Aug. 1990), 11.

1047. -----, "Business Outlook Abroad: German Democratic Republic," *Business America*, 111, no. 7 (9 Apr. 1990), 20-22.

1048. -----, "Grants Help Smaller Firms Do Business in Eastern Europe," *Business America*, 112, no. 22 (4 Nov. 1991), 22.

1049. -----, "Joint Ventures in the Soviet Union," *Business America*, 111, no. 5 (12 Mar. 1990), 2-7.

1050. -----, "Kentucky Plans Mission to Eastern Europe," *Business America*, 112, no. 12 (17 June 1991), 32.

1051. -----, "New Resource Guide Covers Eastern Europe," *Business America*, 12, no. 19 (23 Sept. 1991), 24.

1052. -----, "Trade Watch: `American Store' in Moscow," *Business America*, 112, no. 7 (8 Apr. 1991), ii.

1053. -----, "Trade Watch: Soviet-American Business Internship Training," *Business America*, 112, no. 23 (18 Nov. 1991), ii.

1054. -----, "Trade Watch: U.S.S.R. Railway Joint Ventures," *Business America*, 112, no. 19 (23 Sept. 1991), ii.

1055. -----, "U.S. Midwest Group Opens a Trade Office in Moscow," *Business America*, 112, no. 21 (21 Oct. 1991), 20.

1056. "USSR Currency Market to Be Created," *SEEL: Soviet and East European Law*, 1, no. 6 (Aug. 1990), 8.

1057. "USSR Law on Taxation of Enterprises, Associations and Organizations: What Does It Mean for Western Investment in the Soviet Union?" *Tax Lawyer*, 44 (Summer 1991), 1123-40.

1058. "USSR's New Associations: Why and What Are They?" *Business in Eastern Europe*, 19, no. 7 (12 Feb. 1990), 49-50; no. 8 (19 Feb. 1990), 62-63.

1059. Vlachoutsikos, Charalambos A., "Doing Business with the

Soviets: What, Who, and How?" *Columbia Journal of World Business*, 23, no. 2 (Summer 1988), 67-79.

1060. Weizman, L., "Western Business Opportunities in the Soviet Union: Perestroikian Prospects," *North Carolina Journal of International Law and Commercial Regulation*, 15 (Spring 1990), 172-228.

1061. Welch, J. B., "Investing in Eastern Europe: A Survey of Chief Financial Officers," *International Executive*, 35, no. 1 (1993), 45-72.

1062. "The Western Manager and the Soviet Director: A Talk with N. A. Kaniskin, Director of the `Sibelektrotiazhmash' Scientific-Production Association in Novosibirsk," *Problems of Economics*, 33, no. 11 (Mar. 1991), 87ff.

1063. Wierzbowski, Marek, "Eastern Europe: Observations and Investment Strategies," *Vanderbilt Journal of Transnational Law*, 24, no. 2 (1991), 385-88.

1064. Wilson-Smith, Anthony, "Lavalin Extends its Reach," *Maclean's*, 98 (27 May 1985), 38-39.

1065. Winter, Will, "Sweeping Reforms in Eastern Europe Create New U.S. Opportunities," *Business America*, 111, no. 8 (23 Apr. 1990), 16.

1066. Wolfe, Dan, "Owning and Operating a Moscow Office," *SEEL: Soviet and East European Law*, 1, no. 4 (May 1990), 4.

1067. Work, C. P., "All That's *Glasnost* Does Not Glitter," *U.S. News & World Report*, 104 (4 Apr. 1988), 50-53.

1068. Zabijaka, Val, "U.S.S.R. Ambitious Investment Plans Offer New Opportunities," *Business America* (17 Mar. 1986), 15.

1069. Zack, A. M., "An American Arbitrator in Donetsk, USSR," *Arbitration Journal*, 45 (Sept. 1990), 43-46.

1070. Zaraev, Mikhail, "Making Lots of Money with News for `The New Soviet Businessman'," *World Monitor*, 4, no. 4 (Apr. 1991), 20.

1071. Zeidman, P. F., and M. Avner, "Franchising in Eastern Europe and the Soviet Union," *DePaul Business Law Journal*, 3 (Spring-Summer 1991), 307-38.

1072. Zimbler, Brian L., "Soviet Foreign Investment Laws and Practices," *Transnational Lawyer*, 4, no. 1 (Spring 1991), 85-122.

1073. Zrelov, Pyotr, "Joint Business: A View from Within," *International Affairs* (Moscow), no. 12 (Dec. 1991), 66-76.

VIII. Communist Party Affairs

BOOKS

1074. Bigelow, Ann, Ronald Branch and Frederick Schulze, eds., *Current Soviet Policies X: The Documentary Record of the 19th Conference of the Communist Party of the Soviet Union*, trans. by Erik Carlson *et al.* (Columbus, OH: Current Digest of the Soviet Press, 1988).

1075. Farmer, Kenneth C., *The Soviet Administrative Elite* (New

York: Praeger, 1992).

1076. Frankland, Mark, *The Sixth Continent: Russia and the Making of Mikhail Gorbachev* (New York: Harper & Row, 1987).

1077. Glazov, Yuri, *To Be or Not To Be in the Party: Communist Party Membership in the USSR* (Dordrecht: Kluwer, 1988).

1078. Gorbachev, Mikhail S., *Political Report of the CPSU Central Committee to the 27th Congress of the Communist Party of the Soviet Union* (Moscow: Novosti, 1986).

1079. -----, *An Understanding of the Soviet Union Through His Speeches, with Special Reference to His New Rules of the Communist Party*, ed. by Herbert Axelrod (Neptune, NJ: TFH Publishers, 1986).

1080. Hazan, Barukh, *From Brezhnev to Gorbachev: Infighting in the Kremlin* (Boulder, CO: Westview Press, 1986).

1081. -----, *Gorbachev's Gamble: The 19th All-Union Party Conference* (Boulder, CO: Westview Press, 1990).

1082. Holmes, Leslie, *The End of Communist Power: Anti-Corruption Campaigns and the Legitimation Crisis* (New York: Oxford University Press, 1993).

1083. Karasik, Theodore W., comp., *The CPSU Central Committee: Members, Commissions and Departments; Valid as of May 1, 1989* (Sherman Oaks, CA: T. W. Karasik, 1989).

1084. Kiernan, Brendan, *The End of Soviet Politics: Elections, Legislatures, and the Demise of the Communist Party* (Boulder, CO: Westview Press, 1993).

1085. Laird, Roy D., *The Politburo: Demographic Trends, Gorbachev, and the Future* (Boulder, CO: Westview Press, 1986).

1086. -----, *The Soviet Legacy* (Westport, CT: Greenwood Press, 1993).

1087. Lowenhardt, John, James R. Ozinga and Erik van Ree, *The Rise and Fall of the Soviet Politburo* (New York: St. Martin's Press, 1991).

1088. Marcy, Sam, *Perestroika: A Marxist Critique* (New York: W.W. Publishers, distributed by World View Forum, 1990).

1089. Miller, John, *Mikhail Gorbachev and the End of Soviet Power* (New York: St. Martin's Press, 1993).

1090. Nichol, Jim, *The 28th Soviet Communist Party Congress: Outcomes and Implications* (Washington, DC: Library of Congress, Congressional Research Service, 1990).

1091. Owen, Richard, *Comrade Chairman: Soviet Succession and the Rise of Gorbachev* (New York: Arbor House, 1987).

1092. *Peace and Progress Ahead: The Meaning of the 27th Congress CPSU* (New York: International Publishers, 1986).

1093. Potichnyi, Peter J., ed., *The Soviet Union: Party and Society* (Cambridge: Cambridge University Press, 1988).

1094. Ra'anan, Uri, and Igor Lukes, *Inside the Apparat: Perspec-tives on the Soviet System from Former Functionaries* (Lexington, MA: Lexington Books, 1990).

1095. Rees, E. A., ed., *The Soviet Communist Party in Disarray: The XXVIII Congress of the Communist Party of the Soviet Union* (New York: St. Martin's Press, 1992).

1096. Rigby, T. H., *The Changing Soviet System: Mono-organizational Socialism from Its Origins to Gorbachev's Restructuring* (Brookfield: Edward Elgar, 1990).

1097. Rush, Myron, *The Fate of the Party Apparatus under Gorbachev* (Santa Monica, CA: RAND, 1991).

1098. Schulze, Fred, and Ronald Branch, eds., *Current Soviet Policies XI: Documents from the 28th Congress of the Communist Party of the Soviet Union*, trans. by Bruce Collins et al. (Columbus, OH: Current Digest of the Soviet Press, 1991).

1099. Taras, Raymond C., ed., *Leadership Change in Communist States* (Boston: Unwin Hyman, 1989).

1100. Tsipko, Aleksandr, *Is Stalinism Really Dead?* (New York: HarperCollins, 1990).

1101. Tsypkin, Mikhail, *Gorbachev and the 27th Soviet Party Congress Say Nyet to Change* (Washington, DC: Heritage Foundation, 1986).

1102. Tucker, Robert C., *Political Culture and Leadership in Soviet Russia: From Lenin to Gorbachev* (New York: W. W. Norton & Company, 1987).

1103. Ulam, Adam, *The Communists: A Story of Power and Lost Illusions, 1948-1991* (New York: Macmillan, 1992).

1104. US Central Intelligence Agency. Directorate of Intelligence. *Communist Party of the Soviet Union Central Committee. Executive and Administrative Apparatus* (Springfield, VA: US Department of Commerce, National Technical Information Service, 1989).

1105. US Central Intelligence Agency. Directorate of Intelligence. *CPSU Central Committee and Central Auditing Commission: Members Elected at the 27th Party Congress: A Reference Aid* (Washington, DC: CIA, distributed by Library of Congress, Exchange and Gift Division, Document Expediting Project, 1986).

1106. US Foreign Broadcast Information Service, *Parliamentary Elections in the USSR: Voters Stun Soviet Officialdom* (Washington, DC: FBIS, 1989).

1107. Waller, Michael, *The End of the Communist Party Monopoly* (New York: St. Martin's Press, 1994).

1108. Winiecki, Jan, *Gorbachev's Way Out? A Proposal to Ease Change in the Soviet System by Buying Out the Privileges of the Ruling Stratum* (London: Centre for Research into Communist Economies, 1988).

ARTICLES

1109. Armstrong, John A., "Persistent Patterns of the Ukrainian Apparatus," *Soviet and Post-Soviet Review*, 20, no. 2-3 (1993),

213-31.

1110. Aron, Leon, "After Communism," *National Review*, 43 (23 Sept. 1991), 28-32.

1111. "Atari Communists: From Hardline to Software," *New Perspectives Quarterly*, 5 (Winter 1988-89), 2-60.

1112. Bahry, Donna, and Brian Silver, "Public Perceptions and the Dilemmas of Party Reform in the USSR," *Comparative Political Studies*, 23, no. 2 (July 1990), 171-209.

1113. Beissinger, Mark R., "Leadership and the Soviet Party Congress," *Current History*, 85, no. 513 (Oct. 1986), 309ff.

1114. -----, "The Party and the Rule of Law," *Columbia Journal of Transnational Law*, 28, no. 1 (Spring 1990), 41-58.

1115. Benn, D. W., "Gorbachev's Progress: Confronting the Conservatives," *World Today*, 44, no. 6 (June 1988), 94-95.

1116. Bialer, Seweryn, "The Last Soviet Communist," *U.S. News & World Report*, 109 (8 Oct. 1990), 53-54.

1117. -----, and Joan Afferica, "The Genesis of Gorbachev's World," *Foreign Affairs*, 64, no. 3 (1986), 605-44.

1118. Bilski, A., "The Meaning of the Plan," *Maclean's*, 101 (11 July 1988), 28.

1119. Blitz, James, "Party Fault Lines," *New Republic* (5 Mar. 1990), 15-16.

1120. Brady, A., "All Gorby's Horses and All Gorby's Men...," *Business Week* (2 July 1990), 44-45.

1121. Brovkin, Vladimir, "First Party Secretaries: An Endangered Soviet Species?" *Problems of Communism*, 39, no. 1 (Jan-Feb. 1990), 15-27.

1122. Brucan, Silviu, "Political Reform in the Socialist System," *World Policy Journal*, 4, no. 3 (Summer 1987), 515-26.

1123. Burlatsky, Fyodor M., "Khrushchev, Andropov, Brezhnev: The Issue of Political Leadership," *Perestroika Annual*, 1 (1988), 187-214.

1124. Chengcai, Wan, "Politburo `Cleans House'," *Beijing Review*, 31 (17 Oct. 1988), 14.

1125. Chiesa, Giulietto, "The 28th Congress of the CPSU," *Problems of Communism*, 39, no. 4 (July-Aug. 1990), 24-38.

1126. Chotiner, Barbara A., "Local Party Organizations in the USSR: Organizational Change, Local Party Committees, and Farms," *Studies in Comparative Communism*, 21, no. 1 (Spring 1988), 45-60.

1127. Cioranescu, George, "The Moldavian Clan in the Kremlin Power Struggle," *Journal of the American Romanian Academy of Arts and Sciences*, no. 12 (1989), 160-69.

1128. Clark, William A., "Token Representation in the CPSU Central Committee," *Soviet Studies*, 43, no. 5 (1991), 913-32.

1129. Cockburn, A., "Beat the Devil," *Nation*, 253 (16 Sept. 1991), 292-93.

1130. Colbert James G., "Notes and Comments: On Finessing Perestroika," *Studies in Soviet Thought*, 40, no. 1-3 (Aug-Nov. 1990), 251-55.

1131. Coleman, F., "The People Want to Get Rid of Communism," *Newsweek*, 115 (14 May 1990), 29-30.

1132. Conquest, Robert, "Apparatchiks at Bay," *National Review*, 40 (7 Nov. 1988), 16.

1133. Dahm, Helmut, "What Restoring Leninism Means," *Studies in Soviet Thought*, 39, no. 1 (Feb. 1990), 55-76.

1134. Dale, Patrick, "The Aftermath of the Twenty-Seventh CPSU Congress: Leadership Conflict and Socio-Political Change," *Soviet Union/Union Sovietique*, 14, no. 1 (1987), 19-63.

1135. Dansokho, Amath, "Perestroika Is for Everyone," *World Marxist Review*, 33 (Feb. 1990), 8-14.

1136. DeGeorge, Richard T., "Ideology and the Third Party Programme," *Studies in Soviet Thought*, 34, no. 3 (Oct. 1987), 173-78.

1137. Draper, T., "Who Killed Soviet Communism?" *New York Review of Books*, 39 (11 June 1992), 7ff.

1138. Dunlop, John B., "New National Bolshevik Organization Formed," *Report on the USSR*, 2, no. 37 (14 Sept. 1990), 7-9.

1139. Evans, Alfred B., Jr., "The New Program of the CPSU: Changes in Soviet Ideology," *Soviet Union/Union Sovietique*, 14, no. 1 (1987), 1-18.

1140. Fairbanks, Charles H., Jr., "The Suicide of Soviet Communism," *Journal of Democracy*, 1, no. 2 (Spring 1990), 18-26.

1141. Flacks, Richard, "The Party's Over-So What Is to Be Done?" *Social Research*, 60, no. 3 (Fall 1993), 445-70.

1142. Foye, Stephen, "Maintaining the Union: The CPSU and the Soviet Armed Forces," *Report on the USSR*, 3, no. 23 (7 June 1991), 1-8.

1143. Frank, Peter, "Gorbachev and the `Psychological Restructuring' of Soviet Society," *World Today*, 43, no. 5 (May 1987), 85-87.

1144. Freidin, Gregory, "The Gorbachev Team," *New Republic* (30 July-6 Aug. 1990), 10-12.

1145. Friedgut, Theodore H., "Gorbachev and Party Reform," *Orbis*, 30, no. 2 (Summer 1986), 281-96.

1146. Galuszka, Philip, "Gorbachev Plots an End Run Around the Party Bureaucrats," *Business Week* (27 June 1988), 51.

1147. -----, "Whetting the Soviets' Appetite for Real Results," *Business Week* (18 July 1988), 84-85.

1148. "Good-bye, CPSU," *World Today*, 47, no. 10 (Oct. 1991), 163.

1149. Gooding, John, "The XXVIII Congress of the CPSU in Perspective," *Soviet Studies*, 43, no. 2 (1991), 237-54.

1150. "Gorbachev's Address to the 19th CPSU Conference,"

Survival, 30, no. 6 (Nov-Dec. 1988), 465-68.

1151. Hahn, Jeffrey, "An Experiment in Competition: The 1987 Elections to the Local Soviets," *Slavic Review*, 47, no. 2 (Fall 1988), 434-37.

1152. Hanson, Philip, and Elizabeth Teague, "Soviet Communist Party Loses Members," *Report on the USSR*, 2, no. 20 (18 May 1990), 1-3.

1153. -----, "Gorbachev's Gamble: Voting Out the Foot Draggers," *Commonweal* (18 Nov. 1988), 613-14.

1154. Harasymiw, Bohdan, "Changes in the Party's Composition: The `Destroyka' of the CPSU," *Journal of Communist Studies*, 7, no. 2 (June 1991), 133-60.

1155. -----, "The CPSU in Transition from Brezhnev to Gorbachev," *Canadian Journal of Political Science*, 21, no. 2 (June 1988), 249-66.

1156. -----, "Local Party Organizations in the USSR: Gorbachev's Reorganization and the Gorkom," *Studies in Comparative Communism*, 21, no. 1 (1988), 61-70.

1157. Harrison, Frank, "The Crisis of Soviet Stalinism," *Our Generation*, 21, no. 1 (1990), 185-200.

1158. Heller, Agnes, "The End of Communism," *Thesis Eleven*, no. 27 (1990), 5-19.

1159. Hill, Ronald J., "The CPSU: From Monolith to Pluralist?" *Soviet Studies*, 43, no. 2 (1991), 217-36.

1160. -----, and John Lowenhardt, "Nomenklatura and Perestroika," *Government and Opposition*, 26, no. 2 (Spring 1991), 229-43.

1161. Hoffmann, David L., "A First Glimpse into the Moscow Party Archives," *Russian Review*, 50, no. 4 (Oct. 1991), 484-86.

1162. Holloway, David, "The Soviet Party Congress," *Bulletin of the Atomic Scientists*, 42, no. 5 (May 1986), 15-19.

1163. Howe, Irving, "Soviet Transformation," *Dissent*, 37, no. 2 (Spring 1990), 133-34.

1164. Izyumov, A., "Time to Wind Down the Party," *Newsweek*, 115 (11 June 1990), 27.

1165. Jackson, Marvin R., "Party Assets," *Report on Eastern Europe*, 1, no. 10 (9 Mar. 1990), 52-55.

1166. Jacobs, Margot, "The Party and the People: A Parting of Ways?" *Report on the USSR*, 2, no. 29 (20 July 1990), 8-11.

1167. Jokay, Charles Z., "A Lion in Chains: The CPSU and the Soviet Military," *Crossroads*, no. 24 (1987), 51-63.

1168. Kargalitsky, Boris, "And Thus, the Mossoviet...," *Harriman Institute Forum*, 4, no. 1 (Jan. 1991), 1-4.

1169. Klyamkin, Igor, "Trends in the Political Parties," *Report on the USSR*, 3, no. 42 (18 Oct. 1991), 5-6.

1170. Knight, Amy, "The Party, the KGB, and Soviet Policy-Making," *Washington Quarterly*, 11, no. 2 (Spring 1988), 121-36.

1171. Kramer, Mark, "The Role of the CPSU International Department in Soviet Foreign Relations and National Security Policy," *Soviet Studies*, 42, no. 3 (July 1990), 429-46.

1172. Kraus, Herwig, "Leaders of the Communist and Former Communist Parties of the USSR and the Baltic States," *Report on the USSR*, 2, no. 52 (28 Dec. 1990), 22-23.

1173. Kropiwnicki, Aleksander, "Escaping from Communism... with the Communists," *Uncaptive Minds*, 3, no. 5 (Nov-Dec. 1991), 21-23.

1174. "The Last Rites of Communism," *Maclean's*, 104 (2 Sept. 1991), 22ff.

1175. MacFarquhar, R., "The Anatomy of Collapse," *New York Review of Books*, 38 (26 Sept. 1991), 5ff.

1176. Mann, Dawn, "An Argument for Legalizing Opposition to the CPSU," *Report on the USSR*, 2, no. 11 (16 Mar. 1990), 11-12.

1177. -----, "Authority of Regional Party Leaders Crumbling," *Report on the USSR*, 2, no. 8 (23 Feb. 1990), 1-6.

1178. -----, "The Democratic Party of Communists of Russia," *Report on the USSR* (30 Aug. 1991), 26-30.

1179. -----, "Democratic Party of Communists of Russia Cuts Ties to CPSU," *Report on the USSR*, 3, no. 37 (13 Sept. 1991), 16.

1180. -----, "Divisions within the Communist Party Intensify," *Report on the USSR*, 3, no. 30 (26 July 1991), 1-9.

1181. -----, "Draft Party Program Approved," *Report on the USSR*, 3, no. 32 (9 Aug. 1991), 1-5.

1182. -----, "Gorbachev Meets with Local Party Officials," *Report on the USSR*, 2, no. 9 (2 Mar. 1990), 14-16.

1183. -----, "Gorbachev's Report to the Twenty-eighth Party Congress: Reform of the CPSU," *Report on the USSR*, 2, no. 28 (13 July 1990), 10-12.

1184. -----, "Leadership of Regional Communist Party Committees and Soviets," *Report on the USSR*, 2, no. 51 (21 Dec. 1990), 15-25.

1185. -----, "Leading Bodies of CPSU Transformed," *Report on the USSR*, 2, no. 29 (20 July 1990), 14-20.

1186. Mawsdley, Evan, "The 1990 Central Committee of the CPSU in Perspective," *Soviet Studies*, 43, no. 5 (1991), 897-912.

1187. -----, and Stephen White, "Renewal and Dead Souls: The Changing Soviet Central Committee," *British Journal of Political Science*, 20, part 4 (Oct. 1990), 537-42.

1188. McFaul, Michael, "The Last Hurrah for the CPSU," *Report on the USSR*, 2, no. 30 (27 July 1990), 11-14.

1189. -----, "A Talk with Yuri Skubco," *New Leader*, 73, no. 19 (6-20 Aug. 1990), 14-17.

1190. Methvin, Eugene H., "Yeltsin Spoils the Party," *National Review*, 42 (19 Mar. 1990), 29ff.

1191. Mitchell, R. Judson, "The CPSU Politburo in 1990: A Projection," *Crossroads*, no. 19 (1986), 21-43.

1192. -----, and Teresa Gee, "The Soviet Succession Crisis and Its Aftermath," *Orbis*, 29, no. 2 (Summer 1985), 293-317.

1193. Muray, Leo, "The Soviets in Turmoil," *Contemporary Review*, 253, no. 1472 (Sept. 1988), 122-27.

1194. Nemeth, M., "Is the Party Over?" *Maclean's*, 103 (23 July 1990), 28-29.

1195. "The Next Step for Gorbachev," *Economist*, 320 (3 Aug. 1991), 18-19.

1196. Nicholson, Martin, "Gorbachev's First Congress," *World Today*, 42, no. 2 (Feb. 1987), 23-26.

1197. "19th Conference of the CPSU: A *Soviet Economy* Roundtable," *Soviet Economy*, 4, no. 2 (Apr-June 1988), 103-35.

1198. Oleszczuk, Thomas, "The CPSU as an Integrative Force," *Nationalities Papers*, 19, no. 1 (Spring 1991), 23-26.

1199. "On the Atari Communists," *New Perspectives Quarterly*, 6 (Spring 1989), 60-61.

1200. Ozinga, James R., "The Soviet Political Elite" (Review Article), *Russian Review*, 49, no. 1 (Jan. 1990), 77-88.

1201. Pechenev, V. A., "Kremlin Secrets: Up the Down Staircase," *Soviet Law and Government*, 30, no. 3 (Winter 1991-92), 21-27.

1202. "Perestroika in the USSR and the International Communist Movement," *World Marxist Review*, 31, no. 9 (Sept. 1988), 92-108.

1203. "Perestroika Throws a Party," *Economist*, 309 (1 Oct. 1988), 51-52.

1204. Peretz, Martin, "Great Lenin's Ghost," *New Republic* (5 Mar. 1990), 17-19.

1205. Quinn-Judge, Paul, "Party Spoilers," *New Republic* (23 July 1990), 11-13.

1206. Ra'anan, Uri, "Before and after Chernobyl: Stresses in the Soviet Leadership," *Orbis*, 30, no. 2 (Summer 1986), 249-57.

1207. Rahr, Alexander, "The CPSU after the Twenty-Eighth Party Congress," *Report on the USSR*, 2, no. 45 (9 Nov. 1990), 1-4.

1208. -----, "The CPSU in the 1980s: Changes in the Party Apparatus," *Journal of Communist Studies*, 7, no. 2 (June 1991), 161-69.

1209. -----, "The CPSU Strikes Back," *Report on the USSR*, 3, no. 8 (22 Feb. 1991), 1-3.

1210. -----, "From Politburo to Presidential Council," *Report on the USSR*, 2, no. 22 (1 June 1990), 1-5.

1211. -----, "Inside the Interregional Group," *Report on the USSR*, 2, no. 43 (26 Oct. 1990), 1-4.

1212. -----, "Ligachev Defeated," *Report on the USSR*, 2, no. 29 (20 July 1990), 3-4.

1213. Rice, Condoleezza, "The Party, the Military, and Decision Authority in the Soviet Union," *World Politics*, 40, no. 1 (Oct. 1987), 55-81.

1214. Richmond, N. I., "One Step Forward, Two Steps Back: The USSR Supreme Soviet in the Age of *Perestroika*," *Journal of Communist Studies*, 7, no. 2 (June 1991), 202-16.

1215. Robinson, Neil, "Gorbachev and the Place of the Party in Soviet Reform, 1985-1991," *Soviet Studies*, 44, no. 3 (1992), 423-44.

1216. Rodman, Peter W., "The Last General Secretary," *National Review*, 44 (20 Jan. 1992), 11-12.

1217. "Rules of the Communist Party of the Soviet Union Ratified by the Twenty-Eighth Congress of the CPSU," *Soviet Law and Government*, 30, no. 2 (Fall 1991), 7-25.

1218. Rutland, Peter, "'Democratic Platform' Prepares for CPSU Congress," *Report on the USSR*, 2, no. 26 (29 June 1990), 1-3.

1219. Rywkin, Michael, "The Breakdown of Cadre Policy," *Nationalities Papers*, 28, no. 1 (Spring 1990), 47-48.

1220. Schneider, Eberhard, "The Demise of the CPSU and the Rise of New Political Parties," *Report on the USSR*, 3, no. 42 (18 Oct. 1991), 1-3.

1221. Schorr, Daniel, "Gorbachev's Sinking Ship," *New Leader*, 73, no. 9 (9-23 July 1990), 4.

1222. Scott, Harriet F., "The Party Assembled," *Air Force Magazine*, 69, no. 3 (Mar. 1986), 46-51.

1223. Serrill, M. S., "All Power to the Party," *Time*, 130 (6 July 1987), 96.

1224. Sheehy, Ann, "New Party Rules Give Republican Communist Parties More Autonomy," *Report on the USSR*, 2, no. 29 (29 July 1990), 11-13.

1225. Shevardnadze, Eduard, "Consolidation of the CPSU in a Multiparty System," *Soviet Law and Government*, 29, no. 2 (Spring 1991), 5-20.

1226. Shlapentokh, Vladimir, "The XXVII Congress: A Case Study of the Shaping of a New Party Ideology," *Soviet Studies*, 40, no. 1 (Jan. 1988), 1-20.

1227. Singer, Daniel, "Communism's Great Debate," *Nation*, 250 (26 Mar. 1990), 418ff.

1228. Sneider, Dan, "The Party's Over," *National Review*, 43 (26 Aug. 1991), 21-22.

1229. Socor, Vladimir, "The Moldavian Communists: From Ruling to Opposition Party," *Report on the USSR*, 3, no. 14 (5 Apr. 1991), 15-21.

1230. Solnick, Steven L., "Does the Komsomol Have a Future?" *Report on the USSR*, 38 (21 Sept. 1990), 9-13.

1231. Sosin, G., "Trotsky Redux," *New Leader*, 73 (3 Sept. 1990), 11-12.

1232. Staar, Richard F., "Checklist of Communist Parties in 1989," *Problems of Communism*, 39, no. 2 (Mar-Apr. 1990), 75-84.

1233. Starr, S. Frederick, "Pooped Party," *New Republic* (4 Dec. 1989), 20-21.

1234. "Surviving the Party Congress," *World Press Review*, 202 (5 Mar. 1990), 15-16.

1235. Tatu, Michel, "19th Party Conference," *Problems of Communism*, 37, no. 3-4 (May-Aug. 1988), 1-15.

1236. Teague, Elizabeth, "Gorbachev Discusses Possibility of Multiparty System," *Report on the USSR*, 2, no. 5 (2 Feb. 1990), 3-4.

1237. -----, "Gorbachev Proposes Dropping Communist Party Monopoly," *Report on the USSR*, 2, no. 6 (9 Feb. 1990), 6-8.

1238. -----, "Is the Party Over?" *Report on the USSR*, 2, no. 18 (4 May 1990), 1-4.

1239. -----, "The Twenty-Eighth Party Congress; An Overview," *Report on the USSR*, 2, no. 29 (20 July 1990), 1-3.

1240. -----, and Vera Tolz, "CPSU R.I.P.," *Report on the USSR*, 3, no. 47 (22 Nov. 1991), 1-8.

1241. Thorson, Carla, "Has the Communist Party Been Legally Suspended?" *Report on the USSR*, 3, no. 40 (4 Oct. 1991), 4-8.

1242. Timmermann, M., "The CPSU and the International Communist Party System: A Change of Paradigms in Moscow," *Studies in Comparative Communism*, 22 (Summer-Autumn 1989), 265-77.

1243. Tismaneanu, Vladimir, "Neo-Stalinism and Reform Communism," *Orbis*, 30, no. 2 (Summer 1986), 259-80.

1244. -----, "The Yeltsin Affair," *Orbis*, 32, no. 2 (Spring 1988), 277-86.

1245. Tolz, Vera, "The Emergence of a Multiparty System in the USSR," *Report on the USSR*, 2, no. 17 (27 Apr. 1990), 5-11.

1246. Trimble, J., "Saying Nyet to Communism," *U.S. News & World Report*, 108 (5 Mar. 1990), 46.

1247. Trump, Thomas M., "The Membership Dilemma of the CPSU: Impact on the Party Congress," *Crossroads*, no. 24 (1987), 1-16.

1248. "Turmoil, Panic, Even a New Party," *Economist*, 307 (14 May 1988), 50ff.

1249. Unger, Aryeh L., "The Travails of Intra-Party Democracy in the Soviet Union: The Elections to the 19th Conference of the CPSU," *Soviet Studies*, 43, no. 2 (1991), 329-54.

1250. Urban, Michael E., "From Chernenko to Gorbachev: A Repoliticization of Official Soviet Discourse?" *Soviet Union/Union Sovietique*, 13, no. 2 (1986), 131-61.

1251. Van den Haag, Ernest, "The End of Communism in Italy," *National Review*, 41 (8 Dec. 1989), 21-22.

1252. Vanden Heuvel, Katrina, "Now Is the Time: for the Party to Aid Gorbachev," *Nation* (10 July 1989), 45-48.

1253. "What Kind of Party? Two Points of View," *Soviet Sociology*, 29, no. 5 (Sept-Oct. 1990), 75-83.

1254. White, Stephen, "Rethinking the CPSU," *Soviet Studies*, 43, no. 3 (1991), 405-28.

1255. Wishnevsky, Julia, "Aleksandr Yakovlev Quits the Central Committee," *Report on the USSR*, 2, no. 30 (27 July 1990), 5-8.

1256. -----, "Multiparty System Takes Shape in Moscow," *Report on the USSR*, 2, no. 47 (23 Nov. 1990), 13-14.

1257. -----, and Elizabeth Teague, "Secret Party Directives Said Abolished," *Report on the USSR*, 2, no. 8 (23 Feb. 1990), 11-12.

1258. Yasmann, Viktor, "The KGB and the Party Congress," *Report on the USSR*, 2, no. 31 (3 Aug. 1990), 12-14.

1259. "Yeltsin: Lightning Rod or Leader?" *National Review*, 42 (6 Aug. 1990), 15.

IX. Coup of August 1991

BOOKS

1260. Billington, James, *Russia Transformed: The Breakthrough to Hope* (New York: Free Press, 1992).

1261. Bonnell, Victoria, Ann Cooper and Gregory Freidin, *Russia at the Barricades: Eyewitness Accounts of the August Coup* (Armonk, NY: M. E. Sharpe, 1993).

1262. Frangulov, Vladimir G., *The Coup: Underground Moscow Newspapers from Monday, August 19 to Wednesday, August 21, 1991: A Chronological Compilation of Rare Newspapers Published During the Three-Day Resistance* (Minneapolis: East View Press, 1991).

1263. Gorbachev, Mikhail S., *The August Coup: The Truth and the Lessons* (New York: HarperCollins, 1991).

1264. Loory, Stuart H., and Ann Imse, *Seven Days That Shook the World* (Atlanta: Turner Publishing, 1991).

1265. Pozner, Vladimir, *Eyewitness: A Personal Account of the Unraveling of the Soviet Union* (New York: Random House, 1992).

ARTICLES

1266. Aksyonov, Vassily, "Live Souls," *New Republic* (16-23 Sept. 1991), 12-14.

1267. Alonso, Axel, "U.S. Communist Press and the `August Revolution': A Look at Five Communist Newspapers Around the U.S. and How Each Views the Events in the Soviet Union," *Editor and Publisher*, 124, no. 45 (9 Nov. 1991), 14-17.

1268. Andrejevich, Milan, "The Attempted Coup in the USSR: Eastern European Reactions: Yugoslavia," *Report on Eastern Europe*, 2, no. 35 (30 Aug. 1991), 17-18.

1269. Antic, Oxana, "Church Reaction to the Coup," *Report on the USSR*, 3, no. 38 (20 Sept. 1991), 15-17.

1270. "The August Coup," *New Left Review*, no. 189 (Sept-Oct. 1991).

1271. "The August Revolution," *National Review*, 43 (23 Sept. 1991), 8ff.

1272. "The August Revolution," *New Republic* (16-23 Sept. 1991), 7-8.

1273. Awanohara, Susumu, "Collective Shiver: Coup against Gorbachev Upsets Asian Calculations," *Far Eastern Economic Review*, 153 (29 Aug. 1991), 10-11.

1274. Barnard, Patrick, "The Soviet Coup," *Commonweal*, 118 (13 Sept. 1991), 501.

1275. Barnes, Fred, "White House Watch: Gate Crasher," *New Republic* (16-23 Sept. 1991), 10-12.

1276. Barylski, Robert, "The Soviet Military Before and After the August Coup: Departization and Decentralization," *Armed Forces and Society*, 19, no. 1 (Fall 1992), 27-46.

1277. Beichman, Arnold, "In Retrospect: Labor's Opposition," *Freedom Review*, 22, no. 6 (Nov-Dec. 1991), 14-15.

1278. Beissinger, Mark R., "The Deconstruction of the USSR and the Search for a Post-Soviet Community," *Problems of Communism*, 40, no. 6 (Nov-Dec. 1991), 27-35.

1279. Bond, David F., "Kremlin Cabal's Failure Fuels Defense Budget Debate in U.S.," *Aviation Week & Space Technology*, 135, no. 8 (26 Aug. 1991), 23.

1280. Bonnell, Victoria E., and Gregory Freidin, "*Televorot*: The Role of Television Coverage in Russia's August 1991 Coup," *Slavic Review*, 52, no. 4 (Winter 1993), 810-38.

1281. Bonner, Elena, "We Didn't Defend Gorbachev," *Uncaptive Minds*, 4, no. 3 (Fall 1991), 35-38.

1282. "Boris for President," *Economist*, 320 (24 Aug. 1991), 23-24.

1283. Bradley, Joseph, "Russia after the Coup: Rethinking the Past," *AAASS Newsletter*, 31, no. 5 (Nov. 1991), 5.

1284. Breslauer, George, "Bursting the Dams: Politics and Society in the USSR Since the Coup," *Problems of Communism*, 40, no. 6 (Nov-Dec. 1991), 2-12.

1285. -----, "Reflections on the Anniversary of the August 1991 Coup," *Soviet Economy* (Apr-June 1992), 164-74.

1286. Brown, Bess, "Central Asia: Mixed Reactions," *Report on the USSR*, 3, no. 36 (6 Sept. 1991), 43-47.

1287. "Bush, Major Respond to Soviet Events," *Congressional Quarterly Weekly Report*, 49 (31 Aug. 1991), 2377-78.

1288. "Bush Reacts Daily to Rise, Fall of Three-Day Coup," *Congressional Quarterly Weekly Report*, 49 (24 Aug. 1991), 2330-34.

1289. Calabresi, Massimo, "At Yeltsin's Side," *National Review*, 43 (23 Sept. 1991), 20-21.

1290. Chernyayev, A., "Four Desperate Days," *Time*, 138 (7 Oct. 1991), 28-31.

1291. Cheung, Tai Ming, "Return of the Hard Men," *Far Eastern Economic Review*, 153 (29 Aug. 1991), 13.

1292. Cockburn, Alexander, "Beat the Devil," *Nation*, 253 (16 Sept. 1991), 292-93.

1293. -----, "Unheroic Couplet," *Nation*, 253 (9 Sept. 1991), 254.

1294. Conquest, Robert, "Reflections of the Revolution," *National Review*, 43 (23 Sept. 1991), 24-26.

1295. "The Coup and After," *Report on the USSR*, 3, no. 36 (6 Sept. 1991).

1296. Covault, Craig, "Soviet Defense Ministry Rifts Spurred Coup; Instability Lingers," *Aviation Week & Space Technology*, 135, no. 8 (26 Aug. 1991), 18-19.

1297. "Crisis in the Soviet Union," *Aviation Week & Space Technology*, 137 (26 Aug. 1991), 18-27.

1298. Crow, Suzanne, "Shevardnadze's Vindication," *Report on the USSR*, 3, no. 36 (6 Sept. 1991), 30-31.

1299. Crozier, Brian, "Getting It Wrong About Gorby," *National Review*, 43 (23 Sept. 1991), 22-23.

1300. Cullen, Robert, "After the Coup," *New Yorker* (11 Nov. 1991), 47ff.

1301. Daniels, Robert V., "All That Is Soviet Melts into Air," *New Leader*, 74, no. 14 (30 Dec. 1991), 22-25.

1302. Darski, Jozef, "The Triple Scenario," *Uncaptive Minds*, 4, no. 3 (Fall 1991), 19-23.

1303. Donnelly, Christopher, "The Coup and its Aftermath," *NATO Review*, 39, no. 5 (Oct. 1991), 3-6.

1304. Drew, Elizabeth, "Letter from Washington," *New Yorker* (23 Sept. 1991), 96-101.

1305. Elliot, Iain, "Three Days in August: On-the-Spot Impressions," *Report on the USSR*, 3, no. 36 (6 Sept. 1991), 63-67.

1306. "Europe and the Botched Coup: Anatomy of a Botched Putsch," *Economist*, 320 (24 Aug. 1991), 17-22.

1307. Fairbanks, Charles H., Jr., "After the Moscow Coup," *Journal of Democracy*, 2, no. 4 (Fall 1991), 3-10.

1308. Fischer, Michael S., "For USSR, the Question Is, Will the Union Hold?" *Business International*, 38, no. 34 (26 Aug. 1991), 289-90.

1309. Foye, Stephen, "Leading Plotters in the Armed Forces," *Report on the USSR*, 3, no. 36 (6 Sept. 1991), 12-15.

1310. -----, "A Lesson in Ineptitude: Military-Backed Coup Crumbles," *Report on the USSR*, 3, no. 35 (30 Aug. 1991), 5-8.

1311. Freidin, Gregory, "To the Barricades," *New Republic* (30 Sept. 1991), 8-10.

1312. Friedheim, Jerry W., "Eyewitness to Coup's Collapse: Freedom Forum Official Saw a Free Press in the Soviet Union Prevail," *Editor and Publisher*, 124, no. 35 (31 Aug. 1991), 14-15.

1313. Fulghum, David A., "Failed Coup Could Produce Big Soviet Military Shakeup," *Aviation Week & Space Technology*, 135, no. 8 (26 Aug. 1991), 20.

1314. Gambrell, Jamey, "Seven Days That Shook the World," *New York Review of Books*, 38 (26 Sept. 1991), 56-61.

1315. Gerbner, George, "Instant History: The Case of the Moscow Coup," *Political Communication*, 10, no. 2 (Apr-June 1993), 193ff.

1316. Girnius, Saulius, "Attempted Coup Leads to Recognition of Lithuania," *Report on the USSR*, 3, no. 36 (6 Sept. 1991), 51-54.

1317. Goldman, Marshall I., "Three Days That Shook My World," *World Monitor*, 4 (Oct. 1991), 30-33.

1318. Gooding, John, "Perestroika and the Russian Revolution of 1991," *Slavonic and East European Review*, 71, no. 2 (Apr. 1993), 234-56.

1319. Gorbachev, Mikhail S., "Detention During the Coup," *Vital Speeches of the Day*, 57 (15 Sept. 1991), 11-14.

1320. -----, "I Share the Blame for the Coup," *Vital Speeches of the Day*, 57 (15 Sept. 1991), 14-17.

1321. Hamburg, Roger, "After the Abortive Soviet Coup and `What Is to Be Done'? The Post Soviet Military," *Journal of Political and Military Sociology*, 20, no. 2 (Winter 1992), 305-22.

1322. Harris, David, "Gorbachev with a Human Face," *Freedom Review*, 22, no. 5 (Sept-Oct. 1991), 15ff.

1323. Hellie, Richard, "Russia Before, During and After the `Keystone Coup'," *Russian History/Histoire Russe*, 18, no. 3 (Fall 1991), 255-316.

1324. Hogan, John P., and Bruce MacDonald, "Since the Coup," *Commonweal*, 118 (6 Dec. 1991), 709-10.

1325. Hough, Jerry, "Assessing the Coup," *Current History*, 90, no. 558 (Oct. 1991), 305-10.

1326. Husarka, Anna, "The Apartment," *New Republic* (16-23 Sept. 1991), 14-16.

1327. "The Impact of the Failed Coup in the USSR on Mainland China," *Issues and Studies*, 27, no. 9 (Sept. 1991), 129-31.

1328. Izyumov, A., "Coup Unites Soviet Media," *Quill*, 80 (Jan-Feb. 1992), 27-29.

1329. Kalnins, Ojars, "Coup Document: Three Days in Riga," *American Spectator*, 24, no. 11 (Nov. 1991), 29-31.

1330. Kargalitsky, Boris, "The Coup That Worked," *New Statesman and Society*, 4 (6 Sept. 1991), 18-20.

1331. Kaye, Lincoln, *et al.*, "Bitter Medicine: China on the Defensive after Failed Soviet Coup," *Far Eastern Economic Review*, 153 (5 Sept. 1991), 10-12.

1332. Kenez, Peter, "Debating Democracy in Russia," *New Leader*, 74, no. 10 (9-23 Sept. 1991), 15-18.

1333. Kinsley, Michael, "TRB: Heroes and Wimps," *New Republic* (16-23 Sept. 1991), 4.

1334. Kniffel, L., "Caught in a Coup d'Etat: Historians Witness History at IFLA in Moscow," *American Libraries*, 22 (Oct. 1991), 846ff.

1335. Knight, Amy, "The Coup That Never Was: Gorbachev and the Forces of Reaction," *Problems of Communism*, 40, no. 6 (Nov-Dec. 1991), 36-43.

1336. Kyriakodis, Harry J., "The 1991 Soviet and 1917 Bolshevik Coups Compared: Causes, Consequences, and Legality," *Russian History/Histoire Russe*, 18, no. 3 (Fall 1991), 317-62.

1337. Lapham, Lewis H., "History Lesson," *Harper's*, 283, no. 1698 (Nov. 1991), 13-16.

1338. Laqueur, Walter, "The Empire Strikes Out," *New Republic* (16-23 Sept. 1991), 24-28.

1339. Laski, Wojtek, and Vladimir Sichov, "Great Russians, August `91," *Harper's*, 283, no. 1699 (Dec. 1991), 45.

1340. "Lenin Nyet! The Revolution That Failed," *New Leader*, 74, no. 10 (9-23 Sept. 1991), 3-20.

1341. Lloyd, J., "Hero Boris," *New Statesman and Society*, 4 (23 Aug. 1991), 17.

1342. Lomasky, Loren, "Soviet Union: Coups and Constitution," *Reason*, 23, no. 6 (Nov. 1991), 48ff.

1343. Lotz, C., and S. Massey, "Hundreds Face Sack in Wake of USSR Coup," *The Higher*, 987 (4 Oct. 1991), 11.

1344. Major, J., "Yeltsin Demands Gorbachev Be Freed," *Vital Speeches of the Day*, 57 (15 Sept. 1991), 709.

1345. Malia, Martin, "The August Revolution," *New York Review of Books*, 38 (26 Sept. 1991), 22ff.

1346. Mandelbaum, Michael, "Coup de Grace: The End of the Soviet Union," *Foreign Affairs*, 70, no. 1 (1992), 164-83.

1347. Mann, Dawn, "The Circumstances Surrounding the Conservative Putsch," *Report on the USSR*, 3, no. 36 (6 Sept. 1991), 1-5.

1348. Mayer, Arno J., "Past and Prologue," *Nation*, 253 (16 Sept. 1991), 289-90.

1349. McClellan, Stephen, "Coup Worries, Then Reassures U.S. Companies," *Broadcasting*, 121, no. 9 (26 Aug. 1991), 19-20.

1350. McColm, Bruce R., "Conspiracy Central," *Freedom Review*, 22, no. 6 (Nov-Dec. 1991), 15-17.

1351. McFaul, Michael, "Moscow's Drama: A View from Below," *Freedom Review*, 22, no. 6 (Nov-Dec. 1991), 7-9.

1352. McKay, Betsy, "From Coup to Champagne," *Advertising Age*, 62, no. 35 (1991), 37ff.

1353. -----, "Media Mayhem: Soviet Coup Attempt Leaves TV, Print Reeling," *Advertising Age*, 62 (2 Sept. 1991), 46.

1354. -----, "Moscow Prelude: Warning Signs Ignored," *Report on the USSR*, 3, no. 36 (6 Sept. 1991), 8-11.

1355. Mecham, Michael, "NATO Stresses Political Role During Soviet Union Crisis," *Aviation Week & Space Technology*, 135, no. 8 (26 Aug. 1991), 25.

1356. Meyer, Stephen M., "How the Threat (and the Coup) Collapsed: The Politicization of the Soviet Military," *International Security*, 16, no. 3 (Winter 1991-92), 5-38.

1357. Miller, Stephen, "The Soviet Coup and the Benefits of Breakdown," *Orbis*, 36, no. 1 (Winter 1992), 69-85.

1358. "Moscow, August 1991: The Coup de Grace," *Problems of Communism*, 40, no. 6 (Nov-Dec. 1991), 1-62.

1359. "The Moscow Coup: The Beginning of the End," *National Review*, 43 (9 Sept. 1991), 19-20.

1360. Mullen, Richard, "Historical Reflections on the Revolution in Russia," *Contemporary Review*, 259, no. 1509 (Oct. 1991), 169-73.

1361. "New, Hard Questions," *Nation*, 253 (16 Sept. 1991), 285ff.

1362. Newman, P. C., "A Week That Shook the Communist World," *Maclean's*, 104 (2 Sept. 1991), 44.

1363. Nosov, Fyodor, "How Media Aided Soviet Coup Resisters," *Advertising Age*, 62, no. 43 (7 Oct. 1991), 28.

1364. Novak, Michael, "The Invisible Filament," *Forbes*, 148, no. 7 (30 Sept. 1991), 148-49.

1365. Oberman, Jan, "The Attempted Coup in the USSR: Eastern European Reactions: Czechoslovakia," *Report on Eastern Europe*, 2, no. 35 (3 Aug. 1991), 5-7.

1366. Odom, William E., "Alternative Perspectives on the August Coup," *Problems of Communism*, 40, no. 6 (Nov-Dec. 1991), 13-19.

1367. Perry, Duncan M., "The Attempted Coup in the USSR: Eastern European Reactions: Introduction," *Report on Eastern Europe*, 2, no. 35 (30 Aug. 1991), 1-2.

1368. -----, "The Attempted Coup in the USSR: Eastern European Reactions: Bulgaria," *Report on Eastern Europe*, 2, no. 35 (30 Aug. 1991), 4-5.

1369. Plater-Zyberk, Henry, "The Red Army Blues," *National Review*, 43 (23 Sept. 1991), 34-37.

1370. "Priests of the Putsch," *U.S. News and World Report*, 112 (2 Mar. 1992), 57.

1371. "Publius," "An Open Letter to Mikhail & Boris," *New Leader*, 74, no. 10 (9-23 Sept. 1991), 18-19.

1372. Quade, Quentin L., "Lessons from the Soviet Coup," *Freedom Review*, 22, no. 6 (Nov-Dec. 1991), 11-14.

1373. Quinn, Judy, and Michael Rogers, "IFLA Meeting Interrupted by Attempted Soviet Coup," *Library Journal*, 116, no. 15 (15 Sept. 1991), 14.

1374. "Raisa's Ordeal: Those Were Terrible Days," *Newsweek*, 118 (16 Sept. 1991), 34.

1375. Raleigh, Donald J., "Beyond Moscow and St. Petersburg: Some Reflections on the August Revolution, Provincial Russia and Novostroika," *South Atlantic Quarterly*, 91 (Summer 1992), 603-19.

1376. Rahr, Alexander, "Changes in the El'tsin-Gorbachev Relationship," *Report on the USSR*, 3, no. 36 (6 Sept. 1991), 35-37.

1377 -----, "The Soviet Leadership on the Eve of the Coup," *Report on the USSR*, 3, no. 34 (23 Aug. 1991), 3-8.

1378. "Reacting to the Coup and Counter-Coup," *Economist*, 320 (24 Aug. 1991), 50.

1379. Rich, Vera, "'Shame' over Science Academy's Coup Silence," *The Higher*, 985 (20 Sept. 1991), 12.

1380. Rigby, T. H., "The Road to August 21," *Australian Slavonic and East European Studies*, 5, no. 2 (1991), 85-103.

1381. Rubinfien, Elisabeth, "Exhilaration and Fear in Moscow," *National Review*, 43 (23 Sept. 1991), 18-19.

1382. Rupnick, Jacques, "Emergency Exit," *New Republic* (16-23 Sept. 1991), 16-17.

1383. "The Russian Resolution," *New Republic* (9 Sept. 1991), 7-9.

1384. "The Russian Revolution," *Time*, 138 (2 Sept. 1991), 18ff.

1385. Saar, Andrus, and Liivi Joe, "Polling under the Gun: Political Attitudes in Estonia, Surveyed at the Height of the Soviet Coup Attempt, August 1991," *Public Opinion Quarterly*, 56, no. 4 (Winter 1992), 519-23.

1386. Sakwa, Richard, "A Cleansing Storm: The August Coup and the Triumph of *Perestroika*," *Journal of Communist Studies*, 9, no. 1 (Mar. 1993), 131-49.

1387. "Saved by the Bottle," *Time*, 138 (9 Sept. 1991), 34.

1388. Schoenfeld, Gabriel, "Uniform Failure," *New Republic* (9 Sept. 1991), 9-11.

1389. "The Second Russian Revolution," *Newsweek*, 118 (2 Sept. 1991), 8ff.

1390. Sestanovich, Stephen, "The Hour of the Demagogue," *National Interest*, no. 25 (Fall 1991), 3-15.

1391. Shipler, David K., "After the Coup," *New Yorker* (11 Nov. 1991), 47ff.

1392. Shub, Anatole, "The Fourth Russian Revolution: Historical Perspectives," *Problems of Communism*, 40, no. 6 (Nov-Dec. 1991), 20-26.

1393. Singer, Daniel, "Fast Forward," *Nation*, 253 (16 Sept. 1991), 288-89.

1394. Sloan, K., "Presleystroika," *Michigan Quarterly Review*, 32, no. 1 (Winter 1993), 76-90.

1395. Socor, Vladimir, "The Attempted Coup in the USSR: Eastern European Reactions: Romania," *Report on Eastern Europe*, 2, no. 35 (30 Aug. 1991), 14-16.

1396. -----, "Moldavia Defies Soviet Coup: Removes Vestiges of Communism," *Report on the USSR*, 3, no. 38 (20 Sept. 1991), 18-23.

1397. Solomon, Andrew, "Three Days in August: Building the Barricades with the Artists of Moscow," *New York Times Magazine*, 140 (29 Sept. 1991), 32.

1398. "The Soviet Coup and the Press," *Editor and Publisher*, 124, no. 34 (24 Aug. 1991), 10-11.

1399. Spencer, Metta, "The Colonel and the Coup," *Peace Magazine*, 7, no. 6 (Nov. 1991), 16-17.

1400. Sturua, Melor, "The Real Coup," *Foreign Policy*, no. 85 (Winter 1991-92), 63-72.

1401. Teague, Elizabeth, "Coup d'Etat Represented Naked Interests," *Report on the USSR*, 3, no. 35 (30 Aug. 1991), 1-3.

1402. Thompson, E. P., *et al.*, "What's Next?" *Nation*, 253 (16 Sept. 1991), 323ff.

1403. Thorson, Carla, "Constitutional Issues Surrounding the Coup," *Report on the USSR*, 3, no. 36 (6 Sept. 1991), 19-22.

1404. Tifft, S. E., "Those Days Were Horrible," *Time*, 138 (16 Sept. 1991), 37.

1405. Toffler, Alvin, and Heidi Toffler, "Where Do We Go From Here?" *World Monitor*, 4, no. 10 (Oct. 1991), 34-39.

1406. Tolstaya, Tatyana, "When Putsch Comes to Shove," *New Republic* (16-23 Sept. 1991), 18-24.

1407. Towell, Pat, "A Nuclear Lesson," *Congressional Quarterly Weekly Report*, 49 (14 Sept. 1991), 2632-33.

1408. Tolz, Vera, "Gorbachev Gives Press Conference," *Report on the USSR*, 3, no. 35 (30 Aug. 1991), 9-11.

1409. Trimble, J., and P. Vassiliev, "Three Days That Shook the World," *U.S. News & World Report*, 111 (18 Nov. 1991), 54ff.

1410. Troitsky, Artemy, "Three Days at the Barricades: How Rock 'n Roll, Fax Machines, and the Hip Crowd Helped Crack the Coup," *Rolling Stone*, no. 615 (17 Oct. 1991), 77-81.

1411. Van Atta, Don, "Profile of Coup Leader Vasilii Starodubtsev," *Report on the USSR*, 3, no. 35 (30 Aug. 1991), 3-5.

1412. Vanden Heuvel, Katrina, "Comrade Ligachev Tells His Side," *Nation*, 253 (2 Dec. 1991), 704ff.

1413. -----, "Soviet Voices," *Nation*, 253 (30 Sept. 1991), 359-61.

1414. -----, "Three Days that Shook the Kremlin," *Nation*, 253 (9 Sept. 1991), 249ff.

1415. Vinton, Louisa, "The Attempted Coup in the USSR; Eastern European Reactions: Poland," *Report on Eastern Europe*, 2, no. 35 (30 Aug. 1991), 10-13.

1416. Waller, Douglas, "The CIA Called It-But No One Listened," *Newsweek*, 118 (2 Sept. 1991), 44.

1417. Wedgeworth, R., "An IFLA Conference View of the Soviet Coup," *Wilson Library Bulletin*, 66 (Dec. 1991), 49-53.

1418. Weigel, G., "Death of a Heresy," *National Review*, 44 (20 Jan. 1992), 42ff.

1419. Weiss, Martin, "Neighborly Reactions," *National Review*, 43, (23 Sept. 1991), 21-22.

1420. Wellisz, Christopher, "Soviet Coup Renews Fear of Exodus," *Report on Eastern Europe*, 2, no. 37 (13 Sept. 1991), 18-21.

1421. Wilhelm, M., "The People Say `Nyet'," *People Weekly*, 36 (2 Sept. 1991), 60ff.

1422. "The World Turned Right Side Up," *National Review*, 43 (23 Sept. 1991), 8-12.

1423. Yang, Zhong, "The Transformation of the Soviet Military and the August Coup," *Armed Forces and Society*, 19, no. 1 (Fall 1992), 47-70.

1424. "Yeltsin's Army," *Economist*, 320 (24 Aug. 1991), 11-12.

1425. "Yeltsin's Triumph," *Business Week* (2 Sept. 1991), 20ff.

1426. Young, Cathy, "Soviet Presswatch: Free at Last," *American Spectator*, 24, no. 11 (Nov. 1991), 33-34.

1427. Zanga, Louis, "The Attempted Coup in the USSR: Eastern European Reactions: Albania," *Report on Eastern Europe*, 2, no. 35 (30 Aug. 1991), 2-3.

1428. Zaraev, Mikhail, "An Insider's Guide to the New Russia," *World Monitor*, 4, no. 11 (Nov. 1991), 42-47.

X. Crime, Corruption, Alcoholism and Other Social Problems
BOOKS

1429. Clark, William A., *Crime and Punishment in Soviet Officialdom: Combating Corruption in the Soviet Elite, 1965-1990* (Armonk, NY: M. E. Sharpe, 1993).

1430. Gaddy, Clifford G., *The Size of the Prostitution Market in the USSR* (Berkeley-Duke Occasional Papers on the Second Economy in the USSR; Bala Cynwyd, PA: WEFA Group, 1990).

1431. Holmes, Leslie, *The End of Communist Power, Anti-Corruption Campaigns and Legitimation Crisis* (London: Oxford University Press, 1993).

1432. Jones, Anthony, Walter D. Connor and David E. Powell, eds., *Soviet Social Problems* (Boulder, CO: Westview Press, 1994).

1433. Lampert, Nicholas, *Whistleblowing in the Soviet Union* (London: Macmillan, 1990).

1434. Lee, Rensselaer, *Dynamics of the Soviet Illicit Drug Market* (Washington, DC: Woodrow Wilson International Center for Scholars, 1990).

1435. Los, Maria, ed., *The Second Economy in Marxist States* (New York: St. Martin's Press, 1990).

1436. Meyendorff, Anna, *The Black Market for Foreign Currency in the USSR* (Bala Cynwyd, PA: WEFA Group, 1991).

1437. Neuhauser, Kimberley C., *The Market for Illegal Drugs in the Soviet Union in the Late 1980s* (Berkeley-Duke Occasional Papers on the Second Economy; Bala Cynwyd, PA: WEFA Group, 1990).

1438. Rosner, Lydia S., *The Soviet Way of Crime: Beating the System in the Soviet Union and the United States* (Boston: Bergin and Garvey, 1986).

1439. Segal, Boris M., *The Drunken Society: Alcohol Abuse and Alcoholism in the Soviet Union: A Comparative Study* (New York: Hippocrene, 1990).

1440. Timofeyev, Lev, *Russia's Secret Rulers: How the Government and Criminal Mafia Exercise Their Power* (New York: Knopf, 1992).

1441. Treml, Vladimir G., *Study of Employee Theft of Materials from Places of Employment* (Berkeley-Duke Occasional Papers on the Second Economy in the USSR, no. 20 (Bala Cynwyd, PA: WEFA Group, 1990).

1442. Vaksberg, Arkady, *The Soviet Mafia* (New York: St. Martin's Press, 1991).

ARTICLES

1443. Adams, Nathan M., "Menace of the Russian Mafia," *Reader's Digest*, 141, no. 844 (Aug. 1992), 33-40.

1444. "Alcohol as Solace and Barter," *Survey*, 29, no. 4 (Aug. 1987), 176-78.

1445. Anthony, Lawrence, "Sex and the Soviet Man," *National Review*, 40 (8 July 1988), 24-25.

1446. Ashley, S., "Corruption and Glasnost'," *RFE Research*, 13, no. 14, Part 2 (8 Apr. 1988), 3-7.

1447. Beliaeva, Marina, "New Criminal Sanctions for Soviet Black Marketeers," *SEEL: Soviet and East European Law*, 1, no. 9 (Nov. 1990), 6.

1448. Belikova, G., and A. Shokhin, "The Black Market," *Soviet Sociology*, 28, no. 2 (Mar-Apr. 1989), 50-65.

1449. Bogoliubova, T. A., and K. A. Tolpekin, "Narcotism and Narcomania," *Soviet Law and Government*, 27, no. 1 (Summer 1988), 26-38.

1450. Butler, W. E., "Crime in the Soviet Union: Early Glimpses of the True Story," *British Journal of Criminology*, 32, no. 2 (Spring 1992), 144-59.

1451. Carney, James, "Murder and Mayhem," *Time*, 137 (11 Feb. 1991), 59.

1452. Clark, William A., "Crime and Punishment in Soviet

Officialdom, 1965-1990," *Europe-Asia Studies*, 45, no. 2 (1993), 259-80.

1453. Coleman, Fred, "The Mobsters of Moscow," *Newsweek*, 112 (31 Oct. 1988), 44.

1454. Conroy, Mary Schaeffer, "Abuse of Drugs Other Than Alcohol and Tobacco in the Soviet Union," *Soviet Studies*, 42, no. 3 (July 1990), 447-80.

1455. Critchlow, J., "Corruption, Nationalism and the Native Elites in Soviet Central Asia," *Journal of Communist Studies*, 4, no. 2 (June 1988), 142-61.

1456. "A Dangerous Proclivity: Drugs and Addicts-Three Aspects of the Problem," *Soviet Law and Government*, 26, no. 4 (Spring 1988), 19-35.

1457. Darialova, Natalia, "Vodka: Opiate of the Masses," *Forbes*, 147, no. 4 (18 Feb. 1991), 96-98.

1458. Dashkov, V., "Quantitative and Qualitative Changes in Crime in the USSR," *British Journal of Criminology*, 32, no. 2 (Spring 1992), 160-66.

1459. Davis, Robert B., "Alcohol Abuse and the Soviet Military," *Armed Forces and Society*, 11, no. 3 (Spring 1985), 399-411.

1460. -----, "Ivan Drinks Too Much," *Army Reserve Magazine*, 31, no. 2 (1985), 12-13.

1461. Dorman, Nancy D., and Leland H. Towle, "Initiatives to Curb Alcohol Abuse and Alcoholism in the Former Soviet Union," *Alcohol Health and Research World*, 15, no. 4 (1991), 303-05.

1462. Firkowska-Mankiewicz, Anna, "Soviet Medicine in the Era of `Perestroyka': Some Notes on the Siberian Conference on Human Health as an Indicator of Social Development," *Social Science and Medicine*, 32, no. 1 (1 Jan. 1991), 109-10.

1463. Fishbein, David Joel, "Do Dna: Alcoholism in the Soviet Union," *JAMA: Journal of the American Medical Association*, 266, no. 9 (4 Sept. 1991), 1211-12.

1464. Fletcher, G. P., "In Gorbachev's Courts," *New York Review of Books*, 36 (18 May 1989), 13ff.

1465. Galeotti, Mark, "*Perestroika, Perestrelka, Pereborka*: Policing Russia in a Time of Change," *Europe-Asia Studies*, 45, no. 3 (1993), 769-86.

1466. Galuszka, Philip, "The Paradox of *Perestroika*: A Raging Black Market," *Business Week* (5 June 1989), 66ff.

1467. -----, "Sending a Message Loud and Clear: No More Graft," *Business Week* (6 July 1987), 44-45.

1468. Gambrell, Jamey, "Soviet Art Racket," *Art in America*, 78, no. 11 (Nov. 1990), 45.

1469. "Gangs and *Glasnost*," *U.S. News & World Report*, 109 (19 Nov. 1990), 39.

1470. Georgopoulos, Zach, "Soviet and Chinese Criminal Dissent Laws: Glasnost vs. Tiananmen," *Hastings International and*

Comparative Law Review, 14, no. 2 (Winter 1991), 475-504.

1471. Ginsburgs, George, "The Soviet Union and International Cooperation in Penal Matters," *International and Comparative Law Quarterly*, 41, no. 1 (Jan. 1992), 85-116.

1472. Grossman, Gregory, "The Second Economy: Boom or Bust for the Reform of the First Economy?" *Berkeley-Duke Occasional Papers on the Second Economy in the USSR*, 11, no. 2 (Dec. 1987).

1473. Handelman, Stephen, "The Russian `Mafiya'," *Foreign Affairs*, 73, no. 2 (Mar-Apr. 1994), 83-96.

1474. Harris, P., "Socialist Graft: The Soviet Union and the People's Republic of China-A Preliminary Survey," *Corruption and Reform*, 1, no. 1 (1986), 13-32.

1475. Hofheinz, Paul, "Crime Wave in the Soviet Union," *Fortune*, 123, no. 10 (20 May 1991), 14.

1476. Holden, Constance, "Soviets Seek U.S. Help in Combatting Alcoholism," *Science*, 246 (17 Nov. 1989), 878-79.

1477. Kaminski, A., "Coercion, Corruption and Reform: State and Society in the Soviet-type Socialist Regime," *Journal of Theoretical Politics*, 1, no. 1 (1989), 77-101.

1478. Karpets, I. I., "The Reality of Crime," *Soviet Sociology*, 29, no. 3 (May-June 1990), 63-80.

1479. Klugman, Jeffrey, "The Psychology of Soviet Corruption, Indiscipline and Resistance to Reform," *Political Psychology*, 7, no. 1 (Mar. 1986), 67-82.

1480. Kramer, John M., "Drug Abuse in Eastern Europe: An Emerging Issue of Public Policy," *Slavic Review*, 49, no. 1 (Spring 1990), 19-31.

1481. -----, "Drug Abuse in the Soviet Union," *Problems of Communism*, 38, no. 2 (Mar-Apr. 1988), 28-40.

1482. Kuznetsov, M. T., "Antialcohol Upbringing in the School," *Soviet Education*, 33, no. 2 (Feb. 1991), 78-84.

1483. Land, T., "Soviet Drug War," *New Leader*, 71 (14 Nov. 1988), 4.

1484. Lee, Rensselaer W., III, "Soviet Narcotics Trade," *Society*, 28, no. 5 (July-Aug. 1991), 46-52.

1485. Lee, T. V., and J. Searle-White, "Prisoners Dilemma Meets Glasnost: A Comparative Advantage Solution to the United States Prison Crisis," *Cornell International Law Journal*, 24, no. 2 (1991), 25-56.

1486. Lempert, D., "Soviet Sellout," *Mother Jones*, 16 (Sept-Oct. 1991), 20-21.

1487. Levin, B. M., and M. B. Levin, "Why Do They Drink?" *Soviet Review*, 31, no. 2 (Mar-Apr. 1990), 80ff.

1488. Luryi, Yuri I., "The Use of Criminal Law by the CPSU in the Struggle for the Reinforcement of Its Power and in the Inner-Party Struggle," in Dietrich Andre Loeber, ed., *Ruling Communist Parties and Their Status Under Law* (The Hague: Martinus Nijhoff, 1986).

1489. Martynov, A., "Battles Won-But Not Yet the War," *World Health* (June 1988), 26-27.

1490. Morris, N., "War on Soviet Alcoholism," *Maclean's*, 100 (19 Jan. 1987), 48.

1491. Orland, L., "Insulting the Soviet President and Other Political Crimes in Mikhail Gorbachev's `Rule of Law' State," *Connecticut Journal of International Law*, 5 (Fall 1990), 237-70.

1492. Pavluk, Jonathan, "Amendments to Soviet Law on State Crimes Take Effect," *SEEL: Soviet and East European Law*, 1, no. 1 (Feb. 1990), 6ff.

1493. -----, "The New Soviet Bugbear: Economic Sabotage!" *SEEL: Soviet and East European Law*, 2, no. 1 (Feb. 1991), 9.

1494. -----, "Soviet Legislature Addresses Fears of Public Disorder," *SEEL: Soviet and East European Law*, 1, no. 4 (May 1990), 10.

1495. Quigley, J., "Will the Inquisitorial System Wither Away? Perestroika in the Soviet Lock-up," *St. Louis University Public Law Review*, 8 (1989), 121-39.

1496. Raufer, Xavier, and Pierre Rigoulot, "Lifting the Veil on Crime," *World Press Review*, 35 (June 1988), 16.

1497. "Recognition of Illegalities, Proposals for Reform, and Implemented Reforms in the Soviet Criminal Justice System under Gorbachev, Glasnost and Perestroika," *American University Journal of International Law and Policy*, 5 (Spring 1990), 921-53.

1498. Rekunkov, Aleksandr, "Guarding the Law," *Soviet Law and Government*, 26, no. 1 (Summer 1987), 80-90.

1499. Sagers, Matthew J., "Alcoholism-Related Deaths by Republic Officially Reported," *Soviet Geography*, 29, no. 1 (Jan. 1988), 84-87.

1500. Scully, Michael A., "Autumn Scandals," *National Review*, 37 (13 Dec. 1985), 41.

1501. Shelley, Louise I., "Crime and Criminals in the USSR," in M. P. Sacks and J. G. Pankhurst, eds., *Understanding Soviet Society* (Boston: Unwin Hyman, 1988).

1502. -----, "Policing Soviet Society: The Evolution of State Control," *Law and Social Inquiry*, 15, no. 3 (1990), 479-520.

1503. Solomon, Peter H., "The Case of the Vanishing Acquittal: Informal Norms and the Practice of Soviet Criminal Justice," *Soviet Studies*, 39, no. 5 (1987), 531-55.

1504. "Soviet and Chinese Criminal Dissent Laws: Glasnost v. Tienanmen," *Hastings International and Comparative Law Review*, 14 (Winter 1991), 475-503.

1505. Sudo, P., and S. Goi, "The Soviet Hangover," *Scholastic Update*, 123 (16 Nov. 1990), 14.

1506. Tarchyss, Daniel, "The Success of a Failure: Gorbachev's Alcohol Policy, 1985-88," *Europe-Asia Studies*, 45, no. 1 (1993),

7-26.

1507. Tarkowski, J., "Old and New Patterns of Corruption in Poland and the USSR," *Telos*, no. 80 (1989), 51-62.

1508. Treml, Vladimir, "Alcohol in the Soviet Underground Economy," *Berkeley-Duke Occasional Papers on the Second Economy in the USSR*, 9 (Dec. 1985), no. 5.

1509. Turbiville, Graham H., Jr., "Counternarcotics: International Dimension of Soviet Internal Security Problem," *Military Review*, 70, no. 12 (Dec. 1990), 49-62.

1510. Vaudon, Jean-Pierre, and Pierre Perrin, "Last Days of the Gulag?" *National Geographic*, 177, no. 3 (Mar. 1990), 40-47.

1511. Vlassov, Yuri, "KGB in the Age of Perestroika and Glasnost," *World & I*, 6, no. 8 (Aug. 1991), 537-41.

1512. Welling, Sarah N., "White Collar Crime from Scratch: Some Observations on the East European Experience," *William and Mary Law Review*, 35, no. 1 (Fall 1993), 271-78.

1513. Wilson-Smith, Anthony, "Gang Warfare, Soviet Style," *Maclean's*, 102 (22 May 1989), 44.

1514. -----, "Outlaws in a Red Zone: New Openings for the Soviet Underworld," *Maclean's*, 101 (7 Nov. 1988), N6-8.

1515. Wishnevsky, J., "Gdlyan and Ivanov Expelled from the CPSU," *Report on the USSR*, 2, no. 10 (9 Mar. 1990), 6-8.

1516. -----, "USSR: The Gdlyan-Ivanov Commission Starts Work," *Radio Liberty Research* (21 June 1989).

1517. Wyman, L., "Crime and Punishment in the USSR: How Is It Really Changing?" *Judges' Journal*, 29 (Summer 1990), 14ff.

1518. Yasmann, Viktor, "The Power of the Soviet Internal Security Forces," *Report on the USSR*, 2, no. 43 (26 Oct. 1990), 12-15.

XI. Defense Conversion

BOOKS

1519. Badgett, Lee D., *Defeated by Maze: The Soviet Economy and Its Defense-Industrial Sector* (Santa Monica, CA: RAND, 1988).

1520. Becker, Abraham S., *Sitting on Bayonets: The Soviet Defense Burden and the Slowdown of Soviet Defense Spending* (Santa Monica, CA: RAND/UCLA Center for the Study of Soviet International Behavior, 1986).

1521. Claudon, Michael P., and Kathryn Wittneben, eds., *After the Cold War: Russian-American Defense Conversion for Economic Renewal* (New York: New York University Press, 1993).

1522. Cooper, Julian, *The Soviet Defense Industry: Conversion and Economic Reform* (New York: Council on Foreign Relations Press, 1991).

1523. Maggs, Peter, *Beating Swords into Washing Machines* (New York: Council on Economic Priorities, 1990).

1524. Marlin, John Tepper, and Paul Grenier, eds., *Soviet Conversion 1991: Report and Recommendations of an International Working Group on Economic Demilitarization and Adjustment* (New York: Council on Economic Priorities, 1991).

1525. Rowen, Henry S., Charles Wolfe, Jr., and Jeanne Tayler, *The Soviet Union as Military Giant and Economic Weakling* (Stanford: Hoover Institution Press, 1990).

1526. US Congress. Senate. Committee on Armed Services. *Soviet Military Conversion. Hearing.* 102nd Congress, 1st Session (Washington, DC: Government Printing Office, 1991).

1527. US Congress. Senate. Joint Economic Committee. Subcommittee on National Security Economics. *Allocation of Resources in the Soviet Union and China.* 101st Congress, 1st Session (Washington, DC: Government Printing Office, 1990).

ARTICLES

1528. Adelman, Kenneth L., and Norman R. Augustine, "Defense Conversion: Bulldozing the Management," *Foreign Affairs*, 71, no. 2 (Spring 1992), 26-47.

1529. Barry, John, "All Unhappy on the Eastern Front," *Newsweek*, 118 (5 Aug. 1991), 38.

1530. Bernstein, Alvin H., "Soviet Defense Spending: The Spartan Analogy," *Comparative Strategy*, 9, no. 1 (Jan-Mar. 1990), 33-65.

1531. Brady, Rose, *et al.*, "Can Gorbachev Pound Missiles into Plowshares?" *Business Week* (29 July 1991), 42-43.

1532. Burck, Gordon M., "Chemical Weapons Production Technology and the Conversion to Civilian Production," *Arms Control*, 11, no. 2 (Sept. 1990), 122-63.

1533. Campbell, Robert W., "The Soviet Defense Industry: Conversion and Economic Reform" (Review Article), *Slavic Review*, 51, no. 2 (Summer 1992), 332-36.

1534. Chengjun, Zhu, and Wang Xianju, "Less Arms, More Bread," *Beijing Review*, 31 (26 Dec. 1988), 14-15.

1535. Cohn, Stanley H., "Economic Burden of Soviet Defense Expenditures: Constraints on Productivity," *Studies in Comparative Communism*, 20 (Summer 1987), 145-61.

1536. Cooper, Julian, "Military Cuts and Conversion in the Defense Industry," *Soviet Economy*, 7, no. 2 (Apr-June 1991), 121-42.

1537. -----, "The Soviet Defence Industry and Conversion," *RUSI Journal*, 135, no. 3 (Autumn 1990), 51-56.

1538. -----, "Transforming Russia's Defence Industrial Base," *Survival*, 35, no. 4 (Winter 1993-94), 147-62.

1539. Correa, Hector, and Ji-Won Kim, "A Causal Analysis of the Defense Expenditures of the U.S.A. and the USSR," *Journal of Peace Research*, 29, no. 2 (May 1992), 161-74.

1540. Crawford, M., "Soviets Interested in Study on Economic

Conversion," *Science*, 235 (6 Mar. 1987), 1133.

1541. Cunningham, Ann Marie, "The Soviets Convert-Sort Of," *Technology Review*, 94, no. 5 (July 1991), 14-16.

1542. Fal'tsman, V., "Conversion and Economic Reform," *Problems of Economics*, 34, no. 2 (June 1991), 6-27.

1543. Fish, M. Steven, "Reform and Demilitarization in Soviet Society from Brezhnev to Gorbachev," *Peace and Change*, 15 (Apr. 1990), 150-72.

1544. Glukhikh, Viktor, "The Future of Conversion," *Delovie Liudi*, no. 36 (Aug. 1993), 12-13.

1545. Golway, Terry, "Forget Swords, Try Plowshares: Gorbachev-Era Reforms in the East Bloc Are Changing This Country's Defense Needs: Are New York's Contractors Keeping Pace with the Times?" *Empire State Report*, 16 (Mar. 1990), 13ff.

1546. Gonchar, K., "The Economics of Disarmament-A Difficult Matter," *Problems of Economics*, 33, no. 9 (Jan. 1991), 76-90.

1547. Hanson, Philip, "ANT Revisited: The KGB, the Defense Industry, and Private Enterprise," *Report on the USSR*, 3, no. 17 (26 Apr. 1991), 8-9.

1548. Hardt, John P., "Conversion or Chaos?" *Bulletin of the Atomic Scientists*, 46, no. 1 (Jan-Feb. 1990), 20.

1549. Iakovets, Iu., "The Market and the Strategy of Conversion," *Problems of Economics*, 34, no. 12 (Apr. 1992), 51-64.

1550. Iaremenko, I. V., and V. N. Rassadin, "Conversion and the Structure of the Economy," *Problems of Economic Transition*, 36, no. 3 (July 1993), 80-96.

1551. Iudin, I., "Economic Aspects of Reducing the Armed Forces and Conversion of Military Production," *Problems of Economics*, 32, no. 11 (Mar. 1990), 6-14.

1552. Kapstein, E. B., "From Guns to Butter in the USSR," *Challenge*, 32 (Sept-Oct. 1989), 11-15.

1553. Kelly, Tim, Martin Salamon and Hans-Peter Grassman, "Swords into Ploughshares, Tanks into Telephones," *OECD Observer*, no. 177 (Aug-Sept. 1992), 12-18.

1554. Kincade, William H., and T. Keith Thomson, "Economic Conversion in the USSR: Its Role in *Perestroyka*," *Problems of Communism*, 39, no. 1 (Jan-Feb. 1990), 83-92.

1555. Kireyev, A., "Swords into Ploughshares: Conversion in the USSR," *World Marxist Review*, 32, no. 6 (June 1989), 7-10.

1556. Kiss, Yudit, "Lost Illusions? Defence Industry Conversion in Czechoslovakia, 1989-92," *Europe-Asia Studies*, 45, no. 6 (1993), 1045-70.

1557. Kondakov, Andrei, "Conversion of the Military Industry in the USSR-the Fourth Attempt," *International Affairs* (Moscow), no. 10 (Oct. 1991), 40-44.

1558. Kowalski, Adam, "Swords into Chocolate Truffles," *New Scientist*, 124, no. 1690 (11 Nov. 1989), 30-31.

1559. Kreyev, Alexei, "Swords into Ploughshares: Conversion in the USSR," *World Marxist Review*, 32, no. 6 (June 1989), 7-10.

1560. Kushnirsky, F. I., "Conversion, Civilian Production, and Goods Quality in the Soviet Economy," *Comparative Economic Studies*, 33, no. 1 (Spring 1991), 23-55.

1561. Makushkin, Aleksei, "From Conversion to Deindustrialization?" *Problems of Economic Transition*, 35, no. 9 (Jan. 1993), 34-45.

1562. "Military Outlays Still Slow Soviet Economy, Despite European Force Cuts," *Aviation Week & Space Technology*, 134, no. 22 (2 June 1991), 22-23.

1563. Morrocco, John D., "Avionics Firms Diversify, Seek Western Investment," *Aviation Week & Space Technology*, 135, no. 20 (18 Nov. 1991), 55-56.

1564. Nelson, Daniel N., "The Costs of Demilitarization in the USSR and Eastern Europe," *Survival*, 35, no. 4 (July-Aug. 1991), 312-26.

1565. Nourzad, Farrokh, and Peter G. Toumanoff, "The Effects of the Defense Sector on the Productivity of Civilian Industry in the United States and the USSR," *Journal of Comparative Economics*, 17, no. 4 (Dec. 1993), 768-85.

1566. Ozhegov, A., E. Rogovskii and I. Iaremenko, "Conversion of the Defense Industry and Transformation of the Economy of the USSR," *Problems of Economics*, 34, no. 6 (Oct. 1991), 79ff.

1567. Palmer, Keith, "Developing the Mining Resources of the CIS," *World Today*, 50, no. 6 (June 1994), 102-03.

1568. "The Politics of Peacetime Conversion," *Society*, 30, no. 4 (May-June 1993), 4-40.

1569. Quinn-Judge, Sophie, "Reduction Resistance: Government Fears Military Foot-Dragging on Troop Cuts," *Far Eastern Economic Review*, 143 (16 Mar. 1989), 22.

1570. Richardson, Thomas J., "The Soviet Defense Industry: Conversion and Economic Reform," *Russian Review*, 52, no. 4 (Oct. 1993), 575-76.

1571. Ritter, William S., Jr., "Soviet Defense Conversion: The Votkinsk Machine-Building Plant," *Problems of Communism*, 40, no. 5 (Sept-Oct. 1991), 45-61.

1572. Rosefielde, Steven S., "Assessing Soviet Reforms in the Defense Industry," *Global Affairs*, 4, no. 4 (Fall 1989), 57-73.

1573. Spechler, Martin C., "Conversion of Military Industries in the Successor States of the Soviet Union," in US Congress. Joint Economic Committee. *The Former Soviet Union in Transition*, vol. 2 (Washington, DC: Government Printing Office, 1993), 717-29.

1574. Tedstrom, John, "Industrial Conversion and Consumer Goods Production," *Report on the USSR*, 3, no. 19 (10 May 1991), 3-7.

1575. -----, "Industrial Conversion at the Local Level: Udmurtia," *Report on the USSR*, 3, no. 25 (21 June 1991), 19-23.

1576. -----, "Industrial Conversion in Ukraine: Policies and Prospects," *Report on the USSR*, 3, no. 34 (23 Aug. 1991), 12-16.

1577. -----, "Managing the Conversion of the Defense Industries," *Report on the USSR*, 2, no. 7 (16 Feb. 1990), 11-18.

1578. -----, "The Shatalin Plan and Industrial Conversion," *Report on the USSR*, 2, no. 46 (16 Nov. 1990), 8-10.

1579. Van Metre, Lauren, "Defense Conversion in the Soviet Union: Will It Succeed?" *Soviet Union/Union Sovietique*, 17, no. 2 (1990), 259-80.

1580. Velocci, Anthony L., Jr., "Soviet Coup Collapse to Speed Defense Industry Shift to Civilian Use," *Aviation Week & Space Technology*, 135, no. 9 (2 Sept. 1991), 68-69.

1581. Vid, Leonid, "Guns into Butter, Soviet Style," *Bulletin of the Atomic Scientists*, 46, no. 1 (Jan-Feb. 1990), 16-19.

1582. Weickhardt, John G., "Recent Discussion of Defense Economics," *Report on the USSR*, 2, no. 10 (9 Mar. 1990), 9-14.

1583. Yermishina, Inna, "Defence Privatization: Not Nearly Enough," *Delovie Lyudi*, no. 36 (Aug. 1993), 26-27.

1584. Zaichenko, Alexandr, "The Politics of Conversion," *Delovie Lyudi*, no. 36 (Aug. 1993), 3.

XII. Democratization; Elections

BOOKS

1585. Allison, Graham T., and Grigory Yavlinsky, *Window of Opportunity: The Grand Bargain for Democracy in the Soviet Union* (New York: Pantheon Books, 1991).

1586. Arato, Andrew, *From Neo-Marxism to Democratic Theory: Essays on the Critical Theory of Soviet-Type Societies* (Armonk, NY: M. E. Sharpe, 1993).

1587. Barnard, F. M., *Pluralism, Socialism and Political Legitimacy: Reflections on Opening Up Communism* (New York: Cambridge University Press, 1991).

1588. Bermeo, Nancy, ed., *Liberalization and Democratization: Change in the Soviet Union and Eastern Europe* (Baltimore: The Johns Hopkins University Press, 1992).

1589. Campeanu, Pavel, *Exit: Toward Post-Stalinism* (Armonk, NY: M. E. Sharpe, 1990).

1590. Chiesa, Giulietto, *Transition to Democracy in the USSR: Ending the Monopoly of Power and New Political Forces* (Washington, DC: Woodrow Wilson Center for Scholars, 1990).

1591. -----, *Transition to Democracy: Political Change in the Soviet Union, 1987-1991* (Hanover: University Press of New Hampshire, 1993).

1592. Denitch, Bogdan, *After the Flood: World Politics and Democracy in the Wake of Communism* (Hanover, NH: University Press of New Hampshire, 1993).

1593. Goldfarb, Jeffrey C., *Beyond Glasnost: The Post-Totalitarian Mind* (Chicago: University of Chicago Press, 1989).

1594. Howard, A. E. Dick, *Democracy's Dawn: A Directory of American Initiatives on Constitutionalism, Democracy and the Rule of Law in Central and Eastern Europe* (Charlottesville, VA: University Press of Virginia, 1991).

1595. Institute for East-West Security Studies, *Eastern Europe and Democracy: The Case of Poland* (New York: Institute for East-West Security Studies, 1990).

1596. Khasbulatov, Ruslan, *The Struggle for Russia: Power and Change in the Democratic Revolution* (New York: Routledge, 1993).

1597. Lipset, Martin, *Parliamentary Democracy in the Land of Lenin* (Washington, DC: Progessive Policy Institute, 1990).

1598. McFaul, Michael, *Post-Communist Politics: Democratic Prospects in Russia and Eastern Europe* (Washington, DC: Center for Strategic and International Studies, 1993).

1599. -----, and Sergei Markov, *The Troubled Birth of Russian Democracy: Parties, Personalities and Programs* (Stanford; Hoover Institution Press, 1993).

1600. Mestrovic, Stjepan, with Miroslav Goreta and Slaven Letica, *The Road from Paradise: Prospects for Democracy in Eastern Europe* (Lexington, KY: University of Kentucky Press, 1993).

1601. Milojkovic-Djuric, Jelena, *Aspects of Soviet Culture: The Voices of Glasnost', 1960-1990* (Boulder, CO: East European Monographs, 1991).

1602. Muravchik, Joshua, *Exporting Democracy: Fulfilling America's Destiny* (Washington, DC: AEI Press, 1991).

1603. Nugent, Margaret Latus, ed., *From Leninism to Freedom: The Challenges of Democratization* (Boulder, CO: Westview Press, 1992).

1604. *Red Carnation: A Report on the March 1989 Soviet Elections* (Washington, DC: International Human Rights Law Group, 1989).

1605. Roberts, Brad, and Nina Belyaeva, eds., *After Perestroika: Democracy in the Soviet Union* (Washington, DC: Center for Strategic and International Studies, 1991).

1606. Seligman, Adam B., *The Idea of Civil Society* (New York: Free Press, 1992).

1607. Sergeyev, Victor, and Nikolai Biryukov, *Russia's Road to Democracy: Parliament, Communism and Traditional Culture* (Brookfield, VT: Edward Elgar, 1993).

1608. Soros, George, *Underwriting Democracy* (New York: Free Press, 1991).

1609. Starr, S. Frederick, *Prospects for Stable Democracy in Russia* (Occasional Paper of the Mershon Center; Columbus, OH: Ohio State University, 1992).

1610. Tsipko, Alexander S., *Is Stalinism Really Dead?* (San Francisco: Harper, 1990).

1611. Urban, Michael E., *More Power to the Soviets: The*

Democratic Revolution in the USSR (Brookfield, VT: Gower, 1990).

1612. US Congress. Commission on Security and Cooperation in Europe. *Elections in the Baltic States and the Soviet Republics: A Compendium of Reports on Parliamentary Elections Held in 1990* (Washington, DC: Government Printing Office, 1990).

1613. US Congress. House. Committee on Foreign Affairs. Subcommittee on Europe and the Middle East. *Referendum in the Soviet Union: Implications for Democratization. Hearing.* 102nd Congress, 1st Session (Washington, DC: Government Printing Office, 1991).

1614. US Congress. House. Committee on Foreign Affairs. Subcommittee on Human Rights and International Organizations. *Pace of Democratic Reforms and Status of Human Rights in Eastern Europe and the Soviet Union.* 101st Congress, 4 and 11 Oct. 1990 (Washington, DC: Government Printing Office, 1990).

1615. US Congress. Senate. Committee on Banking, Housing and Urban Affairs. *Report on the Visit to the Soviet Union of the Senate Delegation, Led by Sen John Heinz, 1987: Exploration of the Condition of Human Rights and "Democratization" and Economic Reform Initiatives Undertaken by the Soviet Union.* 100th Congress, 1st Session (Washington, DC: Government Printing Office, 1987).

1616. US Foreign Broadcast Information Service. *Parliamentary Elections in the USSR: Voters Stun Soviet Officialdom* (Washington, DC: FBIS, 1989).

1617. Wilson, Frank L., *European Politics Today: The Democratic Experience* (Englewood Cliffs, NJ: Prentice Hall, 1990).

1618. Woehrel, Steven J., *Soviet Union: An Assessment of Recent Republic and Local Elections* (Washington, DC: Library of Congress, Congressional Research Service, 1990).

1619. Yevtushenko, Yevgeny, *Fatal Half Measures: The Culture of Democracy in the Soviet Union* (Boston: Little, Brown and Co., 1991).

ARTICLES

1620. Adam, Herbert, "Transition to Democracy: South Africa and Eastern Europe," *Telos*, no. 85 (Fall 1990), 33-55.

1621. Almond, M., "Slouching Toward Democracy," *National Review*, 46 (24 Jan. 1994), 22ff.

1622. Avak'ian, S., "Self-Government and Elections," *Soviet Law and Government*, 27, no. 2 (Fall 1988), 73-84.

1623. Bahry, Donna, and Brian D. Silver, "Soviet Citizen Participation on the Eve of Democratization," *American Political Science Review*, 84, no. 3 (Sept. 1990), 821-47.

1624. Barabashev, G. V., "The Election Campaign: Goals and Means," *Soviet Law and Government*, 26, no. 4 (Spring 1988), 5-18.

1625. Baranczak, Stanislaw, "Breakthrough to Democracy: Elections in Poland and Hungary," *Studies in Comparative Communism*, 23, no. 2 (Summer 1990), 191-212.

1626. -----, "Goodbye, Samizdat," *Wilson Quarterly*, 14, no. 2 (Spring 1990), 59-66.

1627. Bates, Robert H., "The Economics of Transitions to Democracy," *PS*, 24, no. 1 (Mar. 1991), 24-27.

1628. Belyaeva, Nina, "Russian Democracy: Crisis as Progress," *Washington Quarterly*, 16, no. 2 (Spring 1993), 5-20.

1629. Berezovskii, V. M., and N. I. Krotov, "Citizens' Movements," *Soviet Sociology*, 29, no. 4 (July-Aug. 1990), 87ff.

1630. Bermeo, Nancy, "Introduction: Liberalization and Democratization in the Soviet Union and Eastern Europe," *World Politics*, no. 55 (Winter 1991), 60-65.

1631. Bodie, William C., "The Threat to America from the Former USSR," *Orbis*, 37, no. 4 (Fall 1993), 509-25.

1632. Borovik, Artyom, "Waiting for Democracy," *Foreign Policy*, no. 84 (Fall 1991), 51-60.

1633. Brovkin, Vladimir, "The Making of Elections to the Congress of People's Deputies (CPD) in March 1989," *Russian Review*, 49, no. 4 (Oct. 1990), 417-42.

1634. -----, "Revolution from Below: Informal Political Associations in Russia 1988-1989," *Soviet Studies*, 42, no. 2 (Apr. 1990), 233-58.

1635. Brumberg, Abraham, "Poland: The Demise of Communism," *Foreign Affairs*, 69, no. 1 (1989-90), 70-88.

1636. Bukovsky, Vladimir, "The Crumbling of the Soviet Bloc: Squaring the Soviet Circle," *Journal of Democracy*, 1, no. 1 (Winter 1990), 86-90.

1637. -----, "Drowning Democracy," *National Review*, 43 (23 Sept. 1991), 32-34.

1638. Bulsys, J. A., and J. J. Mackay, "Gorbachev's Rhetoric of Glasnost: How Openness Intersects with Freedom of Expression," *Free Speech Yearbook*, 27 (1989), 55-67.

1639. Cappelli, Ottorino, "The Soviet Representative System at the Crossroads: Towards Political Representation?" *Journal of Communist Studies*, 7, no. 2 (June 1991), 170-201.

1640. "Case Study: Why the USSR Is `Not Free'," *Freedom at Issue*, no. 112 (Jan-Feb. 1990), 14-15.

1641. Cekuolis, Algimantas, "In the Time of the Hanging (Democracy in the Soviet Union)," *Lituanus*, 37, no. 1 (Spring 1991), 49-52.

1642. Chenoweth, Eric, "The Lessons of Communism," *Uncaptive Minds*, 3, no. 3 (May-July 1990), 1-3.

1643. "Choose! But How? Letters to the Editor," *Soviet Law and Government*, 27, no. 2 (Fall 1988), 93-94.

1644. Chubais, Igor, "The Democratic Opposition: An Insider's View," *Report on the USSR*, 3, no. 18 (3 May 1991), 4-15.

1645. Clark, Terry D., "State-Society Relations in the Soviet

Union: A Model of *Demokratizatsiia*," *Crossroads*, no. 29 (1989), 63-74.

1646. Colton, Timothy J., "The Politics of Democratization: The Moscow Election of 1990," *Soviet Economy*, 6, no. 4 (Oct-Dec. 1990), 285-344.

1647. Coughlin, E. K., "Stirrings of Democracy in China and Russia Astonish Experts," *Chronicle of Higher Education*, 35 (28 June 1989), A1ff.

1648. Crozier, Brian, "Slouching toward Democracy," *National Review*, 42 (1 Apr. 1990), 27.

1649. Czaputowicz, Jacek, "On the Future of Polish Pluralism," *Freedom at Issue*, no. 109 (July-Aug. 1989), 28-31.

1650. Dahl, Robert A., "Democracy, Majority Rule and Gorbachev's Referendum," *Dissent*, 38, no. 4 (Fall 1991), 491-96.

1651. Dahrendorf, Ralf, "Roads to Freedom: Democratization and Its Problems in East Central Europe," *Uncaptive Minds*, 4, no. 2 (Mar-Apr. 1991), 1-6.

1652. -----, "Transitions: Politics, Economics and Liberty," *Washington Quarterly*, 13, no. 3 (Summer 1990), 133-42.

1653. "Democratchniks," *Time*, 139 (22 June 1992), 48-50.

1654. Denisov, Anatoli, "Private Property and the Public Monopoly," *Socialism and Democracy*, no. 10 (Spring-Summer 1990), 43-45.

1655. Di Palma, Giuseppe, "After Leninism: Why Democracy Can Work in Eastern Europe," *Journal of Democracy*, 2, no. 1 (Winter 1991), 21-31.

1656. Drygalski, Jerzy, and Jacek Kwasniewski, "No-Choice Elections," *Soviet Studies*, 42, no. 2 (Apr. 1990), 295-316.

1657. Dudchenko, Mikhail, *et al.*, "From a Mob to a Nation: A Discussion with Four Activists from the Democratic Opposition," *Uncaptive Minds*, 3, no. 5 (Nov-Dec. 1990), 1-6.

1658. Duncan, Peter J. S., "The Democratic Transition in Russia: From Coup to Referendum," *Parliamentary Affairs*, 46, no. 4 (Oct. 1993), 492-505.

1659. "Elections in Eastern Europe" (Special Issue), *Electoral Studies*, 9, no. 4 (Dec. 1990), 277-366.

1660. "The Expanding Frontiers of World Freedom," *Universitas*, 22, no. 6 (Sept. 1991), 3-4.

1661. Favorskaia, A., "Proof in Favor of Democracy," *Soviet Review*, 28, no. 2 (Mar-Apr. 1989), 54-58.

1662. Fedorowicz, Hania M., "Civil Society in Poland: Laboratory for Democratisation in Central Europe," *Plural Societies*, 21, no. 1-2 (June 1991), 155ff.

1663. Filippov, E., "Continuous Education, Democracy, and Society," *Soviet Education*, 32, no. 3 (Mar. 1990), 44-56.

1664. Fomin, Vladimir, "The Value of the Deputy's Mandate," *Soviet Law and Government*, 27, no. 2 (Fall 1988), 95-99.

1665. Forbes, Malcolm S., Jr., "How to Make the Once Evil Empire Safe for Democracy," *Forbes*, 149 (6 Jan. 1992), 23.

1666. Frye, Timothy, "Oktyabr'sky Raion: The Problems of Creating Democracy in One District," *Report on the USSR*, 3, no. 33 (16 Aug. 1991), 26-29.

1667. Gabor, Francis A., "Reflections on the Freedom of Movement in Light of the Dismantled `Iron Curtain'," *Tulane Law Review*, 65, no. 4 (Mar. 1991), 849-82.

1668. Galuszka, Philip, "Gorbachev's Not-So-Secret Weapon: The Ballot Box," *Business Week* (27 Mar. 1989), 51.

1669. -----, "The Vote Heard Round the World," *Business Week* (10 Apr. 1989), 26-27.

1670. Gerchikov, V. I., and B. G. Proshkin, "Elections of Managers: Initial Experience and Problems," *Soviet Sociology*, 28, no. 4 (July-Aug. 1989), 57-71.

1671. Geremek, Bronislaw, "Postcommunism and Democracy in Poland," *Washington Quarterly*, 13, no. 3 (Summer 1990), 125-31.

1672. Gibson, James L., Raymond M. Duch and Kent L. Tedin, "Democratic Values and the Transformation of the Soviet Union," *Journal of Politics*, 54, no. 2 (May 1992), 329-71.

1673. Goldberg, Andrew C., "Russian Democracy's Clouded Future," *World & I*, 6, no. 11 (Nov. 1991), 58-63.

1674. Gooding, John, "Gorbachev and Democracy," *Soviet Studies*, 42, no. 2 (Apr. 1990), 195-232.

1675. Gorbachev, Mikhail S., "Our Ideal Is a Humane, Democratic Socialism," *Vital Speeches of the Day*, 56 (15 Mar. 1990), 322-27.

1676. Grazin, Igor, "On the Influence of Baltic Policy on the Process of Democratization in the U.S.S.R.: The Ethical Aspects," *Lituanus*, 37, no. 2 (Summer 1991), 78-81.

1677. Hahn, Jeffrey W., "Continuity and Change in Russian Political Culture," *British Journal of Political Science*, 21, part 4 (Oct. 1991), 393-421.

1678. Handelman, Stephen, "Remaking the Soviet Union: Euphoria and Fear on the Way to Democracy," *World Press Review*, 38 (Oct. 1991), 9-10.

1679. Hassner, Pierre, "Communism: A Coroner's Inquest," *Journal of Democracy*, 1, no. 4 (Fall 1990), 3-6.

1680. "A Hearty Da! to Democratia," *U.S. News & World Report*, 106 (5 June 1989), 12.

1681. Hirst, Paul, "Soviet Freedom," *New Statesman and Society*, 1 (10 June 1988), 22.

1682. Horner, C., "America the Victorious," *Commentary*, 89 (May 1990), 39-42.

1683. Hosking, Geoffrey, "The Outlook for a Democratic Russia," *Report on the USSR*, 3, no. 41 (11 Oct. 1991), 1-3.

1684. Huntington, Samuel P., "Democracy's Third Wave,"

Journal of Democracy, 2, no. 2 (Spring 1991), 12-34.

1685. -----, "How Countries Democratize," *Political Science Quarterly*, 106, no. 4 (Winter 1991-92), 579-616.

1686. Hurst, Sarrah, "Glasnost Behind the Scenes," *Contemporary Review*, 257, no. 1494 (July 1990), 1-6.

1687. Inglis, F., "Killed By the Cold," *Times Higher Education Supplement*, no. 1043 (30 Oct. 1992), 17ff.

1688. Izyumov, A., "The Need for Competition," *World Press Review*, 37 (Mar. 1990), 13.

1689. Jones, P. M., "Why Soviets Ban Free Expression," *Scholastic Update*, 118 (7 Mar. 1986), 25.

1690. Kapeliush, Ia. S., "The Election of Managers: Yesterday and Today," *Soviet Sociology*, 28, no. 2 (Mar-Apr. 1989), 80-90.

1691. Keane, John, "The Democracy Facing Gorbachev" (Review Article), *New Statesman*, 115 (20 May 1988), 20-21.

1692. Klyamkin, Igor, "The Emergence of Democracy and Russia's New Role," *Report on the USSR*, 3, no. 41 (11 Oct. 1991), 5-6.

1693. Kostin, A. A., "Alienation: Real and Imaginary," *Soviet Sociology*, 28, no. 2 (Mar-Apr. 1989), 91-104.

1694. Kucinskas, Linas, "Lithuania's Independence: The Litmus Test for Democracy in the U.S.S.R.," *Lituanus*, 37, no. 3 (Fall 1991), 5-50.

1695. Kurashvili, B., "Toward Sovereignty of the Soviets," *Soviet Law and Government*, 28, no. 1 (Summer 1989), 37-50.

1696. Kurth, R. J., "Can the Soviet Union Achieve Freedom?" *Vital Speeches of the Day*, 56 (15 Mar. 1990), 331-33.

1697. Laptev, Ivan D., "*Perestroika* in Parliament: Democracy in the USSR: Successes and Setbacks," *Parliamentarian*, 72, no. 3 (July 1991), 172-76.

1698. Lee, Gary, "The Soviet Union Needs a Social Democratic Party," *World & I*, 6, no. 5 (May 1991), 100-05.

1699. Lerner, Michael, "After the Cold War: Possibilities for Human Liberation," *Tikkun*, 5, no. 1 (1990), 16ff.

1700. Lloyd, John, "The Democratic Yardstick," *New Statesman and Society*, 2 (6 Jan. 1989), 18.

1701. -----, "Democracy in Russia," *Political Quarterly*, 64, no. 2 (Apr-June 1993), 147-55.

1702. Lukianov, Anatoly, "Our Course: Democracy, Self-Government, Rule of Law," *World Marxist Review*, 31, no. 11 (Nov. 1988), 14-23.

1703. Makhrin, Yuri, "Dear Pravda: How Do You Handle Democracy?" *World Press Review*, 35 (Jan. 1988), 20-22.

1704. McColm, Bruce R., "The Democratic Moment," *Freedom Review*, 22, no. 1 (Jan-Feb. 1991), 5ff.

1705. McFaul, Michael, "Russia's Emerging Political Parties," *Journal of Democracy*, 3, no. 1 (Jan. 1992), 25-40.

1706. Miljan, Toivo, "Democratization in Estonia," *Lituanus*, 37, no. 2 (Summer 1991), 82-88.

1707. McForan, D. W. J., "*Glasnost'*, Democracy, and *Perestroika*," *International Social Science Review*, 63, no. 4 (Autumn 1988), 165-74.

1708. "Moscow Tries Out Democracy," *Beijing Review*, 32 (10 July 1989), 16-17.

1709. Moses, Joel C., "Democratic Reform in the Gorbachev Era: Dimensions of Reform in the Soviet Union, 1986-1989," *Russian Review*, 48, no. 3 (July 1989), 235-69.

1710. Mudrakov, A., "The First Secretary of a District Party Committee Is Elected by a Secret Ballot," *Soviet Law and Government*, 26, no. 3 (Winter 1987-88), 20-25.

1711. Muravchik, Joshua, "Democratic Transformation in Hungary," *World Affairs*, 151, no. 4 (Spring 1989), 155.

1712. Nakarada, Radmila, "Democratic Alternatives: A Perspective from Eastern Europe," *Alternatives*, 16, no. 2 (Spring 1991), 129-40.

1713. Nikitina, E., "The Plenum of a District Party Committee Elects Its First Secretary," *Soviet Law and Government*, 26, no. 3 (Winter 1987-88), 14-19.

1714. Pataki, Judith, "Journalists Slow to Adjust to Democracy," *Report on Eastern Europe*, 2, no. 49 (6 Dec. 1991), 1-4.

1715. Pehe, Jiri, "Birthing Democracy in Eastern Europe," *Freedom at Issue*, no. 116 (Sept-Oct. 1990), 11-13.

1716. Pei, Minxin, "Societal Takeover in China and the USSR," *Journal of Democracy*, 3, no. 1 (Jan. 1992), 108-18.

1717. Pelham, Ann, "Mikhail Gorbachev Tries to Turn Rubber Stamps into Local Governments," *Governing*, 1 (1988), 30ff.

1718. Pell, Eve, "Growing a Free Press: Yesterday's Dissidents, Today's Editors," *Washington Journalism Review*, 13, no. 3 (Apr. 1991), 43-45.

1719. Phillips, Andrew, "The Scent of Freedom," *Maclean's*, 101 (22 Aug. 1988), 14-19.

1720. Pikcunas, Diane D., "Flames of Freedom Burn Bright in Soviet Union, China," *Universitas*, 22, no. 7 (Oct. 1991), 1.

1721. Popov, Gavril, "Dangers of Democracy," *New York Review of Books*, 37 (16 Aug. 1990), 27-28.

1722. "Power to the People Soviet Style," *U.S. News & World Report*, 108 (26 Feb. 1990), 13.

1723. "Problems of Postcommunism," *Journal of Democracy*, 3, no. 2 (Apr. 1992), 3-69.

1724. "Prospects of Democratization: A Roundtable on the Problems of Political Reform in the USSR," *Soviet Sociology*, 30, no. 2 (Mar-Apr. 1991), 26-65.

1725. Prousis, Theophilus C., "Research in the Soviet Union Under Glasnost," *American Scholar*, 59, no. 2 (Spring 1990), 265-71.

1726. Rahr, Alexander, and William Pomeranz, "Russian Democrats Yesterday and Today," *Report on the USSR*, 3, no. 19 (10 May 1991), 15-17.

1727. Raleigh, Donald J., "The Triumph of Glasnost in Scholarship: Raleigh Reaches Saratov," *AAASS Newsletter*, 30, no. 4 (Sept. 1990), 1-2.

1728. "The Rebirth of Russia... and the Birth of Democracy?" *New Republic* (16-23 Sept. 1991), 7ff.

1729. Reissinger, William M., *et al.*, "Political Values in Russia, Ukraine and Lithuania: Sources and Implications for Democracy," *British Journal of Political Science*, 24, Part 2 (Apr. 1994), 183-223.

1730. Revel, Jean-Francois, "Resurrecting Democracy in Eastern Europe," *Orbis*, 35, no. 3 (Summer 1991), 323-26.

1731. Rubanov, V., "Democracy and National Security," *Soviet Sociology*, 29, no. 3 (May-June 1990), 81ff.

1732. Sakwa, Richard, "Commune Democracy and Gorbachev's Reforms," *Political Studies*, 37 (June 1989), 224-43.

1733. Salisbury, Harrison E., "Groping toward Democracy," *American Heritage*, 43 (Feb-Mar. 1992), 74-77.

1734. Scammon, Richard M., "International Election Notes: Mexico, Russia, Germany, Switzerland," *World Affairs*, 154, no. 1 (Summer 1991), 41-45.

1735. Schifter, Richard, "Glasnost-The Dawn of Freedom?" *Annals of the American Academy of Political and Social Science*, no. 506 (Nov. 1989), 85-97.

1736. Sestanovich, Stephen, "Fiddler on the Roof," *New Republic* (27 May 1991), 19-22.

1737. Shanor, Donald R., "The Shock of Freedom," *World Monitor*, 4, no. 1 (Jan. 1991), 15-19.

1738. Shkaratan, O. I., and E. N. Gurenko, "From Statocracy to the Evolution of Civil Society," *Soviet Sociology*, 30, no. 3 (May-June 1991), 68-88.

1739. Slider, Darrell, "Elections in Eastern Europe: The Soviet Union," *Electoral Studies*, 9, no. 4 (Dec. 1990), 295-302.

1740. -----, "Gorbachev's First Reform Failure: Work-Place Democratization," *Journal of Communist Studies*, 9, no. 2 (June 1993), 62-85.

1741. Solzhenitsyn, Aleksandr, "Our Own Democracy," *National Review*, 43 (23 Sept. 1991), 43ff.

1742. Starr, S. Frederick, "Party Animals: Pluralism Comes to the USSR," *New Republic* (26 June 1989), 18-21.

1743. -----, "A Usable Past: Russia's Democratic Past," *New Republic* (15 May 1989), 24-27.

1744. Stone, Norman, "Real Democracy at Last?" (Review Article), *New Statesman and Society*, 2 (22 Sept. 1989), 32-33.

1745. Strashun, B., "Improving Elections," *Soviet Law and Government*, 27, no. 2 (Fall 1988), 85-92.

1746. Sussman, Leonard R., "Broadcast Democracy in Eastern Europe," *Freedom at Issue*, no. 114 (May-June 1990), 35-37.

1747. -----, "The Distance to Democracy," *World Monitor*, 4, no. 2 (Feb. 1991), 14-18.

1748. Taagepera, Rein, "Elections in Eastern Europe: The Baltic States," *Electoral Studies*, 9, no. 4 (Dec. 1990), 303-11.

1749. Teague, Elizabeth, "Prospects for Democracy," *Report on the USSR*, 3, no. 42 (18 Oct. 1991), 4-5.

1750. Theen, Rolf H. W., "The Appeal of Autocracy and Empire: A Threat to Russian Democracy," *World & I*, 7, no. 9 (Sept. 1992), 583-609.

1751. -----, "On the Prospects for Democracy in the USSR," *World & I*, 6, no. 4 (Apr. 1991), 544-61.

1752. Tikhomirov, Vladimir, "The Prospects for Democratisation in the Soviet Union: A Brief Survey of Modern Soviet History," *Politikon*, 19, no. 2 (June 1992), 99-109.

1753. Tokes, Rudolph L., "Will the Party Survive? Hungary on the Way to Democracy," *New Leader* (18 Sept. 1989), 9-11.

1754. Tolz, Vera, "The Congress of Democratic Forces: Soviet Democrats Make Another Attempt to Unite," *Report on the USSR*, 3, no. 6 (8 Feb. 1991), 6-8.

1755. -----, "The Democratic Opposition in Crisis," *Report on the USSR*, 3, no. 18 (3 May 1991), 1-3.

1756. -----, "Proliferation of Political Parties in the RSFSR," *Report on the USSR*, 3, no. 1 (4 Jan. 1991), 12-15.

1757. "Transitions to Democracy and the Rule of Law," *American University Journal of International Law and Policy*, 5 (Summer 1990), 965-1086.

1758. Ulam, Adam, "What the West Expects," *World & I*, 6, no. 9 (Sept. 1991), 16-17.

1759. Ulc, Otto, "Totalitarian Addiction and Withdrawal Pains," *Freedom at Issue*, no. 114 (May-June 1990), 20-23.

1760. Urnov, M. Iu., "How Ready Are We for Democracy? The Results of a Sociological Study," *Soviet Sociology*, 29, no. 4 (July-Aug. 1990), 6-31.

1761. "The Vote Heard Round the World: The Soviet People Give Gorbachev's Reforms a Huge Boost," *Business Week* (10 Apr. 1989), 26-27.

1762. Walker, M., "Two Party Time in the Soviet Union?" *Rolling Stone* (16 May 1991), 35ff.

1763. Wallis, Victor, "Marxism in the Age of Gorbachev," *Socialism and Democracy*, no. 11 (Sept. 1990), 47-74.

1764. Weigle, Marcia A., "Political Participation and Party Formation in Russia, 1985-1992: Institutionalizing Democracy," *Russian Review*, 53, no. 2 (Apr. 1994), 240-70.

1765. "What's Next for Weimar Russia?" *Glasnost*, 2, no. 6; issues no. 30-31 (Apr-May 1990), 4-27.

1766. White, Stephen, "'Democratization' in the USSR," *Soviet Studies*, 42, no. 1 (Jan. 1990), 3-24.

1767. -----, "Democratizing Eastern Europe: The Elections of 1990," *Electoral Studies*, 9, no. 4 (Dec. 1990), 277-87.

1768. -----, "Post-Communist Politics: Toward Democratic Pluralism?" *Journal of Communist Studies*, 9, no. 1 (Mar. 1993), 18-32.

1769. -----, "Russia's Experiment with Democracy," *Current History*, 91, no. 567 (Oct. 1992), 310-13.

1770. -----, "The Soviet Elections of 1989: From Acclamation to Limited Choice," *Coexistence*, 28, no. 4 (Dec. 1991), 513-40.

1771. -----, and G. Wightman, "Gorbachev's Reforms: The Soviet Elections," *Parliamentary Affairs*, 42 (Oct. 1989), 560-81.

1772. Whitehead, J. C., "The New Freedom in the Soviet Union and Eastern Europe," *Presidential Studies Quarterly*, 20, no. 3 (Summer 1990), 471-76.

1773. Whitney, C. R., "Letter to Gorbachev," *New York Times Magazine* (26 Oct. 1986), 56ff.

1774. Wilson-Smith, Anthony, "New Soviet Democracy," *Maclean's*, 102 (27 Mar. 1989), 18-19.

1775. Wishnevsky, Julia, and Elizabeth Teague, "'Democratic Platform' Created in CPSU," *Report on the USSR*, 2, no. 5 (2 Feb. 1990), 7-9.

1776. Zaslavsky, Ilya, "Pressing for Democracy in the USSR," *Journal of Democracy*, 1, no. 3 (Summer 1990), 123-27.

1777. Zaslavsky, Victor, "Nationalism and Democratic Transition in Postcommunist Societies," *Daedalus*, 121, no. 2 (Spring 1992), 97-121.

1778. Zdravomyslov, A. G., "Changes in Mass Consciousness and the Outlines of Parliamentary Activity," *Journal of Communist Studies*, 7, no. 2 (June 1991), 235ff.

1779. Zubek, Voytek, "Poland's Party Self-Destructs," *Orbis*, 34, no. 2 (Spring (1990), 179-94.

1780. Zuckerman, M. B., "Is Stalin Dead? Yes-At Last," *U.S. News & World Report*, 107 (4 Dec. 1989), 88ff.

XIII. Disarmament and Arms Control

BOOKS

1781. Adams, Valerie, *Chemical Warfare, Chemical Disarmament* (Bloomington: Indiana University Press, 1990).

1782. Adelman, Kenneth, and Norman R. Augustine, *The Defense Revolution: Strategy for the Brave New World* (San Francisco: Institute for Contemporary Studies Press, 1990).

1783. Allison, Graham, et al., eds., *Cooperative Denuclearization: From Pledges to Deeds* (Cambridge, MA: Center for Science and International Affairs, Harvard University, 1993).

1784. Bennett, Paul R., *The Soviet Union and Arms Control: Negotiating Strategy and Tactics* (New York: Praeger, 1989).

1785. Bitzinger, Richard A., *Gorbachev and GRIT: Did Arms Control Succeed Because of Unilateral Actions or in Spite of Them?* (Santa Monica, CA: RAND, 1991).

1786. Blacker, Coit D., *Under the Gun: Nuclear Weapons and the Superpowers* (Stanford: Stanford Alumni Association, 1986).

1787. Blackwill, Robert D., and F. Stephen Larrabee, eds., *Conventional Arms Control and East-West Security* (Durham, NC: Duke University Press, 1989).

1788. Blair, Bruce G., *The Logic of Accidental Nuclear War* (Washington, DC: Brookings Institution, 1993).

1789. Boffey, Philip M., et al., *Claiming the Heavens: The New York Times Complete Guide to the Star Wars Debate* (New York: Time Books, 1988).

1790. Brzezinski, Zbigniew, with Richard Sincere, Martin Strmecki and Peter Wehner, eds., *Promise and Peril: The Strategic Defense Initiative: Thirty-Five Essays by Statesmen, Scholars and Strategic Analysts* (Washington, DC: Ethics and Public Policy Center, 1986).

1791. Bunn, Matthew, *Foundation for the Future: The ABM Treaty and National Security* (Washington, DC: Arms Control Association, 1990).

1792. Burns, Richard Dean, ed., *Encyclopedia of Arms Control and Disarmament*, 3 vols. (New York: Scribner's, 1993).

1793. Caldwell, Dan, *The Dynamics of Domestic Politics and Arms Control: The SALT II Ratification Debate* (Columbia, SC: University of South Carolina Press, 1991).

1794. Calingaert, Daniel, *Soviet Nuclear Policy under Gorbachev: A Policy of Disarmament* (New York: Praeger, 1991).

1795. Campbell, Kurt M., et al., *Soviet Nuclear Fission: Control of the Nuclear Arsenal in a Disintegrating Soviet Union* (Cambridge, MA: Center for Science and International Affairs, Harvard University, 1991).

1796. Carlton, David, and Carlo Schaerf, eds., *The Arms Race in the Era of Star Wars* (New York: St. Martin's Press, 1988).

1797. Carter, April, *Success and Failure in Arms Control Negotiations* (Oxford: Oxford University Press, 1990).

1798. Cimbala, Stephen J., ed., *Strategic Arms Control after SALT* (Wilmington, DE: SR Books, 1989).

1799. Coffey, Joseph I., *Deterrence and Arms Control: American and West German Perspectives on INF* (Denver: University of Denver, Graduate School of International Studies, 1985).

1800. Cox, David, *A Review of the Geneva Negotiations on Strategic Arms Reductions* (Ottawa: Canadian Institute for International Peace and Security, 1987).

1801. CPSU Central Committee, 27th Congress, *The Challenges of Our Time: Disarmament and Social Progress* (New York: International Publishers, 1986).

1802. Cuthbertson, Ian M., and David Robertson, *Enhancing*

European Security: Living in a Less Nuclear World (New York: St. Martin's Press, 1990).

1803. Cuthbertson, Ian M., and Peter Volten, eds., *The Guns Fall Silent: The End of the Cold War and the Future of Conventional Disarmament* (New York: Institute for East-West Security Studies, 1990).

1804. Downs, George W., and David M. Rocke, *Tacit Bargaining, Arms Races and Arms Control* (Ann Arbor: University of Michigan Press, 1990).

1805. Epstein, Joshua M., *Conventional Force Reductions: A Dynamic Assessment* (Washington, DC: Brookings Institution, 1990).

1806. Ferguson, James, *Opening Pandora's Box: From Nuclear Deterrence to Conventional Defence* (Winnipeg: University of Manitoba, 1989).

1807. Fieldhouse, Richard, ed., *Security at Sea: Naval Forces and Arms Control* (New York: Oxford University Press, 1990).

1808. *The First Anniversary of the INF Treaty* (Moscow: Novosti Press Agency Publishing House, 1989).

1809. Freedman, Lawrence, *Arms Control: Management or Reform?* (London: Routledge & Kegan Paul, 1986).

1810. Frei, Daniel, *Perceived Images: US and Soviet Assumptions and Perceptions in Disarmament* (Totowa, NJ: Rowman & Allenheld, 1986).

1811. Garthoff, Raymond L., *Policy versus the Law: The Reinterpretation of the ABM Treaty* (Washington, DC: Brookings Institution, 1987).

1812. George, James L., *The New Nuclear Rules: Strategy and Arms Control after INF and START* (New York: St. Martin's Press, 1990).

1813. Goldman, Andrew, *The Krasnoyarsk Radar: What Is Its Significance?* (Washington, DC: House Republican Research Committee, 1987).

1814. Goller-Calvo, Notburga K., and Michel A. Calvo, *The SALT Agreements: Content, Application, Verification* (Dordrecht-Boston: Martinus Nijhoff, 1987).

1815. Guertner, Gary L., and Donald M. Snow, *The Last Frontier: An Analysis of the Strategic Defense Initiative* (Lexington, MA: Lexington Books, 1986).

1816. Haley, P. Edward, and Jack Merritt, eds., *Strategic Defense Initiative: Folly or Future?* (Boulder, CO: Westview Press, 1986).

1817. Hallenbeck, Ralph A., and David E. Shaver, eds., *On Disarmament: The Role of Conventional Arms Control in National Security Strategy* (New York: Praeger, 1991).

1818. Halloran, Bernard F., ed., *Essays on Arms Control and National Security* (Washington, DC: US Arms Control and Disarmament Agency, Government Printing Office, 1986).

1819. Hannigan, John, *New Dimensions in Canadian-Soviet Arctic Relations* (Ottawa: Canadian Institute for International Peace and Security, 1987).

1820. Haslam, Jonathan, *The Soviet Union and the Politics of Nuclear Weapons in Europe, 1969-1987* (Ithaca: Cornell University Press, 1990).

1821. Hildreth, Steven A., *The Reagan Adminstration Posture toward the ABM Treaty: Possible Implications* (Washington, DC: Library of Congress, Congressional Research Service, 1987).

1822. Hopmann, P. Terrence, and Frank Barnaby, eds., *Rethinking the Nuclear Weapons: The Dilemma in Europe* (New York: St. Martin's Press, 1988).

1823. Johnson, Teresa Pelton, and Steven E. Miller, eds., *Russian Security After the Cold War: Seven Views from Moscow* (Washington, DC: Brassey's, 1993).

1824. Kartchner, Kerry M., ed., *Negotiating START: Strategic Arms Reduction Talks and the Quest for Stability* (New Brunswick, NJ: Transaction Publishers, 1992).

1825. Kolkowicz, Roman, *The Logic of Nuclear Terror* (Boston: Allen & Unwin, 1987).

1826. Lawrence, Marilee, *A Game Worth the Candle: The Confidence- and Security-Building Process in Europe: An Analysis of U.S. and Soviet Negotiating Strategies* (Santa Monica, CA: RAND, 1986).

1827. Lempert, Robert J., *Cruise Missile Arms Control* (Santa Monica, CA: RAND, 1989).

1828. Levine, Robert A., *Still the Arms Debate* (Brookfield, VT: Gower, 1990).

1829. Lewis, K. N., *Possible Soviet Responses to the Strategic Defense Initiative: A Functionally Organized Taxonomy* (Santa Monica, CA: RAND, 1986).

1830. Linam, James, *Setting Limits on Conventional Arms: A New Strategy for U.S. Negotiators* (Washington, DC: Heritage Foundation, 1986).

1831. Lindeman, Mark, with Debra Javeline et al., *The U.S., the Soviets and Nuclear Arms: Choices for the Twenty-First Century* (Providence, RI: Brown University Center for Foreign Policy Development, 1989).

1832. Lucas, Michael R., *The Western Alliance after INF: Redefining U.S. Policy toward Europe and the Soviet Union* (Boulder, CO: L. Rienner, 1990).

1833. Lussoer, Frances M., *Budgetary and Military Effects of a Treaty Limiting Conventional Forces in Europe* (Washington, DC: US Congressional Budget Office, 1990).

1834. Mandelbaum, Michael, ed., *The Other Side of the Table: The Soviet Approach to Arms Control* (New York: Council on Foreign Relations Press, 1990).

1835. Mazarr, Michael J., *START and the Future of Deterrence* (New York: St. Martin's Press, 1990).

1836. Menos, Dennis, *The Superpowers and Nuclear Arms*

Control: Rhetoric and Reality (New York: Praeger, 1991).

1837. Miall, Hugh, *Nuclear Weapons: Who's in Charge* (Basingstoke: Macmillan Press, 1987).

1838. Moodie, Michael, *Conventional Arms Control and Defense Acquisitions: Catching the Caboose?* (Washington, DC: Center for Strategic and International Studies, 1990).

1839. Nitze, Paul H., *Interpreting the ABM Treaty* (Washington, DC: US Department of State, Bureau of Public Affairs, 1987).

1840. -----, *The Nuclear and Space Negotiations: Translating Promise to Progress* (Washington, DC: US Department of State, Bureau of Public Affairs, 1987).

1841. Nunn, Sam, *Sam Nunn on Arms Control*, ed. by Kenneth W. Thompson (Lanham, MD: University Press of America, 1987).

1842. Nye, Joseph S., Jr., *et al.*, *Fateful Visions: Avoiding Nuclear Catastrophe* (Cambridge, MA: Ballinger, 1988).

1843. Ochmanek, D. A., *SDI and/or Arms Control* (Santa Monica, CA: RAND, 1987).

1844. Park, Jae Kyu, and Byungjoon Ahn, eds., *The Strategic Defense Initiative: Its Implications for Asia and the Pacific* (Boulder, CO: Westview Press, 1987).

1845. Parrott, Bruce, *The Soviet Union and Ballistic Missile Defense* (Boulder, CO: Westview, with the Johns Hopkins University School of Advanced International Studies, Foreign Policy Institute, 1987).

1846. Payne, Keith, *Nuclear Peacekeeping: The U.S., the U.S.S.R. and Nuclear Deterrence* (Evanston, IL: McDougal, Littell & Co., 1990).

1847. Potter, William C., with Eve C. Cohen and Edward Kayukov, *Nuclear Profiles of the Soviet Successor States* (Monterey, CA: Program for Nonproliferation Studies, Monterey Institute of International Studies, 1993).

1848. Powaski, Ronald E., *March to Armageddon: The United States and the Nuclear Arms Race, 1939 to the Present* (Oxford: Oxford University Press, 1987).

1849. *The Public, the Soviets and Nuclear Arms: Public Summit '88: Synopsis of Content* (New York: Public Agenda Foundation, 1987).

1850. Purver, Ronald G., *Arctic Arms Control: Constraints and Opportunities* (Ottawa: Canadian Institute for International Peace and Security, 1988).

1851. Rowny, Edward L., *Arms Control: The East Asian and Pacific Focus* (Washington, DC: US Department of State, Bureau of Public Affairs, 1987).

1852. Scheffer, David, *The Reykjavik Talks: Promise or Peril: Report of the Subcommittee on Arms Control, International Security and Science to the Committee on Foreign Affairs, US House of Representatives* (Washington, DC: US Government Printing Office, 1987).

1853. Schwartz, William A., *et al.*, *The Nuclear Seduction: Why the Arms Race Doesn't Matter-And What Does* (Berkeley: University of California Press, 1990).

1854. Scott, Robert T., ed., *The Race for Security: Arms and Arms Control in the Reagan Years* (Lexington, MA: Lexington Books, 1987).

1855. Shcherbak, Igor, *Confidence-Building Measures and International Security: The Political and Military Aspects: A Soviet View* (New York: United Nations, 1991).

1856. Sherr, Alan B., *The Other Side of Arms Control: Soviet Objectives in the Gorbachev Era* (Winchester, MA: Unwin Hyman, 1988).

1857. Stutzle, Walther, Bhupendra Jasani and Regina Cowen, eds., *The ABM Treaty: To Defend or Not to Defend?* (Oxford: Oxford University Press, 1987).

1858. Thompson, Kenneth W., ed., *Arms Control: Moral, Political and Historical Lessons* (Lanham, MD: University Press of America, 1990).

1859. -----, ed., *Negotiating Arms Control: Missed Opportunities and Limited Successes* (Lanham, MD: University Press of America, 1991).

1860. US Arms Control and Disarmament Agency, *Soviet Propaganda Campaign against the US Strategic Defense Initiative* (Washington, DC: US Arms Control and Disarmament Agency, 1986).

1861. US Congress. House. Committee on Armed Services. Defense Policy Panel. *Prospects of U.S.-Soviet Relations with Emphasis on Conventional Arms Control.* 101st Congress, 1st Session (Washington, DC: Government Printing Office, 1989).

1862. US Congress. House. Committee on Armed Services. Defense Policy Panel. *Reykjavik and American Security: Report.* 99th Congress (Washington, DC: Government Printing Office, 1987).

1863. US Congress. House. Committee on Armed Services. Defense Policy Panel. *The Reykjavik Process: Preparation for and Conduct of the Iceland Summit and Its Implications for Arms Control Policy: Report.* 99th Congress (Washington, DC: Government Printing Office, 1987).

1864. US Congress. House. Committee on Armed Services. Procurement and Military Nuclear Systems Subcommittee. Special Panel on Arms Control and Disarmament. *Review of Arms Control and Disarmament Activities: Hearings.* 99th Congress, 10, 12, 18, 20 Sept., 31 Oct., 20 Nov., 12 Dec. 1985 (Washington, DC: Government Printing Office, 1986).

1865. US Congress. House. Committee on Foreign Affairs. Subcommittee on Arms Control, International Security and Science. *Implications of Abandoning SALT: Hearing.* 99th Congress, 15 Apr. 1986 (Washington, DC: Government Printing Office, 1986).

1866. US Congress. House. Committee on Foreign Affairs. Subcommittee on Arms Control, International Security and

Science. *Reaction to the Reykjavik Proposals: Hearing.* 100th Congress, 29 Jan. 1987 (Washington, DC: Government Printing Office, 1987).

1867. US Congress. House. Committee on Foreign Affairs. Subcommittee on Arms Control, International Security and Science. *Review of ABM Treaty Interpretation Dispute and SDI: Hearing.* 100th Congress, 26 Feb. 1987 (Washington, DC: Government Printing Office, 1987).

1868. US Congress. House. Committee on Foreign Affairs. Subcommittee on Arms Control, International Security and Science. *Roundtable Discussion on United States-Soviet Relations and the Future of Arms Control: Hearing.* 101st Congress, 1st Session (Washington, DC: Government Printing Office, 1991).

1869. US Congress. House. Committee on Foreign Affairs. Subcommittee on Arms Control, International Security and Science. *Soviet Compliance with Arms Control Agreements: Hearing.* 100th Congress, 12 Mar. 1987 (Washington, DC: Government Printing Office, 1987).

1870. US Congress. House. Committee on Foreign Affairs. Subcommittee on Arms Control, International Security and Science. *Verifying Arms Control Agreements: The Soviet View: Report.* 100th Congress (Washington, DC: Government Printing Office, 1987).

1871. US Congress. Office of Technology Assessment. *Verification Technologies: Measures for Monitoring Compliance with the START Treaty: Summary* (Washington, DC: Office of Technology Assessment, 1990).

1872. US Congress. Senate. Committee on Armed Services. *Nuclear Testing Issues: Hearing.* 99th Congress, 29 and 30 Apr. 1989 (Washington, DC: Government Printing Office, 1987).

1873. US Congress. Senate. Committee on Foreign Relations. *The ABM Treaty and the Constitution: Joint Hearings.* 100th Congress, 11, 26 Mar. and 29 Apr. 1987 (Washington, DC: Government Printing Office, 1987).

1874. US Congress. Senate. Committee on Foreign Relations. *Nuclear Testing Issues: Hearings.* 99th Congress, 8 May, 19, 26 June 1986 (Washington, DC: Government Printing Office, 1986).

1875. US Congress. Senate. Committee on Foreign Relations. *Test Ban Issues.* 100th Congress, 2nd Session (Washington, DC: Government Printing Office, 1988).

1876. US Congress. Senate. Committee on Foreign Relations. *Threshold Test Ban Treaty and Peaceful Nuclear Explosions Treaty: Hearings.* 100th Congress, 13 and 25 Jan. 1987 (Washington, DC: Government Printing Office, 1987).

1877. US Department of State. Bureau of Public Affairs. *U.S. Arms Control Initiatives: An Update* (Washington, DC: Bureau of Public Affairs, 1987).

1878. US General Accounting Office. *NATO-Warsaw Pact: Issues Related to Implementation of a Conventional Forces Treaty; Report to Congressional Committees* (Washington, DC: General Accounting Office, 1990).

1879. Van Cleave, William R., and S. T. Cohen, *Nuclear Weapons, Policies, and the Test Ban Issue* (New York: Praeger, 1987).

1880. Van Oudenaren, John, *The Role of Shevardnadze and the Ministry of Foreign Affairs in the Making of Soviet Defense and Arms Control Policy* (Santa Monica, CA: RAND, 1990).

1881. *Verifying a CFE Agreement* (Washington, DC: Program on Science, Arms Control and National Security, American Association for the Advancement of Science, 1990).

1882. Weber, Steve, *Cooperation and Discord in U.S.-Soviet Arms Control* (Princeton: Princeton University Press, 1991).

ARTICLES

1883. Adams, G., "Arms Control: Reality and Mirage," *Dissent*, 33, no. 4 (Fall 1986), 396-98.

1884. Adelman, Kenneth L., "Arms Control," *American Defense Annual* (1989-90), 161-73.

1885. -----, "Arms Control and Human Rights," *World Affairs*, 149, no. 3 (Winter 1986-87), 157-62.

1886. -----, "Lessons for the Future: Five Myths in the Arms Control Debate," *Presidential Studies Quarterly*, 18, no. 1 (Winter 1988), 47-53.

1887. -----, "SDI and the Arms Control Process," *Atlantic Community Quarterly*, 23, no. 3 (Fall 1985), 223-27.

1888. -----, "SDI: Setting the Record Straight," *US Department of State. Bulletin*, 85, no. 2103 (Oct. 1985), 42-45.

1889. -----, "START: Just a Sideshow," *Bulletin of the Atomic Scientists*, 47, no. 9 (Nov. 1991), 19-21.

1890. -----, "Why an INF Agreement Makes Sense," *World Affairs*, 149, no. 3 (Winter 1986-87), 143-49.

1891. -----, *et al.*, "Policy Focus: Arms Control Verification Reconsidered," *International Security*, 14, no. 4 (Spring 1990), 140-84.

1892. Adler, Emanuel, "Arms Control, Disarmament, and National Security: A Thirty Year Retrospective and a New Set of Anticipations," *Daedalus*, 120, no. 1 (Winter 1991), 1-20.

1893. "Agreement on the Prevention of Dangerous Military Activities, June 12, 1989, United States-Union of Soviet Socialist Republics," *Harvard International Law Journal*, 31, no. 1 (Winter 1990), 333-38.

1894. Albrecht, Ulrich, "Revive the Reykjavik Dynamism," *Bulletin of the Atomic Scientists*, 43, no. 2 (Mar. 1987), 40-41.

1895. Alexiev, Alex R., "The Soviet Campaign against INF: Strategy, Tactics and Means," *Orbis*, 29, no. 2 (Summer 1985), 319-50.

1896. Allison, Roy, "Current Soviet Views on Conventional Arms Control in Europe," *Arms Control*, 9, no. 2 (Sept. 1988), 134-69.

1897. Almond, Harry H., Jr., "Nuclear Weapons, Nuclear

Strategy, and Law," *Denver Journal of International Law and Policy*, 15, no. 2-3 (Winter-Spring 1987), 283-99.

1898. Arbatov, Alexei G., "Russian Nuclear Disarmament: Problems and Prospects," *Arms Control*, 14, no. 1 (Apr. 1993), 103-15.

1899. -----, "START: Good, Bad or Neutral?" *Survival*, 31, no. 4 (July-Aug. 1989), 291-300.

1900. -----, "We Could Have Done Better," *Bulletin of the Atomic Scientists*, 47, no. 9 (Nov. 1991), 36ff.

1901. Arkin, William M., "Fewer Warheads in Europe," *Bulletin of the Atomic Scientists*, 42, no., 7 (Aug-Sept. 1986), 4-5.

1902. -----, "Happy Birthday, Flexible Response," *Bulletin of the Atomic Scientists*, 43, no. 10 (Dec. 1987), 5-6.

1903. -----, "Navy Autonomy Thwarts Arms Control," *Bulletin of the Atomic Scientists*, 43, no. 7 (Sept. 1987), 14-18.

1904. -----, "Test Ban Fever," *Bulletin of the Atomic Scientists*, 42, no. 8 (Oct. 1986), 4-5.

1905. Barnet, Roger W., "Naval Arms Control: A One-Way Channel," *Strategic Review*, 18, no. 3 (Summer 1990), 35-48.

1906. Barrett, John, "Arms Control and Canada's Security Policy," *International Journal*, 42, no. 4 (Autumn 1987), 731-68.

1907. Beatty, Jack, "Reagan's Gift," *Atlantic Monthly*, 263, no. 2 (Feb. 1989), 59ff.

1908. Beer, Thomas, "Arms Control in Outer Space: Military Technology vs. International Law," *Arms Control*, 6 (September 1985), 183-202.

1909. Berkowitz, Marc J., "Soviet Swords of Damocles," *Global Affairs*, 6, no. 3 (Summer 1991), 101-22.

1910. Bethe, Hans, "Arms Control Frenzy," *National Review*, 39 (23 Oct. 1987), 26ff.

1911. -----, "Chop Down the Nuclear Arsenals," *Bulletin of the Atomic Scientists*, 45, no. 2 (Mar. 1989), 11-15.

1912. Beukel, Erik, "The Fundamental Attribution Error in the Cold War: American Perceptions of the Soviet Union as a Nuclear Superpower," *Arms Control*, 13, no. 3 (Dec. 1993), 396-420.

1913. Bilski, A., "Sounding a Soviet Challenge on Arms," *Maclean's*, 98 (14 Oct. 1985), 44-46.

1914. Borawski, John, "Confidence-Building Measures: Rescuing Arms Control," *Fletcher Forum*, 10, no. 1 (Winter 1986), 111-31.

1915. -----, "Progress in Stockholm Talks," *Bulletin of the Atomic Scientists*, 42, no. 2 (Feb. 1986), 40-42.

1916. -----, Stan Weeks and Charlotte E. Thompson, "The Stockholm Agreement of September 1986," *Orbis*, 30, no. 4 (Winter 1987), 643-62.

1917. Borklund, C. W., "Preventing Nuclear War: Is Western Strategy Changing Again?" *Journal of Social, Political and Economic Studies*, 12, no. 4 (Winter 1987), 443-63.

1918. Bowden, Sharon, and Anita Ramasastry, "Arms Control: Superpower Relations in the New Europe," *Harvard International Law Journal*, 31, no. 2 (Spring 1990), 611-24.

1919. Bowie, Robert R., "Arms Control in the 1990s," *Daedalus*, 120, no. 1 (Winter 1991), 53-68.

1920. Brooks, Linton F., "The Strategic Arms Reduction Treaty: Reducing the Risk of War," *NATO Review*, 39, no. 5 (Oct. 1991), 7-12.

1921. Brown, Neville, "Has SDI a Future?" *Arms Control*, 13, no. 3 (Dec. 1993), 375-95.

1922. Brugioni, Dino A., "The Kyshtym Connection," *Bulletin of the Atomic Scientists*, 46, no. 2 (Mar. 1990), 12.

1923. Brzezinski, Zbigniew, "National Strategy and Arms Control," *Washington Quarterly*, 10, no. 1 (Winter 1987), 5-11.

1924. -----, "A Star Wars Solution," *New Republic* (8 July 1985), 16-18.

1925. Bunn, George, and John B. Rhinelander, "The Arms Control Obligations of the Former Soviet Union," *Virginia Journal of International Law*, 33, no. 2 (Winter 1993), 323-50.

1926. Bunn, Matthew, "Arms Control's Enduring Worth," *Foreign Policy*, no. 79 (Summer 1990), 151-68.

1927. Burant, Stephen R., "Soviet Perspectives on the Legal Regime in Outer Space: The Problem of Space Demilitarization," *Studies in Comparative Communism*, 19, no. 3-4 (Autumn-Winter 1986), 161-75.

1928. Burns, W. F., "Arms Control in Transition: The Reagan Administration's Legacy," *Presidential Studies Quarterly*, 19, no. 1 (Winter 1989), 31-39.

1929. "Bush, Gorbachev Salute Treaty as New Foundation of Peace," *Congressional Quarterly Weekly Report*, 48 (3 Aug. 1991), 2192.

1930. Caldwell, Lawrence T., "United States-Soviet Relations and Arms Control," *Current History*, 86, no. 522 (Oct. 1987), 305ff.

1931. Camesale, Albert, "SDI and Arms Control," *Harvard International Review*, 7, no. 4 (Jan-Feb. 1985), 29-31.

1932. "Change in Soviet Overflight Stance Clears Way for Open Skies Treaty," *Aviation Week & Space Technology*, 135, no. 19 (11 Nov. 1991), 29.

1933. Charles, Daniel, "NATO Looks for Arms Control Loopholes," *Bulletin of the Atomic Scientists*, 43, no. 7 (Sept. 1987), 7-12.

1934. Chayes, Abram, Antonia H. Chayes and Eliot Spitzer, "Space Weapons: The Legal Context," *Daedalus*, 114, no. 3 (Summer 1985), 193-218.

1935. Chernoff, Fred, "Arms Control, European Security and the Future of the Western Alliance," *Strategic Review*, 20, no. 1 (Winter 1992), 19-31.

1936. Clarke, Douglas L., "Arms Control and Security: The Hope of a New Era after a Dramatic Year," *Report on Eastern Europe*, 2, no. 1 (4 Jan. 1991), 54-57.

1937. -----, "The Conventional Armed Forces in Europe Treaty: Limits and Zones," *Report on Eastern Europe*, 2, no. 2 (11 Jan. 1991), 34-39.

1938. -----, "Trouble with the Conventional Forces Treaty," *Report on the USSR*, 3, no. 15 (12 Apr. 1991), 6-10.

1939. -----, "The Unilateral Arms Cuts in the Warsaw Pact," *Report on Eastern Europe*, 1, no. 5 (2 Feb. 1990), 43-47.

1940. "Comparison of U.S. and Soviet Nuclear Cuts," *Arms Control Today*, 21 (Nov. 1991), 27-28.

1941. "Comrades in Arms Control," *Business Week* (21 Dec. 1987), 34-37.

1942. Cotter, Daniel R., "The Emerging INF Agreement: A Case of Strategic Regression," *Strategic Review*, 15, no. 3 (Summer 1987), 11-19.

1943. Covault, Craig, "*Perestroika* in Space, Science Controversial to Soviet Officials," *Aviation Week & Space Technology* (12 Dec. 1988), 34-35.

1944. "Creation of Nuclear Weapons-Free Zone Wins Support," *Aviation Week & Space Technology*, 135, no. 2 (15 July 1991), 26.

1945. Crozier, Brian, "The Arms-Control Morass," *National Review*, 38 (26 Sept. 1986), 25-26.

1946. -----, "Summitry Primer," *National Review*, 38 (21 Nov. 1986), 26ff.

1947. Daalder, Ivo H., "Evaluating SDI Employment Options," *Survival*, 32, no. 1 (Jan-Feb. 1988), 29-46.

1948. Daniels, Robert V., "The Politics of Summitry," *New Leader* (20 Oct. 1986), 6-9.

1949. Danilov, Sergei, "Storming the Chemical Arsenals," *Soviet Military Review*, no. 7 (July 1989), 52-53.

1950. Dean, Jonathan, "Gorbachev's Arms Control Moves," *Bulletin of the Atomic Scientists*, 43, no. 5 (June 1987), 43-40.

1951. -----, "Military Security in Europe," *Foreign Affairs*, 66, no. 1 (Fall 1987), 22-40.

1952. Di, Wan, "Soviets Bite the Bullet in Arms Talks," *Beijing Review*, 30 (16 Nov. 1987), 14-15.

1953. Din, A. M., "Nuclear Test Bans," *Journal of Peace Research*, 24, no. 3 (June 1987), 105-10.

1954. Dixon, William J., and Dale L. Smith, "Arms Control and the Evolution of Superpower Relations," *Social Science Quarterly*, 73, no. 4 (Dec. 1992), 876-89.

1955. "Documentation: Summit Meeting in Reykjavik (1986)," *Survival*, 29, no. 2 (Mar-Apr. 1987), 166-88.

1956. Doty, Paul, "Arms Control: 1960, 1990, 2020," *Daedalus*, 120, no. 1 (Winter 1990), 33-52.

1957. -----, "A Nuclear Test Ban," *Foreign Affairs*, 65, no. 4 (Spring 1987), 750-69.

1958. Downey, Thomas J., Bob Carr and Jim Moody, "Report from Krasnoyarsk," *Bulletin of the Atomic Scientists*, 43, no. 9 (Nov. 1987), 11-14.

1959. Drell, Sidney D., "START: Verification Triumphs," *Bulletin of the Atomic Scientists*, 47, no. 9 (Nov. 1991), 28-29.

1960. Dudney, Robert S., "The ICBM Problem Rolls On," *Air Force Magazine*, 72, no. 10 (Oct. 1989), 46-51.

1961. -----, "Why Gorbachev Needs an Arms Agreement," *U.S. News & World Report*, 98 (1 Apr. 1985), 34.

1962. Earle, Ralph, II, "America Is Cheating Itself," *Foreign Policy*, no. 64 (Fall 1986), 3-16.

1963. -----, "Don't Abandon Salt II," *Bulletin of the Atomic Scientists*, 42, no. 7 (Aug-Sept. 1986), 8-9.

1964. Einhorn, Robert, "Revising the START Process," *Survival*, 32, no. 6 (Nov-Dec. 1990), 497-506.

1965. Eksterowicz, A. J., "The Balance of Power Foundation for Contemporary Arms Control Praxis," *Journal of Social, Political and Economic Studies*, 13, no. 3 (Fall 1988), 315-32.

1966. Ellsberg, Daniel, "Nuclear Security and the Soviet Collapse," *World Policy Journal*, 9, no. 1 (Winter 1991-92), 135-56.

1967. English, Robert, "Offensive Star Wars," *New Republic* (24 Feb. 1986), 13-15.

1968. Epstein, William, "New Hope for a Comprehensive Test Ban," *Bulletin of the Atomic Scientists*, 42, no. 2 (Feb. 1986), 29-30.

1969. Erickson, John, "Arms Negotiations in Europe," *Current History*, 88, no. 541 (Nov. 1989), 369ff.

1970. Evangelista, Matthew A., "Gorbachev's Disarmament Campaign: The New Soviet Approach to Security," *World Policy Journal*, 3, no. 4 (Fall 1986), 561-99.

1971. -----, "Gorbachev's Next Move," *Harper's*, 274, no. 1640 (Jan. 1987), 24ff.

1972. Evans, M. Stanton, "The Common Sense of SDI," *National Review*, 38 (31 Dec. 1986), 32-35.

1973. Feith, Douglas J., "Proposal for Nuclear Test Ban: Failing the Test," *Washington Quarterly*, 9, no. 2 (Spring 1986), 15-21.

1974. Feiveson, Harold A., and Frank N. Von Hippel, "Beyond START: How to Make Much Deeper Cuts," *International Security*, 15, no. 1 (Summer 1990), 154-80.

1975. Felton, J., "In the Bag: Chemical Weapons Pact," *Congressional Quarterly Weekly Report*, 48 (26 May 1990), 1664.

1976. Finder, Joseph, "Biological Warfare, Genetic Engineering and the Treaty That Failed," *Washington Quarterly*, 9, no. 2 (Spring 1986), 5-14.

1977. Fischer, Kristian, "The Modernization of the U.S. Radar Installation at Thule, Greenland," *Journal of Peace Research*, 30, no. 1 (Feb. 1993), 7-20.

1978. Flowerree, Charles C., "On Tending Arms Control Agreements," *Washington Quarterly*, 13, no. 1 (Winter 1990), 199-214.

1979. Foley, Theresa M., "Scientists Urge New Stance on SDI Testing in U.S.-Soviet Arms Talks," *Aviation Week & Space Technology* (14 Sept. 1987), 30-31.

1980. -----, "SDI Stakes Initial Deployment on Success of Four Programs," *Aviation Week & Space Technology* (12 Oct. 1987), 30-31.

1981. Forsberg, Randall, "START: End Arms Control, Begin Disarmament," *Bulletin of the Atomic Scientists*, 47, no. 9 (Nov. 1991), 29-31.

1982. -----, Bob Leavitt and Steve Lilly-Weber, "Conventional Forces Treaty Buries Cold War," *Bulletin of the Atomic Scientists*, 47, no. 1 (Jan-Feb. 1991), 32-37.

1983. Freedman, L., "Star Wars and the Summit," *Government and Opposition*, 21 (Spring 1986), 131-45.

1984. Galbraith, John K., "The Military: A Loose Cannon?" *Harper's*, 273, no. 1638 (Nov. 1986), 13-15.

1985. Galvin, General John R., "Some Thoughts on Conventional Arms Control," *Survival*, 31, no. 2 (Mar-Apr. 1989), 99-108.

1986. Garfinkle, Adam M., "The `INF' Arena after Reykjavik: A Broader U.S. Approach?" *Strategic Review*, 14, no. 4 (Fall 1986), 27-36.

1987. -----, "STARTing Over," *National Interest*, no. 20 (Summer 1990), 71-76.

1988. Garthoff, Raymond L., "Refocusing the SDI Debate," *Bulletin of the Atomic Scientists*, 43, no. 7 (Sept. 1987), 44-50.

1989. -----, "Soviet Snafu: Case of the Wandering Radar," *Bulletin of the Atomic Scientists*, 47, no. 6 (July-Aug. 1991), 7-9.

1990. Gellner, Charles R., with Jeanette Voas, "Arms Control: An Evolving Record of Hope," in Stephen J. Cimbala, ed., *The Reagan Defense Program: An Interim Assessment* (Wilmington, DE: Scholarly Resources, 1986).

1991. Geneste, Mark, "SDI, the Atom and Arms Control," *Atlantic Community Quarterly*, 24, no. 4 (Winter 1986), 300-07.

1992. Geyer, A., "Down From the Summit: The Disarmament Agenda," *Christian Century*, 105 (8-15 June 1988), 566.

1993. Glass, Andrew J., "The Salt II Games," *New Leader* (5-19 May 1986), 3-4.

1994. Goldblat, Jozef, "Will the NPT Survive?" *Bulletin of the Atomic Scientists*, 42, no. 1 (Jan. 1986), 35-38.

1995. Goldman, Marshall I., "Both Reagan and Gorbachev Need an Arms Control Agreement to Divert Attention from Domestic Problems," *Technology Review*, 90, no. 5 (July 1987), 18ff.

1996. Goodby, James E., "Can Arms Control Survive Peace?" *Washington Quarterly*, 13, no. 4 (Autumn 1990), 93-101.

1997. Goodin, R. E., "Mood Matching and Arms Control," *International Studies Quarterly*, 32 (Dec. 1988), 473-81.

1998. Gorbachev, Mikhail S., "The USSR's Disarmament Measures: The Elimination of Tactical Weapons," *Vital Speeches of the Day*, 58 (1 Nov. 1991), 37.

1999. "Gorbachev Proposes Cutback in Aircraft Deployed in Europe," *Aviation Week & Space Technology* (18 July 1988), 25.

2000. Gordon, James K., "Summit Talks Advance New Arms Limitation Possibilities," *Aviation Week & Space Technology* (20 Oct. 1986), 39-40.

2001. Gordon, Michael R., "Dateline Washington: INF: A Hollow Victory?" *Foreign Policy*, no. 68 (Fall 1987), 159-79.

2002. Gore, Albert, Jr., "Stability for Two," *New Republic* (17 Nov. 1986), 19-22.

2003. Graben, Erik K., "Superpower Nuclear Minimalism in the Post-Cold War Era?" *Arms Control*, 13, no. 3 (Dec. 1993), 352-74.

2004. Graham, Daniel O., "A Conservative Deals with *Glasnost'*," *Journal of Social, Political and Economic Studies*, 13, no. 3 (Fall 1988), 227-38.

2005. Gray, Colin S., "Nuclear Delusions: Six Arms Control Fallacies," *Policy Review*, no. 37 (Summer 1986), 48-53.

2006. -----, "Through a Missile Tube Darkly: `New Thinking' about Nuclear Strategy," *Political Studies*, 41, no. 4 (Dec. 1993), 661-71.

2007. Greely, Brendan M., Jr., "Soviets Building Naval Strength While Pursuing Maritime Arms Control," *Aviation Week & Space Technology* (13 Mar. 1989), 63.

2008. Grove, Eric J., "Allied Nuclear Forces Complicate Negotiations," *Bulletin of the Atomic Scientists*, 42, no. 6 (June-July 1986), 18-23.

2009. Guertner, Gary L., "Strategic Arms After Reagan," *SAIS Review*, 10, no. 1 (Winter-Spring 1990), 87-100.

2010. -----, "Three Images of Soviet Arms Control Compliance," *Political Science Quarterly*, 103, no. 2 (Summer 1988), 321-46.

2011. Haley, P. Edward, "`You Could Have Said Yes': Lessons from Reykjavik," *Orbis*, 31, no. 1 (Spring 1987), 75-97.

2012. Hampson, Fen Osler, "Arms Control and East-West Relations," in *Canada Among Nations, 1986: Talking Trade* (Toronto: Lorimer, 1987).

2013. Hardenbergh, Chalmers, "The Other Negotiations," *Bulletin of the Atomic Scientists*, 42, no. 1 (Jan. 1986), 45-47; 42, no. 6 (June-July 1986), 42-44; 43, no. 2 (Mar. 1987), 48-49; and 43, no. 7 (Sept. 1987), 52-53.

2014. Hartung, William, "Star Wars Pork Barrel," *Bulletin of the Atomic Scientists*, 42, no. 1 (Jan. 1986), 20-24.

2015. Hawkins, William R., "The Sub Version of Star Wars," *National Review*, 38 (15 Aug. 1986), 34ff.

2016. Hayward, Dan, "Gorbachev's Murmansk Initiative: New Prospects for Arms Control in the Arctic?" *Northern Perspectives*, 16, no. 4 (1988), 9-11.

2017. Heiss, Klaus P., "Killer Bees, Negative Gates, and Hibernation: An Effective SDI System for Development Now," *Journal of Social, Political and Economic Studies*, 13, no. 3 (Fall 1988), 269-78.

2018. Henderson, Breck W., "Arms Control Pacts May Outpace Advances in Verification Technology," *Aviation Week & Space Technology*, 133, no. 6 (6 Aug. 1990), 51ff.

2019. "Homing in on Krasnoyarsk," *Economist*, 308 (24 Sept. 1988), 39.

2020. Howard, Michael, "Is Arms Control Really Necessary?" *Harper's*, 272, no. 1632 (May 1986), 13-16.

2021. Hulse, Andrew, "Soviet Force Development and Nuclear Arms Reduction," *Parameters*, 17, no. 4 (Dec. 1987), 81-90.

2022. Hyde, Henry, "Trick or Treaty: Excuses for Soviet Treaty Violations," *Policy Review*, no. 40 (Spring 1987), 26-31.

2023. Hylin, Carl F., "Stemming the Arms Race in Outer Space: Suggested Revisions of the Outer Space Treaty Based on Three Successful Arms Control Measures," *California Western International Law Journal*, 16, no. 1 (Winter 1986), 118-37.

2024. Ionescu, Ghita, "A Geopolitical Aspect of an Eminently Geopolitical Crisis," *Government and Opposition*, 22 (Summer 1987), 259-69.

2025. Isaacs, John, "Congress and the Military Revisited," *Bulletin of the Atomic Scientists*, 42, no. 2 (Feb. 1986), 6-7.

2026. -----, "House Challenges Reagan on Arms Control," *Bulletin of the Atomic Scientists*, 42, no. 8 (Oct. 1986), 6-7.

2027. -----, "Using Summitry to Thwart Congress," *Bulletin of the Atomic Scientists*, 42, no. 10 (Dec. 1986), 4-5.

2028. Jamgotch, Nish, Jr., "Assessing the Revolution in Superpower Arms Control and Security Communications," *Coexistence*, 28, no. 3 (Sept. 1991), 351-70.

2029. Jones, David T., "Eliminating Chemical Weapons: Less Than Meets the Eye," *Washington Quarterly*, 12, no. 2 (Spring 1989), 83-92.

2030. Kampelman, Max M., "Negotiating Arms with the Soviets," *Freedom at Issue*, no. 94 (Jan-Feb. 1987), 3-6.

2031. -----, "Negotiating with the Soviet Union," *World Affairs*, 148, no. 4 (Spring 1986), 199-203.

2032. -----, "START: Completing the Task," *Washington Quarterly*, 12, no. 3 (Summer 1989), 5-16.

2033. Kapitsa, Sergei, "A Soviet View of Nuclear Winter," *Bulletin of the Atomic Scientists*, 41, no. 9 (Oct. 1985), 37-39.

2034. Kaplow, David A., "Long Arms and Chemical Arms: Extraterritoriality and the Draft Chemical Weapons Convention," *Yale Journal of International Law*, 15, no. 1 (Winter 1990), 1-83.

2035. Kartchner, Kerry M., "Soviet Compliance with a START Agreement: Prospects under Gorbachev," *Strategic Review*, 17, no. 4 (Fall 1989), 47-57.

2036. Kaufman, Joyce P., "U.S.-Soviet Arms Control and Politics," *Arms Control*, 8, no. 3 (Dec. 1987), 278-94.

2037. Kaysen, Carl, Robert S. McNamara and George W. Rathjens, "Nuclear Weapons after the Cold War," *Foreign Affairs*, 70, no. 4 (Fall 1991), 95-110.

2038. Kemp, Geoffrey, "Regional Security, Arms Control and the End of the Cold War," *Washington Quarterly*, 13, no. 4 (Autumn 1990), 33-51.

2039. Kemp, Jack, "How to Proceed with SDI-Deploy Now," *National Interest*, no. 7 (Spring 1987), 76-79.

2040. -----, "The Politics of SDI," *National Review*, 38 (31 Dec. 1986), 28-31.

2041. Kennedy, Kevin C., "Treaty Interpretation by the Executive Branch: The ABM Treaty and `Star Wars' Testing and Development," *American Journal of International Law*, 80, no. 4 (Oct. 1986), 854-77.

2042. Kinahan, Graham M., "Ratification of START: Lessons from the INF Treaty," *Journal of Social, Political and Economic Studies*, 14, no. 4 (Winter 1989), 387-414.

2043. -----, "Soviet Intentions in Space," *Journal of Social, Political and Economic Studies*, 13, no. 3 (Fall 1988), 247-50.

2044. Kincade, William H., "Arms Control or Arms Coercion?" *Foreign Policy*, no. 62 (Spring 1986), 24-45.

2045. Kirkey, C., "The NATO Alliance and the IMF Treaty," *Armed Forces and Society*, 16, no. 2 (Winter 1990), 287-305.

2046. Kiselyov, Sergei, "Ukraine: Stuck with the Goods," *Bulletin of the Atomic Scientists*, 49, no. 2 (Mar. 1993), 30-33.

2047. Klare, Michael T., "Who's Arming Who? The Arms Trade in the 1990s," *Technology Review*, 93, no. 4 (May-June 1990), 42-50.

2048. Kober, Stanley, "Strategic Defense, Deterrence and Arms Control," *Washington Quarterly*, 10, no. 1 (Winter 1987), 123-35.

2049. Kogut, John, and Michael Weissman, "Taking the Pledge against Star Wars," *Bulletin of the Atomic Scientists*, 42, no. 1 (Jan. 1986), 27-30.

2050. Kokoshin, A. A., "Arms Control: A View from Moscow," *Daedalus*, 120, no. 1 (Winter 1991), 133-43.

2051. Kondracke, Morton, "Testing, Testing," *New Republic* (17 Nov. 1986), 16-17.

2052. Kortunov, Sergei, "Negotiating about Nuclear Weapons in Europe," *Survival*, 33, no. 1 (Jan-Feb. 1991), 45-52.

2053. -----, "START II and Beyond," *Bulletin of the Atomic Scientists*, 46, no. 8 (Oct. 1990), 21-24.

2054. Krass, Allan A., "START: The People, the Debt, and Mikhail," *Bulletin of the Atomic Scientists*, 47, no. 9 (Nov. 1991), 12-17.

2055. Krauthammer, Charles, "A Geneva Guide," *New Republic* (13 Oct. 1986), 16-18.

2056. -----, "Reykjavik and the End of Days," *New Republic* (17 Nov. 1986), 22ff.

2057. Kreamer, Sven F., "The Krasnoyarsk Saga," *Strategic Review*, 18, no. 1 (Winter 1990), 25-38.

2058. Krepon, Michael, "Dormant Threat to the ABM Treaty," *Bulletin of the Atomic Scientists*, 42, no. 1 (Jan. 1986). 31-34.

2059. -----, "High Stakes in INF Verification," *Bulletin of the Atomic Scientists*, 43, no. 5 (June 1987), 14-16.

2060. -----, "INF Agreement in Principle," *Bulletin of the Atomic Scientists*, 43, no. 9 (Nov. 1987), 5-6.

2061. -----, "The Iran/Arms Control Connection," *Bulletin of the Atomic Scientists*, 43, no. 2 (Mar. 1987), 9-10.

2062. -----, "Mixed Signals on Arms Control," *Bulletin of the Atomic Scientists*, 42, no. 7 (Aug-Sept. 1986), 6-7.

2063. -----, "Rocky Road to INF Accord," *Bulletin of the Atomic Scientists*, 43, no. 7 (Sept. 1987), 3-4.

2064. -----, "Ronald Reagan's Hidden Hands," *Bulletin of the Atomic Scientists*, 42, no. 5 (May 1986), 4-5.

2065. Lall, Betty G., "Military Spending, Arms Control, and the U.S. Budget," *New York University Journal of International Law and Politics*, 22, no. 3 (Spring 1990), 589-95.

2066. Lambeth, Benjamin, and Kevin Lewis, "The Kremlin and SDI," *Foreign Affairs*, 66, no. 4 (Spring 1988), 755-70.

2067. Lebow, Richard N., "If I Were Reagan: Stopping the Arms Race," *SAIS Review*, 5, no. 2 (Summer-Fall 1985), 125-32.

2068. Lee, William T., "US-USSR Strategic Arms Control Agreements: Expectations and Reality," *Comparative Strategy*, 19, no. 4 (Oct-Dec. 1993), 415-36.

2069. Legvold, Robert, "Gorbachev's New Approach to Conventional Arms Control," *Harriman Institute Forum*, 1, no. 1 (Jan. 1988), 1-7.

2070. Leitenberg, Milton, "A Return to Sverdlovsk: Allegations of Soviet Activities Related to Biological Weapons," *Arms Control*, 12, no. 2 (Sept. 1991), 161-90.

2071. Lellouche, Pierre, "SDI and the Atlantic Alliance," *Atlantic Community Quarterly*, 23, no. 3 (Fall 1985), 211-21.

2072. Lepingwell, John W. R., "Soviet Early Warning Radars Debated," *Report on the USSR*, 2, no. 33 (17 Aug. 1990), 11-15.

2073. Levin, Carl, "Administration Wrong on ABM Treaty," *Bulletin of the Atomic Scientists*, 43, no. 3 (Apr. 1987), 30-33.

2074. Lodal, J. M., "An Arms Control Agenda," *Foreign Policy*, no. 72 (Fall 1988), 152-72.

2075. Mann, Paul, "Administration Disputes Findings of U.S. Visit to Soviet Radar," *Aviation Week & Space Technology* (14 Sept. 1987), 26-28.

2076. -----, "Arms Control Protests Force Delay in Next Stage of SDI Research," *Aviation Week & Space Technology* (16 Feb. 1987), 16-17.

2077. -----, "CFE Treaty Realigns Forces among Warsaw Pact Countries," *Aviation Week & Space Technology*, 133, no. 22 (26 Nov. 1990), 26.

2078. -----, "CFE Treaty Slashes Weapons, But Huge Armories Remain," *Aviation Week & Space Technology*, 133, no. 22 (26 Nov. 1990), 24.

2079. -----, "Cruise Missile Accord Advances START Treaty," *Aviation Week & Space Technology*, 132, no. 22 (28 May 1990), 18-19.

2080. -----, "President Reagan Terminates U.S. Compliance with SALT 2," *Aviation Week & Space Technology* (2 June 1986), 24-25.

2081. -----, "World Leaders Move Toward New European Security Order," *Aviation Week & Space Technology*, 133, no. 22 (26 Nov. 1990), 24.

2082. Manson, P. D., "*Glasnost'* and Its Impact on the Canadian Forces," *Canadian Defense Quarterly*, 18, no. 6 (1989), 9-12.

2083. Manthrope, William H. J., Jr., "What Is Pushing Gorbachev into Arms Control?" *US Naval Institute Proceedings*, 114, no. 12 (Dec. 1988), 37-43.

2084. -----, "Why Is Gorbachev Pushing Naval Arms Control?" *US Naval Institute Proceedings*, 115, no. 1 (Jan. 1989), 73-77.

2085. Maresca, John J., "Confidence Building and Arms Reduction: The U.S.-Soviet Experience," *Pakistan Horizon*, 45, no. 4 (Oct. 1992), 7-14.

2086. Marsh, Gerald, "START: The Ups and Downs of Downloading," *Bulletin of the Atomic Scientists*, 47, no. 9 (Nov. 1991), 21-23.

2087. Mazarr, Michael J., "Nuclear Weapons after the Cold War," *Washington Quarterly*, 15, no. 3 (Summer 1992), 185ff.

2088. MccGwire, Michael, "Gorbachev's Arms Policy Rooted in the Past," *Bulletin of the Atomic Scientists*, 44, no. 2 (Mar. 1988), 44-46.

2089. -----, "New Directions in Soviet Arms-Control Policy," *Washington Quarterly*, 11, no. 3 (Summer 1988), 185-200.

2090. -----, "Why the Soviets Are Serious About Arms Control," *Proceedings of the Academy of Political Science*, 36, no. 4 (1987), 78-92.

2091. -----, "Why the Soviets Want Arms Control," *Technology Review*, 90, no. 2 (Feb-Mar. 1987), 36-45.

2092. Miller, Gerald E., "Who Needs Arms Control?" *US Naval Institute Proceedings*, 112, no. 1 (Jan. 1986), 39-42.

2093. Miller, Steven E., "Western Diplomacy and the Soviet Nuclear Legacy," *Survival*, 34, no. 3 (Autumn 1992), 28-42.

2094. Morrison, David C., "Back on Course," *National Journal*, 23, no. 35 (31 Aug. 1991), 2074-79.

2095. Nagle, Timothy J., "The Dangerous Military Activities Agreement: Minimum Order and Superpower Relations on the World's Oceans," *Virginia Journal of International Law*, 31, no. 1 (Fall 1990), 125-44.

2096. "NATO to Cut Nuclear Weapons 50% as Part of the New Military Strategy," *Aviation Week & Space Technology*, 135, no. 15 (14 Oct. 1991), 23.

2097. Navias, Martin S., "The Soviet Union and Multilateral Arms Control," *Arms Control*, 10, no. 2 (Sept. 1989), 137-51.

2098. Nitze, Paul H., "SDI and the ABM Treaty," *US Department of State. Bulletin*, 85, no. 2101 (Aug. 1985), 37-39.

2099. -----, and Abraham D. Sofaer, "The ABM Treaty and the SDI Program," *US Department of State. Bulletin*, 85, no. 2105 (Dec. 1985), 37-40.

2100. Nixon, Richard, and Henry Kissinger, "A Real Peace," *National Review*, 39 (22 May 1987), 32-34.

2101. Nolan, Mary L., "The Potemkin Village of *Glasnost'*: CPD Says Soviet Arms Spending Continues Unabated," *Sea Power*, 32, no. 8 (Aug. 1989), 47-48.

2102. "Not Bad at All," *Economist*, 297 (5 Oct. 1985), 13-14.

2103. Nunn, Sam, "The ABM Reinterpretation Issue," *Washington Quarterly*, 10, no. 4 (Autumn 1987), 45-57.

2104. Nye, Joseph S., Jr., "Farewell to Arms Control?" *Foreign Affairs*, 65, no. 1 (Fall 1986), 1-20.

2105. Odom, William E., "The Kremlin's Strategy to De-Nuclearize NATO," *Air Force Magazine*, 72, no. 3 (Mar. 1989), 40-45.

2106. O'Lone, Richard G., "Soviets Encourage Joint Research of Arctic Areas," *Aviation Week & Space Technology* (30 Jan. 1989), 83.

2107. Ooms, Jack A., "Chemical Weapons: Is Revulsion a Safeguard?" *Atlantic Community Quarterly*, 24, no. 2 (Summer 1986), 157-66.

2108. Orlov, Victor, "Red SDI: Gorbachev's Little Secret," *National Review*, 40 (7 Nov. 1988), 46.

2109. Parrott, Bruce, "The Soviet Debate on Missile Defense," *Bulletin of the Atomic Scientists*, 43, no. 3 (Apr. 1987), 9-12.

2110. Perkovich, George, "Counting the Costs of the Arms Race," *Foreign Policy*, no. 85 (Winter 1991-92), 83-105.

2111. Petrie, William, "A Rocky Road to Reduction of Strategic Nuclear Weapons," *Canadian Defence Quarterly*, 16, no. 2 (Autumn 1986), 27-30.

2112. Pfaltzgraff, Robert L., Jr., "Summitry, SDI, and Arms Control," *Fletcher Forum*, 10, no. 1 (Winter 1986), 39-42.

2113. Pick, Otto, "How Serious Is Gorbachev about Arms Control?" *World Today*, 43, no. 4 (Apr. 1987), 66-69.

2114. Pickering, W. L., "The Gorbachev Peace Initiative," *Canadian Defence Quarterly*, 18, no. 4 (Feb. 1989), 74ff.

2115. Pieragostini, Karl, "Arms Control Verification: Cooperating to Reduce Uncertainty," *Journal of Conflict Resolution*, 30, no. 3 (Sept. 1986), 420-44.

2116. Pilat, Joseph, "Star Peace: Soviet Space Arms Control Strategy and Objectives," *Washington Quarterly*, 10, no. 1 (Winter 1987), 137-52.

2117. Posen, Barry R., "Crisis Stability and Conventional Arms Control," *Daedalus*, 120, no. 1 (Winter 1991), 217-32.

2118. Potter, William, "Exodus: Containing the Spread of Soviet Nuclear Weapons," *Harvard International Review*, 14, no. 3 (Spring 1992), 26-30.

2119. Powell, Stewart, "The State of START: After Eight Years of Negotiations, an Agreement Is In Sight," *Air Force Magazine*, 73, no. 6 (June 1990), 84-87.

2120. Quayle, Dan, "Beyond SALT: Arms Control Built Upon Defenses," *Strategic Review*, 14, no. 3 (Summer 1986), 9-16.

2121. Ranger, R., and D. S. Zakheim, "Arms Control Demands Compliance," *Orbis*, 34, no. 2 (Spring 1990), 211-25.

2122. "Reagan, Gorbachev Fail to Agree on Space-Based Weapons Limits," *Aviation Week & Space Technology* (Oct. 1985), 14-15.

2123. "Reason Demands New Political Thinking," *Soviet Law and Government*, 26, no. 1 (Summer 1987), 25-53.

2124. Rhodes, Edward, "Naval Arms Control for the Bush Era," *SAIS Review*, 10, no. 2 (Summer-Fall 1990), 211-29.

2125. Ricigliano, Robert, "The Era of Influence," *New York University Journal of International Law and Politics*, 22, no. 3 (Spring 1990), 557-72.

2126. Riise-Kappen, Thomas, "Star Wars Controversy in West Germany," *Bulletin of the Atomic Scientists*, 43, no. 6 (July-Aug. 1987), 50-52.

2127. Rivkin, David B., Jr., "The Soviet Approach to Nuclear Arms Control: Continuity and Change," *Survival*, 29, no. 6 (Nov-Dec. 1987), 483-510.

2128. -----, "What Does Moscow Think?" *Foreign Policy*, no. 59 (Summer 1985), 85-105.

2129. Roberts, Guthrie, "The New Realism and the Old Rigidities," *Washington Quarterly*, 11, no. 3 (Summer 1988), 213-26.

2130. Roberts, Guy B., "Enforcing the CFE Treaty: Ensuring Compliance Before It's Too Late," *Strategic Review*, 18, no. 4 (Fall 1989), 51-58.

2131. Rogers, Harold E., Jr., "Glasnost and Perestroika," *Denver Journal of International Law and Policy*, 16, no. 2-3 (Winter-Spring 1988), 209-46.

2132. Rogov, Sergey, "The Imperatives of Arms Control: A Soviet Perspective," *Harvard International Review*, 9, no. 5 (May-June 1987), 8-12.

2133. Rose, Francois de, "Brinkmanship at Reykjavik," *Atlantic Community Quarterly*, 24, no. 4 (Winter 1986-87), 295-99.

2134. Rosenberg, Barbara H., "Updating the Biological Weapons Ban," *Bulletin of the Atomic Scientists*, 43, no. 1 (Jan-Feb. 1987), 40-43.

2135. Ross, Michael L., "Disarmament at Sea," *Foreign Policy*, no. 77 (Winter 1989-90), 94-112.

2136. Rostow, Eugene V., "Why the Soviets Want an Arms-Control Agreement, and Why They Want It Now," *Commentary*, 83 (Feb. 1987), 19-26.

2137. Rovit, Sam B., "Arms Control Objectives of the Reagan Administration," *Fletcher Forum*, 11, no. 1 (Winter 1987), 123-45.

2138. Rowny, Edward L., "Arms Control and the Future of U.S.-Soviet Relations," *Strategic Review*, 19, no. 1 (Winter 1991), 17-25.

2139. -----, "Gorbachev's Next 100 Days," *US Department of State. Bulletin*, 85, no. 2103 (Oct. 1985), 17-19.

2140. Rubin, James P., "The Superpower Dispute over Radars," *Bulletin of the Atomic Scientists*, 43, no. 3 (Apr. 1987), 34-37.

2141. Ruehle, Michael, "Anti-Missile Defense in Europe and the ABM Treaty," *Strategic Review*, 15, no. 2 (Spring 1987), 49-57.

2142. Rusakov, Evgeny, "Gorbachev Enters Disarmament Race: Why They Have Shelved the Nukes," *New Times*, no. 41 (1991), 12-15.

2143. Sabirov, A., "Missile Check," *World Press Review*, 36 (Mar. 1989), 40.

2144. Sartori, Leo, "Will SALT II Survive?" *International Security*, 10, no. 3 (Winter 1985-86), 147-74.

2145. Schelling, Thomas C., "What Went Wrong with Arms Control?" *Foreign Affairs*, 64, no. 2 (Winter 1985-86), 219-33.

2146. Scowcroft, Brent, John Deutch and R. James Woolsey, "A Way Out of Reykjavik: Three Strategic Arms Experts Say Reagan's Enthusiasm Must Be Curbed," *New York Times Magazine* (25 Jan. 1987), 40ff.

2147. "Setting a New Agenda for Worldwide Arms Control," *Technology Review*, 93, no. 8 (Nov-Dec. 1990), 32ff.

2148. Sharpe, Jane M. O., "Arms Control and Alliance Commitments," *Political Science Quarterly*, 100, no. 4 (Winter 1985-86), 649-67.

2149. Sherr, Alan B., "Removing the Star Wars Obstacle," *Bulletin of the Atomic Scientists*, 42, no. 10 (Dec. 1986), 11-13.

2150. -----, "Sound Legal Reasoning or Policy Expedient? The `New Interpretation' of the ABM Treaty," *International Security*, 11, no. 3 (Winter 1986-87), 71-93.

2151. Sigal, Leon V., "Getting Over the Summit," *Bulletin of the Atomic Scientists*, 43, no. 1 (Jan-Feb. 1987), 12-13.

2152. Simes, Dmitri K., "Are the Soviets Interested in Arms Control?" *Washington Quarterly*, 8, no. 2 (Spring 1985), 147-57.

2153. Simmons, Susanne, "SDI: A Case Study in Soviet Negotiating Style," *Journal of Social, Political and Economic Studies*, 12, no. 4 (Winter 1987), 355-73.

2154. Sims, Jennifer, "The American Approach to Nuclear Arms Control: A Retrospective," *Daedalus*, 120, no. 1 (Winter 1991), 251-72.

2155. Smart, Christopher, "Amid the Ruins, Arms Makers Raise New Threats," *Orbis*, 36, no. 3 (Summer 1992), 349-64.

2156. Snyder, Jack, "Limiting Offensive Conventional Weapons: Soviet Proposals and Western Opinions," *International Security*, 12, no. 4 (Spring 1988), 48-77.

2157. Sofaer, Abraham D., "The ABM Treaty: Legal Analysis in the Political Cauldron," *Washington Quarterly*, 10, no. 4 (Autumn 1987), 59-75.

2158. "Soviet Views of Arms Control Treaties: Contradiction and the Process of Resolution," *Temple International and Comparative Law Journal*, 2 (Fall 1988), 223-41.

2159. "START" (Special Issue), *Bulletin of the Atomic Scientists*, 47, no. 9 (Nov. 1991), 12-39.

2160. Stephens, Christopher, "Canadian-Soviet Cooperation in the Arctic," *Coexistence*, 27, no. 2 (June 1990), 117-38.

2161. Tanzman, Edward A., and Barry Kellman, "Legal Implementation of the Multilateral Chemical Weapons Convention: Integrating International Security with the Constitution," *New York University Journal of International Law and Politics*, 22, no. 3 (Spring 1990), 475-518.

2162. Teller, Edward, "START: Nuclear Glasnost," *Bulletin of the Atomic Scientists*, 47, no. 9 (Nov. 1991), 34-35.

2163. Tingwei, Huang, and Song Baoxian, "Disarmament: New Aspects of an Old Issue," *Beijing Review*, 30 (19 Jan. 1987), 24-25.

2164. Tirman, John, "Demilitarizing Europe: It Takes Two Not to Tango," *Nation* (17 Apr. 1989), 520-22.

2165. Towell, Pat, "Arms Control No Longer Ranks As the Be-All and End-All," *Congressional Quarterly Weekly Report*, 48 (9 June 1990), 1799-1801.

2166. -----, "Breakthrough Reached on Euromissiles Treaty: Reagan-Gorbachev Summit Planned in the Fall," *Congressional Quarterly Weekly Report*, 45 (19 Sept. 1987), 2233.

2167. -----, "Congress Likely To Be On Board for New Arms-Limit Pact," *Congressional Quarterly Weekly Report*, 47 (9 Dec. 1989), 3383ff.

2168. -----, "Gorbachev Initiative Challenges Bush, NATO," *Congressional Quarterly Weekly Report*, 46 (10 Dec. 1988), 3466-69.

2169. Trachtenberg, Marc, "The Past and Future of Arms Control," *Daedalus*, 120, no. 1 (Winter 1991), 203-16.

2170. Trewhitt, H., "The Next Arms Control Treaty," *U.S. News & World Report*, 105 (12 Dec. 1988), 20-21.

2171. Tsipis, Kosta, "After the Cold War: New Tasks for Arms Controllers," *Bulletin of the Atomic Scientists*, 45, no. 6 (July-Aug. 1989), 7-8.

2172. Ullman, Richard H., "Nuclear Arms: How Big a Cut?" *New York Times Magazine* (16 Nov. 1986), 70ff.

2173. Van Cleave, William R., "Strategic Forces and Arms Control," *Global Affairs*, 3, no. 3 (Summer 1988), 87-91.

2174. -----, "The U.S.-Soviet Military Balance and Arms Control," *Global Affairs*, 4, no. 2 (Spring 1989), 1-18.

2175. Von Hippel, Frank, "Taking Apart the Doomsday Machine," *Bulletin of the Atomic Scientists*, 45, no. 4 (May 1989), 10-12.

2176. -----, "A U.S. Scientist Addresses Gorbachev," *Bulletin of the Atomic Scientists*, 43, no. 4 (May 1987), 12-13.

2177. Wales, Jane, and Morton H. Halperin, "Advice to the President: Don't Count on Nuclear Weapons," *Bulletin of the Atomic Scientists*, 45, no. 2 (Mar. 1989), 7-8.

2178. Walker, William, "Nuclear Weapons and the Former Soviet Republics," *International Affairs*, 68, no. 2 (Apr. 1992), 255-78.

2179. Wallerstein, Immanuel, "The World-System after the Cold War," *Journal of Peace Research*, 30, no. 1 (Feb. 1993), 1-6.

2180. Wallop, Malcolm, "SDI and Arms Control," *Harvard International Review*, 9, no. 5 (May-June 1987), 22ff.

2181. Warnke, Paul, "Gorbachev's American Ways," *Harper's*, 272, no. 1633 (June 1986), 20ff.

2182. Weber, Steve, "Realism, Detente and Nuclear Weapons," *International Organization*, 44, no. 1 (Winter 1990), 55-82.

2183. Weigel, George, "America's Peace Movement, 1900-1986: A Long March," *Wilson Quarterly*, 11, no. 1 (1987), 122-43.

2184. Weinberger, Caspar W., "Arms Reductions and Deterrence," *Foreign Affairs*, 66, no. 3 (Spring 1988), 700-19.

2185. Weinrod, W. Bruce, "Strategic Defense and the ABM Treaty," *Washington Quarterly*, 9, no. 2 (Summer 1986), 73-87.

2186. Wiesner, Jerome B., Philip Morrison and Kosta Tsipis, "Ending Overkill," *Bulletin of the Atomic Scientists*, 49, no. 2 (Mar. 1993), 12-23.

2187. Yost, David S., "The Reykjavik Summit and European Security," *SAIS Review*, 7, no. 2 (Summer-Fall 1987), 1-22.

2188. Zhang, Yunwen, "Gorbachev Keeps the Ball Rolling," *Beijing Review*, 30 (10 Aug. 1987), 13.

2189. Zheutlin, Peter, "Nevada, U.S.S.R.," *Bulletin of the Atomic Scientists*, 46, no. 2 (Mar. 1990), 10-12.

XIV. Dissent

BOOKS

2190. Bilocerkowycz, Jaroslaw, *Soviet Ukrainian Dissent: A Study of Political Alienation* (Boulder, CO: Westview Press, 1988).

2191. Goricheva, Tatiana, *Talking about God Is Dangerous: The Diary of a Russian Dissident* (New York: Crossroad, 1987).

2192. Hughes, H. Stuart, *Sophisticated Rebels: The Political Culture of European Dissent, 1968-1987* (Cambridge, MA: Harvard University Press, 1988).

2193. Johnson, A. Ross, *Political Change and Dissent in Eastern Europe* (Santa Monica, CA: RAND, 1987).

2194. Lampert, Nicholas, *Whistleblowing in the Soviet Union: A Study of Complaints and Abuses under State Socialism* (New York: Schocken Books, 1985).

2195. Parchomenko, Walter, *Soviet Images of Dissidents and Nonconformists* (New York: Praeger, 1986).

2196. Pontuso, James F., *Solzhenitsyn's Political Thought* (Charlottesville: University Press of Virginia, 1990).

2197. Rubenstein, Joshua, *Soviet Dissidents: Their Struggle for Human Rights*, 2nd rev. ed. (Boston: Beacon Press, 1985).

2198. US Congress. Commission on Security and Cooperation in Europe. *Implementation of the Helsinki Accords. Hearings on Irina Ratushinskaya.* 100th Congress, 31 Mar. 1987 (Washington, DC: Government Printing Office, 1987).

2199. US Congress. House. Committee on Foreign Affairs. Subcommittee on Human Rights and International Organizations. *Developments Concerning Dr. Andre Sakharov.* Joint Hearing, 99th Congress, 18 Mar. 1986 (Washington, DC: Government Printing Office, 1986).

ARTICLES

2200. Afanasyev, Yuri, and Tatyana Zaslavskaya, "Socialist Voices in the Soviet Union," *Dissent*, 37, no. 2 (Spring 1990), 192-93.

2201. Anderson, Stuart, "Gorbie's Choices: *Perestroika*'s Dissident Roots," *New Republic* (17 Apr. 1989), 11-12.

2202. Ashley, Richard K., and R. B. J. Walker, "Speaking the Language of Exile: Dissident Thought in International Studies," *International Studies Quarterly*, 34, no. 3 (Sept. 1990), 259-68.

2203. Banionis, Asta, "The Summer of 1988 and the Molotov-Ribbentrop Pact in Lithuania," *Lituanus*, 35, no. 1 (Spring 1989), 75-96.

2204. Brudny, Yitzhak, "The Heralds of Opposition to *Perestroika*," *Soviet Economy*, 5, no. 2 (Apr-June 1989), 162-200.

2205. Bukovskii, V. K., "Who Resists Gorbachev?" *Washington Quarterly*, 12, no. 1 (Winter 1989), 5-19.

2206. Delfs, Robert, "Watershed for Glasnost: The Government Accepts Public Expression of Dissent," *Far Eastern Economic Review*, 144 (18 May 1989), 10-11.

2207. Dunlop, John B., "Russian Reactions to Solzhenitsyn's Brochure," *Report on the USSR*, 2, no. 50 (14 Dec. 1990), 3-8.

2208. -----, "Solzhenitsyn Calls for the Dismemberment of the Soviet Union," *Report on the USSR*, 2, no. 40 (5 Oct. 1990), 9-12.

2209. Fireside, Harvey, "Dissent and Soviet Society" (Review Article), *Problems of Communism*, 35, no. 4 (July-Aug. 1986), 93-98.

2210. -----, "Perestroika Radicals: The Origins and Ideology of the Soviet New Left," *Monthly Review*, 40, no. 4 (Sept. 1988), 19-33.

2211. Haraszti, Miklos, "The Dialectics of Dissent," *Harper's*, 275, no. 1651 (Dec. 1987), 28ff.

2212. Holden, Constance, "Release of Soviet Dissidents Continues," *Science*, 235 (27 Feb. 1987), 968.

2213. Howe, Irving, "Notes from the Left," *Dissent*, 37, no. 3 (Summer 1990), 300-02.

2214. Karklins, Rasma, "The Dissent/Coercion Nexus in the USSR," *Studies in Comparative Communism*, 20, no. 3-4 (Autumn-Winter 1987), 321-41.

2215. Kowalewski, David, "Protest Militancy in the USSR: When Does It Work?" *Social Science Journal*, 24, no. 2 (1987), 169-79.

2216. Kusin, Vladimir V., "Reform and Dissidence in Czechoslovakia," *Current History*, 86, no. 523 (Nov. 1987), 361ff.

2217. Muraka, Dev, "Gorbachev's Opposition: The Foes of *Perestroika* Sound Off," *Nation* (21 May 1988), 697ff.

2218. O'Clery, Conor, "Back in the USSR," *New Republic* (19 Nov. 1990), 22-23.

2219. Pakulski, Jan, "Legitimacy and Mass Compliance: Reflections on Max Weber and Soviet-Type Societies," *British Journal of Political Science*, 16, part 1 (Jan. 1986), 35-56.

2220. Rabinovich, Abraham, "Larger Than the Myth: Shcharansky Comes Home," *Present Tense*, 13, no. 3 (Spring 1986), 44-45.

2221. Sainer, Arthur, "An Open Letter to Natan Sharansky," *Midstream*, 33, no. 2 (Feb. 1987), 38-40.

2222. Sakharov, Andrei, "On Accepting a Prize," *New York Review of Books*, 34 (13 Aug. 1987), 49.

2223. Satter, David, "A Test Case," *New York Review of Books*, 34 (12 Feb. 1987), 3-4.

2224. Sharansky, Natan, "Free," *Partisan Review*, 56, no. 1 (Winter 1989), 7-20.

2225. -----, "The Triumph of Natan Sharansky," *Reader's Digest*, 134, no. 801 (Jan. 1989), 75-80.

2226. Sharlet, Robert, "Dissent and the Contra-System in East Europe," *Current History*, 84, no. 505 (Nov. 1985), 353ff.

2227. -----, "Soviet Dissent since Brezhnev," *Current History*, 85, no. 513 (Oct. 1986), 321ff.

2228. Shcharansky, Anatoly, Yelena Bonner and Ludmilla Alexeyeva, "The Tenth Year of the Watch," *New York Review of Books*, 33 (26 June 1986), 5-6.

2229. Shlapentokh, Vladimir, "The Justification of Political Conformism: The Mythology of Soviet Intellectuals," *Studies in Soviet Thought*, 39, no. 2 (Mar. 1990), 111-35.

2230. Shtromas, Alexander, "Dissent, Nationalism and the Soviet Future," *Studies in Comparative Communism*, 20, no. 3-4 (Autumn-Winter 1987), 277-86.

2231. Siegelman, Philip, "Paul Flory & His Work," *Freedom at Issue*, no. 89 (Mar-Apr. 1986), 5-12.

2232. Simpson, John, "Moscow Cops," *World Monitor*, 3, no. 1 (Jan. 1990), 52ff.

2233. Smith, Fred, "Sakharov and Solzhenitsyn: Dissidents with a Different World View," *Journal of Social, Political and Economic Studies*, 16, no. 4 (Winter 1991), 469-76.

2234. "Soviets to Let Chemist Tarnopolsky Emigrate," *Chemical and Engineering News*, 65 (12 Jan. 1987), 6.

2235. Syrkin, Marie, "Peace and Human Rights: The Link," *Midstream*, 32, no. 2 (Feb. 1986), 34-36.

2236. Tolz, Vera, "Solzhenitsyn Proposes a Plan for the Reconstruction of Russia," *Report on the USSR*, 2, no. 40 (5 Oct. 1990), 12-14.

2237. Tumarkin, Nina, "Truth Teller," *World Monitor*, 3, no. 2 (Feb. 1990), 22-23.

2238. "Ukrainian Dissident on Hunger Strike," *Human Rights Internet Reporter*, 12, no. 1 (Fall 1987), 50.

2239. Uzzell, Lawrence A., "Solzhenitsyn the Centrist," *National Review*, 42 (28 May 1990), 28-29.

2240. Wolfer, Barbara, "Five Poems That Spelled Danger: The Fate of Irina Ratushinskaya," *Commonweal* (27 Feb. 1987), 107-11.

XV. Eastern Europe, Liberation of

BOOKS

2241. Abel, Elie, *The Shattered Bloc: Behind the Upheaval in Eastern Europe* (Boston: Houghton Mifflin, 1990).

2242. Aldcroft, D. H., and Stephen Morewood, *Economic Change in Eastern Europe since 1918* (Brookfield, VT: Edward Elgar, 1994).

2243. Almond, Mark, *Decline Without Fall: Romania Under Ceausescu* (London: Institute for European Defence and Strategic Studies, 1988).

2244. Aron, Leon, and Douglas Seay, *George Bush's Trip to*

Poland and Hungary, July 9-13, 1989: Bringing the American Agenda to Eastern Europe (Washington, DC: Heritage Foundation, 1989).

2245. Asmus, Ronald D., J. F. Brown and Keith Crane, *Soviet Foreign Policy and the Revolutions of 1989 in Eastern Europe* (Santa Monica, CA: RAND, 1991).

2246. Atkinson, Anthony B., and John Micklewright, *Economic Transformation in Eastern Europe and the Distribution of Income* (Cambridge: Cambridge University Press, 1992).

2247. Balassa, Bela A., *Economic Integration in Eastern Europe* (Washington, DC: World Bank, Office of the Vice President, 1991).

2248. -----, *Perestroika and Its Implications for European Socialist Countries* (Washington, DC: The World Bank, 1990).

2249. Banac, Ivo, ed., *Eastern Europe in Revolution* (Ithaca: Cornell University Press, 1992).

2250. Batt, Judy, *East Central Europe: From Reform to Transformation* (New York: Chatham House Papers; Council on Foreign Relations Press, 1991).

2251. -----, *Economic Reform and Political Change in Eastern Europe: Studies in Soviet History and Society* (Basingstoke and London: Macmillan Press, in association with CREES, University of Birmingham, 1988).

2252. Baylis, Thomas A., *The West and Eastern Europe: Economic Statecraft and Political Change* (New York: Praeger, 1993).

2253. Behr, Edward, *Kiss the Hand You Cannot Bite: The Rise and Fall of the Ceausescus* (New York: Villard, 1991).

2254. Berglund, Sten, and Jan Ake Dellebrant, eds., *The New Democracies in Eastern Europe: Party Systems and Political Cleavages* (Brookfield, VT: Edward Elgar, 1991).

2255. Blanchard, Olivier, *et al.*, *Reform in Eastern Europe* (Cambridge, MA: MIT Press, 1991).

2256. Bornstein, Jerry, *The Wall Came Tumbling Down: The Berlin Wall and the Fall of Communism* (New York: Arch Cape Press, distributed by Outlet Book Co., 1990).

2257. Bradley, John F. N., *Politics in Czechoslovakia, 1945-1990* (Boulder, CO: East European Monographs, distributed by Columbia University Press, 1991).

2258. Braun, Aurel, ed., *The Soviet-East European Relationship in the Gorbachev Era: The Prospects for Adaptation* (Boulder, CO: Westview Press, 1990).

2259. Brinton, William M., and Alan Rinzler, eds., *Without Force or Lies: Voices from the Revolution of Central Europe in 1989-90* (San Francisco: Mercury House Books, 1990).

2260. Brown, J. F., *Surge to Freedom: The End of Communist Rule in Eastern Europe* (Durham, NC: Duke University Press, 1991).

2261. Brus, Wlodzimierz, and Kazimierz Laski, *From Marx to the Market: Socialism in Search of an Economic System* (Oxford: Oxford University Press, 1991).

2262. Bugajski, Janusz, and Maxine Pollack, *East European Fault Lines: Dissent, Opposition, and Social Activism* (Boulder, CO: Westview Press, 1989).

2263. Chafetz, Glenn R., *Gorbachev, Reform and the Brezhnev Doctrine: Soviet Policy Toward Eastern Europe, 1985-1990* (Westport, CT: Praeger, 1993).

2264. Chirot, Daniel, ed., *The Crisis of Communism and the Decline of the Left: The Revolutions of 1989* (Seattle: University of Washington Press, 1989).

2265. Cipkowski, Peter, *Revolution in Eastern Europe: Understanding the Collapse of Communism in Poland, Hungary, East Germany, Czechoslovakia, Romania, and the Soviet Union* (New York: Wiley, 1991).

2266. Clark, John, and Aaron Wildavsky, *The Moral Collapse of Communism: Poland as Cautionary Tale* (San Francisco: Institute for Contemporary Studies Press, 1990).

2267. Codrescu, Andrei, *The Hole in the Flag: A Romanian Exile's Story of Return and Revolution* (New York: Morrow, 1991).

2268. Corbo, Vittorio, Fabrizio Coriceli and Jan Bossak, eds., *Reforming Central and Eastern European Economies: Initial Results and Challenges* (Washington, DC: World Bank, 1991).

2269. Csaba, Laszlo, *Systemic Change and Stabilization in Eastern Europe* (Brookfield, VT: Dartmouth, 1991).

2270. Cviic, Christopher, *Remaking the Balkans* (New York: Council on Foreign Relations Press, 1991).

2271. Dagne, Theodore S., *East European Developments: A Summary of Major Issues and Chronology, January-April 1990* (Washington, DC: Library of Congress, Congressional Research Service, 1990).

2272. Dahrendorf, Ralph, *Reflections on the Revolution in Europe: In a Letter Intended to Have Been Sent to a Gentleman in Warsaw* (New York: Time Books, 1990).

2273. De Soto, Hermine G., and David G. Anderson, eds., *The Curtain Rises: Rethinking Culture, Ideology and the State in Eastern Europe* (Atlantic Highlands, NJ: Humanities Press, 1993).

2274. Dawisha, Karen, *Eastern Europe, Gorbachev and Reform: The Great Challenge*, 2nd ed. (Cambridge: Cambridge University Press, 1990).

2275. East, Roger, *Revolutions in Eastern Europe* (New York: St. Martin's Press, 1992).

2276. Echikson, William, *Lighting the Night: Revolution in Eastern Europe* (New York: W. Morrow, 1990).

2277. Feher, Ferenc, and Andrew Arato, eds., *Crisis and Reform in Eastern Europe* (New Brunswick, NJ: Transaction, 1991).

2278. Fowkes, Ben, *The Rise and Fall of Communism in Eastern*

Europe (New York: St. Martin's Press, 1993).

2279. Frydman, Roman, Andrzej Rapaczynski and John S. Earle et al., *The Privatization Process in East Central Europe* (London: Central European University Press, 1993).

2280. Gamer, Robert E., *East Europe's Search for Freedom without Disruption: Avoiding the China Syndrome* (Indianapolis: Universities Field Staff International, 1990).

2281. Garton Ash, Timothy, *The Magic Lantern: The Revolution of '89 Witnessed in Warsaw, Budapest, Berlin and Prague* (New York: Random House, 1990).

2282. -----, *The Polish Revolution: Solidarity*, rev., updated ed. (New York: Viking Penguin, 1991).

2283. -----, *The Uses of Adversity: Essays on the Fate of Central Europe* (New York: Random House, 1989).

2284. Gati, Charles, *The Bloc That Failed: Soviet-East European Relations in Transition* (Bloomington: Indiana University Press, 1990).

2285. Giersch, Herbert, ed., *Towards a Market Economy in Central and Eastern Europe* (New York: Springer-Verlag, 1991).

2286. Gilberg, Trond, *Nationalism and Communism in Romania: The Rise and Fall of Ceausescu's Personal Dictatorship* (Boulder, CO: Westview Press, 1990).

2287. Glenny, Misha, *The Rebirth of History: Eastern Europe in the Age of Democracy* (New York: Viking Penguin, 1990).

2288. Griffith, William E., ed., *Central and Eastern Europe: The Opening Curtain?* (Boulder, CO: Westview Press, 1989).

2289. Hankiss, Elemer, *East European Alternatives* (New York: Oxford University Press, 1990).

2290. Havel, Vaclav, *et al.*, *The Power of the Powerless: Citizens Against the State in Central Eastern Europe* (Armonk, NY: M. E. Sharpe, 1985).

2291. Havlik, Peter, ed., *Dismantling the Command Economy in Eastern Europe* (Boulder, CO: Westview Press, 1991).

2292. Held, Joseph, ed., *The Columbia History of Eastern Europe in the Twentieth Century* (New York: Columbia University Press, 1993).

2293. Jarausch, Konrad H., *The Rush to German Unity* (Oxford: Oxford University Press, 1994).

2294. Johnson, A. Ross, *The Impact of Eastern Europe on Soviet Policy toward Western Europe* (Santa Monica, CA: RAND, 1986).

2295. Kaminski, Bartlomiej, *The Collapse of State Socialism: The Case of Poland* (Princeton: Princeton University Press, 1991).

2296. Kemme, David, *Economic Transitions in Eastern Europe and the Soviet Union: Issues and Strategies* (New York: Institute for East-West Security Studies, 1991).

2297. Kennan, George F., *The German Problem: A Personal View* (Washington, DC: American Institute for Contemporary German Studies, 1989).

2298. Keren, Michael, and Gur Offer, eds., *Trials of Transition: Economic Reform in the Former Soviet Bloc* (Boulder, CO: Westview Press, 1992).

2299. Kittrie, Nicholas N., and Ivan Volgyes, eds., *The Uncertain Future: Gorbachev's Eastern Bloc* (New York: Paragon House, 1988).

2300. Kovrig, Bennett, *Of Walls and Bridges: The United States and Eastern Europe* (New York: New York University Press, 1991).

2301. Larrabee, F. Stephen, ed., *The Two German States and European Security* (New York: St. Martin's Press, with the Institute for East-West Security Studies, 1989).

2302. Lewis, Paul G., ed., *Democracy and Civil Society in Eastern Europe* (New York: St. Martin's Press, 1992).

2303. Liska, George, *Fallen Dominions, Reviving Powers* (Washington, DC: Johns Hopkins Foreign Policy Institute, 1990).

2304. Maier, Charles, *Across the Wall: Revolution and the Reunification of Germany* (Princeton: Princeton University Press, 1994).

2305. Mason, David S., *Revolution in East-Central Europe: The Rise and Fall of Communism and the Cold War* (Boulder, CO: Westview Press, 1992).

2306. Merkl, Peter H., *German Unification in the European Context* (University Park, PA: Penn State Press, 1993).

2307. Michta, Andrew A., and Ilya Prizel, eds., *Postcommunist Eastern Europe: Crisis and Reform* (New York: St. Martin's Press, in association with the Johns Hopkins Foreign Policy Institute, 1992).

2308. Murrell, Peter, *The Nature of Socialist Economies: Lessons from Eastern European Foreign Trade* (Princeton: Princeton University Press, 1990).

2309. Myant, Martin, *Transforming Socialist Economies: The Case of Poland and Czechoslovakia* (Brookfield, VT: Edward Elgar, 1993).

2310. Neckerman, Peter, *The Unification of Germany, or, The Anatomy of a Peaceful Revolution* (Boulder, CO: East European Monographs, 1991).

2311. Nee, Victor, and David Stark, eds., *Remaking the Economic Institutions of Socialism: China and Eastern Europe* (Stanford: Stanford University Press, 1989).

2312. Page, Benjamin, *Four Summers: A Czech Kaleidoscope* (Washington, DC: International Research & Exchanges Board, 1993).

2313. Pavlyshyn, Marko, ed., *Glasnost' in Context: On the Recurrence of Liberalizations in Central and Eastern European Literatures and Cultures* (New York: Berg, 1990).

2314. Philipsen, Dirk, *We Were the People: Voices from East Germany's Revolutionary Autumn of 1989* (Durham, NC: Duke

University Press, 1993).

2315. Pilon, Juliana Geran, *The Bloody Flag: Post-Communist Nationalism in Eastern Europe, Spotlight on Romania* (New Brunswick, NJ: Transaction Publishers, 1992).

2316. Pinder, John, *The European Community and Eastern Europe* (New York: Council on Foreign Relations Press, for the Royal Institute of International Affairs, 1991).

2317. Pittman, Avril, *From Ostpolitik to Reunification: West German-Soviet Political Relations since 1974* (New York: Cambridge University Press, 1992).

2318. *Political Parties in Eastern Europe* (Munich: Radio Free Europe, 1990).

2319. Poznanski, Kazimierz Z., ed., *Stabilization and Privatization in Poland: An Economic Evaluation of the Shock Therapy Program* (Boston: Kluwer Academic Publishers, 1993).

2320. Pressler, Larry, *Trip Report: A Visit to Eastern Europe in the Wake of the Twenty-seventh Soviet Party Congress and the Chernobyl Nuclear Accident (Czechoslovakia, Hungary, Yugoslavia and Romania) on June 28, 1986 : A Report to the Committee on Foreign Relations, United States Senate* (Washington, DC: Government Printing Office, 1987).

2321. Prins, Gwyn, ed., *Spring in Winter: The 1989 Revolutions* (Manchester: Manchester University Press, 1990).

2322. Pryor, Frederick L., *East European Economic Reforms: The Rebirth of the Market* (Stanford: Hoover Institution, Stanford University, 1990).

2323. Ramet, Sabrina P., *Social Currents in Eastern Europe: The Sources and Meaning of the Great Transformation* (Durham, NC: Duke University Press, 1991).

2324. Rapoport, Roger, *Into the Sunlight: Life After the Iron Curtain* (Berkeley: Heyday, 1990),

2325. Ratesh, Nestor, *Romania: The Entangled Revolution* (New York: Praeger, with the Center for Strategic and International Studies, 1991).

2326. Revesz, Gabor, *Perestroika in Eastern Europe: Hungary's Economic Transformation, 1945-1988* (Boulder, CO: Westview Press, 1989).

2327. Rollo, J. M. C., *et al.*, *The New Eastern Europe: Western Response* (New York: Council on Foreign Relations Press, 1990).,

2328. Rothschild, Joseph, *Return to Diversity: A Political History of East Central Europe Since World War II*, 2nd ed. (New York: Oxford University Press, 1993).

2329. Rumer, Eugene B., *The German Question in Moscow's "Common European Home": A Background to the Revolutions of 1989* (Santa Monica, CA: RAND, 1991).

2330. Scanlan. Michael D., *East European Developments: A Summary of Major Issues and Chronology, May-August 1990* (Washington, DC: Library of Congress, Congressional Research Service, 1990).

2331. Schopflin, George, ed., *The Soviet Union and Eastern Europe*, rev., updated ed. (New York: Facts on File, 1986).

2332. Seay, Douglas, *How George Bush Can Help Lech Walesa Succeed* (Washington, DC: Heritage Foundation, 1989).

2333. Smolar, Aleksander, and Pierre Kende, *The Role of Opposition: The Role of Opposition Groups on the Eve of Democratization in Poland and Hungary (1987-1988)* (Munich: Projekt, 1989).

2334. Staar, Richard F., ed., *East Central Europe and the USSR* (New York: St. Martin's Press, 1991).

2335. Staniszkis, Jadwiga, *The Dynamics of the Breakthrough in Eastern Europe* (Berkeley: University of California Press, 1991).

2336. Stokes, Gale, ed., *From Stalinism to Pluralism: A Documentary History of Eastern Europe Since 1945* (New York: Oxford University Press, 1991).

2337. -----, *The Walls Came Tumbling Down: The Collapse of Communism in Eastern Europe* (Oxford: Oxford University Press, 1993).

2338. Szabo, Stephen F., *The Diplomacy of German Unification* (New York: St. Martin's Press, 1992).

2339. Szelenyi, Ivan, with Robert Manchin *et al.*, *Socialist Entrepreneurs: Embourgeoisement in Rural Hungary* (Madison: University of Wisconsin Press, 1988).

2340. Taras, Raymond, ed., *The Road to Disillusion: From Critical Marxism to Post-Communism in Eastern Europe* (Armonk, NY: M. E. Sharpe, 1992).

2341. Tismaneanu, Vladimir, *Reinventing Politics: Eastern Europe from Stalin to Havel* (New York: The Free Press, 1993).

2342. Tokes, Laszlo, and David Porter, *The Fall of Tyrants: The Incredible Story of One Pastor's Witness, the People of Romania and the Overthrow of Ceausescu* (Wheaton, IL: Crossway Books, 1990).

2343. *Toward a Europe Whole and Free: Goals and Guidelines for U.S. Policy in Central and Eastern Europe: The Report of the CSIS Potomac Council and the CSIS Congressional Study Group on Central and Eastern Europe* (Washington, DC: Center for Strategic and International Studies, 1991).

2344. US Congress. Commission on Security and Cooperation in Europe. *Elections in Central and Eastern Europe: A Compendium of Reports on the Elections Held from March through June 1990* (Washington, DC: Government Printing Office, 1990).

2345. US Congress. Commission on Security and Cooperation in Europe. *Implementation of the Helsinki Accords: East European Perestroika: U.S. and Soviet Foreign Policy Options. Hearing.* 100th Congress, 2nd Session, 15 Mar. 1988 (Washington, DC: Government Printing Office, 1988).

2346. US Congress. Commission on Security and Cooperation in Europe. *Implementation of the Helsinki Accords: Gorbachev,*

"Glasnost" and Eastern Europe. Hearing. 100th Congress, 18 June 1987 (Washington, DC: Government Printing Office, 1987).

2347. US Congress. Commission on Security and Cooperation in Europe. *Reform and Human Rights in Eastern Europe: Report* (Washington, DC: Government Printing Office, 1989).

2348. US Congress. Conference Committees, 1989. *Support for East European Democracy (SEED) Act of 1989: Conference Report to Accompany H.R. 3402.* 101st Congress, 1st Session, 1989, H Rept 101-377.

2349. US Congress. House. Committee on Foreign Affairs. *Democracy in Eastern Europe Act of 1989: Report to Accompany H.R. 2550... .* 101st Congress, 1st Session, 1989. H Rept 101-92, Part 1-2.

2350. US Congress. House. Committee on Foreign Affairs. Subcommittee on Europe and the Middle East. *Developments in Eastern Europe, June 1989,* 101st Congress, 1st Session (Washington, DC: Government Printing Office, 1989).

2351. US Congress. House. Committee on Foreign Affairs. Subcommittee on Europe and the Middle East. *Eastern Europe in the Gorbachev Era: Implications for U.S. Policy.* 101st Congress, 1st Session (Washington, DC: Government Printing Office, 1990).

2352. US Congress. House. Committee on Foreign Affairs. Subcommittee on Europe and the Middle East. *Roundtable Discussion on Recent Developments in East Germany.* 101st Congress, 1st Session, 21 Nov. 1989 (Washington, DC: Government Printing Office, 1990).

2353. US Congress. House. Committee on Small Business. *Economic Restructuring in Eastern Europe: American Interests.* 101st Congress, 1st Session (Washington, DC: Committee Printing, 1989).

2354. *The U.S. Looks at the Revolutions of 1989* (Winchester, MA: Americans Talk Security, 1990).

2355. Valdez, Jonathan C., *Internationalism and the Ideology of Soviet Influence in Eastern Europe* (New York: Cambridge University Press, 1993).

2356. Volten, Peter, ed., *Uncertain Futures: Eastern Europe and Democracy* (New York: Institute for East-West Security Studies, 1990).

2357. Weilemann, Peter R., Georg Brunner and Rudolf L. Tokes, eds., *Upheaval against the Plan: Eastern Europe on the Eve of the Storm* (New York: Berg, distributed by St. Martin's Press, 1991).

2358. Welfens, Paul, *Market-Oriented Systemic Transformations in Eastern Europe* (Heidelberg: Springer Verlag, 1992).

2359. Wheaton, Bernard, and Zdenek Kavan, *The Velvet Revolution: Czechoslovakia, 1988-91* (Boulder, CO: Westview Press, 1992).

2360. Williamson, John, ed., *Currency Convertibility in Eastern Europe* (Washington, DC: Institute for International Economics,

1991).

2361. -----, *The Economic Opening of Eastern Europe* (Washington, DC: Institute for International Economics, 1991).

2362. Zeman, Z. A. B., *The Making and Breaking of Communist Europe* (Cambridge, MA: B. Blackwell, 1991).

ARTICLES

2363. Adomeit, Hannes, "Gorbachev and German Unification: Revision of Thinking, Realignment of Power," *Problems of Communism*, 39, no. 4 (July-Aug. 1990), 1-23.

2364. Agocs, Sandor, "The Collapse of the Communist Ideology in Hungary: November 1988 to February 1989," *East European Quarterly*, 27, no. 2 (Summer 1992), 187-211.

2365. Allen, Bruce, "Poland's New Generation of Oppositionists," *Our Generation*, 21, no. 1 (1989), 153-84.

2366. "Apostle of Glasnost Visits Prague," *America*, 156 (25 Apr. 1987), 333.

2367. Arato, Andrew, "Interpreting 1989," *Social Research*, 60, no. 3 (Fall 1993), 609ff.

2368. -----, and Sveta Stojanovic, eds., "Thinking the Present: Revolution in Eastern Europe" (Special Section), *Praxis International*, 10, nos. 1-2 (Apr-July 1990), 24-103.

2369. Asmus, Ronald D., "A United Germany," *Foreign Affairs*, 69, no. 2 (Spring 1990), 63-76.

2370. Baranczyk, Stanislaw, "Eastern Europe: Annus Mirabilis," *Salmagundi*, no. 85-86 (Winter-Spring 1990), 5-11.

2371. Barany, Zoltan D., "East European Armed Forces in Transitions and Beyond," *East European Quarterly*, 26, no. 1 (Spring 1992), 1-30.

2372. -----, "A Hungarian Dream Comes True: Soviet Troops to Leave after 45 Years," *Report on Eastern Europe*, 1, no., 13 (30 Mar. 1990), 23-28.

2373. Bigler, Robert M., "From Communism to Democracy: Hungary's Transition Thirty-Five Years After the Revolution," *East European Quarterly*, 25, no. 4 (Winter 1991), 437-61.

2374. Bingham, Sam, "Scenes from a Peaceful Revolution," *World Monitor*, 3, no. 3 (Mar. 1990), 48-52.

2375. Bogdan, Corneliu, "Crossing the European Divide," *Foreign Policy*, no. 75 (Summer 1989), 56-75.

2376. Bogdanor, Vernon, "Founding Elections and Regime Change," *Electoral Studies*, 9, no. 4 (Dec. 1990), 288-94.

2377. Bowers, Stephen R., "The East European Revolution," *East European Quarterly*, 25, no. 2 (Summer 1991), 129-43.

2378. -----, "*Perestroika* in Eastern Europe," *Journal of Social, Political and Economic Studies*, 14, no. 2 (Summer 1989), 149-87.

2379. Brown, J. F., "Hope and Uncertainty in Eastern Europe," *SAIS Review*, 10, no. 1 (Winter-Spring 1990), 117-32.

2380. Brumberg, Abraham, "Poland: The Demise of Communism," *Foreign Affairs*, 69, no. 1 (1989-90), 70-88.

2381. -----, and Irving Howe, "An Immensity of Change: Perestroika, Poland, Politics in Eastern Europe," *Dissent*, 37, no. 1 (Winter 1990), 3-7.

2382. Bugajski, Janusz, "The Bird in Moscow's Cage: Eastern Europe and *Perestroika*," *National Interest*, no. 12 (Summer 1988), 57-68.

2383. -----, "Eastern Europe in the Post-Communist Era," *Columbia Journal of World Business*, 26, no. 1 (Spring 1991), 5-9.

2384. -----, "The Fate of Nationalities in Eastern Europe," *Journal of Democracy*, 4, no. 4 (Oct. 1993), 85-99.

2385. -----, "Skeptical Satellites," *New Republic* (4 May 1987), 15-16.

2386. Bunce, Valerie, "Decline of a Regional Hegemon: The Gorbachev Regime and Reform in Eastern Europe," *Eastern European Politics and Societies*, 3, no. 2 (Spring 1989), 235-66.

2387. -----, "Rising Above the Past," *World Policy Journal*, 7, no. 3 (Summer 1990), 395-430.

2388. Burawoy, Michael, "The Future of Socialism in Eastern Europe," *Socialism and Democracy*, no. 9 (Fall-Winter 1989), 43-48.

2389. Calinescu, Matei, and Vladimir Tismaneanu, "The 1989 Revolution and Romania's Future," *Problems of Communism*, 40, no. 1-2 (Jan-Apr. 1991), 42-59.

2390. Campeanu, Pavel, "Transition in Eastern Europe," *Social Research*, 57, no. 3 (Fall 1990), 587-90.

2391. Childs, David, "East Germany: Coping with Gorbachev," *Current History*, 88, no. 541 (Nov. 1989), 385ff.

2392. -----, "East Germany: Glasnost' and Globetrotting," *World Today*, 43, no. 10 (Oct. 1987), 177-79.

2393. Chirot, Daniel, "What Happened in Eastern Europe in 1989?" *Praxis International*, 10, nos. 3-4 (Oct. 1990-Jan. 1991), 278-305.

2394. Clarke, Douglas L., "The Military Implications of a Soviet Troop Withdrawal from Czechoslovakia," *Report on Eastern Europe*, 1, no. 5 (2 Feb. 1990), 48-51.

2395. -----, "Soviet Troop Withdrawals from Eastern Europe," *Report on Eastern Europe*, 1, no. 13 (30 Mar. 1990), 41-46.

2396. -----, "Soviets Withdraw Headquarters from Poland," *Report on Eastern Europe*, 1, no. 33 (17 Aug. 1990), 21-22.

2397. Cohen, Mitchell, "The Withering Away of a Communist State?" *Dissent*, 36, no. 4 (Fall 1989), 455-61.

2398. Colton, Timothy J., "The USSR and Eastern Europe: Gorbachev at the Helm," *Freedom at Issue*, no. 94 (Jan-Feb. 1987), 12-14.

2399. Crowe, Suzanne, "Soviet Reaction to the Crisis in Yugoslavia," *Report on the USSR*, 3, no. 31 (2 Aug. 1991), 9-12.

2400. -----, "Who Lost Eastern Europe?" *Report on the USSR*, 3, no. 15 (12 Apr. 1991), 1-5.

2401. Cynkin, Thomas M., "*Glasnost, Perestroika* and Eastern Europe," *Survival*, 30, no. 4 (July-Aug. 1988), 310-31.

2402. D'Anastasio, M., "Gorbachev's Agenda: Housecleaning First, Economic Reform Later," *Business Week* (24 June 1985), 61.

2403. Dawisha, Karen, "Gorbachev and Eastern Europe: A New Challenge for the West?" *World Policy Journal*, 3, no. 2 (Spring 1986), 277-300.

2404. Dennis, Mike, "The Collapse of the German Democratic Republic: The Economic Dimension," *East Central Europe/L'Europe du Centre-Est*, 19, no. 1 (1992), 81-114.

2405. -----, and Sally Luxton, "A Selected Bibliography of Articles and Books on the Collapse of the GDR and the Process of German Reunification (1989-1991)," *East Central Europe*, 18, no. 2 (1991), 177-250.

2406. Dorough, Felix, "The Economics of Eastern Europe under Gorbachev's Influence," *NATO Review*, 36, no. 3 (June 1988), 18-24.

2407. "Eastern Europe" (Special Issue), *World Press Review*, 35 (Apr. 1988), 33-35.

2408. "Eastern Europe Begins Its Long Climb," *Harvard International Review*, 13, no. 1 (Fall 1990), 6-7.

2409. "East-West Relations and Eastern Europe," *Problems of Communism*, 37, no. 3-4 (May-Aug. 1988), 55-70.

2410. Ellis, Mark S., "Central and East European Law Initiative," *International Lawyer*, 25, no. 1 (Spring 1991), 299-303.

2411. Ellison, Herbert J., "The Rebirth of Politics after the Revolution," *World & I* (May 1990), 22-33.

2412. Falls, Donald R., "Soviet Decision-Making and the Withdrawal of Soviet Troops from Romania," *European Quarterly*, 27, no. 4 (Winter 1993), 489-502.

2413. Farrar, John H., "Gorbachev and Eastern Europe," *World & I* (May 1990), 34-37.

2414. Finn, James, "The History of the End," *Freedom at Issue*, no. 112 (Jan-Feb. 1990), 5.

2415. Fischer, David A. V., "Eastern Europe after Pax Sovietica," *Bulletin of the Atomic Scientists*, 46, no. 6 (July-Aug. 1990), 23-27.

2416. Fisher, William, "Fighting Change: Romania in the Age of Glasnost," *New Leader* (29 June 1987), 11-13.

2417. Galbraith, John Kenneth, "Which Capitalism for Eastern Europe?" *Harper's*, 280, no. 1679 (Apr., 1990), 19-21.

2418. Garton Ash, Timothy, "Apres le Deluge, Nous," *New York Review of Books*, 37 (16 Aug. 1990), 51-57.

2419. -----, "Eastern Europe: The Year of Truth," *New York Review of Books*, 37 (15 Feb. 1990), 17-22.

2420. -----, "The Empire in Decay," *New York Review of Books*, 35 (29 Sept. 1988), 53-60.

2421. -----, "Poland After Solidarity" (Review Article), *New York Review of Books*, 38 (13 June 1991), 46-58.

2422. Gati, Charles, "East-Central Europe: The Morning After," *Foreign Affairs*, 69, no. 5 (Winter 1990-91), 129-45.

2423. -----, "Eastern Europe on Its Own," *Foreign Affairs*, 68, no. 1 (1989), 99-119.

2424. -----, "Gorbachev and Eastern Europe," *Foreign Affairs*, 65, no. 5 (Summer 1987), 958-75.

2425. -----, "USSR and Eastern Europe: Can Gorbachev Make a Difference?" *Freedom at Issue*, no. 88 (Jan-Feb. 1986), 40-42.

2426. Geipel, Gary L., "The Meaning of German Unification," *International Executive*, 32, no. 2 (Sept-Oct. 1990), 23-26.

2427. Gilberg, Trond, "Eastern Europe in Flux" (Review Article), *Problems of Communism*, 39, no. 3 (May-June 1990), 99-103.

2428. Gitelman, Zvi, "The Roots of Eastern Europe's Revolution" (Review Article), *Problems of Communism*, 39, no. 3 (May-June 1990), 89-94.

2429. "Glasnost Comes to East Germany: Each Country Chooses its Own Solution-An Interview with Kurt Hager," *World Affairs*, 152, no. 4 (Spring 1990), 198-200.

2430. Goldfarb, Jeffrey C., "Post-Totalitarian Policy: Ideology Ends Again," *Social Research*, 57, no. 3 (Fall 1990), 533-37.

2431. "Gorbachev's Prague Spring," *Maclean's*, 100 (20 Apr. 1987), 18-19.

2432. Griffith, William E., "Superpower Problems in Europe: A Comparative Assessment," *Orbis*, 29, no. 4 (Winter 1986), 735-52.

2433. Gross, Jan T., "Between Russia and the United States-Reflections of an East European," *Polish Review*, 33, no. 2 (1988), 191-205.

2434. -----, "The First Soviet Sponsored Election in Eastern Europe," *Eastern European Politics and Societies*, 1, no. 1 (Winter 1987), 4-29.

2435. Gyarmati, Istvan, "Hungarian Says Keep Soviets on German Soil," *Bulletin of the Atomic Scientists*, 46, no. 5 (June 1990), 10-11.

2436. Harries, Owen, "Credit Ratings," *National Interest*, no. 20 (Summer 1990), 109-12.

2437. Havel, Vaclav, "People, Your Government Has Returned to You!" *Journal of Democracy*, 1, no. 2 (Spring 1991), 99-105.

2438. -----, "The Velvet Hangover," *Harper's*, 281 no. 1685 (Oct. 1990), 18-21.

2439. Heilbronner, Robert, "Rethinking the Past, Rehoping the Future," *Social Research*, 57, no. 3 (Fall 1990), 579-87.

2440. Heller, Agnes, and Ferenc Feher, "Gorbachev and Eastern Europe: *Perestroika* and Historical Compromise," *Dissent*, 35, no. 4 (Fall 1988), 415-21.

2441. Horn, N., "The Lawful German Revolution: Privatization and Market Economy in a Re-unified Germany," *American Journal of Comparative Law*, 39, no. 4 (Fall 1991), 725-46.

2442. "Hungary after *Glasnost*': A Symposium," *Partisan Review*, 56, no. 2 (Spring 1989), 179-92.

2443. "International Boundaries: Ex-Soviet Union and Eastern Europe," *World Today*, 48, no. 3 (Mar. 1992), 38-40.

2444. Jedlicki, Jerzy, "A Colloquium: The Revolution of 1989: The Unbearable Burden of History," *Problems of Communism*, 39, no. 4 (July-Aug. 1990), 39-44.

2445. Jones, Christopher, "Gorbachev and the Warsaw Pact," *Eastern European Politics and Societies*, 3, no. 2 (Spring 1989), 215-34.

2446. -----, "Gorbachev Seeks a Trade-off," *World & I* (Feb. 1990), 42-47.

2447. Judt, Tony, "What Prospects for Eastern Europe?" *Tikkun*, 5, no. 2 (1990), 11-18.

2448. Kaplan, Morton A., "The Challenge of History," *World & I* (Feb. 1990), 48-51.

2449. Keep, John, "Zheleznovodsk and After: Towards a New Russo-German Relationship," *East European Quarterly*, 26, no. 4 (Winter 1992), 431-47.

2450. Kennan, George F., "On the Soviet Union and Eastern Europe," *New York Review of Books*, 37 (1 Mar. 1990), 7.

2451. Keuhnelt-Leddihn, Erik von, "Rusting Iron Curtain," *National Review*, 41 (10 Nov. 1989), 25ff.

2452. Kolakowski, Leszek, "The Postrevolutionary Hangover," *Journal of Democracy*, 2, no. 3 (Summer 1991), 70-74.

2453. Komisar, L., "The East's Summit," *Nation*, 241 (23 Nov. 1985), 540.

2454. Kosela, Krzysztof, "The Polish Catholic Church and the Elections of 1989," *Religion in Communist Lands*, 18, no. 2 (Summer 1990), 124-37.

2455. Kovacs, Dezso, and Sally Ward Maggard, "The Human Face of Political, Economic and Social Change in Eastern Europe," *East European Quarterly*, 27, no. 3 (Fall 1993), 317-45.

2456. Kovrig, Bernard, "Moving Time: The Emancipation of Eastern Europe," *International Journal*, 46, no. 2 (Spring 1991), 242-66.

2457. Kramer, John M., "Eastern Europe and the `Energy Shock' of 1990-91," *Problems of Communism*, 40, no. 3 (May-June 1991), 85-96.

2458. Kramer, Mark, "Beyond the Brezhnev Doctrine: A New Era in Soviet-East European Relations," *International Security*,

14, no. 3 (Winter 1989-90), 25-67.

2459. Kraus, Michael, "Gorbachev's Challenge: The USSR and Eastern Europe," *Freedom at Issue*, no. 106 (Jan-Feb. 1989), 23-26.

2460. -----, "Soviet Policy toward East Europe," *Current History*, 86, no. 523 (Nov. 1987), 353ff.

2461. -----, "The Soviet Union and Eastern Europe in Mid-Crisis," *Freedom at Issue*, no. 112 (Jan-Feb. 1990), 27-30.

2462. Kuran, Timur, "The East European Revolution of 1989: Is It Surprising That We Were Surprised?" *American Economic Review*, 81, no. 2 (May 1991), 121-25.

2463. -----, "Now Out of Never: The Element of Surprise in the East European Revolutions of 1989" (Review Article), *World Politics*, 44, no. 1 (Oct. 1991), 7-48.

2464. Kuron, Jacek, "From Russia with Glasnost: A New Look at What Is to Be Done: Reform in the Reform," *New Perspectives Quarterly*, 4, no. 2 (Spring 1987), 43-45.

2465. Kusin, V. V., "Gorbachev and Eastern Europe," *Problems of Communism*, 35, no. 1 (Jan-Feb. 1986), 39-53.

2466. -----, "Gorbachev: The View from Warsaw," *Harper's*, 275, no. 1646 (July 1987), 26-27.

2467. Kux, Ernst, "Change in Central and Eastern Europe and the End of the Soviet Union," *Aussenpolitik*, 44, no. 2 (1993), 135-43.

2468. -----, "Revolution in Eastern Europe-Revolution in the West?" *Problems of Communism*, 40, no. 3 (May-June 1991), 1-15.

2469. Kux, Stephan, "Report from Eastern Europe: Soviet Oil and Economic Reform in Eastern Europe," *International Economic Insights*, 2, no. 1 (Jan-Feb. 1991), 36-37.

2470. Laber, Jeri, "Slouching toward Democracy," *New York Review of Books*, 40 (14 Jan. 1993), 24-27.

2471. Lamper, Ivan, "Was the Gentle Revolution Too Gentle?" *Uncaptive Minds*, 3, no. 2 (Mar-Apr. 1990), 23.

2472. Larrabee, F. Stephen, "Eastern Europe: A Generational Change," *Foreign Policy*, no. 70 (Spring 1988), 42-64.

2473. -----, "*Perestroika* Shakes Eastern Europe," *Bulletin of the Atomic Scientists*, 45, no. 2 (Mar. 1989), 25-29.

2474. -----, "`Rollback' in Eastern Europe," *Contemporary Review*, 253, no. 1475 (Dec. 1988), 281-86.

2475. -----, "Soviet Policy toward Germany: New Thinking and Old Realities," *Washington Quarterly*, 12, no. 3 (Summer 1989), 33-51.

2476. Lewis, Flora, "Bringing in the East," *Foreign Affairs*, 69, no. 4 (Fall 1990), 15-26.

2477. Lewis, Paul G., "Chips Off the Old Bloc: The Changing Character of Eastern Europe" (Review Article), *Studies in Comparative Communism*, 23, no. 1 (Spring 1990), 101-08.

2478. Lipton, David, and Jeffrey Sachs, "Creating a Market Economy in Eastern Europe," *Brookings Papers on Economic Activity* (1990), 75-147.

2479. Loory, S. H., "New Kid on the Bloc: Gorbachev's Reforms Spill into Eastern Europe," *Progressive*, 51, no. 6 (June 1987), 21-23.

2480. Luers, William H., "Czechoslovakia: Road to Revolution," *Foreign Affairs*, 69, no. 2 (Spring 1990), 77-98.

2481. -----, "The U.S. and Eastern Europe," *Foreign Affairs*, 65, no. 5 (Summer 1987), 976-94.

2482. Lukes, Igor, "To Reform or Not to Reform: Gorbachev's Initiatives and Their Impact on Czechoslovakia," *Harvard International Review*, 10, no. 1 (Nov. 1987), 14-17.

2483. Lynch, Allen, "Changing Contours of Soviet-East European Relations," *Journal of International Affairs*, 42 (Spring 1989), 423-34.

2484. Mason, David S., "Glasnost, Perestroika and Eastern Europe," *International Affairs*, 64 (Summer 1988), 431-48.

2485. McAdams, A. James, "Crisis in the Soviet Empire: Three Ambiguities in Search of a Prediction," *Comparative Politics*, 20, no. 1 (Oct. 1987), 107-18.

2486. -----, "Gorbachev's Gamble: A New Deal for Eastern Europe," *Nation* (13 June 1987), 799ff.

2487. McCauley, Martin, "Glasnost in Eastern Europe," *Contemporary Review*, 253, no. 1471 (Aug. 1988), 57-60.

2488. -----, "Soviet-GDR Relations under Gorbachev," *East Central Europe/L'Europe du Centre-Est*, 14-15 (1987-88), 461ff.

2489. Mearsheimer, John J., "Back to the Future: Instability in Europe after the Cold War," *International Security*, 15, no. 1 (Summer 1990), 5-56.

2490. Michielson, Peter, "Glasnost: How Eastern Europe Looks at Glasnost," *World & I*, 2, no. 6 (June 1987), 44-53.

2491. Michnik, Adam, "Notes on the Revolution," *New York Times Magazine* (11 March 1990), 39ff.

2492. Milenkovitch, Deborah, "The Politics of Economic Transformation," *Journal of International Affairs*, 45 (Summer 1991), 151-64.

2493. Mislivetz, Ferenc, "The Unfinished Revolutions of 1989: The Decline of the Nation-State," *Social Research*, 58, no. 4 (Winter 1991), 781-804.

2494. Morton, Brian, "Glasnost in Eastern Europe," *Dissent*, 35, no. 2 (Spring 1988), 235-36.

2495. -----, and Joanne Landy, "East European Activists Test Glasnost," *Bulletin of the Atomic Scientists*, 44, no. 3 (May 1988), 18-26.

2496. Nagorski, Andrew, "The Intellectual Roots of Eastern Europe's Upheavals," *SAIS Review*, 10, no. 2 (Summer-Fall 1990), 89-100.

2497. "New Romanian Association for the Defense of Human Rights under Attack," *Human Rights Internet Reporter*, 11, no. 5-6 (Winter-Spring 1987), 37-38.

2498. Olivier, Maurice J., "Eastern Europe: The Path to Success," *Columbia Journal of World Business*, 26, no. 1 (Spring 1991), 10-14.

2499. Pascal, Nina S., "East European-Soviet Relations in a Changing Economic Environment," *East European Quarterly*, 23, no. 1 (Spring 1989), 99-107.

2500. Pehe, Jiri, "Birthing Democracy in Eastern Europe," *Freedom at Issue*, no. 116 (Sept-Oct. 1990), 11-13.

2501. -----, "The Prague Spring-in 1988," *Freedom at Issue*, no. 102 (May-June 1988), 17-23.

2502. Peng, Yali, "Privatization in Eastern European Countries," *East European Quarterly*, 26, no. 4 (Winter 1992), 471-84.

2503. Perth-Grabowska, Alina, "Why `Glasnost' Isn't Working in Poland," *Studium Papers*, 11, no. 4 (Oct. 1987), 67-68.

2504. Pick, Otto, "Probems of Adjustment: The Gorbachev Effect in Eastern Europe," *SAIS Review*, 8, no. 1 (Winter-Spring 1988), 57-73.

2505. -----, "Reassuring Eastern Europe," *NATO Review*, 40, no. 2 (Apr. 1992), 27ff.

2506. Pogany, Peter, "Transition to Market-Based Trading between Eastern Europe and the Soviet Union Is Proving Painful," *International Economic Review* (June 1991), 9-10.

2507. "Polish League for Human Rights Proscribed," *Human Rights Internet Reporter*, 11, no. 5-6 (Winter-Spring 1987), 37.

2508. "Political Prisoners in Wroclaw," *Studium Papers*, 10, no. 3 (July 1986),97-100.

2509. Pond, Elizabeth, "A Wall Destroyed: The Dynamics of German Unification in the GDR," *International Security*, 15, no. 1 (Summer 1990), 35-66.

2510. Precan, Vilem, "The Crumbling of the Soviet Bloc: The Democratic Revolution," *Journal of Democracy*, 1, no. 1 (Winter 1990), 79-85.

2511. Rachwald, Arthur R., "Soviet-East European Relations," *Current History*, 88, no. 541 (Nov. 1989), 377ff.

2512. Reisch, Alfred, "New Prospects for Hungarian-Soviet Relations," *Report on Eastern Europe*, 2, no. 39 (27 Sept. 1991), 5-11.

2513. Remington, Robin Alison, "Eastern Europe after the Revolutions," *Current History*, 90, no. 559 (Nov. 1991), 379-83.

2514. "Report from Eastern Europe: Preventing Regional Trade Collapse," *International Economic Insights*, 2, no. 1 (Jan-Feb. 1991), 38-40.

2515. Roskin, Michael G., "The Emerging Party Systems of Central and Eastern Europe," *East European Quarterly*, 27, no. 1 (Spring 1993), 47-63.

2516. Ross, Jeffrey A., "Religion, Nationalism and the Decommunization of Eastern Europe," *Religion in Communist Dominated Areas*, 29, no. 1 (Winter 1990), 2-3.

2517. Rupnik, Jacques, "Bloc Busters: Poland and Hungary, Perestroika's Mad Scientists," *New Republic* (22 May 1989), 18-23.

2518. "The Scent of Freedom," *Maclean's*, 101 (22 Aug. 1988), 12ff.

2519. Scheye, Eric, "Psychological Notes on Central Europe 1989 and Beyond," *Political Psychology*, 12, no. 2 (June 1991), 331-44.

2520. Seroka, Jim, "The New Politics, Change and Political Pluralism in East Central Europe," *Crossroads*, no. 25 (1987), 31-41.

2521. Seymour, Jack M., Jr., "Gorbachev's Impact on East Europe," *Religion in Communist Dominated Areas*, 28, no. 1 (Winter 1989), 18-21.

2522. Shoup, Paul, "National Communism in Eastern Europe Revisited," *Canadian Review of Studies in Nationalism*, 16, no. 1-2 (1989), 251-62.

2523. Shumaker, David, "The Origins and Development of Central European Cooperation, 1989-1992," *East European Quarterly*, 27, no. 3 (Fall 1993), 351-73.

2524. Sobell, Vladimir, "The Eastern European Economies in 1989," *Report on Eastern Europe*, 1, no. 1 (5 Jan. 1990), 37-38.

2525. -----, "The Politics of Economic Reform," *Report on Eastern Europe*, 1, no. 12 (23 Mar. 1990), 34-36.

2526. "Solidarity Forms a New Above-Ground Leadership and a New Investigative Commission," *Human Rights Internet Reporter*, 12, no. 1 (Fall 1987), 42-43.

2527. Stanglin, D., "Reforms? Few Fans in East Bloc," *U.S. News & World Report*, 102 (23 Feb. 1987), 26.

2528. Staniszkis, Jadwiga, "Patterns of Change in Eastern Europe," *Eastern European Politics and Societies*, 4, no. 1 (Winter 1990), 77-97.

2529. Stokes, Gale, "Lessons of the East European Revolutions of 1989," *Problems of Communism*, 40, no. 5 (Sept-Oct. 1991), 17-22.

2530. "Student Section of Polish League for Human Rights," *Human Rights Internet Reporter*, 12, no. 1 (Fall 1987), 43.

2531. "A Survey of Opinion on the East European Revolution," *Eastern European Politics and Societies*, 4, no. 2 (Spring 1990), 153-207.

2532. Svec, M., "The Prague Spring: 20 Years Later," *Foreign Affairs*, 66 (Summer 1988), 981-1001.

2533. Szayna, S. Thomas, "Ultra-Nationalism in Central Europe," *Orbis*, 37, no. 4 (Fall 1993), 527-52.

2534. Terry, Sarah Meiklejohn, "Gorbachev, *Glasnost* and

Eastern Europe," *Fletcher Forum*, 12, no. 2 (Summer 1988), 253-64.

2535. -----, "Thinking about Post-Communist Transitions; How Different Are They?" *Slavic Review*, 52, no. 2 (Summer 1993), 333-37.

2536. "Thinking the Present: Symposium on the Meaning of 1989 and the Future of the Left," *Praxis International*, 10, nos. 3-4 (Oct. 1990-Jan. 1991), 185-240.

2537. "The Timisoara Proclamation," *Uncaptive Minds*, 3, no. 3 (May-July 1990), 5-7.

2538. Tismaneanu, Vladimir, "Nascent Civil Society in the German Democratic Republic," *Problems of Communism*, 38, no. 2-3 (Mar-June 1989), 90-111.

2539. Varga, Ivan, "Opaque Glasnost? Eastern Europe and Gorbachev's Reforms," *International Journal*, 43, no. 1 (Winter 1987-88), 18-34.

2540. Vinton, Louisa, "Soviet Union Begins Withdrawing Troops-But on Its Own Terms," *Report on Eastern Europe*, 2, no. 17 (26 Apr. 1991), 19-25.

2541. Volgyes, Ivan, "Between the Devil and the Deep Blue Sea: The Foreign Policies of Eastern Europe during the Gorbachev Era," *International Journal*, 43, no. 1 (Winter 1987-88), 127-41.

2542. -----, "Gorbachev and Eastern Europe," *Harvard International Review*, 10, no. 1 (Nov. 1987), 6-9.

2543. -----, "Troubled Friendship or Mutual Dependence? Eastern Europe and the USSR in the Gorbachev Era," *Orbis*, 30, no. 2 (Summer 1986), 343-53.

2544. Waller, Michael, "Peace, Power and Protest: Eastern Europe in the Gorbachev Era," *Conflict Studies*, no. 209 (Mar. 1988), 1-26.

2545. Weinberger, Caspar W., "A NonCommunist Eastern Europe Is Not Here Yet," *Forbes*, 145 (5 Feb. 1990), 31.

2546. Wesolowski, Wlodzimierz, "Transition from Authoritarianism to Democracy," *Social Research*, 57, no. 2 (Summer 1990), 435-62.

2547. Wolchik, Sharon L., "Czechoslovakia's `Velvet Revolution'," *Current History*, 89, no. 551 (Dec. 1990), 413ff.

2548. Zinam, Oleg, "The Revolution of Rising Expectations, Nationalism and the Prospects for Freedom in the Soviet Bloc," *Journal of Social, Political and Economic Studies*, 13, no. 1 (Spring 1988), 87-96.

2549. Zubek, Voytek, "The Threshold of Poland's Transition: 1989 Electoral Campaign as the Last Act of a United Solidarity," *Studies in Comparative Communism*, 24, no. 4 (Dec. 1991), 355-76.

XVI. Economic Policy and Economic Reform
BOOKS

2550. Adam, Jan, *Economic Reforms in the Soviet Union and Eastern Europe since the 1960's* (New York: St. Martin's Press, 1989).

2551. Aganbegyan, Abel, *The Challenge: The Economics of Perestroika* (London: Hutchinson, for the Second World Series, 1988).

2552. -----, *Inside Perestroika: The Future of the Soviet Economy* (New York: Harper & Row, 1989).

2553. -----, *The Economic Challenge of Perestroika* (Bloomington: Indiana University Press, 1988).

2554. -----, and Timor Timofeyev, *The New Stage of Perestroika* (New York: Institute for East-West Security Studies, 1988).

2555. Anderson, Richard, *et al.*, *The Soviet Economy in the Wake of the Moscow Coup: Symposium Report* (Santa Monica, CA: RAND, 1991).

2556. Aslund, Anders, *Differences over Economics in the Soviet Leadership, 1988-1990* (Santa Monica, CA: RAND, 1991).

2557. -----, *Gorbachev's Struggle for Economic Reform: Equality vs. Efficiency*, updated ed. (Washington, DC: Brookings Institution, 1991).

2558. -----, ed., *The Post-Soviet Economy: Soviet and Western Perspectives* (New York: St. Martin's Press, 1992).

2559. -----, and Richard Layard, eds., *Changing the Economic System in Russia* (New York: St. Martin's Press, 1993).

2560. Atkinson, A. B., and J. Micklewright, *Economic Transformation in Eastern Europe and the Distribution of Income* (New York: Cambridge University Press, 1992).

2561. Bahry, Donna L., and Joel C. Moses, eds., *Political Implications of Economic Reform in Communist Systems: Communist Dialectic* (New York: New York University Press, 1990).

2562. Boettke, Peter J., *Why Perestroika Failed: The Politics and Economics of Socialist Transformation* (New York: St. Martin's Press, 1993).

2563. Brine, Jenny, comp., *Comecon: The Rise and Fall of an International Socialist Organization* (New Brunswick, NJ: Transaction Publishers, 1992).

2564. -----, comp., *COMECON: Selective, Critical, Annotated Bibliographies* (Oxford: Clio Press, 1992).

2565. Brus, Wlodzimierz, and Kazimierz Laski, *From Marx to the Market: Socialism in Search of an Economic System* (Oxford: Clarendon Press, 1991).

2566. Bush, Keith, *From the Command Economy to the Market: A Collection of Interviews* (Brookfield, VT: Dartmouth, 1991).

2567. Campbell, Robert W., *The Failure of Soviet Economic Planning* (Bloomington: Indiana University Press, 1992).

2568. -----, *The Socialist Economies in Transition: A Primer on Semi-Reformed Systems* (Bloomington: Indiana University Press, 1991).

2569. Commander, Simon, ed., *Managing Inflation in Socialist Economies in Transition* (Washington, DC: World Bank, 1991).

2570. Cooper, William H., *Soviet Economic Reform and the U.S. Role* (Washington, DC: Library of Congress, Congressional Research Service, 1990).

2571. Copetas, A. Craig, *Bear Hunting with the Politburo: A Gritty First-Hand Account of Russia's Young Entrepreneurs-and Why Soviet-Style Capitalism Can't Work* (New York: Simon & Schuster, 1991).

2572. Desai, Padma, *Perestroika in Perspective: The Design and Dilemmas of Soviet Reform*, rev. ed. (Princeton: Princeton University Press, 1990).

2573. Duch, Raymond M., *Privatizing the Economy: Tele-communications Policy in Comparative Perspective* (Ann Arbor: University of Michigan Press, 1991).

2574. Dyker, David A., *Restructuring the Soviet Economy* (New York: Routledge, 1992).

2575. Ellman, Michael, *Socialist Planning*, 2nd ed. (Cambridge: Cambridge University Press, 1989).

2576. Fischer, Stanley, and Allan Gelb, *Issues in Socialist Economy Reform* (Washington, DC: The World Bank, 1990).

2577. Flakierski, Henryk, *Income Inequalities in the Former Soviet Union and Its Republics* (Armonk, NY: M. E. Sharpe, 1993).

2578. Freidzon, Sergei, *Patterns of Soviet Economic Decision-Making: An Inside View of the 1985 Reform* (Falls Church, VA: Delphic Associates, 1987).

2579. Frydman, Roman, Andrzej Rapaczynski and John S. Earle, *The Privatization Process in Russia, Ukraine, and the Baltic States* (Bucharest: Central European University Press, 1993).

2580. Gabrisch, Robert, ed., *Economic Reforms in Eastern Europe and the Soviet Union* (Boulder, CO: Westview Press, 1989).

2581. Gey, Peter, Jiri Kosta and Wolfgang Quaisser, eds., *Crisis and Reform in Socialist Economies* (Boulder, CO: Westview Press, 1987).

2582. Goldman, Marshall I., *Gorbachev's Challenge: Economic Reform in the Age of High Technology* (New York: Norton, 1987).

2583. -----, *What Went Wrong with Perestroika?* (New York: Norton, 1991).

2584. Gregory, Paul R., *Restructuring the Soviet Economic Bureaucracy* (Cambridge: Cambridge University Press, 1990).

2585. -----, and Robert C. Stuart, *Soviet Economic Structure and Performance*, 5th ed. (New York: HaperCollins, 1994).

2586. Gros, Daniel, and Alfred Steinherr, *Economic Reform in the Soviet Union: Pas de Deux Between Disintegration and Macroeconomic Destablization* (Princeton: Department of Economics, Princeton University, 1991).

2587. -----, *From Centrally-Planned to Market Economies: Issues for the Transition in Central Europe and the Soviet Union* (Elmsford, NY: Brassey's Maxwell House, 1991).

2588. Grossman, Gregory, *Inflationary, Political and Social Implications of the Current Economic Slowdown* (Berkeley: G. Grossman, 1985).

2589. -----, and Bohdan Wiznikiewicz, *The Second Economy in the USSR and Eastern Europe: A Bibliography (with a Bibliography of Recent Polish-Language Works on the Second Economy of Poland, by Bohdan Wiznikiewicz)* (Berkeley-Duke Occasional Papers on the Second Economy in the USSR, no. 21; Bala Cynwyd, PA: WEFA Group, 1990).

2590. Gustafson, Thane, *Crisis Amid Plenty: The Politics of Soviet Energy under Brezhnev and Gorbachev* (Princeton: Princeton University Press, 1991).

2591. -----, *Gorbachev's Dilemma: Toward a Radical Reform for Soviet Energy* (Cambridge, MA: Cambridge Energy Research Associates, 1989).

2592. Hall, Derek R., ed., *Tourism and Economic Development in Eastern Europe and the Soviet Union* (New York: Halsted Press, 1991).

2593. Hanson, Philip, *From Stagnation to Catastroika: Commentaries on the Soviet Economy, 1983-1991* (New York: Praeger, 1992).

2594. Hewett, Ed A., *Reforming the Soviet Economy* (Washington, DC: Brookings Institution, 1988).

2595. Hildebrandt, Gregory G., and Peter B. Staugaard, *The Changing Soviet Priority Economy: Modeling the Conflict between Gold and the Sword* (Santa Monica, CA: RAND, 1991).

2596. Hill, Ronald J., and Jan Ake Dellenbrant, eds., *Gorbachev and Perestroika: Towards a New Socialism?* (Aldershot, England: Edward Elgar, 1989).

2597. Hough, Jerry F., *Opening Up the Soviet Economy* (Washington, DC: Brookings Institution, 1988).

2598. International Monetary Fund, *et al.*, *The Economy of the USSR: Summary and Recommendations* (Washington, DC: The World Bank, 1990).

2599. Ioffe, Olimpiad S., *Gorbachev's Economic Dilemma: An Insider's View* (St. Paul: Merrill/Magnus Publishing Corp., 1989).

2600. Islam, Shafiqul, and Michael Mandelbaum, eds., *Making Markets: Economic Transformation in Eastern Europe and the Post-Soviet States* (New York: Council on Foreign Relations, 1993).

2601. Jeffries, Ian, *Socialist Economies and the Transition to the Market: A Guide* (New York: Routledge, 1993).

2602. Johnson, Paul M., *Redesigning the Communist Economy: The Politics of Economic Reform in Eastern Europe* (Boulder, CO: East European Monographs; New York: distributed by Columbia University Press, 1989).

2603. Jones, Anthony, and William Moskoff, *Ko-ops: The Rebirth of Entrepreneurship in the Soviet Union* (Bloomington: Indiana University Press, 1991).

2604. -----, eds., *The Great Market Debate in Soviet Economics: An Anthology* (Armonk, NY: M. E. Sharpe, 1991).

2605. -----, eds., *Perestroika and the Economy: New Thinking in Soviet Economics* (Armonk, NY: M. E. Sharpe, 1989).

2606. Kahan, Arcadius, *Studies and Essays on the Soviet and Eastern European Economies*, 2 vols. (Newtonville, MA: Oriental Research Partners, 1991).

2607. Kemme, David M., *Economic Transition in Eastern Europe and the Soviet Union: Issues and Strategies* (New York: Institute for East-West Security Studies, 1991, distributed by Westview Press).

2608. -----, and Claire E. Gordon, eds., *The End of Central Planning? Socialist Economies in Transition: The Cases of Czechoslovakia, Hungary, China and the Soviet Union* (New York: Institute for East-West Security Studies, distributed by Westview Press, 1990).

2609. Kornai, Janos, *The Road to a Free Economy* (New York: Norton, 1992).

2610. -----, *Vision and Reality: Market and State: Contradictions and Dilemmas Revisited* (New York: Routledge, 1990).

2611. Kroll, Heidi, *Reform and Monopoly in the Soviet Economy* (Providence, RI: Brown University, 1990).

2612. Lavigne, Marie, *Financing the Transition: The Shatalin Plan and the Soviet Economy* (New York: Institute for East-West Security Studies, and Boulder, CO: Westview Press, 1990).

2613. Linz, Susan J., and William Moskoff, eds., *Reorganization and Reform in the Soviet Economy* (Armonk, NY: M. E. Sharpe, 1987).

2614. McKinnon, Ronald T., *The Order of Economic Liberalization: Financial Control in the Transition to a Market Economy* (Baltimore: The Johns Hopkins University Press, 1991).

2615. McLure, Charles E., Jr., *Income Tax Policy for the Russian Republic* (Stanford: Hoover Institution, 1991).

2616. Miko, Francis T., and Kerry Dumbaugh, *Gorbachev's Reform Strategy: Comparisons with the Hungarian and Chinese Experience* (Washington, DC: Library of Congress, Congressional Research Service, 1987).

2617. Milanovic, Branko, *Liberalization and Entrepreneurship: Dynamics of Reform in Socialism and Capitalism* (Armonk, NY: M. E. Sharpe, 1989).

2618. Milner, Boris Z., and Dmitry S. Lvov, eds., *Soviet Market Economy: Challenges and Reality* (New York: North-Holland, distributed by Elsevier Science Pub. Co., 1991).

2619. Moore, Stephen, and Julian L. Simon, *Communism, Capitalism, and Economic Development: Implications for U.S. Economic Assistance* (Washington, DC: Heritage Foundation, 1988).

2620. Moskoff, William, *Hard Times; Impoverishment and Protest in the Perestroika Years* (Armonk, NY: M. E. Sharpe, 1993).

2621. Nelson, Lynn D., and Irina Y. Kuzes, *Property to the People: The Struggle for Radical Economic Reform in Russia* (Armonk, NY: M. E. Sharpe, 1993).

2622. Nove, Alec, *An Economic History of the U.S.S.R. 1917-1991: New and Final Edition* (New York: Penguin USA, 1993).

2623. Peck, Merton J., and Thomas J. Richardson, eds., *What Is To Be Done? Proposals for the Soviet Transition to the Market* (New Haven: Yale University Press, 1991).

2624. Purvis, Douglas D., *Economic Developments in the Soviet Union and Eastern Europe* (Kingston, Ontario: John Deutsch Institute for the Study of Economic Policy, 1990).

2625. Roberts, Paul Craig, *Alienation and the Soviet Economy: The Collapse of the Socialist Era*, rev. 2nd ed. (New York: Holmes & Meier, 1990).

2626. Rutland, Peter, *The Politics of Economic Stagnation in the Soviet Union* (Cambridge: Cambridge University Press, 1993).

2627. Shmelev, Nikolai, and Vladimir Popov, *The Turning Point: Revitalizing the Soviet Economy* (New York: Doubleday, 1989).

2628. Spulber, Nicholas, *Restructuring the Soviet Economy: In Search of the Market* (Ann Arbor: University of Michigan Press, 1991).

2629. Steinberg, Dmitri, *The Soviet Economy, 1970-90: A Statistical Analysis* (San Francisco: International Trade Press, 1990).

2630. Sutela, Pekka, *Economic Thought and Economic Reform in the Soviet Union* (Cambridge: Cambridge University Press, 1991).

2631. -----, ed., *The Soviet Economy in Crisis and Transition* (Helsinki: Bank of Finland, 1993).

2632. Tedstrom, John, ed., *Perestroika and the Private Sector of the Soviet Economy* (Boulder, CO: Westview Press, 1990).

2633. -----, ed., *Socialism, Perestroika and the Dilemmas of Soviet Economic Reform* (Boulder, CO: Westview Press, 1990).

2634. Ticktin, Hillel, *Origins of the Crisis in the USSR: Essays on the Political Economy of a Disintegrating System* (Armonk, NY: M. E. Sharpe, 1992).

2635. United Nations Economic Commission for Europe. *Economic Reforms in the European Centrally Planned Economies: Proceedings of a Symposium Conducted in Association with the Vienna Institute for Comparative Economic Studies* (New York: United Nations, 1989).

2636. US Central Intelligence Agency and US Defense Intelligence Agency. *The Soviet Economy under a New Leader: A Report Presented to the Subcommittee on Economic Resources, Competitiveness and Security Economics of the Joint Economic Committee* (Washington, DC: Central Intelligence Agency, 1986).

2637. US Central Intelligence Agency. Directorate of Intelligence. *Measuring Soviet GNP: Problems and Solutions: A Conference Report* (Washington, DC: CIA, 1990).

2638. US Congress. House. Committee on Small Business. *East Germany's Time of Crisis*, 101st Congress, 2nd Session (Washington, DC: Government Printing Office, 1990).

2639. US Congress. Joint Economic Committee. *Gorbachev's Economic Plans: Study Papers* 2 vols. (Washington, DC: Government Printing Office, 1987).

2640. US Congress. Joint Economic Committee. *The Soviet Economic Crisis: Hearing...*, 101st Congress, 2nd Session (Washington, DC: Government Printing Office, 1991).

2641. US Congress. Joint Economic Committee. Subcommittee on National Security Economics. *Allocation of Resources in the Soviet Union and China-1987*, 100th Congress, 2nd Session, 1989, S Hrg 100-599, Part 13.

2642. US Congress. Senate. Committee on Foreign Relations. *Estimating the Size and Growth of the Soviet Economy: Hearing...*, 101st Congress, 2nd Session (Washington, DC: Government Printing Office, 1991).

2643. US Defense Intelligence Agency, *Gorbachev's Modernization Program: A Status Report* (Washington, DC: USDIA, 1987).

2644. Wiles, Peter, ed., *The Soviet Economy on the Brink of Reform: Essays in Honor of Alec Nove* (Boston: Unwin Hyman, 1988).

2645. Williamson, John, and Oleh Havrylyshyn, *From Soviet DisUnion to Eastern Economic Community* (Washington, DC: Institute for International Economics, 1991).

2646. Winiecki, Jan, *Resistance to Change in the Soviet Economic System: A Property Rights Approach* (London: Routledge, 1991).

2647. Wolf, Charles, Jr., *et al.*, *Gorbachev's Allocative Choices: Constraints, Dilemmas and Policy Directions* (Santa Monica, CA: RAND, 1990).

2648. Yavlinsky, G., *et al.*, *500 Days: Transition to the Market* (New York: St. Martin's Press, 1991).

2649. Zwass, Adam, *Market, Plan and State: The Strengths and Weaknesses of the Two World Economic Systems* (Armonk, NY: M. E. Sharpe, Inc., 1987).

ARTICLES

2650. Abalkin, Leonid Ivanovich, "The Current Crisis and Prospects for the Development of the Soviet Economy," *Problems of Economic Transition*, 35, no. 2 (June 1992), 6-13.

2651. -----, "Relying on the Lessons of the Past," *Problems of Economics*, 31, no. 2 (June 1988), 6-18.

2652. -----, *et al.*, "The New Model of Economic Development," *Soviet Economy*, 3, no. 4 (Oct-Dec. 1987), 298-312.

2653. Abouchar, Alan, "The Soviet Economy: Whence, Where, Whither, Why?" *Comparative Economic Studies*, 33, no. 3 (Fall 1991), 67-93.

2654. Ackland, L., "The *Perestroika* Experiment," *Bulletin of the Atomic Scientists*, 44 (Dec. 1988), 2.

2655. Aganbegyan, Abel G., *et al.*, "Basic Directions of Perestroyka," *Soviet Economy*, 3, no. 4 (Oct-Dec. 1987), 277-97.

2656. -----, "Economic Reforms," *Perestroika Annual*, 1 (1988), 73-105.

2657. -----, "Economics of Perestroika," *International Affairs*, 64, no. 2 (Spring 1988), 177-85.

2658. -----, "Phased Acceleration," *World Marxist Review*, 31, no. 1 (Jan. 1988), 103-13.

2659. -----, "The Program of Radical Restructuring," *Soviet Review*, 29, no. 3 (Fall 1988), 3-20.

2660. -----, "The Soviet Economy in Transition," *World & I* (Jan. 1990), 42-49.

2661. Amodio, Nicoletta, "From Ministries to Corporations," *Journal of Communist Studies*, 9, no. 1 (Mar. 1993), 227ff.

2662. Aslund, Anders, "Gorbachev, *Perestroyka*, and Economic Crisis," *Problems of Communism*, 40, no. 1-2 (Jan-Apr. 1991), 18-41.

2663. -----, "Gorbachev's Economic Advisors," *Soviet Economy*, 3, no. 3 (July-Sept. 1987), 246-69.

2664. -----, "The Making of Economic Policy in 1989 and 1990," *Soviet Economy*, 6, no. 1 (Jan-Mar. 1990), 65-94.

2665. -----, "Soviet and Chinese Reforms: Why They Must Be Different," *World Today*, 45, no. 11 (Nov. 1989), 188-91.

2666. -----, "The Soviet Economy after the Coup," *Problems of Communism*, 40, no. 6 (Nov-Dec. 1991), 44-52.

2667. Bahry, Donna, "The Contradictions of Economic Reform," *Nationalities Papers*, 28, no. 1 (Spring 1990), 10-13.

2668. -----, "*Perestroika* and the Debate over Territorial Economic Decentralization," *Harriman Institute Forum*, 2, no. 5 (May 1989), 1-8.

2669. -----, "The Union Republics and Contradictions in Gorbachev's Economic Reform," *Soviet Economy*, 7, no. 3 (July-Sept. 1991), 215-55.

2670. Bartel, R. D., "The Gorbachev Revolution," *Challenge*, 30 (Sept-Oct. 1987), 26-33.

2671. Becker, G. S., "The Last Thing the Soviets Need Is a Foreign-Aid Package," *Business Week* (4 Nov. 1991), 21.

2672. Belkin, V. G., *et al.*, "Is the Economy As Bad As the Soviets Say?" *Orbis*, 34, no. 4 (Fall 1990), 509-26.

2673. Bell, Daniel, "Behind the Soviet Economic Crisis," *Dissent*, 38, no. 1 (Winter 1991), 46-49.

2674. Bergson, A., "Economics of Perestroika: An Inauspicious

Beginning," *Challenge*, 32 (May-June 1989), 10-15.

2675. Bethell, Tom, "Why Gorbachev Is Worried," *National Review*, 37 (4 Oct. 1985), 34ff.

2676. Bialer, Seweryn, "The Curtain Rises on Gorbachev's Act II," *U.S. News & World Report*, 103 (13 July 1987), 36-37.

2677. Birman, Igor, "The State of Soviet Economic Affairs," *Russia*, no. 11 (1985), 56-67.

2678. Blough, Roger A., and Philip D. Stewart, "Political Obstacles to Reform and Innovation in Soviet Economic Policy: Brezhnev's Political Legacy," *Comparative Political Studies*, 20, no. 1 (Apr. 1987), 72-97.

2679. Blumenfeld, G., "Problems of the Soviet Economy-Alleged and Real," *Monthly Review*, 40, no. 12 (May 1988), 43-45.

2680. Bond, Andrew R., "Spatial Dimensions of Gorbachev's Economic Strategy," *Soviet Geography*, 28, no. 7 (Sept. 1987), 490-523.

2681. Boretsky, Michael, "The Tenability of the CIA Estimates of Soviet Economic Growth," *Journal of Comparative Economics*, 11, no. 4 (Dec. 1987), 517-42.

2682. Bornstein, Morris, "Soviet Price Policies," *Soviet Economy*, 3, no. 2 (Apr-June 1987), 96-134.

2683. Boycko, Maxim, Andrei Shleiffer and Robert W. Vishny, "Privatizing Russia," *Brookings Papers on Economic Activity*, no. 2 (1993), 139-92.

2684. Brady, Rose, "This Time, Gorbachev May Really Turn the Economy Upside Down," *Business Week* (27 Aug. 1990), 49.

2685. -----, and M. McNamee, "Is the Soviet Economy Too Sick for *Perestroika*?" *Business Week* (16 Oct. 1989), 33.

2686. -----, and Philip Galuszka, "The Soviet Lurch toward Capitalism," *Business Week* (21 Oct. 1991), 50-51.

2687. -----, and R. Boyle, "Going Private: The Soviets Can Hardly Wait," *Business Week* (10 June 1991), 49-50.

2688. Brand, H., "Reforming the Soviet Economy," *Dissent*, 39, no. 1 (Winter 1992), 12-15.

2689. -----, "Why the Soviet Economy Failed," *Dissent*, 39, no. 2 (Spring 1992), 232-44.

2690. Bredenkamp, Hugh, "Reforming the Soviet Economy," *Finance and Development*, 28, no. 2 (June 1991), 18-21.

2691. Brus, Wlodzimierz, "Marketisation and Democratisation: The Sino-Soviet Divergence," *Cambridge Journal of Economics*, 17, no. 4 (Dec. 1993), 423-40.

2692. Burks, R, V., "Reform in the Soviet Union" (Review Article), *Washington Quarterly*, 8, no. 1 (Winter 1985), 177-81.

2693. "Capitalist Road," *Nation*, 253 (2 Dec. 1991), 692.

2694. Cardani, Angelo M., "Recent Developments of the Economic Reform in the USSR," *Il Politico*, 56, no. 3 (July-Sept. 1991), 443-72.

2695. Carrington, Samantha, "The Remonetization of the Commonwealth of Independent States," *American Economic Review*, 82, no. 2 (May 1992), 22-26.

2696. Clark, Andrew, "The Biggest Aid Program Ever," *World Monitor*, 4, no. 4 (Apr. 1991), 34ff.

2697. Clark, John, and Aaron Wildavsky, "Why Communism Collapsed: The Moral and Material Failures of Command Economies Are Intertwined," *Journal of Public Policy*, 10, no. 4 (Oct-Dec. 1989), 361-90.

2698. Colton, Timothy J., "Approaches to the Politics of Systematic Economic Reform in the Soviet Union," *Soviet Economy*, 3, no. 2 (Apr-June 1987), 145-70.

2699. Cornwell, R., "Is Gorbachev's Economy Doomed to Collapse?" *World Press Review*, 36 (Sept. 1989), 20ff.

2700. Costa, Alexandra, "Will Soviet Private Enterprise Survive?" *World & I*, 5, no. 6 (June 1990), 136-42.

2701. "Countdown to Capitalism," *World Press Review*, 37 (Nov. 1990), 11ff.

2702. Day, Richard, "The Political Economy of Perestroika: Thinking about the `New Thinking' in the Soviet Union" (Review Article), *Canadian Slavonic Papers*, 31, no. 3-4 (Sept-Dec. 1989), 316-22.

2703. "Delusions Before Dawn," *Nation*, 251 (15 Oct. 1990), 401.

2704. Dentzer, S., "No Free-Market Magic," *U.S. News & World Report*, 109 (29 Oct. 1990), 85-87.

2705. Desai, Padma, "*Perestroika*, Prices, and the Ruble Problem," *Harriman Institute Forum*, 2, no. 11 (Nov. 1989), 1-8.

2706. -----, "Soviet Economic Reform: A Tale of Two Plans," *Harriman Institute Forum*, 3, no. 12 (Dec. 1990), 1-12.

2707. Dienes, Leslie, "Regional Planning and the Development of Soviet Asia," *Soviet Geography*, 28, no. 5 (May 1987), 287-314.

2708. Dragadze, P., "Russia's Embryonic Capitalists," *Forbes*, 144 (16 Oct. 1989), 90ff.

2709. Dudney, Robert S., "Gorbachev's Economy," *Air Force Magazine*, 71, no. 3 (Mar. 1988), 40-47.

2710. Dyker, David, "Gorbachev's Economic Revolution: The Realities of Perestroika," *Conflict Studies*, no. 218 (Feb. 1989), 1-21.

2711. Ellman, Michael, "Convertibility of the Rouble," *Cambridge Journal of Economics*, 15, no. 4 (Dec. 1991), 481-97.

2712. -----, "A Note on the Distribution of Income in the USSR under Gorbachev," *Soviet Studies*, 42, no. 1 (Jan. 1990), 147-48.

2713. Ericson, Richard E., "Soviet Economic Reforms: The Motivation and Content of *Perestroika*," *Journal of International Affairs*, 42 (Spring 1989), 317-31.

2714. -----, "Soviet Numbers Game Threatens *Perestroika*,"

Bulletin of the Atomic Scientists, 44, no. 10 (Dec. 1988), 20-25.

2715. -----, "What Is To Be Done?" *New Republic* (5 Mar. 1990), 34-38.

2716. Evstigneeva, L., and V. Perlamutrov, "*Perestroika*: Social Capital and the Market," *Problems of Economics*, 33, no. 11 (Mar. 1991), 7-31.

2717. Fairlamb, David, "Financing Perestroika," *Institutional Investor*, 22 (May 1988), 94-98.

2718. Fallenbuchl, Zbigniew M., "Soviet Economic Reform," *Canadian Slavonic Papers*, 30, no. 3 (Sept. 1988), 305-22.

2719. Feige, Edgar L., "A Message to Gorbachev: Redistribute the Wealth," *Challenge*, 33 (May-June 1990), 46-53.

2720. -----, "Perestroika and Ruble Convertibility," *Cato Journal*, 10, no. 3 (Winter 1991), 631-54.

2721. -----, "Perestroika and Socialist Privatization: What Is To Be Done? And How?" *Comparative Economic Studies*, 32, no. 3 (Fall 1990), 1-54.

2722. -----, "Socialist Privatization: Response," *Comparative Economic Studies*, 32, no. 3 (Fall 1990), 71-81.

2723. Fennell, T., "Supply-Side Theory Is Alive and Well-in Moscow," *Business Week* (24 July 1989), 10.

2724. Filatotchev, Igor, Trevor Buck and Mike Wright, "Privatisation and Buy-outs in the USSR," *Soviet Studies*, 44, no. 2 (Mar. 1992), 265-82.

2725. "Financial Perestroika: A Look at the Recent Soviet Banking Reforms," *Law and Policy in International Business*, 21 (1989), 53-69.

2726. "500 Days: Shatalin at Columbia," *Harriman Institute Forum*, 3, no. 12 (Dec. 1990), 13-20.

2727. Floroff, O., and S. W. Tiefenbrun, "A Legal Framework for Soviet Privatization," *Pepperdine Law Review*, 18 (May 1991), 849-92.

2728. Foner, Eric, "Soviet Yuppies: The Romance of the Market," *Nation*, 251 (24 Dec. 1990), 796ff.

2729. Francis, D., "The Spectre of Soviet Profits," *Maclean's*, 101 (23 May 1988), 9.

2730. Gaidar, Egor, "At the Beginning of a New Phase: An Economic Review," *Problems of Economics*, 34, no. 6 (Oct. 1991), 6-23.

2731. Galbraith, John K., "Can the Russians Reform? The Soviet Economy: Prospects for Change," *Harper's*, 274, no. 1645 (June 1987), 52-55.

2732. Galuszka, Philip, "Gorbachev Has Planted the Seeds, But Will They Grow?" *Business Week* (2 Feb. 1987), 44-45.

2733. -----, "Gorbachev Is Making a Bold Bid to Get His Reforms Moving," *Business Week* (29 June 1987), 49.

2734. Goble, Paul, "Ethnicity and Economic Reform," *Report on the USSR*, 2, no. 7 (16 Feb. 1990), 23-24.

2735. Goldberg, Paul, "Economic Reform and Product Quality Improvement Efforts in the Soviet Union," *Soviet Studies*, 44, no. 1 (Jan. 1992), 113-22.

2736. Goldman, Marshall I., "The Chinese Model: The Solution to Russia's Economic Ills?" *Current History*, 92, no. 576 (Oct. 1993), 320-24.

2737. -----, "Diffusion of Development: The Soviet Union," *American Economic Review*, 81, no. 2 (May 1991), 276-81.

2738. -----, "The Future of Soviet Economic Reform," *Current History*, 88, no. 540 (Oct. 1989), 329ff.

2739. -----, "Gorbachev and Economic Reform," *Foreign Affairs*, 64, no. 1 (Fall 1985), 56-73.

2740. -----, "Gorbachev the Economist," *Foreign Affairs*, 69, no. 2 (1990), 28-44.

2741. -----, "Helping Gorbachev: The Right Thing To Do?" *World & I* (Jan. 1990), 110-17.

2742. -----, "The Hunt for Red Enterprise," *World Monitor*, 3, no. 12 (Dec. 1990), 50-52.

2743. -----, "Moscow's Money Troubles," *World Monitor*, 3, no. 10 (Oct. 1990), 26-28.

2744. -----, "Needed: A Russian Economic Revolution," *Current History*, 91, no. 567 (Oct. 1992), 314-20.

2745. -----, "The Soviet Economy and the Need for Reform," *Annals of the American Academy of Political and Social Science*, no. 507 (Jan. 1990), 26-34.

2746. -----, "Soviet Perceptions of Chinese Economic Reforms and the Implications for Reform in the U.S.S.R.," *Journal of International Affairs*, 39 (Winter 1986), 41-55.

2747. -----, and Merle Goldman, "Soviet and Chinese Economic Reform," *Foreign Affairs*, 63, no. 3 (1988), 551-73.

2748. Goldstein, Shirley, "Leasing and Cooperatives Play Important Role in Denationalization of Property in the USSR," *SEEL: Soviet and East European Law*, 1, no. 9 (Nov. 1990), 8ff.

2749. -----, "Russian Privatization: Rough Sailing Ahead," *SEEL: Soviet and East European Law*, 2, no. 8 (Oct. 1991), 8-10.

2750. "Gorbachev's Economic Policy-A Psychological Illusion?" *Soviet Analyst*, 17 (14 Sept. 1988), 5-7.

2751. "Gorbachev's Economic Reforms: A *Soviet Economy* Roundtable," *Soviet Economy*, 3, no. 1 (Jan-Mar. 1987), 40-53.

2752. Gorbunov, E., "On the Idea of Developing Small Business in the USSR," *Problems of Economics*, 35, no. 1 (May 1992), 47-60.

2753. Gorlin, Alice C., "The Soviet Economy," *Current History*, 85, no. 513 (Oct. 1986), 325ff.

2754. Graham, Loren, "The Limits of Change: Science and Technology," *Nation* (13 June 1987), 804-08.

2755. Gray, M., "Capitalism, Soviet Style," *Maclean's*, 104 (29 Apr. 1991), 25-26.

2756. "Great Expectations," *Progressive*, 54, no. 7 (July 1990), 7-8.

2757. Gregory, Paul R., "The Impact of *Perestroika* on the Soviet Planned Economy: Results of a Survey of Moscow Economic Officials," *Soviet Studies*, 43, no. 5 (1991), 859-74.

2758. -----, "Soviet Bureaucratic Behaviour: Khozyaistvenniki and Apparatchiki," *Soviet Studies*, 41 (Oct. 1990), 511-25.

2759. Grossman, Gregory, "Sub-Rosa Privatization and Marketization in the USSR," *Annals of the American Academy of Political and Social Science*, no. 507 (Jan. 1990), 44-52.

2760. Guetta, B., "The Road Back from Serfdom," *Orbis*, 34, no. 3 (Summer 1990), 424-30.

2761. Hagler, Marian M., "Financial *Perestroika*: A Look at the Recent Soviet Banking Reforms," *Law Policy in International Business*, no. 1 (1989), 53-69.

2762. Hallick, Stephen P., Jr., "*Caveat Emptor*: Gorbachev's *Glasnost*," *Ukrainian Quarterly*, 43, no. 1-2 (Spring-Summer 1987), 100-13.

2763. Hamilton, John Maxwell, "Capitalism's Young Pioneers," *World Monitor*, 4, no. 8 (Aug. 1991), 34-39.

2764. Hanke, Steve H., and Kurt Schuler, "Ruble Reform: A Lesson from Keynes," *Cato Journal*, 10, no. 3 (Winter 1991), 655-66.

2765. Hanson, Philip, "Creating Private Companies," *Report on the USSR*, 2, no. 19 (11 May 1990), 3-5.

2766. -----, "Faster Economic Reform?" *Report on the USSR*, 2, no. 18 (4 May 1990), 7-8.

2767. -----, "Nikolai Petrakov: Gorbachev's New Economics Aide," *Report on the USSR*, 2, no. 4 (26 Jan. 1990), 18-20.

2768. -----, "The Novosibirsk Paper," in Voytech Mastny, ed., *Soviet/East European Survey, 1983-1984* (Durham, NC: Duke University Press, 1985), 22-24.

2769. -----, "Property Rights in the New Phase of Reforms," *Soviet Economy*, 6, no. 2 (Apr-June 1990), 95-124.

2770. -----, "Prospects for Reform: Three Key Issues in 1990," *Report on the USSR*, 2, no. 4 (26 Jan. 1990), 1-4.

2771. -----, "Russia: Economic Reform and Local Politics," *World Today*, 49, no. 4 (Apr. 1993), 64-66.

2772. -----, "The Shape of Gorbachev's Economic Reform," *Soviet Economy*, 2, no. 4 (Oct-Dec. 1986), 313-26.

2773. Hardt, John P., "Gorbachev's Economic Strategy," *Towson State Journal of International Affairs*, 22 (Fall 1987), 1-7.

2774. Hewett, Ed A., "Economic Reform in the USSR, Eastern Europe, and China: The Politics of Economics," *American Economic Review*, 79, no. 2 (May 1989), 16-20.

2775. -----, "Gorbachev at Two Years: Perspectives on Economic Reforms," *Soviet Economy*, 2, no. 4 (Oct-Dec. 1986), 283-88.

2776. -----, "Gorbachev's Economic Strategy: A Preliminary Assessment," *Soviet Economy*, 1, no. 4 (Oct-Dec. 1985), 285-305.

2777. -----, "Is It Reform or Rhetoric?" *Current*, 291 (Mar-Apr. 1987), 21-27.

2778. -----, "Is Soviet Socialism Reformable?" *SAIS Review*, 10, no. 2 (Summer-Fall 1990), 75-88.

2779. -----, "The New Soviet Plan," *Foreign Affairs*, 69, no. 5 (Winter 1990-91), 146-67.

2780. -----, "*Perestroyka* and the Congress of People's Deputies," *Soviet Economy*, 5, no. 1 (Jan-Mar. 1989), 47-69.

2781. -----, "Perestroika Plus: The Abalkin Reforms," *PlanEcon Report*, 5 (1 Dec. 1989), 146-66.

2782. -----, "Reform or Rhetoric: Gorbachev and the Soviet Economy," *Brookings Review*, 4, no. 4 (Fall 1986), 13-20.

2783. -----, "Up Against the System: Reforming the Economy," *Nation* (13 June 1987), 802-04.

2784. -----, et al., "1986 Panel on the Soviet Economic Outlook," *Soviet Economy*, 2, no. 1 (Jan-Mar. 1986), 3-18.

2785. -----, et al., "1987 Panel on the Soviet Economic Outlook: Perceptions on a Confusing Set of Statistics," *Soviet Economy*, 3, no. 1 (Jan-Mar. 1987), 332-52.

2786. Heymann, Hans, Jr., "Russia's Economic Reform," *Soviet Economy*, 8, no. 1 (Jan-Mar. 1992), 42-45.

2787. Hofheinz, Paul, "Gorbachev's Double Burden: Economic Reform and Growth Acceleration," *Millennium*, 15 (Spring 1987), 21-53.

2788. -----, "Who to Call in the Soviet Union Now," *Fortune*, 124 (2 Dec. 1991), 163ff.

2789. Holtzman, Franklyn D., "Moving Toward Ruble Convertibility," *Comparative Economic Studies*, 33, no. 3 (Fall 1991), 3-66.

2790. Horvath, J., "Soviet Economic Reforms Are Destined to Fizzle," *Challenge*, 31 (Mar-Apr. 1988), 50-52.

2791. Hough, Jerry F., "The Gorbachev Reform: A Maximal Case," *Soviet Economy*, 2, no. 4 (Oct-Dec. 1986), 302-12.

2792. -----, "The Politics of Successful Economic Reform," *Soviet Economy*, 5, no. 1 (Jan-Mar. 1989), 26-41.

2793. Ickes, Barry W., "Obstacles to Economic Reform of Socialism: An Institutional-Choice Approach," *Annals of the American Academy of Political and Social Science*, no. 507 (Jan. 1990), 53-64.

2794. "Is Economic Reform Possible Without Restructuring Politics? A Roundtable Discussion," *Problems of Economics*, 31, no. 10 (Feb. 1989), 26-59.

2795. Islam, Shafiqul, "Russia's Rough Road to Capitalism,"

Foreign Affairs, 72, no. 2 (Spring 1993), 57-66.

2796. Javetski, B., and J. Pearson, "Gorbachev's Das Kapitalism," *Business Week* (13 July 1987), 30-31.

2797. Jenkins, Helmut W., "Gorbachev's Economic Reforms: A Structural or a Technical Alteration?" *International Journal of Social Economics*, 15, no. 1 (1988), 3-32.

2798. Johnson, Simon, and Heidi Kroll, "Managerial Strategies for Spontaneous Privatization," *Soviet Economy*, 7, no. 4 (Oct-Dec. 1991), 281-316.

2799. Johnstone, Diana, "Of Transforming and Being Transformed," *World Policy Journal*, 8, no. 3 (Summer 1991), 525-36.

2800. Kaser, M., "'One Economy, Two Systems': Parallels Between Soviet and Chinese Reforms," *International Affairs*, 63 (Summer 1987), 395-412.

2801. -----, "The Technology of Decontrol: Some Macroeconomic Issues," *Economic Journal*, 100 (June 1990), 596-615.

2802. Kavass, Igor, "Gorbachev Insists He's the Boss," *SEEL: Soviet and East European Law*, 1, no. 9 (Nov. 1990), 7.

2803. Khanin, G. I., "Economic Growth in the USSR in the Eighties," *Problems of Economics*, 34, no. 12 (Apr. 1992), 30-39.

2804. Khorev, B. S., "Economic Decentralization and Regionalism," *Soviet Geography*, 31, no. 9 (Sept. 1990), 509-16.

2805. Kirkland, Richard I., Jr., "Russia: Where Gorbanomics Is Leading," *Fortune*, 116 (28 Sept. 1987), 82ff.

2806. -----, "Why Russia Is Still in the Red," *Fortune*, 119 (30 Jan. 1989), 173ff.

2807. Kolko, Joyce, "Global Restructuring and Economic Reforms," *Socialism and Democracy*, no. 10 (Spring-Summer 1990), 23-36.

2808. Konstantinov, Yuri, "Can the Ruble Become Convertible Currency?" *International Affairs* (Moscow), 7 (Mar. 1988), 56-63.

2809. Kotz, David, "The Direction of Soviet Economic Reform: From Socialist Reform to Capitalist Transition," *Monthly Review*, 44, no. 4 (Sept. 1992), 14-34.

2810. Kriegel, Annie, "Survival Mode," *New Republic* (14 May 1990), 12-13.

2811. Kroll, Heidi, "Monopoly and Transition to the Market," *Soviet Economy*, 7 (Apr-June 1991), 167-75.

2812. -----, "Property Rights and the Soviet Enterprise: Evidence from the Law of Contract," *Journal of Comparative Economics*, 13, no. 1 (Mar. 1989), 115-33.

2813. -----, "The Role of Contracts in the Soviet Economy," *Soviet Studies*, 40, no. 3 (July 1988), 349-66.

2814. Kroncher, Allen, "What Sort of Market Does Gorbachev Want?" *Soviet Analyst*, 19 (Oct. 1990), 4-6.

2815. Krug, Barbara, "Blood, Sweat, or Cheating: Politics and the Transformation of Socialist Economies in China, the USSR and Eastern Europe," *Studies in Comparative Communism*, 24, no. 2 (June 1991), 137-50.

2816. Kushnirsky, F. I., "The New Role of Normatives in Soviet Economic Planning," *Soviet Studies*, 41, no. 4 (Oct. 1989), 526-42.

2817. Kvint, Vladimir L., "Confronting the Soviet Management Structure: Bureaucratic But Workable," *International Executive*, 32, no. 3 (Nov-Dec. 1990), 3-6.

2818. Landy, Joanne, "One Step Forward, Two Steps Back: The East Chases the Worst of the West," *Progressive*, 55, no. 6 (June 1991), 17-21.

2819. Lane, Cleveland, "Russia's Economy: Achilles Heel of the USSR," *American Legion Magazine*, 118, no. 3 (1985), 24ff.

2820. Latsis, Otto, "Economic Reform Debates in the Soviet Union," *World Marxist Review*, 31, no. 7 (July 1988), 106-13.

2821. -----, "Progress of Economic Reform in the USSR," *World Marxist Review*, 32, no. 12 (Dec. 1989), 24-28.

2822. Lei, Xi, "Economic Reform in the USSR: An Overview," *Beijing Review*, 30 (16 Mar. 1987), 18-21.

2823. Leontieff, W. W., "Some Soviet Lessons," *Challenge*, 33 (Sept-Oct. 1990), 14-15.

2824. Levine, Herbert S., "Why Did Soviet Central Planning Fail?" *AAASS Newsletter*, 32, no. 1 (Jan. 1992), 1-2.

2825. Levinson, M., "The Market Comes to Moscow," *Newsweek*, 117 (15 Apr. 1991), 38-39.

2826. Litvin, Valentin, "On *Perestroyka*: Reforming Economic Management," *Problems of Communism*, 36, no. 4 (July-Aug. 1987), 87-92.

2827. Litwack, John M., "Discretionary Behaviour and Soviet Economic Reform," *Soviet Studies*, 43, no. 2 (Apr. 1991), 255-80.

2828. -----, "Legality and Market Reform in Soviet-Type Economies," *Journal of Economic Perspectives*, 5, no. 4 (Fall 1991), 77-89.

2829. -----, "Ratcheting and Economic Reform in the USSR," *Journal of Comparative Economics*, 14, no 2 (June 1990), 254-68.

2830. Loginov, V., "Special Features of the Transition to a Market in the USSR," *Problems of Economics*, 34, no. 9 (Jan. 1992), 65-81.

2831. Luke, Tim, "Postcommunism in the USSR: The McGulag Archipelago," *Telos*, no. 84 (Summer 1980), 33-42.

2832. Makarov, Valery L. "On the Strategy for Implementing Economic Reform in the USSR," *American Economic Review*, 78, no. 2 (May 1988), 457-60.

2833. Maltsev, Y. M., "When Reform Collides with Ideology," *American Enterprise*, 1 (Mar-Apr. 1990), 88-91.

2834. Manevich, E., "Means of Restructuring the Economic Mechanism," *Soviet Review*, 28, no. 3 (Fall 1987), 3-19.

2835. Manezhev, Sergei, "Free Economic Zones in the Context of Economic Changes in Russia," *Europe-Asia Studies*, 45, no. 4 (1993), 609-25.

2836. Marrese, Michael, "Perestroika and Socialist Privatization: A Comment," *Comparative Economic Studies*, 32, no. 3 (Fall 1990), 55-61.

2837. McAuley, Alastair, "The Economic Consequences of Soviet Disintegration," *Soviet Economy*, 7, no. 3 (July-Sept. 1991), 189-214.

2838. -----, "*Perestroika* and Privatization," *Journal of Communist Studies*, 9, no. 21 (Mar. 1993), 213-26.

2839. McKinney, Judith Record, "Confusion in Soviet Economic Reform," *Current History*, 89, no. 549 (Oct. 1990), 317ff.

2840. McKinnon, Ronald I., "Financial Control in the Transition from Classical Socialism to Market Economy," *Journal of Economic Perspectives*, 5, no. 4 (Fall 1991), 107-22.

2841. Melcher, R. A., "How Gorby Took the Money-Before Bashing the Baltics," *Business Week* (4 Feb. 1991), 66.

2842. Millar, James R., "Perestroika and Socialist Privatization: What Is To Be Done? A Comment: There Is No Quick Fix," *Comparative Economic Studies*, 32, no. 3 (Fall 1990), 62-70.

2843. Moltz, James Clay, "Divergent Learning and the Failed Politics of Soviet Economic Reform," *World Politics*, 45, no. 2 (Jan. 1993), 301-25.

2844. Montias, J. M., "The Sequencing of Reforms," *Challenge*, 33 (Sept-Oct. 1990), 12-14.

2845. Moody, Stephen S., "Fallen Star," *New Republic* (9 Sept. 1991), 21-25.

2846. Moroz, Valentyn, "The Lvov Oblast Soviet Attempts to Introduce a Market Economy," *Report on the USSR*, 2, no. 46 (16 Nov. 1990), 22-23.

2847. Nazarov, M., "The Market and Statistics," *Problems of Economics*, 34, no. 7 (Nov. 1991), 69-81.

2848. Newcity, Michael, "An IRS for the USSR?" *SEEL: Soviet and East European Law*, 1, no. 6 (Aug. 1990), 7.

2849. Nikiforov, L., and T. Kuznetsova, "Conceptual Foundations of Destatization and Privatization," *Problems of Economics*, 34, no. 7 (Nov. 1991), 6-24.

2850. Noren, James H., "The FSU Economies: First Year of Transition," *Post-Soviet Geography*, 34, no. 7 (Sept. 1993), 419-52.

2851. -----, "The Russian Economic Reform: Progress and Prospects," *Soviet Economy* (Jan-Mar. 1992), 3-41.

2852. -----, "The Soviet Economic Crisis: Another Perspective," *Soviet Economy*, 6, no. 1 (Jan-Mar. 1990), 3-55.

2853. Nove, Alec, "The Problems of Perestroika: Portrait of an Economy in Transition," *Dissent*, 36, no. 4 (Fall 1989), 462-74.

2854. -----, "'Radical Reform': Problems and Prospects," *Soviet Studies*, 39, no. 3 (July 1987), 452-67.

2855. Nuti, Domenico Mario, "Perestroika: Transition from Central Planning to Market Socialism," *Economic Policy: A European Forum* (Oct. 1988), 352-89.

2856. Odell, Peter, "Gorbachev's New Economic Strategy: The Role of Gas Exports to Western Europe," *World Today*, 43, no. 7 (July 1987), 123-25.

2857. Odom, W. E., "How Far Can Soviet Reform Go?" *Problems of Communism*, 36, no. 6 (Nov-Dec. 1987), 18-33.

2858. Ofer, Gur, "Budget Deficit, Market Disequilibrium and Soviet Economic Reforms," *Soviet Economy*, 5, no. 2 (Apr-June 1989), 107-61.

2859. -----, "Economic Aspects of the Modernization of Russia and China," in *Patterns of Modernity*, vol 2: *Beyond the West*, ed. by S. N. Eisenstadt (New York: New York University Press, 1987), 37-64.

2860. "On the Banks of the Volga, Russia's Rudimentary Banking System Is Being Revolutionised as Part of-and to Promote-Perestroika," *Economist*, 311 (22 Apr. 1989), 71-72.

2861. Paalberg, Harry, "On the Origins of Soviet Economic Mechanisms and the Need for Radical Reform: An Essay," *Journal of Baltic Studies*, 20, no. 2 (Summer 1989), 191-95.

2862. Palei, L. V., and K. L. Radzivanovich, "How to Carry Out Economic Reform: Points of View and Reality," *Soviet Studies*, 42, no. 1 (Jan. 1990), 25-38.

2863. Parker, Richard, "Gorbanomics," *New Republic* (27 Feb. 1989), 18-20.

2864. -----, "Inside the `Collapsing' Soviet Economy," *Atlantic*, 265 (June 1990), 68-75.

2865. Pasour, E. C., Jr., "Perestroika and the Socialist Calculation Debate," *Journal of Social, Political and Economic Studies*, 15, no. 4 (Winter 1990), 483-94.

2866. Pechota, Vratislav, and Marina Beliaeva, "A Plan to End All Plans: The 500-Day Plan for Economic Reform in the Soviet Union," *SEEL: Soviet and East European Law*, 1, no. 7 (Sept. 1990), 1ff.

2867. Peel, Quentin, "Walled In," *New Republic* (15 Oct. 1990), 13-18.

2868. Pellicani, Luciano, "Preconditions for Soviet Economic Development," *Telos*, no. 84 (Summer 1990), 43-57.

2869. "Perestroika Meets the Payments System," *Economist*, 321 (5 Oct. 1991), 91.

2870. Pervushin, S., "On One of the Deep-Seated Causes of the Soviet Economy's State of Crisis," *Problems of Economics*, 34, no. 12 (Apr. 1992), 40-50.

2871. Peterhoff, Reinhard, "Obstacles to the Transformation of the Soviet Economy," *Aussenpolitik*, 42, no. 3 (1991), 221-30.

2872. Peterson, P. G., "Gorbachev's Bottom Line," *New York*

Review of Books, 34 (25 June 1987), 29-33.

2873. Petr, Jerry L., "Economic Reforms in Socialist Economies: An Evolutionary Perspective," *Journal of Economic Issues*, 24, no. 1 (Mar. 1990), 1-15.

2874. -----, "'New Thinking' in the Soviet Economy: Lessons for Western Political Economists," *Journal of Economic Issues*, 24, no. 4 (Dec. 1990), 981-94.

2875. Pfouts, Ralph W., "The Gorbachev Economic Proposals and the USSR," *Atlantic Economic Journal*, 18 (Mar. 1988), 1.

2876. Picone, Paul, "Paradoxes of *Perestroika*," *Telos*, no. 84 (Summer 1990), 3-32.

2877. Plofchan, Thomas K., Jr., "Beyond Collectivism," *World & I*, 6, no. 10 (Oct. 1991), 586-601.

2878. Popkova-Pijasheva, Larissa, "Why Is the Plan Incompatible with the Market?" *Annals of the American Academy of Political and Social Science*, no. 507 (Jan. 1990), 80-90.

2879. "A Pragmatists's Approach to the Soviet Economy: A Conversation with Nikolai Shmelev and Ed A. Hewett," *Brookings Review*, 8, no. 1 (Winter 1989-90), 27-32.

2880. Pryor, Frederic L., "The Performance of Agricultural Production in Marxist and Non-Marxist Nations," *Comparative Economic Studies*, 3, no. 3 (Fall 1991), 95-127.

2881. Puddington, Arch, "Economic Restructuring in the Soviet Union," *Atlantic Community Quarterly*, 25, no. 4 (Winter 1987-88), 492-98.

2882. Raiklin, Ernest, "The Soviet Budget Deficit: Reality ... Or Myth?" *Journal of Social, Political and Economic Studies*, 14, no. 3 (Fall 1989), 299-349.

2883. Rhodes, Mark, "Food Supply in the USSR," *Report on the USSR*, 3, no. 41 (11 Oct. 1991), 11-16.

2884. Roberts, Paul Craig, "Privileged Privatization," *Reason*, 23 (July 1991), 26-27.

2885. -----, "'Property Owners' Are Rising from Russia's Economic Rubble," *Business Week* (13 May 1991), 16.

2886. -----, "Seven Days That Shook the World," *National Review*, 42 (15 Oct. 1990), 26-28.

2887. Rosefielde, Stephen, "The Illusion of Material Progress: The Analytics of Soviet Economic Growth Revisited," *Soviet Studies*, 43, no. 4 (1991), 597-612.

2888. -----, and R. W. Pfouts, "Ruble Convertibility: Demand Response Exchange Rates in a Goal-Directed Economy," *European Economic Review*, 34 (Nov. 1990), 1377-97.

2889. Rubenstein, Ed, "Perestroika Stumbles," *National Review*, 42 (9 July 1990), 13.

2890. Rubin, M., "Self-Interest and the Kosygin Reforms: Finding New Wine in Old Bottles," *Journal of Comparative Economics*, 14 (Sept. 1990), 473-92.

2891. Rumer, Boris, "The 'Abalkinization' of Soviet Economic

Reform," *Problems of Communism*, 39, no. 1 (Jan-Feb. 1990), 74-82.

2892. -----, "Investment Performance in the 12th Five-year Plan," *Soviet Studies*, 43, no. 3 (1991), 451-72.

2893. -----, "Realities of Gorbachev's Economic Program," *Problems of Communism*, 35, no. 3 (May-June 1986), 20-31.

2894. Sacks, Jeffrey D., "Spontaneous Privatization: A Comment," *Soviet Economy*, 7, no. 4 (Oct-Dec. 1991), 317-21.

2895. -----, and Wing Thye Woo, "Structural Factors in the Economic Reforms of China, Eastern Europe, and the Former Soviet Union," *Economic Policy: A European Forum* (Apr. 1994), 101-46.

2896. Schroeder, Gertrude E., "Anatomy of Gorbachev's Economic Reform," *Soviet Economy*, 3, no. 3 (July-Sept. 1987), 219-41.

2897. -----, "Consumer Malaise in the Soviet Union: Perestroika's Achilles Heel?" *PlanEcon Report*, 4, no. 11 (10 Mar. 1988), 1-12.

2898. -----, "Crisis in the Consumer Sector: A Comment," *Soviet Economy*, 6, no. 1 (Jan-Mar. 1990), 56-64.

2899. -----, "A Critical Time for Perestroika," *Current History*, 90, no. 558 (Oct. 1991), 323-27.

2900. -----, "Gorbachev: 'Radically' Implementing Brezhnev's Reforms," *Soviet Economy*, 2, no. 4 (Oct-Dec. 1986), 289-301.

2901. -----, "Perestroika in the Aftermath of 1990," *Soviet Economy*, 7, no. 1 (Jan-Mar. 1991), 3-13.

2902. -----, "Soviet Economic Reform: From Resurgence to Retrenchment?" *Russian Review*, 48, no. 3 (July 1989), 305-19.

2903. -----, "The Soviet Economy under Gorbachev," *Current History*, 86, no. 522 (Oct. 1987), 317ff.

2904. Scully, G. W., "The Institutional Framework and Economic Development," *Journal of Political Economy*, 96 (June 1988), 652-62.

2905. Seligman, D., "The Main Point of Communism," *Fortune*, 116 (7 Dec. 1987), 183ff.

2906. Shabad, Theodore, "Geographic Aspects of the New Soviet Five-Year Plan, 1986-90," *Soviet Geography*, 27, no. 1 (Jan. 1986), 1-16.

2907. -----, "Siberian Development under Gorbachev," in *Soviet Geography Studies in Our Time: A Festschrift for Paul E. Lydolph*, ed. by Lutz Holzner and Jeane M. Knapp (Milwaukee: University of Wisconsin-Milwaukee and American Geographical Society Collection of the Golda Meir Library, 1987), 163-73.

2908. Shanin, T., "Soviet Economic Crisis: The Most Immediate Stumbling Block and the Next Step," *Monthly Review*, 41, no. 5 (Oct. 1989), 18-21.

2909. Shmelev, Nikolai, "On Urgent Measures to Prevent the Collapse of the Soviet Economy," *Problems of Economics*, 33, no. 6 (Oct. 1990), 29-39.

2910. Simmons, Rebecca, J., "A New Approach to Banking in the USSR," *SEEL: Soviet and East European Law*, 1, no. 8 (Oct. 1990), 7.

2911. Simonov, V., "Credit Reform in the USSR: From Total Regulation to Total Deregulation?" *Problems of Economic Transition*, 35, no. 2 (June 1992), 77ff.

2912. Singer, Daniel, "The Perils of Perestroika," *Nation*, 251 (2 July 1990), 15-18.

2913. Smirnov, Alexander D., and Emil B. Ershov, "Perestroika: A Catastrophic Change of Economic Reform Policy," *Journal of Conflict Resolution*, 36, no. 3 (Sept. 1992), 415-53.

2914. Smith, Hedrick, "On the Road with Gorbachev's Guru" [Aganbegian], *New York Times Magazine* (10 Apr. 1988), 36ff.

2915. Sobell, Vlad, "The Formation of the New Soviet-East European Economic Order," *Harvard International Review*, 13, no. 1 (Fall 1990), 20ff.

2916. "Soviet Economy Near Crisis: Bad Luck Is Aggravating Problems Caused by Bad Planning and Bad Policy," *Air Force Magazine*, 73, no. 7 (July 1990), 25-39.

2917. "The Soviet Growth Slowdown: Three Views," *American Economic Review*, 76, no. 2 (May 1986), 170-85.

2918. Spechler, Martin C., "Gorbachev's Economic Reforms: Early Assessments" (Review Article), *Problems of Communism*, 38, no. 5 (Sept-Oct. 1989), 116-20.

2919. Steinberg, B., "Reforming the Soviet Economy," *Fortune*, 112 (25 Nov. 1985), 90ff.

2920. "Streetwise Mikhail," *Economist*, 300 (26 July 1986), 7-8.

2921. Summers, Jeffrey A., "The Macroeconomic Correlates of Investment Growth in the Soviet Union," *Soviet Studies*, 42, no. 4 (Oct. 1990), 795-810.

2922. Summers, L. H., "Soviet Federalism," *Challenge*, 33 (Sept-Oct. 1990), 15-16.

2923. Svejnar, Jan, "Microeconomic Issues in the Transition to a Market Economy," *Journal of Economic Perspectives*, 5, no. 4 (Fall 1991), 123-38.

2924. "Symposium on Regional Aspects of Economic Restructuring in the Former Soviet Union," *International Regional Science Review*, 15, no. 2 (1993), 229-316.

2925. "A Tale of Strange Bedfellows: Individual Private Enterprise and Planned Economy in the U.S.S.R.," *New York University Journal of International Law and Policy*, 21, no. 2 (Winter 1989), 353-77.

2926. Tarasov, Artem, "Horror Tales from Central Planning," *Orbis*, 34, no. 4 (Fall 1990), 527-30.

2927. Tedstrom, John E., "Economic Slide Continues," *Report on the USSR*, 2, no. 37 (14 Sept. 1990), 9-12.

2928. -----, "The Fate of Economic Reform in the Soviet Union," *Report on the USSR*, 2, no. 40 (5 Oct. 1990), 4-5.

2929. -----, "First Quarter Economic Results: Can It Get Any Worse?" *Report on the USSR*, 2, no. 22 (1 June 1990), 5-6.

2930. -----, "Gorbachev Redefines Socialist Economics," *Report on the USSR*, 2, no. 41 (12 Oct. 1990), 8-10.

2931. -----, "Goskomstat Report for 1989: An Economy Out of Control," *Report on the USSR*, 2, no. 7 (16 Feb. 1990), 1-5.

2932. -----, "On *Perestroyka*: Analyzing the `Basic Provisions'," *Problems of Communism*, 36, no. 4 (July-Aug. 1987), 93-98.

2933. -----, "Party to Play Smaller Role in Making Economic Policy," *Report on the USSR*, 2, no. 29 (20 July 1990), 4-6.

2934. -----, "Russia's Radical Reform Program," *Report on the USSR*, 3, no. 20 (17 May 1991), 22-26.

2935. -----, "What to Expect in the New Stage of Economic Reform," *Report on the USSR*, 2, no. 16 (20 Apr. 1990), 1-3.

2936. Thorniley, Daniel, "Soviet Reform Bogs Down: Acceleration in the Autumn?" *Business in Eastern Europe*, 19, no. 31 (30 July 1990), 249-50.

2937. Vanous, Jan, "Some Thoughts on Western Economic Strategy vis-a-vis the Soviet Union," *Global Affairs*, 3, no. 3 (Summer 1988), 137-41.

2938. Vickers, John, and George Yarrow, "Economic Perspectives on Privatization," *Journal of Economic Perspectives*, 5, no. 2 (Spring 1991), 111-32.

2939. Vitebsky, P., "Perestroika among the Reindeer Herders," *Geography Magazine*, 61 (June 1989), 22-25.

2940. Volkov, A., "Financial Statistics and the Transition to a Market Economy," *Problems of Economics*, 34, no. 7 (Nov. 1991), 82-91.

2941. Vol'skii, A., "The Market and Economic Stabilization," *Problems of Economics*, 34, no. 9 (Jan. 1992), 48-64.

2942. Wagener, H-J., "The Market and the State under Perestroika," *Kyklos*, 43, no. 3 (1990), 359-83.

2943. Wanniski, Jude, "The Future of Russian Capitalism," *Foreign Affairs*, 71, no. 2 (Spring 1990), 17-25.

2944. Wegren, Stephen K., "Food Prices in the USSR," *Report on the USSR*, 2, no. 12 (23 Mar. 1990), 13-15.

2945. -----, "Market Reform and Public Opinion," *Report on the USSR*, 2, no. 48 (30 Nov. 1990), 4-8.

2946. Weickhardt, George G., "Capitalists for *Perestroika*," *Bulletin of the Atomic Scientists*, 44, no. 5 (June 1988), 30-34.

2947. -----, "Gorbachev's Record on Economic Reform," *Soviet Union/Union Sovietique*, 12, no. 3 (1985), 251-76.

2948. "The West's Prescription for the Soviet Union," *Economist*, 317 (22 Dec. 1990), 61-62.

2949. Whitesell, Robert S., "Why Does the Soviet Economy Appear to be Allocatively Efficient?" *Soviet Studies*, 42, no. 2 (Apr. 1990), 259-68.

2950. Wilhelm, John Howard, "The Soviet Economic Failure: Brutzkus Revisited," *Europe-Asia Studies*, 45, no. 2 (1993), 343ff.

2951. Young, Cathy, "'Bombzh' Away," *New Republic* (29 Jan. 1990), 18-21.

2952. -----, "Creeping Capitalism in the Soviet Union," *American Spectator*, 23, no. 3 (Mar. 1990), 12-14.

2953. Zaslavskaia, Tatiana [anonymously], "The Novosibirsk Report," *Survey*, 28 (Spring 1984), 88-108.

2954. -----, "Urgent Problems in the Theory of Economic Sociology," *Soviet Sociology*, 27 (1988), 7-27.

2955. Zaslavsky, Victor, "Three Years of *Perestroika*," *Telos*, no. 74 (Winter 1987-88), 31-41.

XVII. Education and Social Studies

BOOKS

2956. Avis, George, ed., *The Making of the Soviet Citizen: Character Formation and Civic Training in Soviet Education* (New York: Croom Helm, 1987).

2957. -----, *Soviet Higher and Vocational Education from Khrushchev to Gorbachev* (Bradford: University of Bradford, Modern Languages Centre, 1987).

2958. Dunstan, John, ed., *Soviet Education under Scrutiny* (Glasgow: Jordanhill College Publications, 1987).

2959. Eklof, Ben, and Edward Dneprov, eds., *Democracy in the Russian School: The Reform Movement in Education Since 1984* (Boulder, CO: Westview Press, 1993).

2960. Jones, Anthony, ed., *Education and Society in the New Russia* (Armonk, NY: M. E. Sharpe, 1994).

2961. Muckle, James, *Education in Russia Past and Present: An Introductory Study Guide and Select Bibliography* (Nottingham: Bramcote Press, 1993).

2962. -----, *A Guide to the Soviet Curriculum: What the Russian Child Is Taught in School* (London: Croom Helm, Ltd., 1988).

2963. -----, *Portrait of a Soviet School Under Glasnost* (New York: St. Martin's Press, 1990).

2964. Pearson, Landon, *Children of Glasnost: Growing up Soviet* (Seattle: University of Washington Press, 1990).

2965. Puffer, Sheila M., ed., *The Russian Management Revolution: Preparing Managers for the Market Economy* (Armonk, NY: M. E. Sharpe, 1992).

2966. Sorrentino, Frank M., and Frances R. Curcio, eds., *Soviet Politics and Education* (Lanham, MD: University Press of America, 1986).

2967. Yanowitch, Murray, ed., *New Directions in Soviet Social Thought* (Armonk, NY: M. E. Sharpe, 1989).

ARTICLES

2968. Ailes, Catherine P., and Francis W. Rushing, "Soviet Math and Science Educational Reforms During *Perestroika*," *Technology in Society*, 13, no. 1-2 (1991), 109-22.

2969. Alexander, John C. T., "Education and the Former Soviet Republics," *AAASS Newsletter*, 32, no. 3 (May 1992), 3.

2970. Avis, G., "The Soviet Higher Education Reform: Proposals and Reactions," *Comparative Education*, 26, no. 1 (1990), 5-12.

2971. Balzer, Harley, "From Hypercentralization to Diversity: Continuing Efforts to Restructure Soviet Education," *Technology in Society*, 13, no. 1-2 (1991), 123-50.

2972. Black, J. L., "Perestroika and the Soviet General School: The CPSU Loses Control of the Ideological Dimension of *Vospitanie*," *Canadian Slavonic Papers*, 33, no. 1 (Mar. 1991), 1-18.

2973. Bolkhovitinov, N. N., "Improving the Quality of American Studies in the Post-Soviet Era," *Chronicle of Higher Education*, 38 (19 Feb. 1992), A40.

2974. Bollag, Burton, "Baltic Republics Ask New Education Leaders to Rid Their Universities of Soviet Influence," *Chronicle of Higher Education*, 36, no. 42 (5 July 1990), A31.

2975. -----, "For Educators in the Baltics, Overcoming Soviet Legacy Is Harder Than Expected," *Chronicle of Higher Education*, 38, no. 10 (30 Oct. 1991), A40-42.

2976. -----, "Lithuanian Scholar Leads Effort to Save Country's Jewish History," *Chronicle of Higher Education*, 38, no. 17 (18 Dec. 1991), A37-38.

2977. -----, "Lithuania to Give University Full Autonomy and Academic Freedom," *Chronicle of Higher Education*, 36, no. 39 (13 June 1990), A33ff.

2978. -----, "Reform of Eastern Europe's Universities Proving to Be a Tough, Long-Term Task," *Chronicle of Higher Education*, 37, no. 46 (31 July 1991), A1ff.

2979. -----, and Susannah Massey, "Soviet Crackdown in Baltic Republic Ends Optimism for Higher-Education Reforms," *Chronicle of Higher Education*, 37, no. 19 (23 Jan. 1991), A1ff.

2980. Brodinsky, Ben, "The Changing Role of the Soviet Secondary School Principal under Perestroika," *NASSP Bulletin*, 75, no. 535 (May 1991), 59-70.

2981. -----, "The Impact of *Perestroika* on Soviet Education," *Phi Delta Kappan*, 73 (Jan. 1992), 378-85.

2982. -----, "Soviet Secondary Principals under *Perestroika*: Changing Roles," *Education Digest*, 57 (Oct. 1991), 7-11.

2983. Brown, Archie, "Tat'yana Zaslavskaya and Soviet Sociology: An Introduction," *Social Research*, 55, no. 1-2 (Spring-Summer 1988), Part 2, 261-66.

2984. Buchholz, Arnold, "The Ongoing Deconstruction of Marxism-Leninism," *Studies in Soviet Thought*, 40, no. 1-3 (Aug-Nov. 1990), 231-40.

2985. Craig, Diane, "Estonian Business School Pioneers," *AABS Newsletter*, 13, no. 3 (Aug. 1989), 13-14.

2986. "A Destiny Born of *Perestroika*: An Interview with Lidiia Vasil'evna Kiriachkova," *Soviet Education*, 32, no. 8 (Aug. 1990), 17-26.

2987. Drechsler, Wolfgang "Reuniting German Higher Education and Research," *World Affairs*, 154, no. 1 (Summer 1991), 5-8.

2988. "Emphasis Has Shifted from the Expansion of Higher and Specialized Secondary Education to Their Qualitative Improvement," *Higher Education in Europe*, 14, no. 1 (1989), 108-11.

2989. Georgeoff, John, "Eastern Europe: Survey of Events, 1989," *Comparative Education Review*, 34, no. 2 (May 1990), 285-86.

2990. Gershunsky, Boris S., and Robert T. Pullin, "Current Dilemmas for Soviet Secondary Education: An Anglo-Soviet Analysis," *Comparative Education*, 26, nos. 2-3 (1990), 307-18.

2991. Gleazer, E. J., Jr., "Perestroika in Soviet Education," *Community, Technical and Junior College Journal*, 58 (Feb-Mar. 1988), 47-48.

2992. Hilkes, Peter, "The Estonian SSR as an Example of Soviet School Reform in the 1980s," *Journal of Baltic Studies*, 18, no. 4 (1987), 349-66.

2993. Hollander, Paul, "Communism's Collapse Won't Faze the Marxists in Academe," *Chronicle of Higher Education*, 36, no. 36 (23 May 1990), A44.

2994. Iagodin, G. A., "'Only a Free School Will Educate a Free Person...," *Soviet Review*, 32, no. 6 (Nov-Dec. 1991), 76-88.

2995. -----, "The Restructuring of the Higher Education System and Continuing Education," *Soviet Education* (July-Aug. 1987), 94-117.

2996. "Information: USSR," *Higher Education in Europe*, 14, no. 2 (1989), 99-103; no. 3 (1989), 88-91.

2997. James, W. A., "A Promising Future: The Fulbright Program with the USSR," *Annals of the American Academy of Political and Social Science*, no. 491 (May 1987), 118-25.

2998. Kaser, Michael, Ronald Amann and Robert Porter, "Area Studies in a Changing World: Three Views," *Journal of Communist Studies*, 7, no. 3 (Sept. 1991), 376ff.

2999. Katznelson, Y., "What the 'Znanye' Society Should Be Like," *Religion in Communist Dominated Areas*, 30, no. 2 (1991), 27-28.

3000. Kerr, Stephen T., "Educational Reform and Technological Change: Computing Literacy in the Soviet Union," *Comparative Education Review*, 35, no. 2 (May 1991), 222-54.

3001. -----, "Reform in Soviet and American Education: Parallels and Contrasts," *Phi Delta Kappan*, 71 (Sept. 1989), 19-28.

3002. -----, "Soviet Applications of Microcomputers in Education: Developments in Research and Practice during the Gorbachev Era," *Journal of Educational Computing Research*, 3, no. 1 (1987), 1-17.

3003. -----, "Soviet Union-Survey of Events, 1989," *Comparative Education Review*, 34, no. 2 (May 1990), 283-84.

3004. -----, "Will Glasnost Lead to Perestroika? Directions of Educational Reform in the USSR," *Educational Researcher*, 19 (Oct. 1990), 26-31.

3005. King, Gundar T., and David McNabb, "Education for Business in Latvia," *Lituanus*, 36, no. 1 (Spring 1990), 59-70.

3006. Kondakov, M. I., "The Road to Educational Reform in the USSR," *Prospects*, 17, no. 1 (1987), 27-35.

3007. Kostin, L. A., "The Development of Vocational Guidance in the USSR," *International Labour Review*, 125, no. 6 (Nov-Dec. 1986), 715-29.

3008. Kuebart, Friedrich, "Soviet Education and Comparative Research: A German View," *Comparative Education*, 25, no. 3 (1989), 283-317.

3009. Kuritsyn, Alexander, "Progress Is Difficult and Slow, But 'Perestroika' Is Changing the Lives of Soviet Scholars," *Chronicle of Higher Education*, 36, no. 22 (14 Feb. 1990), A44.

3010. Long, Delbert H., "Continuity and Change in Soviet Education under Gorbachev," *American Educational Research Journal*, 27, no. 3 (Fall 1990), 403-23.

3011. Massey, Susannah, "Amid Economic Clamor, Gorbachev Issues Decree Granting Autonomy to Academic Institutions," *Chronicle of Higher Education*, 37, no. 8 (24 Oct. 1990), A35ff.

3012. -----, "Education Official in Russian Republic Wants to End Moscow's Control of Academic System," *Chronicle of Higher Education*, 36, no. 45 (25 July 1990), A31.

3013. -----, "Soviet Plans for a Market Economy Already in Focus at Some of Moscow's Higher-Education Institutes," *Chronicle of Higher Education*, 37, no. 4 (26 Sept. 1990), 49ff.

3014. Merkuriev, S., "'Soviet' Higher Education in a Changing Political, Social and Economic Context: A Scenario for the Future," *Prospects*, 21, no. 3 (1991), 413-20.

3015. "The New Vytautas Didysis University in Lithuania," *AABS Newsletter*, 13, no. 4 (Dec. 1989), 15.

3016. Nikandrov, Nikolai D., "What to Compare, When and Why: A Soviet Perspective," *Comparative Education*, 25, no. 3 (1989), 275-82.

3017. Onushkin, Victor Grigorievich, "Social Progress, Scientific and Technological Progress, and Education," *Soviet Education*, 30, no. 6 (June 1988), 11-33.

3018. Orlov, A., and Iu. Tkachenko, "How to Teach About the Market Economy," *Soviet Education*, 33, no. 11 (Nov. 1991), 11-14.

3019. Peschar, Jules L., and Roel Popping, "Educational Opportunity in Five East European Countries," *Comparative Education Review*, 35, no. 1 (Feb. 1991), 154-69.

3020. Popov, N. P., *et al.*, "Soviet and American Secondary School Students on War and Peace," *Soviet Sociology*, 28, no. 4 (July-Aug. 1989), 81ff.

3021. Rainer, Stephan, "Helplessness at a System Left in a Shambles," *World Affairs*, 154, no. 1 (Summer 1991), 34-35.

3022. Read, Gerald H., "Education in the Soviet Union: Has *Perestroika* Met Its Match?" *Phi Delta Kappan*, 70 (Apr. 1989), 606-13.

3023. Reszel, Daniel, "Building Bridges in Nursing: How American and Russian Nursing Educators Are Sharing Their Knowledge," *Vocational Education Journal*, 66, no. 5 (May 1991), 32-33.

3024. Riabchenko, A., "Cost Accounting: Dictatorship or Freedom?" *Soviet Review*, 32, no. 5 (Sept-Oct. 1991), 74-81.

3025. Riabov, V., "The Restructuring of Education: Ways to Accelerate It," *Soviet Education*, 33, no. 7 (July 1991), 3-25.

3026. Rossabi, Mary J., "Education in Leningrad as the Berlin Wall Fell," *Education Digest* (May 1991), 19-21.

3027. Seymore, J. W., "The Instructors and Principal at a Leningrad School Challenge Rigidities in Soviet Education," *People Weekly*, 27 (6 Apr. 1987), 104-07.

3028. Shalin, Dmitri N., "Sociology for the Glasnost Era: Institutional and Substantive Changes in Recent Soviet Sociology," *Social Forces*, 68, no. 4 (June 1990), 1019-40.

3029. "Soviet Ministry [of Education] Takes Rap For Failing to Push Perestroika," *Times Higher Education Supplement*, no. 800 (4 Mar. 1988), 8.

3030. Spence Richards, P., "Education and Training for Information Science in the Soviet Union," *Annual Review of Information Science and Technology*, 27 (1992), 267-90.

3031. "Stacking the Texts," *Progressive*, 54, no.7 (July 1990), 8.

3032. Stein, Jonathan, "Central and Eastern Europe Civic Education Project," *PS*, 24, no. 4 (Dec. 1991), 798.

3033. Stern, Paul C., and Jo L. Husbands, "Liberating Soviet Social Science," *Bulletin of the Atomic Scientists*, 45, no. 7 (Sept. 1989), 28-31.

3034. Sukharev, A. Y., "The Legal Education of Workers and Managers in the USSR," *International Labour Review*, 127, no. 5 (1988), 613-26.

3035. Tamm, Boris, "Moving Towards a Real University Education," *AABS Newsletter*, 13, no. 4 (Dec. 1989), 1-2.

3036. Tolz, Vera, "Russian Academy of Sciences to Be Set Up," *Report on the USSR*, 2, no. 7 (16 Feb. 1990), 19-20.

3037. -----, "The USSR Academy of Sciences in Crisis," *Report on the USSR*, 2, no. 23 (8 June 1990), 9-12.

3038. Tomiak, Janusz, "Education in the Baltic States, Ukraine, Belarus', and Russia," *Comparative Education*, 28, no. 1 (1992), 33-44.

3039. Traver, N., "Restructuring the 3 R's," *Time*, 133 (10 Apr. 1989), 96-97.

3040. Treml, Vladimir G., "*Perestroika* and Soviet Statistics," *Soviet Economy*, 4, no. 1 (Jan-Mar. 1988), 65-94.

3041. -----, "Soviet Statistics and Gorbachev's Reforms," *AAASS Newsletter*, 29, no. 3 (May 1989), 5-6.

3042. Trout, Thomas, "The Educational Challenge of Gorbachev's *Perestroika*: What Do We Know? What Can We Teach?" *Educational Leadership*, 46, no. 4 (Dec. 1988-Jan. 1989), 72-74.

3043. -----, "The Soviet Challenge to American Education," *Education Digest*, 54 (Apr. 1989), 35-37.

3044. Tselishcheva, T., "Experimental Sites: The Path to the New School," *Russian Social Science Review*, 33, no. 2 (Mar-Apr. 1992), 57-82.

3045. Van der Veer, Rene, "The Reform of Soviet Psychology: A Historical Perspective," *Studies in Soviet Thought*, 40, no. 1-3 (Aug-Nov. 1990), 205-21.

3046. Vikhanskii, O. S., "Let's Train Managers for the Market Economy," *Soviet Education*, 33, no. 11 (Nov. 1991), 37-44.

3047. Vinokurova, U. A., "The Role of School Education in the Modern Life of the Nationalities of the North," *Soviet Education*, 32 (May 1990), 93-103.

3048. Walker, P., "Soviets to Launch Far-Reaching Reforms," *Times Higher Education Supplement*, no. 739 (2 Jan. 1987), 2.

3049. -----, "USSR Set to Start Ambitious Reform of Education System," *Chronicle of Higher Education*, 33 (28 Jan. 1987), 1ff.

3050. Wellington, Jerry, "Mixed Brew," *Times Educational Supplement*, no. 3910 (7 June 1991), 45.

3051. White, John, "Values Education for the Age of Perestroika," *Oxford Review of Education*, 15, no. 1 (1989), 29-40.

3052. Zaslavskaia, Tatiana, "*Perestroika* and Sociology," *Social Research*, 55, no. 2 (Spring-Summer 1988), Part 2, 267-76.

XVIII. Environmental Matters; Chernobyl

BOOKS

3053. Bailey, C. C., *The Aftermath of Chernobyl: History's Worst Nuclear Reactor Accident* (Dubuque, Iowa: Kendall/Hunt Publishing Co., 1989).

3054. Barr, Brenton M., and Kathleen E. Braden, *The Disappearing Russian Forest: A Dilemma in Soviet Resource Management* (London: Hutchison Education, 1988).

3055. DeBardeleben, Joan, ed., *To Breathe Free: Eastern Europe's Environmental Crisis* (Washington, DC: The Woodrow Wilson Center Press, 1991).

3056. Feshbach, Murray, and Alfred Friendly, Jr., *Ecocide in the USSR: Health and Nature under Siege* (New York: Basic Books, 1992).

3057. Flavin, Christopher, *Reassessing Nuclear Power: The*

Fallout from Chernobyl (Washington, DC: Worldwatch Institute, 1987).

3058. Gale, Robert P., and Thomas Hauser, *Final Warning: The Legacy of Chernobyl* (New York: Warner Books, 1988).

3059. Gould, Jay M., Benjamin A. Goldman and Kate Millpointer, *Deadly Deceit: Low Level Radiation, High Level Cover-Up* (New York: Four Walls Eight Windows, 1990).

3060. Gould, Peter, *Fire in the Rain: The Democratic Consequences of Chernobyl* (Baltimore: Johns Hopkins University Press, 1990).

3061. Green, Eric, *Ecology and Perestroika: Environmental Protection in the Soviet Union* (Washington, DC: American Committee on US-Soviet Relations, n. d.).

3062. Hamman, Henry, and Stuart Parrott, *Mayday at Chernobyl: One Year On, The Facts Revealed* (London: New English Library, 1987).

3063. Hawkes, Nigel, *Chernobyl: The End of the Nuclear Dream* (New York: Vintage, 1987).

3064. Haynes, Viktor, and Marko Bojcun, *The Chernobyl Disaster: The True Story of a Catastrophe-an Unanswerable Indictment of Nuclear Power* (London: Hogarth Press, 1988).

3065. Jancar, Barbara, *Environmental Management in the Soviet Union and Yugoslavia* (Durham, NC: Duke University Press, 1987).

3066. Khabibullov, Marat R., Joan T. DeBardeleben and Arthur B. Sacks, *New Trends in Soviet Environmental Policy* (Indianapolis: Universities Field Staff International, 1990).

3067. Lemeshev, Mikhail, *Bureaucrats in Power: Ecological Collapse* (Moscow: Progress, 1990).

3068. Mangan, Bonnie F., *Chernobyl Accident and Its Aftermath* (Washington, DC: Library of Congress, Congressional Research Service, 1987).

3069. Marples, David R., *Chernobyl and Nuclear Power in the USSR* (New York: St. Martin's Press, 1986).

3070. -----, *The Social Impact of the Chernobyl Disaster* (New York: St. Martin's Press, 1988).

3071. Medvedev, Grigory, *No Breathing Room: The Aftermath of Chernobyl* (New York: Basic Books, 1993).

3072. -----, *The Truth About Chernobyl* (New York: Basic Books, 1991).

3073. Medvedev, Zhores A., *The Legacy of Chernobyl* (New York: W. W. Norton, 1990).

3074. Micklin, Philip P., *The Water Management Crisis in Soviet Central Asia*, The Carl Beck Papers in Russian and East European Studies, no. 905 (Pittsburgh: University of Pittsburgh Center for Russian and East European Studies, 1991).

3075. Mould, Richard F., *Chernobyl: The Real Story* (New York: Pergamon Press, 1988).

3076. Park, Chris C., *Chernobyl: The Long Shadow* (London: Routledge, 1989).

3077. Peterson, D. J., *Troubled Lands: The Legacy of Soviet Environmental Destruction* (Boulder, CO: Westview Press, 1993).

3078. Pryde, Philip R., *Environmental Management in the Soviet Union* (Cambridge: Cambridge University Press, 1991).

3079. Read, Piers Paul, *Ablaze: The Story of the Heroes and Victims of Chernobyl* (New York: Random House, 1993).

3080. Rozengurt, Michael, *The Soviet Water Crisis: Exposing an Environmental Disaster* (Boulder, CO: Westview Press, 1991).

3081. Sandberg, Mikael, ed., *Baltic Sea Region Environmental Protection: "Eastern" Perspectives and International Cooperation* (Goteborg: Almqvist & Wiksell International, 1992).

3082. Segerstahl, Boris, ed., *Chernobyl: A Policy Response Study* (New York: Springer-Verlag, 1991).

3083. Shcherbak, Iurii, *Chernobyl: A Documentary Story* (London: Macmillan, 1989).

3084. Silver, L. Ray, *Fallout from Chernobyl* (Toronto: Deneau, 1987).

3085. Singleton, Fred, ed., *Environmental Problems in the Soviet Union & Eastern Europe* (Boulder, CO: Lynne Rienner Publishers, Inc., 1987).

3086. Stewart, John Massey, ed., *The Soviet Environment: Problems, Policies and Politics* (New York: Cambridge University Press, 1992).

3087. Turnbull, Mildred, *Soviet Environmental Policies and Practices: The Most Critical Investment* (Brookfield, VT: Dartmouth Publishing Co., 1991).

3088. US Central Intelligence Agency, Directorate of Intelligence, *Soviet Energy Resource Handbook: A Reference Aid* (Washington, DC: CIA, 1990).

3089. US Congress. House. Committee on Energy and Commerce. Subcommittee on Energy Conservation and Power. *Soviet Nuclear Accident at Chernobyl: Briefing and Hearing.* 99th Congress, 1 and 7 May 1987 (Washington, DC: Government Printing Office, 1987).

3090. US Congress. House. Committee on Energy and Commerce. Subcommittee on Energy Research and Production. *Positive Safety Features of U.S. Nuclear Reactors: Technical Lessons Confirmed at Chernobyl. Hearing.* 99th Congress, 14 May 1986 (Washington, DC: Government Printing Office, 1986).

3091. US Congress. House. Committee on Energy and Commerce. Subcommittee on Oversight and Investigations. *Report of the Delegation to Latvia on the State of the Environment (March 30 to April 10, 1990).* 101st Congress, 2nd Session (Washington, DC: Government Printing Office, 1990).

3092. US Congress. Joint Economic Committee. Subcommittee on Agriculture and Transportation. *The Chernobyl Disaster: Implications for World Food Security and the U.S. Farm*

Economy. Hearing, 99th Congress, 5 May 1986 (Washington, DC: Government Printing Office, 1987).

3093. US Congress. Senate. Committee on Energy and Natural Resources. *The Chernobyl Accident: Hearing.* 99th Congress, 19 June 1986 (Washington, DC: Government Printing Office, 1986).

3094. US Congress. Senate. Committee on Labor and Human Resources. *The Chernobyl, Russia, Nuclear Accident: Hearing.* 100th Congress, 20 Jan. 1987 (Washington, DC: Government Printing Office, 1987).

3095. US Department of Energy. *Report on the Accident at the Chernobyl Nuclear Power Station* (Washington, DC: US Nuclear Regulatory Commission, 1987).

3096. US Department of Energy. Assistant Secretary for Nuclear Energy. *Report of the U.S. Department of Energy's Team Analyses of the Chernobyl 1-4 Atomic Energy Station Accident Sequence* (Washington, DC: US Department of Energy, 1986).

3097. US Department of Energy. Office of Energy Research. Office of Health and Environmental Research. *Health and Environmental Consequences of the Chernobyl Nuclear Power Plant Accident* (Washington, DC: US Department of Energy, and Springfield, VA: US Department of Commerce, National Technical Information Center, 1987).

3098. US General Accounting Office. *Nuclear Safety: Comparison of DOE's Hanford N-Reactor with the Chernobyl Reactor: Briefing Report to Congressional Requesters, August 1986* (Washington, DC: General Accounting Office, 1986).

3099. US Nuclear Regulatory Commission. *Implications of the Accident at Chernobyl for Safety Regulations of Commercial Nuclear Power Plants in the United States: Final Report*, 2 vols. (Washington, DC: Nuclear Regulatory Agency, 1989).

3100. Weiner, Douglas R., *Models of Nature: Ecology, Conservation, and Cultural Revolution in Soviet Russia* (Bloomington: Indiana University Press, 1988).

3101. Worley, Norman, and Jeffrey Lewins, eds., *The Chernobyl Accident and Its Implications for the United Kingdom* (New York: Elsevier Applied Science Publishers, 1988).

3102. Ziegler, Charles E., *Environmental Policy in the USSR* (Amherst: University of Massachusetts Press, 1987).

ARTICLES

3103. Abrams, Herbert L., "Chernobyl-The Emerging Story: How Radiation Victims Suffer," *Bulletin of the Atomic Scientists*, 42, no. 7 (Aug-Sept. 1986), 13.

3104. Albright, David, "Chernobyl and the U.S. Nuclear Industry," *Bulletin of the Atomic Scientists*, 42, no. 9 (Nov. 1986), 38-40.

3105. Amerisov, Alexander, "Chernobyl-The Emerging Story: A Chronology of Soviet Media Coverage," *Bulletin of the Atomic Scientists*, 42, no. 7 (Aug-Sept. 1986), 38-39.

3106. Anspaugh, L. R., *et al.*, "The Global Impact of the Chernobyl Reactor Accident," *Science*, 242 (16 Dec. 1988), 1513-19.

3107. Arbatov, Georgi A., "The Chernobyl Boomerang," *World Press Review*, 33 (July 1986), 47-48.

3108. "As the Dust Settles from Chernobyl, Carl Sagan Sounds a Warning About Technological Recklessness," *People Weekly*, 25 (19 May 1986), 57ff.

3109. Ausubel, Jesse H., "Chernobyl After *Perestroika*: Reflections on a Recent Visit," *Technology in Society*, 14, no. 2 (1992), 187-98.

3110. Barringer, Felicity, "Chernobyl, Five Years Later the Danger Persists," *New York Times Magazine* (14 Apr. 1991), 28-32.

3111. Baskaran, M., *et al.*, "Environmental Radiocesium in Subarctic and Arctic Alaska Following Chernobyl," *Arctic*, 44, no. 4 (1991), 346-50.

3112. Bennett, J., "A New Chernobyl Debate," *Maclean's*, 101 (21 Mar. 1988), 6.

3113. Beroset, D., "The Children of Chernobyl & Other Stories from Inside Russia Today," *Ladies Home Journal*, 103 (Oct. 1986), 116ff.

3114. Bethe, Hans A., "U.S. Panel Assesses Chernobyl," *Bulletin of the Atomic Scientists*, 42, no. 10 (Dec. 1986), 45-46.

3115. Bohatiuk, Yurii, "The Chernobyl Disaster," *Ukrainian Quarterly*, 42, no. 1-2 (Spring-Summer 1986), 5-21.

3116. Bond, Andrew R., and Kurt Piepenburg, "Land Reclamation after Surface Mining in the USSR: Economic, Political and Legal Issues," *Soviet Geography*, 31, no. 5 (May 1990), 332-65.

3117. Bowers, Stephen R., "Soviet and Post-Soviet Environmental Problems," *Journal of Social, Political and Economic Studies*, 18, no. 2 (Summer 1993), 131-58.

3118. Brown, Bess, "The Strength of Kazakhstan's Antinuclear Lobby," *Report on the USSR*, 3, no. 4 (18 Jan. 1991), 23-24.

3119. Bungs, Dzintra, "Latvia's Major River Suffers Disastrous Pollution," *Report on the USSR*, 2, no. 47 (23 Nov. 1990), 19-21.

3120. Chalidze, Francheska, "Nitrate Pollution in the USSR," *Freedom at Issue*, no. 115 (July-Aug. 1990), 27-28.

3121. "The Chernobyl Lessons," *America*, 154 (17 May 1986), 393.

3122. "Chernobyl: New Estimates of Deaths, Concerns for Food Chain," *Environment*, 28 (Sept. 1986), 22.

3123. "Chernobyl: 3 Years After," *FDA Consumer*, 23 (Apr. 1989), 38-39.

3124. "Chernobyl's Legacy" (Special Section), *World Press Review*, 33 (July 1986), 35-41.

3125. "Chornobyl Report," *Ukrainian Quarterly*, 48, no. 3 (Fall 1982), 288-308.

3126. Clines, Francis X., "A New Arena for Nationalism: Chernobyl," *New York Times* (30 Dec. 1990), 1, 8.

3127. "The Cloud Over Gorbachev," *Economist*, 299 (24 May 1986), 13-14.

3128. Cochran, Thomas, and Frank von Hippel, "Chernobyl-The Emerging Story: Estimating Long-Term Health Effects," *Bulletin of the Atomic Scientists*, 42, no. 7 (Aug-Sept. 1986), 18-24.

3129. "Correspondence: Two Views on Chernobyl," *Contemporary Review*, 250, no. 1454 (Mar. 1987), 158-60.

3130. Cortese, A., "Glasnost, Perestroika, and the Environment," *Environmental Science and Technology*, 23, no. 10 (Oct. 1989), 1212-13.

3131. Critchlow, James, "Uzbek Writer on Threat Posed by Radioactive Waste," *Report on the USSR*, 2, no. 10 (9 Mar. 1990), 19-21.

3132. Darst, Robert G., Jr., "Environmentalism in the USSR: The Opposition to the River Diversion Projects," *Soviet Economy*, 4, no. 3 (July-Sept. 1988), 223-52.

3133. Davis, L., "Concern Over Chernobyl Tainted Birds," *Science News*, 130 (26 July 1986), 54.

3134. DeBardeleben, Joan, "Economic Reform and Environmental Protection in the USSR," *Soviet Geography*, 31, no. 4 (Apr. 1990), 237-56.

3135. Dejevsky, Mary, "The Soviets and Chernobyl," *World Press Review*, 33 (Aug. 1986), 61.

3136. Demko, George J., "Report on Reports: Two Reports on the Environment of the USSR," *Environment*, 32 (Dec. 1990), 25-26.

3137. Dickman, S., "Chernobyl's Effects Not as Bad as Feared," *Nature*, 351 (30 May 1991), 335.

3138. Dickson, D., "*Glasnost* and the Soviet Environment," *Science*, 236 (5 June 1987), 1180.

3139. -----, "Soviets Admit 1957 Nuclear Mishap," *Science*, 244 (23 June 1989), 1435.

3140. -----, "Soviet Union Suspends Plans to Divert Four Rivers," *Science*, 233 (5 Sept. 1986), 1036.

3141. D'Monte, Darryl, "Gorbachev Goes Goes (Pale) Green," *World Press Review*, 40 (July 1993), 52.

3142. Dorman, William A., and Daniel Hirsch, "Chernobyl-The Emerging Story: The U.S. Media's Slant," *Bulletin of the Atomic Scientists*, 42, no. 7 (Aug-Sept. 1986), 54-56.

3143. Edwards, Mike, "Chernobyl-One Year After," *National Geographic*, 171, no. 5 (May 1987), 633-53.

3144. Elliot, I., "Deadly Winds: One Year After Chernobyl," *Reader's Digest*, 130 (May 1987), 129-33.

3145. Ellis, William S., "The Aral: A Soviet Sea Lies Dying," *National Geographic*, 177, no. 2 (Feb. 1990), 73-92.

3146. "An Environment of Desolation," *Glasnost*, 3, no. 3 (Jan-Apr. 1991), 34-47.

3147. "Environmental Law Developments in the Soviet Union," *Pace Environmental Law Review*, 5 (Spring 1988), 345-546.

3148. "Environmental Law in the USSR and the United Kingdom: A Symposium," *Connecticut Journal of International Law*, 4 (Winter 1989), 261-511.

3149. Finder, Susan, "The Price of Progress," *Wilson Quarterly*, 9, no. 4 (Autumn 1985), 68-69.

3150. Fischer, David A. V., "Chernobyl-The Emerging Story: The International Response," *Bulletin of the Atomic Scientists*, 42, no. 7 (Aug-Sept. 1986), 46-48.

3151. French, Hilary F., "Eastern Europe's Clean Break," *World Watch*, 4, no. 2 (Mar-Apr. 1991), 21-27.

3152. -----, "Environmental Problems and Policies in the Soviet Union," *Current History*, 90, no. 558 (Oct. 1991), 333-37.

3153. -----, "Green Revolutions: Environmental Reconstruction in Eastern Europe and the Soviet Union," *Columbia Journal of World Business*, 26, no. 1 (Spring 1991), 28-52.

3154. Galazii, Grigori, "Lake Baikal Reprieved," *Endeavor*, 15, no. 1 (Winter 1991), 13-18.

3155. Gale, Robert P., "Calculated Risk: Radiation and Chernobyl," *Journal of Communication*, 37, no. 3 (Summer 1987), 68-73.

3156. -----, "Chernobyl: Answers Slipping Away," *Bulletin of the Atomic Scientists*, 46, no. 7 (Sept. 1990), 144-45.

3157. Glantz, Michael, and Igor Zonn, "A Quiet Chernobyl," *World & I*, 6, no. 9 (Sept. 1991), 324-29.

3158. Glazovskiy, N. F., "Ideas on an Escape from the `Aral Crisis'," *Soviet Geography*, 32, no. 2 (Feb. 1991), 73-89.

3159. Gleason, Gregory, "The Struggle for Control over Water in Central Asia: Republican Sovereignty and Collective Action," *Report on the USSR*, 3, no. 25 (21 June 1991), 11-19.

3160. Goldman, Marshall I., "Keeping the Cold War Out of Chernobyl," *Technology Review*, 89, no. 5 (July 1986), 18-19.

3161. -----, "Soviet Energy Runs Out of Gas," *Current History*, 89, no. 549 (Oct. 1990), 313ff.

3162. Gorbachev, Mikhail S., "The Chernobyl Accident," *Vital Speeches of the Day*, 52 (15 June 1986), 514-17.

3163. "The Greening of the Soviet Union," *Glasnost*, 3, no. 2 (Oct-Dec. 1990), 34-43.

3164. Grinevetskiy, V. T., *et al.*, "Regional Ecological Problems of the Ukraine: Theoretical and Methodological Aspects," *Soviet Geography*, 32, no. 8 (Oct. 1991), 533-37.

3165. Gros, Daniel, and Erik Jones, "Soviet Energy Reforms: A Key to Success," *International Economic Insights*, 2, no. 5 (Sept-Oct. 1991), 15-17.

3166. Hall, Barbara Welling, "Soviet Perceptions of Global Ecological Interdependence: Some Implications of `New Political Thinking'," *Soviet Union/Union Sovietique*, 15, no.1 (1988), 31-43.

3167. Halverson, Thomas, "Ticking Time Bombs: East European Reactors," *Bulletin of the Atomic Scientists*, 49, no. 6 (July-Aug. 1993), 43ff.

3168. Hamilton, John Maxwell, "Will Pollution Kill the Revolution?" *Bulletin of the Atomic Scientists*, 47, no. 5 (June 1991), 12-18.

3169. Hewett, Ed A., *et al.*, "Panel on the Economic and Political Consequences of Chernobyl'," *Soviet Economy*, 2, no. 2 (Apr-June 1986), 97-130.

3170. Hodkova, Iveta, "Is There a Right to a Healthy Environment in the International Legal Order?" *Connecticut Journal of International Law*, 7, no. 1 (Fall 1991), 65-80.

3171. Hoffmann, Eric P., "Chernobyl-The Emerging Story: Nuclear Deception: Soviet Information Policy," *Bulletin of the Atomic Scientists*, 42, no. 7 (Aug-Sept. 1986), 32-37.

3172. Hohenemser, C., *et al.*, "Chernobyl: An Early Report," *Environment*, 28 (June 1986), inside cover, 6ff.

3173. Homaday, A., "Dr. Alice Stewart: Straight Talk About Chernobyl," *Ms.*, 15 (Aug. 1986), 83ff.

3174. Huda, Walter, "Medical Consequences of Chernobyl," *Journal of Ukrainian Studies*, 11, no. 1 (Summer 1986), 35-52.

3175. Ianitskii, O. N., "The Environmental Movement," *Soviet Sociology*, 29, no. 6 (Nov-Dec. 1990), 39-57.

3176. Ivleva, Victoria, "Into the White-Hot Center," *New York Times Magazine* (14 Apr. 1991), 34-35.

3177. Jankowski, M. W., *et al.*, "Onsite Response to the Accident at Chernobyl," *Nuclear Safety*, 28, no. 1 (1987), 36-42.

3178. Jones, Ellen, and Benjamin L. Woodbury II, "Chernobyl' and Glasnost'," *Problems of Communism*, 35, no. 6 (Nov-Dec. 1986), 28-38.

3179. Josephson, Paul R., "Chernobyl and Its Aftermath" (Review Article), *Slavic Review*, 50, no. 3 (Fall 1991), 680-82.

3180. -----, "The Historical Roots of the Chernobyl Disaster," *Soviet Union/Union Sovietique*, 13, no. 3 (1986), 275-99.

3181. Kabala, Stanley J., "The Hazardous Waste Problem in Eastern Europe," *Report on Eastern Europe*, 2, no. 25 (21 June 1991), 27-33.

3182. Kapitza, Sergei P., "Lessons of Chernobyl," *Foreign Affairs*, 72, no. 3 (Summer 1993), 7-11.

3183. Knox, C. E., "Chernobyl Health Effects May Never Be Seen," *Science News*, 134 (17 Dec. 1988), 391.

3184. -----, "Fresh Surface Waters Decline in Black Sea," *Science News*, 134 (29 Oct. 1988), 279.

3185. Kohak, Erazim, "The Relevance of Tolstoy: Or, Europe after Chernobyl," *Dissent* (Winter 1987), 5-9.

3186. Kolata, G., "The UCLA-Occidental-Gorbachev Connection," *Science*, 233 (4 July 1986), 19-21.

3187. Kotlyakov, V. M., "The Aral Sea Basin," *Environment*, 33 (Jan-Feb. 1991), inside cover, 2ff.

3188. Kouts, H. J., "Nuclear Power after Chernobyl," *Physics Today*, 39 (Dec. 1986), 136.

3189. Kress, T. S., *et al.*, "The Chernobyl Accident Sequence," *Nuclear Safety*, 28, no. 1 (1987), 1-9.

3190. Kruglov, V. V., "Problems of Improving Ecological Control at the Enterprise," *Connecticut Journal of International Law*, 4 (1989), 325-32.

3191. Land, Thomas, "Meltdown of Authority: Soviet-Designed Nuclear Plants Court Disaster," *Contemorary Review*, 260, no. 1516 (May 1992), 249-51.

3192. Lapidus, Gail Warshofsky, "KAL 007 and Chernobyl: The Soviet Management of Crises," *Survival*, 29, no. 3 (May-June 1987), 215-23.

3193. Lavrov, S. B., "Regional and Environmental Problems of the USSR: A Synopsis of Views from the Soviet Parliament," *Soviet Geography*, 31, no. 7 (Sept. 1990), 477-99.

3194. Lax, Eric, "The Chernobyl Doctor," *New York Times Magazine* (13 July 1986), 22ff.

3195. Legasov, Valery, "A Soviet Expert Discusses Chernobyl," *Bulletin of the Atomic Scientists*, 43, no. 6 (July-Aug. 1987), 32-34.

3196. Lemeshev, M., "Economics and Ecology: A Fatal Conflict and the Path to Resolving It," *Problems of Economics*, 34, no. 4 (Aug. 1991), 38-51.

3197. Leventhal, Paul L., and Milton M. Hoenig, "The Hidden Danger: Risks of Nuclear Terrorism," *Terrorism*, 10, no. 1 (1987), 1-21.

3198. Levi, Barbara Gross, "International Team Examines Health in Zones Contaminated by Chernobyl," *Physics Today*, 44, no. 8 (Aug. 1991), 20-22.

3199. Lewis, W., "Report on Reports: The Accident at the Chernobyl Nuclear Power Plant and Its Consequences," *Environment*, 28 (Nov. 1986), 25-27.

3200. Lvovich, Mark I., "Passing on the Trend of Hydroecology into the Twenty-First Century," *Soviet Geography*, 32, no. 9 (Nov. 1991), 604-15.

3201. MacLeish, William H., "Ways to Beat the Noxious `90s," *World Monitor*, 3, no. 6 (June 1990), 16ff.

3202. Malinauskas, Anthony P., *et al.*, "Calamity at Chernobyl," *Mechanical Engineering* (Feb. 1987), 50-53.

3203. Marcus, S. J., "Environmental Management, Market-Style," *Technology Review*, 95, no. 1 (Jan. 1992), 63-68.

3204. Marples, David R., "After Chernobyl: Ukraine Fallout Debate," *Bulletin of the Atomic Scientists*, 45, no. 10 (Dec. 1989), 9-11.

3205. -----, "Chernobyl' and Ukraine," *Problems of Communism*,

35, no. 6 (Nov-Dec. 1986), 17-27.

3206. -----, "Chernobyl: A Six-Month Review," *Journal of Ukrainian Studies*, 11, no. 1 (Summer 2986), 3-19.

3207. -----, "The Chernobyl Disaster" *Current History*, 86, no. 522 (Oct. 1987), 325ff.

3208. -----, "Chernobyl: Five Years Later," *Soviet Geography*, 32, no. 5 (May 1991), 291-313.

3209. -----, "Chernobyl: Observations on the Fifth Anniversary," *Soviet Economy*, 7, no. 2 (Apr-June 1991), 175-88.

3210. -----, "Chernobyl, Past and Future," *Freedom at Issue*, no. 99 (Nov-Dec. 1987), 22-27.

3211. -----, "Chernobyl's Lengthening Shadow," *Bulletin of the Atomic Scientists*, 49, no. 7 (Sept. 1993), 38-43.

3212. -----, "Chernobyl' Sparks New Disputes in Ukraine," *Report on the USSR*, 2, no. 42 (19 Oct. 1990), 28-29.

3213. -----, "Decree on Ecology Adopted in Ukraine," *Report on the USSR*, 2, no. 14 (6 Apr., 1990), 15-16.

3214. -----, "Ecological Issues Discussed at Founding Congress of `Zelenyi svit'," *Report on the USSR*, 2, no. 5 (2 Feb. 1990), 21-22.

3215. -----, "The Ecological Situation in Ukraine," *Report on the USSR*, 2, no. 3 (19 Jan., 1990), 23-25.

3216. -----, "Glasnost' and Ecology," *Soviet Analyst* (17 Aug. 1988).

3217. -----, "The Greens and the `Ecological Catastrophe' in Ukraine," *Report on the USSR*, 2, no. 44 (22 June 1990), 23-25.

3218. -----, "Growing Influence of Anti-nuclear Movement in Ukraine," *Report on the USSR*, 2, no. 25 (22 June 1990), 17-19.

3219. -----, "An Insider's View of Chernobyl'," *Report on the USSR*, 2, no. 42 (19 Oct. 1990), 23-27.

3220. -----, "Narodichi and `The Big Lie' about the Effects of Chernobyl'," *Report on the USSR*, 2, no. 3 (19 Jan. 1990), 21-23.

3221. -----, "One Million Ukrainians Affected by Chernobyl'," *Report on the USSR*, 2, no. 13 (30 Mar. 1990), 19-21.

3222. -----, "Revelations of a Chernobyl Insider," *Bulletin of the Atomic Scientists*, 46, no. 10 (Dec. 1990), 16-21.

3223. -----, "Zhitomir Residents Express Concern over Radioactive Fallout," *Report on the USSR*, 2, no. 4 (26 Jan. 1990), 25-27.

3224. Marshall, E., "Recalculating the Cost of Chernobyl," *Science*, 236 (8 May 1987), 658-59.

3225. Matthiessen, Peter, "The Blue Pearl of Siberia," *New York Review of Books*, 38 (14 Feb. 1991), 37-46.

3226. Matzko, John R., "Underground Nuclear Testing on Novaya Zemlya: The Physical Background," *Post-Soviet Geography*, 35, no. 3 (Mar. 1994), 123-41.

3227. McCally, Michael, "Chernobyl-The Emerging Story: Hospital Number Six: A First Hand Report," *Bulletin of the Atomic Scientists*, 42, no. 7 (Aug-Sept. 1986), 10-12.

3228. McDonald, Hamish, "Fallout from Glasnost: Opposition Springs from Poisoned Environment," *Far Eastern Economic Review*, 148 (24 May 1990), 28ff.

3229. Metzer, Bernhard H., and Kempton Dunn III, "Cleaning Up the CIS," *Crossborders* (Winter 1994), 28-31.

3230. Micklin, Philip P., ed., "The Aral Sea Crisis" (Special Issue), *Post-Soviet Geography*, 33, no. 5 (May 1992), 269-331.

3231. -----, "Dessication of the Aral Sea: A Water Management Disaster in the Soviet Union," *Science*, 241, no. 4870 (2 Sept. 1988), 1170-76.

3232. -----, "The Status of the Soviet Union's North-South Water Transfer Projects Before Their Abandonment in 1985-86," *Soviet Geography*, 27, no. 5 (May 1986), 287-329.

3233. -----, "Touring the Aral: Visit to an Ecological Disaster Zone," *Soviet Geography*, 32, no. 2 (Feb. 1991), 90-105.

3234. -----, "The Vast Diversion of Soviet Rivers," *Environment*, 27 (Mar. 1985), 12ff., and "Correction," 27 (June 1985), 43.

3235. -----, and Andrew R. Bond, "Reflections on Environmentalism and the River Diversion Projects," *Soviet Economy*, 4, no. 3 (July-Sept. 1988), 253-74.

3236. Mihalisko, Kathleen, "Belorussian Supreme Soviet Abolishes Chernobyl' Investigatory Commission," *Report on the USSR*, 3, no. 28 (12 July 1991), 19-20.

3237. "Mikhail Gorbachev on the Environment," *Population and Development Review*, 16, no. 1 (Mar. 1990), 198-203.

3238. Milne, Roger, "Chernobyl Disaster Zone to Become National Park," *New Scientist*, 119, no. 1630 (15 Sept. 1988), 34.

3239. Monroe, Scott D., "Chelyabinsk: The Evolution of Disaster," *Post-Soviet Geography*, 33, no. 8 (Oct. 1992), 533-45.

3240. Neporozhniy, P. S., and V. B. Kozlov, "Environmental Problems Associated with the Soviet Electric Power Industry: A Survey," *Energy Problems and Policy*, 14, no. 1 (Jan-Mar. 1990), 1-36.

3241. Nikitina, Elena N., "New Soviet Environmental Policy: Approaches to Global Change," *International Studies Notes*, 16, no. 1 (Winter 1991), 31-36.

3242. Norman, C., "Chernobyl: Errors and Design Flaws," *Science*, 233 (5 Sept. 1986), 1029-31.

3243. -----, and D. Dickson, "The Aftermath of Chernobyl," *Science*, 233 (12 Sept. 1986), 1141-43.

3244. "On Gorbachev and Bush," *Environment*, 32 (May 1990), 2ff.

3245. Osherenko, Gail, "Environmental Cooperation in the Arctic: Will the Soviets Participate?" *International Environmental Affairs*, 1 (Summer 1989), 203-21.

3246. "Out of Control," *Progressive*, 50, no. 6 (June 1986), 9-10.

3247. "Panel on Patterns of Disintegration in the Former Soviet Union," *Post-Soviet Geography*, 33, no. 6 (June 1992), 347-404.

3248. "Panel on the State of the Soviet Environment at the Start of the Nineties," *Soviet Geography*, 31, no. 6 (June 1990), 401-68.

3249. Patterson, Walter C., "Chernobyl-The Official Story," *Bulletin of the Atomic Scientists*, 42, no. 9 (Nov. 1986), 34-36.

3250. Perera, Judith, "Kremlin Moves to Save the Aral Sea," *New Scientist*, 120, no. 1640 (26 Nov. 1988), 20.

3251. Perrow, C., "The Habit of Courting Disaster," *Nation*, 243 (11 Oct. 1986), 329ff.

3252. Peterson, D. J., "Baikal: A Status Report," *Report on the USSR*, 2, no. 2 (12 Jan. 1990), 1-4.

3253. -----, "Bleeding Arteries: Pipelines in the USSR," *Report on the USSR*, 2, no. 24 (15 June 1990), 1-32.

3254. -----, "An Environmental Disaster Unfolds," *Report on the USSR*, 2, no. 27 (6 July 1990), 11-12.

3255. -----, "Environmental Protection and the State of the Union," *Report on the USSR*, 3, no. 12 (22 Mar. 1991), 6-8.

3256. -----, "Hard Times for the Environment," *Report on the USSR*, 3, no. 46 (15 Nov. 1991), 15-19.

3257. -----, "The Impact of the Environmental Movement on the Soviet Military," *Report on the USSR*, 3, no. 11 (15 Mar. 1991), 9-12.

3258. -----, "The State of the Environment: An Overview," *Report on the USSR*, no. 8 (23 Feb. 1990), 13-17.

3259. -----, "The State of the Environment: The Air," *Report on the USSR*, 2, no. 9 (2 Mar. 1990), 5-10.

3260. -----, "The State of the Environment: The Land," *Report on the USSR*, 2, no. 22 (1 June 1990), 8-12.

3261. -----, "The State of the Environment: Solid Wastes," *Report on the USSR*, 2, no. 19 (11 May 1990), 11-14.

3262. -----, "The State of the Environment: The Water," *Report on the USSR*, 2, no. 11 (16 Mar. 1990), 14-19.

3263. -----, "A Wave of Environmentalism Sweeps the Soviet Union," *Report on the USSR*, 2, no. 25 (22 June 1990), 8-9.

3264. Plotnikov, Aleksandr, "The Army and Ecology," *Soviet Military Review*, no. 7 (July 1989), 50-51.

3265. Potter, William C., "The Impact of Chernobyl on Nuclear Power Safety in the Soviet Union," *Studies in Comparative Communism*, 24, no. 2 (June 1991), 191-210.

3266. -----, and Lucy Kerner, "The Soviet Military's Performance at Chernobyl," *Soviet Studies*, 43, no. 6 (1991), 1027-48.

3267. Powers, D. A., *et al.*, "The Chernobyl Source Term," *Nuclear Safety*, 28, no. 1 (1987), 10-28.

3268. Powers, T., "Chernobyl as a Paradigm of a Faustian Bargain," *Discover*, 7 (June 1986), 33-35.

3269. Precoda, Norman, "Leningrad's Protective Barrier against Flooding Project," *Soviet Geography*, 29, no. 8 (Oct. 1988), 725-35.

3270. Quinn-Judge, Sophie, "All the Gold in the Waters," *Far Eastern Economic Review*, 141 (18 Aug. 1988), 54-63.

3271. Raloff, J., "A Melt-Down But No Melt-Through," *Science News*, 129 (17 May 1986), 308.

3272. -----, "Soviets Unveil Lessons from Chernobyl," *Science News*, 130 (30 Aug. 1986), 135.

3273. Ramberg, Bennett, "Learning from Chernobyl," *Foreign Affairs*, 65, no. 2 (Winter 1986-87), 304-28.

3274. Rasputin, Valentin G., "Hopes and Despair, and Hopes...," *Perestroika Annual*, 2 (1989), 255-72.

3275. Reed, Cordell, "After Chernobyl: Where Do We Go From Here?" *USA Today*, 116, no. 2510 (Nov. 1987), 48-51.

3276. Reed, Susan E., "Atomic Lake," *New Republic* (28 Oct. 1991), 12-13.

3277. -----, "Siberian Writer Valentin Rasputin Fears for the Planet's Fate," *People Weekly*, 27 (6 Apr. 1987), 123-29.

3278. Reiffel, Leonard, "Chernobyl Five Years Later," *National Review*, 43 (13 May 1991), 24-26.

3279. Reisch, Frigyes, "The Chernobyl Accident: Its Impact on Sweden," *Nuclear Safety*, 28, no. 1 (1987), 29-36.

3280. -----, "Technical Note: How Chernobyl Happened: A Second Opinion," *Nuclear Safety*, 28, no. 1 (1987), 43-45.

3281. Rich, Vera, "Byelorussian Criticism," *Nature*, 341, no. 6237 (7 Sept. 1989), 8.

3282. -----, "Byelorussia Still Alarmed by the Effects of Chernobyl Fallout," *Nature*, 337, no. 6209 (23 Feb. 1989), 683.

3283. -----, "Chernobyl's Psychological Legacy," *Lancet*, 337, no. 8749 (4 May 1991), 1086.

3284. -----, "Mapping Pollution," *Lancet*, 338, no. 8777 (16 Nov. 1991), 1261.

3285. -----, "Pollution Takes Its Toll," *Lancet*, 339, no. 8788 (1 Feb. 1992), 295-96.

3286. -----, "Protest by Chernobyl Workers," *Lancet*, 336, no. 8730 (22-29 Dec. 1990), 1570.

3287. -----, "Theft of Chernobyl Data," *Lancet*, 336, no. 8717 (22 Sept. 1990), 736.

3288. Rinehart, D., "Chernobyl's Legacy," *Maclean's*, 102 (29 May 1989), 52.

3289. Robinson, N. A., "Soviet Environmental Protection: The Challenge for Legal Studies," *Pace Environmental Law Review*, 7 (Fall 1989), 117ff.

3290. Rosenblatt, Sabine, "Is Poland Lost? Pollution and Politics in Eastern Europe," *Greenpeace*, 13, no. 6 (Nov-Dec. 1988), 14-19.

3291. Rosencranz, Armin, and Antony Scott, "Siberia, Environmentalism, and Problems of Environmental Protection," *Hastings International and Comparative Law Review*, 14 (Symposium 1991), 929-47.

3292. Sabau, M. N., and C. S. Sabau, "Assessment of the Impact of the Chernobyl Nuclear Accident in Europe," *Journal of the American Romanian Academy of Arts and Sciences*, no. 12 (1989), 118-32.

3293. Sagers, Matthew J., "News Notes: Environmental Concerns Stop Development of Phosphorite Deposit in Estonia," *Soviet Geography*, 29, no. 10 (Dec. 1988), 951-53.

3294. Salisbury, Harrison, "Gorbachev's Dilemma," *New York Times Magazine* (27 July 1986), 18ff.

3295. Sander, G. F., "No Friend to the Fir," *Sierra*, 76 (May-June 1991), 36-39.

3296. Sanders, Alan, "The Glow of Glasnost: Mongolia Discloses Existence of Uranium Mine," *Far Eastern Economic Review*, 146 (30 Nov. 1989), 73.

3297. Sands, P., "Burying Chernobyl," *Nation*, 246 (30 Apr. 1988), 593.

3298. Schoenfeld, Gabriel, "A Dosimeter for Every Dacha," *Bulletin of the Atomic Scientists*, 45, no. 6 (July-Aug. 1989), 13-15.

3299. -----, "The Soviet Union: Rad Storm Rising," *Atlantic*, 266 (Dec. 1990), 44-58.

3300. Schreiber, Helmut, "The Threat from Environmental Destruction in Eastern Europe," *Journal of International Affairs*, 44 (Winter 1991), 359-91.

3301. Shabad, Theodore, "News Notes: Geographic Aspects of the Chernobyl' Nuclear Accident," *Soviet Geography*, 27, no. 7 (Sept. 1986), 504-26.

3302. Sheehan, James M., "The Greening of Eastern Europe," *Global Affairs*, 7, no. 2 (Spring 1992), 153-72.

3303. Shulman, S., "Chernobyl Fallout," *Technology Review*, 92, no. 2 (Feb-Mar. 1989), 73.

3304. Shultz, George, "Soviet Nuclear Reactor Accident at Chernobyl," *Department of State Bulletin*, 86 (July 1986), 71-76.

3305. Sieff, M., "The Ecology Crisis," *National Review*, 41 (7 Apr. 1989), 28.

3306. Sikora, Veniamin D., "Ukraine: The Locomotive Force in Soviet Environmental Reform," *Harvard International Review*, 13, no. 1 (Fall 1990), 29-31.

3307. Sirotenko, O. D., *et al.*, "Global Warming and the Agroclimatic Resources of the Russian Plain," *Soviet Geography*, 32, no. 5 (May 1991), 337-48.

3308. Smith, David R., "Change and Variability in Climate and Ecosystem Decline in Aral Sea Basin Deltas," *Post-Soviet Geography*, 35, no. 3 (Mar. 1994), 142-65.

3309. -----, "Growing Pollution and Health Concerns in the Lower Amu Dar'ya Basin, Uzbekistan," *Soviet Geography* 32, no. 8 (Oct. 1991), 553-65.

3310. "The Soviet Environment," *Glasnost*, 3, no. 1 (July-Sept. 1990), 52-55.

3311. "Soviet Union Planned Paddy Fields for Aral Sea," *New Scientist*, 122, no. 1665 (20 May 1989), 27.

3312. "Special Politburo Meeting on Chernobyl'," *Soviet Economy*, 2, no. 2 (Apr-June 1986), 180-85.

3313. Stebelsky, Ihor, "Soil Management in Ukraine: Responding to Environmental Degradation," *Canadian Slavonic Papers*, 31, no. 3-4 (Sept-Dec. 1989), 247-66.

3314. Stein, George, "Chernobyl' Mortality Issue Resurfaces at IAEA Conference," *Report on the USSR*, 3, no. 22 (31 May 1991), 17.

3315. -----, "Controversy of Chernobyl' Mortality Figures," *Report on the USSR*, 3, no. 22 (31 May 1991), 13-17.

3316. -----, "Where Is the Chernobyl' Fallout Now?" *Report on the USSR*, 3, no. 23 (14 June 1991), 6-11.

3317. Stewart, John Massey, "The Great Lake Is in Peril," *New Scientist*, 126, no. 1723 (30 June 1990), 58-63.

3318. Stringer, W. J., and J. E. Groves, "Location and Areal Extent of Polynyas in the Bering and Chukchi Seas," *Arctic*, 44, no. 1 (1991), 164-74.

3319. Sun, M., "Environmental Awakening in the Soviet Union," *Science*, 241 (26 Aug. 1988), 1033-35.

3320. "Swedish Moose a la Cesium 137," *Environment*, 31 (May 1989), 22-23.

3321. Sweet, W., "Chernobyl: What Really Happened," *Technology Review*, 92, no. 5 (July 1989), 42-52.

3322. "Ten Years in Stir for Chernobyl's Scapegoats," *Newsweek*, 110 (10 Aug. 1987), 47.

3323. Thompson, Gordon, "Chernobyl-The Emerging Story: What Happened at Reactor Four," *Bulletin of the Atomic Scientists*, 42, no. 7 (Aug-Sept. 1986), 26-31.

3324. Thorniley, Daniel, "Companies Face Heightened USSR Environmental Concern," *Business in Eastern Europe*, 19, no. 32 (6 Aug. 1990), 257-58.

3325. Timoshenko, A. S., "Developments in Environmental Law in the Soviet Union," *Journal of Environmental Law and Litigation*, 4 (1989), 131-41.

3326. "Trends: Perestroika and Energy," *Technology Review*, 93, no. 1 (Jan. 1990), 20-22.

3327. Tumarkin, Nina, "The Gadfly of Chernobyl," *World Monitor*, 3, no. 10 (Oct. 1990), 61-62.

3328. "Two World Leaders on Global Environmental Policy," *Environment*, 32 (Apr. 1990), inside cover, 13ff.

3329. Vardy, Nicholas A., "Eastern Europe: The Rocky Road to Privatization," *World & I*, 6, no. 9 (Sept. 1991), 80-89.

3330. Wall, Patrick, "The Fallout from Chernobyl," *Sea Power*, 29, no. 8 (July 1986), 24-26.

3331. Wasserman, Harvey, "Chernobyl Fallout: Time to Dispel the Nuclear Cloud," *Nation* (24 May 1986), 721-24.

3332. Weinberg, Alvin M., "Chernobyl-The Emerging Story. A Nuclear Power Advocate Reflects on Chernobyl," *Bulletin of the Atomic Scientists*, 42, no. 7 (Aug-Sept. 1986), 57-60.

3333. Weinberg. Steve, "Chernobyl-The Emerging Story: Armand Hammer's Unique Diplomacy," *Bulletin of the Atomic Scientists*, 42, no. 7 (Aug-Sept. 1986), 50-52.

3334. Wickens, B., "A Deadly Explosion," *Maclean's*, 102 (19 June 1989), 46-47.

3335. Wilson, David, "USSR Environmentalists Threaten the Energy Industry," *Petroleum Review*, 44, no. 519 (Apr. 1990), 191-94.

3336. Wilson, R., "A Visit to Chernobyl," *Science*, 236 (26 June 1987), 1636-40.

3337. Wynne, B., "Sheepfarming after Chernobyl," *Environment*, 31 (May 1989), 22-23.

3338. Yosie, Terry F., "Environmental Perestroika," *Environmental Forum*, 5 (May-June 1988), 9-12.

3339. Zaharchenko, T., "The Environmental Movement and Ecological Law in the Soviet Union: The Process of Transformation," *Ecology Law Quarterly*, 17 (1990), 455-75.

3340. Ziegler, Charles E., "The Bear's View: Soviet Environmentalism," *Technology Review*, 90, no. 3 (Apr. 1987), 44-51.

XIX. Foreign Commerce and International Trade

BOOKS

3341. Baldwin, David A., and Helen V. Milner, eds., *East-West Trade and the Atlantic Alliance* (New York: St. Martin's Press, 1991).

3342. Bertsch, Gary, and Steven Elliott-Gower, eds., *The Impact of Governments on East-West Economic Relations* (New York: New York University Press, 1991).

3343. Bloed, Arie, *The External Relations of the Council for Mutual Economic Assistance* (Dordrecht: Martinus Nijhoff Publishers, 1988).

3344. Boguslavskii, M. M., and P. S. Smirnov, *The Reorganization of Soviet Foreign Trade: Legal Aspects*, ed. by Serge A. Levitsky (Armonk, NY: M. E. Sharpe, 1992).

3345. Brada, Josef C., and Michael P. Claudon, eds., *The Emerging Russian Bear: Integrating the Soviet Union into the World Economy* (New York: New York University Press, 1991).

3346. Bubnov, Boris, *Foreign Trade with the USSR: A Manager's Guide to Recent Reforms* (New York: Pergamon Press, 1987).

3347. Collins, Susan M., and Dani Rodrik, *Eastern Europe and the Soviet Union in the World Economy* (Washington, DC: Institute for International Economics, 1991).

3348. Cullen, Robert, ed., *The Post-Containment Handbook: Key Issues in U.S.-Soviet Economic Relations* (Boulder, CO: Westview Press, 1990).

3349. *Directory of Foreign Trade Organizations in Eastern Europe: Bulgaria, Czechoslovakia, East Germany, Hungary, Poland, Romania, and the U.S.S.R.*, 3rd ed. (San Francisco: International Trade Press, 1990).

3350. *East-West Trade and the Congress: Proceedings of a CRS Seminar* (Washington, DC: Library of Congress, Congressional Research Service, 1990).

3351. Evenko, Leonid I., John L. Graham and Mahesh N. Rajan, *An Empirical Study of Marketing Negotiations in the Soviet Union* (Cambridge, MA: Marketing Science Institute, 1990).

3352. Feinberg, Richard E., *The Soviet Union and the Breton Woods Institutions: Risks and Rewards of Membership* (New York: Institute for East-West Security Studies, 1989).

3353. -----, *et al.*, *Economic Reform in Three Giants: U.S. Foreign Policy and the U.S.S.R., China and India* (New Brunswick, NJ: Transaction, 1990).

3354. Geron, Leonard, *Soviet Foreign Economic Policy under Perestroika* (New York: Council on Foreign Relations Press, 1990).

3355. Greenwald, G. Jonathan, and Leonard Sullivan, Jr., *The Western Stake in the Future of the Soviet Economy* (Washington, DC: Atlantic Council of the United States, 1987).

3356. Hansen, Carl R., *U.S.-Soviet Trade Policy* (Washington, DC: Johns Hopkins University, School of Advanced International Studies, Foreign Policy Institute, distributed by University Press of America, 1988).

3357. Haus, Leah, *Globalizing the GATT: The Soviet Union's Successor States, Eastern Europe and the International Trading System* (Washington, DC: Brookings Institution, 1992).

3358. Hunter, David W., *Western Trade Pressure on the Soviet Union: An Interdependence Perspective on Sanctions* (New York: St. Martin's Press, 1991).

3359. Kaser, Michael, and Aleksandar M. Vacic, eds., *Reforms in Foreign Economic Relations of Eastern Europe and the Soviet Union: Proceedings of a Symposium Conducted in Association with Osteuropa-Institut, Munich and Sudost-Institut, Munich* (New York: United Nations Economic Commission for Europe, 1991).

3360. Kiser, John W., III, *Communist Entrepreneurs: Unknown Innovators in the Global Economy* (New York: Watts, 1989).

3361. Kraus, Michael, and Ronald D. Liebowitz, eds., *Perestroika and East-West Economic Relations: Prospects for the 1990s* (New York: New York University Press, 1990).

3362. Malmgren, Harald B., *The Soviet Union and the GATT:*

Benefits and Obligations of Joining the World Trade Club (New York: Institute for East-West Security Studies, 1989).

3363. Meredith, Mark, ed., *Trading with Uncertainty: Foreign Investment Trends in the Soviet Union* (New York, distributed by Scientific and Technical Book, 1991).

3364. Neu, Carl R., and John Lund, *Toward a Profile of Soviet Behavior in International Financial Markets* (Santa Monica, CA: RAND, 1987).

3365. Pregelj, Vladimir N., *Jackson-Vanik Amendment and Granting Most-Favored Nation Treatment and Access to U.S. Financial Programs to the Soviet Union* (Washington, DC: Library of Congress, Congressional Research Service, 1989).

3366. Sanders, Sol, *Living Off the West: Gorbachev's Secret Agenda and Why It Will Fail* (Lanham, MD: Madison Books, 1990).

3367. Smith, Alan, *Russia and the World Economy: Problems of Integration* (New York: St. Martin's Press, 1993).

3368. Starr, Robert, and Sally March, *Practical Aspects of Trading with the Soviets* (New York: Worldwide Information, distributed by STBS, 1990).

3369. Stern, Jonathan P., *Soviet Oil and Gas Exports to the West: Commercial Transaction or Security Threat?* (Aldershot: Gower Publishing Co., 1987).

3370. Stubbs, Eric, ed., *Soviet Foreign Economic Policy and International Security* (Armonk, NY: M. E. Sharpe, 1991).

3371. United Nations. Conference on Trade and Development. *Manual on Trading with the Socialist Countries of Eastern Europe* (New York: United Nations, 1985).

3372. United Nations. Conference on Trade and Development. *USSR: New Management Mechanism in Foreign Economic Relations* (New York: United Nations, 1989).

3373. United Nations. Economic Commission for Europe. *Economic Bulletin for Europe*, vol. 43 (New York: United Nations, 1991).

3374. United Nations. Economic Commission for Europe. *U.S.S.R.: New Management Mechanism in Foreign Economic Relations* (New York: United Nations, 1988).

3375. US Central Intelligence Agency. Directorate of Intelligence. *Selected Countries' Trade with the USSR and Eastern Europe* (Washington, DC: CIA, National Technical Information Service, 1990).

3376. US Congress. House. Committee on Energy and Commerce. Subcommittee on Commerce, Transportation and Tourism. *U.S. Trade Relations with the Soviet Union: Hearing*. 99th Congress, 25 June 1986 (Washington, DC: Government Printing Office, 1986).

3377. US Congress. House. Committee on Foreign Affairs. Subcommittee on Europe and the Middle East. *United States-Soviet Trade Relations*. 101st Congress, 1st Session (Washington, DC: Government Printing Office, 1989).

3378. US Congress. House. Committee on Foreign Affairs. Subcommittee on International Economic Policy and Trade. *Commercial Lending to the Soviet Bloc*. 100th Congress, 1st Session (Washington, DC: Government Printing Office, 1989).

3379. US Congress. House. Committee on Small Business. *Perestroika and Its Implications for the United States*. 100th Congress, 2nd Session (Washington, DC: Government Printing Office, 1988).

3380. US Congress. House. Committee on Small Business. Subcommittee on Regulation, Business Opportunities and Energy. *Pacific Northwest Trade with the Eastern Bloc: Opportunities and Obstacles for Timber and Electronics*. 101st Congress, 2nd Session, 12 Feb. 1990 (Washington, DC: Government Printing Office, 1990).

3381. US Congress. House. Committee on Ways and Means. Subcommittee on Trade. *Report on Trade Mission to Europe and the Soviet Union*. 102nd Congress, 1st Session (Washington, DC: Government Printing Office, 1991).

3382. US Congress. House. Committee on Ways and Means. Subcommittee on Trade. *Written Comments on H.R. 1724, a Bill to Normalize U.S. Trade Relations with Hungary and Czechoslovakia, and on Trade Agreements between the United States and Bulgaria and the United States and Mongolia*. 102nd Congress, 1st Session (Washington, DC: Government Printing Office, 1991).

3383. US Congress. Joint Economic Committee. Subcommittee on Trade, Productivity and Economic Growth. *Prospects for Improved American-Soviet Trade: Hearings*. 99th Congress, 9 Oct. 1985 (Washington, DC: Government Printing Office, 1986).

3384. US Congress. Senate. Committee on Finance. *US-USSR Economic Relations*. 101st Congress, 1st Session (Washington, DC: Government Printing Office, 1990).

3385. US Congress. Senate. Committee on Finance. Subcommittee on International Trade. *Enforcement of U.S. Prohibitions on the Importation of Goods Produced by Convict Labor: Hearing*. 99th Congress, 9 July 1985 (Washington, DC: Government Printing Office, 1986).

3386. US Congress. Senate. Committee on Foreign Relations. *Workshop on US-USSR Commercial Relations, 17 Apr. 1989*. 101st Congress, 2nd Session (Washington, DC: Government Printing Office, 1990).

3387. US President. *Agreement on Trade Relations between the United States and the Union of Soviet Socialist Republics: Communication from the President of the United States Transmitting a Copy of a Proclamation That Extends Nondiscriminatory Treatment to the Products of the Union of Soviet Socialist Republics...* . 102nd Congress, 1st Session (Washington, DC: Government Printing Office, 1991).

3388. US President. *Extension of Waiver Authority: Message from the President of the United States Transmitting Notification of His Determination That a Continuation of Waiver Currently in Effect for the Republic of Bulgaria, the Czech and Slovak Federal Republic, the Soviet Union, and the Mongolian People's*

Republic Will Substantially Promote the Objectives of Article 402, of the Trade Act of 1974, Pursuant to 19 U.S.C. 2432 (c), (d). 102nd Congress, 1st Session (Washington, DC: Government Printing Office, 1991).

3389. US President and US Congress. House. Committee on Foreign Affairs. *Waiving Certain Emigration Practices with Respect to the Soviet Union: Communication from the President of the United States Transmitting Notification of His Determination That a Waiver with Respect to the Emigration Practices of the Soviet Union Will Substantially Promote the Objectives of Section 402 of the Trade Act of 1974, Pursuant to 19 U.S.C. 2432(c), (d).* 102nd Congress, 1st Session (Washington, DC: Government Printing Office, 1991).

3390. Wilson, Arlene, *Currency Convertibility in Eastern Europe and the Soviet Union* (Washington, DC: Library of Congress, Congressional Research Service, 1990).

3391. Wolf, Thomas A., *Foreign Trade in the Centrally Planned Economy* (Chur: Harwood Academic Publishers, 1988).

3392. Zloch-Christy, Iliana, *East-West Financial Relations: Current Problems and Future Prospects* (New York: Cambridge University Press, 1991).

ARTICLES

3393. Aganbegyan, Abel, and Ivan D. Ivanov, "Profitable for Us and Our Partner: *Perestroika,* Foreign Economic Ties, and International Economic Relations," *Perestroika Annual,* 2 (1989), 143-57.

3394. "Agreement Includes Provisions to Expand Market Access," *Congressional Quarterly Weekly Report,* 47 (9 June 1989), 1823-24.

3395. Aho, C. Michael, and Bruce Stokes, "The Year the World's Economy Turned," *Foreign Affairs,* 70, no. 1 (1990-91), 179-205.

3396. Anikin, A. V., "The Soviet Union Joins the International Economy," *Challenge,* 32 (May-June 1989), 4-9.

3397. Arefyev, V., and Z. Mieczkowski, "International Tourism in the Soviet Union in the Era of Glasnost and Perestroyka," *Journal of Travel Research,* 29, no. 4 (Spring 1991), 2-6.

3398. Aslund, Anders, "The New Soviet Policy Towards International Economic Organizations," *World Today,* 44, no. 2 (Feb. 1988), 27-30.

3399. "Bartering with the Bolsheviks: A Guide to Countertrading with the Soviet Union," *Dickinson Journal of International Law,* 8 (Winter 1990), 269-89.

3400. Beaglehole, J. H., "The New Zealand-USSR/CIS Economic Relationship: Problems and Prospects in a Time of Change," *Soviet and Post-Soviet Review,* 19, no. 1-3 (1992), 163-83.

3401. "Beggar's Opera," *New Republic* (1 July 1991), 7-8.

3402. Bergsten, Fred C., "From Cold War to Trade War?" *International Economic Insights,* 1, no. 1 (July-Aug. 1990), 2-6.

3403. Brada, Josef C., "The Soviet Union and the GATT: A Framework for Western Policy," *Soviet Economy,* 5, no. 4 (Oct-Dec. 1989), 360-71.

3404. Brandenberg, Mary, "Glasnost Spells Openness for East-West Trade," *Accountancy,* 100 (Dec. 1987), 99.

3405. Brougher, Jack, "Trade Agreement Would Improve U.S.-Soviet Commercial Relationship," *Business America,* 111, no., 13 (2 July 1990), 2-4.

3406. Brown, Leslie C., "USSR: Commercial Accords Build Solid Business Foundation," *Business America,* 111, no. 8 (23 Apr. 1990), 16-17.

3407. Burchfield, Lisa, "Directory of Periodicals on U.S.-U.S.S.R. Trade and Investment," *Business America,* 111, no. 23 (3 Dec. 1990), 26-27.

3408. "Bush and Gorbachev Sign Commercial Agreement," *Congressional Quarterly Weekly Report,* 48 (2 June 1990), 1721.

3409. "Change in the Soviet Foreign Trade System" (Special Issue), *Soviet and Eastern European Foreign Trade,* 24, no. 4 (Winter 1988-89), 3-94.

3410. Chanis, J. A., "United States Trade Policy toward the Soviet Union: A More Commercial Orientation," *Proceedings of the Academy of Political Science,* 37, no. 4 (1990), 110-21.

3411. Cloud, D. S., "Rethinking Soviet Trade," *Congressional Quarterly Weekly Report,* 49 (29 May 1991), 1359.

3412. -----, "Trading with Moscow," *Congressional Quarterly Weekly Report,* 49 (29 Nov. 1991), 3517.

3413. Cooper, Mary H., "Soviet Trade: In America's Best Interest?" *Editorial Research Reports* (10 Feb. 1989), 74-87.

3414. Copetas, A. Craig, "Ruble without a Cause," *Regardie's,* 9, no. 5 (May 1989), 75ff.

3415. Critchlow, James, "Uzbeks Looking to World Market," *Report on the USSR,* 1, no. 13 (30 Mar. 1990), 14-16.

3416. Dallmeyer, D., *et al.,* "U.S.S.R.'s Entry into the International Economic System: A Panel," *American Society of International Law Proceedings,* 83 (1989), 183-204.

3417. Dessauer, John P., "Getting in on Europe's Boom," *World Monitor,* 3, no. 3 (Mar. 1990), 22ff.

3418. "Developing the Foreign Economic Ties of Siberia: From an Address by M. S. Gorbachev in Krasnoiarsk, September 16, 1988," *Soviet and Eastern European Foreign Trade,* 25, no. 3 (Fall 1989), 68-69.

3419. "East-West Economic Relations," *International Economy,* 2 (July-Aug. 1988), 26ff.

3420. Elving, R. D., "Bush and Gorbachev Sign Commercial Agreement," *Congressional Quarterly Weekly Report,* 48 (2 June 1990), 1721.

3421. -----, "Warning on Soviet Trade," *Congressional Quarterly Weekly Report,* 48 (5 May 1990), 1334.

3422. Feldman, Jan, "Trade Policy and Foreign Policy," *Washing-*

ton *Quarterly*, 8, no. 1 (Winter 1985), 65-75.

3423. Fischer, Michael, "US-Soviet Trade in the Post-Malta Era," *Business International*, 36, no. 50 (18 Dec. 1989), 385ff.

3424. Galuszka, Philip, and J. Pearson, "Can Gorbachev Blast Open the Doors to Soviet Trade?" *Business Week* (29 Sept. 1986), 52-53.

3425. Goldman, Marshall I., "Will Gorbachev's Policy of Encouraging Trade with the West Work?" *Technology Review*, 90, no. 1 (Jan. 1987), 18ff.

3426. Gorbachev, Mikhail S., "Remarks on US-USSR Trade," *Harvard Business Review*, 64 (May-June 1986), 56-58.

3427. "Gorbachev Holds Q&A Session with Congressional Leaders," *Congressional Quarterly Weekly Report*, 48 (9 June 1990), 1827-30.

3428. Grishchenko, Dmitri I., and Marian G. Dent, "Barter Trade Operations with the USSR and Recent Changes in Hard Currency Policy," *SEEL: Soviet and East European Law*, 2, no. 4 (June 1991), 3ff.

3429. "Half a Loaf for Gorbachev," *Economist*, 311 (13 May 1989), 32.

3430. Hamilton, George, "Export Controls Will Still Hinder Trade with USSR," *Business in Eastern Europe*, 19, no. 46 (12 Nov. 1990), 369-70.

3431. Hanson, Philip, "New Exchange Rate to Govern Ruble for Trade and Investment," *Report on the USSR*, 2, no. 46 (16 Nov. 1990), 3-5.

3432. Hardt, J. P., and J. F. Boone, "The Soviet Union's Trade Policy," *Current History*, 87 (Oct. 1988), 329ff.

3433. Haus, Leah, "The East European Countries and GATT: The Role of Realism, Mercantilism and Regime Theory in Explaining East-West Trade Negotiations," *International Organizations*, 45, no. 2 (Spring 1991), 163-82.

3434. Hewett, Ed A., "The Foreign Economic Factor in *Perestroika*," *Harriman Institute Forum*, 1, no.8 (Aug. 1988), 1-8.

3435. Hoffmann, Erik P., "Gorbachev's Trade Reforms: Something Old, Something New," *Bulletin of the Atomic Scientists*, 44, no. 5 (June 1988), 22-25.

3436. Ivanov, Ivan D., "*Perestroika* and Foreign Economic Relations," *Perestroika Annual*, 1 (1988), 145-64.

3437. -----, "Restructuring the Mechanism of Foreign Economic Relations in the USSR," *Soviet Economy*, 3, no. 3 (July-Sept. 1987).

3438. "Jackson-Vanik and Other Trade Barriers," *SEEL: Soviet and East European Law*, 1, no. 3 (Apr. 1990), 8-9.

3439. Kemen, Beat R., "The Politics of the Soviet-American Grain Trade," *Crossroads*, no. 19 (1986), 45-71.

3440. Klimczak, Edward, "Trade with the Soviets: Veiled Exploitation? Interview with Edmund Krasowski and Czeslaw Nowak," *Uncaptive Minds*, 4, no. 1 (Spring 1991), 65-71.

3441. Kovalev, A., "A Legal Base for Soviet International Trade," *New Zealand Law Journal* (Dec. 1991), 440-42.

3442. Kraljic, Pewter, "The Economic Gap Separating East and West," *Columbia Journal of World Business*, 25, no. 4 (Winter 1990), 14-19.

3443. Kraus, James R., "U.S. Leaders Take Cautious Tack in Dealings with Soviet Union," *American Banker*, 152 (20 Dec. 1987), 1-2.

3444. Lieberman, Edward, Jeffrey M. Colon and Dariusz Oleszczuk, "New Soviet Tax Laws Attract Foreign Investors," *Journal of International Taxation*, 1, no. 5 (May-June 1990), 278-83.

3445. McCarthy, P., "Seven Steps to Expand East-West Trade," *Bulletin of the Atomic Scientists*, 44 (9 June 1988), 26-29.

3446. McMillan, Carl H., "Canada's Response to the `New Detente' in East-West Economic Relations," in Maureen Appel Molot and Fen Osler Hampson, eds., *Canada Among Nations 1989* (Ottawa: Carleton University Press, 1990), 59-77.

3447. Melcher, R. A., "Point Man in London for *Perestroika*," *Business Week* (3 Oct. 1988), 52.

3448. Mendes, Errol P., "The Soviet Union: Open for Business?" *Review of International Business Law*, 1 (1987), 357-71.

3449. Mendez, Jose A., and Donald J. Rousslang, "Liberalizing U.S. Trade with the Eastern Bloc: What Are the Consequences?" *Journal of Comparative Economics*, 13, no. 4 (Dec. 1989), 491-507.

3450. Menshikov, S. M., "Problems in East-West Trade: Frank Discussion with an American Businessman," *World Marxist Review*, 32, no. 1 (Jan. 1989), 21-25.

3451. Moe, A., "The Future of Soviet Oil Supplies to the West," *Soviet Geography*, 32, no. 3 (Mar. 1991), 137-67.

3452. Onorato, William T., "West-East Foreign Investment in the International Petroleum Sector: The Sakhalin Continental Shelf Oil and Gas Project," *ICSID Review: Foreign Investment Law Journal*, 3 (1988), 326-37.

3453. Osakwe, C., "The Harmonization of Soviet and EEC Trade Laws in Anticipation of 1992," *Whittier Law Review*, 12 (1991), 151-57.

3454. Pavluk, Jonathan, "Enterprise Secularization Opens Way for Soviets' Integration into Global Financial Markets," *SEEL: Soviet and East European Law*, 1, no. 8 (Oct. 1990), 4ff.

3455. Pettibone, Peter J., "U.S.-Soviet Trade Agreement," *SEEL: Soviet and East European Law*, 1, no. 6 (Aug. 1990), 6.

3456. Quigley, John, "Legal Implications of the Dismantling of the Soviet Foreign Trade Monopoly," *International Tax and Business Lawyer*, 7 (Summer 1989), 275-98.

3457. Ray, Steven R., "The Effects of Gorbachev's Perestroika on U.S.-Soviet Trade," *Global Trade*, 108 (June 1988), 26-28.

3458. Reisinger, William M., "The International Regime of

Soviet-East European Economic Relations," *Slavic Review*, 49, no. 4 (Winter 1990), 554-67.

3459. Reisman, M., "For a Permanent U.S.-Soviet Claims Commission," *American Journal of International Law*, 83, no. 1 (Jan. 1989), 51-56.

3460. Renaud, Jean-Claude, "East-West Economic Relations in the Context of Perestroika," *NATO Review*, 36, no. 4 (Autumn 1988), 17-19.

3461. "Resolution of International Trade Disputes: An Analysis of the Soviet Foreign Trade Arbitration Commission's Decisions Concerning the Doctrine of Force Majeure as an Excuse to the Performance of Private International Trade Agreements," *Maryland Journal of International Law and Trade*, 10 (Spring 1986), 135-65.

3462. Rossant, J., "Gorbachev's Reforms Whip Up Continental Trade Winds," *Business Week* (31 Oct. 1988), 50.

3463. Sagers, M. J., et al., "Prospects for Soviet Gas Exports: Opportunities and Constraints," *Soviet Geography*, 29, no. 12 (Dec. 1988), 881-908.

3464. Sanders, Jonathan, "Introduction: A New Era in Soviet-American Trade," *Columbia Journal of World Business*, 23, no. 2 (Summer 1988), 5-6.

3465. Schmickle, William E., "New Political Thinking and the Foreign Trade Reform," *Crossroads*, no. 28 (1989), 35-52.

3466. Seppain, H., "The Divided West: Contrasting German and US Attitudes to Soviet Trade," *Political Quarterly*, 61, no. 1 (Jan-Mar. 1990), 51-65.

3467. Snyder, Jack, "International Leverage on Soviet Domestic Change," *World Politics*, 42 (Oct. 1989), 1-30.

3468. "Soviet `Participation' in GATT: A Case for Accession," *New York University Journal of International Law and Politics*, 20, no. 2 (Winter 1988), 477-523.

3469. "Soviet Union Seeks to Renew Industry Relations with China," *Aviation Week & Space Technology* (26 Oct. 1987), 29.

3470. Stanfield, Rochelle L., "Shaky Soviets," *National Journal*, 22, no. 23 (9 June 1990), 1412-13.

3471. Stern, Paula, "U.S.-Soviet Trade: The Question of Leverage," *Washington Quarterly*, 12, no. 4 (Autumn 1989), 183-97.

3472. Stevenson, Adlai E., and Alton Frye, "Trading with the Communists," *Foreign Affairs*, 68, no. 2 (Spring 1989), 53-71.

3473. Stokes, Bruce, "Opening Eastern Gates," *National Journal*, 22, no. 25 (23 June 1990), 1531-34.

3474. Sutela, Pekka, "Exporting to the Soviet Union: Microeconomic Aspects for Finland," *Osteuropa-Wirtschaft*, 36, no. 4 (Dec. 1991), 301-15.

3475. Taylor, William, "Two Soviet Scholars Encourage USSR Accession to GATT," *SEEL: Soviet and East European Law*, 1, no. 1 (Feb. 1990), 7.

3476. Tedstrom, John, "Credit Problems Plague Foreign Business Deals," *Report on the USSR*, 2, no. 23 (8 June 1990), 6.

3477. -----, "Soviet Membership of GATT," *Report on the USSR*, 2, no. 12 (23 Mar. 1990), 7-9.

3478. Tishcenko, Anatoly S., "Soviet Oil and East-West Trade," *Petroleum Review*, 43, no. 504 (Jan. 1989), 4-6.

3479. Trinich, Fridrikh A., "Trade and Economic Cooperation between the USSR and Asia-Pacific Region Countries," *Journal of Northeast Asian Studies*, 6, no. 4 (Winter 1987-88), 61-69.

3480. US Department of Commerce, "Exporting Pays Off," *Business America*, 111, no. 20 (22 Oct. 1990), 27.

3481. -----, "Food Processing Trade Opportunities in Leningrad," *Business America*, 111, no. 13 (2 July 1990), 14.

3482. -----, "Soviet Payment Delays Now Require That Companies Use Caution in Arranging Terms," *Business America*, 111, no. 13 (2 July 1990), 12.

3483. -----, "Soviet Reforms Create Opportunities and Risks," *Business America*, 111, no. 23 (3 Dec. 1990), 22-24.

3484. -----, "Trade Watch: Foreign Business in the Soviet Union," *Business America*, 111, no. 20 (5 Nov. 1990), ii.

3485. -----, "Trade Watch: Soviet Stock Market," *Business America*, 111, no. 20 (22 Oct. 1990), ii.

3486. -----, "Trade Watch: Soviet Union/Market Economy," *Business America*, 111, no. 19 (8 Oct. 1990), ii.

3487. Van Ham, Peter, "Soviet Economic Reform and East-West Relations," *Problems of Communism*, 40, no. 1-2 (Jan-Apr. 1991), 144-49.

3488. Vause, W. G., "Perestroika and Market Socialism: The Effects of Communism's Slow Thaw on East-West Economic Relations," *Northwestern Journal of International Law and Business*, 9 (Fall 1988), 231-76.

3489. Vernikov, Andrei, "New Entrants in Soviet Foreign Trade: Behaviour Patterns and Regulation in the Transitional Period," *Soviet Studies*, 43, no. 5 (1991), 823-36.

3490. Vlachoutsicos, Charalambos A., "Gorbachev's Trade Reforms: Treadmill or Dynamo?" *Harvard International Review*, 9, no. 4 (Apr. 1987), 42-46.

3491. Zabijaka, Val, "Soviet Foreign Trade Reforms Offer New Challenges for U.S. Business," *Business America* (17 Aug. 1987), 6-9.

3492. -----, "U.S.S.R.: Summit Leaders Support Mutually Beneficial Trade," *Business America* (25 Apr. 1988), 17-18.

XX. Foreign Policy and International Affairs

BOOKS

3493. Aron, Leon, *Khrushchev, Gorbachev and the West* (Washington, DC: Heritage Foundation, 1987).

3494. -----, *The Search for "Socialist Pluralism": Gorbachev's*

Vision of the Future (Washington, DC: Heritage Foundation, 1988).

3495. Beichman, Arnold, *The Long Pretense: Soviet Treaty Diplomacy from Lenin to Gorbachev* (New Brunswick, NJ: Transaction Publishers, 1991).

3496. Benn, David Wedgwood, *From Glasnost to Freedom of Speech: Russian Openness and International Relations* (New York: Council on Foreign Relations Press, 1992).

3497. Beschloss, Michael R., and Strobe Talbott, *At the Highest Levels: The Inside Story of the End of the Cold War* (Boston: Little, Brown and Co., 1993).

3498. Beyme, Klaus von, *The Soviet Union in World Politics* (Aldershot, England: Gower, 1987).

3499. Bowker, Mike, and Robin Brown, eds., *From Cold War to Collapse: Theory and World Politics in the 1980s* (New York: Cambridge University Press, 1992).

3500. Denitch, Bogdan Denis, *The End of the Cold War: European Unity, Socialism, and the Shift in Global Power* (Minneapolis: University of Minnesota Press, 1990).

3501. Fleron, Frederic J. Jr., Erik P. Hoffmann and Robbin F. Laird, eds., *Contemporary Issues in Soviet Foreign Policy: From Brezhnev to Gorbachev* (New York: Aldine de Gruyter, 1991).

3502. Flynn, Gregory, and Richard E. Greene, eds., *The West and the Soviet Union: Politics and Policy* (New York: St. Martin's Press, 1990).

3503. Gelman, Harry, *Gorbachev's Policies toward Western Europe* (Santa Monica, CA: RAND, 1987).

3504. Golan, Galia, *Gorbachev's "New Thinking" on Terrorism* (New York: Praeger, 1990).

3505. Gorodetsky, Gabriel, ed., *Soviet Foreign Policy: A Retrospective 1917-1991* (London: Frank Cass and Co. Ltd., 1994).

3506. Hemsley, John, ed., *The Lost Empire: Perceptions of Soviet Policy Shifts in the 1990s* (Washington, DC: Brassey's, 1991).

3507. Hirsch, Steve, ed., *MEMO 2: Soviets Examine Foreign Policy for a New Decade* (Washington, DC: Bureau of National Affairs, 1991).

3508. Imam, Zafar, *Soviet Foreign Policy, 1917-1990* (New York: Sterling, distributed by Apt Books, 1991).

3509. Institute for National Strategic Studies, *Understanding Soviet Foreign Policy* (Washington, DC: Institute for National Strategic Studies, 1990).

3510. Jacobsen, Carl G., ed., *Soviet Foreign Policy: New Dynamics, New Themes* (London: Macmillan, 1989).

3511. Jervis, Robert, and Jack Snyder, eds., *Dominoes and Bandwagons: Strategic Beliefs and Great Power Competition in the Eurasian Rimland* (New York: Oxford University Press, 1991).

3512. Jones, Robert A., *The Soviet Concept of "Limited Sovereignty" from Lenin to Gorbachev: The Brezhnev Doctrine* (New York: St. Martin's Press, 1990).

3513. Katz, Mark N., *Anti-Soviet Insurgencies: Growing Trend or Passing Phase?* (Washington, DC: Woodrow Wilson International Center for Scholars, Kennan Institute, 1986).

3514. Laird, Robbin F., and Erik P. Hoffmann, eds., *Soviet Foreign Policy in a Changing World* (New York: Aldine, 1986).

3515. Leonhard, Wolfgang, *The Kremlin and the West; A Realistic Approach* (New York: W. W. Norton, 1986).

3516. Levgold, Robert, and the Task Force on Soviet New Thinking, *Gorbachev's Foreign Policy: How Should the U.S. Respond?* (New York: Foreign Policy Association, 1988).

3517. Livermore, Gordon, ed., *Soviet Foreign Policy Today: Reports and Commentaries from the Soviet Press*, 2nd ed. (Columbus, OH: Current Digest of the Soviet Press, 1986).

3518. Lynch, Allen, *Gorbachev's International Outlook: Intellectual Origins and Political Consequences* (New York: Institute for East-West Security Studies, distributed by Westview Press, 1989).

3519. MacKenzie, David, *From Messianism to Collapse: Soviet Foreign Policy, 1917-1991* (New York: Harcourt Brace, 1994).

3520. Malik, Hafeez, ed., *Domestic Determinants of Soviet Foreign Policy towards South Asia and the Middle East* (New York: St. Martin's Press, 1990).

3521. Marantz, Paul, *New Concepts of East-West Relations* (Kingston: Centre for International Relations, Queen's University, 1989).

3522. Miko, Francis T., *Soviet Foreign Policy under Gorbachev: Determinants, Prospects and Implications* (Washington, DC: US Library of Congress, Congressional Research Service, 1987).

3523. Miller, Robert F., *Soviet Foreign Policy Today: Gorbachev and the New Political Thinking* (New York: Unwin Hyman, 1991).

3524. Mlynar, Zdenek, *Can Gorbachev Change the Soviet Union? The International Dimensions of Political Reform* (Boulder, CO: Westview Press, 1990).

3525. Morris, Michael A., ed., *Great Power Relations in Argentina, Chile and Antarctica* (New York: St. Martin's Press, 1990).

3526. Nichol, James P., *Perestroika of the Soviet Ministry of Foreign Affairs during the Gorbachev Period* (University of Massachusetts of Amherst: Program in Soviet and East European Studies, Occasional Papers Series, no. 16, 1988).

3527. Pyadyshev, Boris, ed., *Russia and the World: New Views on Russian Foreign Policy* (New York: Carol, 1991).

3528. Shevardnadze, Eduard, *A New World Vision: Soviet Foreign Policy in the Age of Perestroika* (New York: Pantheon, 1991).

3529. Sodaro, Michael, *Moscow, Germany, and the West from*

Khrushchev to Gorbachev (Ithaca: Cornell University Press, 1990).

3530. Sperry, Mary Elizabeth, ed., *The USSR in the New World Order: Symposium Report* (Santa Monica, CA: RAND/UCLA Center for Soviet Studies, 1991).

3531. Staar, Richard F., *Foreign Policies of the Soviet Union* (Stanford: Hoover Institution Press, 1991).

3532. -----, *USSR Foreign Policies after Detente*, rev. ed. (Stanford: Hoover Institution Press, 1987).

3533. Thom, Francoise, *Moscow's 'New Thinking' as an Instrument of Foreign Policy* (Toronto: Mackenzie Institute for the Study of Terrorism, Revolution and Propaganda, 1987).

3534. US Congress. Senate. Committee on Foreign Relations. Subcommittee on European Affairs. *Soviet Imperatives for the 1990's: Hearing.* 99th Congress (Washington, DC: Government Printing Office, 1986).

3535. Walters, Vernon A., *Reflections on Gorbachev's Policies and East-South Relations* (Coral Gables, FL: Institute for Soviet and East European Studies, 1988).

3536. Weeks, John F., ed., *Beyond Superpower Rivalry: Latin America and the Third World* (New York: New York University Press, 1991).

3537. Woodby, Sylvia, *Gorbachev and the Decline of Ideology in Soviet Foreign Policy* (Boulder, CO: Westview Press, 1989).

3538. Zwick, Peter, *Soviet Foreign Relations: Process and Policy* (Englewood Cliffs, NJ: Prentice Hall, 1990).

ARTICLES

3539. "Address of E. A. Shevardnadze to a Conference of the USSR Ministry of Foreign Affairs, June 25-27, 1988," *Soviet Law and Government*, 28, no. 2 (Fall 1989), 6-56.

3540. Allison, Graham T., "Testing Gorbachev," *Foreign Affairs*, 67 (Fall 1988), 18-32.

3541. Alvares, S., "We Were Right in Rejecting the Brezhnev Doctrine," *World Marxist Review*, 33, no. 2 (Feb. 1990), 85-88.

3542. Aspaturian, Vernon V., "Farewell to Soviet Foreign Policy," *Problems of Communism*, 40, no. 6 (Nov-Dec. 1991), 53-62.

3543. "The Battle for Gorbachev's Ear," *Economist*, 295 (29 June 1985), 43-44.

3544. Bessmertnykh, Alexander A., "Foreign Policy-A New Course," *Perestroika Annual*, 2 (1989), 43-64.

3545. Bialer, Seweryn, "'New Thinking' and Soviet Foreign Policy," *Survival*, 30, no. 4 (July-Aug. 1988), 291-309.

3546. Blum, Douglas W., "The Soviet Foreign Policy Belief System: Beliefs, Politics, and Foreign Policy Outcomes," *International Studies Quarterly*, 37, no. 4 (Dec. 1993), 373-94.

3547. Bochkarev, Andrei G., "The Policy of New Thinking in the Changing World," *India Quarterly*, 47, no. 1-2 (Jan-June 1991), 1-26.

3548. Brazier, W. F., and J. S. Hellman, "Gorbachev's New World View," *Social Policy*, 18 (Summer 1987), 4-12.

3549. Breslauer, George, "Linking Gorbachev's Domestic and Foreign Policies," *Journal of International Affairs*, 42 (Spring 1989), 267-82.

3550. Bunce, Valerie, "Domestic Reform and International Change: The Gorbachev Reforms in Historical Perspective," *International Organization*, 47 (Winter 1993), 107-38.

3551. Bundy, McGeorge, "From Cold War Toward Trusting Peace," *World Affairs*, 153, no. 1 (1989-90), 197-212.

3552. Burke, James F., "Gorbachev's Eurasian Strategy," *World Affairs*, 155, no. 4 (Spring 1993), 156-68.

3553. Butler, William E., "International Law, Foreign Policy and the Gorbachev Style," *Journal of International Affairs*, 42 (Spring 1989), 363-75.

3554. Checkel, Jeff, "Ideas, Institutions, and the Gorbachev Foreign Policy Revolution," *World Politics*, 45, no. 2 (Jan. 1993), 271-300.

3555. Clark, Mark T., "Gorbachev's New Line: Twenty Years After the Brezhnev Doctrine," *Global Affairs*, 3, no. 4 (Fall 1988), 71-86.

3556. Clemens, Walter C., Jr., "Gorbachev's Role in International Detente: True Grit?" *Soviet and Post-Soviet Review*, 20, no. 1 (1993), 51-75.

3557. -----, "The Republics as International Actors," *Nationalities Papers*, 19, no. 1 (Spring 1991), 73-76.

3558. Crow, Suzanne, "Another Conservative Attack on Soviet Foreign Policy," *Report on the USSR*, 3, no. 10 (8 Mar. 1991), 6-7.

3559. -----, "Restructuring the Soviet Foreign Ministry: The Foreign Ministry Survey," *Report on the USSR*, 2, no. 20 (18 May 1990), 3-5.

3560. -----, "*Vestnik MID*: The Soviet Foreign Ministry's Window on Itself," *Report on the USSR*, 2, no. 24 (15 June 1990), 13-14.

3561. Crozier, Brian, "Strategy for the Gorbachev Era," *Global Affairs*, 3, no. 4 (Fall 1988), 1-14.

3562. Cullen, Robert, "The Soviet Union: Laying That Burden Down," *Atlantic*, 265 (Mar. 1990), 32-39.

3563. Dawisha, Karen, "*Perestroika, Glasnost* and Soviet Foreign Policy," *Harriman Institute Forum*, 3, no. 1 (Jan. 1990), 1-8.

3564. Despard, Lucy E., ed., "Recent Books on International Relations," *Foreign Affairs*, 65, no. 5 (Summer 1987), 1097-1121; 66, no. 1 (Fall 1987), 189-208; and 66, no. 2 (Winter 1987-88), 429-52.

3565. Dobrynin, Anatoly, "Soviet Foreign Policy: Basic Principles and New Thinking," *World Marxist Review*, 31, no. 3 (Mar.

1988), 15-27.

3566. Evangelista, Matthew, "Give Peace a Chance: `New Thinking' in Foreign Policy," *Nation* (13 June 1987), 795-99.

3567. Fairbanks, Charles, "Gorbachev's Global Doughnut: The Empire with a Hole in the Middle," *National Interest*, no. 19 (Winter 1990), 21-33.

3568. Franck, Thomas M., "Soviet Initiatives: U.S. Responses-New Opportunities for Reviving the United Nations System," *American Journal of International Law*, 83, no. 3 (July 1989), 531-43.

3569. -----, "United Nations Based Prospects for a New Global Order," *New York University Journal of International Law and Politics*, 22, no. 4 (Summer 1990), 601-40.

3570. Galuszka, Philip, *et al.*,"Gorbachev Is Trying to Outflank Reagan in Europe and Asia," *Business Week* (22 Sept. 1986), 52.

3571. Garthoff, Raymond L., "Soviet `New Thinking' on the World and Foreign Policy," *Fletcher Forum*, 12, no. 2 (Summer 1989), 231-38.

3572. Gelman, Harry, "Gorbachev's Dilemmas and His Conflicting Foreign-Policy Goals," *Orbis*, 30, no. 2 (Summer 1986), 231-47.

3573. "Gorbachev and Glasnost: Soviet Foreign Policy for the Future," *Loyola of Los Angeles International and Comparative Law Journal*, 11 (1989), 377-97.

3574. "The Gorbachev Options," *Economist*, 294 (30 Mar. 1985), 12-13.

3575. Gordon, Nancy, "Better Late Than Never, Moscow Courts the UN," *Peace and Security*, 4, no. 1 (1989), 8-9.

3576. Gorin, A., and P. Mishchenko, "New Political Thinking as a Philosophy and a Tool of Soviet Foreign Policy," *Journal of Legislation*, 17 (Winter 1990), 13-21.

3577. Green, William C., "Are There `Hawks' and `Doves' in the Soviet Leadership?" *Strategic Review*, 15, no. 1 (Winter 1987), 31-42.

3578. Gustafson, Thane, "Will Soviet Foreign Policy Change under Gorbachev?" *Washington Quarterly*, 9, no. 4 (Fall 1986), 153-57.

3579. Gusterson, Hugh, "Realism and the International Order after the Cold War," *Social Research*, 60, no. 2 (Summer 1993), 279-300.

3580. Gvosdev, Nikolas K., "Their Proclamation Has Gone Out into All the World: Soviet Messianism and the International System," *Canadian Slavonic Papers*, 32, no. 4 (Dec. 1990), 431-43.

3581. Hoffmann, Stanley, "The Case for Leadership," *Foreign Policy*, no. 81 (Winter 1990-91), 20-38.

3582. Holloway, David, "Gorbachev's New Thinking," *Foreign Affairs*, 68, no. 1 (1989), 66-81.

3583. Howe, Sir Geoffrey, "Soviet Foreign Policy under Gorbachev," *World Today*, 45, no. 3 (Mar. 1989), 40-45.

3584. Hunter, Shireen T., "The Muslim Republics of the Former Soviet Union: Policy Challenges for the United States," *Washington Quarterly*, 15, no. 3 (Summer 1992), 57-74.

3585. Jonsson, Christer, "The Superpower Factor in Soviet Foreign Policy-Making," *Crossroads*, no. 24 (1987), 17-28.

3586. Jowitt, Ken, "Moscow `Centre'," *Eastern European Politics and Societies*, 1, no. 3 (Fall 1987), 296-348.

3587. Kagan, Donald, "World War I, World War II, World War III," *Commentary*, 83 (Mar. 1987), 21-40.

3588. Kanet, Roger E., "New Political Thinking and Soviet Foreign Policy," *Crossroads*, no. 28 (1989), 5-22.

3589. Kirschbaum, Stanislav J., "The Gorbachev Gambit: A Grand Master's Next Move," in Brian MacDonald, ed., *The Canadian Strategic Forecast 1989* (Toronto: Canadian Institute of Strategic Studies, 1989), 3-15.

3590. Kozyrev, Andrei V., "The New Soviet Attitude toward the United Nations," *Washington Quarterly*, 13, no. 3 (Summer 1990), 41-53.

3591. Kramer, Mark, "Soviet Foreign Policy after the Cold War," *Current History*, 90, no. 558 (Oct. 1991), 317-22.

3592. Laird, Robert F., ed., "Soviet Foreign Policy," *Proceedings of the Academy of Political Science*, 36, no. 4 (1987), 1-272.

3593. Laqueur, Walter, "*Glasnost'* Abroad: New Thinking in Foreign Policy," *Washington Quarterly*, 11, no. 4 (Autumn 1988), 75-93.

3594. Leggett, J., "Gorbachev at an Historic Crossroads," *New Statesman*, 113 (27 Feb. 1987), 8ff.

3595. Legvold, Robert, "The Revolution in Soviet Foreign Policy," *Foreign Affairs*, 68, no. 1 (1989), 82-98.

3596. "Life After Gorbachev," *Economist*, 321 (21 Dec. 1991), 55-56.

3597. Lowenkron, Barry F., "The New Political Thinking: Pax Sovietica with a Human Face," *SAIS Review*, 8, no. 2 (Summer 1992), 83-101.

3598. Lynch, Allen, "The Continuing Importance of Ideology in Soviet Foreign Policy," *Harriman Institute Forum*, 3, no. 7 (July 1990), 1-8.

3599. -----, "The Restructuring of Soviet Foreign Policy," *Bulletin of the Atomic Scientists*, 44 (Mar. 1988), 40-43.

3600. Lyne, R., "Making Waves: Mr Gorbachev's Public Diplomacy, 1985-6," *International Affairs*, 63 (Spring 1987), 205-24.

3601. Malcolm, N., "Gorbachev's New Thinking," *New Statesman*, 112 (24 Oct. 1986), 12-13.

3602. Marantz, Paul, "Soviet New Thinking and East West Relations," *Current History*, 87, no. 531 (Oct. 1988), 309-12.

3603. McBride, Ken, "Treaty Verification with the `Evil Empire'," *Queen's Quarterly*, 95, no. 3 (1988), 608-11.

3604. "New Style or Substance in Soviet Foreign Policy?" *Soviet Analyst*, 17 (29 June 1988), 3-5.

3605. "New Thinking: Questions and Answers," *PS*, 23 (Mar. 1990), 29-32.

3606. Nichol, Jim, "The Question of Legitimate Representation of the Soviet Union in Signing Interstate Treaties: A Research Note," *Soviet Studies*, 42, no. 2 (Apr. 1990), 341-54.

3607. Ostreng, Willy, "The Northern Sea Route: A New Era in Soviet Policy?" *Ocean Development and International Law*, 22, no. 3 (1991), 259-87.

3608. Park, A., "Global Security, Glasnost and the Retreat Dividend," *Government and Opposition*, 26 (Winter 1991), 75-85.

3609. "Perestroika, the 19th Party Conference and Foreign Policy," *International Affairs* (Moscow), 7 (July 1988), 3-18.

3610. Perle, Richard N., and Michael Mandelbaum, "Three Perestroikians Explain the Link Between Reform and Foreign Policy," *U.S. News & World Report*, 104 (13 June 1988), 42-43.

3611. Peterson, Bo, "Essay and Reflection: On the Soviet Union and the Neutrals," *International History*, 11, no. 2 (May 1989), 291-302.

3612. Petrov, Vladimir, "In Search of a Foreign Policy," *World & I*, 6, no. 8 (Aug. 1991), 38-43.

3613. Pines, B. Y., "Waiting for Mr. X: And a Strategy of Liberation for Post-Cold War Europe," *Policy Review*, no. 49 (Summer 1989), 2-6; Discussion, no. 50 (Fall 1989), 77-83.

3614. Popov, Nikolai, "We're All in the Same Boat: Polemical Thoughts on the World's Trust in Us and Mistrust in Us," *Soviet Law and Government*, 28, no. 4 (Spring 1990), 74-81.

3615. Raditsa, Leo, "Sense in Chaos: Europe, Middle East, South Africa," *Midstream*, 37, no. 9 (Dec. 1991), 11-12.

3616. Roberts, Cynthia, "The New Realism and the Old Realities: Gorbachev's Strategy in Perspective," *Washington Quarterly*, 11, no. 3 (Summer 1988), 213-26.

3617. Roberts, W. R., "Germany: The Gorbachev Memorandum," *World Today*, 46, no. 10 (Oct. 1990), 180-81.

3618. Rogov, Sergey M., "Detente Is Not Enough." *Foreign Policy*, no. 74 (Spring 1989), 86-102.

3619. Rubinstein, Alvin Z., "The Soviet Union's Foreign Policy Environment to the Year 2000," *Naval War College Review*, 40, no. 3 (Summer 1987), 19-36.

3620. Sestanovich, Stephen, "Gorbachev's Foreign Policy: A Diplomacy of Decline," *Problems of Communism*, 37, no. 1 (Jan-Feb. 1988), 1-15.

3621. Simes, Dimitri K., "Gorbachev: A New Foreign Policy?" *Foreign Affairs*, 65, no. 3 (1987), 477-500.

3622. Stewart, Philip D., "Gorbachev and Obstacles toward Detente," *Political Science Quarterly*, 101, no. 1 (1986).

3623. Taubman, William, "Sources of Soviet Foreign Conduct," *Problems of Communism*, 35, no. 5 (Sept-Oct. 1986), 47-52.

3624. Titov, Vladimir, "The Union's Foreign Policy: Will There Be Any Future?" *International Affairs* (Moscow), no. 12 (Dec. 1991), 29.

3625. Vartanov, Raphael V., and Alexei Yu. Roginko, "New Dimensions of Soviet Arctic Policy: Views from the Soviet Union," *Annals of the American Academy of Political and Social Science*, no. 512 (Nov. 1990), 69-78.

3626. Waever, O., "Three Competing Europes: German, French, Russian," *International Affairs*, 66 (July 1990), 477-93.

3627. Weickhardt, George G., "Foreign Policy Disputes in the Gorbachev Succession," *Soviet Union/Union Sovietique*, 16, no. 1 (1989), 29-54.

3628. Weiss, Thomas G., "Moscow's U.N. Policy," *Foreign Policy*, no. 79 (Summer 1990), 94-112.

3629. Weisser, Ulrich, "The Superpowers on the Way to a Settlement of Regional Conflicts: A German Perspective," *Naval War College Review*, 42, no. 3 (Summer 1989), 63-77.

3630. Wise, Sallie, "Foreign Ministry Adrift," *Report on the USSR*, 3, no. 36 (6 Sept. 1991), 28-30.

3631. Wofsy, Leon, "Gorbachev's New Thinking and World Politics," *Monthly Review*, 40, no. 5 (Oct. 1988), 18-31.

3632. Ximin, Song, "Changes in International Relations," *Beijing Review*, 30 (2 May 1988), 28-32.

3633. Zhi, Rong, and Zhang Wuzhuan, "Gorbachev's `New Thinking' and Foreign Policy Adjustment," *Beijing Review*, 31 (15 Aug. 1988), 23-28.

3634. Zimmerman, William, "Soviet Foreign Policy and World Politics," *Journal of International Affairs*, 44 (Spring 1990), 125-38.

3635. Zwick, Peter, "New Thinking and New Foreign Policy Under Gorbachev," *PS*, 21 (June 1989), 215-24.

3636. Zubok, Vladislav, "Tyranny of the Weak: Russia's New Foreign Policy," *World Policy Journal*, 9, no. 2 (Spring 1992), 191-217.

A. Africa
BOOKS

3637. Bark, Dennis L., *Red Orchestra: The Case of Africa* (Stanford: Hoover Institution Press, 1990).

3638. Campbell, Kurt M., *Soviet Policy towards South Africa* (New York: St. Martin's Press, 1986).

3639. Clough, Michael, ed., *Reassessing the Soviet Challenge in Asia* (Berkeley: University of California, Institute of International Studies, 1986).

3640. Coker, Christopher, *NATO, the Warsaw Pact and Africa*

(New York: St. Martin's Press, 1985).

3641. Gromyko, Anatoly A., and C. S. Whitaker, eds., *Agenda for Action: African-Soviet-U.S. Cooperation* (Boulder, CO: L. Rienner, 1990).

3642. Henze, Paul B., *Glasnost about Building Socialism in Ethiopia: Analysis of a Critical Soviet Article* (Santa Monica, CA: RAND, 1990).

3643. Jordan, Donald, *Changing American Assessments of the Soviet Threat in Sub-Saharan Africa* (Lanham, MD: University Press of America, 1987).

3644. Kempton, Daniel R., *Soviet Strategy toward Southern Africa: The National Liberation Movement Connection* (New York: Praeger, 1989).

3645. Korn, David A., *Ethiopia, the United States and the Soviet Union* (Carbondale, IL: Southern Illinois University Press, 1986).

3646. Laidi, Zaki, *The Superpowers and Africa: The Constraints of a Rivalry, 1960-90* (Chicago: University of Chicago Press, 1990).

3647. Pascoe, William W., III, *Moscow's Strategy in Southern Africa: A Country by Country Review* (Washington, DC: Heritage Foundation, 1986).

3648. Patman, Robert G., *The Soviet Union in the Horn of Africa: The Diplomacy of Intervention and Disengagement* (Cambridge: Cambridge University Press, 1990).

3649. Phillips, Howard, *Moscow's Challenge to U.S. Vital Interests in Southern Africa* (Vienna, VA: Policy Analysis, Inc., 1987).

3650. Radu, Michael, and Arthur Jay Klinghoffer, *The Dynamics of Soviet Policy in Sub-Saharan Africa* (New York: Holmes & Meier, 1990).

ARTICLES

3651. "All You Need to Know about South Yemen," *National Review*, 38 (28 Feb. 1986), 20.

3652. Anderson, Lisa, "Qadhdhafi and the Kremlin," *Problems of Communism*, 34, no. 5 (Sept.-Oct. 1985), 29-44.

3653. Bender, Gerald J., "The Eagle and the Bear in Angola," *American Academy of Political and Social Science. Annals*, 489 (1987), 123-32.

3654. Campbell, Kurt M., "The Soviet-South African Connection," *Africa Report*, 31, no. 2 (Mar-Apr. 1986), 72-75.

3655. Clute, R. E., "The American-Soviet Confrontation in Africa: Its Impact on the Politics of Africa," *Journal of Asian and African Studies*, 24 (July-Oct. 1989), 159-69.

3656. Coker, Christopher, "Moscow and Pretoria: A Possible Alignment?" *World Today*, 44, no. 1 (Jan. 1988), 6-8.

3657. Collins, Robert F., "Soviet Influence in Sub-Saharan Africa," *Military Review*, 65, no. 4 (Apr. 1985), 46-57.

3658. Crozier, Brian, "Moscow's Libyan Tool," *National Review*, 38 (6 June 1986), 26.

3659. Deeb, Mary-Jane, "Qaddafi's Calculated Risks," *SAIS Review*, 6, no. 2 (Summer-Fall 1986), 151-62.

3660. Dhada, Mustafah, "Post-*Perestroika* Africa: Changing Relationships with the Outside World," *Africa Today*, 38, no. 3 (1991), 5-6.

3661. Falk, Pamela S., "Cuba in Africa," *Foreign Affairs*, 65, no. 5 (Summer 1987), 1077-96.

3662. Francis, Samuel T., "Communism, Terrorism, and the African National Congress," *Journal of Social, Political and Economic Studies*, 11, no. 1 (Spring 1986), 55-71.

3663. Goldstein, Lyle, "The Collapse of Soviet Power: Implications for Southern Africa," *Harvard International Review*, 14, no. 2 (Winter 1991-92), 42-44.

3664. Gordon, David F., "Southern Africa: Demise of the Centrist Consensus," *SAIS Review*, 6, no. 2 (Summer-Fall 1986), 117-36.

3665. Gusarov, Vladilen, "Russia-Africa: The Far Continent," *Delovie Lyudi*, no. 37 (Sept. 1993), 40-41.

3666. Habib, Henry, "Changing Patterns in Libyan Foreign Policy," *Journal of South Asian and Middle Eastern Studies*, 10, no. 2 (Winter 1986), 3-15.

3667. Henze, Paul B., "Eritrea: The Endless War," *Washington Quarterly*, 9, no. 2 (Spring 1986), 23-36.

3668. Hull, Richard W., "United States Policy in Southern Africa," *Current History*, 89, no. 547 (May 1990), 193-200.

3669. Johns, Michael, "Gorbachev's Holocaust: Soviet Complicity in Ethiopia's Famine," *Policy Review*, no. 45 (Summer 1988), 74-75.

3670. -----, "The Winds of Democracy," *World & I* (Aug. 1990), 32-39.

3671. Jolliffe, J., "Getting Out of Angola," *World Press Review*, 35 (Aug. 1988), 19-20.

3672. Kauppi, Mark V., "Moscow and the Congo," *Problems of Communism*, 39, no. 2 (Mar-Apr. 1990), 42-60.

3673. Keller, Edmond J., "The Politics of State Survival: Continuity and Change in Ethiopian Foreign Policy," *American Academy of Political and Social Science. Annals*, 489 (Jan. 1987), 76-87.

3674. Kempton, Daniel R., "Africa in the Age of *Perestroika*," *Africa Today*, 38, no. 3 (1991), 7-30.

3675. Kitchen, Helen, "Africa: Year of Ironies," *Foreign Affairs*, 64, no. 3 (1986), 562-82.

3676. Klinghoffer, Arthur J., "US-Soviet Relations in Angola," *Harvard International Review*, 8, no. 3 (Jan-Feb. 1986), 15-19.

3677. Knight, R., "West's Aid Fails to Sway Ethiopia from East's Orbit," *U.S. News & World Report*, 99 (29 July 1985), 35ff.

3678. MacFarlane, S. Neil, "The Soviet Union and Southern African Security," *Problems of Communism*, 38, no. 2-3 (Mar-June 1988), 71-89.

3679. Marcus, Howard G., "The Politics of Famine," *Worldview*, 28, no. 3 (Mar. 1985), 20-21.

3680. Massing, Michael, "Upside Down in Angola," *New Republic* (3 Mar. 1986), 16-18.

3681. Nel, Philip R., "Soviet Fortunes in Southern Africa" (Review Article), *Problems of Communism*, 34, no. 3 (May-June 1985), 74-78.

3682. Ottaway, Marina, "African Marxist Regimes and U.S. Policy: Ideology and Interest," *SAIS Review*, 6, no. 2 (Summer-Fall 1986), 137-49.

3683. Pateman, Roy, "The Eritrean War," *Armed Forces & Society*, 17, no. 1 (Fall 1990), 81-98.

3684. Popov, Yuri, "Africa and the Soviet Perestroika," *International Affairs* (Moscow), no. 3 (Mar. 1991), 40-50.

3685. Pork, A., "The Concept of `Ideological Struggle': Some Soviet Interpretations," *Government and Opposition*, 24 (Summer 1989), 283-93.

3686. Puddington, Arch, "Ethiopia: The Communist Uses of Famine," *Commentary*, 81 (Apr. 1986), 30-38.

3687. Remnek, Richard B., "The Horn of Africa: Retrospect and Prospect," *Strategic Review*, 18, no. 4 (Fall 1990), 39-50.

3688. Rossant, J., "Moving Further and Further into Moscow's Embrace," *Business Week* (3 Feb. 1986), 44.

3689. Sarris, Louis G., "Soviet Military Policy and Arms Activities in Sub-Saharan Africa," in William J. Foltz and Henry S. Bienen, eds., *Arms and the African: Military Influences on Africa's International Relations* (New Haven: Yale University Press, 1985).

3690. Schultz, Barry M., "Soviet Designs on Africa," *Problems of Communism*, 35, no. 1 (Jan-Feb. 1986), 77-83.

3691. Schumacher, Edward, "The United States and Libya," *Foreign Affairs*, 65, no. 2 (Winter 1986-87), 329-48.

3692. Shepherd, G. W., "Dominance and Conflict on the Horn: Notes on U.S.-Soviet Rivalry," *Africa Today*, 32, no. 3 (1985), 7-21.

3693. Smith, Wayne, "A Trap in Angola," *Foreign Policy*, no. 62 (Spring 1986), 61-74.

3694. Solarz, Stephen J., "Next Stop, Angola," *New Republic* (2 Dec. 1985), 18ff.

3695. "The States of the Unions," *New Republic* (26 Feb. 1990), 7-9.

3696. Thomas, Maria, "A State of Permanent Revolution: Ethiopia Bleeds Red," *Harper's*, 274, no. 1640 (Jan. 1987), 53ff.

3697. Webber, M., "Soviet Policy in Sub-Saharan Africa: The Final Phase," *Journal of Modern African Studies*, 30 (Mar. 1992), 1-30.

3698. Weitz, Richard, "Moscow and Its African Allies," *Report on the USSR*, 3, no. 6 (8 Feb. 1991), 8-15.

3699. -----, "The Reagan Doctrine Defeated Moscow in Angola," *Orbis*, 36, no. 1 (Winter 1992), 57-68.

3700. Worthington, Peter, "Time Is on UNITA's Side," *National Review*, 38 (20 June 1986), 44-45.

B. Asia, the Far East and the Pacific

BOOKS

3701. Babbage, Ross, ed., *The Soviets in the Pacific in the 1990s* Canberra: Brassey's, 1989).

3702. Bark, Dennis L., and Owen Harries, eds., *The Red Orchestra*, vol. 3: *The Case of the Southwest Pacific* (Stanford: Hoover Institution Press, 1989).

3703. Beresford, Melanie, *Vietnam: Politics, Economics and Society* (London: Pinter Publishers, 1988).

3704. -----, *National Unification and Economic Development in Vietnam* (London: Macmillan, 1989).

3705. Billington, James H., and Herbert J. Ellison, *The Soviet Crisis and Foreign Policy toward East Asia: Essays* (Seattle: National Bureau of Asian and Soviet Research, 1991).

3706. Blank, Stephen J., *Moscow, Seoul and Soviet Strategy in the Asia-Pacific Region* (Carlisle Barracks, PA: Strategy Studies Institute, US Army War College, 1991).

3707. Buszynski, Leszek, *Gorbachev and Southeast Asia* (London: Routledge, 1992).

3708. -----, *Soviet Foreign Policy and Southeast Asia* (New York: St. Martin's Press, 1986).

3709. Chung, Yung Il, ed., *Korea and Russia: Toward the 21st Century* (Seoul: The Sejong Institute, 1992).

3710. Cline, Ray, James Miller and Roger Kanet, eds., *Asia in Soviet Global Strategy* (Boulder, CO: Westview Press, 1987).

3711. Drysdale, Peter, ed., *The Soviets and the Pacific Challenge* (Armonk, NY: M. E. Sharpe, 1991).

3712. Ellison, Herbert J., *The Soviet Union and Northeast Asia* (Lanham, MD: University Press of America, 1989).

3713. Harrison, Selig S., and K. Subrahmanyam, eds., *Superpower Rivalry in the Pacific Ocean: Indian and American Perspectives* (New York: Oxford University Press, 1989).

3714. Horelick, Arnold L., *U.S.-Soviet Relations in the Post-Cold War Era: Implications for Korea* (Santa Monica, CA: RAND/UCLA Center for Soviet Studies, 1990).

3715. Horn, R. C., *Alliance Politics Between Comrades: The Dynamics of Soviet-Vietnamese Relations* (Santa Monica, CA: RAND, 1987).

3716. Johnson, Dion W., *Bear Tracks in Indochina: An Analysis of Soviet Presence in Vietnam* (Maxwell Air Force Base, AL: Air University Press, 1987).

3717. Kim, Young C., and Gaston J. Sigur, eds., *Asia and the Decline of Communism* (New Brunswick, NJ: Transaction Publishers, 1992).

3718. Longmire, R. A., *Soviet Relations with Southeast Asia* (London: Kegan Paul, 1989).

3719. Malik, Hafeez, ed., *Soviet-American Relations with Pakistan, Iran and Afghanistan* (Basingstoke: Macmillan Press, 1987).

3720. Nishihara, Masashi, *East Asian Security and the Trilateral Countries: A Report to the Trilateral Commission* (New York: New York University Press, 1985).

3721. Pike, Douglas, *Vietnam and the Soviet Union: Anatomy of an Alliance* (Boulder, CO: Westview Press, 1987).

3722. Plunk, Daryl M., *Sino-Soviet Rivalry Threatens Korean Truce* (Washington, DC: Heritage Foundation, 1986).

3723. Rich, Michael D., and Mary E. Morris, *Security Issues in East Asia* (Santa Monica, CA: RAND, 1986).

3724. Robinson, Thomas W., *Is the Soviet Union Really a Threat to Asia?* (Washington, DC: Woodrow Wilson International Center for Scholars, Kennan Institute, 1986).

3725. Scalapino, Robert A., *Major Power Relations in Northeast Asia* (New York: Asia Society, and Lanham, MD: University Press of America, 1987).

3726. Segal, Gerald, *The Soviet Union and the Pacific* (Boston: Unwin Hyman, 1990).

3727. Sicker, Martin, *Soviet Strategy in Asia* (Washington, DC: Heritage Foundation, 1987).

3728. -----, ed., *Siberia and the Soviet Far East: Strategic Dimensions in Multinational Perspective* (Stanford: Hoover Institution Press, 1987).

3729. Thakur, Ramesh, and Carlyle A. Thayer, eds., *The Soviet Union as an Asian Pacific Power: Implications of Gorbachev's 1986 Vladivostok Initiative* (Boulder, CO: Westview Press, 1988).

3730. Thambipillai, Pushpa, and Daniel C. Matuszewski, eds., *The Soviet Union and the Asian Pacific Region: Views from the Region* (New York: Praeger, 1989).

3731. US Congress. House. Committee on Foreign Affairs. Subcommittee on Asian and Pacific Affairs. *Developments in the South Pacific Region. Hearing.* 99th Congress, 10 Sept. 1986 (Washington, DC: Government Printing Office, 1987).

3732. Woodrow Wilson International Center for Scholars, Kennan Institute for Advanced Russian Studies, *The USSR and Marxist Revolutions in the Third World: A Conference Report* (Washington, DC: Woodrow Wilson International Center for Scholars, Kennan Institute, 1987).

3733. Ziegler, Charles E., *Foreign Policy and East Asia: Learning and Adaptation in the Gorbachev Era* (New York:

Cambridge University Press, 1993).

ARTICLES

3734. Ahn, Byung-joon, "South Korean-Soviet Relations: Contemporary Issues and Prospects," *Asian Survey*, 31, no. 9 (Sept. 1991), 816-25.

3735. Alagappa, Muthiah, "Soviet Policy in Southeast Asia: Towards Constructive Engagement," *Pacific Affairs*, 63, no. 3 (Fall 1990), 321-50.

3736. Alexander, Michael, "The Political Challenge from the East," *NATO Review*, 36, no. 3 (June 1988), 7-12.

3737. Ali, Salamat, "Circular Arguments: Separate Goals Hinder Soviet-Pakistan Relations," *Far Eastern Economic Review*, 147 (29 Mar. 1990), 17.

3738. Anderson, H., "Breaking Ice in the Pacific," *Newsweek*, 115 (18 June 1990), 24-26.

3739. Arkin, William M., "Red Herring in the Pacific," *Bulletin of the Atomic Scientists*, 43, no. 3 (Apr. 1987), 6-7.

3740. Atkinson, Scott, "The Struggle for the Soviet Far East: Political, Military and Economic Trends under Gorbachev," *Soviet Union/Union Sovietique*, 17, no. 3 (1990), 205-33.

3741. -----, "The USSR and the Pacific Century," *Asian Survey*, 30, no. 7 (July 1990), 629-45.

3742. Bach, William, "A Chance in Cambodia," *Foreign Policy*, no. 62 (Spring 1986), 75-95.

3743. Bae, Young-shik, "Soviet-South Korea Economic Cooperation Following Rapprochement," *Journal of Northeast Asian Studies*, 10, no. 1 (Spring 1991), 19-34.

3744. Bagley, Worth H., "Toward a Sino-Soviet Compact," *Global Affairs*, 4, no. 3 (Summer 1989), 1-11.

3745. Bazhanov, Eugene, and Natasha Bazhanov, "Russia and Asia in 1992: A Balancing Act," *Asian Survey*, 33, no. 1 (Jan. 1993), 91-102.

3746. -----, "Soviet Views on North Korea: The Domestic Scene and Foreign Policy," *Asian Survey*, 31, no. 12 (Dec. 1991), 1123-38.

3747. Bell, Coral, "The Unquiet Pacific," *Conflict Studies*, no. 205 (Nov. 1987), 1-27.

3748. Blacker, Coit D., "The U.S.S.R. and Asia in 1989: Recasting Relationships," *Asian Survey*, 30, no. 1 (Jan. 1990), 1-12.

3749. Blank, Stephen, "Soviet Perspectives on Asian Security," *Asian Survey*, 31, no. 7 (July 1991), 646-61.

3750. -----, "Violins with a Touch of Brass: The Soviet Design for Collective Security in Asia," *Conflict*, 10, no. 4 (1991), 281-306.

3751. Bodansky, Yossef, "Countering the Soviet Threat in South Asia," *Global Affairs*, 3, no. 3 (Summer 1989), 188-91.

3752. Brady, Rose, *et al.*, "Gorbachev's Charm Offensive, Asian Style," *Business Week* (12 Feb. 1990), 45.

3753. Buszynski, Leszek, "Russia and the Asia-Pacific Region," *Pacific Affairs*, 65 (Winter 1992-93), 486-509.

3754. -----, "Soviet Foreign Policy and Southeast Asia: Prospects for the Gorbachev Era," *Asian Survey*, 26, no. 5 (May 1986), 590-609.

3755. Chanda, Nayan, "The Glasnost Gap: US Tries to Counter Improved Soviet Image in Asia," *Far Eastern Economic Review*, 145 (8 July 1989), 23-24.

3756. -----, "A Troubled Friendship: Moscow Loses Patience with Hanoi over Economy and Cambodia," *Far Eastern Economic Review*, 140 (9 June 1988), 16-17.

3757. Cheow, Eric T. C., "New Omnidirectional Overtures in Thai Foreign Policy," *Asian Survey*, 26, no. 7 (July 1986), 745-58.

3758. Cheung, T. M., "Lifting the Curtain: Asians Hard to Convince about Soviet Sincerity," *Far Eastern Economic Review*, 145 (31 Aug. 1989), 31.

3759. -----, "Opening Gambit: Soviets Relax Guard along Asian Land Frontier," *Far Eastern Economic Review*, 145 (31 Aug. 1989), 28-30.

3760. Chufrin, Gennady, "The U.S.S.R. and Asia-Pacific in 1990," *Asian Survey*, 31, no. 1 (Jan. 1991), 14-20.

3761. -----, "The USSR and Asia in 1991: Domestic Priorities Prevail," *Asian Survey*, 32, no. 1 (Jan. 1992), 11-18.

3762. Clifford, Mark, "Gamble on Glasnost: South Korea Announces US$3 Billion Loan Package for Soviets," *Far Eastern Economic Review*, 151 (7 Feb. 1991), 44-45.

3763. Correll, John T., "Power Players on the Rim of Asia," *Air Force Magazine*, 70, no. 11 (Nov. 1987), 60ff.

3764. Cotton, James, "North Korea and the Costs of Isolation," *World & I* (July 1990), 44-51.

3765. Crow, Suzanne, "Mongolia: Still the Sixteenth Republic?" *Report on the USSR*, 2, no. 34 (24 Aug. 1990), 3-4.

3766. -----, "Shevardnadze's Asian Tour: Mixed Results," *Report on the USSR*, 2, no. 37 (14 Sept. 1990), 5-7.

3767. -----, "Soviet-North Korean Rapprochement," *Report on the USSR*, 2, no. 24 (15 June 1990), 11-13.

3768. -----, "Will the Moscow-Hanoi Alliance Survive Aid and Arms Cutbacks?" *Report on the USSR*, 2, no. 45 (9 Nov. 1990), 14-17.

3769. Dorrance, John C., "The Soviet Union and the Pacific Islands: A Current Assessment," *Asian Survey*, 30, no. 9 (Sept. 1990), 908-25.

3770. Duiker, William J., "Vietnam Moves toward Pragmatism," *Current History*, 86, no. 519 (Apr. 1987), 148ff.

3771. Ekedahl, Carolyn M., and Melvin A. Goodman, "Gorba-chev's `New Directions' in Asia," *Journal of Northeast Asian Studies*, 8, no. 3 (Fall 1989), 3-24.

3772. Evans, Roland, and Robert D. Novak, "Pakistan: Moscow's Terror Target," *Reader's Digest*, 133 (July 1988), 124-28.

3773. Falkenheim, Peggy L., "The Soviet Union, Japan, and East Asia: The Security Dimension," *Journal of Northeast Asian Studies*, 8, no. 4 (Winter 1989), 43-59.

3774. Finkelstein, David M., "Vietnam: A Revolution in Crisis," *Asian Survey*, 27, no. 9 (Sept. 1987), 973-90.

3775. Fitzgerald, David M., "The Soviets in Southeast Asia," *US Naval Institute Proceedings*, 112, no. 2 (Feb. 1986), 48-57.

3776. Fukuyama, Francis, "Asia in a Global War," *Comparative Strategy*, 6, no. 4 (Oct-Dec. 1987), 387-413.

3777. Garrett, Banning N., "Ending the United States-Soviet Cold War in East Asia: Prospects for Changing Military Strategies," *Washington Quarterly*, 14, no. 2 (Spring 1991), 163-78.

3778. Garrett, Stephen A., "The Changing Face of Security in Asia," *World & I* (June 1990), 120-26.

3779. Gelman, Harry, "Gorbachev's Policies in East Asia after Two Years," *Journal of Northeast Asian Studies*, 7, no. 1 (Spring 1988), 47-54.

3780. Gill, Graeme, "The Soviet Union in Southeast Asia: A New Beginning?" *Contemporary South East Asia*, 10, no. 1 (June 1988), 69-81.

3781. Glaubitz, Joachim, "The Soviet Union and the Korean Peninsula," *Aussenpolitik*, 43, no. 1 (1992), 82-91.

3782. Gorbachev, Mikhail S., "International Affairs," *Vital Speeches of the Day*, 52 (15 Sept. 1986), 706-11.

3783. -----, "USSR Foreign Relations with Japan: A Peaceful World Order Depends on Perestroika," *Vital Speeches of the Day*, 57 (15 May 1991), 453-55.

3784. Gordon, Bernard K., "The Third Indochina Conflict," *Foreign Affairs*, 65, no. 1 (Fall 1986), 66-85.

3785. Ha, Yong-Chool, "Soviet Perceptions of Soviet-North Korean Relations," *Asian Survey*, 26, no. 5 (May 1986), 573-90.

3786. Haas, Richard N., "The `Europeanization' of Moscow's Asia Policy," *SAIS Review*, 7, no. 2 (Summer-Fall 1987), 127-41.

3787. Harrison, Selig S., "Cut a Regional Deal," *Foreign Policy*, no. 62 (Spring 1986), 126-47.

3788. Hayward, Thomas B., "Asia Is Still Living Up to Its Dynamic Reputation," *Sea Power*, 30, no. 2 (Jan. 1987), 52ff.

3789. -----, "The Pacific: The Inscrutable Far East Is Now the Dynamic Far West," *Sea Power*, 29, no. 4 (Mar. 1986), 44-49.

3790. Hiebert, M., "Carping about Cam Ranh: Hanoi Is Unhappy Over Moscow's Offer on the Base," *Far Eastern Economic Review*, 142 (27 Oct. 1988), 27.

3791. -----, "Hammer Blow for Hanoi: Vietnam and Cambodia

Feel the Pinch from Soviet Cutbacks," *Far Eastern Economic Review*, 149 (5 July 1990), 44-45.

3792. Horn, R. C., "Soviet Policy in East Asia," *Current History*, 86 (Oct. 1987), 321ff.

3793. Hua Di, "The Soviet Threat to the Northern Pacific Region from an Overall Point of View," *Atlantic Community Quarterly*, 24, no. 1 (Spring 1986), 28-38.

3794. Hyman, Anthony, "The Thaw in Moscow's Relations with Pakistan," *Report on the USSR*, 2, no. 3 (19 Jan. 1990), 12-14.

3795. Ivanov, Vladimir, "Perestroika in the Pacific," *Far Eastern Economic Review*, 147 (22 Feb. 1990), 24-25.

3796. -----, "Reducing Tensions: The View from Moscow," *World & I* (July 1990), 30-35.

3797. Ji Guoxing, "Current Security Issues in Southeast Asia," *Asian Survey*, 26, no. 9 (Sept. 1986), 973-90.

3798. Kennedy, William V., "Moving West: The New Theater of Decision," *Naval War College Review*, 42, no. 1 (Winter 1989), 19-32.

3799. Kimura, Hiroshi, "Soviet Focus on the Pacific," *Problems of Communism*, 36, no. 3 (May-June 1987), 1-16.

3800. Kiste, Robert C., and R. A. Herr, "The Potential for Soviet Penetration of the South Pacific Islands: An Assessment," *Bulletin of Concerned Asian Scholars*, 18, no. 2 (Apr-June 1986), 42-59.

3801. Kreisberg, Paul H., "Containment's Last Gasp," *Foreign Policy*, no. 75 (Summer 1989), 146-63.

3802. Lapidus, Gail W., "The USSR and Asia in 1986: Gorbachev's New Initiatives," *Asian Survey*, 27, no. 1 (Jan. 1987), 1-9.

3803. Legvold, Robert, "Soviet Policy in East Asia," *Washington Quarterly*, 14, no. 2 (Spring 1991), 129-42.

3804. Leighton, Marian, "Asia and the INF," *Global Affairs*, 4, no. 3 (Summer 1989), 30-51.

3805. Manning, Robert A., "Moscow's Pacific Future: Gorbachev Rediscovers Asia," *World Policy Journal*, 5, no. 1 (Winter 1987-88), 55-78.

3806. McNeill, Terry, "Soviet Policy in the Far East," *Report on the USSR*, 2, no. 42 (19 Oct. 1990), 14-16.

3807. Menon, Rajan, "New Thinking and Northeast Asian Security," *Problems of Communism*, 38, no. 2-3 (Mar-June 1989), 1-29.

3808. -----, and Daniel Abele, "Security Dimensions of Soviet Territorial Disputes with China and Japan," *Journal of Northeast Asian Studies*, 8, no. 1 (Spring 1989), 3-19.

3809. Meyer, Peggy Falkenheim, "Gorbachev and Post-Gorbachev Policy toward the Korean Peninsula: The Impact of Changing Russian Perceptions," *Asian Survey*, 32, no. 8 (Aug. 1992), 757-72.

3810. Mikheyev, Vasily V., "New Soviet Approaches to North Korea," *Korea and World Affairs*, 15, no. 3 (Fall 1991), 446ff.

3811. Miller, Elisa, "The USSR's Asia-Pacific Rim," *Pacific Northwest Executive*, 4 (July 1988), 20-25.

3812. Mossov, Mikhail G., "The USSR and the Security of the Asia-Pacific Region: From Vladivostok to Krasnoyarsk," *Asian Survey*, 29, no. 3 (Mar. 1989).

3813. Nakarmi, L., "South Korea Is Warming Up to China and Russia," *Business Week* (18 Apr. 1988), 42-43.

3814. -----, and Rose Brady, "The Handshake Felt Round East Asia," *Business Week* (28 June 1990), 43.

3815. -----, et al., "The Olympic Torch Took the Chill Out of Seoul-Moscow Relations," *Business Week* (3 Oct. 1988), 57.

3816. Nathan, K. S., "Malaysia and the Soviet Union: A Relationship with a Distance," *Asian Survey*, 27, no. 10 (Oct. 1987), 1059-73.

3817. Nations, Richard, "Moscow's New Tack," *Far Eastern Economic Review*, 133 (14 Aug. 1986), 30-40.

3818. Nolan, Mary I., "Gorbachev Mends Fences in Asia: Soviets Offer Political and Trade Incentives," *Sea Power*, 32, no. 10 (Oct. 1989), 41-42.

3819. O'Ballance, Edgar, "Pakistan: On the Front Porch of Conflict," *Military Review*, 66, no. 3 (Mar. 1986), 68-75.

3820. Odom, William E., "Pakistan and the Asian Balance," *National Interest*, no. 15 (Spring 1989), 104-09.

3821. Okonogi, Masao, "The Korean Peninsula: The Revival of the Old Equilibrium in the New Context," *Journal of North East Asian Studies*, 8, no. 1 (Spring 1989), 56-69.

3822. Olsen, Ed, "The Post-Cold War Era: An American Perspective," *World & I* (July 1990), 36-43.

3823. Paik, Keun-Wook, "Japan, Korea, and the Development of Russian Far Eastern Energy Resources," *Journal of Energy Development*, 16, no. 2 (Spring 1991), 227-46.

3824. "Pakistan and the Bear," *National Review*, 37 (19 Apr. 1985), 14-15.

3825. Palmer, Norman, D., "Setting Priorities in a Changing Asia," *World & I* (Jan. 1990), 126-32.

3826. Palmer, Ronald D., "The Soviet Union and Southeast Asia," *Washington Quarterly*, 9, no. 4 (Fall 1986), 169-73.

3827. Paranjpe, Shrikant, "Gorbachev's Asia-Pacific Security and the Regional State System of South Asia," *India Quarterly*, 46, no. 2-3 (Apr-Sept. 1990), 113-126.

3828. Perkovich, George, "The Soviets' Asian Dimension: Moscow Turns East," *Current* (Washington), 303 (June 1988), 15-24.

3829. -----, "The Soviet Union: Moscow Turns East," *Atlantic Monthly*, 260, no. 5 (Dec. 1987), 30ff.

3830. Plunk, Daryl, "Springtime for Soviet-Korean Relations,"

World & I (May 1990), 124-29.

3831. Pollack, D., "Moscow takes a Hard Look at Ties with Vietnam," *Far Eastern Economic Review*, 141 (22 Sept. 1988), 26-27.

3832. Pringle J., "Room to Breathe: Nationalist Upsurge as Soviets Pull Out" [of Mongolia], *Far Eastern Economic Review*, 145 (24 Aug. 1989), 24-25.

3833. Quinn-Judge, Sophie, "Ten Year Itch: Soviets Admit Much of Economic Aid to Hanoi Was Wasted," *Far Eastern Economic Review*, 142 (10 Nov. 1988), 23.

3834. Randolph, R. Sean, "The Soviet Economic Role in Asia and the Pacific: A Business Perspective," *Asian Survey*, 30, no. 12 (Dec. 1990), 1169-85.

3835. Reppy, Judith, "Reagan's Security Legacy: More for the Military," *Bulletin of the Atomic Scientists*, 45, no. 1 (Jan-Feb. 1989), 46-48.

3836. "The Road to Pakistan," *National Review*, 38 (15 Aug. 1986), 16-17.

3837. Robinson, Thomas W., "American Russian Relations in Asia: Cooperation or Competition?" *American Asian Review*, 8, no. 3 (Fall 1990), 75-94.

3838. ------, "U.S.-Soviet Relations in Asia: Cooperation or Competition?" *American Enterprise*, 1 (July-Aug. 1990), 56-61.

3839. Romberg, Alan D., "New Stirrings in Asia," *Foreign Affairs*, 64, no. 3 (1986), 515-38.

3840. Rosario, Louise, "The Soviet Far East: Perestroika Heads East: Coup's Defeat Brings Hope for Speedy Reform," *Far Eastern Economic Review*, 153 (Sept. 1991), 28ff.

3841. Rose, Leo E., "United States and Soviet Policy toward South Asia," *Current History*, 85, no. 509 (Mar. 1986), 97ff.

3842. Samuel, Peter, "Defense Flips Down Under," *Washington Quarterly*, 10, no. 4 (Autumn 1987), 113-27.

3843. ------, "Dibb Defense Doctrine in Australia," *Atlantic Community Quarterly*, 25, no. 1 (Spring 1987), 35-46.

3844. Sanders, A. J. K., "Mongolia in 1989: Year of Adjustment," *Asian Survey*, 30, no. 1 (Jan. 1990), 59-66.

3845. Scalapino, Robert A., "Asia's Future," *Foreign Affairs*, 66, no. 1 (Fall 1987), 77-108.

3846. Segal, Gerald, "Soviet Options in the Pacific," *Civilisations*, 40, no. 1 (1990), 43-100.

3847. ------, "The USSR and Asia in 1987: Signs of a Major Effort," *Asia Survey*, 28, no. 1 (Jan. 1988), 1-9.

3848. Sejong Institute, "The Dissolution of the Soviet Union and Its Impact on Northeast Asia" (Special Issue), *Sejong Review* (Oct. 1992), 1-311.

3849. Seung-ho, Joo, "South Korea's *Nordpolitik* and the Soviet Union," *Journal of East Asian Affairs*, 7, no. 2 (Summer-Fall 1993), 404-50.

3850. Shim, Jae Hoon, "Perestroika Pay Off: North Korea Outflanked as Gorbachov Meets Roh," *Far Eastern Economic Review*, 148 (14 June 1990), 10-11.

3851. Sigur, Gaston, Jr., "An East Asia-Pacific Prognosis: The Vital Signs Are Strong," *Strategic Review*, 14, no. 2 (Spring 1986), 36-43.

3852. Simeone, Matthew J., and Vladimir Wozniuk, "Selling Perestroika and New Thinking to Southeast Asia: Gorbachev at His Persuasive Best," *Political Communication and Persuasion*, 7 (July-Sept. 1990), 129-45.

3853. Soedjati, Djiwandono, "Indonesia's Changing Perception of the Soviet Union," *Indonesia Quarterly*, 15, no. 1 (1987).

3854. Stephan, John J., "Far Eastern Conspiracies? Russian Separatism on the Pacific," *Australian Slavonic and East European Studies*, 4, no. 102 (1990), 135-52.

3855. ------, "Perestroika on the Pacific: The Intellectual Dimension," *Pacifica*, 2, no. 1 (Jan. 1990), 1-15.

3856. Syrkin, Marie, "Moscow's Salute to Marcos," *Midstream*, 32, no. 5 (May 1986), 45-47.

3857. Szymanderski, J., and J. Winiecki, "The Gorbachev Challenge: The View from the East," *World Today*, 45, nos. 8-9 (Aug-Sept. 1989), 145-48.

3858. Titarenko, Mikhail L., "The Soviet Concept of Security and Cooperation in the Asia-Pacific Region," *Journal of Northeast Asian Studies*, 7, no. 1 (Spring 1988), 55-69.

3859. Trainor, Bernard, "Southeast Asia Ten Years after the Fall of Saigon," *Naval War College Review*, 39, no. 4 (Autumn 1986), 39-50.

3860. Van der Kroef, Justus M., "Crafting a Cambodian Compromise: `Eight Points,' `Three Points,' `No Point'," *Asian Thought and Society*, 11, no. 32-33 (July-Nov. 1986), 231-44.

3861. Vatikiotis, Michael, "Glasnost or 100 Flowers: Suharto's Openness Call Evokes Mixed Reviews," *Far Eastern Economic Review*, 150 (18 Oct. 1990), 23-24.

3862. Whiting, Allen, "The Peninsula and Perestroika," *World & I* (July 1990), 22-29.

3863. Williams, Michael C., "New Soviet Policy Toward Southeast Asia: Reorientation and Change," *Asian Survey*, 31, no. 4 (Apr. 1991), 364-77.

3864. Wolpert, Stanley, "Superpower Politics and South Asia," *Harvard International Review*, 9, no. 6 (July-Aug. 1987), 4-7.

3865. Yakovlev, Alexander G., "Role of the PRC and North Korea in Soviet-South Korean Relations," *Sino-Soviet Affairs* (Seoul), 13, no. 3 (Fall 1990), 94ff.

3866. Young, Stephen M., "Gorbachev's Asian Policy: Balancing the New and the Old," *Asian Survey*, 28, no. 3 (Mar. 1988), 317-39.

3867. Zagoria, Donald S., "Soviet-American Rivalry in Asia," in James W. Morley, ed., *The Pacific Basin: New Challenges for* the United States (New York: Academy of Political Science and Columbia University East Asian Institute and Center on Japanese Economy and Business, 1986).

3868. -----, "Soviet Policy in East Asia: A New Beginning?" *Foreign Affairs*, 68, no. 1 (1989), 120-38.

3869. -----, "The USSR and Asia in 1985," *Asian Survey*, 26, no. 1 (Jan. 1986), 15-29.

3870. Zaitsev, Valery K., "Problems of Russian Economic Reforms and Prospects for Economic Cooperation Between the Russian Far East and Northwest Pacific Countries," *Journal of Northeast Asian Studies*, 10, no. 4 (Winter 1991-92), 35-42.

3871. Zarsky, L., et al., "Is the Pacific a Nuclear Flashpoint?" *Utne Reader* (Mar-Apr. 1988), 50-51.

3872. Ziebart, Geoffrey, "Soviet Naval Developments in East Asia," *Journal of International Affairs*, 42 (Spring 1989), 457-75.

3873. Ziegler, Charles F., "Soviet Strategies for Development: East Asia and the Pacific Basin," *Pacific Affairs*, 63, no. 4 (Winter 1990-91), 451-69.

C. China
BOOKS

3874. Brick, Andrew B., *How the U.S. Should Prepare for a Sino-Soviet Summit* (Washington, DC: Heritage Foundation, Asian Studies Center, 1989).

3875. Chang, Gordon H., *Friends and Enemies: The United States, China and the Soviet Union* (Stanford: Stanford University Press, 1990).

3876. Harris, Lillian C., and Robert L. Worden, eds., *China and the Third World: Champion or Challenger?* (Dover, MA: Auburn House Publishing Co., 1986).

3877. Hart, Thomas, *Sino-Soviet Relations: Reexamining the Prospects for Normalization* (Aldershot: Gower Publishing Co., 1987).

3878. Holmes, Kim R., *U.S.-Soviet-China Relations and Strategic Defense* (Washington, DC: Heritage Foundation, 1986).

3879. Johnston, Alastair I., *China and Arms Control: Emerging Interests and Issues in the 1980s* (Ontario: Canadian Centre for Arms Control and Disarmament, 1986).

3880. Kim, Ilpyong I., ed., *The Strategic Triangle: China, the United States and the Soviet Union* (New York: Paragon House, 1987).

3881. Stoessinger, John G., *Nations in Darkness: China, Russia and America*, 5th ed. (New York: McGraw-Hill, 1990).

3882. Stolper, Thomas E., *China, Taiwan and the Offshore Islands: Together with an Implication for Mongolia and Sino-Soviet Relations* (Armonk, NY: M. E. Sharpe, 1985).

3883. Uhalley, Stephen, Jr., ed., *Sino-Soviet Documents Annual* (Gulf Breeze, FL: Academic International Press, 1993, and annually).

3884. US Congress. Senate. Committee on Foreign Relations. Subcommittee on East Asian and Pacific Affairs. *Sino-Soviet Relations after the Summit: A Workshop Sponsored by the Senate Foreign Relations Committee and the Congressional Research Service-15 May 1989*. 101st Congress, 2nd Session (Washington, DC: Government Printing Office, 1990).

ARTICLES

3885. "As the Gorbachev Wave Heads East," *Economist*, 314 (10 Feb. 1990), 31-32.

3886. Bagley, Worth H., "Toward a Sino-Soviet Compact," *Global Affairs*, 4, no. 3 (Summer 1989), 1-11.

3887. Becker, J., et al., "Deng Is Playing Hard-to-Get with Gorbachev," *Business Week* (20 June 1988), 67.

3888. Bilski, A., "In Search of Asian Peace," *Maclean's*, 101 (25 Jan. 1988), 18-19.

3889. Bonavia, David, "Deng and Gorbachov Face Demands of Materialism," *Far Eastern Economic Review*, 136 (9 Apr. 1987), 28-29.

3890. Chanda, Nayan, "A Summit in the Offing: Peking and Moscow Prepare for Deng-Gorbachev Meeting," *Far Eastern Economic Review*, 142 (13 Oct. 1988), 16-18.

3891. "China Welcomes Soviet Decision" [on Mongolia], *Beijing Review*, 31 (19 Dec. 1988), 10-11.

3892. Chu, Wellington, "Increased Military Sales to China: Problems and Prospects," *Journal of International Affairs*, 39 (Winter 1986), 133-47.

3893. Crozier, Brian, "The Moscow/Peking Dilemma," *National Review*, 39 (18 Dec. 1987), 26.

3894. D'Anastasio, M., et al., "Where a Soviet-Chinese Thaw Would Leave the U.S.," *Business Week* (6 May 1985), 65.

3895. Delfs, Robert, "One Stage, Two Plays: Deng's Position Undercut at Moment of History," *Far Eastern Economic Review*, 144 (25 May 1989), 12-14.

3896. Doder, Dusko, "China Snipes at One Summit but Readies for Another," *U.S. News & World Report*, 104 (13 June 1988), 45.

3897. Dreyer, June T., "The Xinjiang Uygur Autonomous Region at Thirty: A Report Card," *Asian Survey*, 26, no. 7 (July 1986), 721-44.

3898. Eikenberry, Karl W., "China on Arms Control and Disarmament," *Parameters*, 16, no. 3 (Autumn 1986), 68-75.

3899. Ellison, Herbert J., "Changing Sino-Soviet Relations," *Problems of Communism*, 36, no. 3 (May-June 1987), 17-29.

3900. -----, "Sino-Soviet Rapprochement," *Global Affairs*, 4, no. 3 (Summer 1989), 12-29.

3901. Ferdinand, Peter, "Russian and Soviet Shadows over China's Future?" *International Affairs*, 68, no. 2 (Apr. 1992), 279-92.

3902. Friedman, Edward, "Moscow and Beijing: Together Again?" *Telos*, no. 69 (Fall 1986), 32-48.

3903. Garver, John W., "The Chinese Communist Party and the Collapse of Soviet Communism," *China Quarterly*, no. 133 (Mar. 1993), 1-26.

3904. Ginsburgs, George, "The End of Sino-Russian Territorial Disputes?" *Journal of East Asian Affairs*, 7, no. 1 (Winter-Spring 1993), 261ff.

3905. Goldstein, Joseph S., and John R. Freeman, "U.S.-Soviet-Chinese Relations; Routine, Reciprocity, or Rational Expectations?" *American Political Science Review*, 85, no. 1 (Mar. 1991), 17-35.

3906. Gliksman, Alex, "Emerging Technology and China's Changing Security Requirements," *Washington Quarterly*, 10, no. 3 (Summer 1987), 133-44.

3907. Goldstein, Steven M., "Diplomacy amid Protest: The Sino-Soviet Summit," *Problems of Communism*, 38, no. 5 (Sept-Oct. 1989), 49-71.

3908. Green, Elizabeth E., "China and Mongolia: Recurring Trends and Prospects for Change," *Asian Survey*, 26, no. 12 (Dec. 1986), 1337-63.

3909. Gu, Xuewu, "China's Policy towards Russia," *Aussenpolitik*, 44, no. 3 (1993), 288-97.

3910. Hopkins, Mark, "Exploiting the `Three Obstacles': Beijing Plays Coy with Moscow," *New Leader* (10-24 Aug. 1987), 8-9.

3911. -----, "Beijing Plays Coy with Moscow," *New Leader*, 70 (10-24 Aug. 1987), 8-9.

3912. Horn, Robert C., "Soviet Leadership Changes and Sino-Soviet Relations," *Orbis*, 30, no. 4 (Winter 1987), 683-99.

3913. -----, "Soviet Policy in East Asia," *Current History*, 86, no. 522 (Oct. 1987), 321ff.

3914. -----, "Vietnam and Sino-Soviet Relations: What Price Rapprochement?" *Asian Survey*, 27, no. 7 (July 1987), 729-47.

3915. Hsiung, J. C., "Sino-Soviet Detente," *Current History*, 84 (Oct. 1985), 329-33.

3916. -----, "Sino-Soviet Detente and Chinese Foreign Policy," *Current History*, 87 (Sept. 1988), 245ff.

3917. Hsueh, Chun-tu, "Sino-Soviet Relations As Viewed from Moscow: An Account of a Meeting with Soviet Deputy Foreign Minister Kapitsa," *International Studies Notes*, 12, no. 3 (Fall 1986), 64-66.

3918. Huan Guocang, "Dynamics of Sino-Soviet Relations," *Atlantic Community Quarterly*, 24, no. 1 (Spring 1986), 39-49.

3919. -----, "The Dynamics of Sino-Soviet Relations," *Washington Quarterly*, 14, no. 2 (Spring 1991), 143-62.

3920. Hummel, Arthur W., Jr., "China's Changing Relations with the U.S. and the U.S.S.R.," *American Philosophical Society Proceedings*, 133, no. 1 (Mar. 1989), 75-83.

3921. Knight, Gregory D., "China's Soviet Policy in the Gorbachev Era," *Washington Quarterly*, 9, no. 2 (Spring 1986), 97-108.

3922. Lee, D., "Diplomacy, Gorbachev-Style, Looks Like a Winner in Beijing," *Business Week* (15 May 1989), 55.

3923. Levine, Steven I., "The End of Sino-Soviet Estrangement," *Current History*, 85, no. 512 (Sept. 1986), 245ff.

3924. -----, "Second Chance in China: Sino-Soviet Relations in the 1990s," *Annals of the American Academy of Political and Social Science*, 519 (Jan. 1992), 26-38.

3925. Long, Simon, "Gorbachev and Turmoil in China," *World Today*, 45, no. 7 (July 1989), 110-11.

3926. Lukin, Alexander, "The Initial Soviet Reaction to the Events in China in 1989 and the Prospects for Sino-Soviet Relations," *China Quarterly*, no. 125 (Mar. 1991), 119-36.

3927. Mahnken, Thomas G., "Current Sino-Soviet Military Relations," *Asian Affairs, An American Review*, 14, no. 2 (Summer 1987), 91-105.

3928. McCormick, Samuel D., "China's Security Involvement in Southwest Asia," *Air University Review*, 37, no. 3 (Mar-Apr. 1986), 31-41.

3929. Meaney, Constance S., "Is the Soviet Present China's Future?" *World Politics*, 39, no. 2 (Jan. 1987), 203-30.

3930. Mills, William deB., "Baiting the Chinese Dragon: Soviet Relations after Vladivostok," *Journal of Northeast Asian Studies*, 6, no. 3 (Fall 1987), 3-30.

3931. -----, "Gorbachev and the Future of Sino-Soviet Relations," *Political Science Quarterly*, 101, no. 4 (1986), 535-57.

3932. Nguyen, Hung P., "Russia and China: The Genesis of an Eastern Rapallo," *Asian Survey*, 33, no. 3 (Mar. 1993), 285-301.

3933. Oksenberg, Michel, "China's Confident Nationalism," *Foreign Affairs*, 65, no. 3 (1987), 501-23.

3934. Palmer, Norman D., "The United States and the Soviet Union in the Western Pacific," in *Westward Watch: The United States and the Changing Western Pacific* (Washington, DC: Pergamon-Brassey's International Defense Publications, 1987), 36-51.

3935. Pike, Douglas, and Benjamin Ward, "Losing and Winning: Korea and Vietnam as Success Stories," *Washington Quarterly*, 10, no. 3 (Summer 1987), 77-85.

3936. Pollack, Jonathan D., "China's Changing Perceptions of East Asian Security and Development," *Orbis*, 29, no. 4 (Winter 1986), 771-94.

3937. -----, "Gorbachov in Peking," *Far Eastern Economic Review*, 144 (1 June 1989), 22-23.

3938. Quinn-Judge, Sophie, "A Model for Reform: China's Example Inspires Soviet Reformers," *Far Eastern Economic Review*, 144 (25 May 1989), 16.

3939. -----, "The Soviets Cash in on the Rift with Peking," *Far Eastern Economic Review*, 128 (2 May 1985), 34.

3940. Robinson, Thomas W., "The New Era in Sino-Soviet Relations," *Current History*, 86, no. 521 (Sept. 1987), 241ff.

3941. Schiff, Daniel, "China: A New Challenge," *Harvard International Review*, 8, no. 4 (Mar. 1986), 41-44.

3942. Segal, Gerald, "Sino-Soviet Detente: How Far, How Fast?" *World Today*, 43, no. 5 (May 1987), 87-91.

3943. -----, "Sino-Soviet Relations: The New Agenda," *World Today*, 44, no. 6 (June 1988), 95-99.

3944. -----, "Taking Sino-Soviet Detente Seriously," *Washington Quarterly*, 12, no. 3 (Summer 1989), 53-63.

3945. "Shanghai's Gorbachev," *Economist*, 315 (16 June 1990), 79.

3946. Shao, Wenguang, "China's Relations with the Super-Powers," *Survey*, 32, no. 2 (Mar-Apr. 1990), 157-73.

3947. Shen Shouyuan, "Sino-European Relations in the Global Context: Increased Parallels in an Increasingly Plural World," *Asian Survey*, 26, no. 11 (Nov. 1986), 1164-83.

3948. Sing, Lam Lai, "From Mikhail Gorbachev's Policy to China's Regional Role," *Journal of East Asian Affairs*, 7, no. 2 (Summer-Fall 1993), 587ff.

3949. Speltz, Michael J., "Chinese Territorial Claims on the Soviet Far East," *Military Review*, 65, no. 8 (Aug. 1985), 63-73.

3950. Strode, Dan L., "Soviet China Policy in Flux," *Survival*, 30, no. 4 (July-Aug. 1988), 332-50.

3951. Suter, Keith D., "The Soviet Union and China: All Quiet on the Eastern Front?" *Contemporary Review*, 256, no. 1493 (June 1990), 287-94.

3952. Sutter, Robert G., "Changes in Eastern Europe and Soviet Union: The Effects on China," *Journal of Northeast Asian Studies*, 9, no. 2 (Summer 1990), 33-45.

3953. -----, "Sino-Soviet Relations: Recent Developments and Implications for the United States," *Journal of Northeast Asian Studies*, 6, no. 1 (Spring 1987), 62-75.

3954. Talbott, Strobe, "Swords into Sample Cases," *Time*, 132 (18 July 1988), 32-34.

3955. "Thunder Out of China," *Maclean's*, 102 (29 May 1989), 28ff.

3956. Trewhitt, H., "Why the Sino-Soviet Summit Was Important," *U.S. News & World Report*, 106 (29 May 1989), 36.

3957. Walsh, J. Richard, "China and the New Geopolitics of Central Asia," *Asian Survey*, 33, no. 3 (Mar. 1993), 272-84.

3958. "What's Behind the Soviet-Chinese Thaw," *Business Week* (24 Oct. 1988), 45.

3959. Woods, Lawrence T., "Delicate Diplomatic Debuts: Chinese and Soviet Participation in the Pacific Economic Cooperation Conference," *Pacific Affairs*, 63, no. 2 (Summer 1990), 210-27.

3960. Yahuda, Michael B., "Chinese Foreign Policy and the Collapse of Communism," *SAIS Review*, 12, no. 1 (Winter-Spring 1992), 125-38.

3961. Ying-hsien, Pi, "Chiang Tse-min's Visit to Moscow and Peking-Moscow Relations," *Issues and Studies*, 27, no. 12 (Dec. 1991), 100-11.

3962. Yu, Bin, "Sino-Russian Military Relations: Implications for Asian-Pacific Security," *Asian Survey*, 33, no. 3 (Mar. 1993), 302-16.

D. India

BOOKS

3963. Duncan, Peter J. S., *The Soviet Union and India* (New York: Council on Foreign Relations Press, 1989).

3964. Gooptu, Amiya, *An Image of the Contemporary World* (New York: Oxford University Press, 1987).

3965. Mehrota, Santosh, *India and the Soviet Union: Trade and Technology Transfer* (Cambridge: Cambridge University Press, 1990).

3966. Nihal Singh, S., *The Yogi and the Bear: Story of Indo-Soviet Relations* (London: Mansell, 1986).

3967. Rais, Rasul B., *The Indian Ocean and the Superpowers: Economic, Political and Strategic Perspectives* (Totowa, NJ: Barnes & Noble Books, Imports, 1987).

3968. Workshop on the Indian Ocean, *The Indian Ocean as a Zone of Peace* (Norwell, MA: Kluwer Academic Publishers, 1986).

ARTICLES

3969. Ahmar, Moonis, "India and Its Role in the New Central Asia," *Pakistan Horizon*, 45, no. 3 (July 1992), 57-70.

3970. Ali, Salamat, "A Shot in the Arm: Gorbachev Reassures Gandhi over China Rapprochement," *Far Eastern Economic Review*, 142 (1 Dec. 1988), 38.

3971. Banerjee, Jyotirmoy, "Moscow's Indian Alliance," *Problems of Communism*, 36, no. 1 (Jan-Feb. 1987), 1-12.

3972. Bhardwaj, Ram Dev, "Super-Power Rivalry in the Indian Ocean," *Political Science Review*, 28, no. 1-2 (Jan-June 1989), 9-40.

3973. Bouton, Marshall M., "Foreign Relations: Elusive Regional Security," in *India Briefing* (Boulder, CO: Westview Press, 1987), 159-83.

3974. Brown, D. A., "India Nearing Full Production of Soviet MiG-27M Fighter," *Aviation Week & Space Technology*, 124 (28 Apr. 1986), 22.

3975. Chadda, Maya, "India and the United States: Why Detente Won't Happen," *Asian Survey*, 26, no. 10 (Oct. 1986), 1118-36.

3976. Frankel, Francine R., "Play the India Card," *Foreign Policy*, no. 62 (Spring 1986), 148-66.

3977. Garver, John W., "The Indian Factor in Recent Sino-Soviet Relations," *China Quarterly*, no. 125 (Mar. 1991), 55-85.

3978. Jayawardane, Amal, "The Soviet Attitude toward the Indo-Sri Lankan Problem," *Pacific Affairs*, 64, no. 2 (Summer 1991), 194-207.

3979. Kreisberg, Paul H., "India after Indira," *Foreign Affairs*, 63, no. 4 (Spring 1985), 873-91.

3980. Malik, J. Mohan, "India Copes with the Kremlin's Fall," *Orbis*, 37, no. 1 (Winter 1993), 69-87.

3981. Modak, A. G., "The Gorbachevian Policy of Openness," *India Quarterly*, 45, no. 1 (Jan-Mar. 1989), 46-70.

3982. Mukerjee, Dilip, "India and the Soviet Union," *Washington Quarterly*, 9, no. 2 (Spring 1986), 109-22.

3983. -----, "U.S. Weaponry for India," *Asian Survey*, 27, no. 6 (June 1987), 595-614.

3984. Raghavulu, C. V., and K. C. Suri, "Perestroika, Developments in East Europe, and Indian Reaction," *Indian Journal of Political Science*, 52, no. 2 (Apr-June 1991), 165-84.

3985. Sahai-Achuthan, Nisha, "Soviet Presence in the Indian Ocean: Significance of the South Asian Littoral States," *Journal of South Asian and Middle Eastern Studies*, 10, no. 3 (Spring 1987), 3-37.

3986. Sedov, Leonid, "USSR-India: Dialogue in the Name of Peace," *Soviet Military Review*, no. 2 (Feb. 1987), 53-54.

3987. Shahi, Agha, "Pakistan-India Relations and Superpower Presence," *Journal of South Asian and Middle Eastern Studies*, 10, no. 4 (Summer 1987), 3-16.

3988. Subrahmanyam, K., "Eradicate the Nuclear Cult," *Bulletin of the Atomic Scientists*, 43, no. 2 (Mar. 1987), 36-39.

3989. Thakur, Ramesh, "The Impact of the Soviet Collapse on Military Relations with India," *Europe-Asia Studies*, 45, no. 5 (1993), 831-50.

3990. -----, "India and the Soviet Union: Conjunctions and Disjunctions of Interests," *Asian Survey*, 31, no. 9 (Sept. 1991), 826-46.

3991. Thornton, Thomas R., "Gorbachev's Courtship of India: India and the Soviet Union," *Round Table* (Oct. 1987), 457-66.

3992. Tongchang, Gui, "India-USSR: Gorbachev Affirms Special Friendship," *Beijing Review*, 31 (5 Dec. 1988), 16.

3993. Tully, M., "India and the Developments in the Soviet Union," *Asian Affairs*, 23 (June 1992), 142-51.

3994. Wriggins, W. Howard, "South Asia and the Gulf: Linkages, Gains and Limitations," *Middle East Review*, 18, no. 2 (Winter 1985-86), 25-35.

E. Japan

BOOKS

3995. Ellison, Herbert J., ed., *Japan and the Pacific Quadrille: The Major Powers in East Asia* (Boulder, CO: Westview, 1987).

3996. Falkenheim, Peggy L., *Japan and Arms Control: Tokyo's Response to SDI and INF* (Ottawa: Canadian Centre for Arms Control and Disarmament, 1988).

3997. Gelman, Harry, *Russo-Japanese Relations and the Future of the US-Japanese Alliance* (Santa Monica, CA: RAND Project Air Force, 1993).

3998. Hasegawa, Tsuyoshi, Jonathan Haslam and Andrew C. Kuchins, eds., *Russia and Japan: An Unresolved Dilemma between Distant Neighbors* (Berkeley: University of California Press, 1993).

3999. Jacob, Jo Dee Catlin, ed., *Beyond the Hoppo Ryodo: Japanese-Soviet-American Relations in the 1990s* (Washington, DC: AEI Press, Lanham, MD, distributed by University Press of America, 1991).

4000. Kim, Roy, *Japanese-Soviet Relations under Gorbachev* (Carl Beck Papers in Russian and East European Studies, no. 608; Pittsburgh: University of Pittsburgh Center for Russian and East European Studies, 1988).

4001. McGuire, Sumiye O., *Soviet-Japanese Economic Relations* (Santa Monica, CA: RAND, 1990).

4002. Nimmo, William F., *Japan and Russia: A Revolution in the Post-Soviet Era* (Westport, CT: Greenwood Press, 1994).

4003. Rozman, Gilbert, *Japan's Response to the Gorbachev Era, 1985-1991: A Rising Superpower Views a Declining One* (Princeton: Princeton University Press, 1992

ARTICLES

4004. Berton, Peter, "Soviet-Japanese Relations: Perceptions, Goals, Interactions," *Asian Survey*, 26, no. 12 (Dec. 1986), 1259-83.

4005. Blank, Stephen, "We Can Live Without You: Rivalry and Dialogue in Russo-Japanese Relations," *Comparative Strategy*, 12, no. 2 (Apr-June 1993), 173-98.

4006. Borrus, A., "Now, Gorbachev Is Building a Bridge to Japan," *Business Week* (25 Dec. 1989), 70.

4007. Bridges, Brian, "Japan: Waiting for Gorbachev," *Pacific Review*, 4, no. 1 (1991), 56-62.

4008. Buszynski, Leszek, "Russia and Japan: The Unmaking of a Territorial Settlement," *World Today*, 49, no. 3 (Mar. 1993), 50-53.

4009. Clark, Susan L., "Moscow's Opening to Japan," *Report on the USSR*, 2, no. 3 (19 Jan. 1990), 9-12.

4010. -----, "The Soviets and Japan's Defense Efforts," *Soviet Union/Union Sovietique*, 13, no. 2 (1986), 187-215.

4011. Crowe, Suzanne, "The Soviet-Japanese Summit: Expectations Unfulfilled," *Report on the USSR*, 3, no. 17 (26 Apr. 1991), 1-6.

4012. Dienes, Leslie, "Soviet-Japanese Economic Relations: Are They Beginning to Fade?" *Soviet Geography*, 26, no. 7 (Sept. 1985), 509-25.

4013. Falkenheim, Peggy Levine, "Evolving Regional Ties in Northeast Asia: Japan, the U.S. and the U.S.S.R.," *Asian Survey*, 28, no. 12 (Dec. 1988), 1229-44.

4014. -----, "Gorbachev's Japan Policy," in *International Symposium 86: Prospects for the International Situation and the Future of Japan-Soviet Relations* (Tokyo: Hokuku, 1987), 313-31.

4015. -----, "Japan, the Soviet Union and the Northern Territories: Prospects for Accommodation," in Lawrence E. Grinter and Young Whan Kihl, eds., *East Asian Conflict Zones: Prospects for Regional Stability and Deescalation* (New York: St. Martin's Press, 1987), 47-69.

4016. -----, "Moscow and Tokyo," *World Policy Journal*, 8, no. 1 (Winter 1990-91), 159-80.

4017. -----, "The Soviet Union, Japan and the Northern Territories Dispute: Incentives for and Obstacles to Its Resolution," *Korean Journal of International Studies*, 17, no. 4 (1986), 73-99.

4018. Foell, Earl W., "Yeltsin's Yen," *World Monitor*, 4, no. 2 (Feb. 1991), 80.

4019. Giblin, James F., "National Strategies and Japan's Northern Territories," *Naval War College Review*, 40, no. 1 (Winter 1987), 53-68.

4020. Gorbachev, Mikhail S., "USSR Foreign Relations with Japan," *Vital Speeches of the Day*, 57 (15 May 1991), 453-57.

4021. "Gorbachev-san," *Economist*, 319 (13 Apr. 1991), 13-14.

4022. Griffiths, D., "Soviet Saber-Rattling Speeds Japan's Rearmament," *Business Week* (9 Sept. 1985), 51.

4023. Gross, N., *et al.*, "Can Gorbachev Break a 40-Year Deadlock with Japan?" *Business Week* (5 Oct. 1987), 57.

4024. Helm, L., "Hands across the Tundra: Why Japan and Russia Are Talking Trade," *Business Week* (25 Feb. 1985), 48.

4025. Horne, Mari K., "The Northern Territories: Source or Symptom?" *Journal of North East Asian Studies*, 8, no. 4 (Winter 1989), 60-76.

4026. Hunter, Robert, "The United States, Japan, and the Future of Russia," *SAIS Review*, 12, no. 2 (Summer-Fall 1992), 65-71.

4027. "Islands Small, Problems Big," *U.S. News & World Report*, 100 (27 Jan. 1986), 31.

4028. Ito, Kenichi, "Japan and the Soviet Union: Entangled in the Deadlock of the Northern Territories," *Washington Quarterly*, 11, no. 1 (Winter 1988), 34-44.

4029. "Japan, Gorbachev and the Price of Peace," *Economist*, 318 (30 Mar. 1991), 33-34.

4030. Johnson, Chalmers, "Japanese-Soviet Relations in the Early Gorbachev Era," *Asian Survey*, 27, no. 11 (Nov. 1987), 1145-60.

4031. -----, "Reflections on the Dilemma of Japanese Defense," *Asian Survey*, 26, no. 5 (May 1986), 557-72.

4032. Kato, Koichi, "An Emerging Consensus: The Evolution of Japan's Defense Posture," *Atlantic Community Quarterly*, 23, no. 4 (Winter 1985-86), 325-29.

4033. Kim, Roy, "Gorbachev's Challenge to Japan," *Atlantic Community Quarterly*, 25, no. 3 (Fall 1987), 351-66.

4034. -----, "Warming Up Soviet-Japanese Relations," *Washington Quarterly*, 9, no. 2 (Spring 1986), 85-96.

4035. Kimura, Hiroshi, "Gorbachev's Japan Policy: The Northern Territories Issue," *Asian Survey*, 31, no. 9 (Sept. 1991), 798-815.

4036. -----, "The Soviet-Japanese Territorial Dispute," *Harriman Institute Forum*, 2, no. 6 (June 1989), 1-8.

4037. Langdon, Frank, "The Security Debate in Japan," *Pacific Affairs*, 58, no. 3 (Fall 1985), 397-410.

4038. Mack, Andrew, and Martin O'Hare, "Moscow-Tokyo and the Northern Territories Dispute," *Asian Survey*, 30, no. 4 (Apr. 1990), 380-94.

4039. Mazzocco, William, "Japan, the USSR, and Eurasia," *Global Affairs*, 4, no. 1 (Winter 1989), 187-202.

4040. Mendl, Wolf, "Japan and the Soviet Union: Towards a Deal?" *World Today*, 47, no. 11 (Nov. 1991), 196ff.

4041. -----, "Japan's Northern Territories: An Asian Falklands?" *World Today*, 43, no. 6 (June 1987), 99-102.

4042. Menon, Rajan, "Gorbachev's Japan Policy," *Survival*, 33, no. 2 (Mar-Apr. 1991), 158-72.

4043. -----, "Soviet-Japanese Relations-More of the Same," *Current History*, 90, no. 555 (Apr. 1991), 160-63.

4044. Mochizuki, Mike, "Japan's Foreign Policy," *Current History*, 84, no. 506 (Dec. 1985), 401ff.

4045. Nakayama, Taro, "Japan's Stance in Eastern Europe," *Harvard International Review*, 13, no. 1 (Fall 1990), 15ff.

4046. Neff, R., "Will Gorbachev Ask Tokyo to Play `Let's Make a Deal'?" *Business Week* (8 Apr. 1991), 46-47.

4047. Nemeth, M., "No Islands, No Money: Gorbachev Appeals in Vain for Japanese Aid," *Maclean's*, 104 (29 Apr. 1991), 27.

4048. Njoroge, Lawrence M., "The Japan-Soviet Union Territorial Dispute," *Asian Survey*, 25, no. 5 (May 1985), 499-511.

4049. O'Connell, John, "Strategic Implications of the Japanese SSM-1 Cruise Missile," *Journal of Northeast Asian Studies*, 6, no. 2 (Summer 1987), 53-66.

4050. Olsen, Edward A., "Determinants of Strategic Burden-sharing in East Asia: The U.S.-Japanese Conflict," *Naval War College Review*, 39, no. 3 (May-June 1986), 4-21.

4051. Powell, B., and F. Coleman, "Gorbachev Goes to Tokyo:

No Deal," *Newsweek*, 117 (29 Apr. 1991), 40.

4052. Rehbein, Robert E., "The Japan-Soviet Far East Trade Relationship: A Case of the Cautious Buyer and the Over-confident Seller," *Journal of Northeast Asian Studies*, 8, no. 2 (Summer 1989), 38-64.

4053. Saito, M., "Japanese and the Russian Struggle toward a New System," *Japan Quarterly*, 39 (Apr-June 1989), 76-85.

4054. Song, Allan Y., "A Half-Step Forward: An Assessment of the April 1991 Soviet-Japanese Summit," *Asian Perspectives*, 16 (Spring-Summer 1992), 103-28.

4055. "Soviet Japanese Relations in the 1980s: More of the Same," *Korea and World Affairs*, 11, no. 2 (Summer 1987), 264-67.

4056. Spandaryan, Victor, "Economic Relations with Japan: How to Fix Them Up?" *International Affairs* (Moscow), no. 5 (1991), 63-71.

4057. Stokes, Bruce, "National Security: Making Eyes at Moscow," *National Journal*, 22, no. 3 (20 Jan. 1990), 116-20.

F. Latin America, Central America, Cuba and the Caribbean
BOOKS

4058. Adams, Jan. S., *A Foreign Policy in Transition: Moscow's Retreat from Central America and the Caribbean, 1985-1992* (Durham, NC: Duke University Press, 1992).

4059. Cirincione, Joseph, ed., *Central America and the Western Alliance* (New York: Holmes & Meier, 1985).

4060. Falk, Pamela S., *Cuban Foreign Policy: Caribbean Tempest* (Lexington, MA: Lexington Books, 1986).

4061. Gonzalez, Edward, and David Ronfeldt, *Castro, Cuba and the World* (Santa Monica, CA: RAND, 1986).

4062. Kirkpatrick, Evron M., ed., *The Rising Soviet Presence in Latin America* (Washington, DC: American Peace Society, 1986).

4063. Larkin, Bruce, *Vital Interests: The Soviet Issue in U.S. Central American Policy* (Boulder, CO: Lynne Rienner Publishers, 1988).

4064. Mesa-Lago, Carmelo, *Cuba-After the Cold War* (Pittsburgh: University of Pittsburgh Press, 1993).

4065. Miller, Nicola, *Soviet Relations with Latin America, 1959-1987* (New York: Cambridge University Press, 1989).

4066. Mujal-Leon, Eusebio, ed., *The USSR and Latin America: A Developing Relationship* (Boston: Unwin Hyman, 1989).

4067. Sand, G. W., *Soviet Aims in Central America: The Case of Nicaragua* (New York: Praeger, 1989).

4068. Shearman, Peter, *The Soviet Union and Cuba* (London: Routledge & Kegan Paul, 1987),

4069. Smith, Wayne S., *The Closest of Enemies: A Personal and Diplomatic Account of U.S.-Cuban Relations since 1957* (New York: W. W. Norton, 1987).

4070. -----, ed., *The Russians Aren't Coming: New Soviet Policy in Latin America* (Boulder, CO: Lynne Rienner, 1992).

4071. Suchlicki, Jaime, *The Crisis in Central America* (Washington, DC: Washington Institute Press, 1987).

4072. Tagor, Sergei, *Perestroika and Soviet-Latin American Relations* (Washington, DC: Latin American Program, The Wilson Center, 1991).

4073. US Congress. House. Committee on Foreign Affairs. Subcommittee on Europe and the Middle East. *Cuba in a Changing World: The United States-Soviet-Cuban Triangle. Hearings.* 102nd Congress, 1st Session (Washington, DC: Government Printing Office, 1991).

4074. Wiarda, Howard J., and Mark Falcoff, with Ernest Evans et al., *The Communist Challenge in the Caribbean and Central America* (Washington, DC: American Enterprise Institute for Public Policy Research, 1987).

ARTICLES

4075. Adams, Jan S., "Change and Continuity in Soviet Central American Policy," *Problems of Communism*, 38, no. 2-3 (Mar-June 1989), 112-20.

4076. Armbrister, Trevor, "Central America: It Would Appear Tide Is Turning the Wrong Way," *Sea Power*, 29, no. 4 (Mar. 1986), 60-65.

4077. Ashby, Timothy, "Has Gorbachev Turned His Back?" *US Naval Institute Proceedings*, 116, no. 1 (Jan. 1990), 79-82.

4078. Black, George, "Fidel Holds Fast," *Nation*, 250 (1 Jan. 1990), 4-5.

4079. Blasier, Cole, "Moscow's Retreat from Cuba," *Problems of Communism*, 40, no. 6 (Nov-Dec. 1991), 91-99.

4080. Brady, Rose, *et al.*, "Will Moscow Someday Decide `Yanqui Si, Fidel No'?" *Business Week* (17 June 1991), 52.

4081. Brooke, James, "Cuba's Strange Mission in Angola," *New York Times Magazine* (1 Feb. 1987), 24ff.

4082. Brooks, David, "Fidel and His Masters," *National Review*, 38 (25 Apr. 1986), 26.

4083. -----, "Latin America Is Not East of Here" *National Review*, 38 (14 Mar. 1986), 32ff.

4084. Bryan, Anthony T., "A Tropical Perestroika? Cuba, the Soviet Union and the Caribbean," *Caribbean Affairs*, 2, no. 2 (1989), 92-103.

4085. Burman, R., "Reaching Out to Latin America," *World Press Review*, 35 (Aug. 1988), 20-21.

4086. Bustamante, Fernando, "Soviet Policy toward Latin America: Time for Renewal," *Journal of Interamerican Studies and World Affairs*, 32, no. 4 (Winter 1990), 35-65.

4087. Castaneda, Jorge G., "Latin America and the End of the

Cold War," *Cross Currents: Religion & Intellectrual Life*, 41, no. 2 (1991), 195-219.

4088. Colbum, Forrest D., "Embattled Nicaragua," *Current History*, 86, no. 524 (Dec. 1987), 405ff.

4089. Coll, Alberto R., "Soviet Arms and Central American Turmoil," *World Affairs*, 148, no. 1 (Summer 1985), 7-17.

4090. -----, "Why Grenada Was Important," *Naval War College Review*, 40, no. 3 (Summer 1987), 4-18.

4091. Cox, Tom, "The Cold War Endgame in Central America," *World & I* (May 1990), 130-34.

4092. Cross, Sharyl, "Gorbachev's Policy in Latin America: Origins, Impact, and the Future," *Communist and Post-Communist Studies*, 26, no. 3 (Sept. 1993), 315-34.

4093. Crozier, Brian, "The Protracted Conflict: Fidel and His Masters," *National Review*, 38 (25 Apr. 1986), 26.

4094. Depalo, William A., "The Military Situation in Nicaragua," *Military Review*, 66, no. 8 (Aug. 1986), 28-41.

4095. Dominguez, Jorge I., "Cuba: Charismatic Communism," *Problems of Communism*, 34, no. 5 (Sept-Oct. 1985), 102-07.

4096. Duncan, W. Raymond, "Castro and Gorbachev: Politics of Accommodation," *Problems of Communism*, 35, no. 2 (Mar-Apr. 1986), 45-57.

4097. -----, "Castro's Cuba: The Odd Partners," *Wilson Quarterly*, 12, no. 5 (Winter 1988), 75-83.

4098. Ellison, Katherine, "Cuba Succeeding Castro," *Atlantic*, 265 (June 1990), 34-39.

4099. Farber, Samuel, "Castro under Siege," *World Policy Journal*, 9, no. 2 (Spring 1992), 329-48.

4100. Goble, Paul, "Is Moscow About to Cut Castro Loose?" *Report on the USSR*, 2, no.2 (12 Jan. 1990), 4-6.

4101. Gonzalez, Edward, and David Ronfeldt, "Castro, Cuba and the World," *Conflict*, 7, no. 4 (1987), 403-30.

4102. Grabendorff, Wolf, "Central America: A Dilemma for US-European Relations," *Harvard International Review*, 9, no. 1 (Nov-Dec. 1986), 37-39.

4103. Grenier, R., "The Albania of the Caribbean," *National Review*, 41 (5 May 1989), 41-43.

4104. Gunn, Gillian, "Cuba's Search for Alternatives: Excerpts from an Interview with Fidel Castro," *Current History*, 91, no. 562 (Feb. 1992), 59-64.

4105. Haggerty, Brian C., "U.S. Policy in Latin America: Assessing the Balance Sheet," *Air University Review*, 37, no. 5 (July-Aug. 1986), 17-25.

4106. Haglund, David G., "The Missing Link: Canada's Security Interests and the Central American Crisis," *International Journal*, 42, no. 4 (Autumn 1987), 789-820.

4107. Hamburg, Roger, "Soviet-Latin American Relations" (Review Article), *Problems of Communism*, 39, no. 5 (Sept-Oct. 1990), 99-107.

4108. -----, "Soviet Perspectives on the Cuban, Chilean and Nicaraguan Revolutions," *Crossroads*, no. 24 (1987), 65-76.

4109. Kapcia, Tony, "Cuba After Thirty Years: The Gorbachev Visit and After," *Contemporary Review*, 255, no. 1483 (Aug. 1989), 68-74.

4110. Kirkpatrick, Jeane J., "Our Cuban Misadventures," *Atlantic Community Quarterly*, 24, no. 2 (Summer 1986), 155-56.

4111. Kline, Michael, "Castro and `New Thinking' in Latin America," *Journal of Interamerican Studies and World Affairs*, 32, no. 1 (Spring 1990), 83-118.

4112. Krauss, Clifford, "Revolution in Central America?" *Foreign Affairs*, 65, no. 3 (1987), 564-81.

4113. Lane, Charles, "Low Fidelity: How Long Can Cuban Communism Last?" *New Republic* (7 Jan. 1991), 25-28.

4114. LeMoyne, James, "A Region in Conflict," *New York Times Magazine* (6 Apr. 1986), 14ff.

4115. Leonard, Thomas M., "Central America: A Microcosm of U.S. Cold War Policy," *Air University Review*, 37, no. 5 (July-Aug. 1986), 39-55.

4116. Marcella, Gabriel, "Security, Democracy, and Development: The United States and Latin America in the Next Decade," *Air University Review*, 37, no. 5 (July-Aug. 1986), 2-14.

4117. McColm, R. Bruce, "Castro's Ambitions Amid New Winds from Moscow," *Strategic Review*, 14, no. 3 (Summer 1986), 48-57.

4118. -----, "Nicaragua, Facing the Issues," *Freedom at Issue*, no. 92-93 (Nov-Dec.1986), 3-8.

4119. Michel, James H., "Soviet Activities in Latin America and the Caribbean," *Department of State Bulletin*, 85 (July 1985), 80-85.

4120. Mikoyan, Sergo A., "Soviet Foreign Policy and Latin America," *Washington Quarterly*, 13, no. 3 (Summer 1990), 179-91.

4121. Montaner, Carlos Alberto, "Cuba: The Twelfth Hour," *World & I* (June 1990), 41-45.

4122. -----, "*Glasnost'*, *Perestroika* and the Soviet Union: Castro's Cuba in Gorbachev's Era," *Society*, 25, no. 4 (May-June 1988), 27-30.

4123. Moore, John N., "Global Order, Low Intensity Conflict and a Strategy of Deterrence," *Naval War College Review*, 39, no. 1 (Jan-Feb. 1986), 30-46.

4124. -----, "The Secret War in Central America and the Future of World Order," *American Journal of International Law*, 80, no. 1 (Jan. 1986), 43-127.

4125. Mujal-Leon, Eusebio M., "Perspectives on Soviet-Latin American Relations," *Washington Quarterly*, 9, no. 4 (Fall 1986),

165-68.

4126. Oborotova, Marina, "Russian Policy in Latin America: Past, Present, and Future" (Review Article), *Latin American Research Review*, 28, no. 3 (1993), 183-88.

4127. Ortega, Daniel, and Tomas Borge, "From Russia with Glasnost: A New Look at What Is To Be Done: Revolution and the Reform," *New Perspectives Quarterly*, 4, no. 2 (Spring 1987), 38-43.

4128. Packenham, Robert A., "Capitalist vs. Socialist Dependency: The Case of Cuba," *Journal of Inter-American Studies and World Affairs*, 28, no. 1 (Spring 1986), 59-92.

4129. Padelford, Edward A., "Caribbean Security and U.S. Political-Military Presence," *Strategic Review*, 14, no. 4 (Fall 1986), 54-62.

4130. Pastor, Robert A., "Does the United States Push Revolutions to Cuba? The Case of Grenada," *Journal of Inter-American Studies and World Affairs*, 28, no. 1 (Spring 1986), 1-34.

4131. Payne, Douglas W., "Fidel Castro versus Perestroika," *Report on the USSR*, 2, no. 2 (12 Jan. 1990), 6-10.

4132. -----, and Antonio Ybarra-Rojas, "Crisis in Chile: Scenarios and Gameplans," *Strategic Review*, 14, no. 3 (Summer 1986), 27-47.

4133. Pearson, John, and Gail DeGeorge, "Mr. Castro Goes to Market: Suddenly, Western Investment Is Replacing Soviet Aid," *Business Week* (20 Apr. 1992), 46-47.

4134. Perez-Lopez, Jorge F., "Swimming against the Tide: Implications for Cuba of Soviet and Eastern European Reforms in Foreign Economic Relations," *Journal of Interamerican Studies and World Affairs*, 33, no. 2 (Summer 1991), 81-140.

4135. Quiros, Daniel O., "Central America and the Western Alliance," *Harvard International Review*, 9, no. 1 (Nov-Dec. 1986), 26ff.

4136. "Reading Between the Lines in Havana," *U.S. News & World Report*, 106 (17 Apr. 1989), 13.

4137. Riefe, Robert H., "Gorbachev, Castro and National Liberation in Latin America," *Journal of Social, Political and Economic Studies*, 14, no. 3 (Fall 1989), 259-82.

4138. Ritter, A. R. M., "The Cuban Economy in the 1990s: External Challenges and Policy Imperatives," *Journal of Interamerican Studies and World Affairs*, 32, no. 3 (Fall 1990), 117-49.

4139. Robertson, J. Michael, "Latin American Revolutionaries in the Post-Soviet Era: The Case of Sendero Luminoso," *Strategic Review*, 20, no. 1 (1992), 32-41.

4140. Schorr, Daniel, "A Coup Dividend (Pullout of Troops from Cuba)," *New Leader*, 74, no. 11 (7-21 Oct. 1991), 4.

4141. -----, "Top-Level Talk in Havana," *New Leader*, 72 (3-17 Apr. 1989), 4.

4142. Stanchenko, Vladimir I., "The Soviet Role in Central America," *Washington Quarterly*, 13, no. 3 (Summer 1990), 193-202.

4143. Stoiko, Michael, and George Luedeke, Jr., "Advancing South with Advanced Vehicles," *US Naval Institute Proceedings*, 112, no. 2 (Feb. 1986), 81-88.

4144. Szulc, Tad, "Can Castro Last?" *New York Review of Books*, 37 (31 May 1990), 12-15.

4145. Valenta, Jiri, "'New Thinking' and Soviet Policy in Latin America," *Washington Quarterly*, 13, no. 2 (Spring 1990), 135-51.

4146. Waghelstein, John D., "A Latin-American Insurgency Status Report," *Military Review*, 67, no. 2 (Feb. 1987), 42-47.

4147. "Who's Man in Havana?" *Nation*, 248 (24 Apr. 1989), 541.

4148. Wiarda, Howard J., "Updating U.S. Strategic Policy: Containment in the Caribbean Basin," *Air University Review*, 37, no. 5 (July-Aug. 1986), 27-38.

4149. Zimbalist, Andrew, "Cuba in the Age of Perestroika," *Latin American Perspectives*, 20 (Winter 1993), 47-57.

4150. Zubek, Voytek, "Soviet 'New Thinking' and the Central American Crisis," *Journal of Inter-American Studies and World Affairs*, 29, no. 3 (Fall 1987), 87-106.

G. Middle East

BOOKS

4151. Allen, Robert L., *Middle Eastern Economic Relations with the Soviet Union, Eastern Europe and Mainland China* (Westport, CT: Greenwood Press, 1985).

4152. Breslauer, George W., *Soviet Strategy in the Middle East* (Boston: Unwin Hyman, 1990).

4153. Cossa, Ralph A., *Iran: Soviet Interests, US Concerns* (Washington, DC: Institute of National Strategic Studies, National Defense University, 1990).

4154. Efrat, Moshe, and Bercovitch, Jacob, eds., *Superpowers and Client States in the Middle East: The Imbalance of Influence* (London: Routledge, 1991).

4155. Freedman, Robert O., *Moscow and the Middle East: Soviet Policy since the Invasion of Afghanistan* (Cambridge: Cambridge University Press, 1987).

4156. -----, *Soviet Policy toward Israel Under Gorbachev* (New York: Praeger, 1991).

4157. Golan, Galia, *Moscow and the Middle East: New Thinking on Regional Conflict* (New York: Council on Foreign Relations Press, 1992).

4158. -----, *Soviet Middle East Policy under Gorbachev* (Santa Monica, CA: RAND, 1990).

4159. -----, *Soviet Policies in the Middle East: From World War II to Gorbachev* (New York: Cambridge University Press, 1990).

4160. Goldman, Stuart D., *Soviet Policy toward Iran and the*

Strategic Balance in Southeast Asia (Washington, DC: Library of Congress, Congressional Research Service, 1987).

4161. Hollis, Rosemary, ed., *The Soviets, Their Successors and the Middle East: Turning Point* (New York: St. Martin's Press, 1994).

4162. International Security Council, *The Soviet-Syrian Alliance and Security of the Middle East, Jerusalem, Israel, October 19-21, 1986*, CAUSA International Seminar Series, vol. 24 (New York: International Security Council, 1987).

4163. Karp, Aaron, *The United States and the Soviet Union and the Control of Ballistic Missile Proliferation in the Middle East* (New York: Institute for East-West Security Studies, 1990).

4164. Karsh, Efraim, *Soviet Policy toward Syria since 1970* (New York: St. Martin's Press, 1991).

4165. -----, *The Soviet Union and Syria: The Asad Years* (London: Routledge, for the Royal Institute of International Affairs, 1988).

4166. Katz, Mark N., *Russia and Arabia: Soviet Foreign Policy toward the Arabian Peninsula* (Baltimore: Johns Hopkins University Press, 1986).

4167. Keddie, Nikki R., and Mark J. Gasiorowski, eds., *Neither East nor West: Iran, the Soviet Union and the United States* (New Haven: Yale University Press, 1990).

4168. McNaugher, Thomas L., *Arms and Oil: Military Strategy and the Persian Gulf* (Washington, DC: Brookings Institution, 1985).

4169. Phillips, James A., *Responding to the Soviet Challenge in the Persian Gulf* (Washington, DC: Heritage Foundation, 1989).

4170. Ramet, Pedro, *Soviet Policy toward Syria, 1976-1986: Factionalism and the Limits of Influence* (Washington, DC: Woodrow Wilson International Center for Scholars, Kennan Institute, 1986).

4171. Ramet, Sabrina P., *The Soviet-Syrian Relationship since 1955: A Troubled Alliance* (Boulder, CO: Westview Press, 1990).

4172. Saivetz, Carol, *The Soviet Union and the Gulf in the 1980s* (Boulder, CO: Westview Press, 1989).

4173. Sella, Amnon, *The USSR's Interests Along Its Southern Borders and Beyond* (College Station, TX: Texas A&M University System, Center for Strategic Technology, 1986).

4174. Sicker, Martin, *The Bear and the Lion: Soviet Imperialism and Iran* (New York: Praeger, 1988).

4175. Smolansky, Oles M., with Bettie M. Smolansky, *The USSR and Iraq: The Soviet Quest for Influence* (Durham, NC: Duke University Press, 1991).

4176. Taylor, Alan R., *The Superpowers and the Middle East* (Syracuse: Syracuse University Press, 1991).

4177. US Foreign Broadcast Information Service. *Moscow's Posture on the Arab-Israeli Conflict: Evolving Flexibility* (Washington, DC: FBIS, 1989).

4178. Zabih, Sepehr, *The Left in Contemporary Iran: Ideology, Organisation, and the Soviet Connection* (Stanford: Hoover Institution Press, 1986).

ARTICLES

4179. Abir, Mordechai, "Saudi-Soviet Relations and the Iran-Iraq War," *Middle East Journal*, 22, no. 1 (Winter 1989), 10-16.

4180. Abrir, M. E., "Moscow and the Middle East: The Future of Strategic Relationships," *Journal of South Asian and Middle Eastern Studies*, 17, no. 4 (Summer 1994), 1-20.

4181. Ahrari, Mohammed E., "Iran and the Superpowers in the Gulf," *SAIS Review*, 7, no. 1 (Winter-Spring 1987), 157-68.

4182. -----, and Omar Khalidi, "The Emerging Shape of Strategic Competition in the Persian Gulf," *Strategic Review*, 18, no. 4 (Fall 1990), 23-28.

4183. Alexandrova, Olga, "Soviet Policy in the Gulf Conflict," *Aussenpolitik*, 42, no. 3 (1991), 231-40.

4184. Anderson, H., "*Glasnost* in the Persian Gulf," *Newsweek*, 111 (11 Jan. 1988), 124-28.

4185. Arens, Moshe, "Interview with Moshe Arens, Minister without Portfolio of the State of Israel," *Crossroads*, no. 22 (1986), 61-72.

4186. Atherton, Alfred L., Jr., "The Soviet Role in the Middle East: An American View," *Middle East Journal*, 39, no. 4 (Autumn 1985), 688-715.

4187. Atkin, Muriel, "Rethinking the Iranian Revolution," *Problems of Communism*, 35, no. 2 (Mar-Apr. 1986), 86-92.

4188. Bennett, Alexander J., "Arms Transfer as an Instrument of Soviet Policy in the Middle East," *Middle East Journal*, 39, no. 4 (Autumn 1985), 745-74.

4189. Bruner, Whitley, "Soviet New Thinking and the Middle East: Gorbachev's Arab-Israeli Options," *Comparative Strategy*, 9, no. 4 (Oct-Dec. 1990), 385-401.

4190. Brzoska, Michael, "Profiteering on the Iran-Iraq War," *Bulletin of the Atomic Scientists*, 43, no. 5 (June 1987), 42-45.

4191. "Bush, Gorbachev Call on Iraq to Withdraw from Kuwait," *Congressional Quarterly Weekly Report*, 48 (15 Sept. 1990), 2957-60.

4192. Christopher, Ian, "The Soviet Union Lost the Arms Race in the Gulf War," *Contemporary Review*, 258, no. 1504 (May 1991), 230-32.

4193. Cigar, Norman, "South Yemen and the USSR: Prospects for the Relationship," *Middle East Journal*, 39, no. 4 (Autumn 1985), 775-95.

4194. -----, "Soviet-South Yemeni Relations: The Gorbachev Years," *Journal of South Asian and Middle Eastern Studies*, 12, no. 4 (Summer 1989), 3-38.

4195. Clarke, Douglas L., "Warsaw Pact Arms in Iraq," *Report on Eastern Europe*, 1, no. 33 (17 Aug. 1990), 23-26.

4196. Critchlow, James, "Ties with Turkey: A Lifeline for the Central Asians?" *Report on the USSR*, 3, no. 6 (8 Feb. 1991), 19-21.

4197. Crow, Suzanne, "The Gulf Conflict and Debate over Soviet `National' Interests," *Report on the USSR*, 3, no. 6 (8 Feb. 1991), 15-17.

4198. -----, "Legislative Considerations and the Gulf Crisis," *Report on the USSR*, 2, no. 50 (14 Dec. 1990), 1-3.

4199. -----, "Moscow Struggles with Decision on UN Force," *Report on the USSR*, 2, no. 48 (30 Nov. 1990), 1-4.

4200. -----, "Primakov and the Soviet Peace Initiative," *Report on the USSR*, 3, no. 9 (1 Mar. 1991), 14-17.

4201. -----, "Restoration of Ties with Israel," *Report on the USSR*, 3, no. 44 (1 Nov. 1991), 1-4.

4202. -----, "Soviet Union Pursues Dual Policy on Iraq," *Report on the USSR*, 2, no. 40 (5 Oct. 1990), 6-8.

4203. Crozier, Brian, "The Protracted Conflict: The Problem of Crazy States," *National Review*, 38 (14 Mar. 1986), 24.

4204. -----, "Saddam's Soviet Connection," *National Review*, 43 (18 Mar. 1991), 40.

4205. Dannreuther, Roland, "Russia, Central Asia and the Persian Gulf," *Survival*, 35, no. 4 (Winter 1993-94), 92-112.

4206. Dickey, Christopher, "Assad and His Allies: Irreconcilable Differences?" *Foreign Affairs*, 66, no. 1 (Fall 1987), 58-76.

4207. Eickelman, Dale F., and Kamran Pasha, "Muslim Societies and Politics: Soviet and US Approaches-A Conference Report," *Middle East Journal*, 45, no. 4 (Autumn 1991), 630-48.

4208. Epstein, Edward Jay, "Virtual Ally," *New Republic* (3 Dec. 1990), 19-20.

4209. Evans, Roland, and Robert D. Novak, "High Drama in the Persian Gulf," *Reader's Digest*, 131 (Dec. 1987), 133-36.

4210. "Faking the Red Menace," *Nation*, 244 (24 Jan. 1987), 65.

4211. Freedman, Robert O., "Moscow and the Gulf War," *Problems of Communism*, 40, no. 4 (July-Aug. 1991), 1-17.

4212. -----, "Soviet Jewry as a Factor in Soviet-Israeli Relations," in his *Soviet Jewry in the 1980s: The Politics of Anti-Semitism and Emigration and the Dynamics of Resettlement* (Durham, NC: Duke University Press, 1989), 61-96.

4213. Fuller, Graham E., "The Middle East in United States-Soviet Relations," *Middle East Journal*, 44, no. 3 (Summer 1990), 415-30.

4214. -----, "Moscow and the Gulf War," *Foreign Affairs*, 70, no. 1 (Summer 1991), 55-76.

4215. Galloway, J. L., "Mideast: Moscow on a Roll," *U.S. News & World Report*, 102 (18 May 1987), 32-33.

4216. Gawad, Atef A., "Moscow's Arms-for-Oil Diplomacy," *Foreign Policy*, no. 63 (Summer 1986), 147-68.

4217. Golan, Galia, "Gorbachev's Difficult Time in the Gulf," *Political Science Quarterly*, 107, no. 2 (Summer 1992), 213-30.

4218. -----, "Gorbachev's Middle East Strategy," *Foreign Affairs*, 66, no. 1 (Fall 1987), 41-57.

4219. -----, "The Soviet Union and the PLO since the War in Lebanon," *Middle East Journal*, 40, no. 2 (Spring 1986), 285-306.

4220. Goodman, Melvin A., "Trends in Soviet Policy in the Middle East and the Gulf," *International Journal*, 45, no. 3 (Summer 1990), 603-30.

4221.-----, and Carolyn McGiffert Ekedahl, "Gorbachev's `New Directions' in the Middle East," *Middle East Journal*, 42, no. 2 (Autumn 1988).

4222. Haass, Richard N., "Paying Less Attention to the Middle East," *Commentary* (Aug. 1986), 22-26.

4223. Halliday, Fred, "Gorbachev and the `Arab Syndrome': Soviet Policy in the Middle East," *World Policy Journal*, 4, no. 3 (Summer 1987), 415-42.

4224. -----, "The Shevardnadze Shuttle: Moscow's New Role in the Middle East," *Nation* (20 Mar. 1989), 361ff.

4225. Hearmsro, Dilip, "The Ayatollahs and the Bear: Russia and Iran Make Up," *Nation* (16 Oct. 1989), 414-16.

4226. Hehir, J. B., "A Study in Contrast: Central America and the Persian Gulf," *Commonweal*, 114 (14 Aug. 1987), 439.

4227. Herrmann, Richard, "Soviet Policy and the Arab-Israeli Conflict: Actions, Patterns and Interpretations," *Political Science Quarterly*, 102, no. 3 (Fall 1987), 417-40.

4228. Hess, Andrew C., "The Gulf as a No-Man's Land," *Washington Quarterly*, 9, no. 4 (Fall 1986), 41-49.

4229. Hiro, Dilip, "The Ayatollahs and the Bear: Russia and Iran Make Up," *Nation* (16 Oct. 1989), 414-16.

4230. Hunter, Shireen T., "After the Ayatollah," *Foreign Policy*, no. 66 (Spring 1987), 77-97.

4231. -----, "Between Iraq and a Hard Place: After the Ayatollah," *Foreign Policy*, no. 66 (Spring 1987), 77-97.

4232. Hyman, Anthony, "Soviet Interests in the Persian Gulf," *Report on the USSR*, 2, no. 11 (16 Mar. 1990), 12-14.

4233. -----, "Soviet-Iranian Relations and the Two Azerbaijans," *Report on the USSR*, 2, no. 2 (12 Jan. 1990), 15-17.

4234. -----, "Soviet-Iranian Relations: The End of Rapprochement?" *Report on the USSR*, 2, no. 4 (26 Jan. 1990), 17-18.

4235. Indyk, Martin, "Reagan and the Middle East: Learning the Art of the Possible," *SAIS Review*, 7, no. 1 (Winter-Spring 1987), 111-38.

4236. Ishmael, Tareq Y., "The Soviet Union and the Middle East," in *International Relations of the Contemporary Middle East: A Study in World Politics* (Syracuse: Syracuse University Press, 1989), 167-98.

4237. Kanet, Roger E., "Soviet Strategy in Southwest Asia and the Persian Gulf Region," *Crossroads*, no. 20 (1986), 1-20.

4238. Karsh, Efraim, "Influence through Arms Suplies: The Soviet Experience in the Middle East," *Conflict Quarterly*, 6, no. 1 (Winter 1986), 45-55.

4239. -----, "Soviet-Israeli Relations: A New Phase?" *World Today*, 41, no. 12 (Dec. 1985), 214-17.

4240. Katz, M. N., "Gorbachev and the Middle East: A Policy of Continuity," *Current* (Washington), 303 (4 June 1988), 30-34.

4241. -----, "Soviet Policy in the Middle East," *Current History*, 87 (Feb. 1988), 57ff.

4242. Keddie, Nikki R., "Iranian Imbroglios: Who's Irrational?" *World Policy Journal*, 5, no. 1 (Winter 1987-88), 29-54.

4243. Kessler, Martha N., "New Strategies and the Soviets," in *Syria: Fragile Mosaic of Power* (Washington, DC: Government Printing Office, 1987).

4244. Khomeini, Ruhollah, "Gorbachev's Crisis of Faith," *Harper's*, no. 1667 (Apr. 1989), 21-22.

4245. Klinghoffer, Arthur J., "The Dynamics of Quiet Diplomacy: The Soviet Union and Israel," *Middle East Review* 18, no. 4 (Summer 1986), 34-42.

4246. -----, "Soviet-Israeli Relations and a Middle East Peace Settlement," *Crossroads*, no. 23 (1987), 1-13.

4247. Kondracke, Morton, "Interested Parties," *New Republic* (24 Sept. 1990), 16-18.

4248. Konoplyanik, Andrei A., "Crisis in the Gulf: Losses and Benefits for the Soviet Economy," *Petroleum Review*, 45, no. 528 (Jan. 1991), 16-19.

4249. Kriesberg, Louis, "Carrots, Sticks, De-escalation: Soviet-American and Arab-Israeli Relations," *Armed Forces and Society*, 13, no. 3 (Spring 1987), 403-23.

4250. Kuniholm, Burei, "Retrospect and Prospects in the Middle East," *Middle East Journal*, 41, no. 1 (Winter 1987), 7-25.

4251. Landau, Jacob M., "Soviet Works on Middle Eastern Minorities," *Middle Eastern Studies*, 28, no. 1 (Jan. 1992), 216ff.

4252. Legvold, Robert, "The Gulf Crisis and the Future of Gorbachev's Foreign Policy Revolution," *Harriman Institute Forum*, 3, no. 10 (Oct. 1990), 1-8.

4253. Mann, Paul, "Study Finds Rapid Deployment Force Could Thwart Soviet Attack on Iran," *Aviation Week & Space Technology*, 126 (12 Jan. 1987), 85ff.

4254. Menicucci, Garay, "*Glasnost*, the Coup, and Soviet Arabist Historians," *International Journal of Middle Eastern Studies*, 24 (Nov. 1992), 559-77.

4255. Nelson, Daniel, "Keep an Eye on Turkey," *National Interest*, no. 19 (Spring 1990), 117-21.

4256. "Opportunism Knocks," *New Republic* (11 Mar. 1991), 7-8.

4257. Page, Stephen, "The Soviet Impact on the Arabian Peninsula since 1979," *Middle East Focus*, 11, no. 4 (1990), 12ff.

4258. Perlmutter, Amos, "Can Glasnost Bring Peace in the Middle East?" *World & I* (July 1990), 137-41.

4259. Phillips, James A., "Gorbachev's `Newthink' on the Middle East," *Midstream*, 35, no. 6 (Aug-Sept. 1989), 12-15.

4260. -----, "Responding to Gorbachev's `New Thinking' in the Middle East," *Jewish Spectator*, 54, no. 2 (Fall 1989), 32-38.

4261. Pipes, Daniel, "Fundamentalist Muslims between America and Russia," *Foreign Affairs*, 64, no. 5 (Summer 1986), 939-59.

4262. -----, "Syria: The Cuba of the Middle East?" *Commentary* (July 1986), 15-22.

4263. Pollock, David, "Moscow and Aden: Coping with a Coup," *Problems of Communism*, 35, no. 3 (May-June 1986), 50-70.

4264. Pope, S., "Superpowers in the Gulf," *World Press Review*, 34 (Aug. 1987), 39.

4265. Potter, William C., and Stulberg, Adam, "The Soviet Union and the Spread of Ballistic Missiles," *Survival*, 32, no. 6 (Nov-Dec. 1990), 543-57.

4266. Ramati, Yohanan, "Moscow and Damascus," *Global Affairs*, 4, no. 2 (Spring 1989), 97-110.

4267. -----, "The Soviet Union and the Gulf Crisis," *Midstream*, 36, no. 9 (Jan. 1991), 2-8.

4268. Ramet, Pedro, "The Soviet-Syrian Relationship," *Problems of Communism*, 36, no. 5 (Sept-Oct. 1986), 35-46.

4269. "The Red Flag Is Hoisted in Israel," *U.S. News & World Report*, 103 (27 July 1987), 9.

4270. Rubin, Barry, "Drowning in the Gulf," *Foreign Policy*, no. 69 (Winter 1987-88), 120-34.

4271. -----, "Middle East: Search for Peace," *Foreign Affairs*, 64, no. 3 (1986), 583-604.

4272. Saivetz, Carol R. "Islam and Gorbachev's Policy in the Middle East," *Journal of International Affairs*, 42 (Spring 1989), 435-44.

4273. -----, "Superpowers in the Middle East" (Review Article), *Problems of Communism*, 36, no. 5 (Sept-Oct. 1987), 77-84.

4274. Sanz, Timothy L., "Middle East Conflicts: An Annotated Bibliography from the Soviet Press," *Military Review*, 70, no. 12 (Dec. 1990), 80-84.

4275. Shoumikhin, Andrey U., "Soviet Perceptions of U.S. Middle East Policy," *Middle East Journal*, 43, no. 1 (Winter 1989), 16-19.

4276. Sick, Gary, "Iran's Quest for Superpower Status," *Foreign Affairs*, 65, no. 4 (Spring 1987), 697-715.

4277. Singer, Daniel, "The New Holy Alliance," *Nation*, 251 (5 Nov. 1990), 520ff.

4278. Smith, W. E., "Welcoming Back the Bear," *Time*, 130 (13 July 1987), 38-39.

4279. "Soviet Peace Plan Weighed as Gulf Ground War Looms," *Aviation Week & Space Technology*, 134, no. 8 (25 Feb. 1991), 20-22.

4280. Spiegel, Steven L., "U.S. Relations with Israel: The Military Benefits," *Orbis*, 30, no. 3 (Fall 1986), 475-97.

4281. Stanfield, Rochelle L., "In the New Game, Moscow's a Wild Card," *National Journal*, 23, no. 12 (23 Mar. 1991), 677-78.

4282. -----, "Mixed Soviet Goals in the Persian Gulf," *National Journal*, 23, no. 8 (23 Feb. 1991), 459.

4283. -----, "Role for Moscow?" *National Journal*, 22, no. 38 (22 Sept. 1990), 2278-79.

4284. Stein, George, "Soviet Muslims Divided on Gulf War," *Report on the USSR*, 3, no. 8 (22 Feb. 1991), 13-15.

4285. Stein, Janice G., "Extended Deterrence in the Middle East: American Strategy Reconsidered," *World Politics*, 39, no. 3 (Apr. 1987), 326-52.

4286. Story, Christopher, "Winning the War Without Fighting," *Midstream*, 37, no. 3 (Apr. 1991), 2-9.

4287. Vasilyev, A., "Rx: A Conference," *World Press Review*, 34 (July 1987), 13-14.

4288. Wehling, Fred, "Three Scenarios for Russia's Middle East Policy," *Communist and Post-Communist Studies*, 26, no. 2 (June 1993), 182-204.

4289. Weitz, Richard, "The Gulf Conflict and the USSR's Changing International Position," *Report on the USSR*, 2, no. 41 (12 Oct. 1990), 1-5.

4290. -----, "The USSR and the Confrontation in the Gulf," *Report on the USSR*, 3, no. 33 (17 Aug. 1990), 1-7.

4291. Whitaker, M., "Gorbachev's Gulf Game," *Newsweek*, 110 (20 July 1987), 32-33.

4292. Zenchew, Vladimir, "The Soviet Union and Gulf Crisis," *Harvard International Review*, 13, no. 2 (Winter 1990-91), 25.

H. Third World

BOOKS

4293. Albright, David E., *Vanguard Parties & Revolutionary Change in the Third World: Soviet Perspectives and Their Implications* (Berkeley: Institute of International Studies, University of California, 1990).

4294. Allison, Roy, *The Soviet Union and the Strategy of Non-Alignment in the Third World* (New York: Cambridge University Press, 1988).

4295. -----, and Phil Williams, eds., *Superpower Competition and Crisis Prevention in the Third World* (Cambridge: Cambridge University Press, 1990).

4296. Becker, Abraham S., *The Soviet Union and the Third World: The Economic Dimension* (Santa Monica, CA: RAND, 1986).

4297. Brun, Ellen, and Jacques Hirsch, *Soviet-Third World Relations in a Capitalist World: The Political Economy of Broken Promises* (New York: St. Martin's Press, 1990).

4298. Campbell, Kurt M., and S. Neil MacFarlane, eds., *Gorbachev's Third World Dilemmas* (New York: Routledge, 1989).

4299. David, Stephen R., *Third World Coups d'Etat and International Security* (Baltimore: Johns Hopkins University Press, 1987).

4300. Duncan, W. Raymond, and Carolyn McGiffert Ekedahl, *Moscow and the Third World under Gorbachev* (Boulder, CO: Westview Press, 1990).

4301. Feinberg, Richard, *et al.*, *U.S. and Soviet Aid to Developing Countries: From Confrontation to Cooperation?* (New Brunswick, NJ: Transaction, 1991).

4302. Fukuyama, Francis, *Gorbachev and the New Soviet Agenda in the Third World* (Santa Monica, CA: RAND, 1989).

4303. -----, *Military Aspects of the U.S.-Soviet Competition in the Third World* (Santa Monica, CA: RAND, 1985).

4304. -----, *Moscow's Post-Brezhnev Assessment of the Third World* (Santa Monica, CA: RAND, 1986).

4305. -----, *The Soviet Civil-Military Relations and the Power Projection Mission* (Santa Monica, CA: RAND, 1987).

4306. -----, S. A. Bruckner and Sally W. Stoecker, *Soviet Political Perspectives on Power Projection* (Santa Monica, CA: RAND, 1987).

4307. Golan, Galia, *The Soviet Union and National Liberation Movements in the Third World* (Boston: Unwin Hyman, 1988).

4308. Goodman, Melvin A., *Gorbachev's Retreat: The Third World* (New York: Praeger 1991).

4309. Graziani, Giovanni, *Gorbachev's Economic Strategy in the Third World* (New York: Praeger, 1990).

4310. Hough, Jerry F., *The Struggle for the Third World: Soviet Debates and American Options* (Washington, DC: Brookings Institution, 1986).

4311. Katz, Mark N., *Gorbachev's Military Policy in the Third World* (New York: Praeger, 1989).

4312. -----, ed., *Soviet-American Conflict Resolution in the Third World* (Washington, DC: US Institute of Peace Press, 1991).

4313. -----, ed., *The USSR and Marxist Revolution in the Third World* (Cambridge: Woodrow Wilson International Center for Scholars and the Cambridge University Press, 1988).

4314. Kolodziej, Edward A., and Roger E. Kanet, eds., *Limits of Soviet Power in the Developing World* (Baltimore: Johns Hopkins University Press, 1989).

4315. Korbonski, Andrzej, and Francis Fukuyama, eds., *The*

Soviet Union and the Third World: The Last Three Decades (Ithaca: Cornell University Press, 1987).

4316. Laidi, Zaki, ed., *The Third World and the Soviet Union* (London: Zed Books, Ltd., 1988).

4317. Light, Margot, ed., *Troubled Friendships: Moscow's Third World Ventures* (New York: St. Martin's Press, 1994).

4318. Mesbahi, Mohiaddin, ed., *Russia and the Third World in the Post-Soviet Era* (Gainesville, FL: University Press of Florida, 1994).

4319. Neuman, Stephanie G., *Military Assistance in Recent Wars: The Dominance of the Superpowers* (New York: Praeger, 1986).

4320. Rubinstein, Alvin Z., *Moscow's Third World Strategy* (Princeton: Princeton University Press, 1990).

4321. Saivetz, Carol, ed., *The Soviet Union in the Third World* (Boulder, CO: Westview Press, 1989).

4322. Schultz, Richard H., *et al.*, *Guerrilla Warfare and Counterinsurgency: U.S.-Soviet Policy in the Third World* (Lexington, MA: Lexington Books, 1989).

4323. Shulman, Marshall D., ed., *East-West Tensions in the Third World* (New York: W. W. Norton, 1986).

4324. Thornton, Thomas P., *The Challenge to U.S. Policy in the Third World: Global Responsibilities and Regional Devolution* (Boulder, CO: Westview, with the Johns Hopkins University Foreign Policy Institute, School of Advanced International Studies, 1986).

4325. Valenta, Jiri, and Frank Cibulka, eds., *Gorbachev's New Thinking and Third World Conflicts* (New Brunswick, NJ: Transaction, 1990).

4326. Whelan, Joseph G., and Michael J. Dixon, new ed. *The Soviet Union in the Third World: Threat to World Peace?* (Washington, DC: Pergamon-Brassey's, 1989).

ARTICLES

4327. Albright, David E., "The USSR and the Third World in the 1980s," *Problems of Communism*, 38, no. 2-3 (Mar-June 1989), 50-70.

4328. Anderson H., "Moscow's Third World Game," *Newsweek*, 109 (23 Mar. 1987), 34.

4329. Armacost, M. H., "U.S.-Soviet Relations: Coping with Conflicts in the Third World," *Department of State Bulletin*, 86 (Dec. 1986), 57-61.

4330. Asopa, Sheel K., "Soviet Economy and the Third World: A Multifaceted Collaboration," *Political Science Review*, 27, no. 1-4 (1988), 66-97.

4331. Becker, Abraham S., "Soviet Union and the Third World: The Economic Dimension," *Soviet Economy*, 2, no. 3 (July-Sept. 1986), 233-60.

4332. Breslauer, George, "The Empire's New Clothes: The Soviet Union and the Third World after Afghanistan. All Gorbachev's

Men," *National Interest*, no. 122 (Summer 1988), 91-100.

4333. -----, "Ideology and Learning in Soviet Third World Policy," *World Politics*, 39, no. 3 (Apr. 1987), 429-48.

4334. Bugajski, Janusz, "Perestroika in the Third World," *Fletcher Forum of World Affairs*, 15, no. 1 (Winter 1991), 93-110.

4335. -----, "The Soviet Union and the Third World," *Washington Quarterly*, 9, no. 4 (Fall 1986), 141-45.

4336. Burke, James F., "Western Assessments of Gorbachev's Policies in the Third World," *World Affairs*, 155, no. 1 (Summer 1992), 31-39.

4337. Casey, Francis M., "The Theory and Tactics of Soviet Third World Strategy," *Journal of Social, Political and Economic Studies*, 12, no. 3 (Fall 1987), 243-58.

4338. "Changing Soviet Policy toward the Third World," *World Press Review*, 35 (June 1988), 18-21.

4339. Clemens, Walter C., Jr., "The Price of Intervention," *Harvard International Journal*, 8, no. 3 (Jan-Feb. 1986), 20ff.

4340. Croan, Melvin, "Soviet Policy toward the Third World: The Long Road to Thermidor-and Beyond?" (Review Article), *Russian Review*, 49, no. 3 (July 1990), 317-20.

4341. David, Steven R., "Soviet Involvement in Third World Coups," *International Security*, 11, no. 1 (Summer 1986), 3-36.

4342. Debray, R., "From Kalashnikovs to God and Computers," *New Perspectives Quarterly*, 5 (Fall 1988), 42-45.

4343. Denitch, Bogdan, "Return to the Third World," *Dissent*, 38, no. 3 (Summer 1991), 360-68.

4344. Ellison, Herbert J., "Soviet-American Intervention," *Harvard International Review*, 8, no. 3 (Jan-Feb. 1986), 3-6.

4345. Fukuyama, Francis, "Gorbachev and the Third World," *Foreign Affairs*, 64, no. 4 (Spring 1986), 715-31.

4346. -----, "Gorbachev's New Politics: Soviet Third World Policy," *Current* (Washington), 303 (June 1988), 15-24.

4347. -----, "Patterns of Soviet Third World Policy," *Problems of Communism*, 36, no. 5 (Sept-Oct. 1987), 1-13.

4348. Golan, Galia, "Moscow and the Third World National Liberation Movements: The Soviet Role," *Journal of International Affairs*, 40 (Winter-Spring 1987), 303-24.

4349. Hagerty, Randy, and Roger E. Kanet, "US and Soviet Involvement in the Third World," *Harvard International Review*, 8, no. 3 (Jan-Feb. 1986), 11-14.

4350. Hossein-zadeh, Esmail, "Perestroika and the Third World," *Review of Radical Political Economics*, 22, no. 2-3 (1990), 252-74.

4351. Hough, Jerry F., "The Revolutionary Road Runs Out," *Nation*, 240 (1 June 1985), 666-68.

4352. Kanet, Roger E., "Economic Aspects of Soviet Policy in the Third World: A Comment," *Soviet Economy*, 2, no. 3 (July-Sept. 1986), 261-68.

4353. Katz, Mark N., "Soviet Military Policy toward the Third World," *Washington Quarterly*, 9, no. 4 (Fall 1986), 159-63.

4354. -----, "Soviet Third World Policy" (Review Article), *Problems of Communism*, 35, no. 4 (July-Aug. 1986), 87-92.

4355. -----, "The Soviet Union and the Third World," *Current History*, 85, no. 513 (Oct. 1986), 329ff.

4356. Kramer, Mark N., "Soviet Arms Transfers to the Third World," *Problems of Communism*, 36, no. 5 (Sept-Oct. 1987), 52-68.

4357. Landau, Saul, "Rethinking the Idea of Revolution," *Progressive*, 54, no. 11 (Nov. 1990), 30.

4358. Lavigne, Marie, "Comment on the Economic Dimension of Soviet Interaction with the Third World," *Soviet Economy*, 2, no. 3 (July-Sept. 1986), 269-76.

4359. Litwak, Robert S., and S. Neil MacFarlane, "Soviet Activism in the Third World," *Survival*, 29, no. 1 (Jan-Feb. 1987), 21-39.

4360. MacFarlane, S. Neil, "The USSR and the Third World: Continuity and Change under Gorbachev," *Harriman Institute Forum*, 1, no. 3 (Mar. 1988), 1-7.

4361. Mendras, Marie, "Soviet Policy Toward the Third World," *Proceedings of the Academy of Political Science*, 36, no. 4 (July 1987), 164-75.

4362. Modak, A. G., "New Trends in Soviet Relations with the Third World," *India Quarterly*, 47, no. 3 (July-Sept. 1991), 39-68.

4363. Neuman, Stephanie G., "Arms and Superpower Influence: Lessons from Recent Wars," *Orbis*, 30, no. 4 (Winter 1987), 711-29.

4364. Rubinstein. Alvin Z., "The Changing Strategic Balance and Soviet Third World Risk-Taking," *Naval War College Review*, 38, no. 2 (Mar-Apr. 1985), 5-17.

4365. -----, "A Third World Policy Waits for Gorbachev," *Orbis*, 30, no. 2 (Summer 1986), 355-64.

4366. Saivetz, Carol R., "'New Thinking' and Soviet Third World Policy," *Current History*, 88, no. 540 (Oct. 1989), 325ff.

4367. Savimbi, Jonas, "The War Against Soviet Colonialism: The Strategy and Tactics of Anti-Communist Resistance," *Policy Review*, no. 35 (Winter 1986), 18-25.

4368. Shultz, Richard, "Soviet Use of Surrogates to Project Power into the Third World," *Parameters*, 16, no. 3 (Autumn 1986), 32-42.

4369. "The Soviet Union and the Third World," *Washington Quarterly*, 9, no. 4 (Fall 1986), 139ff.

4370. Stollar, Lawrence B., "Recent Writings on the USSR and the Third World: Abundant Harvest, Much Fine Fruit" (Review Article), *Studies in Comparative Communism*, 23, no. 1 (Spring 1990), 89-100.

4371. Valkenier, Elizabeth, "Glasnost' and Perestroika in Soviet-Third World Economic Relations," *Harriman Institute Forum*, 5, no. 2 (Oct. 1991), 1-12.

4372. -----, "New Soviet Thinking about the Third World," *World Policy Journal*, 4, no. 4 (Fall 1987), 651-74.

4373. Walker, M., "Gorbachev Plots a 'Southern' Course," *World Press Review*, 35 (June 1988), 15-16.

4374. Wallander, Celeste A., "Third-World Conflict in Soviet Military Thought: Does the 'New Thinking' Grow Prematurely Grey?" *World Politics*, 42, no. 1 (Oct. 1989), 31-63

I. United States and the West

BOOKS

4375. Amundsen, Kirsten, *Soviet Strategic Interests in the North* (New York: St. Martin's Press, 1990).

4376. Aron, Leon, and Jay P. Kosminsky, *The Bush-Gorbachev Washington Summit, May 30-June 2, 1990: Maintaining the Momentum of Change* (Washington, DC: Heritage Foundation, 1990).

4377. Beliaev, Igor, and John Marks, eds., *Common Ground on Terrorism: Soviet-American Cooperation Against the Politics of Terror* (New York: W. W. Norton, 1991).

4378. Bernstein, Henry T., *And None Afraid: Soviet-Western Suspicion and Trusting from Red October to Glasnost* (Oxford: Blackwell, 1991).

4379. Bernstein, Jerome S., *Power and Politics: The Psychology of Soviet-American Partnership* (New York: Random House, 1989).

4380. Bialer, Seweryn, and Michael Mandelbaum, eds., *Gorbachev's Russia and American Foreign Policy* (Boulder, CO: Westview Press, 1988).

4381. Black, J. L., and Norman G. Hillmer, eds., *Nearly Neighbours: Canada and the Soviet Union, from Cold War to Detente and Beyond* (Kingston: R.P. Frye, 1989).

4382. Bowles, W. Donald, and Elena B. Arefieva, *Tripartite Projects: Proposals for Joint U.S.-U.S.S.R. Cooperation with Developing Countries* (Washington, DC: Development Council, 1990).

4383. Boyle, Peter G., *American-Soviet Relations: From the Russian Revolution to the Fall of Communism* (London: Routledge, 1993).

4384. Brement, Marshall, *Reaching Out to Moscow: From Confrontation to Cooperation* (New York: Praeger, 1991).

4385. Breslauer, George W., and Philip Tetlock, ed., *Learning in US and Soviet Foreign Policy* (Boulder, CO: Westview Press, 1991).

4386. Brzezinski, Zbigniew, *Game Plan: A Geostrategic Frame-*

work for the Conduct of the U.S.-Soviet Contest (Boston: Atlantic Monthly Press, 1986).

4387. Bush, George, *Agreement with the Union of Soviet Socialist Republics on the Maritime Boundary*, 101st Congress, 2nd Session (Washington, DC: Government Printing Office, 1990).

4388. Clark, Michael T., and Simon Serfaty, eds., *New Thinking & Old Realities: America, Europe, and Russia* (Washington, DC: Seven Locks Press, 1991).

4389. Cockburn, Patrick, *Getting Russia Wrong: The End of Kremlinology* (New York: Verso, 1989).

4390. Cohen, Lenard J., *Canada in the Soviet Elite Mindset: A Case of "New Political Thinking"* (Toronto: Centre for Russian and East European Studies, University of Toronto, 1989).

4391. Cohen, Stephen F., *Sovieticus: American Perceptions and Soviet Realities*, 1st ed., expanded (New York: W. W. Norton, 1986).

4392. Cohen, Warren I., *Cambridge History of American Foreign Relations*, vol. 4: *America in the Age of Soviet Power, 1945-1991* (New York: Cambridge University Press, 1993).

4393. Cox, Michael, ed., *Beyond the Cold War: Superpowers at the Crossroads* (Lanham, MD: University Press of America, 1990).

4394. Dean, Jonathan, *Meeting Gorbachev's Challenge: How to Build Down the NATO-Warsaw Pact Confrontation* (New York: St. Martin's Press, 1989).

4395. Dennis, Everette E., George Gerbner and Yassen N. Zassoursky, eds., *Beyond the Cold War: Soviet and American Media Images* (Newbury Park, CA: Sage, 1991).

4396. Dobell, Peter, ed., *The Changing Soviet Union: Implications for Canada and the World* (Toronto: James Lorimer, 1991).

4397. Eliot, Theodore L., et al., eds., *The Red Army on Pakistan's Border: Policy Implications for the United States* (Washington, DC: Pergamon-Brassey's International Defense Publications, 1986).

4398. Feffer, John, *Beyond Detente: Soviet Foreign Policy and U.S. Options* (New York: Noonday Press, 1990).

4399. Froman, Michael B., *The Development of the Idea of Detente: Coming to Terms* (New York: St. Martin's Press, 1991).

4400. Glynn, Patrick, *Closing Pandora's Box: Arms Races, Arms Control, and the History of the Cold War* (New York: Basic Books, 1993).

4401. Gorbachev, Mikhail, *Reykjavik, Results and Lessons* (Madison, CT: Sphinx Press, 1987).

4402. -----, *Perestroika and Soviet-American Relations* (Madison, CT: Sphinx Press, 1990).

4403. Gottstein, Klaus, ed., *Mutual Perceptions of Long-Range Goals: Can the United States and the Soviet Union Cooperate Permanently?* (Frankfurt am Main: Campus Verlag, and Boulder,

CO: Westview Press, 1991).

4404. -----, ed., *Western Perceptions of Soviet Goals: Is Trust Possible?* (Boulder, CO: Westview Press, 1989).

4405. Halliday, Fred, *From Kabul to Managua: Soviet-American Relations in the 1980s: The Gorbachev Era* (New York: Pantheon, 1990).

4406. Harle, Vilho, and Jyrki Iivonen, eds., *Gorbachev and Europe* (London: Pinter Publishers Ltd., 1990).

4407. Hendrickson, David C., *The Future of American Strategy* (New York: Holmes & Meier, 1987).

4408. Herman, Paul F., *Thinking about Peace: The Conceptualization and Conduct of U.S.-Soviet Detente* (Lanham, MD: University Press of America, 1987).

4409. Heyns, Terry L., *American and Soviet Relations since Detente: The Framework* (Washington, DC: National Defense University Press, Government Printing Office, 1987).

4410. Hogan, Michael J., ed., *The End of the Cold War: Its Meaning and Implications* (Cambridge, Cambridge University Press, 1993).

4411. Homet, Roland S., Jr., *The New Realism: A Fresh Beginning in U.S.-Soviet Relations* (New York: HarperCollins, 1990).

4412. Horelick, Arnold L., *U.S.-Soviet Relations: From a 'Post-Cold War' to a 'Post-Communism' Era?* (Santa Monica, CA: RAND/UCLA Center for Soviet Studies, 1991).

4413. -----, ed., *U.S.-Soviet Relations: The Next Phase* (Ithaca: Cornell University Press, 1986).

4414. Hyland, William, *The Cold War Is Over* (New York: Times Books/Random House, 1990).

4415. Institute for East-West Security Studies, *How Should America Respond to Gorbachev's Challenge? A Report of the Task Force on Soviet New Thinking* (New York: Institute for East-West Security Studies, 1987).

4416. Jamgotch, Nish, Jr., ed., *Sectors of Mutual Benefit in U.S.-Soviet Relations* (Durham, NC: Duke University Press, 1985).

4417. -----, ed., *U.S.-Soviet Cooperation: A New Future* (New York: Praeger, 1989).

4418. Jervis, Robert, and Seweryn Bialer, eds., *Soviet-American Relations After the Cold War* (Durham, NC: Duke University Press, 1991).

4419. Jordan, Robert, ed., *Europe and the Superpowers: Essays on European International Politics* (London: Pinter, 1991).

4420. Kaldor, Mary, Gerald Holden and Richard Falk, eds., *The New Detente: Rethinking East-West Relations* (New York: Verso, 1989).

4421. Kanet, Roger, and Edward A. Kolodziej, eds., *The Cold War as Cooperation* (Baltimore: Johns Hopkins University Press, 1991).

4422. Keeble, Curtis, *Britain and the Soviet Union, 1917-1989*

(New York: St. Martin's Press, 1990).

4423. Kelley, Donald R., and Hoyt Purvis, eds., *Old Myths and New Realities in United States-Soviet Relations* (New York: Praeger, 1990).

4424. Keohane, Robert O., Joseph S. Nye and Stanley Hoffmann, eds., *After the Cold War: International Institutions and State Strategies in Europe, 1989-1991* (Cambridge, MA: Harvard University Press, 1993).

4425. Keyssar, Helene, and Vladimir Pozner, comps., *Remembering War: A US-Soviet Dialogue* (New York: Oxford University Press, 1990).

4426. Knelman, Fred H., *Reagan, God, and the Bomb: From Myth to Policy in the Nuclear Arms Race* (Buffalo: Prometheus Books, 1985).

4427. Krickus, Richard J., *The Superpowers in Crisis: Implications of Domestic Discord* (Washington, DC: Pergamon-Brassey's International Defense Publications, 1987).

4428. Laird, Robbin F., and Susan L. Clark, eds., *The USSR and the Western Alliance* (Boston: Unwin Hyman, 1990).

4429. Levering, Ralph B., *The Cold War, 1945-1991: A Post-Cold War History* (Arlington Heights, IL: Harlan Davidson, 1993).

4430. Liska, George, *Rethinking U.S.-Soviet Relations* (Oxford: Basil Blackwell, 1987).

4431. Lynch, Allen, *The Cold War Is Over-Again* (Boulder, CO: Westview Press, 1992).

4432. Lynn-Jones, Sean, and Steven E. Miller, eds., *The Cold War and After: Prospects for Peace*, expanded ed. (Cambridge, MA: MIT Press, 1993).

4433. Magstadt, Thomas M., *Gorbachev and Glasnost'-A New Soviet Order? Implications for U.S. Foreign Policy* (Washington, DC: Cato Institute, 1987).

4434. Malcolm, Neil, *Russia and Europe: An End to Confrontation?* (London: Pinter Publishers, for RIIA, 1993).

4435. Mandelbaum, Michael, and Strobe Talbott, *Reagan and Gorbachev* (New York: Vintage Books, 1987).

4436. Marantz, Paul, *From Lenin to Gorbachev: Changing Soviet Perspectives on East-West Relations* (Ottawa: Canadian Institute for International Peace and Security, 1988).

4437. McDougall, Derek, *Soviet-American Relations Since the 1940s* (New York: E. Arnold, 1990).

4438. McLeod, J. David, ed., *The End of the Cold War? Prospects for East-West Security in the 1990s: Papers Presented at the 1990 Political Science Students' Conference* (Winnipeg: University of Manitoba, 1990), 125-37.

4439. McNamara, Robert S., *Out of the Cold: New Thinking for American Foreign and Defense Policy in the Twenty-First Century* (New York: Simon & Schuster, 1989).

4440. Menges, Constantine, *The Twilight Struggle: The Soviet Union v. the United States Today* (Washington, DC: AEI Press, 1990).

4441. Miko, Francis T., *The 1987 Reagan-Gorbachev Summit Agenda* (Washington DC: Library of Congress, Congressional Research Service, 1987).

4442. Mills, Richard M., *As Moscow Sees Us: American Politics and Society in the Soviet Mindset* (New York: Oxford University Press, 1990).

4443. Nelsen, Harvey W., *Power and Insecurity: Beijing, Moscow and Washington, 1949-88* (Boulder, CO: Lynne Rienner 1989).

4444. Nelson, Daniel N., and Roger B. Anderson, eds., *Soviet-American Relations: Understanding Differences, Avoiding Conflicts* (Wilmington, DE: SR Books, 1989).

4445. Nissani, Moti, *Lives in the Balance: The Cold War and American Politics, 1945-1991* (Wakefield: Hollowbrook, 1992).

4446. Oberdorfer, Don, *The Turn: From the Cold War to a New Era: The United States and the Soviet Union, 1983-1990* (New York: Poseidon, 1991).

4447. Paterson, Thomas G., *On Every Front: The Making and Unmaking of the Cold War* (New York: W. W. Norton, 1992).

4448. Pisar, Samuel, *Dealing with Russia: Weapons of Peace* (New York: Scribner's, 1991).

4449. Reagan, Ronald, *The Current State of Soviet-American Relations* (Washington, DC: US Department of State, Bureau of Public Affairs, 1987).

4450. -----, *On the Eve of My Meeting with Gorbachev*, Heritage Lectures, no. 141 (Washington, DC: Heritage Foundation, 1987).

4451. -----, *The Washington Summit: Progress toward Peace* (Washington, DC: US Department of State, Bureau of Public Affairs, 1987).

4452. Ryavec, Karl M., *United States-Soviet Relations* (New York: Longman, 1989).

4453. Savigear, Peter, *Cold War or Detente in the 1980s: The International Politics of American-Soviet Relations* (New York: St. Martin's Press, 1987).

4454. Schweizer, Peter, *Victory: The Reagan Administration's Secret Strategy That Hastened the Collapse of the Soviet Union* (New York: Atlantic Monthly Press, 1994).

4455. Serfaty, Simon, ed., *The Future of U.S.-Soviet Relations* (Washington, DC: Foreign Policy Institute, 1989).

4456. Sestanovich, Stephen, *et al.*, *Coping with Gorbachev's Soviet Union* (Washington, DC: Center for Strategic and International Studies, 1988).

4457. Shavit, David, *United States Relations with Russia and the Soviet Union: A Historical Dictionary* (Westport, CT: Greenwood Press, 1993).

4458. Shimko, Keith, *Images and Arms Control: Perceptions of the Soviet Union in the Reagan Administration* (Ann Arbor: University of Michigan Press, 1991).

4459. Simons, Thomas W., Jr., *The End of the Cold War?* (New York: St. Martin's Press, 1990).

4460. *Soviet-U.S. Relations: A Briefing Book, by the Congressional Research Service* (Washington, DC: Library of Congress, Congressional Research Service, 1986-90).

4461. Spiers, Ronald I., *U.S.-Soviet Agreement on Embassy Construction in Washington* (Washington, DC: US Department of State, Bureau of Public Affairs, 1987).

4462. *Strengthening the U.S.-Soviet Communications Process to Reduce the Risks of Misunderstandings and Conflicts* (Washington, DC: National Academy of Public Administration, 1987).

4463. US Congress. House. Committee on Armed Services. Defense Policy Panel. *Process and Implications of the Iceland Summit. Hearings.* 99th Congress (Washington, DC: Government Printing Office, 1987).

4464. US Congress. House. Committee on Armed Services. Defense Policy Panel. *The Soviet Succession: Implications for U.S. Policy. Hearings.* 99th Congress, 1 Apr. 1985 (Washington, DC: Government Printing Office, 1985).

4465. US Congress. House. Committee on Foreign Affairs. *The "Congress Factor" in Superpower Relations: Soviet Views of the U.S. Congress: Report of a Staff Study Mission to the Soviet Union, 25 May-6 June 1987* (Washington, DC: Government Printing Office, 1987).

4466. US Congress. House. Committee on Foreign Affairs. *The First Post-Cold War Summit, May 1990.* 101st Congress, 2nd Session (Washington, DC: Government Printing Office, 1990).

4467. US Congress. House. Committee on Foreign Affairs. *The Reagan-Gorbachev Summit and Its Implications for United States-Soviet Relations. Hearing.* 99th Congress, 31 Oct. 1985 (Washington, DC: Government Printing Office, 1986).

4468. US Congress. House. Committee on Foreign Affairs. *The Reagan-Gorbachev Summit and Its Implication for United States-Soviet Relations.* 100th Congress, 1st Session, 16 Dec. 1987 (Washington, DC: Government Printing Office, 1988).

4469. US Congress. House. Committee on Foreign Affairs. Subcommitte on Arms Control, International Security and Science. *The Reykjavik Talks: Promise or Peril: Report.* 100th Congress (Washington, DC: Government Printing Office, 1987).

4470. US Congress. House. Committee on Foreign Affairs. Subcommittee on Europe and the Middle East. *Developments in Europe, October 1990.* 101st Congress, 2nd Session, 9 Oct. 1990 (Washington, DC: Government Printing Office, 1991).

4471. US Congress. House. Committee on Foreign Affairs. Subcommittee on Europe and the Middle East. *United States-Soviet Relations, 1988,* 2 vols. (Washington, DC: Government Printing Office, 1988).

4472. US Congress. Senate. Committee on Foreign Relations. *The Future of Soviet-U.S. Relations.* 101st Congress, 1st Session (Washington, DC: Government Printing Office, 1990).

4473. US Congress. Senate. Committee on Foreign Relations. Subcommittee on European Affairs. *The Future of Europe. Hearings.* 101st Congress, 2nd Session (Washington, DC: Government Printing Office, 1991).

4474. US Congress. Senate. Committee on Foreign Relations. Subcommittee on European Affairs. *The Soviet Crisis and the U.S. Interest: Future of the Soviet Military and Future of the Soviet Economy. Hearings.* 102nd Congress, 1st Session (Washington, DC: Government Printing Office, 1991).

4475. US Congress. Senate. Committee on Foreign Relations. Subcommittee on European Affairs. *Soviet Disunion: The American Response. Hearings.* 102nd Congress, 1st Session (Washington, DC: Government Printing Office, 1991).

4476. US General Accounting Office. *Overseas Construction: Design and Construction of the U.S. Embassy Complex in Moscow: Briefing Report to the Chairman, Committee on the Budget, United States Senate* (Washington, DC: General Accounting Office, 1987).

4477. Wessell, Nils H., Jr., *The New Europe: Revolution in East-West Relations* (New York: Academy of Political Science, 1991).

4478. Wettig, Gerhard, *Changes in Soviet Policy Towards the West* (Boulder, CO: Westview Press, 1991).

4479. Whelan, Joseph G., *The Moscow Summit, 1988: Reagan and Gorbachev in Negotiation* (Boulder, CO: Westview Press, 1990).

4480. -----, *Soviet Diplomacy and Negotiating Behavior: Fall of Gorbachev and Collapse of the Soviet Union* (Buffalo: William S. Hein, 1993)

4481. -----, and the Library of Congress, *Soviet Diplomacy and Negotiating Behavior-1988-90: Gorbachev-Reagan-Bush Meetings at the Summit* (Washington, DC: Government Printing Office, 1991).

4482. White, Colin, *Russia and America: The Roots of Economic Divergence* (New York: Croom Helm, 1987).

4483. Yergin, Daniel, and Thane Gustafson, *Russia 2010: And What It Means to the West* (New York: Random House, 1993).

ARTICLES

4484. "A Conversation with Alexander M. Haig, Jr.," *Crossroads,* no. 19 (1986), 1-11.

4485. Adelman, Kenneth L., "The Road from Reykjavik," *World Affairs,* 149 (Summer 1986), 11-14.

4486. Allison, Graham, and Robert Blackwill, "America's Stake in the Soviet Future," *Foreign Affairs,* 70, no. 3 (Summer 1991), 77-97.

4487. Anderson, H., "Gorbomania in Germany," *Newsweek,* 113 (26 June 1989), 31.

4488. Anderson, William D., and Sterling J. Kernek, "How `Realistic' Is Reagan's Diplomacy?" *Political Science Quarterly*, 100, no. 3 (Fall 1985), 389-409.

4489. Arbatov, Georgi A., "The Cold War Is Ending," *World Marxist Review*, 31, no. 8 (Aug. 1988), 43-46.

4490. ——, "Such Different Meetings... ; Soviet-American Relations and the Four Summit Meetings," *Perestroika Annual*, 1 (1988), 217-33.

4491. Archer, Clive, "The North as a Multidimensional Strategic Arena," *Annals of the American Academy of Political and Social Science*, no. 512 (Nov. 1990), 22-32.

4492. Arkin, William M., "Long on Data, Short on Intelligence," *Bulletin of the Atomic Scientists*, 43, no. 5 (June 1987), 5-6.

4493. Armacost, Michael, "Implications of Gorbachev for U.S.-Soviet Relations," *Journal of International Affairs*, 42 (Spring 1989), 445-56.

4494. Aspin, Les, "The Bush Quick Fix Foreign Policy," *Vital Speeches of the Day*, 58 (1 Feb. 1992), 235-37.

4495. Avery, P. A., "First Ladies at the Summit: Matching Charm and Style," *U.S. News & World Report*, 99 (25 Nov. 1985), 42.

4496. Badruddin, "Bush-Gorbachev Summit: Alternatives to Peace Building," *Pakistan Horizon*, 43, no. 3 (July 1990), 33-40.

4497. Baker, James A., III, "America and the Collapse of the Soviet Union," *Vital Speeches of the Day*, 58 (1 Jan. 1992), 162-68.

4498. Barnes, Fred, "Gorbachev Envy," *New Republic* (21 Oct. 1985), 12-14.

4499. ——, "White House Watch: Be Nice to Gorby," *New Republic* (25 June 1990), 12-13.

4500. Barnet, Richard J., "Reflections: After the Cold War," *New Yorker* (1 Jan. 1990), 46-60.

4501. Bethell, T., "Reagan, Armand, Gorby & Cockburn," *American Spectator*, 21, no. 8 (Aug. 1988), 9ff.

4502. Beukel, Erik, "The Fundamental Attribution Error in the Cold War: American Perceptions of the Soviet Union as a Nuclear Superpower," *Arms Control*, 13, no. 3 (Dec. 1992), 396-420.

4503. "Beyond Summitry," *Nation*, 250 (18 June 1990), 843-44.

4504. Billington, James H., "Realism and Vision in American Foreign Policy," *Foreign Affairs*, 65, no. 3 (1987), 630-52.

4505. ——, "Soviet Power and the Unity of the Industrial Democracies," *Atlantic Community Quarterly*, 24, no. 4 (Winter 1986), 374-79.

4506. Blacker, Coit D., "The Collapse of Soviet Power in Europe," *Foreign Affairs*, 70, no. 1 (1990-91), 88-102.

4507. ——, "The New United States-Soviet Detente," *Current History*, 88, no. 540 (Oct. 1989), 321ff.

4508. Blumenthal, Sidney, "The Moscow Primary," *New Republic* (25 June 1990), 13-16.

4509. Bluth, Christoph, "American-Russian Strategic Relations: From Confrontation to Cooperation?" *World Today*, 49, no. 3 (Mar. 1993), 47-49.

4510. Bodie, William C., "How Gorbachev Saved Reagan...," *National Interest*, no. 23 (Spring 1991), 101-04.

4511. Bonner, Elena, "Looking to the Future," *Current History*, 91, no. 567 (Oct. 1992), 305-09.

4512. Borawski, John, "U.S.-Soviet Move toward Risk Reduction," *Bulletin of the Atomic Scientists*, 43, no. 6 (July-Aug. 1987), 16-18.

4513. Borrus, A., "Bush Takes a Gamble on Gorbachev," *Business Week* (18 June 1990), 28-29.

4514. Brahm, Heinz, "The Disintegrating Soviet Union and Europe," *Aussenpolitik*, 43, no. 1 (1992), 43-53.

4515. Brandenburg, Ulrich, "The `Friends' Are Leaving: Soviet and Post-Soviet Troops in Germany," *Aussenpolitik*, 44, no. 1 (1993), 77-88.

4516. Brement, Marshall, "Reaching Out to Moscow," *Foreign Policy*, no. 80 (Fall 1990), 56-76.

4517. ——, "U.S.-U.S.S.R.: Possibilities in Partnership," *Foreign Policy*, no. 84 (Fall 1991), 107-24.

4518. Brooks, Thomas A., "The Soviet Navy: In the Wake of the Visits," *US Naval Institute Proceedings*, 115, no. 11 (Nov. 1989), 138-39.

4519. Brown, Archie, "Soviet Political Developments and Prospects," *World Policy Journal*, 4, no. 1 (Winter 1986-87), 55-87.

4520. Brzezinski, Zbigniew, "America's New Geostrategy," *Foreign Affairs*, 66 (Spring 1988), 680-99.

4521. ——, "Beyond Chaos: A Policy for the West," *National Interest*, no. 19 (Spring 1990), 3-12.

4522. ——, "Ending the Cold War," *Washington Quarterly*, 12, no. 4 (Autumn 1989), 29-34.

4523. ——, "The U.S.-Soviet Relationship: Paradoxes and Prospects," *Strategic Review*, 15, no. 2 (Spring 1987), 11-18.

4524. Bukovskii, V. K., "What To Do About the Soviet Collapse," *Commentary*, 92 (Sept. 1991), 19-24.

4525. Bundy, McGeorge, "Prospects for Soviet-American Relations After the Cold War," *New York University Journal of International Law and Politics*, 22, no. 3 (Spring 1990), 381-87.

4526. Bush, George, "Future United States-Soviet Relations," *Vital Speeches of the Day*, 57 (1 Sept. 1991), 74-76.

4527. ——, "President Bush Remarks on Mikhail S. Gorbachev's Resignation," *Vital Speeches of the Day*, 58 (15 Jan. 1992), 195-96.

4528. -----, and Mikhail Gorbachev, "The Moscow Summit," *US Department of State Dispatch*, 2 (12 Aug. 1991), 591-98.

4529. "Bush and Gorbachev Discuss Results of Talks," *Congressional Quarterly Weekly Report*, 49 (3 Aug. 1991), 2193-94.

4530. "The Bush-Gorbachev Summit," *World Press Review*, 37 (Jan. 1990), 8ff.

4531. Caldwell, Lawrence T., "Soviet-American Relations: The Cold War Ends," *Current History*, 89, no. 549 (Oct. 1990), 305ff.

4532. -----, "Washington and Moscow: A Tale of Two Summits," *Current History*, 87 (Oct. 1988), 305ff.

4533. Campbell, Kurt M., "The Soldiers' Summit," *Foreign Policy*, no. 75 (Summer 1989), 76-91.

4534. -----, "The Soviet Diusunion: The New Challenges for American Foreign Policy," *Harvard International Review*, 14, no. 1 (Fall 1991), 15ff.

4535. Carlucci, Frank C., "Prospects for the U.S.-Soviet Dialogue," *Vital Speeches of the Day*, 54 (1 Oct. 1988), 738-40.

4536. Clarke, Michael, ed., "The Soviet Union and Eastern Europe," in Peter Byrd, ed., *British Foreign Policy under Thatcher* (New York: St. Martin's Press, 1988), 54-75.

4537. Cockburn, Alexander, "The Epstein Interrogation," *Nation*, 251 (1990), 118-19.

4538. Cohen, Stephen, "The Malchik Meets the Lone Ranger," *New Statesman*, 110 (15 Nov. 1985); 21-22.

4539. Comes, F. J., "Europe Wants to Believe in a Kinder, Gentler Kremlin," *Business Week* (26 Dec. 1988), 60.

4540. -----, and M. D'Anastasio, "Gorbachev Is Regaining Ground in Western Europe," *Business Week* (5 Aug. 1985), 45.

4541. Copson, Raymond D., and Richard P. Cronin, "The `Reagan Doctrine' and Its Prospects," *Survival*, 29, no. 1 (Jan-Feb. 1987), 40-55.

4542. Corddry, Charles W., "Scenes from Sevastopol: Goodwill Mission to a Hero City," *Sea Power*, 32, no. 10 (Oct. 1989), 43ff.

4543. Crow, Suzanne, "US-Soviet Relations: How Deep Is the Chill?" *Report on the USSR*, 3, no. 9 (1 Mar. 1991), 12-14.

4544. Crozier, Brian, "The Protracted Conflict: Post-Summit Optimism," *National Review*, 38 (31 Jan. 1986), 30.

4545. Dallin, Alexander, "America's Search for a Policy toward the Former Soviet Union," *Current History*, 91, no. 567 (Oct. 1992), 321-26.

4546. D'Anastasio, M., and B. France, "The Moscow Shakeup: Gorbachev Girds for the Summit," *Business Week* (15 July 1985), 53.

4547. Daniels, Robert V., "The Star Wars Summit," *New Leader*, 68 (23 Sept. 1985), 3-6.

4548. Darrach, B., "Ronald Reagan & Mikhail Gorbachev," *People Weekly*, 32, special issue (Fall 1989), 44-46.

4549. Deming, A., "Gorbachev's European Card," *Newsweek*, 106 (7 Oct. 1985), 27ff.

4550. De Santis, Hugh, "An Anti-Tactical Missile Defense for Europe," *SAIS Review*, 6, no. 2 (Summer-Fall 1986), 99-116.

4551. Dixon, W. J., "Reciprocity in United States-Soviet Relations: Multiple Symmetry or Issue Linkage?" *American Journal of Political Science*, 30 (May 1986), 421-45.

4552. Dobell, W. M., "Soviet Relations and Canadian Defence," *International Journal*, 46, no. 3 (Summer 1991), 536-65.

4553. Dolan, Anthony R., "Impressions: Premeditated Prose: Reagan's Evil Empire," *American Enterprise*, 4, no. 2 (Mar-Apr. 1993), 24-28.

4554. Dole, Bob, "Grappling with the Bear: A Strategy for Dealing with Moscow," *Policy Review*, no. 38 (Fall 1986), 2-7.

4555. Drew, Elizabeth, "Letter from Washington," *New Yorker* (2 July 1990), 62-67.

4556. Feshbach, Murray, "How Gorbachev Has Changed Them," *American Enterprise*, 1 (Jan-Feb. 1990), 29-33.

4557. Fesler, Pamela, "Yeltsin Charges onto Capital Hill, Charms the Life Out of Cold War," *Congressional Quarterly Weekly Report*, 92 (20 June 1992), 1813-18.

4558. Fischer, Stanley, "The West's Challenge: Coordinating Soviet Aid," *International Economic Insights*, 2, no. 5 (Sept-Oct. 1991), 2-5.

4559. "The Flickering Glow from the Fireside Summit," *Economist*, 297 (23 Nov. 1985), 31-32.

4560. Foell, Earl W., "Teddy and Bear," *World Monitor*, 4, no. 4 (Apr. 1991), 80.

4561. "Follow-Up Measures of the Initiatives Advanced by Presidents George Bush and Mikhail Gorbachev," *International Affairs* (Moscow), no. 12 (Dec. 1991), 135ff.

4562. Fossedal, G. A., and A. Lieberman, "The Gorbachev Rating," *National Review*, 40 (22 July 1988), 39ff.

4563. Foye, Stephen, "US Congressional Report on Soviet Committee for Defense and State Security," *Report on the USSR*, 2, no. 19 (11 May 1990), 6-8.

4564. Frolic, Michael, "The Collapse of Communism," *Behind the Headlines*, 49, no. 2 (Winter 1991-92), 16-23.

4565. Gaddis, John L., "How the Cold War Might End," *Atlantic Monthly*, 260, no. 5 (Nov. 1987), 88ff.

4566. Galvin, J. R., "Perestroika and NATO," *Atlantic Community Quarterly*, 26, no. 3-4 (Fall-Winter 1988), 225-32.

4567. Garfinkle, Adam, "Coping with Collapse," *Reason*, 23, no. 3 (July 1991), 32-35.

4568. Garthoff, Raymond L., "American-Soviet Relations in Perspective," *Political Science Quarterly*, 100, no. 4 (Winter

1985-86), 541-59.

4569. -----, "The Bush Administration's Policy toward the Soviet Union," *Current History*, 90, no. 558 (Oct. 1991), 311-16.

4570. Gelb, N., "Moscow's Perilous Charms," *New Leader*, 69 (5-19 May 1986), 5-6.

4571. Gellner, Ernest, "Perestroika Observed," *Government and Opposition*, 25 (Winter 1990), 3-15.

4572. George, A. L., "US-Soviet Global Rivalry: Norms of Competition," *Journal of Peace Research*, 23, no. 3 (June 1986), 247-62.

4573. Geyer, A., "The Summit and Revised History," *Christian Century*, 105 (6-13 Jan. 1988), 4-5.

4574. Gibson, Andrew E., "Negotiating with the Soviets," *Naval War College Review*, 42, no. 1 (Winter 1989), 121-23.

4575. Gilpin, Robert, "American Policy in the Post-Reagan Era," *Daedalus*, 116, no. 3 (Summer 1987), 33-67.

4576. Glenny, Michael, "Gorbachev Courts the President," *New Statesman*, 111 (27 June 1986), 19-20.

4577. Goble, Paul A., "Ten Issues in Search of a Policy: America's Failed Approach to the Post-Soviet States," *Current History*, 92, no. 576 (Oct. 1993), 305-08.

4578. Goetze, B. A., "NATO Strategy after Reykjavik: Challenges and Opportunities," *Canadian Defence Quarterly*, 17, no. 2 (Autumn 1987), 43ff.

4579. Goldstein, Joshua S., "Reciprocity in Super-Power Relations," *International Studies Quarterly*, 35, no. 2 (June 1991), 195-209.

4580. Gorbachev, Mikhail S., "The Geneva Meeting," *Vital Speeches of the Day*, 52 (15 Jan. 1986), 194-203.

4581. -----, "New Opportunities in US-Soviet Relations," *US Department of State Dispatch*, 2 (16 Sept, 1991), 681-83.

4582. -----, "Summit Meeting," *Vital Speeches of the Day*, 54 (15 Feb. 1988), 266-71.

4583. -----, "U.S.S.R. and U.S. Relations," *Vital Speeches of the Day*, 57 (15 Dec. 1990), 130-32.

4584. "Gorbachev Holds QandA Session with Congressional Leaders," *Congressional Quarterly Weekly Report*, 48 (9 June 1990), 1827-30.

4585. Greider, W., "Understanding the Summit," *Rolling Stone* (28 Jan. 1988), 20ff.

4586. Halliday, F., "Fireside Chat That Doused the 3rd World," *New Statesman*, 110 (20-27 Dec. 1985), 37-39.

4587. -----, "Future Tense: The Changed US-USSR Relationship Not Only Heralds a New Global Order, But a World Slipping Beyond the Grasp of the Two Superpowers," *New Statesman and Society*, 3 (14 Sept. 1990), 14-15.

4588. Hansen, Roger D., "The Reagan Doctrine and Global Containment: Revival or Recessional?" *SAIS Review*, 7, no. 1 (Winter-Spring 1987), 39-66.

4589. Harries, Owen, "Is the Cold War Really Over?" *National Review*, 41 (10 Nov. 1989), 40ff.

4590. Hassner, Pierre, "Gorbachev and the West," *Washington Quarterly*, 11, no. 4 (Autumn 1988), 95-103.

4591. Helmer, O., "The Future Relationship Between the Super Powers," *Futures*, 18 (Aug. 1986), 484-92.

4592. Holbrooke, R., "Giving Gorbachev a Boost: Soviet Reform Is in the U.S. National Interest," *Newsweek*, 114 (25 Sept. 1989), 28.

4593. Holzman, Franklyn D., "Reforms in the USSR: Implications for U.S. Policy," *American Economic Review*, 79, no. 2 (May 1989), 26-30.

4594. Horelick, Andrew L., "U.S.-Soviet Relations: The Threshold of a New Era," *Foreign Affairs*, 69, no. 1 (1989-90), 51-69.

4595. Hough, Jerry F., "The End of Russia's `Khomeini' Period: Dilemmas for U.S. Foreign Policy," *World Policy Journal*, 4, no. 4 (Fall 1987), 583-604.

4596. -----, "The Future of Soviet-American Relations," *Current History*, 85, no. 513 (Oct. 1986), 305ff.

4597. -----, "Managing the U.S.-Soviet Relationship," *World Policy Journal*, 3, no. 1 (Winter 1985-86), 1-28.

4598. Huan, Guocang, "The New Relationship with the Former Soviet Union," *Current History*, 91, no. 566 (Sept. 1992), 253-56.

4599. Hunter, Robert E., "The Cold War Has Ended," *World & I* (Feb. 1990), 21-27.

4600. Hurwitz, John, and Mark Peffley, "Public Images of the Soviet Union: The Impact on Foreign Policy Attitudes," *Journal of Politics*, 52, no. 1 (Feb. 1990), 3-28.

4601. Hyland, William G., "Reagan-Gorbachev III," *Foreign Affairs*, 66, no. 1 (Fall 1987), 7-21.

4602. Javetski, B., "Bush May Have to Choose Between Perestroika and Its Creator," *Business Week* (2 Apr. 1990), 57.

4603. Johnson, Lena, "Soviet Policy towards Sweden and the Region of Northern Europe under Gorbachev," *Cooperation and Conflict*, 25, no. 1 (1990), 1-19.

4604. "Joint Document Underlines Progress, Good Relations," *Congressional Quarterly Weekly Report*, 46 (4 June 1988), 1546-47.

4605. Jones, David T., "How to Negotiate with Gorbachev's Team," *Orbis*, 33, no. 3 (Summer 1989), 357-73.

4606. Jordan, Amos A., "Explosive Change in China and the Soviet Union: Implications for the West," *Washington Quarterly*, 12, no. 4 (Autumn 1989), 97-111.

4607. -----, "A National Strategy for the 1990s," *Washington Quarterly*, 10, no. 3 (Summer 1987), 15-24.

4608. Kanet, Roger E., and David E. Albright, "New Challenges in the Study of American-Soviet Relations: The Implications of the Gorbachev Reforms," *International Studies Notes*, 16-17, no. 3-1 (Fall-Winter 1991-92), 20-24.

4609. Kass, Ilana, "The U.S.-Soviet Strategic Relationship," *Annals of the American Academy of Political and Social Science*, no. 517 (Sept. 1991), 25-39.

4610. Katz, Mark N., "Can the Superpowers Plot Peace?" *Bulletin of the Atomic Scientists*, 46, no. 4 (May 1990), 38-39.

4611. -----, "Evolving Soviet Perceptions of U.S. Strategy," *Washington Quarterly*, 12, no. 3 (Summer 1989), 157-67.

4612. -----, "Superpower Conflict Resolution: Lessons for the Future," *Annals of the American Academy of Political and Social Science*, no. 518 (Nov. 1991), 177-87.

4613. Kelly, P., "The Wall, *Glasnost*, and Marlboros," *New Perspectives Quarterly*, 4 (Winter 1988), 46-48.

4614. Kempton, M., "At the Summit," *New York Review of Books*, 35 (30 June 1988), 53-54.

4615. Kennan, George F., "America and the Russian Future," *Foreign Affairs*, 69, no. 2 (Spring 1990), 157-66.

4616. -----, "Containment Then and Now," *Foreign Affairs*, 65, no. 4 (Spring 1987), 885-90.

4617. -----, "Morality and Foreign Policy," *Parameters*, 16, no. 1 (Spring 1986), 76-82.

4618. Knight, R., "Wooing of the West," *U.S. News & World Report*, 99 (14 Oct. 1985), 22-23.

4619. Kozyrev, Andrei, "The Lagging Partnership," *Foreign Affairs*, 73, no. 3 (May-June 1994), 59-71.

4620. Krauthammer, C., "When to Call Off the Cold War," *New Republic* (16 Nov. 1987), 18-21.

4621. Kristol, Irving, and Eugene V. Rostow, "NATO: Do We Still Need It?" *Freedom at Issue*, no. 95 (Mar-Apr. 1987), 5-11.

4622. Kupperman, Robert H., "Using SDI to Reshape Soviet Strategic Behavior," *Washington Quarterly*, 8, no. 3 (Summer 1985), 77-84.

4623. Kusin, Vladimir V., "Western Europe and Reforms in the Soviet Bloc," *Harvard International Review*, 10, no. 1 (Nov. 1987), 10-13.

4624. Larrabee, F. Stephen, and Allen Lynch, "Gorbachev: The Road to Reykjavik," *Foreign Policy*, no. 65 (Winter 1986-87), 3-28.

4625. Layne, Christopher, "The Eclipse of a Great Power: America's Stake in Soviet Stability," *World Policy Journal*, 8, no. 1 (Winter 1990-91), 61-88.

4626. -----, "Superpower Disengagement," *Foreign Policy*, no. 77 (Winter 1989-90), 17-31.

4627. Ledeen, Michael, "The Beginning of the Beginning," *American Spectator*, 23, no. 2 (Feb. 1990), 14-16.

4628. Lenczowski, John, "The Soviet Union and the United States: Myths, Realities, Maxims," *Global Affairs*, 4, no. 1 (Winter 1989), 38-82.

4629. Lind, W. S., "Western Reunion: Our Coming Alliance with Russia?" *Policy Review*, no. 49 (Summer 1989), 18-21.

4630. Liska, George, "From Containment to Concert," *Foreign Policy*, no. 62 (Spring 1986), 3-23.

4631. Luck, Edward C., and Toby T. Gati, "Gorbachev, the United Nations and U.S. Policy," *Washington Quarterly*, 11, no. 4 (Autumn 1988), 19-35.

4632. Lugar, Richard G., "A Republican Looks at Foreign Policy," *Foreign Affairs*, 66, no. 2 (Winter 1987-88), 249-62.

4633. Lukacs, J., "America and Russia, Americans and Russians," *American Heritage*, 43 (Feb-Mar. 1992), 64-73.

4634. Luttwack, E. N., "Gorbachev's Strategy and Ours," *Commentary*, 88 (July 1989), 29-36.

4635. MacFarlane, S. Neil, "Soviet Strategy: Implications for Canada," *International Journal*, 45, no. 1 (Spring 1990), 58-80.

4636. Magstadt, T. M., "Is Communism Changing? Implications for U.S. Foreign Policy," *USA Today*, 117 (July 1988), 66-68.

4637. Mandelbaum, Michael, "Ending the Cold War," *Foreign Affairs*, 68, no. 2 (Spring 1989), 16-36.

4638. -----, and Strobe Talbott, "Reykjavik and Beyond," *Foreign Affairs*, 65, no. 2 (Winter 1986-87), 215-35.

4639. Manion, Christopher, "Can Foreign Policy Be Based on Morality?" *USA Today*, 118, no. 2538 (Mar. 1990), 36-38.

4640. Marantz, Paul, "Gorbachev's Road to Reykjavik and Beyond," in *Les grands puissances au lendemain de Reykjavik: Colloque 1987* (Que: Centre quebecois de re-lations internationales, L'Universite Laval, 1987), 107-28.

4641. Marzani, C., "On Interring Communism and Exalting Capitalism," *Monthly Review*, 41, no. 8 (Jan. 1990), suppl. 1-32; Discussion: 42, no. 12 (May 1990), 53-54.

4642. Massing, M., "Gorbaphobes in the U. S. Media," *Nation*, 247 (26 Dec. 1988), 13ff.

4643. Matlock, Jack F., "U.S.-Soviet Relations: Background and Prospects," *Department of State Bulletin*, 86 (Dec. 1986), 61-65.

4644. Matthews, Christopher, "The Teflon Comrade," *New Republic* (28 Oct. 1985), 16-17.

4645. Maynes, Charles W., "Change in Russia: America's Chance," *Foreign Policy*, no. 68 (Fall 1987), 88-99.

4646. McNeill, John H., "America's Maritime Boundary with the Soviet Union," *Naval War College Review*, 44, no. 3 (Summer 1991), 46-57.

4647. "Meetings Between President Bush and Gorbachev," *US Department of State Dispatch*, 2 (4 Nov. 1991), 805-06.

4648. Methvin, Eugene, "The Evil Empire Strikes Back: The

Politics of Hate, Soviet Style," *Policy Review*, no. 37 (Summer 1986), 63-65.

4649. Meyerson, Adam, "Ronald Reagan's Peace Offensive: Containing the Soviets without Going to War," *Policy Review*, no. 38 (Fall 1986), 66-67.

4650. Miko, Francis T., "The 27th Soviet Party Congress and the West," *Survival*, 28, no. 4 (July-Aug. 1986), 291-305.

4651. "Mission to Moscow," *New Republic* (16-23 Sept. 1991), 9-10.

4652. Moro, D. A., "The National Rebirth of Russia: A U.S. Strategy for Lifting the Soviet Siege," *Policy Review*, no. 43 (Winter 1988), 2-13.

4653. Mroz, John Edwin, "Russia and Eastern Europe: Will the West Let Them Fail?" *Foreign Affairs*, 72, no. 1 (1993), 44-57.

4654. Nelson, Daniel N., "The Soviet Union and Europe," *Telos*, no. 84 (Summer 1990), 142-54.

4655. Neuchterlein, Donald E., "The Reagan Doctrine in Perspective," *Perspectives on Political Science*, 19, no. 1 (Winter 1990), 43-49.

4656. "News Conference of President Bush and President Mikhail Gorbachev of the Soviet Union, September 9, 1990," *Weekly Compilation of Presidential Documents*, 26 (17 Sept. 1990), 1345-53.

4657. Nincic, Miroslav, "U.S. Soviet Policy and the Electoral Connection," *World Politics*, 43, no. 3 (Apr. 1990), 370-96.

4658. Nixon, Richard M., "Dealing with Gorbachev," *New York Times Magazine* (13 Mar. 1988), 30ff.

4659. -----, "Should the U.S. Help Gorbachev?" *Time*, 134 (18 Dec. 1989), 94.

4660. Novak, Michael, "Tell Gorbachev For Me," *National Review*, 37 (Oct. 1985), 46.

4661. Obukhov, Alexei, "The U.S. President's State Visit to the USSR," *International Affairs* (Moscow), no. 10 (Oct. 1991), 3-17.

4662. Odom, William E., "Only Ties to America Provide the Answer," *Orbis*, 34, no. 4 (Fall 1990), 483-504.

4663. "Paris Summit: `A Grand Turn in the Course of History'," *Foreign Policy Bulletin*, 1 (Jan-Apr. 1991), 70-82.

4664. Peretz, M., "The Gorbachev Tease," *New Republic* (10 July 1989), 14ff.

4665. Petersen, E. F., "The End of the Cold War: A Review of Recent Literature," *History Teacher*, 26 (Aug. 1993), 471-85.

4666. Pipes, Richard, and the Heritage Foundation Task Force, "Paper *Perestroika*: Gorbachev and American Strategy," *Policy Review*, no. 47 (Winter 1989), 14-20.

4667. Podlesnyi, Pavel T., "The Agenda of U.S.-Soviet Relations for the 1990s," *New York University Journal of International Law and Politics*, 22, no. 3 (Spring 1990), 389-406.

4668. Porter, Bruce D., "A Country Instead of a Cause: Russian Foreign Policy in the Post-Soviet Era," *Washington Quarterly*, 15, no. 3 (Summer 1992), 41-56.

4669. "Potemkin Summit," *New Republic* (25 June 1990), 7-8.

4670. "President Reagan and General Secretary Gorbachev Meet in Geneva," *Department of State Bulletin*, 86 (Jan. 1986), 58-60.

4671. "President Reagan and General Secretary Gorbachev Meet in Reykjavik," *Department of State Bulletin*, 86 (Dec. 1986), 1-21.

4672. Prina, L. Edgar, "Politics and *Perestroika*: President Bush Takes Command of `The Post-Reagan Revolution'," *Sea Power*, 32, no. 2 (Feb. 1989), 18ff.

4673. Prins, G., "Soviet Might and Western Blindness" (Review Article), 114 (24 July 1987), 15.

4674. Pytte, Alyson, "Jackson-Vanik Limits on Trade Come under New Scrutiny," *Congressional Quarterly Weekly Report*, 47 (25 Feb. 1989), 400-04.

4675. Qubing, Zhuang, "A Review of the Development of US-Soviet Relations," *Beijing Review*, 33 (4 Dec. 1989), 34-35.

4676. Ravenal, Earl C., "The Case for Adjustment," *Foreign Policy*, no. 81 (Winter 1990-91), 3-19.

4677. Razuvayev, Vladimir, "The Future of Europe Is Linked with Russia," *International Affairs* (Moscow), no. 12 (Dec. 1991), 30-42.

4678. Reagan, Ronald, "The Elements of Peace," *Vital Speeches of the Day*, 52 (1 Dec. 1985), 98-100.

4679. -----, "The Geneva Summit Meeting," *Vital Speeches of the Day*, 52 (15 Dec. 1985), 130-32.

4680. -----, "News Conference of September 17, 1985," *Department of State Bulletin*, 85 (Nov. 1985), 3-6.

4681. -----, "U.S.-Soviet Relations," *Department of State Bulletin*, 86 (Feb. 1986), 23.

4682. "Reagan and Gorbachev" (Special Section), *Foreign Affairs*, 64 (Fall 1985), 1-73.

4683. "Realism in Geneva," *National Review*, 37 (31 Dec. 1985), 16-18.

4684. Reissky de Dubnic, Vladimir, "Gorbachev's Policy toward Europe," *Global Affairs*, 4, no. 3 (Summer 1989), 68-82.

4685. "Rev. Jackson's `Mini-Summit' with Gorbachev Brings Praise from Jewish Group," *Jet*, 69 (9 Dec. 1985), 4ff.

4686. Richardson, R. C., "Risks and Implications of a Fading Threat," *Journal of Social, Political and Economic Studies*, 14, no. 4 (Winter 1989), 415-32.

4687. Roche, John P., "From Reykjavik All Roads Led Down," *National Review*, 39 (22 May 1987), 27-30.

4688. Rodman, Peter W., "Is the Cold War Over?" *Wilson Quarterly*, 13, no. 1 (1989), 39-42.

4689. Rose, Francois de, "Brinkmanship at Reykjavik," *Atlantic Community Quarterly*, 24, no. 4 (Winter 1986), 295-99.

4690. Rosefielde, Steven, "The Grand Bargain: Underwriting Catastroika," *Global Affairs*, 7, no. 1 (Winter 1992), 15-35.

4691. Rostow, Eugene V., "The Next Step in Soviet-American Relations: Modus Vivendi or Peace?" *Atlantic Community Quarterly*, 23, no. 2 (Summer 1985), 123-28.

4692. Rostow, W. W., "On Ending the Cold War," *Foreign Affairs*, 65, no. 4 (Spring 1987), 831-51.

4693. Russell, G., "Gorbachev's `Charm Offensive'," *Time*, 126 (14 Oct. 1985), 30-32.

4694. Russett, Bruce, "Doves, Hawks, and U.S. Public Opinion," *Political Science Quarterly*, 105, no. 4 (Winter 1990-91), 515-38.

4695. "Russophilia," *Economist*, 315 (9 June 1990), 21-22.

4696. Sanders, Sol W., "A `Common European House'-or a New Design for Soviet Hegemony?" *Strategic Review*, 17, no. 2 (Spring 1989), 18-31.

4697. Schlesinger, Arthur, Jr., "A Democrat Looks at Foreign Policy," *Foreign Affairs*, 66, no. 2 (Winter 1987-88), 263-83.

4698. Schlesinger, James, "Reykjavik and Revelations: A Turn of the Tide?" *Foreign Affairs*, 65, no. 3 (1987), 426-46.

4699. Schneider, William, "Bush's Goal Is to Stay Out of Trouble," *National Journal*, 22, no. 18 (5 May 1990), 1126.

4700. Schorr, Daniel, "Getting Ready for the Summit," *New Leader*, 71 (2 May 1988), 3-4.

4701. -----, "Selling Capitalism," *New Leader*, 74, no. 8 (15-29 July 1991), 4.

4702. Sempa, Francis P., "Geopolitics and American Strategy: A Reassessment," *Strategic Review*, 15, no. 2 (Spring 1987), 27-38.

4703. Senigallia, S. F., "Italy's Reaction to `Glasnost'," *New Leader*, 70 (23 Mar. 1987), 7.

4704. Shallhorn, Steve, "Canadian Defense: Standing Up to the United States," *Bulletin of the Atomic Scientists*, 43, no. 8 (Oct. 1987), 16-17.

4705. Sherwin, Martin J., "Gorby and Z," *Nation*, 250 (12 Feb. 1990), 189.

4706. Shevardnadze, Eduard, "Cooperation between the Soviet Union and the United States to Resolve Regional Conflicts," *Yearbook of Finnish Foreign Policy* (1991), 7.

4707. Shulman, Marshall D., "Four Decades of Irrationality: U.S.-Soviet Relations," *Bulletin of the Atomic Scientists*, 43, no. 9 (Nov. 1987), 15-25.

4708. Shultz, George P., "News Conference: July 3, 1985," *Department of State Bulletin*, 85 (Aug. 1985), 29-33.

4709. -----, "Reykjavik: A Watershed in U.S.-Soviet Relations," *Department of State Bulletin*, 86 (Dec. 1986), 22-25.

4710. Simard, Camil, "Soviet Sovereignty in the Arctic Seas," *Northern Perspectives*, 16, no. 4 (1988), 24-28.

4711. Smith, Hedrick, "Gorbachev's Shrewd Summitry," *New York Times Magazine* (6 Dec. 1987), 50ff.

4712. "Soviets and Americans," *Wilson Quarterly*, 13, no. 1 (1989), 38-66.

4713. Spiers, R. I., "U.S.-Soviet Agreement on Embassy Construction in Washington," *Department of State Bulletin*, 87 (July 1987), 34-35.

4714. Stanglin, D., "Dealing Warily with a Sick Bear," *U.S. News & World Report*, 107 (25 Sept. 1989), 32ff.

4715. Stavrakis, Peter J., "Challenge to the U.S.: Gorbachev's Opening to the West," *New Leader* (12 Dec. 1988), 5-7.

4716. Stent, Angela, "The Soviet Union and Western Europe: Divided Continent or Common House?" *Harriman Institute Forum*, 2, no. 9 (Sept. 1989), 1-8.

4717. Stewart, Philip D., "Gorbachev and the Obstacles toward Detente," *Political Science Quarterly*, 101, no. 1 (1986), 1-22.

4718. Stokes, Bruce, "While America Slept: Ignoring History's Lessons," *National Journal*, 23, no. 37 (14 Sept. 1991), 2240.

4719. Tatu, Michel, "Gorbachev and the West," *Fletcher Forum*, 12, no. 2 (Summer 1988), 265-70.

4720. Templeman, J., and G. E. Schares, "Gorbachev Lays the Cornerstone for His `Common European House'," *Business Week* (26 June 1989), 84.

4721. Tombs, George, "Canada's New Arctic," *World Monitor*, 3, no. 7 (July 1990), 42ff.

4722. Towell, Pat, "Gorbachev Initiative Challenges Bush, NATO," *Congressional Quarterly Weekly Report*, 46 (10 Dec. 1988), 3466-69.

4723. -----, "Gorbachev Raises Stakes, Proposes Joint Defense," *Congressional Quarterly Weekly Report*, 49 (12 Oct. 1991), 2965.

4724. Trofimenko, Henry, "The End of the Cold War, Not History," *Washington Quarterly*, 13, no. 2 (Spring 1990), 21-35.

4725. Udalov, Vadim V., "The Concept of Balance of Interests and U.S.-Soviet Interaction," *Annals of the American Academy of Political and Social Science*, no. 518 (Nov. 1991), 165-76.

4726. Ullman, Richard H., "Ending the Cold War," *Foreign Policy*, no. 72 (Fall 1988), 130-51.

4727. US Department of Commerce, "President/Prime Minister on Aid for Soviet Union, Republics," *Business America*, 112, no. 18 (9 Sept. 1991), ii.

4728. -----, "White House Initiative for Central and Eastern Europe," *Business America*, 112, no. 4 (25 Mar. 1991), ii.

4729. "U.S. Lawmakers Size Up Gorbachev," *U.S. News & World Report*, 99 (16 Sept. 1985), 27.

4730. Vassallo, A., "The End of the Cold War: Reflections Following the Soviet-American Summit," *World Marxist Review*,

33, no. 2 (Feb. 1990), 2-4.

4731. "Visit of General Secretary Gorbachev of the Soviet Union," *Department of State Bulletin*, 88 (Feb. 1988), 1-21.

4732. Vogel, H., "The Gorbachev Challenge: To Help or Not to Help?" *World Today*, 45, nos. 8-9 (Aug-Sept. 1989), 142-45.

4733. Vtorov, A., "USSR-France: Through a Dialogue to Greater Understanding and Detente," *International Affairs* (Dec. 1985), 3-8.

4734. Wade, Rex A., *et al.*, "Seminar: The United States, Russia and the Republics," *Soviet and Post-Soviet Review*, 20, nos. 2-3 (1993), 115-68.

4735. Wall, J. M., "Playing for Peace on the World Stage," *Christian Century*, 102 (4 Dec. 1985), 1107-08.

4736. Ward, Michael D., and Sheen Rajmaira, "Reciprocity and Norms in U.S.-Soviet Foreign Policy," *Journal of Conflict Resolution*, 36, no. 2 (June 1992), 342-68.

4737. "Wary Antagonists Reagan and Gorbachev Reach Out for Peace with a Handshake," *People Weekly*, 28 (21 Dec. 1987), 37ff.

4738. "Washington Summit," *Weekly Compilation of Presidential Documents*, 26 (4 June 1990), 847-94.

4739. Weinrod, W. B., "Soviet 'New Thinking' and U.S. Foreign Policy," *World Affairs*, 151 (Fall 1988), 59-65.

4740. Weiss, Seymour, "U.S.-Soviet Detente: The Collision of Hope and Experience," *Strategic Review*, 17, no. 1 (Winter 1989), 16-24.

4741. Whitney, Craig R., "Letter to Gorbachev," *New York Times Magazine* (26 Oct. 1986), 56ff.

4742. Williams, P., "Soviet-American Relations," *Proceedings of the Academy of Political Science*, 36, no. 4 (1987), 54-66.

4743. Wolfe, James H., "Soviet Challenge to the West," *USA Today*, 118, no. 2536 (Jan. 1990), 27.

4744. Wrong, Dennis, "The Waning of the Cold War: A Turning Point in Modern History," *Dissent*, 36, no. 2 (Spring 1989), 192-97.

4745. Yakovlev, Alexander N., "From Russia with Glasnost: A New Look at What Is To Be Done: We Will Astonish You," *New Perspectives Quarterly*, 4, no. 2 (Spring 1987), 32-38.

4746. Zakaria, Fareed, "The Reagan Strategy of Containment," *Political Science Quarterly*, 105, no. 3 (Fall 1990), 373-96.

4747. Zemtsov, Ilya, and John Farrar, "The Pendulum of Reykjavik or One More Attempt to Reverse History," *Crossroads*, no. 24 (1987), 29-50.

XXI. General Studies; Analysis; Reflection

BOOKS

4748. Aanason, Johann P., *The Future That Failed: Origins and Destinies of the Soviet Model* (London: Routledge, 1993).

4749. Ackerman, Bruce, *The Future of Liberal Revolution* (New Haven: Yale University Press, 1993).

4750. Bialer, Seweryn, *The Soviet Paradox: External Expansion, Internal Decline* (London: I. B. Tauris & Co., 1986).

4751. Bryson, Philip P., *Perestroika, Phase III: Can the USSR Learn from the Only Successful Reform*, Carl Beck Papers in Russian and East European Studies, no. 904 (Pittsburgh: University of Pittsburgh Center for Russian and East European Studies, 1991).

4752. Brzezinski, Zbigniew, *The Grand Failure: The Birth and Death of Communism in the Twentieth Century* (New York: Charles Scribner's Sons, 1989).

4753. Clemens, Walter C., Jr., *Can Russia Change? The Soviet Union Confronts Global Interdependence* (New York: Routledge, 1990).

4754. Cockburn, Patrick, *Getting Russia Wrong: The End of Kremlinology* (New York: Verso, 1989).

4755. Cohen, Stephen F., and Katrina vanden Heuvel, *Voices of Glasnost* (New York: W. W. Norton, 1989).

4756. Cooper, Leo, *Soviet Reforms and Beyond* (New York: St. Martin's Press, 1991).

4757. Crozier, Brian, *The Gorbachev Phenomenon: "Peace" and the Secret War* (London: Claridge Press, 1990).

4758. Dibb, Paul, *The Soviet Union: The Incomplete Superpower*, 2nd ed. (London: Macmillan, 1988).

4759. Dowlah, Abu Faij, *Perestroika: An Inquiry into Its Historical, Ideological and Intellectual Roots* (San Marcos, TX: Southwest Texas State University and Bethany Books, 1990).

4760. Ellman, Michael, *The USSR in the 1990s: Struggling Out of Stagnation* (London: The Economist Intelligence Unit, 1989).

4761. Evans, Alfred B., Jr., *Soviet Marxism-Leninism: The Decline of an Ideology* (New York: Praeger, 1993).

4762. Faid, Robert W., *Gorbachev: Has the Real Antichrist Come?* (Tulsa: Victory House, 1988).

4763. Feher, Ferenc, and Andrew Arato, eds., *Gorbachev-The Debate* (Atlantic Highlands, NJ: Humanities Press International, 1989).

4764. Fleron, Frederic J., and Erik P. Hoffmann, eds., *Post-Communist Studies and Political Science: Methodology and Empirical Theory in Sovietology* (Boulder, CO: Westview Press, 1993).

4765. Fukuyama, Francis, *The End of History and the Last Man* (New York: Free Press, 1992).

4766. Gorbachev, Mikhail, *The Coming Century of Peace* (New York: Richardson & Steirman, 1986).

4767. Gunlicks, Arthur B., and John D. Treadway, *The Soviet Union Under Gorbachev: Assessing the First Year* (New York: Praeger, 1987).

4768. Gwertzman, Bernard, and Michael T. Kaufman, *The Collapse of Communism; By Correspondents of the New York Times*, rev. and updated ed. (New York: New York Times Co., 1992).

4769. Hart, Gary, *Russia Shakes the World: The Second Russian Revolution and Its Impact on the West* (New York: Cornelia & Michael Bessie Books, 1991).

4770. Hirsch, Steve, ed., *MEMO: New Voices on Soviet Foreign and Economic Policy* (Washington, DC: Bureau of National Affairs, 1989).

4771. Hosking, Geoffrey, *The Awakening of the Soviet Union*, enlarged ed. (Cambridge, MA: Harvard University Press, 1991).

4772. Hough, Jerry, *Russia and the West: Gorbachev and the Politics of Reform* (New York: Simon and Schuster, 1988).

4773. Huber, Robert T., and Donald E. Kelley, *Perestroika-Era Politics* (Armonk, NY: M. E. Sharpe, 1991).

4774. Hudelson, Richard H., *The Rise and Fall of Communism* (Boulder, CO: Westview Press, 1993).

4775. Jowitt, Ken, *New World Disorder: The Leninist Extinction* (Berkeley: University of California Press, 1993).

4776. Juviler, Peter, and Hiroshi Kimura, eds., *Gorbachev's Reforms: U.S. and Japanese Assessments* (New York: Aldine, 1988).

4777. Kaiser, Robert G., *Why Gorbachev Happened: His Triumphs and His Failure* (New York: Simon & Schuster, 1991).

4778. Kelley, Donald R., and Shannon G. Davis, eds., *The Sons of Sergei: Khrushchev and Gorbachev as Reformers* (New York: Praeger, 1992).

4779. Kerblay, Basile H., *Gorbachev's Russia* (New York: Pantheon Books, 1989).

4780. Kirkpatrick, Jeane J., *The Withering Away of the Totalitarian State-And Other Surprises* (Washington, DC: AEI Press, distributed by National Book Network, 1990).

4781. Krasnov, Vladislav, *Russia Beyond Communism: A Chronicle of National Rebirth* (Boulder, CO: Westview Press, 1991).

4782. Kubalkova, V., and A. A. Cruickshank, *Thinking about Soviet "New Thinking"* (Berkeley: University of California Institute of International Studies, 1989).

4783. Lapeyrouse, Stephen Ludger, *Towards the Spiritual Convergence of America and Russia: American Mind and Russian Soul, American Individuality and Russian Community, and the Potent Alchemy of National Characteristics* (Santa Cruz, CA: S. Lapeyrouse, 1990).

4784. Lesourne, Jacques, and Bernard Lecomte, *After Communism: From the Atlantic to the Urals* (Philadelphia: Harwood Academic, 1991).

4785. Levy, David, *Reflections of a Moscow Correspondent* (Toronto: Mackenzie Institute for the Study of Terrorism, Revolution and Propaganda, 1989).

4786. Likhachev, Dmitri, *Reflections on Russia* (Boulder, CO: Westview Press, 1991).

4787. Linden, Carl A., *Khrushchev and the Soviet Leadership: With an Epilogue on Gorbachev*, updated ed. (Baltimore: Johns Hopkins University Press, 1990).

4788. Ludwikowski, Rett R., *The Crisis of Communism: Its Meaning, Origins and Phases* (Washington, DC: Pergamon-Brassey's International Defense Publications, 1987).

4789. Martin, Lawrence, *Breaking with History: The Gorbachev Revolution: An Eyewitness Account* (Toronto: Doubleday Canada, 1989).

4790. Medvedev, Roy, and Giulietto Chiesa, *Time of Change: An Insider's View of Russia's Transformation* (New York: Pantheon, 1989).

4791. Mikheyev, Dimitry, *The Rise and Fall of Gorbachev* (Indianapolis: Hudson Institute, 1993).

4792. Murphy, Kenneth, *Retreat from the Finland Station: Moral Odysseys in the Breakdown of Communism* (New York: Free Press, 1992).

4793. Naishul, V. A., *The Supreme and Last Stage of Socialism* (London: CRCE, 1991).

4794. Nixon, Richard, *Beyond Peace* (New York: Random House, 1994).

4795. Pokorny, Dusan, *Efficiency and Justice in the Industrial World*, vol. 1: *The Failure of the Soviet Experiment* (Armonk, NY: M. E. Sharpe, 1993).

4796. Remnick, Richard, *Lenin's Tomb: The Last Days of the Soviet Empire* (New York: Random House, 1993).

4797. Sakwa, Richard, *Gorbachev and His Reforms* (Englewood Cliffs, NJ: Prentice-Hall, 1990).

4898. Sallnow, John, *Reform in the Soviet Union: Glasnost and the Future* (New York: St. Martin's Press, 1989).

4899. Sestanovich, Stephen, *Rethinking Russia's National Interests* (Washington, DC: Center for Strategic and International Studies, 1994).

4800. Shlapentokh, Vladimir, with Dmitry Shlapentokh, *Soviet Ideologies in the Period of Glasnost: Responses to Brezhnev's Stagnation* (New York: Praeger, 1988).

4801. Shlapentokh, Vladimir, with Neil F. O'Donnell, *The Last Years of the Soviet Union: Snapshots from 1985-1991* (Westport, CT: Praeger, 1993).

4802. Solzhenitsyn, Alexander, *Rebuilding Russia: Reflections and Tentative Proposals* (New York: Farrar, Straus and Giroux, 1991).

4803. Stern, Geoffrey, *The Rise and Decline of International Communism* (Brookfield, VT: Gower, 1990).

4804. Thom, Francoise, *The Gorbachev Phenomenon: A History of Perestroika* (London: Pinter Publishers, 1989).

4805. Vogt-Downey, Marilyn, *The Soviet Union 1987-1991: Marxist Perspectives* (New York: Humanities Press, 1993).

4806. Walker, Rachel, *Six Years That Shook the World: Perestroika-The Impossible Project* (New York: St. Martin's Press, 1993).

4807. Wren, Christopher S., *The End of the Line: The Failure of Communism in the Soviet Union and China* (New York: Simon & Schuster, 1990).

4808. Yanov, Alexander, *The Russian Challenge and the Year 2000* (New York: Basil Blackwell, 1987).

ARTICLES

4809. Acker, Kevin, "'Poisoning of the Soul': New Leaders of Russia and Central Europe Talk About the Evil Empire," *Policy Review*, no. 55 (Winter 1991), 60-65.

4810. Adelman, Kenneth L., "How Gorbachev Has Changed Us," *American Enterprise*, 1 (Jan-Feb. 1990), 22-28.

4811. Agh, Attila, "Comparative Communism: Toward a Third Generation?" (Review Article), *Studies in Comparative Communism*, 23, no. 2 (Summer 1990), 213-22.

4812. Akselrod, Yulia, "Why My Grandfather Leon Trotsky Must Be Turning in His Grave," *Commentary*, 87 (Apr. 1989), 39-43.

4813. Alexeev, Michael, Clifford Gaddy and Jim Leitzel, "Getting the Picture Right: Soviet Collapse, Transition Problems, and Western Aid," *Brookings Review*, 10, no. 1 (Winter 1992), 14-17.

4814. Amalric, J., "The Gorbachev Era," *World Press Review*, 32 (May 1985), 46.

4815. Amann, Ronald, "The Empire Strikes Back: The Interplay of Economic and Political Change in the Soviet Union," *World Today*, 43, nos. 8-9 (Aug-Sept. 1987), 132-37.

4816. Aron, Leon, "Two Requiems for Perestroika" (Review Article), *World Affairs*, 155, no. 1 (Summer 1992), 40-44.

4817. Avineri, Shlomo, "Capitalism Has Not Won, Socialism Is Not Dead," *Dissent*, 39, no. 1 (Winter 1992), 7-11.

4818. Barnathan, J., "Gorbachev: What Makes Him Run?" *Newsweek*, 106 (18 Nov. 1985), 50ff.

4819. Barnet, Richard J., "Reflections: Defining the Moment," *New Yorker* (16 July 1990), 46-60.

4820. Bauman, Zygmunt, "A Revolution in the Theory of Revolutions?" *International Political Science Review*, 15, no. 1 (Jan. 1994), 15-24.

4821. Bell, Daniel, "On the Fate of Communism," *Dissent*, 37, no. 2 (Spring 1990), 187-88.

4822. Bergson, Abram, "The USSR Before the Fall: How Poor and Why," *Journal of Economic Perspectives*, 5, no. 4 (Fall 1991), 29-44.

4823. Besancon, Alain, "Gorbachev without Illusions," *Commentary*, 85 (Apr. 1988), 47-57.

4824. Bialer, Seweryn, "Can Gorbachev Radicalize *Perestroika*?" *U.S. News & World Report*, 107 (7 Aug. 1989), 39-40.

4825. -----, "The Death of Soviet Communism," *Foreign Affairs*, 70, no. 5 (Winter 1991-92), 166ff.

4826. -----, "Domestic and International Factors in the Formation of Gorbachev's Reforms," *Journal of International Affairs*, 42 (Spring 1989), 283-97.

4827. -----, "Interview: Aleksandr Yakovlev: Redefining Socialism at Home and Abroad," *Journal of International Affairs*, 42 (Spring 1989), 333-55.

4828. -----, "The Passing of the Soviet Order?" *Survival*, 32, no. 2 (Mar-Apr. 1990), 107-20.

4829. Billington, James H., "Russia's Fever Break," *Wilson Quarterly*, 15, no. 4 (Autumn 1991), 58-65.

4830. Blaney, John, and Mike Gfoeller, "Lessons from the Failure of Perestroika," *Political Science Quarterly*, 108, no. 3 (Fall 1993), 481-96.

4831. Blank, Stephen, "Paying for Lenin's Illusions: The Economic Dimension of Soviet Foreign Policies," *Comparative Strategy*, 10, no. 4 (Oct-Dec. 1991), 365-92.

4832. Bogomolov, Oleg, "The Socialist World on the Path of Restructuring," *Soviet Review*, 29, no. 3 (Fall 1988), 68-83.

4833. Bolman, Leo G., "Leadership Lessons from Mikhail Gorbachev," *Human Resources Development Quarterly*, 3, no. 1 (Spring 1992), 3-28.

4834. Bonner, Elena, "The Myth of Gorbachev," *Freedom at Issue*, no. 115 (July-Aug. 1990), 25-26.

4835. Braun, Aurel, and Richard B. Day, "Gorbachevian Contradictions," *Problems of Communism*, 39, no. 3 (May-June 1990), 36-50.

4836. Breslauer, George, "Evaluating Gorbachev as Leader," *Soviet Economy*, 5, no. 4 (Oct-Dec. 1989), 299-340.

4837. -----, "How to Think About the New Political Thinking," *Crossroads*, no. 28 (1989), 53-59.

4838. -----, "Understanding Gorbachev: Diverse Perspectives," *Soviet Economy*, 7, no. 2 (Apr-June 1991), 110-20.

4839. Brown, Archie, "Gorbachev: New Man in the Kremlin," *Problems of Communism*, 36, no. 3 (May-June 1985).

4840. -----, "Soviet Political Developments and Prospects," *World Policy Journal*, 4, no. 1 (Winter 1986), 55-87.

4841. Brucan, Silviu, "Can the Soviet System Be Changed?" *Current* (May 1988), 34-41.

4842. Brumberg, Abraham, "Changes in Russia and the American Right," *Dissent*, 39, no. 1 (Winter 1992), 16-22.

4843. Brzezinski, Zbigniew, "On the USSR Empire Today: The Imperial Relationship-A Conversation with Zbigniew Brzezinski,"

Freedom at Issue, no. 98 (Sept-Oct. 1987), 20-22.

4844. Buckley, William F., "The Case for Gorbachev," *National Review*, 43 (1 Apr. 1991), 55.

4845. Bukovsky, Vladimir, "What to Do About the Soviet Collapse," *Commentary*, 92 (Sept. 1991), 19-24.

4846. Bunce, Valerie, "The Soviet Union under Gorbachev: Ending Stalinism and Ending the Cold War," *International Journal*, 46, no. 2 (Spring 1991), 220-41.

4847. Burlatskii, Fedor, "A Frank Conversation (A Polemical Dialogue on Restructuring)," *Soviet Law and Government*, 26, no. 1 (Summer 1987), 5-24.

4848. "Can the Soviet Union Survive?" *Progressive*, 55, no. 10 (Oct. 1991), 7-9.

4849. Castoriadis, Cornelius, "The Gorbachev Interlude," *Thesis Eleven*, no. 20 (1988), 5-29.

4850. -----, "The Pulverization of Marxism-Leninism," *Salmagundi*, no. 88-89 (Fall 1990-Winter 1991), 371-84.

4851. Cohen, Stephen F., "Sovieticus," *Nation*, 239 (17 Nov. 1984), 503; 240 (4 May 1985), 522; 241 (14 Sept. 1985), 199; 242 (18 Jan. 1986), 409; 242 (15 Feb. 1986), 168; 242 (3 May 1986), 607; 242 (31 May 1986), 750; 242 (11 Oct. 1986), 336; 242 (15 Nov. 1986), 511;

4852. -----, "What's Really Happening in Russia," *Nation* (2 Mar. 1992), 259-68.

4853. Coleman, F., and R. Watson, "*Perestroika* Isn't Working," *Newsweek*, 113 (13 Mar. 1989), 28ff.

4854. Colton, Timothy J., "Taking Gorbachev's Measure," *Peace and Security*, 2, no. 2 (1987), 8-9.

4855. Conquest, Robert, "Soviet Communism (1917-1991)," *New Leader*, 74, no. 10 (9-23 Sept. 1991), 3.

4856. "Consequences of Soviet Decline: A Faltering Economy and a Strong Military Could Be a Volatile Mix," *Futurist*, 23 (Jan-Feb. 1989), 39-40.

4857. Corelli, R., "A Warning to Gorbachev," *Maclean's*, 102 (25 Sept. 1989), 30.

4858. Crozier, Brian, "All Over? Not Quite," *National Review*, 42 (5 Nov. 1990), 71-73.

4859. -----, "Getting Gorbachev Wrong," *Midstream*, 37, no. 2 (Feb-Mar. 1991), 17-19.

4860. Dahl, Robert A., and Ian Shapiro, "Impressions from the Soviet Union," *Dissent*, 38, no. 3 (Summer 1991), 342-45.

4861. Daniels, Robert V., "The Riddle of Russian Reform," *Dissent*, 40, no. 4 (Fall 1993), 489-96.

4862. Day, Richard B., "The Political Economy of Perestroika: Thinking about the `New Thinking' in the Soviet Union," *Canadian Slavonic Papers*, 21, no. 3-4 (1989), 316-22.

4863. Dejevsky, Mary, "The Gorbachev Era Begins," *World Today*, 42, no. 4 (Apr. 1986), 56-57.

4864. Desai, Padma, "Perestroika: Is It on Track?" *Canadian Business Law Journal*, 17 (Dec. 1990), 226-37.

4865. Deudney, Daniel, and G. John Ikenberry, "Soviet Reform and the End of the Cold War: Explaining Large-Scale Historical Change," *Review of International Studies*, 17, no. 3 (July 1991), 225-50.

4866. Di Leo, Rita, "The Soviet Union 1985-1990: After Communist Rule the Deluge?" *Soviet Studies*, 43, no. 3 (1991), 429-50.

4867. Draper, Theodore, "Soviet Reformers: From Lenin to Gorbachev," *Dissent*, 34, no. 3 (Summer 1987), 287-301.

4868. "Eastern Europe: Who Will Benefit from Reform?" *USA Today: Special Newsletter Edition*, 120, no. 2555 (Aug. 1991), 12.

4869. Edwards, Mike, "Mother Russia on a New Course," *National Geographic*, 179, no. 2 (Feb. 1991), 2-37.

4870. Evanier, D., "Will the Soviet Union Survive until 1994?" *National Review*, 41 (7 Apr. 1989), 24ff.

4871. Evans, Alfred, Jr., "Gorbachev's Unfinished Revolution" (Review Article), *Problems of Communism*, 40, no. 1-2 (Jan-Apr. 1991), 133-43.

4872. Evans, Charles, "In Search of Mother Russia," *Contemporary Review*, 256, no. 1491 (Apr. 1990), 191-94.

4873. Fairbanks, Charles H., and Richard Pipes, "Dangers from a Dying Bear: Two Perspectives on the Soviet Union," *American Enterprise*, 2, no. 3 (May-June 1991), 62-71.

4874. Falin, Valentin M., "*Glasnost'*: Getting at the Roots," *Perestroika Annual*, 1 (1988), 281-305.

4875. Feher, Ferenc, "Crisis and Crisis-Solving in the Soviet System Under Gorbachev's New Course," *Thesis Eleven*, no. 21 (1988), 5-19.

4876. Feldmesser, Robert A., "The Origins of Soviet Political Pathology," *International Journal of Comparative Sociology*, 32, no. 3-4 (Sept-Dec. 1991), 304-09.

4877. Feshbach, Murray, "How Gorbachev Has Changed Them," *American Enterprise*, 1 (Jan-Feb. 1990), 29-33.

4878. Finn, James, "On the New World (Dis)Order," *Freedom Review*, 22, no. 4 (July-Aug. 1991), 5-6.

4879. Frank, Peter, "The End of Perestroika," *World Today*, 46, no. 5 (May 1990), 87-89.

4880. Franklin, Daniel, "Gorbachev's Progress: Is the Perestroikamobile Moving?" *World Today*, 44, no. 6 (June 1988), 92-93.

4881. Freidin, Gregory, "Reform or Else," *New Republic* (13 Aug. 1990), 16-18.

4882. Frost, Gerald, "Margaret and Mikhail: The Odyssey of an Odd Couple," *National Interest*, no. 13 (Fall 1988), 93-99.

4883. Fukuyama, Francis, "Are We at the End of History?" *Fortune*, 121 (15 Jan. 1990), 75ff.

4884. -----, "The End of History?" *National Interest*, 16 (Summer 1989), 3-18.

4885. Galloway, J. L., "A Troubled Land on the Edge," *U.S. News & World Report*, 108 (5 Feb. 1990), 42-47.

4886. Gallup, George, Jr., and Frank Newport, "Americans Still Ambivalent about Soviet Union, Gorbachev," *Gallup Poll Monthly* (May 1990), 18-20.

4887. Gewen, Barry, "Sobering Views of the USSR," *New Leader*, 71, no. 11 (27 June 1988), 17-18.

4888. Gitlin, Todd, "Sisyphus After the Putsch," *Tikkun*, 6, no. 6 (Nov-Dec. 1991), 17-19.

4889. Glazov, Yuri, "Gorbachev Is Gone, Yeltsin...?" *Dalhousie Review*, 72, no. 2 (Summer 1992), 150-66.

4890. Goble, Paul, "Forget the Soviet Union," *Foreign Policy* (Spring 1992), 56-66.

4891. Goldhagen, Erich, "The Ideological Beliefs of Mikhail Gorbachev," *Midstream*, 36, no. 2 (Feb-Mar. 1990), 3-9.

4892. Goldman, Marshall I., "Gorbachev and *Perestroika*," *Fletcher Forum*, 132, no. 2 (Summer 1988), 216-20.

4893. -----, "Grand Bargain or Grand Illusion?" *World & I*, 6, no. 9 (Nov. 1991), 28-35.

4894. -----, "Losing Ground," *World Monitor*, 4, no. 3 (Mar. 1991), 42-43.

4895. Gooding, John, "Perestroika as Revolution from Within: An Interpretation," *Russian Review*, 51, no. 1 (Jan. 1992), 36-57.

4896. Gorbachev, Mikhail, "Subjectivism and an Unsystematic Approach," *Delovie Lyudi*, no. 40 (Dec. 1993), 20.

4897. -----, "We Are the Makers of Our Own Future," *New Times*, no. 27 (July 1988), 4-8.

4898. "Gorbachev or Yeltsin? The Lords of Misrule," *Economist*, 319 (6 Apr. 1991), 17ff.

4899. "The Gorbachev Record: The Rise and Fall of Perestroika," *Economist*, 318 (19 Jan. 1991), 39-41.

4900. "Gorbymania, Gorbyphobia," *Nation*, 252 (8 Apr. 1991), 433.

4901. Gordon, David M., "Socialism: What's Left After the Collapse of the Soviet System?" *Social Research*, 60, no. 3 (Fall 1993), 471-92.

4902. Gordon, L., and A. Nazimova, "Perestroika in Historical Perspective: Possible Scenarios," *Government and Opposition*, 25 (Winter 1990), 16-29.

4903. Greenfield, Meg, "The Many Faces of Gorbachev," *Newsweek*, 117 (4 Mar. 1991), 72.

4904. Greider, W., "Is Bush Bold Enough to Answer Gorbachev?" *Rolling Stone* (9 Feb. 1989), 48ff.

4905. Gruliow, Leo, "Changing Times in the USSR" (Review Article), *Antioch Review*, 49, no. 4 (Fall 1991), 607-09.

4906. -----, "The Unfinished Revolution II," *Antioch Review*, 49, no. 2 (Spring 1991), 288-95.

4907. Hammer, Darrell P., "Alternative Visions of the Russian Future: Religious and Nationalist Alternatives," *Studies in Comparative Communism*, 20, no. 3-4 (Autumn 1987), 265-75.

4908. Hanson, Philip, "Is There a `Third Way' Between Capitalism and Socialism?" *Report on the USSR*, 3, no. 35 (30 Aug. 1991), 15-19.

4909. Hazard, J. N., "The Gorbachev Era in the USSR: The Best and Worst of Times," *Syracuse Journal of International Law and Commerce*, 15 (Fall 1988), 1-12.

4910. Heilbroner, Robert L., "After Communism," *New Yorker* (10 Sept. 1990), 91-100.

4911. Heleniak, Tim, and Albert Motivans, "A Note on *Glasnost'* and the Soviet Statistical System," *Soviet Studies*, 43, no. 3 (1991), 473-90.

4912. Heller, Agnes, "Can Glasnost Become Permanent?" *New Statesman*, 116 (13 May 1988), 23.

4913. -----, and Ferenc Feher, "Khrushchev and Gorbachev: A Contrast," *Dissent*, 35, no. 1 (Winter 1988), 6-10.

4914. Hemans, Simon, "Whither the Soviet Union?" *RUSI Journal*, 135, no. 3 (Autumn 1990), 21-25.

4915. Hergesheimer, John, "The End of the Soviet Union," *Sunburst*, 17, no. 3 (9 Feb. 1992), 8.

4916. Hill, Ronald J., "Gorbachev's Reforms: Prospects of Success," *Contemporary Review*, 250, no. 1457 (Jan. 1987), 286-92.

4917. Hofheinz, P., "Can the Soviet Union Survive Gorbachev?" *Fortune*, 123 (14 Jan. 1991), 37-38.

4918. Howard, Michael, "Russia Rethinks the Revolution," *World Today*, 43, no. 11 (Nov. 1987), 185-86.

4919. Howell, Llewellyn D., "The End of Ideology," *USA Today*, 120, no. 2554 (July 1991), 39.

4920. Huber, Robert T., "Gorbachev's First Five Years," *Items*, 44, no. 2-3 (June-Sept. 1990), 25-30.

4921. Ignatius, David, "What's So Good About Gorbachev?" *Atlantic*, 262 (July 1988), 14-17.

4922. Jameson, Lisa, and Mitchell Reiss, "The New Soviet Union: An Unfinished Revolution," *RUSI Journal*, 136, no. 4 (Winter 1991), 29-32.

4923. Janos, Andrew C., "Social Science, Communism, and the Dynamics of Political Change," *World Politics*, 44, no. 1 (Oct. 1991), 81-112.

4924. Kagan, Frederick, "The Secret History of Perestroika," *National Interest*, no. 23 (Spring 1991), 33-42.

4925. Kaiser, Robert G., "Gorbachev: Triumph and Failure," *Foreign Affairs*, 70, no. 2 (Spring 1991), 160-74.

4926. -----, "The Soviet Pretense," *Foreign Affairs*, 65, no. 2 (Winter 1986-87), 236-51.

4927. Kaminski, Bartlomiej, and Karol Soltan, "The Evolution of Communism," *International Political Science Review*, 10, no. 4 (1989), 371-91.

4928. Kaplinski, Jaan, "When Attila Is Dead," *National Review*, 43 (15 Apr. 1991), 41-42.

4929. Kemme, David M., "The Houston Report: The Failure of Perestroika," *International Economic Insights*, 2, no. 1 (Jan-Feb. 1991), 9-12.

4930. Kennan, George F., "The Gorbachev Prospect," *New York Review of Books* (21 Jan. 1988).

4931. Kinsley, Michael, "TRB: Perestroika Bailout?" *New Republic* (25 June 1990), 4.

4932. Kintner, W. R., "Soviet Global Strategy," *Conservative Digest*, 14 (Sept. 1988), 89-93.

4933. Kirkpatrick, Jeane J., "Beyond the Cold War," *Foreign Affairs*, 69, no. 1 (1990), 1-16.

4934. Kissinger, Henry, "How to Deal with Gorbachev," *Newsweek*, 109 (2 Mar. 1987), 39ff.

4935. Kliamkin, Igor, "Gorbachev versus Gorbachev," *Global Affairs*, 7, no. 1 (Winter 1992), 1-14.

4936. "Kohl on Gorbachev: Too Much Candor?" *Newsweek*, 108 (17 Nov. 1987), 58.

4937. Kondracke, Morton, "Revolution `91," *New Republic* (24 June 1991), 18-21.

4938. Korionov, V., "Glasnost: Bane or Boom?" *World Marxist Review*, 30, no. 12 (Dec. 1987), 92-93.

4939. Korotich, V., "Gorbachev: The Saint That Failed," *New Perspectives Quarterly*, 8 (Spring 1991), 64-65.

4940. Krizan, Mojmir, "The Ideological Impasse of Gorbachev's Perestrojka," *Studies in Soviet Thought*, 40, no. 1-3 (Aug-Nov. 1990), 113-35.

4941. Krol, Marcin, "Being a Conservative in a Postcommunist Country," *Social Research*, 60, no. 3 (Fall 1993), 589-608.

4942. Kuehnelt-Leddihn, E. von, "Gorbachev's Inheritance," *National Review*, 37 (19 Apr. 1985), 40.

4943. Kvint, V., "The Myth of Good Czar Gorbachev," *Forbes*, 147 (4 Feb. 1991), 36-37.

4944. Lambakis, Steven, "Churchill versus Gorbachev: The Bout of the Century," *Comparative Strategy*, 12, no. 2 (Apr-June 1993), 225-32.

4945. Landy, Joanne, "Politics and the Economy: What's to Come in the USSR?" *Social Policy*, 22, no. 2 (Fall 1991), 17-34.

4946. Laqueur, Walter, "Gorbachev and Epimetheus: The Origins of the Russian Crisis," *Journal of Contemporary History*, 28, no. 3 (July 1993), 387-420.

4947. -----, "The World as Seen by Gorbachev," *Washington Quarterly*, 9, no. 4 (Fall 1986), 147-51.

4948. Lasky, M. J., "Is Russia Really Changing?" *Reader's Digest*, 132 (June 1988), 71-74.

4949. Lea, J. F., "Gorbachev as Roosevelt?" *USA Today*, 118 (Mar. 1990), 35.

4950. Leach, Rodney, "Should We Save Gorbachev?" *National Review*, 42 (19 Feb. 1990), 27-29.

4951. Lewis, Flora, "Communism without Marx," *New York Times Magazine* (7 June 1987), 44ff.

4952. Lieven, Dominic, "Assessing the Gorbachev Revolution," *Conflict Studies*, no. 200 (June 1987), 1-30.

4953. Linden, Carl, "Gorbachev's New Course at Home and Abroad: Renovation or Transformation?" *Towson State Journal of International Affairs*, 22 (Fall 1987), 19-30.

4954. Lipton, David, "Reform Endangered," *Foreign Policy*, no. 90 (Spring 1993), 57-78.

4955. Loone, Eero, "Marxism and *Perestroika*," *Soviet Studies*, 42, no. 4 (Oct. 1990), 779-94.

4956. Lubin, Peter, "How to Dismantle Communism," *National Review*, 41 (8 Dec. 1989), 29-33.

4957. Ludwikowski, Rett R., "*Glasnost* as a Conservative Revolution," *Intercollegiate Review*, 25, no. 1 (Fall 1989), 25-32.

4958. Lukacs, John, "The Stirrings of History: A New World Rises from the Ruins of Empire," *Harper's*, 281, no. 1683 (Aug. 1990), 41-48.

4959. Lyakhouchuk, Victor, "Reflecting on Perestroika," *World Marxist Review*, 31, no. 8 (Aug. 1988), 60-67.

4960. Malia, Martin, "Why Amalrik Was Right," *TLS: Times Literary Supplement*, no. 4675 (6 Nov. 1992), 9.

4961. Martz, L., "Who's Going to Be `Mr. X'?" *Newsweek*, 115 (15 Jan. 1990), 44.

4962. McLaughlin, John, "Gorby Fever," *National Review*, 38 (10 Oct. 1986), 22.

4963. Mead, Walter Russell, "On the Road to Ruin: Winning the Cold War, Losing the Economic Peace," *Harper's*, 280, no. 1678 (Mar. 1990), 59-64.

4964. Mearsheimer, John J., "Why We Will Soon Miss the Cold War," *Atlantic*, 266 (Aug. 1990), 35ff.

4965. Medvedev, Roy, and Giulietto Chiesa, "In a Time of Change," *Dissent*, 37, no. 3 (Summer 1990), 315-25.

4966. Medvedev, Vadim A., "The Ideology of *Perestroika*," *Perestroika Annual*, 2 (1989), 23-40.

4967. Meyerson, Adam, "The Ash Heap of History: Why Communism Failed," *Policy Review*, no. 58 (Fall 1991), 4-5.

4968. -----, "Ronald Reagan: Terminator," *Policy Review*, no. 59 (Winter 1992), 53-54.

4969. Mohieddin, K., "A Revolution That Is Transforming the World," *World Marxist Review*, 30, no. 11 (Nov. 1987), 137-39.

4970. Morrison, David C., "The New Russian Revolution," *National Journal*, 23, no. 31 (3 Aug. 1991), 1908-17.

4971. Moynihan, Daniel P., "End of the Marxist Epoch," *New Leader* (23 Jan. 1989), 9-11.

4972. Mshvenieradze, Vladimir V., "New Political Thinking," *Soviet Law and Government*, 26, no. 2 (Fall 1987), 50-65.

4973. Muravchik, Joshua, "Glasnostrums: Five Ways to Help Gorbo and Us," *New Republic* (30 Jan. 1989), 16-18.

4974. -----, "Gorbachev's Intellectual Odyssey," *New Republic* (5 Mar. 1990), 20-25.

4975. -----, "Gorbachev, the True Communist: The Intellectual Odyssey That May Lead to a Rejection of Marx and Lenin," *American Enterprise*, 1 (Mar-Apr. 1990), 38-45.

4976. Muray, Leo, "Gorbachov: The 12 Months' Test," *Contemporary Review*, 255, no. 1486 (Nov. 1989), 237-41.

4977. -----, "The Great Upheaval," *Contemporary Review*, 256, no. 1490 (Mar. 1990), 113-18.

4978. -----, "A Look at Leningrad," *Contemporary Review*, 256, no. 1488 (Jan. 1990), 26-29.

4979. -----, "Studying Soviet Realities," *Contemporary Review*, 258, no. 1504 (May 1991), 233-36.

4980. Naylor, T. H., "Gorbachev in Perspective," *Christian Century*, 108 (4-11 Sept. 1991), 797-98.

4981. "1917-1991: A Suicide," *Maclean's*, 104 (16 Sept. 1991), 24ff.

4982. "Nixon on Gorbachev: Not a Quitter," *Newsweek*, 117 (15 Apr. 1991), 38-39.

4983. Nixon, Richard M., "Should We Help Gorbachev?" *American Spectator*, 23, no. 3 (Mar. 1990), 18-21.

4984. Oates, Joyce C., "Intellectual Seduction: Meeting with Gorbachev," *New York Times Magazine* (3 Jan. 1988), 16ff.

4985. O'Brien, John Conway, "Communism Now and Then" (Special Issue), *International Journal of Social Economics*, 20, nos. 5-7 (1993), 3-212.

4986. -----, "The Evils of Communism and Other Critical Essays" (Special Issue), *International Journal of Social Economics*, 21, nos. 2-4 (1994), 2-152.

4987. Orlov, Yuri, "Before and After Glasnost," *Commentary*, 86 (Oct. 1988), 24-34.

4988. Pankin, Boris, "The World Does Not Want to Be Left without a Second Superpower," *International Affairs* (Moscow), no. 12 (Dec. 1991), 3-10.

4989. Paperny, Zinovy, "Today and Always: The Role of Jokes in Russian Humor," *World & I*, 8, no. 1 (Jan. 1993), 653-63.

4990. Park, Andus, "Gorbachev and the Role of Personality in History," *Studies in Comparative Communism*, 25, no. 1 (Mar. 1992), 43-56.

4991. Pearson, Geoffrey, "So Gorbachev Is Serious... Now What?" *Peace and Security*, 3, no. 2 (1988), 4-5.

4992. Peifer, George, "The New God Will Fail Moscow," *Harper's*, 277 (Oct. 1988), 43-50.

4993. Pereira, N. G. O., "M. S. Gorbachev's Liberalism in Historical Perspective," *Dalhousie Review*, 72, no. 2 (Summer 1992), 167-83.

4994. Peretz, Martin, "The Gorbachev Tease: Haven't We Seen This Act Before?" *New Republic* (10 July 1989), 14-18.

4995. Piccone, Paul, "Paradoxes of *Perestroika*," *Telos*, no. 84 (Summer 1990), 3-32.

4996. Pipes, Richard, "The Soviet Union Adrift," *Foreign Affairs*, 70, no. 1 (1991), 70-87.

4997. Pireni, Felix, "The Dark Side of Glasnost," *New Statesman and Society*, 1 (9 Dec. 1988), 20.

4998. Powell, David E., "Soviet Glasnost: Definitions and Dimensions," *Current History*, 87, no. 531 (Oct. 1988), 321-24.

4999. Poznanski, Kazimierz, "An Interpretation of Communist Decay: The Role of Evolutionary Mechanisms," *Communist and Post-Communist Studies*, 26, no. 1 (Mar. 1993), 3-24.

5000. Pradhan, S. V., "Perestroika and Its Implications for Marxist-Leninist Criticism," *Bombay Review*, no. 1 (1989), 50-55.

5001. Puddington, Arch, "The U.S.S.R. and Eastern Europe: A Turbulent Year One of the Post-Communist Era," *Freedom Review*, 22, no. 1 (Jan-Feb. 1991), 51-54.

5002. -----, "The Wounds of *Glasnost*," *National Review*, 41 (24 Nov. 1989), 26-28.

5003. Quatras, Jean, "New Soviet Thinking Is Not Good News," *Washington Quarterly*, 11, no. 3 (Summer 1988), 171-83.

5004. Rand, Robert, "*Perestroika* Up Close," *Wilson Quarterly*, 13, no. 2 (Spring 1989), 51-58.

5005. Ratford, David, "Development in the Soviet Union," *RUSI Journal*, 134, no. 1 (Spring 1989), 15-18.

5006. Remnick, Richard, "What's It All About, Gorby?" *Vanity Fair*, 55 (Aug. 1992), 92ff.

5007. "The Requiem for Marxism-Leninism," *Ukrainian Quarterly*, 46, no. 3 (Fall 1990), 229-32.

5008. "Restructuring: Quality and Duration," *Soviet Review*, 29, no. 1 (Spring 1988), 9-28.

5009. Rinehart, D., "How Much Longer Can Gorbachev Keep Putting Out Fires?" *Business Week* (7 Aug. 1989), 41.

5010. Roberts, P. C., "Go Ahead, Give Gorbachev Money-And Kill Soviet Reform," *Business Week* (8 July 1991), 16.

5011. Rogers, H. E., Jr., "Glasnost and Perestroika: An Evaluation of the Gorbachev Revolution and Its Opportunities for the West," *Denver Journal of International Law and Policy*, 16 (Winter-Spring 1988), 209-46.

5012. Rozek, Edward J., "Glasnost: Fiction or Reality?" *Survey*, 30, no. 3 (Oct. 1988), 121-23.

5013. Rush, Myron, "Fortune and Fate," *National Interest*, no. 31 (Spring 1993), 19-26.

5014. Russell, Cosmo, "Gorbachov at Strasbourg," *Contemporary Review*, 255, no. 1487 (Dec. 1989), 286-87.

5015. Rutland, Peter, "Gauging Glasnost: Soviet Studies and the Gorbachev Phenomenon" (Review Article), *International Studies*, 66 (Jan. 1990), 137-41.

5016. Sagan, Carl, and Vitaly Korotich, "Opening the Soviet Mind: A Conversation," *New Perspectives Quarterly*, 4 (Winter 1988), 50-54.

5017. Sanna, Mark, "Public Management in Russia: Old Failures," *Public Manager*, 22, no. 2 (Summer 1993), 35-38.

5018. Satter, David, "*Homo Sovieticus*: Can Attitudes Change?" *Survey*, 30, no. 3 (Oct. 1990), 92-105.

5019. -----, "Moscow Believes in Tears," *National Review*, 43 (29 Apr. 1991), 30-34.

5020. Schloflin, George, "Why Communism Collapsed," *International Affairs* (Jan. 1990), 3-16.

5021. Schmemann, Serge, "Glasnost: Between Hope and History," *New York Review of Books*, 92 (26 Apr. 1987), 12-13.

5022. Schmidt-Hauer, C., "The Gorbachev Enigma," *World Press Review*, 32 (Oct. 1985), 31-33.

5023. Selucky, Radoslav, "Mr. Gorbachev's Perestroika," *New Federation*, 1, no. 1 (1988), 5-6.

5024. Service, Robert, "Soviet Marxism's Obituary?" *History Today*, 41 (Oct. 1991), 45-48.

5025. Shakhnazarov, Georgi Kh., "The New Political Thinking: Principle Ideas and Guidelines," *Perestroika Annual*, 2 (1989), 81-98.

5026. Sharansky, Natan, "As I See Gorbachev," *Commentary*, 85 (Mar. 1988), 29-34.

5027. Shatalin, Stanislav, "What Shatalin Would Have Done: `Socialism Belongs in the Garbage'" (Interview), *World Press Review*, 38 (May 1991), 15-16.

5028. Shatrov, Mikhail, "The Trust as a Constructive Factor," *International Affairs* (Moscow), 7 (July 1988), 49-60.

5029. Shelley, Louise I., "The World: The Soviet System on Trial," *American Enterprise*, 4, no. 2 (Mar-Apr. 1993), 12-17.

5030. Shevardnadze, Eduard Amvrosievich, "No One Can Isolate Us, Save Ourselves. Self-Isolation Is the Ultimate Danger," *Slavic Review*, 51, no. 1 (Spring 1991), 117-21.

5031. Shmelev, Nikolai, "The System Must Give Way," *Survey*, 29 (Aug. 1987), 135-38.

5032. "Should There Be a Soviet Union? A Conversation between George Urban and Dominic Lieven," *Report on the USSR*, 3, no. 29 (19 July 1991), 14-19; 3, no. 30 (26 July 1991), 16-21.

5033. Simonov, Boris, "Changes in the Ownership of the Means of Production," *Survey*, 29 (Aug. 1987), 125-28.

5034. Smart, Christopher, "In Search of a Vision for Gorbachev's Soviet Union," *World & I* (Sept. 1990), 122-27.

5035. Snyder, Jack, "Russian Backwardness and the Future of Europe," *Daedalus*, 123, no. 2 (Spring 1994), 179-201.

5036. Sokolov, Vladimir, "To the Market-Under the Cover of the Army? Reflections on Alternatives to Our Upcoming Future," *Soviet Law and Government*, 30, no. 1 (Summer 1991), 68-79.

5037. "The Soviet Union, 1991," *Current History*, 90 (Oct. 1991).

5038. Stewart, L. H., "The World Cycle of Leadership," *Journal of Analytical Psychology*, 36, no. 4 (Oct. 1991), 449-59.

5039. Stone, I. F., "The Rights of Gorbachev," *New York Review of Books*, 36 (16 Feb. 1989), 3ff.

5040. Story, Christopher, "`When Strong, Look Weak': Soviet `Reforms'," *Midstream*, 37, no. 7 (Oct. 1991), 2-8.

5041. Surovell, Jeffrey, "Gorbachev's Last Year: Leftist or Rightist?" *Europe-Asia Studies*, 46, no. 3 (1994), 465-88.

5042. Sweezy, Paul M., "Is This Then the End of Socialism?" *Nation*, 250 (26 Feb. 1990), 257ff.

5043. Swoboda, Viktor, "Was the Soviet Union Really Necessary?" *Soviet Studies*, 44, no. 5 (1992), 761-84.

5044. Talbott, Strobe, "Now for a Moscow Peace Conference...," *Time*, 138 (11 Nov. 1991), 63.

5045. -----, "Russia vs Gorbachev," *Time*, 140 (26 Oct. 1992), 58.

5046. Tanenhaus, Sam, "What the Anti-Communists Knew," *Commentary*, 90 (July 1990), 32-36.

5047. Tavasiev, A., "Is a `Socialist Choice' Possible for Our Country Today?" *Problems of Economics*, 34, no. 7 (Nov. 1991), 38-52.

5048. Tetlock, Philip E., "Monitoring the Integrative Complexity of American and Soviet Policy Rhetoric: What Can Be Learned?" *Journal of Social Issues*, 44, no. 2 (Summer 1988), 101-31.

5049. Thaler, Joshua, "Confronting Crises: The Nature of Change in the Soviet Union," *Harvard International Review*, 12, no. 3 (Spring 1991), 38-42.

5050. Tiegang, Zhang, "Soviet Reform Programme Faces Test," *Beijing Review*, 30 (11 Jan. 1988), 120-22.

5051. Tiersky, Ronald, "Perestroika and Beyond," *Problems of Communism*, 39, no. 2 (Mar-Apr. 1990), 109-14.

5052. "A Time for Reflection," *Nation*, 250 (19 Mar. 1990), 365.

5053. Tismaneanu, Vladimir, "Is Gorbachev a Revolutionary?" *Orbis*, 32, no. 3 (Summer 1988), 420-25.

5054. Tompson, W. J., "Khrushchev and Gorbachev as Reformers: A Comparison," *British Journal of Political Science*, 23, part 1 (Jan. 1993), 77-105.

5055. "Towards 2017: Gorbachev's New World," *Soviet Analyst*, 16 (11 Nov. 1987), 3.

5056. Trimble, J., "Can Gorbachev Last?" *U.S. News & World Report*, 110 (22 Apr. 1991), 31-32.

5057. -----, "*Perestroika* on the Ropes," *U.S. News & World Report*, 109 (17 Sept. 1990), 37-38.

5058. -----, "Reform Is Risky Business," *U.S. News & World Report*, 106 (19 June 1989), 27-28.

5059. "Twilight of the Dinosaurs," *U.S. News & World Report*, 106 (8 May 1989), 46.

5060. Tyrrell, R. E., "The Great Bungler," *American Spectator*, 25, no. 2 (Feb. 1992), 12.

5061. Ulam, Adam, "Looking at the Past: The Unraveling of the Soviet Union," *Current History*, 91, no. 567 (Oct. 1992), 339-46.

5062. "Undoing Lenin's Legacy," *Time*, 135 (19 Feb. 1990), 28-38.

5063. Urban, G. R., "Djilas on Gorbachev," *Encounter*, 71 (Sept-Oct. 1988), 3-19; 71 (Nov. 1988), 21-31.

5064. Urban, Joan B., "Gorbachev and the Communist World: Collapse or Perestroyka?" (Review Article), *Problems of Communism*, 37, no. 5 (Sept-Oct. 1988), 71-76.

5065. Vacca, Giuseppe, "Perestroika, Socialism, and Europe," *Rethinking Marxism*, 3, no. 2 (Summer 1990), 64-110.

5066. Vickers, Simon, "Travelling through Perestroika: Across the USSR by Bicycle," *Contemporary Review*, 259, no. 1508 (Sept. 1991), 113-18.

5067. Vogel, H., J. Szymanderski and J. Winiecki, "The Gorbachev Challenge," *World Today*, 45, nos. 8-9 (Aug-Sept. 1989), 142-48.

5068. Vujacic, Veljko, and Victor Zaslavsky, "The Causes of Disintegration in the USSR and Yugoslavia," *Telos*, no. 88 (Summer 1991), 120-40.

5069. Wall, J. M., "Waking Up at Last to Gorbachev's Strategy," *Christian Century*, 107 (21 Feb. 1990), 171-72.

5070. Wallace, W. V., "The Soviet Union and Eastern Europe: Thinking About Their Likely Future," *Futures*, 22 (June 1990), 451-61.

5071. Weinberger, Caspar W., "Can We Trust This Nice Mr. Gorbachev?" *Forbes*, 143 (9 Jan. 1989), 37.

5072. "Why Did Soviet Communism Fail?" *Wilson Quarterly*, 17, no. 4 (Summer 1993), 123-24.

5073. Winter, David G., *et al.*, "The Personalities of Bush and Gorbachev Measured at a Distance: Procedures, Portraits, and Policy," *Political Psychology*, 12, no. 2 (June 1991), 215-45.

5074. -----, "The Personalities of Bush and Gorbachev at a Distance: Follow-up on Predictions," *Political Psychology*, 12, no. 3 (Sept. 1991), 457-64.

5075. Woods, Randall B., "Cold War or Cold Peace" (Review Article), *International History Review*, 16, no. 1 (Feb. 1994), 81-91.

5076. Yakovlev, Alexander, "The Humanistic Choice of Perestroika," *World Marxist Review*, 32, no. 2 (Feb. 1989), 8-13.

5077. Yanov, Alexander, "*Perestroika* and Its American Critics" (Review Article), *Slavic Review*, 47, no. 4 (Winter 1988), 716-25.

5078. Yevtushenko, Yevgeni A., "Civic Timidity Is Killing Perestroika," *World Press Report*, 35 (July 1988), 26-28.

5079. Zhukov, Vladimir, "`We Want to Be Understood': Readers' Conference on Mikhail Gorbachev's Book," *Soviet Military Review*, no. 4 (Apr. 1988), 2-4.

5080. Zuckerman, Mortimer B., "The Irony of Mikhail Gorbachev," *U.S. News & World Report*, 111, no. 25 (16 Dec. 1991), 96.

XXII. Government and Domestic Policies

BOOKS

5081. Babkina, M. A., *New Political Parties in the Soviet Union* (Commack, NY: Nova Science, 1991).

5082. Brown, Archie, ed., *Political Leadership in the Soviet Union* (Bloomington: Indiana University Press, 1990).

5083. Colton, Timothy, *The Dilemma of Reform in the Soviet Union*, rev., expanded ed. (New York: Council on Foreign Relations, 1986).

5084. Crouch, Martin, *Revolution and Evolution: Gorbachev and Soviet Politics* (New York: Prentice-Hall, 1989).

5085. Daniels, Robert V., *The End of the Communist Revolution* (New York: Routledge, 1993).

5086. -----, *Is Russia Reformable? Change and Resistance from Stalin to Gorbachev* (Boulder, CO: Westview Press, 1988).

5087. Daycock, Davis W., *The Pattern of Soviet Leadership Politics: Perestroika, De-Stalinization and the Cartel of Anxiety* (Winnipeg: University of Manitoba, Programme in Strategic Studies, 1989).

5088. DeBardeleben, Joan, *Soviet Politics in Transition* (Lexington, MA: D. C. Heath and Company, 1992).

5089. Eklof, Ben, *Soviet Briefing: Gorbachev and the Reform Period* (Boulder, CO: Westview Press, 1989).

5090. Gelman, Harry, *Gorbachev's First Five Years in the Soviet Leadership: The Clash of Personalities and the Remaking of Institutions* (Santa Monica, CA: RAND, 1990).

5091. Gorbachev, Mikhail S., *Perestroika: New Thinking for Our*

Country and the World (New York: Harper and Row, 1987).

5092. -----, *Speeches and Writings* (Oxford: Pergamon, 1987).

5093. -----, *A Time for Peace* (New York: Richardson & Steirman, 1985).

5094. Hahn, Jeffrey W., *Soviet Grassroots: Citizen Participation in Local Soviet Government* (Princeton: Princeton University Press, 1988).

5095. Hammer, Darrell P., *USSR: The Politics of Oligarchy* (Boulder, CO: Westview Press, 1990).

5096. Hazan, Baruch, *Gorbachev and His Enemies: The Struggle for Perestroika* (Boulder, CO: Westview Press, 1990).

5097. Hill, Ronald J., *Communist Politics under the Knife: Surgery or Autopsy?* (London: Pinter Publishers, 1990).

5098. Hosking, Geoffrey, Jonathan Aves and P. J. S. Duncan, eds., *The Road to Post-Communism: Independent Political Movements in the Soviet Union, 1985-1991* (London: Pinter Publishers, 1992).

5099. Kargalitsky, Boris, *Farewell, Perestroika: A Soviet Chronicle* (New York: Verso, 1990).

5100. Kelley, Donald R., *Soviet Politics from Brezhnev to Gorbachev* (New York: Praeger, 1987).

5101. Krawczyk, Rafal H., *The Communist Bloc: Transformation in Progress* (Washington, DC: Heritage Foundation, 1989).

5102. Kux, Ernst, *Gorbachev's Revolutionary Changes* (Washington, DC: Woodrow Wilson International Center for Scholars, Kennan Institute, 1986).

5103. Kux, Stephen, *Soviet Federalism: A Comparative Perspective* (New York: The Institute for East-West Security Studies, 1990).

5104. Landis, Lincoln, *Gorbachev's Hidden Agenda: Glimpses of the Soviet Mind* (New York: Vantage, 1991).

5105. Laqueur, Walter, *The Long Road to Freedom: Russia and Glasnost'* (London: Unwin Hyman, 1989).

5106. Legro, J. W., *Soviet Crisis Decisionmaking and the Gorbachev Reforms* (Santa Monica, CA: RAND, 1989).

5107. Little, D. Richard, *Governing the Soviet Union* (New York: Longman, 1989).

5108. Mandel, Ernest, *Beyond Perestroika: The Future of Gorbachev's USSR*, rev. ed. (New York: Verso, 1991).

5109. Martin, Lawrence, *Breaking with History: The Gorbachev Revolution* (Toronto: Doubleday Canada, 1989).

5110. Matthews, Mervyn, ed., *Party, State, and Citizen in the Soviet Union: A Collection of Documents* (Armonk, NY: M. E. Sharpe, 1989).

5111. McAuley, Mary, *Soviet Politics, 1917-1991* (New York: Oxford University Press, 1992).

5112. Mitchell, R. Judson, *Getting to the Top in the USSR:*

Cyclical Patterns in the Leadership Succession Process (Stanford: Hoover Institution Press, 1990).

5113. Nove, Alec, *Glasnost' in Action: Cultural Renaissance in Russia* (Boston: Unwin Hyman, 1989).

5114. Parker, John W., *Kremlin in Transition*, vol. 2: *Gorbachev, 1985-1989* (Boston: Unwin Hyman, 1990).

5115. Rigby, T. H., *Political Elites in the USSR: Central Leaders and Local Cadres from Lenin to Gorbachev* (Brookfield: Edward Elgar, 1990).

5116. Roeder, Philip G., *Red Sunset: The Failure of Soviet Politics* (Princeton: Princeton University Press, 1993).

5117. Rollins, Patrick J., ed., *First Congress of People's Deputies of the USSR. 25 May-9 June 1989. Stenographic Record* (Gulf Breeze, FL: Academic International Press, 1993).

5118. Roxburgh, Angus, *The Second Russian Revolution* (London: BBC Books, 1991).

5119. Schmidt-Hauer, Christian, *Gorbachev: The Path to Power* (London: Tauris, 1986).

5120. Solovyov, Vladimir, and Elena Klepikova, *Behind the High Kremlin Walls* (New York: Dodd, Mead, 1986).

5121. Szajkowski, Bohdan, ed., *New Political Parties of Eastern Europe and the Soviet Union* (Detroit: Gale Research, 1991).

5122. Tatu, Michel, *Mikhail Gorbachev: The Origins of Perestroika* (Boulder, CO: East European Monographs, 1991).

5123. Theen, Rolf H. W., *The U.S.S.R. First Congress of People's Deputies: Complete Documents and Records, May 25, 1989-June 10, 1989*, 4 vols. (New York: Paragon House, 1991).

5124. Tolz, Vera, *The USSR's Emerging Multi-Party System* (New York: Praeger, 1990).

5125. US Central Intelligence Agency. *The New Soviet Legislature: A Reference Aid* (Washington, DC: Central Intelligence Agency, 1989).

5126. US Commission on Security and Cooperation in Europe. *Implementation of the Helsinki Accords: A Changing Soviet Society* (Washington, DC: Government Printing Office, 1989).

5127. US Congress. House. Committee on Post Office and Civil Service. Subcommittee on Postal Operations. *Disruption of Mail in the Soviet Union: Hearing.* 99th Congress, 19 June 1986 (Washington, DC: Government Printing Office, 1987).

5128. Vlahos, Michael, director, *The Soviet Union: The Gorbachev Reforms-Preparing for the Thirteenth Five Year Plan* (Washington, DC: US Department of State, Foreign Service Institute, 1989).

5129. White, Stephen, *After Gorbachev*, 4th ed. (Cambridge: Cambridge University Press, 1993).

5130. -----, *Gorbachev in Power* (Cambridge: Cambridge University Press, 1990); reissued in an updated and enlarged paperback edition entitled *Gorbachev and After* (Cambridge:

Cambridge University Press, 1991).

5131. -----, *Soviet Communism: Programme and Rules* (New York: Routledge & Kegan Paul, 1989).

5132. -----, *et al.*, *Communist and Post-Communist Political Systems: An Introduction* (New York: St. Martin's Press, 1990).

5133. -----, and Alex Pravda, eds., *Ideology and Soviet Politics* (New York: St. Martin's Press, 1988).

5134. -----, Graeme Gill and Darrell Slider, *The Politics of Transition: Shaping a Post-Soviet Future* (New York: Cambridge University Press, 1993).

5135. -----, Alex Pravda and Zvi Gitelman, *Developments in Soviet Politics* (Durham, NC: Duke University Press, 1990).

5136. Yakovlev, Alexander, *The Fate of Marxism in Russia*, trans. by Catherine A. Fitzpatrick (New Haven: Yale University Press, 1993).

5137. Yin, John, *Government of the USSR under Perestroika* (Sudbury, Ontario: Northernmost View Press).

5138. Zacek, J. S., ed., *The Gorbachev Generation: Issues in Soviet Domestic Policy* (New York: Paragon, 1989).

5139. Zaslavskaia, Tatiana, *The Second Socialist Revolution: An Alternative Soviet Strategy* (Bloomington: Indiana University Press, 1990).

5140. -----, *A Voice of Reform: Essays by Tat'iana Zaslavskaia*, ed. by Murray Yanowitch (Armonk, NY: M. E. Sharpe, 1989).

5141. Zinoviev, Aleksandr, *Gorbachevizm* (New York: Liberty Publishing House, 1988).

ARTICLES

5142. Afanasyev, Yuri, "The Coming Dictatorship," *New York Review of Books*, 38 (31 Jan. 1991), 36-39.

5143. Aksyonov, Vassily, "Through the Glasnost, Darkly: A Cool Reaction to Gorbachev's Thaw," *Harper's*, 274, no. 1643 (Apr. 1987), 65-67.

5144. Alksnis, Viktor, "Suffering from Self-Determination," *Foreign Policy* (Fall 1991), 61-71.

5145. Amann, Ronald, "Soviet Politics in the Gorbachev Era: The End of Hesitant Modernization," *British Journal of Political Science*, 20, part 3 (July 1990), 289-310.

5146. "An Alternative to the Break-up of the Forces of the Left: A Movement for Social Democracy (Interview with Sergei Alekseev, Fedor Burlatskii and Stanislav Shatalin)," *Soviet Law and Government*, 30, no. 3 (Winter 1991-92), 6-20.

5147. Armstrong, G. Patrick, "Gorbachev's Nightmare," *Crossroads*, no. 29 (1989), 21-30.

5148. Aron, Leon, "The Search for `Socialist Pluralism'," *Global Affairs*, 4, no. 1 (Winter 1989), 104-18.

5149. -----, "Waiting for Yeltsin," *National Interest*, no. 20 (Summer 1990), 39-53.

5150. -----, "What Glasnost Has Destroyed," *Commentary*, 88 (Nov. 1989), 30-34.

5151. -----, "Yeltsin's Chess Game," *Reason*, 23, no. 3 (July 1991), 36-39.

5152. Axelrod, Robert, "Building a Strong Legislature: The Western Experience," *PS*, 24, no. 3 (Sept. 1991), 474-78.

5153. Barnathan, J., and S. Strasser, "The Mystery of Ligachev," *Newsweek*, 111 (2 May 1988), 28-29.

5154. Barnes, Fred, "Washington Diarist: Gorby's Demons," *New Republic* (12 Feb. 1990), 43.

5155. Barnett, Anthony, Boris Kargalitsky and Hans Magnus Enzensberger, "Can *Perestroika* Be Salvaged?" *Harper's*, 280, no. 1676 (Feb. 1990), 28-33.

5156. Battle, John M., "*Uskorenie, Glasnost'* and *Perestroika*: The Pattern of Reform under Gorbachev," *Soviet Studies*, 40, no. 3 (July 1988), 367-84.

5157. Bell, David A., "Is Gorbo Another Louis XIV? Paristroika," *New Republic* (11 July 1988), 21ff.

5158. Bennett, R., "Prospects for Economic and Democratic Reform in the Soviet Union," *Social Policy*, 19 (Summer 1988), 48-56.

5159. Berard-Zarzicka, Ewa, "The Authoritarian *Perestroika* Debate," *Telos*, no. 84 (Summer 1990), 115-24.

5160. Bernstam, Mikhail, "Anatomy of the Soviet Reform," *Global Affairs*, 3, no. 2 (Spring 1988), 63-88.

5161. -----, "The Enduring Gorbachev Era," *Global Affairs*, 4, no. 3 (Summer 1989), 52-67.

5162. Betaneli, N. I., and V. V. Lapaeva, "The Sociological Service for the First Congress of People's Deputies of the USSR," *Soviet Sociology*, 30, no. 2 (Mar-Apr. 1991), 64-80.

5163. Bialer, Seweryn, "Change in Russia: Gorbachev's Move," *Foreign Policy*, no. 68 (Fall 1987), 58-87.

5164. -----, "Domestic and International Factors in the Formation of Gorbachev's Reforms," *Journal of International Affairs*, 42 (Spring 1989), 283-97.

5165. -----, "Gorbachev's Program of Change: Sources, Significance, Prospects," *Political Science Quarterly*, 103, no. 3 (Fall 1988), 403-60.

5166. -----, "How Far Can Gorbachev Go? Crisis, Reform and Limits," *Dissent* (Spring 1987), 188-94.

5167. -----, "Inside *Glasnost'*," *Atlantic Monthly*, 261, no. 2 (Feb. 1988), 64ff.

5168. -----, "Interview: Aleksandr Yakovlev: Redefining Socialism at Home and Abroad," *Journal of International Affairs*, 42 (Spring 1989), 333-55.

5169. Blitz, James, "President's Thorn," *New Republic* (2 Apr. 1990), 9-10.

5170. Bodie, William C., "The Secret Police and Soviet Politics" (Review Article), *Problems of Communism*, 39, no. 1 (Jan-Feb. 1990), 101-08.

5171. Bouis, Antonina W., and Y. Afanasyev, "The Coming Dictatorship," *New York Review of Books*, 38 (31 Jan. 1991), 36-39.

5172. Bova, Russell, "Political Dynamics of the Post-Communism Transition: A Comparative Perspective," *World Politics*, 44, no. 1 (Oct. 1991), 113-38.

5173. Brady, Rose, "A Bloody Roadblock for *Perestroika*," *Business Week* (29 Jan. 1990), 49-50.

5174. -----, "For Gorbachev, *Perestroika* II May Mean Survival," *Business Week* (25 Sept. 1989), 60ff.

5175. -----, "Gorbachev's Hollow Victory," *Business Week* (1 Apr. 1991), 38-39.

5176. -----, "Will President Gorbachev Succeed Where Comrade Gorbachev Failed?" *Business Week* (23 July 1990), 47.

5177. Breslauer, George W., "Can Gorbachev's Reforms Succeed?" *AAASS Newsletter*, 29, no. 5 (Nov. 1989), 1ff.

5178. -----, "Provincial Party Leaders Demand Articulation and the Nature of Center-Periphery Relations in the USSR," *Slavic Review*, 45, no. 4 (Winter 1986), 650-72.

5179. Brown, Archie, "Change in the Soviet Union," *Foreign Affairs*, 64, no. 5 (Summer 1986), 1048-65.

5180. -----, "Gorbachev: New Man in the Kremlin," *Problems of Communism*, 34, no. 3 (May-June 1985), 1-23.

5181. -----, "Gorbachev's Leadership: Another View," *Soviet Economy*, 6, no. 2 (Apr-June 1990), 141-54.

5182. -----, "Gorbachev's Policy Innovations," *Bulletin of the Atomic Scientists*, 41, no. 10 (Nov. 1985), 18-22.

5183. -----, "Political Change in the Soviet Union," *World Policy Journal*, 6, no. 3 (Summer 1989), 469-501.

5184. -----, "Power and Policy: A Reformer in the Kremlin," *Nation* (13 June 1987), 792-95.

5185. -----, "Soviet Politics in the 1980s" (Review Article), *Slavonic and East European Review*, 68, no. 4 (Oct. 1990), 725-30.

5186. Brumberg, Abraham, "The Turning Point," *New York Review of Books*, 37 (28 June 1990), 52-59.

5187. Brzezinski, Zbigniew, "The Crisis of Communism: The Paradox of Political Participation," *Washington Quarterly*, 10, no. 4 (Autumn 1987), 167-74.

5188. Buchholz, Arnold, "*Perestroika* and Ideology: Fundamental Questions as to the Maintenance of and Change in the Soviet System," *Studies in Soviet Thought*, 36, no. 3 (Oct. 1988), 149-68.

5189. Buckley, Mary, "Political Groups and Crisis," *Journal of Communist Studies*, 9, no. 1 (Mar. 1993), 173-91.

5190. Buckley, William F., "A Future for Gorbachev," *National Review*, 43 (28 Jan. 1991), 70-71.

5191. Bugayev, V. K., "Improving the Administrative-Territorial Division of the USSR," *Soviet Geography*, 32, no. 8 (Oct. 1991), 545-50.

5192. Bukovsky, Vladimir, "Will Gorbachev Reform the Soviet Union?" *Commentary* (Sept. 1986), 19-24.

5193. Bush, George, "President Bush Remarks on Mikhail S. Gorbachev's Resignation," *Vital Speeches of the Day*, 58 (15 Jan. 1992), 195-96.

5194. Byrnes, Robert F., "Change in the Soviet Political System: Limits and Likelihoods," *Review of Politics*, 46 (Oct. 1984), 502-15.

5195. Byzov, L. G., L. A. Gordon and I. E. Mintusov, "Reflections of Sociologists on the Political Reforms," *Soviet Sociology*, 30, no. 1 (Jan-Feb. 1991), 26-42.

5196. Campbell, Adrian, "Local Government Policymaking and Management in Russia: The Case of St. Petersburg (Leningrad)," *Policy Studies Journal*, 21, no. 1 (Spring 1993), 133-43.

5197. Canan, James W., "Watching Mr. Gorbachev," *Air Force Magazine*, 70, no. 12 (Dec. 1987), 86-89.

5198. Cappelli, Ottorino, "The Short Parliament 1989-1991: Political Elites, Social Cleavages and the Weakness of Party Politics," *Journal of Communist Studies*, 9, no. 1 (Mar. 1993), 109-30.

5199. Chalidze, V., "Perestroika, Socialism and the Constitution," *Annals of the American Academy of Political and Social Science*, 506 (Nov. 1989), 98-108.

5200. Clem, Ralph S., "The Soviet Union: Crisis, Stability or Renewal?" *Air University Review*, 38, no. 1 (Nov-Dec. 1986), 2-13.

5201. Cockburn, Patrick, "Gorbachev and Soviet Conservatism," *World Policy Journal*, 6, no. 1 (Winter 1988-89), 81-106.

5202. Cohen, Stephen, "Gorbachev Struggles for Power," *New Statesman*, 110 (27 Sept. 1985), 22-23.

5203. Coleman, F., "Gorbachev Faces Down a Gang of Four," *Newsweek*, 118 (1 July 1991), 35.

5204. -----, "Gorbachev's New Grip on the Kremlin," *Newsweek*, 114 (2 Oct. 1989), 22-23.

5205. Colton, Timothy J., "The Cultural Factor and the Soviet Future," *Studies in Comparative Communism*, 20, no. 3-4 (Autumn-Winter 1987), 287-90.

5206. -----, "Moscow Politics and the El'tsin Affair," *Harriman Institute Forum*, 1, no. 6 (June 1988), 1-8.

5207. -----, "Political Reform in the Soviet Union: How Much Is Enough?" *Canadian Business Law Journal*, 17 (Dec. 1990), 173-78.

5208. -----, "The Resignation of Mikhail Gorbachev," *Soviet*

Economy, 7, no. 3 (July-Sept. 1991), 277-80.

5209. -----, "The Soviet Union under Gorbachev," *Current History*, 84, no. 504 (Oct. 1985), 305ff.

5210. Connor, Walter D., "Fast Forward, Rewind: Politics in the Gorbachev Era" (Review Article), *Studies in Comparative Communism*, 25, no. 1 (Mar. 1992), 75-88.

5211. Costa, Alexandra, "Boris Yeltsin: Russia's Abe Lincoln?" *World & I*, 6, no. 11 (Nov. 1991), 70-77.

5212. -----, "Gorbachev and Yeltsin: Room for Two at the Top?" *World & I* (Nov. 1990), 124-34.

5213. Covington, Stephen R., and John Lough, "Russia's Post-Revolution Challenge: Reform of the Soviet Superpower Paradigm," *Washington Quarterly*, 15, no. 1 (Winter 1992), 5-26.

5214. Cracraft, James, "The Gorbachev Regime after Two Years," *Bulletin of the Atomic Scientists*, 43, no. 4 (May 1987), 31-33.

5215. Crouch, J. D., II, and William R. Van Cleave, "An International Security Council Conference: The Politics of Reform in Russia," *Global Affairs*, 8, no. 3 (Summer 1993), 185ff.

5216. Crow, Suzanne, "The Resignation of Shevardnadze," *Report on the USSR*, 3, no. 2 (11 Jan. 1991), 6-8.

5217. -----, "Shevardnadze's Vindication," *Report on the USSR*, 3, no. 36 (6 Sept. 1991), 30-31.

5218. Crozier, Brian, "The Force of Myth," *National Review*, 38 (29 Aug. 1986), 24.

5219. -----, "Gorbachev's Many Voices," *National Review*, 37 (3 May 1985), 25.

5220. -----, "The Protracted Conflict: The Leopard's Spots," *National Review*, 38 (28 Feb. 1986), 26.

5221. Cullen, R. B., "Letter from Rostov-on-Don," *New Yorker* (12 June 1989), 107-20.

5222. Dallin, Alexander, "Gorbachev: A Premature Postmortem," *New Leader*, 74 (9-23 Sept. 1991), 4-6.

5223. -----, "Standing Lenin on His Head," *New Leader*, 73 (5-19 Feb. 1990), 7-10.

5224. Daniels, Robert V., "Building a Power Base: Gorbachev's Cultural Revolution," *New Leader*, 71 (11 July 1988), 5-7.

5225. -----, "Gorbachev Buys Time: The Perils of *Perestroika*," *New Leader*, 71 (31 Oct. 1988), 6-8.

5226. -----, "Gorbachev Consolidates His Rule," *New Leader*, 69 (24 Feb. 1986), 6-8.

5227. -----, "The Limits of Gorbachev's Reform," *New Leader*, 74, no. 2 (28 Jan. 1991), 7-9.

5228. -----, "The Making of a Kremlin Transition," *New Leader*, 68 (11 Mar. 1985), 4-5.

5229. Daniloff, Nicholas, "Gorbachev's Firmer Grip: What It Means for U.S.," *U.S. News & World Report*, 99 (15 July 1985), 35-37.

5230. -----, "Gorbachev's Kremlin: What Now?" *U.S. News & World Report*, 98 (25 Mar. 1985), 22-32.

5231. Dejevsky, Mary, "The Soviet Succession," *World Today*, 41, no. 5 (May 1985), 85-86.

5232. -----, "What Makes Russia Tick?" (Review Article), *World Today*, 41, no. 10 (Oct. 1985), 191-92.

5233. Duncan, J. P. S., "Towards a Pluralistic Society in the Soviet Union," *Slavonic and East European Review*, 69, no. 1 (Jan. 1991), 107-21.

5234. Dunlop, John B., "The Leadership of the Centrist Bloc," *Report on the USSR*, 3, no. 6 (8 Feb. 1991), 4-6.

5235. -----, "Moscow at a Turning Point," *Report on the USSR*, 2, no. 24 (15 June 1990), 8-11.

5236. -----, "Moscow Report: Russia's Surprising Reactionary Alliance," *Orbis*, 35, no. 3 (Summer 1991), 423-26.

5237. -----, and Henry S. Rowen, "Gorbachev versus Ligachev: The Kremlin Divided," *National Interest*, no. 11 (Spring 1988), 18-29.

5238. Eberstadt, Nick, "The Latest Myths about the Soviet Union" (Review Article), *Commentary*, 83 (May 1987), 17-27.

5239. Eggers, William, "The New Opposition," *Reason*, 23, no. 3 (July 1991), 40-43.

5240. Elliot, I., "And Now Gorbachov, the Great Reformer," *Survey*, 29 (Spring 1985), 1-11.

5241. Ellison, Herbert, "Gorbachev's Revolution," *World & I*, 6, no. 1 (Jan. 1991), 28-35.

5242. Embree, Gregory, "RSFSR Election Results and Roll Call Votes," *Soviet Studies*, 43, no. 6 (1991), 1065-84.

5243. Evans, Alfred B., Jr., "Problems of Conflict Management in Russian Politics," *Journal of Communist Studies*, 9, no. 2 (June 1993), 1-19.

5244. Fairbanks, Charles H., Jr., "Russian Roulette: The Dangers of a Collapsing Empire," *Policy Review*, no. 57 (Summer 1991), 2-13.

5245. Falin, Valentin M., "*Glasnost'*: Getting at the Roots," *Perestroika Annual*, 1 (1988), 281-305.

5246. "The First President," *New Times*, no. 12 (1990), 4-6.

5247. Flaherty, Patrick, "The Making of the New Soviet Left," *Telos*, no. 84 (Summer 1990), 88-114.

5248. Foell, Earl W., "Why Gorby Zigzags," *World Monitor*, 4, no. 7 (July 1991), 64.

5249. Forbes, Malcolm S., Jr., "There Are Two Fundamental Questions," *Forbes*, 140 (30 Nov. 1987), 25.

5250. Friedberg, Maurice, "Does Gorbachev *Really* Mean Business? Twelve Reforms That Could Make a Difference,"

Present Tense, 14, no. 2 (Jan-Feb. 1987), 21ff.

5251. Galuszka, Philip, "Gorbachev Is Scoring Points Abroad to Win Support at Home," *Business Week* (8 Sept. 1986), 43.

5252. Gankovsky, Yuri V., "Who Rules the Soviet Union?" *Journal of South Asian and Middle Eastern Studies*, 14, no. 3 (Spring 1991), 77-85.

5253. Genaite, Sarah, "Can Anyone Save the USSR?" *Peace Magazine*, 7, no. 1 (Jan. 1991), 24.

5254. Gill, Graeme, "The Sources of Political Reform in the Soviet Union," *Studies in Comparative Communism*, 24, no. 3 (Sept. 1991), 235-58.

5255. Gitlin, Todd, "The Bureaucracy That Failed: Boris Kargalitsky on the Soviet Quagmire," *Tikkun*, 6, no. 4 (July-Aug. 1991), 11ff.

5256. "Glasnost, Perestroika and the Soviet Empire," *Society*, 25 (May-June 1988), 7-30.

5257. Glass, Andrew J., "Lenin's New Apostle," *New Leader* (24 Feb. 1986), 3-6.

5258. Gleason, Gregory, "The Federal Formula and the Collapse of the USSR," *Publius*, 22, no. 3 (Summer 1992), 141-62.

5259. Goldberg, Joseph E., "Regime Considerations in the Soviet Union," *Comparative Strategy*, 9, no. 4 (Oct-Dec. 1990), 371-83.

5260. Goldfarb, Alex, "Testing Glasnost: An Exile Visits His Homeland," *New York Times Magazine* (6 Dec. 1987), 46ff.

5261. Goldman, Marshall I., "The Amazing Gorbachev and His High-Risk Reforms," *World Monitor*, Prototype Issue (1989), 28-35.

5262. -----, "Gorbachev at Risk," *World Monitor*, 3, no. 6 (June 1990), 34ff.

5263. -----, "Losing Ground," *World Monitor*, 4 (Mar. 1991), 42-43.

5264. -----, "*Perestroika* Comes to the Soviet Union," *Harvard International Review*, 10, no. 1 (Nov. 1987), 3ff.

5265. -----, "What to Expect from Gorbachev," *Bulletin of the Atomic Scientists*, 41, no. 5 (May 1985), 8-9.

5266. -----, "Yeltsin's Reforms: Gorbachev II?" *Foreign Policy*, no. 88 (Fall 1992), 76-90.

5267. "Goodbye, Gorbachev," *Newsweek*, 118 (23 Dec. 1991), 18ff.

5268. "Goodbye Gorbachev, Hello Yeltsin," *World Press Review*, 39 (Feb. 1992), 20.

5269. Gorbachev, Mikhail S., "Document: The Revolution and Perestroika," *Foreign Affairs*, 66, no. 2 (Winter 1987-88), 410-25.

5270. -----, "The Most Responsible Phase of *Perestroika*," *Vital Speeches of the Day*, 56 (15 Aug. 1990), 642-48.

5271. -----, "*Perestroika* Is Marked by Pitfalls," *Vital Speeches of the Day*, 57 (15 Jan. 1991), 194-200.

5272. -----, "Resignation of President Mikhail S. Gorbachev," *Vital Speeches of the Day*, 58 (15 Jan. 1992), 194-95.

5273. "Gorbachev and Yeltsin," *World Press Review*, 38 (June 1991), 7-8.

5274. "Gorbachev and Yeltsin: The Lords of Misrule," *Economist*, 319 (6 Apr. 1991), 17ff.

5275. "Gorbachev's Russia," *Business Week* (11 Nov. 1985), 82ff.

5276. "Gorbachev-Yeltsin Feud Worsens," *Facts on File*, 52, no. 2708 (15 Oct. 1992), 778.

5277. Goure, Leon, "The Kremlin Shakeup," *Global Affairs*, 4, no. 1 (Winter 1989), 1-17.

5278. Grenier, Richard, "Gorbachev's Long Journey," *National Review*, 41 (31 Dec. 1989), 27-29.

5279. "Grinding Down Gorbachev: Suffocation Rather Than Coup Will Be the Likely Cause of Perestroika's Death," *Economist*, 313 (21 Oct. 1989), 15-16.

5280. Grondona, M., "The Enlightened Patriot," *World Press Review*, 36 (Apr. 1989), 64.

5281. Gustafson, Thane, and Dawn Mann, "Gorbachev's First Year: Building Power and Authority," *Problems of Communism*, 35, no. 3 (May-June 1986), 1-19.

5282. -----, "Gorbachev's Next Gamble," *Problems of Communism*, 36, no. 4 (July-Aug. 1987), 1-20.

5283. Hahn, Gordon M., "Opposition Politics in Russia," *Europe-Asia Studies*, 46, no. 2 (1994), 305-35.

5284. Hahn, Jeffrey W., "Boss Gorbachev Confronts His New Congress," *Orbis*, 34, no. 2 (Spring 1990), 163-78.

5285. -----, "Gorbachev's Uncertain Reformation: What Has Changed and What Has Not," *Commonweal* (23 Oct. 1987), 586-92.

5286. -----, "Local Politics and Political Power in Russia: The Case of Yaroslavl," *Soviet Economics*, 7, no. 4 (Oct-Dec. 1991), 322-41.

5287. -----, "Yuri's Usurpers: Why Gorbachev Matters," *Commonweal*, 112 (22 Mar. 1985), 165-66.

5288. Harris, Jonathan, "Ligachev on Glasnost and Perestroika," in *The Carl Beck Papers in Russian and East European Studies*, no. 706 (Pittsburgh: Pittsburgh University Center for Russian and East European Studies, Mar. 1991).

5289. -----, "The Public Policies of Aleksandr Nikolaevich Yakovlev, 1983-1989," in *The Carl Beck Papers in Russian and East European Studies*, no. 901 (Pittsburgh: Pittsburgh University Center for Russian and East European Studies, Dec. 1990).

5290. "Heading for a Crackup?" *Newsweek*, 117 (7 Jan. 1991), 36ff.

5291. Heller, Agnes, "Can Glasnost Become Permanent?" *New Statesman*, 115 (13 May 1988), 23.

5292. Hertzberg, Hendrick, "Washington Diarist: Gorbo In, Gorbo Out," *New Republic* (29 Apr. 1991), 42.

5293. Hill, Ronald J., "Soviet Political Development and the Culture of the Apparatchiki," *Studies in Comparative Communism*, 19, no. 1 (Spring 1986), 25-39.

5294. -----, "The Soviet Union: From `Federation' to `Commonwealth'," *Regional Politics and Policy*, 3, no. 1 (Spring 1993), 96-122.

5295. -----, and J. Lowenhardt, "Nomenklatura and Perestroika," *Government and Opposition*, 26 (Spring 1991), 229-43.

5296. Horowitz, Irving Louis, "The New Generation of Soviet Intellectuals," *Freedom Review*, 22, no. 2 (Mar-Apr. 1991), 22-25.

5297. Hosking, Geoffrey A., "The Soviet Union: The Paradox of Perestroika," *Atlantic*, 265 (Feb. 1990), 20-25.

5298. Hough, Jerry F., "Gorbachev's Endgame," *World Policy Journal*, 7, no. 4 (Fall 1990), 639-72.

5299. -----, "Gorbachev's Politics," *Foreign Affairs*, 68 (Winter 1989-90), 26-41.

5300. -----, "Gorbachev's Strategy," *Foreign Affairs*, 64, no. 1 (Fall 1985), 33-55.

5301. -----, "Understanding Gorbachev: The Importance of Politics," *Soviet Economy*, 7, no. 2 (Apr-June 1991), 89-109.

5302. Howe, Irving, "A New Political Situation," *Dissent*, 37, no. 1 (Winter 1990), 87-90.

5303. Hutchings, R. L., "'Leadership Drift' in the Communist Systems of the Soviet Union and Eastern Europe," *Studies in Comparative Communism*, 22 (Spring 1989), 5-9.

5304. Huyn, Hans, "Glasnost: Desperately Seeking Stability," *World & I*, 2, no. 6 (June 1987), 34-43.

5305. Hyland, William G., "The Gorbachev Succession," *Foreign Affairs*, 63, no. 4 (Spring 1985), 800-09.

5306. Ianitskii, O. N., "The Arguments Underlying Urban Development Decisions under *Glasnost'*," *Soviet Sociology*, 28, no. 5 (Sept-Oct. 1989), 67-86.

5307. Jay, Martin, "Force Fields: No Power to the Soviets," *Salmagundi*, no. 88-89 (Fall 1990-Winter 1991), 64-69.

5308. Judy, Richard W., "The World's Most Powerful President?" *World & I* (Mar. 1990), 55-59.

5309. Kargalitsky, Boris, "On Neo-Liberalism and Socialism in the Soviet Union," *Socialism and Democracy*, no. 12 (Jan. 1991), 11-18.

5310. Karklins, Rasma, "Explaining Regime Change in the Soviet Union," *Europe-Asia Studies*, 46, no. 1 (1994), 29-46.

5311. Kasparov, Gary, "Your Move, *Perestroika*!" *Perestroika Annual*, 1 (1988), 129-42.

5312. Katsenelinboigen, Aron, "Will Glasnost Bring the Reac-

tionaries to Power?" *Orbis*, 32, no. 2 (Spring 1988), 217-30.

5313. Kennedy, Paul, "What Gorbachev Is Up Against," *Atlantic Monthly*, 259, no. 6 (June 1987), 29ff.

5314. Kennedy, W. R., "The Evil Empire Is Not Run by Rebecca of Sunnybrook Farm," *Conservative Digest*, 14 (Feb. 1988), 127-28.

5315. Kiernan, Brendan, and Joseph Aistrup, "The 1989 Elections to the Congress of People's Deputies in Moscow," *Soviet Studies*, 43, no. 6 (1991), 1049-64.

5316. Kissinger, Henry, "Gorbachev: The Price of Survival," *Newsweek*, 115 (18 June 1990), 37.

5317. Knight, R., "Dismantling Lenin's Legacy," *U.S. News & World Report*, 109 (9 July 1990), 26-28.

5318. -----, "The KGB Decided to Stop Gorbachev," *U.S. News & World Report*, 110 (25 Mar. 1991), 40-41.

5319. Kohan, J., "A Chastened Character in Search of a Role," *Time*, 138 (9 Sept. 1991), 42-43.

5320. -----, and Y. Shchekochikhin, "Tambov: *Perestroika* in the Provinces," *Time*, 133 (10 Apr. 1989), 86ff.

5321. Kondracke, Morton M., "The World Turned Upside Down: Gorbachev Throws Left and Right for a Loop," *New Republic* (18-25 Sept. 1989), 26-29.

5322. Kozyrev, Andrei, "Inside the USSR: Facing Realities," *World & I*, 6, no. 1 (Jan. 1991), 36-41.

5323. Kraus, Herwig, "Membership of the USSR Council of the Federation," *Report on the USSR*, 2, no. 24 (15 June 1990), 14-15.

5324. Kudryavtsev, Vladimir N., "Political Reform in the USSR: The First Stage," *Perestroika Annual*, 2 (1989), 67-78.

5325. Kulikowski, Mark, "Gorbachev and Glasnost': American Perceptions and Soviet Realities," *SUNY Research*, 7, no. 3 (1987), 22-23.

5326. Lane, David, and Cameron Ross, "The Social Background and Political Allegiance of the Political Elite of the Supreme Soviet of the USSR: The Terminal Stage, 1984 to 1991," *Europe-Asia Studies*, 46, no. 3 (1994), 437-64.

5327. Lapidus, Gail W., "The Crisis of Perestroika," *Journal of Democracy*, 2, no. 2 (Spring 1991), 47-53.

5328. -----, "*Glasnost'*: Its Multiple Roles in Gorbachev's Reform Strategy," *Fletcher Forum*, 12, no. 2 (Summer 1988), 271-78.

5329. -----, "Gorbachev and the Reform of the Soviet System," *Daedalus*, 116, no. 2 (Spring 1987), 1-30.

5330. Latey, M., "Gorbachev's Gamble," *World Today*, 44, no. 10 (Oct. 1988), 166-68.

5331. Lea, James F., "Gorbachev as Roosevelt," *USA Today*, 118, no. 2538 (Mar. 1990), 35.

5332. Ledeen, Michael, "Mr. Gorbachev's Bizarreries," *American*

Spectator, 23, no. 6 (June 1990), 12-14.

5333. Legro, Jeffrey W., "Soviet Crisis Decision-Making in the Gorbachev Reforms," *Survival*, 31, no. 4 (July-Aug. 1989), 339-75.

5334. Lempert, David, "Changing Russian Political Culture in the 1990s: Parasites, Paradigms, and Perestroika," *Comparative Studies in Society and History*, 35, no. 3 (July 1993), 628-46.

5335. "Lenin's Legacy," *Nation*, 250 (26 Feb. 1990), 251-52.

5336. Lentini, Peter, "Reforming the Electoral System: The 1989 Elections to the USSR Congress of People's Deputies," *Journal of Communist Studies*, 7, no. 1 (Mar. 1991), 69ff.

5337. Levada, Yuri, Leonid Sedov and Lev Timofeev, "Is a New Revolution in the Making?" *Uncaptive Minds*, 4, no. 1 (Spring 1991), 86-96.

5338. Lih, Lars T., "Gorbachev and the Reform Movement," *Current History*, 86, no. 522 (Oct. 1987), 309ff.

5339. -----, "Soviet Politics: Breakdown or Renewal?" *Current History*, 89, no. 549 (Oct. 1990), 309ff.

5340. -----, "The Transition Era in Soviet Politics," *Current History*, 88, no. 540 (Oct. 1989), 333ff.

5341. Lynch, Allen, "Does Gorbachev Matter Anymore?" *Foreign Afffairs*, 69, no. 3 (Summer 1990), 19-29.

5342. Lyne, Roderic, "Making Waves: Gorbachev's Public Diplomacy, 1985-86," *Proceedings of the Academy of Political Science*, 36, no. 4 (1987), 235-53.

5343. Makarenko, V. P., "The Crisis of Power and the Political Opposition," *Soviet Law and Government*, 30, no. 3 (Winter 1991-92), 66-77.

5344. Malia, Martin, "A New Russian Revolution?" *New York Review of Books*, 38 (18 July 1991), 29-31.

5345. Mann, Dawn, "Bringing the Congress of People's Deputies to Order," *Report on the USSR*, 2, no. 3 (19 Jan. 1990), 1-5.

5346. -----, "Gorbachev Sworn in as President," *Report on the USSR*, 2, no. 12 (23 Mar. 1990), 1-4.

5347. -----, "The Trend towards Public Initiative in Local Government," *Report on the USSR*, 2, no. 15 (13 Apr. 1990), 7-8.

5348. Mathews, T., "Yeltsin's Challenge," *Newsweek*, 115 (11 June 1990), 20ff.

5349. McAuley, Mary, "Soviet Political Reform in a Comparative Context," *Harriman Institute Forum*, 2, no. 10 (Oct. 1989), 1-8.

5350. McGrath, P., "How to Help Gorbachev," *Newsweek*, 117 (17 June 1991), 34ff.

5351. McLaughlin, John, `Glasnosting Gorbachev," *National Review*, 40 (22 Jan. 1988), 26.

5352. Meerovich, Aleksandr, "The Emergence of Russian Multiparty Politics," *Report on the USSR*, 2, no. 34 (1990), 8-16.

5353. Methvin, Eugene H., "Gorbachev's Dilemma," *National Review*, 39 (4 Dec. 1987), 42ff.

5354. Michnik, Adam, "Gorbachev: The Great Counter-Reformer," *Harper's*, 275, no. 1650 (Nov. 1987), 19-20.

5355. Migranian, Andranik, "Gorbachev's Leadership: A Soviet View," *Soviet Economy*, 6, no. 2 (Apr-June 1990), 155-59.

5356. -----, Igor Kliamkin and Irina Zorina, "An Authoritarian Perestroika? A Roundtable," *Telos*, no. 84 (Summer 1990), 125-41.

5357. Mitchell, J. K., and V. A. Kolosov, "The Geography of Elections of USSR People's Deputies by National-Territorial Districts and the Nationalities Issue," *Soviet Geography*, 31, no. 12 (Dec. 1990), 753-66.

5358. Moffitt, Larry R., "New Dimensions for Perestroika," *World & I* (June 1990), 98-101.

5359. Moses, Joel C., "Soviet Provincial Politics in an Era of Transition and Revolution, 1989-91," *Soviet Studies*, 44, no. 3 (1992), 479-510.

5360. Mote, Max E., "Electing the USSR Congress of People's Deputies," *Problems of Communism*, 37, no. 6 (Nov-Dec. 1989), 51-56.

5361. Motyl, Alexander J., "Policing *Perestroika*: The Indispensable KGB," *Harriman Institute Forum*, 2, no. 6 (Aug. 1989), 1-8.

5362. -----, "Reassessing the Soviet Crisis: Big Problems, Muddling Through, Business as Usual," *Political Science Quarterly*, 104, no. 2 (Summer 1989), 269-80.

5363. Nadell, Bernhardt, "The Presidency and Congress of People's Deputies in the Soviet Union," *Harvard International Review*, 13, no. 3 (Spring 1991), 40-42.

5364. Navrozov, Lev, "The More the Kremlin Changes...," *Midstream*, 37, no. 8 (Nov. 1991), 16-20.

5365. Nelan, B. W., "Boris vs. Mikhail," *Time*, 137 (25 Mar. 1991), 26-31.

5366. "The Not-Quite Tsar: Decisions the Apparently Decisive Mr. Gorbachev Has Yet to Take," *Economist*, 298 (15 Feb. 1986), 12-13.

5367. Novak, Michael, "Toward an Open Soviet Union," *Freedom at Issue*, no. 96 (May-June 1987), 9-12.

5368. Obolonskii, A. V., "The Bureaucratic Deformation of Consciousness and the Struggle Against Bureaucratism," *Soviet Law and Government*, 27, no. 1 (Summer 1988), 39-54.

5369. Odom, William E., "How Far Can the Soviet Union Go?" *Problems of Communism*, 36, no. 6 (Nov-Dec. 1987), 18-33.

5370. Oliver, Dawn, "`Perestroika' and Public Administration in the USSR," *Public Administration*, 66 (Winter 1988), 411-28.

5371. Ollman, Bertell, "The Regency of the Proletariat: A Job for Perestroika," *PS*, 24, no. 3 (Sept. 1991), 456-60.

5372. Parrott, Bruce, "Gorbachev's Gamble: Political, Economic and Ethnic Challenges to Soviet Reform," *SAIS Review*, 10, no. 2 (Summer-Fall 1990), 57-74.

5373. Peterson, Peter G., "Gorbachev's Bottom Line," *New York Review of Books*, 33 (25 June 1987), 29-33.

5374. Petrovsky, Vladimir, "New Thinking: Questions and Answers," *PS*, 23, no. 1 (Mar. 1990), 29-32.

5375. Pipes, Richard, "Gorbachev's Russia: Breakdown or Crackdown?" *Commentary*, 89 (Mar. 1990), 13-25.

5376. Piskotin, M. I., and V. V. Smirnov, "Political Reform and Political Science," *Soviet Law and Government*, 30, no. 1 (Summer 1991), 50-67.

5377. Ploss, Sidney I., "A New Soviet Era?" *Foreign Policy*, no. 62 (Spring 1986), 46-60.

5378. Popov, Gavril, "*Perestroika* and the Primacy of Politics," *Dissent*, 37, no. 1 (Winter 1990), 91-96.

5379. "Power Tools," *New Republic* (2 Apr. 1990), 8.

5380. Price, Garrett, "Gorbachev's New Course," *Harvard International Review*, 11, no. 3 (Spring 1989), 45-47.

5381. Primakov, Yevgeny, "A New Stage of Political Reform," *World Marxist Review*, 32, no. 9 (Sept. 1989), 13-15.

5382. -----, Vladlen Martynov and Herman Diligensky, "New Thinking: Some Problems," *Social Sciences*, no. 3 (1990), 8-24.

5383. Quigley, John, "The Soviet Presidency," *American Journal of Comparative Law*, 39, no. 1 (Winter 1991), 67-93.

5384. Raeff, Marc, "Consequences of *Glasnost*" (Review Article), *Problems of Communism*, 39, no. 2 (Mar-Apr. 1990), 105-08.

5385. Rahr, Alexander, "Further Restructuring of the Soviet Political System," *Report on the USSR*, 3, no. 14 (5 Apr. 1991), 1-4.

5386. -----, "Gorbachev and the Post-Chebrikov KGB," *Report on the USSR* (22 Dec. 1989), 16-20.

5387. -----, "KGB Attack on Gorbachev and His Reforms," *Report on the USSR*, 2, no. 15 (13 Apr. 1990), 4-6.

5388. -----, "Russia's `Young Turks' in Power," *Report on the USSR* (22 Nov. 1991), 20-23.

5389. "Reassessing Glasnost," *Harvard International Review*, 13, no. 3 (Spring 1991), 37ff.

5390. Reddaway, Peter, "Empire on the Brink," *New York Review of Books*, 38 (31 Jan. 1991), 7-9.

5391. -----, "The Quality of Gorbachev's Leadership," *Soviet Economy*, 6, no. 2 (Apr-June 1990), 125-40.

5392. Redden, C., "The Second Revolution," *Maclean's*, 100 (9 Nov. 1987), 19ff.

5393. -----, "Slowing Down *Glasnost*," *Maclean's*, 100 (16 Nov. 1987), 30-31.

5394. "Reform and Upheaval in the Soviet Union," *Scholastic Update*, 123, special issue (7 Dec. 1990), 2-23.

5395. Reid, Carl, "Gorbachev the Efficient?" *International Perspectives* (May-June 1985), 10-13.

5396. Remington, Thomas, "A Socialist Pluralism of Opinions: *Glasnost'* and Policy-Making under Gorbachev," *Russian Review*, 48, no. 3 (July 1989), 271-304.

5397. Robinson, Neil, "Parliamentary Politics under Gorbachev: Opposition and the Failure of Socialist Pluralism," *Journal of Communist Studies*, 9, no. 1 (Mar. 1993), 91-108.

5398. Rodman, P. W., "The Last General Secretary," *National Review*, 44 (20 Jan. 1992), 11ff.

5399. Roeder, Philip G., "Do New Soviet Leaders Really Make a Difference? Rethinking the `Succession Connection'," *American Political Science Review*, 79, no. 4 (Dec. 1985), 958-76.

5400. "Russia: Economic Reform and Local Politics," *World Today*, 49, no. 4 (Apr. 1993), 64-65.

5401. "The Russia Housekeeper," *Nation*, 252 (21 Jan. 1991), 37.

5402. Rutland, Peter, "From *Perestroika* to Paralysis: The Stalemate in Leningrad," *Report on the USSR*, 3, no. 12 (22 Mar. 1991), 12-17.

5403. -----, "The Search for Stability: Ideology, Discipline and the Cohesion of the Soviet Elite," *Studies in Comparative Communism*, 24 (Mar. 1991), 27-57.

5404. Samhoun, R., and G. Orchibat, "The Thrust of Political Reform in the USSR," *World Marxist Review*, 31, no. 9 (Sept. 1988), 57-65.

5405. Samuylov, Sergei M., "The Gorbachev Presidency: On the Way to Dictatorship?" *Presidential Studies Quarterly*, 22, no. 2 (Spring 1992), 239-59.

5406. Santore, John, "The Soviet Crisis of the Early 1980s and Gorbachev's Rise to Power," *Socialism and Democracy*, no. 11 (Sept. 1990), 1-16.

5407. -----, "Why Gorbachev Lost," *National Review*, 43 (23 Sept. 1991), 38-41.

5408. Schifter, R., "The Soviet Constitution: Myth and Reality," *Department of State Bulletin*, 87 (Oct. 1987), 34-37.

5409. Schmemann, Serge, "The Emergence of Gorbachev," *New York Times Magazine* (3 Mar. 1985), 40ff.

5410. Schorr, Daniel, "The Gorbachev Paradox," *New Leader*, 73, no. 5 (19 Mar. 1990), 3-4.

5411. Sestanovich, Stephen, "Inventing the Soviet National Interest," *National Interest*, no. 20 (Summer 1990), 3-16.

5412. -----, "What Gorbachev Wants: Russia's Answer to Nixon," *New Republic* (25 May 1987), 20-23.

5413. Shama, A., and S. Sementsov, "The Collapse of the Soviet Ministries: Economic and Legal Transformation," *International Executive*, 34, no. 2 (1992), 131-50.

5414. Sheehy, Gail, "Red Star Falling," *Vanity Fair*, 54 (Dec. 1991), 234ff.

5415. "Shevardnadze and Gorbachev," *World Press Review*, 38 (Feb. 1991), 9.

5416. Shipler, David K., "The Politics of Neighborhood," *New Yorker* (3 June 1991), 45ff.

5417. -----, "A Reporter at Large: Between Dictatorship and Anarchy," *New Yorker* (25 June 1990), 42-70.

5418. Shoup, Paul, "Leadership Drift in the Soviet Union and Yugoslavia," *Studies in Comparative Communism*, 22 (Spring 1989), 43-55.

5419. Shub, Anatole, "Russia at the Crossroads," *New Leader*, 73, no. 3 (5-19 Feb. 1990), 3-6.

5420. Sigov, J., "The Return of Gorby," *New Statesman and Society*, 5 (24 Jan. 1992), 19.

5421. Simes, Dimitri, "Gorbachev's Time of Troubles," *Foreign Policy*, no. 82 (Spring 1991), 97-117.

5422. Simis, Konstantin M., "The Gorbachev Generation," *Foreign Policy*, no. 59 (Summer 1985), 3-21.

5423. Singer, Daniel, "Gorbachev-Two Steps Backward?" *Nation*, 252 (18 Feb. 1991), 198-201.

5424. Singer, Max, "The Decline and Fall of the Soviet Empire," *National Review*, 42 (9 July 1990), 26-28.

5425. Slider, Darrell, "More Power to the Soviets? Reform and Local Government in the Soviet Union," *British Journal of Political Science*, 16, part 4 (Oct. 1986), 35-56.

5426. Smart, Christopher, "Time to Look Beyond Gorbachev," *World & I*, 6, no. 2 (Feb. 1991), 113-19.

5427. Smiley, Xan, "Beyond Gorbachev," *National Review*, 42 (28 May 1990), 25-29.

5428. Smith, Gordon, "Gorbachev and the Council of Ministers: Leadership Consolidation and Its Policy Implications," *Soviet Union/Union Sovietique*, 14, no. 3 (1987), 343-63.

5429. Snyder, Jack, "International Leverage on Soviet Domestic Change," *World Politics*, 42, no. 1 (Oct. 1989), 1-30.

5430. "Soviet Prospects: `Not Absolutely Hopeless': Interview with L. A. Gordon," *Challenge*, 34 (May-June 1991), 23-31.

5431. Stanfield, Rochelle L., "Gorbachev Foes Look Abroad," *National Journal*, 23, no. 10 (9 Mar. 1991), 583.

5432. Stankevich, Sergei, "The USSR's Protracted Crisis," *Journal of Democracy*, 2, no. 3 (Summer 1991), 55-57.

5433. Stepanov, Dmitri, "Where Do the Long Lines of Leningrad Lead?" *Freedom Review*, 22, no. 2 (Mar-Apr. 1991), 5-7.

5434. Suny, Ronald Grigor, "Soviet Centrism," *Nation*, 253 (11 Nov. 1991), 576.

5435. Surovell, Jeffrey, "Ligachev and Soviet Politics," *Soviet Studies*, 43, no. 2 (1991), 355-74.

5436. Talbott, Strobe, "The General Secretary in His Labyrinth," *Time*, 136 (10 Dec. 1990), 63.

5437. Taubman, Philip, "Gorbachev's Gamble," *New York Times Magazine* (19 July 1987), 28ff.

5438. Teague, Elizabeth, "The Powers of the Soviet Presidency," *Radio Liberty Report on the USSR*, 2 (23 Mar. 1990), 4-7.

5439. -----, "The Presidential Council Starts Its Work," *Report on the USSR*, 2, no. 14 (6 Apr. 1990), 1-3.

5440. -----, and Dawn Mann, "Gorbachev's Dual Role," *Problems of Communism*, 39, no. 1 (Jan-Feb. 1990), 1-14.

5441. Templeman, J., "How the Fallout from Romania Could Burn Gorbachev," *Business Week* (8 Jan. 1990), 57.

5442. Tetlock, Philip E., and Richard Boettger, "Cognitive and Rhetorical Styles of Traditionalist and Reformist Soviet Politicians: A Content Analysis Study," *Political Psychology*, 10, no. 2 (June 1989), 209-32.

5443. "They Did What He Said: The Changes Mikhail Gorbachev Has Set in Motion Are Moving Beyond His Control," *Economist*, 312 (9 Sept. 1989), 16.

5444. Thom, Francoise, "The Second Echelon," *Uncaptive Minds*, 4, no. 4 (Winter 1991-92), 5-9.

5445. -----, "We're Still Playing with Our Toys: An Interview with Aleksandr Podrabinek," *Uncaptive Minds*, 3, no. 5 (Nov-Dec. 1990), 7-8.

5446. Thorson, Carla, "The Collapse of Constitutional Order," *Report on the USSR*, 3, no. 42 (18 Oct. 1991), 15-18.

5447. Tiersky, Ronald, "*Perestroyka* and Beyond" (Review Article), *Problems of Communism*, 39, no. 2 (Mar-Apr. 1990), 109-14.

5448. Tismaneanu, Vladimir, "Neo-Stalinism and Reform Communism," *Orbis*, 30, no. 3 (Summer 1986), 259-80.

5449. Toffler, Alvin, "Moscow's Dark Colonel," *World Monitor*, 4, no. 7 (July 1991), 29-35.

5450. Tolstaia, Tatiana, "President Potemkin," *New Republic* (27 May 1991), 27ff.

5451. Tucker, Robert C., "Gorbachev and the Fight for Soviet Reform," *World Policy Journal*, 4, no. 2 (Spring 1987), 179-206.

5452. Urban, M. E., "Boris Yeltsin, Democratic Russia and the Campaign for the Russian Presidency," *Soviet Studies*, 44, no. 2 (1992), 187-207.

5453. Vanden Heuvel, Katrina, "The Young Fight for the `Three Ds'," *Nation* (29 May 1989), 729-31.

5454. Walker, Martin, "Punk *Perestroika*: The Mad Max Mood of Moscow," *New Republic* (4 Dec. 1987), 22-27.

5455. Weber, S., "Cooperation and Interdependence," *Daedalus*, 120, no. 1 (Winter 1991), 183-201.

5456. "Where *Perestroika* Makes Strange Bedfellows," *U.S. News*

& World Report, 107 (28 Aug. 1989), 77ff.

5457. White, Stephen, Ian McAllister and Olga Kryshtanovskaya, "El'tsin and His Voters: Popular Support in the 1991 Russian Presidential Elections and After," *Europe-Asia Studies*, 46, no. 2 (1994), 185-303.

5458. Wiener, Jon, "Yeltsin's American `Advisers'," *Nation*, 253, (16 Dec. 1991), 761ff.

5459. Willerton, John P., "Reforms, the Elite and Soviet Center-Periphery Relations," *Soviet Union/Union Sovietique*, 17, no. 1-2 (1990), 55-94.

5460. ----, and William Reisinger, "Troubleshooters, Political Machines, and Moscow's Regional Control," *Slavic Review*, 50, no. 2 (Summer 1991), 347-58.

5461. Wilson-Smith, Anthony, "Challenging Gorbachev," *Maclean's*, 103 (22 Jan. 1990), 18-20.

5462. ----, "Gorbachev's Bold Gamble," *Maclean's*, 103 (19 Feb. 1990), 24-32.

5463. Wishnevsky, Julia, "Vadim Medvedev Joins the Presidential Council," *Report on the USSR*, 2, no. 30 (27 July 1990), 8-10.

5464. ----, "Will the Conservatives Join the Liberals Against Gorbachev?" *Report on the USSR*, 3, no. 6 (8 Feb. 1991), 1-3.

5465. "Without Hypnosis: Supervising the KGB-Myth or Reality?" *Soviet Law and Government*, 30, no. 2 (Fall 1991), 76-87.

5466. Yasmann, Victor, "Elite Think Tank Prepares `Post-Perestroika' Strategy," *Report on the USSR*, 3, no. 21 (24 May 1991), 1-6.

5467. Young, C., "The Strategy of Political Liberalization: A Comparative View of Gorbachev's Reforms," *World Politics*, 45 (Oct. 1992), 47-65.

5468. Zaraev, Mikhail, "What Makes Boris Yeltsin Run?" *World Monitor*, 3, no. 8 (Aug. 1990), 16-22.

5469. Zemtsov, Ilya. "The Interregnum in the Kremlin," *Crossroads*, no. 15 (1985), 1-34.

5470. ----, and S. Mogilevsky, "First Congress of the People's Deputies of the USSR: Expectations and Disillusionments," *Crossroads*, no. 30 (1989), 1-18.

5471. Zuckerman, Mortimer B., "The Gorbachev Effect," *U.S. News & World Report*, 109 (9 July 1990), 29-30.

XXIII. Health Reform, Medicine, Psychiatry

BOOKS

5472. Fitzpatrick, Catherine A., *Soviet Abuse of Psychiatry for Political Reasons: A Helsinki Watch Report Update* (New York: US Helsinki Watch Committee, 1987).

5473. Ryan, Michael, *Doctors and the State in the Soviet Union* (New York: St. Martin's Press, 1990).

5474. US Commission on Security and Cooperation in Europe. *Implementation of the Helsinki Accords: Soviet Psychiatric Practices* (Washington, DC: Government Printing Office, 1989).

5475. US Congress. House. Committee on Energy and Commerce. *US and USSR Psychiatric Care Practices*. 101st Congress, 1st Session, 1989 (Washington, DC: Government Printing Office, 1989).

ARTICLES

5476. "AIDS Outbreak at Soviet Hospital Traced to Blood Transfusion," *New Scientist*, 121, no. 1654 (4 Mar. 1989), 27.

5477. Belitsky, Viktor, "Children Infect Mothers in AIDS Outbreak at a Soviet Hospital," *Nature*, 337, no. 6207 (9 Feb. 1989), 493.

5478. Body, W., "Life in the Wasteland," *International Health*, 5 (May-June 1991), 60-70.

5479. Bohen, Halcyone H., "A Glimpse of Family Therapy in the Soviet Union," *Family Systems Medicine*, 5, no. 1 (1987), 31-51.

5480. Bonner, Elena, "Health Care in the Soviet Union," *Freedom at Issue*, no. 117 (Nov-Dec. 1990), 10-14.

5481. Bower, B., "Soviets Reenter World Psychiatry Society," *Science News*, 136, no. 18 (28 Oct. 1989), 278.

5482. Brahams, Diana, "Soviet Union: The Leningrad Experiment," *Lancet*, 335, no. 8681 (13 Jan. 1990), 101-02.

5483. ----, "USSR: Abuses of Legal and Medical Systems," *Lancet*, no. 8638 (18 Mar. 1989), 608.

5484. Corwin, J., "Soviet Medicine," *U.S. News & World Report*, 109 (8 Oct. 1990), 16.

5485. Cromley, Ellen K., and Peter R. Craumer, "Regional Patterns of Medical Care Availability in the Former Soviet Union," *Post-Soviet Geography*, 33, no. 4 (Apr. 1992), 203-18.

5486. Cunningham, Ann Marie, "Downwind from Polygon: The Toll at a Soviet Test Site," *Progressive*, 54, no. 1 (Jan. 1990), 27-29.

5487. Davis, C. M., "The Soviet Health System: A National Health System in a Socialist Society," in Mark G. Field, ed., *Success and Crisis in National Health Systems: A Comparative Approach* (London: Routledge, 1989).

5488. Desrosiers, Muriel C., "Impressions from a Soviet-American Educational Tour," *Journal of School Health*, 57 (Feb. 1987), 51-52.

5489. "Enterprise Redemption Funds: Key to Soviet Health Sector," *Business in Eastern Europe*, 19, no. 15 (9 Apr. 1990), 121-22.

5490. "Exchanges in the Medical Sciences," *AABS Newsletter*, 13, no. 1-2 (Mar-Apr. 1989), 18.

5491. Feshbach, Murray, and A. Rubin, "Health Care in the USSR," in *Economic Reforms and Welfare Systems in the USSR, Poland and Hungary* (New York: St. Martin's Press, 1991), 68-84.

5492. Field, Mark G., "In Sickness and in Health," *Wilson Quarterly*, 9, no. 4 (Autumn 1985), 47-60.

5493. -----, "Noble Purpose, Grand Design, Flawed Execution, Mixed Results: Soviet Socialized Medicine after Seventy Years," *American Journal of Public Health*, 80, no. 2 (Feb. 1990), 144-45.

5494. -----, "The Position of the Soviet Physician: The Bureaucratic Professional," *Milbank Quarterly*, 66, no. 2 (Summer 1988), S182-201.

5495. Fonkalsrud, E. W., "Humanism and the Profession of Surgery in the Era of Medical Perestroika," *Archives of Surgery*, 125, no. 10 (Oct. 1990), 1252-55.

5496. Forest, James, "*Perestroika* Links Church and Hospital," *Christian Century*, 105 (9 Nov. 1988), 1004-05.

5497. "Getting Russia Well Again," *Economist*, 305 (21 Nov. 1987), 51-52.

5498. "*Glasnost* Comes to Psychiatric Asylums," *U.S. News & World Report*, 104 (18 Jan. 1988), 13.

5499. Greenberg, J., and B. Bower, "Soviet Psychiatrist Describes Abuses," *Science News*, 131 (23 May 1987), 328.

5500. Groopman, Jerome E., "Red Scare: AIDS in the U.S.S.R.," *New Republic* (17 Apr. 1989), 25-27.

5501. "Health Sector Reform in the Former Soviet Union," *Lancet*, 341, no. 8839 (23 Jan. 1993), 210.

5502. Herd, M. M., "Redkino to Rutland: A Glimmer of *Glasnost*," *British Dental Journal*, 168, no. 5 (10 Mar. 1990), 217.

5503. Herxheimer, Andrew, "Soviet Union: Supplying Essential Medicines," *Lancet*, 338, no. 8775 (2 Nov. 1991), 1135-36.

5504. Holden, Constance, "Koryagin Skeptical on *Glasnost*," *Science*, 238 (23 Oct. 1987), 476.

5505. -----, "Politics and Soviet Psychiatry," *Science*, 239 (5 Feb. 1988), 551-53.

5506. -----, "Psychiatrists Examine Soviet System," *Science*, 243, no. 4898 (24 Mar. 1989), 1547.

5507. Holowinsky, Ivan Z., "Perestroika (Restructuring) of Soviet Psychology in the Context of Gorbachev's Glasnost," *American Psychologist*, 44, no. 12 (Dec. 1989), 1547-48.

5508. Jacobs, Margot, "Minister of Health Talks about Reform," *Report on the USSR*, 2, no. 35 (31 Aug. 1990), 6-7.

5509. Jones, P. M., "Compare Two Nations' Care: The Soviet Union and Nigeria," *Scholastic Update*, 119 (20 Apr. 1987), 24-25.

5510. Kozlova, N., "Giving Birth in Tadzhikistan," *Survey*, 29, no. 4 (Aug. 1987), 160-62.

5511. "Law, Theory and Politics: The Dilemma of Soviet Psychiatry," *Yale Journal of International Law*, 11, no. 2 (Spring 1986), 297-361.

5512. "Lethal Injection," *Wilson Quarterly*, 15, no. 2 (Winter 1991), 134-35.

5513. Lewenz, Susan M. H., Michael Fuchs and Irena Staniak, "U.S. Health Care Mission Tours the Soviet Union: A Personal Perspective," *Business America*, 111, no. 123 (2 July 1990), 5-7.

5514. Light, D. W., "Russia: Perestroika for Health Care?" *Lancet*, 339, no. 8787 (25 Jan. 1992), 236.

5515. Marples, David, "The Medical Consequences of Chemobyl," *Report on the USSR*, 2, no. 10 (9 Mar. 1990), 21-23.

5516. Marshall, Eliot, "AIDS in the U.S.S.R.," *Science*, 240 (22 Apr. 1988), 384.

5517. -----, "Sverdlovsk: Anthrax Capital?" *Science*, 240 (22 Apr. 1988), 383-85.

5518. Miller, Susan Katz, "Secret Samples Reveal Truth About Anthrax," *New Scientist*, 137, no. 1865 (20 Mar. 1993), 4.

5519. Navarro, Vicente, "Has Socialism Failed? An Analysis of Health Indicators under Capitalism and Socialism," *Science and Society*, 57, no. 1 (Spring 1993), 6-30.

5520. Neuhauser, Kimberley, "New Statistics on Maternal Mortality in the USSR," *Report on the USSR*, 2, no. 14 (6 Apr. 1990), 6-9.

5521. Nichols, Mark, "Deadly Shortages: Decay Sabotages Care in the Soviet Union," *Maclean's*, 104, no. 32 (12 Aug. 1991), 38.

5522. Offerhaus, Leo, "Russia: Emergency Drugs Aid Goes Awry," *Lancet*, 339, no. 8793 (7 Mar. 1992), 606.

5523. Patrushev, Pyotr, "AIDS Tests Soviet Tolerance," *World Press Review*, 35 (Dec. 1988), 54.

5524. Peterson, D. J., "Study Indicates Infant Mortality Higher Than Reported," *Report on the USSR*, 2, no. 32 (10 Aug. 1990), 17.

5525. -----, "Understanding Soviet Infant Mortality Statistics," *Report on the USSR*, 2, no. 14 (6 Apr. 1990), 4-6.

5526. -----, "The USSR: Coming to Terms with AIDS," *Report on the USSR*, 2, no. 25 (22 June 1990), 10-16.

5527. Phillips, C., "A Brave Soviet Deputy Speaks Up for a Forgotten Minority" [the Handicapped], *People Weekly*, 32 (9 Oct. 1989), 109-10.

5528. Pompey, Carmen, "The AIDS Epidemic," *Report on Eastern Europe*, 1, no. 33 (17 Aug. 1990), 16-20.

5529. Powell, David E., "The Emerging Health Crisis in the Soviet Union," *Current History*, 84, no. 504 (Oct. 1985), 325ff.

5530. Reddaway, Peter, "Civil Society and Soviet Psychiatry," *Problems of Communism*, 40, no. 4 (July-Aug. 1991), 41-48.

5531. -----, "Reform of Soviet Psychiatry: Is the Establishment Beginning to Panic?" *Report on the USSR*, 2, no. 44 (2 Nov. 1990), 1-14.

5532. -----, "Soviet Psychiatry: An End to Abuse?" *Survey*, 30, no. 3 (June 1988), 25-38.

5533. Remennick, Larissa I., "Epidemiology and Determinants of Induced Abortion in the U.S.S.R.," *Social Science and Medicine*, 33, no. 7 (1 Oct. 1991), 841-48.

5534. Remensnyder, John P., MD, "Pipeline Disaster: Treating Soviet Burn Victims," *Harvard Medical Journal* (Summer 1990), 33-36.

5535. Repin, E. N., "Can We Properly Calculate the Economic Efficiency of Health Care Activities?" *Problems of Economics*, 31, no. 7 (Nov. 1988), 58-71.

5536. Rhein, Reginald, "Bright Prognosis for the Health Care Industry in Eastern Europe," *Journal of European Business*, 2, no. 4 (Mar-Apr. 1991), 47-51.

5537. Rich, Vera, "Anthrax in the Urals," *Lancet*, 339, no. 8790 (15 Feb. 1992), 409-10.

5538. -----, "Russia: Changes for Forensic Psychiatry?" *Lancet*, 34, no. 8816 (15 Aug. 1992), 419-20.

5539. -----, "Soviet Minister Warns of HIV Epidemic Within 10 Years," *New Scientist*, 126, no. 1717 (19 May 1990), 24.

5540. -----, "Soviet Union Admits to Abuses of Psychiatry," *New Scientist*, 132, no. 1795 (16 Nov. 1991), 13.

5541. -----, "Soviet Union: Crumbling Edifice of Medical Research," *Lancet*, 338, no. 8778 (23 Nov. 1991), 1323.

5542. -----, "Soviet Union: Diphtheria Tightens Its Grip," *Lancet*, 338, no. 8773 (19 Oct. 1991), 1004.

5543. -----, "Soviet Union: A Healthier Army?" *Lancet*, 338, no. 8770 (28 Sept. 1991), 810.

5544. -----, "Soviet Union: Living Near Nuclear Power Stations," *Lancet*, 337, no. 8738 (16 Feb. 1991), 420.

5545. -----, "Soviet Union: Psychiatry on Probation," *Lancet*, 337, no. 8743 (23 Mar. 1991), 723-24.

5546. -----, "Ukraine: New Health Care System Planned," *Lancet*, 340, no. 8820 (12 Sept. 1992), 663.

5547. -----, "USSR: Doubts about Psychiatric Reform," *Lancet*, 336, no. 8715 (8 Sept. 1990), 616-17.

5548. Rimashevskaia, Natal'ia, "The Individual's Health Is the Health of Society," *Russian Social Science Review*, 34, no. 4 (July-Aug. 1993), 56-68.

5549. Robbins, Anthony, *et al.*, "Financing Medical Care in the New Soviet Economy," *Journal of the American Medical Association*, 264, no. 9 (5 Sept. 1990), 1097-98.

5550. Rogers T., and T. Brown, "Letter from Leningrad," *Lancet*, 336, no. 8706 (7 July 1990), 42.

5551. Rothman, David J., and Sheila M. Rothman, "How AIDS Came to Romania," *New York Review of Books*, 37 (8 Nov. 1990), 5-7.

5552. Rowland, D., and A. V. Telyukov, "Soviet Health Care from Two Perspectives," *Health Affairs*, 10, no. 3 (Fall 1991).

5553. "Sales to Soviet Health Sector Look Promising," *Business in Eastern Europe*, 19, no. 7 (12 Feb. 1990), 53.

5554. Schecter, Kate, "Soviet Socialized Medicine and the Right to Health Care in a Changing Soviet Union," *Human Rights Quarterly*, 14, no. 2 (May 1992), 206-15.

5555. Schultz, Daniel S., and Michael P. Rafferty, "Soviet Health Care and Perestroika," *American Journal of Public Health*, 80, no. 2 (Feb. 1990), 193-97.

5556. Selby, Philip, "Soviet Union: Medicine Crisis," *Lancet*, 335, no. 8687 (24 Feb. 1990), 463.

5557. Shabad, Steven, "Fighting AIDS," *World Press Review*, 36 (Oct. 1989), 53.

5558. "The Sick Man of Eurasia," *Economist*, 316, no. 7673 (22 Sept. 1990), 19-22.

5559. "The Soviet Psychiatric Assistance Statute of 1988: An Uncertain Prognosis," *American University Journal of International Law and Policy*, 4 (Summer 1989), 617-53.

5560. "Soviet Straitjacket Psychiatry: New Legislation to End the Psychiatric Reign of Terror in the U.S.S.R.," *Syracuse Journal of International Law and Commerce*, 16 (Spring 1990), 271-91.

5561. "A Soviet Tragedy: Shortages Help Spread AIDS," *Fortune*, 121 (7 May 1990), 120.

5562. Starostina, E. G., and M. B. Antsiferov, "Diabetes Education in the USSR: How to Begin?" *Diabetic Medicine*, 7, no. 8 (Sept-Oct. 1990), 744-49.

5563. Storey, P. B., J. G. Freymann and D. M. Macfadyen, "Cooperation Between Health Professionals from the United States and the Union of Soviet Socialist Republics: Conclusions Drawn from a Trip to the Soviet Union," *Annals of Internal Medicine*, 113, no. 11 (1 Dec. 1990), 882-84.

5564. Stroot, E., "The Elektrostal Project: Better Nutrition for Soviet Workers," *World Health* (May-June 1991), 28-29.

5565. Teague, Elizabeth, "Hospice Movement to Expand in RSFSR," *Report on the USSR*, 3, no. 30 (26 July 1991), 24-26.

5566. Telyukov, Alexander V., "A Concept of Health-Financing Reform in the Soviet Union," *International Journal of Health Services*, 21, no. 3 (1991), 493-504.

5567. Terris, M., "Restructuring and Accelerating the Development of the Soviet Health Service," *Journal of Public Health Policy* (Winter 1988), 537-43.

5568. Teryaev, Vladislav G., "The Whole World Gave Us a Helping Hand: The Phase of Isolation," *Perestroika Annual*, 2 (1989), 197-207.

5569. Thompson, Lori M., "Soviet Straitjacket Psychiatry: New Legislation to End the Psychiatric Reign of Terror in the USSR," *Syracuse Journal of International Law and Commerce*, 16, no. 2 (Spring 1990), 271-91.

5570. Thomiley, Daniel, "Offices, Countertrade Aid Soviet Health Sales," *Business in Eastern Europe*, 19, no. 49 (3 Dec. 1990), 396.

5571. Trofimov, N., "Numbers Instead of Patients," *World Affairs*, 15, no. 2 (Summer 1989), 43-44.

5572. -----, et al., "Medical Care," *World Affairs*, 15, no. 1 (Summer 1989), 39-70.

5573. Tsaregorodtsev, G. I., and A. Y. A. Ivanyushkin, "Trends in the Development of Medical Ethics in the USSR," *Journal of Medicine and Philosophy*, 14, no. 3 (June 1989), 301-14.

5574. Ullyot, J., "Fit in the USSR?" *Women's Sports*, 7 (May 1985), 3ff.

5575. US Department of Commerce, "Soviet Health Care Group Comes Prepared for Business," *Business America*, 111, no. 5 (12 Mar. 1990), 8-10.

5576. -----, "U.S. Health Care Industry Gears Up to `Cure' Soviet Health Care Woes," *Business America*, 111, no. 13 (2 July 1990), 8-9.

5577. "USSR: Top Psychiatrist Denounced," *Lancet*, no. 8634 (18 Feb. 1989), 374.

5578. Veatch, Robert M., "Medical Ethics in the Soviet Union," *Hastings Center Report*, 19, no. 2 (Mar-Apr. 1989), 11-14.

5579. Velimirovic, B., "Plague and *Glasnost*: First Information About Human Cases in the USSR in 1989 and 1990," *Infection*, 18, no. 6 (Nov-Dec. 1990), 388-93.

5580. Weiss, L. D., and S. A. Theno, "Perestroika and Health Care in the USSR: Innovations in State Financing," *Journal of Public Health Policy*, 12, no. 2 (Summer 1991), 229-40.

5581. Weiss, R., "Soviet Describes AIDS Errors," *Science News*, 135 (17 June 1989), 382.

5582. Will, George F., "The Sickening Soviet Reality," *Newsweek*, 109 (19 Jan. 1987), 68.

5583. Witt, K., "Abortion in the Soviet Union," *World Press Review*, 36 (August 1989), 55.

5584. Wittenberg, C. K., "*Glasnost* and Cancer: Information Flows to Eastern European Nations," *Journal of the National Cancer Institute*, 82, no. 13 (4 July 1990), 1090-91.

XXIV. Historiography, History and Archival Matters

BOOKS

5585. Adler, Nanci, *Victims of Soviet Terror: The Story of the Memorial Movement* (Westport, CT: Praeger, 1993).

5586. Bergmann, Theodor, Gert Schaefer and Mark Selden, eds., *Bukharin in Retrospect* (Armonk, NY: M. E. Sharpe, 1993).

5587. D'Agostino, Anthony, *Soviet Succession Struggles: Kremlinology and the Russian Question from Lenin to Gorbachev* (Boston: Allen & Unwin, 1988).

5588. Dallin, Alexander, and Bertrand M. Patenaude, eds., *Soviet Scholarship under Gorbachev* (Stanford: Center for Russian and East European Studies, Stanford University, 1988).

5589. Davies, R. W., *Soviet History in the Gorbachev Revolution* (Bloomington: Indiana University Press, 1989).

5590. Grimsted, Patricia Kennedy, *Archives in Russia, 1993* (Washington, DC: IREX Research Services, 1993).

5591. -----, *Russian Archives in Transition: Caught Between Political Crossfire and Economic Crisis* (Washington, DC: IREX Research Services, 1993).

5592. Heller, Agnes, and Terence Feher, *From Yalta to Glasnost': Dismantling Stalin's Empire* (Oxford: Basil Blackwell, 1991).

5593. Hochschild, Adam, *Russia Faces Its Past* (New York: Viking, 1994).

5594. Iggers, Georg, *Marxist Historiography in Transformation: East German Social History in the 1980s* (New York: Berg, distributed by St. Martin's Press, 1991).

5595. Ito, Takayuki, ed., *Facing Up to the Past: Soviet Historiography under Perestroika* (Sapporo: Hokkaido University, Slavic Research Center, 1989).

5596. Kozicki, Henry, ed., *Western and Soviet Historiography: Recent Views* (New York: St. Martin's Press, 1993).

5597. Kozlov, Nicholas N., and Eric D. Weitz, eds., *Nikolai Ivanovich Bukharin: A Centenary Appraisal* (New York: Praeger, 1990).

5598. Laqueur, Walter, *Stalin: The Glasnost Revelations* (New York: Scribner's, 1991).

5599. Lewin, Moshe, *The Gorbachev Phenomenon: An Historical Interpretation*, rev. and expanded ed. (Berkeley: University of California Press, 1991).

5600. Lewis, Jonathan, and Philip Whitehead, *Stalin: A Time for Judgement* (New York: Pantheon, 1990).

5601. Merridale, Catherine, and Chris Ward, eds., *Perestroika: The Historical Perspective* (New York: Routledge, 1993).

5602. Nichol, Jim, *Stalin's Crimes against the Non-Russian Nations: The 1987-1990 Revelations and Debate*. The Carl Beck Papers in Russian and East European Studies, no. 906 (Pittsburgh: University of Pittsburgh Center for Russian and East European Studies, 1991).

5603. Raleigh, Donald J., ed., *Soviet Historians and Perestroika: The First Phase* (Armonk, NY: M. E. Sharpe, 1989).

5604. Solomon, Susan Gross, ed., *Beyond Sovietology: Essays in Politics and History* (New York: M. E. Sharpe, 1993).

5605. Stojanovich, Svetozar, *Perestroika: From Marxism and Bolshevism to Gorbachev* (Buffalo: Prometheus Books, 1988).

5606. Takayuki, Ito, ed., *Facing Up to the Past: Soviet Historiography Under Perestroika* (Hokkaido: Sapporo Slavic Research Center of Hokkaido University, 1989).

5607. Velychenko, Stephen, *Shaping Identity in Eastern Europe and Russia: Soviet and Polish Accounts of Ukrainian History, 1914-1991* (New York: St. Martin's Press, 1991).

5608. Volkogonov, Dimitrii, *Stalin: Triumph and Tragedy* (New York: Grove Weidenfeld, 1991).

ARTICLES

5609. "About Khrushchev, Brezhnev and Others: Interview with Shelest," *Soviet Law and Government*, 28, no. 4 (Spring 1990), 60-65.

5610. Afanas'ev, Yuri, "Perestroika and Historical Knowledge," *Michigan Quarterly Review*, 28, no. 4 (Fall 1989), 532-48.

5611. Aizlewood, R., "The Return of the `Russian Idea' in Publications, 1988-91," *Slavonic and East European Review*, 71, no. 3 (July 1993), 490-99.

5612. Allyn, Bruce J., James G. Blight and David A. Welch, "Essence of Revision: Moscow, Havana and the Cuban Missile Crisis," *International Security*, 14, no. 3 (Winter 1989-90), 136-72.

5613. Altstadt, Audrey L., "Rewriting Turkic History in the Gorbachev Era," *Journal of Soviet Nationalities*, 2, no. 2 (Summer 1991), 73-90.

5614. Amiel, B., "Straight from the Horse's Mouth," *Maclean's*, 101 (19 Sept. 1988), 9.

5615. Angotti, T., "The Stalin Period: Opening Up History," *Science and Society*, 52, no. 1 (Spring 1988), 5-34.

5616. Artizov, A. N., "To Suit the Views of the Leader: The 1936 Competition for the [Best] Textbook on the History of the USSR," *Russian Social Science Review*, 34, no. 3 (May-June 1993), 73-93.

5617. "Back to the Future," *Economist*, 303 (27 June 1987), 16.

5618. Bacon, E., "Glasnost' and the Gulag: New Information on Soviet Forced Labour around World War II," *Soviet Studies*, 44, no. 6 (1992), 1069-86.

5619. Bolkhovitinov, Nikolai Nikolaevich, "New Thinking and the Study of the History of the United States in the Soviet Union," *Reviews in American History*, 19, no. 2 (June 1991), 155-65.

5620. -----, *et al.*, "Glasnost' in Archives? Commentary by Soviet Historians," *American Archivist*, 53, no. 3 (Summer 1990), 468-75.

5621. Bowen, E., "A Fresh Breath of Heresy," *Time*, 32 (25 July 1988), 74.

5622. Boyer, John W., and Julius Kirshner, "Perestroika, History and Historians," *Journal of Modern History*, 62, no. 4 (Dec. 1990), 782-830.

5623. Brown, Edward J., "*Glasnost'* in Historical Perspective," *Soviet Union/Union Sovietique*, 15, no. 2-3 (1988), 139-50.

5624. Burlatskii, Fedor, "After Stalin: Notes on the Political Thaw," *Soviet Law and Government*, 28, no. 3 (Winter 1989-90),

5-80.

5625. -----, "Khrushchev: Strokes on a Political Portrait," *Soviet Law and Government*, 27, no. 3 (Winter 1988-89), 31-43.

5626. Bushnell, John, "Making History out of Current Events: The Gorbachev Era," *Slavic Review*, 51, no. 3 (Fall 1992), 557-63.

5627. Byrnes, Robert F., "The Ferment of History in the Soviet Union," *AAASS Newsletter*, 27, no. 4 (Sept. 1987), 1-2.

5628. Campbell, Kurt M., "Gorbachev's Challenge: The Ghost of Stalin," *New Leader* (2 Nov. 1987), 9-14.

5629. Cohen, Stephen F., "Bukharin Redux," *Nation* (20 Feb. 1988), 222.

5630. Condee, P., and V. Padunov, "Reforming Soviet Culture/Retrieving Soviet History," *Nation*, 244 (13 June 1987), 815-20.

5631. Conquest, Robert, "Skeletons from the Closets of the Kremlin," *Mother Jones*, 13, no. 5 (June 1988), 40-41.

5632. Cooper, N., "The Ghost of an Old Bolshevik," *Newsweek*, 110 (16 Nov. 1987), 76.

5633. Daniels, Robert V., "Gorbachev's Reforms and the Reversal of History," *History Teacher*, 23, no. 3 (May 1990), 237-54.

5634. Danilov, Viktor P., "The Issue of Alternatives and History of the Collectivisation of Agriculture," *Journal of Historical Sociology*, 2, no. 1 (1989), 1-13.

5635. Davis, R. W., "Soviet History in the Gorbachev Revolution: The First Phase," *Social Register* (1988), 62ff.

5636. Day, Richard B., "The Blackmail of the Single Alternative: Bukharin, Trotsky and Perestrojka," *Studies in Soviet Thought*, 40, no. 1-3 (Aug-Nov. 1990), 159-88.

5637. "De-Stalinizing the Soviet Past," *Harper's*, 279, no. 1673 (Oct. 1989), 32ff.

5638. Dukes, Paul, "From Soviet to Russian History," *History Today*, 43 (Aug. 1993), 9-11.

5639. -----, "Glasnost and the Russian Revolution," *History Today*, 37 (Oct. 1987), 11-14.

5640. Enteen, George M., "Problems of CPSU Historiography," *Problems of Communism*, 38, no. 5 (Sept-Oct. 1989), 72-80.

5641. Erickson, John, "Stalin Revisited," *RUSI Journal*, 136, no. 1 (Spring 1991), 69-72.

5642. Feldman, Gayle, "London's Verso to Form Joint Venture with Soviet House," *Publishers Weekly*, 235, no. 24 (16 June 1989), 14.

5643. Filatova, Irina, "Some Thoughts on Soviet South African Studies under `Stagnation' and Perestroika," *International Journal of African Historical Studies*, 25, no. 1 (1992), 15-23.

5644. Fitzpatrick, Sheila, "New Perspectives on Stalinism," *Russian Review*, 45, no. 4 (Oct. 1986), 357-413; Discussion: 46

(Oct. 1987), 375-431.

5645. Fleron, Frederic J., Jr., and Erik P. Hoffmann, "Sovietology and Perestroika: Methodology and Lessons from the Past," *Harriman Institute Forum*, 5, no. 1 (Sept. 1991), 1-12.

5646. Foner, Erich, "Restructuring Yesterday's News: The Russians Write a New History," *Harper's*, 281, no. 1687 (Dec. 1990), 70-78.

5647. Gammer, Moshe, "Shamil in Soviet History," *Middle Eastern Studies*, 28, no. 4 (1992), 729-77.

5648. Gellner, Ernest, "Stalin Takes the Stand: Pushing the Limits of *Glasnost'*," *New Republic* (20 Mar. 1989), 20-24.

5649. Gimius, Kestutis, "The Historiography of the Molotov-Ribbentrop Pact," *Lituanus*, 35, no. 2 (Summer 1989), 67-88.

5650. "*Glasnost'* and Soviet Historians," *Soviet Studies in History*, 27, no. 1 (Summer 1988), 2-91.

5651. "*Glasnost'* and the October Revolution," *Soviet Studies in History*, 27, no. 2 (Fall 1988), 3-113.

5652. Gleason, Gregory, "Lenin, Gorbachev, and 'National-Statehood': Can Leninism Countenance the New Soviet Federal Order?" *Studies in Soviet Thought*, 40, no. 1-3 (Aug-Nov. 1990), 137-58.

5653. Gooding, John, "Lenin in Soviet Politics, 1985-1991," *Soviet Studies*, 44, no. 3 (1992), 403-22.

5654. Gorbachev, Mikhail, "The Revolution and Perestroika," *Foreign Affairs*, 66 (Winter 1987-88), 410-25.

5655. Grimsted, Patricia, "*Perestroika* in the Archives: Further Efforts at Soviet Archival Reform," *American Archivist*, 54, no. 1 (Winter 1991), 70-95.

5656. Hahn, Gordon M., "Researching Perestroika in the TsK KPSS Archives," *Russian Review*, 53, no. 3 (July 1994), 419-23.

5657. Hargreaves, John D., "The Comintern and Anti-colonialism: New Research Opportunities," *African Affairs*, 92, no. 367 (Apr. 1993), 255-62.

5658. Heller, M., "Current Politics and Current Historiography," *Survey*, 30, no. 3 (June 1989), 1-6.

5659. ------, ed., "Perestroika and Soviet History," *Survey*, 30, no. 3 (June 1989), 1-130.

5660. Herminghouse, Patricia, "Confronting the 'Blank Spots of History': GDR Culture and the Legacy of Stalinism," *German Studies Review*, 14, no. 2 (May 1991), 345-66.

5661. Hochman, J., "The Soviet Historical Debate," *Orbis*, 32, no. 3 (Summer 1988), 369-83.

5662. Howard, M., "Russia Rethinks the Revolution," *World Today*, 43, no. 11 (Nov. 1987), 185-86.

5663. Howe, Irving, "Gorbachev Meets Up with History," *Dissent*, 35, no. 2 (Spring 1988), 160-63.

5664. Husband, William B., "Secondary School History Texts in

the USSR: Revising the Soviet Past," *Russian Review*, 50, no. 4 (Oct. 1991), 458-80.

5665. Johns, Michael, "Seventy Years of Evil: Soviet Crimes from Lenin to Gorbachev," *Policy Review*, no. 42 (Fall 1987), 10-23.

5666. Kan, Aleksander, "Norwegian Sovietology 1922-1992," *Scandinavian Journal of History*, 18, no. 3 (1993), 199-216.

5667. Keep, John L. H., "Restructuring Soviet History: A New 'Great Turn'," *Studies in Soviet Thought* (Aug. 1989), 117-45.

5668. Kenez, Peter, "(Re)Making History in Moscow," *New Leader*, 73, no. 6 (16 Apr. 1990), 10-11.

5669. Kennan, George, "Communism in Russian History," *Foreign Affairs*, 69, no. 5 (Winter 1990-91), 168-86.

5670. Kliamkin, Igor', "Why It Is Difficult to Speak the Truth," *Soviet Law and Government*, 29, no. 1 (Summer 1990), 31-101.

5671. Knight, Amy, "The Fate of the KGB Archives," *Slavic Review*, 52, no. 3 (Fall 1993), 582-86.

5672. Kononenko, V. P., "The Truth about Pavlik Morozov (A Chronicle of a Journalist's Investigation of a Court Case)," *Soviet Education*, 32, no. 8 (Aug. 1990), 69-92.

5673. Kozlov, V. A., "The Historian and *Perestroika*," *Soviet Review*, 28, no. 2 (Mar-Apr. 1989), 19-38.

5674. Kull, Steven, "Dateline Moscow: Burying Lenin," *Foreign Policy*, no. 78 (Spring 1990), 172-91.

5675. Kuraev, M., "Perestroika: The Restructuring of the Past or the Invention of the Future?" *South Atlantic Quarterly*, 90 (Spring 1991), 227-36.

5676. Labedz, Leopold, "E. H. Carr: An Historian Overtaken by History," *Survey*, 30, no. 2 (Mar. 1988), 94-111.

5677. Lapham, Lewis, "History Lesson," *Harper's*, 283, no. 1698 (Nov. 1991), 13-16.

5678. Lewin, Moshe, "*Perestroika*: A New Historical Stage," *Journal of International Affairs*, 42 (Spring 1989), 299-315.

5679. Lisson, Paul, "History, Change and Libraries in the Soviet Union," *Canadian Library Journal*, 48, no. 1 (Feb. 1991), 47-50.

5680. Loenhard, W., "The Bolshevik Revolution Turns 70," *Foreign Affairs*, 66 (Winter 1987-88), 388-409.

5681. "Luther, Calvin, Gorbachev," *Economist*, 307 (25 June 1988), 49-51.

5682. Maslov, N. N., "*Short Course of the History of the All-Russian Communist Party (Bolshevik)*-An Encyclopedia of Stalin's Personality Cult," *Soviet Review*, 31, no. 2 (Mar-Apr. 1990), 50-79.

5683. McClamand, Elaine, "The Debate Continues: Views on Stalinism from the Former Soviet Union," *Soviet and Post-Soviet Review*, 20, no. 1 (1993), 11-33.

5684. McLaughlin, Sigrid, "Rybakov's *Deti Arbata*: Reintegrating

Stalin into Soviet History," *Slavic Review*, 50, no. 1 (Spring 1991), 90-99.

5685. Menashe, Louis, "From Stalin to Gorbachev: Moshe Lewin on Soviet History" (Review Article), *International Labor and Working Class History*, no. 35 (Spring 1989), 53-61.

5686. Merridale, Catherine, "Glasnost and Stalin: New Material, Old Questions," *Historical Journal*, 36 (Mar. 1993), 233-43.

5687. Methvin, Eugene H., "The Unquiet Ghosts of Stalin's Victims," *National Review*, 41 (1 Sept. 1989), 24ff.

5688. Meyerson, Adam, "The Battle for the History Books: Who Won the Cold War?" *Policy Review*, no. 52 (Spring 1990), 2-3.

5689. Miasnikov, A. L., "The End," *Soviet Law and Government*, 29, no. 3 (Winter 1990-91), 53-61.

5690. Monas, Sidney, "Perestroika in Reverse Perspective: The Reforms of the 1860s," *South Atlantic Journal*, 90 (Spring 1991), 255-67.

5691. Murarka, Dev, "A New Revolution in Consciousness," *Nation*, 245 (31 Oct. 1987), 486ff.

5692. -----, "Recovering the Buried Stalin Years," *Nation*, 245 (24 Oct. 1987), 433ff.

5693. -----, "Soviet History: A New Revolution in Consciousness," *Nation* (31 Oct. 1987), 486ff.

5694. Nekrich, Aleksandr M., "Past Tense," *New Republic* (29 Apr. 1991), 14-16.

5695. -----, "Perestroika in History: The First Stage," *Survey*, 30, no. 3 (June 1989), 22-43.

5696. "A 1921 Lesson for Russia," *Economist*, 302 (24 Jan. 1987), 45.

5697. Norlander, David, "Khrushchev's Image in Light of Glasnost and Perestroika," *Russian Review*, 52, no. 2 (Apr. 1993), 248-64.

5698. Nove, Alec, "Terror Victims-Is the Evidence Complete?" *Europe-Asia Studies*, 46, no. 3 (1994), 535-38.

5699. O'Brien, C., "Hello, History, Get Me Rewrite," *Newsweek*, 120 (9 Nov. 1992), 74-75.

5700. "On the Russian Archives: An Interview with Sergei V. Mironenko," *Slavic Review*, 52, no. 4 (Winter 1993), 839-46.

5701. Orlovsky, Daniel T., "The New Soviet History" (Review Article), *Journal of Modern History*, 62, no. 4 (Dec. 1990), 831-50.

5702. Park, A., "Gorbachev and the Role of Personality in History," *Studies in Comparative Communism*, 25 (Mar. 1992), 47-56.

5703. "*Perestroika* and the Journal *Voprosy istorii KPSS*," *Soviet Studies in History*, 27, no. 3 (Winter 1988-89), 3-90.

5704. Phillips, Hugh, "*Glasnost'* and the History of Soviet Foreign Policy" (Review Article), *Problems of Communism*, 40,

no. 4 (July-Aug. 1991), 63-68.

5705. Pope, Victoria, "Rewriting Soviet History," *U.S. News and World Report*, 111, no. 17 (21 Oct. 1991), 52.

5706. Powell, David E., "'History' and the Recent Histories of the USSR" (Review Article), *Studies in Comparative Communism*, 20 (Autumn-Winter 1987), 343-57.

5707. Raeff, Marc, "Consequences of Glasnost" (Review Article), *Problems of Communism*, 39, no. 2 (Mar-Apr. 1990), 105-08.

5708. Raun, Toivo U., "Perestroika and Baltic Historiography," *Journal of Soviet Nationalities*, 2, no. 2 (Summer 1991), 52-62.

5709. Reed, S. K., "Tearing a Veil from Soviet History: Anatoli Rybakov Tries to Exorcize the Monstrous Spirit of Stalin," *People Weekly*, 29 (27 June 1988), 73-74.

5710. "Reforming Russia: In the Light of History," *Economist*, 314 (10 Feb. 1990), 15ff.

5711. Richards, H., "Soviet Historians Begin to Dismantle Lenin," *Times Higher Education Supplement*, 931 (7 Sept. 1990), 1ff.

5712. Rinehart, D., "Denouncing Stalin and `Stagnation'," *Maclean's*, 101 (11 July 1988), 27.

5713. "A Roundtable on Soviet Historians and *Perestroika*," *Soviet Studies in History*, 27, no. 4 (Spring 1989), 3-98.

5714. Sancton, T. A., "Lifting the Veil on History," *Time*, 130 (16 Nov. 1987), 45ff.

5715. Senn, Alfred Erich, "Lighting the Road Behind: Soviet Historiography of the Russian Revolutionary Movement," in Terry L. Thompson and Richard Sheldon, eds., *Soviet Society and Culture: Essays in Honor of Vera S. Dunham* (Boulder, CO: Westview Press, 1990), 195-205.

5716. -----, "*Perestroika* in Lithuanian Historiography: The Molotov-Ribbentrop Pact," *Russian Review*, 49, no. 1 (Jan. 1990), 43-56.

5717. "Sentencing Lenin to the *Gulag*," *Glasnost*, 2, no. 6, issues no. 30-31 (Apr-May 1990), 28-33.

5718. Shabad, Steven, "Gaps in History," *World Press Review*, 34 (Oct. 1987), 42.

5719. Shapiro, J., "Soviet History Writing: Toward Normalization" (Review Article), *Slavonic and East European Review*, 68, no. 3 (July 1990), 516-20.

5720. Sherlock, Thomas, "Politics and History under Gorbachev," *Problems of Communism*, 37, no. 3 (May-Aug. 1988), 16-42.

5721. Shishkin, Vladimir I., and Alan Wood, "The October Revolution and Perestroika: A Critical Analysis of Recent Soviet Historiography," *European History Quarterly*, 22, no. 4 (Oct. 1992), 517-40.

5722. Shlapentokh, Vladimir, "Alexander II and Mikhail Gorbachev: Two Reformers in Historical Perspective," *Russian History/Histoire Russe*, 17, no. 4 (Winter 1990), 395-408.

5723. Shukman, Harold, "Lenin or Alexander?" *Times Higher Education Supplement*, 904 (2 Mar. 1990), 15.

5724. Shulman, Marshall D., "How to Respond to Gorbachev: Some Right and Wrong Lessons from History," *Michigan Quarterly Review*, 28, no. 4 (Fall 1989), 468-80.

5725. Siegelbaum, Lewis H., "Historical Revisionism in the USSR," *Radical History Review*, 44 (1989), 32-61.

5726. Sikorski, R., "Haunting Russia" [Gulag Camps], *National Review*, 46 (2 May 1994), 23-24.

5727. Singer, D., "On Recapturing the Soviet Past," *Nation*, 245 (12 Dec. 1987), 716-18.

5728. Smart, Christopher, "Gorbachev's Lenin: The Myth in Service to Perestroika," *Studies in Comparative Communism*, 23, no. 1 (Spring 1990), 5-22.

5729. Smirnov, G., "Perestroika's Impact on Soviet History," *History Today*, 38 (Apr. 1988), 8-10.

5730. Snyder, Jack, "The Gorbachev Revolution: A Waning of Soviet Expansionism?" *International Security*, 12, no. 3 (Winter 1987-88), 93-131.

5731. Solchanyk, Roman, "Filling in the `Blank Spots' in Ukrainian History: An Interview with Stanislav V. Kul'chyts'kyi," *Report on the USSR*, 2, no. 16 (20 Apr. 1990), 18-24.

5732. Starr, S. Frederick, "A Peculiar Pattern," *Wilson Quarterly*, 13, no. 3 (Spring 1989), 37-50.

5733. -----, "A Usable Past: Russia's Democratic Past," *New Republic* (15 May 1989), 24-27.

5734. Startsev, V., "The 70th Anniversary of the October Revolution: Echo of History" (Review Article), *World Marxist Review*, 30, no. 7 (July 1987), 153-60.

5735. Suziedelis, Saulius, "The Molotov-Ribbentrop Pact and the Baltic States: An Introduction and Interpretation," *Lituanus*, 35, no. 1 (Spring 1989), 8-46.

5736. Sysyn, Frank E., "Three Works on the Russian Question" (Review Article), *Canadian Slavonic Papers*, 34, no. 1-2 (Mar-June 1992), 143-52.

5737. Thompson, W. J., "Khrushchev and Gorbachev as Reformers: A Comparison," *British Journal of Political Science*, 23 (Jan. 1993), 77-105.

5738. Tikhvinskii, S. L., "Soviet Questions Regarding the Work of Soviet Historians," *Soviet Review*, 29, no. 3 (Fall 1988), 36-50.

5739. Timmermann, Heinz, "Is Gorbachev a Bukharinist? Moscow's Reappraisal of the NEP Period," *Journal of Communist Studies*, 5, no. 1 (Mar. 1989), 1-17.

5740. Timofeyev, Lev, "How Stephen Cohen Re-Thinks the Soviet Experience" (Review Article), *Survey*, 30, no. 4 (June 1989), 189-95.

5741. Tolz, Vera, "`Memorial' Society Launches New Series of Historical Anthologies," *Report on the USSR*, 3, no. 50 (13 Dec. 1991), 8-10.

5742. Tsipko, A., "The Sources of Stalinism," *Soviet Law and Government*, 29, no. 1 (Summer 1990), 5-30.

5743. -----, "The Sources of Stalinism (Cont'd)," *Soviet Law and Government*, 29, no. 2 (Fall 1990), 5-58.

5744. Tucker, Robert C., "The Gorbachev-Stalin Leadership Struggle: Giving Up the Ghost," *New Republic* (17 Oct. 1988), 20ff.

5745. -----, "International Conference of Historians in Moscow," *AAASS Newsletter*, 30, no. 3 (May 1990), 1-3.

5746. Valkenier, Elizabeth Kridl, "Filling in Blank Spots: Soviet-Polish History and Polish Renewal," *Harriman Institute Forum*, 2, no. 12 (Dec. 1989), 1-8.

5747. -----, "Stalinizing Polish Historiography: What Soviet Archives Disclose," *East European Politics and Societies*, 7, no. 1 (Winter 1993), 109ff.

5748. -----, "To Tell the Truth," *New Republic* (22 May 1989), 20-21.

5749. Vasetskii, N., "Liquidation: Who Killed Trotsky and Why: Evidence and Versions from Various Years," *Soviet Law and Government*, 28, no. 3 (Winter 1989-90), 81ff.

5750. Von Hagen, Mark, "History and Politics under Gorbachev: Professional Autonomy and Democratization," *Harriman Institute Forum*, 1, no. 11 (Nov. 1989), 1-8.

5751. -----, "Soviet Historiography and the Nationality Question," *Nationalities Papers*, 28, no. 1 (Spring 1990), 53-56.

5752. Wheatcroft, S. G., "Steadying the Energy of History," *Australian Slavonic and East European Studies*, 1, no. 2 (1987), 57-114.

5753. Woll, Josephine, "Fruits of Glasnost: A Sampling from the Soviet Press," *Dissent*, 36, no. 1 (Winter 1989), 24-38.

5754. "Z" [Martin Malia], "To the Stalin Mausoleum," *Daedalus*, 119, no. 1 (Winter 1990), 295-344.

5755. Zilper, Nadia, "The Consequences of Glasnost," *Library Journal*, 116, no. 9 (15 May 1991), 44-49.

5756. Zweerde, Evert van der, "Recent Developments in Soviet Historiography of Philosophy," *Studies in Soviet Thought*, 39, no. 1 (Feb. 1990), 1-53.

XXV. Industry

BOOKS

5757. Almquist, Peter, *Red Forge: Soviet Military Industry since 1965* (New York: Columbia University Press, 1990).

5758. Amann, Robert, and Julian Cooper, eds., *Technical Progress and Soviet Economic Development* (New York: Basil Blackwell, 1986).

5759. Berliner, Joseph S., *Soviet Industry from Stalin to Gorbachev: Essays on Management and Innovation* (Ithaca:

Cornell University Press, 1988).

5760. Blackwell, William L., *The Industrialization of Russia: A Historical Perspective*, 3rd ed. (Arlington Heights, IL: Harlan Davidson, 1993).

5761. Burawoy, Michael, and Kathryn Hendley, *Strategies of Adaptation: A Soviet Enterprise under Perestroika and Privatization* (Bala Cynwyd, PA: WEFA Group, 1991).

5762. Cantor, David J., *The Steel Industries of Eastern Europe: Can They Compete with the West?* (Washington, DC: Library of Congress, Congressional Research Service, 1990).

5763. Economist Intelligence Unit, *The East European Motor Industry: Prospects and Developments* (New York: Economist Intelligence Unit, 1989).

5764. Heath, John, ed., *Revitalizing Socialist Enterprise: A Race Against Time* (London: Routledge, 1993).

5765. Jeffries, Ian, ed., *Industrial Reform in Socialist Countries: From Restructuring to Revolution* (Brookfield, VT: Edward Elgar, 1992).

5766. Kapitany, Zsuzsa, and Laszlo Kallay, *The Motor Industry of Eastern Europe: Prospects to 2000 and Beyond* (New York: Economist Intelligence Unit, 1991).

5767. Lawrence, P. R., *et al.*, *Behind the Factory Walls: Decision Making in Soviet and U.S. Enterprises* (Boston: Harvard Business School Press, 1990).

5768. Lewarne, Stephen, *Soviet Oil: The Move Offshore* (Boulder, CO: Westview Press, 1988).

5769. Nellis, John, *Improving the Performance of Soviet Enterprises* (Washington, DC: World Bank, 1991).

5770. Popper, Steven W., *Modernizing the Soviet Textile Industry: Implications for Perestroika* (Santa Monica, CA: RAND, 1989).

5771. -----, *The Prospects for Modernizing Soviet Industry* (Santa Monica, CA: RAND, 1990).

5772. Rumer, Boris Z., *Soviet Steel: The Challenge of Industrial Modernization in the USSR* (Ithaca: Cornell University Press, 1989).

5773. Sagers, Matthew J., and Theodore Shabad, *The Chemical Industry in the USSR: An Economic Geography* (Boulder, CO: Westview Press, 1990).

5774. US Congress. Senate. Committee on Foreign Relations and US General Accounting Office. National Security and International Affairs Division. *Soviet Energy: U.S. Attempts to Aid Oil Production Are Hindered by Many Obstacles: Report to the Chairman, Committee on Foreign Relations, U.S. Senate* (Washington, DC: General Accounting Office, 1991).

5775. Van Winkle, Jeannette, and Benjamin Zycher, *Future Soviet Investment in Transportation, Energy and Environmental Protection* (Santa Monica, CA: RAND, 1991).

5776. Whitefield, Stephen, *Industrial Power and the Soviet State*

(Oxford: Clarendon Press, 1993).

ARTICLES

5777. Achilles, Todd, and Rick Frye, "Russia's Ample Forests Interest Pacific Traders," *Forest Industries*, 118, no. 9 (Nov. 1991), 19-21.

5778. Aganbegian, Abel G., "What Perestroika Means for Soviet Enterprises," *International Labour Review*, 128, no. 1 (1989), 85-101.

5779. Arnot, B., "Contradictions of Soviet Industrialization" (Review Article), *Capital Class*, 33 (Winter 1987), 156-67.

5780. "At Factories, It's Do-or-Die Time," *Business Week* (25 June 1989), 56-57.

5781. Banks, Howard, "Can Bob Strauss Save the Soviet Oil Industry?" *Forbes*, 148, no. 1 (8 July 1991), 35.

5782. Belkindas, M. V., "Review of the New Soviet Industry Statistical Handbook," *Soviet Geography*, 30, no. 4 (May 1989), 389-94.

5783. Bilski, A., "Gorbachev's Latest Plan," *Maclean's*, 101 (18 Jan. 1988), 29-30.

5784. Black, Clayton, "Party Crisis and the Factory Shop Floor," *Europe-Asia Studies*, 46, no. 1 (1994), 107-26.

5785. Bond, Andrew R., with Richard M. Levine and Gordon T. Austin, "Russian Diamond Industry in State of Flux," *Post-Soviet Geography*, 33, no. 10 (Dec. 1992), 635-44.

5786. Bradac, C., "Change Is Slow for Soviet Enterprise,' *World Press Review*, 35 (Sept. 1988), 51.

5787. Brown, Bess, "Can Kazakhstan's Oil Help to Fuel Economic Autonomy?" *Report on the USSR*, 2, no. 25 (22 June 1990), 19-20.

5788. Burawoy, Michael, and Kathryn Hendley, "Between Perestroika and Privatisation: Divided Strategies and Political Crisis in a Soviet Enterprise," *Soviet Studies*, 44, no. 3 (1992), 371-402.

5789. Chandler, Alfred D., Jr., "Organizational Capabilities and Industrial Restructuring: A Historical Analysis," *Journal of Comparative Economics*, 17, no. 2 (June 1993), 309-37.

5790. Clarke, Simon, *et al.*, "The Privatisation of Industrial Enterprises in Russia: Four Case-Studies," *Europe-Asia Studies*, 46, no. 2 (1994), 179-214.

5791. Cole, J. P., "Is the USSR Entering the Post-Materials Age? Trends in Per Capita Production of Primary Products," *Soviet Geography*, 29, no. 4 (May 1988), 476-500.

5792. Cook, Linda J., "The Politics of Soviet Enterprise Insolvency," *Soviet Union/Union Sovietique*, 17, no. 3 (1990), 235-58.

5793. Covault, Craig, "U.S., Soviet Negotiators Agree on Space Cooperation Pact," *Aviation Week & Space Technology* (10 Nov. 1986), 27-28.

5794. -----, "White House, Kremlin May Revive Cooperative Space Programs," *Aviation Week & Space Technology* (6 Oct. 1986), 23-24.

5795. Danilin, V. I., *et al.*, "Measuring Enterprise Efficiency in the Soviet Union: A Stochastic Frontier Analysis," *Economica*, 52 (May 1985), 225-33.

5796. "Decision Making in Soviet and U.S. Enterprises," *International Executive*, 33, no. 3 (Nov-Dec. 1991), 54-56.

5797. Dejevsky, Nikolai, "Free-Wheeling in Bear Country: Automotive Manufacturing and Trading in the Former Soviet Union" (Special Issue), *International Automotive Review*, 13, no. 2 (Winter 1993-94), 3-44.

5798. Ebel, Robert E., "Out of Gas: Jimmy Carter Meets Mikhail Gorbachev in the Great Coming Soviet Energy Crisis," *International Economy*, 5 (July-Aug. 1991), 63-67.

5799. Filtzer, Donald A., "The Contradictions of the Marketless Market: Self-Financing in the Soviet Industrial Enterprise, 1986-90," *Soviet Studies*, 43, no. 6 (1991), 989-1010.

5800. Flory, Paul J., "Science in a Divided World: Conditions for Cooperation," *Freedom at Issue*, no. 89 (Mar-Apr. 1986), 3ff.

5801. Galuszka, Philip, "A Tractor Factory Tries to Pull Its Own Weight," *Business Week* (7 Dec. 1987), 79.

5802. Goddy, D., "Revitalizing Industry," *Scholastic Update*, 118 (7 Mar. 1986), 11.

5803. Gost, Isabel, "The Challenge Ahead for Soviet Gas," *Petroleum Review*, 44, no. 527 (Dec. 1990), 616-18.

5804. Graham, Loren R., "Red Elephants," *Technology Review*, 96, no. 8 (Nov-Dec. 1993), 26-27.

5805. Gray, Malcolm, "Switching Gears," *Maclean's*, 104 (4 Nov. 1991), 46-47.

5806. Greenwald, J., "At the Point of No Return," *Time* 131 (25 Jan. 1988), 46.

5807. Grosfeld, Irena, "Privatization of State Enterprises in Eastern Europe: The Search for a Market Environment," *East European Politics and Societies*, 5, no. 1 (Winter 1991), 142-61.

5808. Jennings, Paul, "A Western Oilman's View of the Soviet Union," *Petroleum Review*, 45, no. 532 (May 1991), 218-19.

5809. Kotkin, Stephen, "Perestroika in the Russian Rustbelt," *Harriman Institute Forum*, 4, no. 2 (Feb. 1991), 1-16.

5810. Kroll, Heidi, "Decentralization and the Precontract Dispute in Soviet Industry," *Soviet Economy*, 2, no. 1 (Jan-Mar. 1986), 51-71.

5811. -----, "Property Rights and the Soviet Enterprise: Evidence from the Law of Contract," *Journal of Comparative Economics*, 13 (Mar. 1989), 115-33.

5812. Kuhnert, Caroline, "More Power for the Soviets: *Perestroika* and Energy," *Soviet Studies*, 43, no. 3 (1991), 491-506.

5813. Lavrovskii, B., "The Paralysis of Soviet Industry: Techno-

logical Sources," *Problems of Economics*, 35, no. 1 (May 1992), 61-73.

5814. Leary, Neil A., and Judith Thornton, "Are Socialist Industries Inoculated against Innovation? A Case Study of Technological Change in Steelmaking," *Comparative Economic Studies*, 31, no. 2 (Summer 1989), 42-65.

5815. Lenorovitz, Jeffrey M., "Military, Aerospace Industry in USSR Undergo Shakeup," *Aviation Week & Space Technology*, 135, no. 9 (2 Sept. 1991), 20-21.

5816. -----, "Soviets Urge International Effort Leading to Manned Mars Mission," *Aviation Week & Space Technology* (24 Mar. 1986), 76-77.

5817. Maremont, Mark, "Why Soviet Oil Wells Won't Be Gushing Soon," *Business Week* (9 Sept. 1991), 36-37.

5818. Marples, David R., "Nuclear Power: A Fading Soviet Energy Alternative?" *Soviet Analyst* (7 Dec. 1988).

5819. Matosich, Andrew J., and Bonnie K. Matosich, "Machine Building: *Perestroyka*'s Sputtering Engine," *Soviet Economy*, 4, no. 2 (Apr-June 1988), 144-76.

5820. Mitchell, Jay K., "Chemical Industry of the Former U.S.S.R.," *Chemical and Engineering News*, 70, no. 15 (13 Apr. 1992), 46-58.

5821. Moe, Arild, and Valeriy Kryukov, "Observations on the Reorganization of the Russian Oil Industry," *Post-Soviet Geography*, 35, no. 2 (Feb. 1994), 89-101.

5822. Moore, T., "Managers: Russia's New Elite," *Fortune*, 112 (25 Nov. 1985), 98ff.

5823. Morrocco, John D., "Five Research Facilities Band Together to Form Independent Association," *Aviation Week & Space Technology*, 135, no. 20 (18 Nov. 1991), 48-49.

5824. -----, "Soviet Aviation Control Shifting to Republics as Industry Privatizes," *Aviation Week & Space Technology*, 135, no. 12 (23 Sept. 1991), 27.

5825. -----, "Soviets Face Grim Prospects in Selling Aircraft Internationally," *Aviation Week & Space Technology*, 135, no. 20 (18 Nov. 1991), 45ff.

5826. -----, "Soviets Grope for Order with New Industry Alliances," *Aviation Week & Space Technology*, 135, no. 20 (18 Nov. 1991), 42-44.

5827. Pearson, J., "Now a Soviet Manager Can Start Thinking for Himself," *Business Week* (11 Nov. 1985), 93.

5828. "Perestroika in the Factory," *Economist*, 315 (9 June 1990), 70.

5829. "Perestroika That Succeeded," *Delovie Lyudi*, no. 35 (July 1993), 33.

5830. Pomorski, S., "The Future of the State Enterprise and the `Restructuring' of the National Economy in the USSR," *Tulane Law Review*, 61 (June 1987), 1383-95.

5831. "Red Metal," *Economist*, 320 (17 Aug. 1991), 73.

5832. Rosefielde, Stephen S., "State-Directed Market Socialism: The Enigma of Gorbachev's Radical Industrial Reforms," *Soviet Union/Union Sovietique*, 16, no. 1 (1989), 1-27.

5833. -----, and Ralph W. Pfouts, "Economic Optimization and Technical Efficiency in Soviet Enterprises Jointly Regulated by Plans and Incentives," *European Economic Review*, 32 (July 1988), 1285-99.

5834. Ryavec, Karl W., "Soviet Economic Mismanagement" (Review Article), *Problems of Communism*, 40, no. 1-2 (Jan-Apr. 1991), 150-54.

5835. Sagers, Matthew J., "The Aluminum Industry in the Former USSR in 1992," *Post-Soviet Geography*, 33, no. 9 (Nov. 1992), 591-601.

5836. -----, "The Energy Industries of the Former USSR: A Mid-Year Survey," *Post-Soviet Geography*, 34, no. 6 (June 1993), 341-418.

5837. -----, "News Notes," *Soviet Geography*, 31, no. 3 (Mar. 1990), 224-34; no. 5 (May 1990), 388-99; no. 6 (June 1990), 469-75; no. 10 (Dec. 1990), 770-75.

5838. -----, "Regional Industrial Structures and Economic Prospects in the Former USSR," *Post-Soviet Geography*, 33, no. 8 (Oct. 1992), 487-515.

5839. -----, "The Soviet Industrial Modernization Program in the Petroleum Refining Industry, 1986-1990," *Soviet Geography*, 28, no. 5 (May 1987), 315-29.

5840. -----, and Valeriy Kryuchkov, "The Hydrocarbon Processing Industry in West Siberia," *Post-Soviet Geography*, 34, no. 2 (Feb. 1993), 127-52.

5841. Sanjian, A. S., "Constraints on Modernization: The Case of Administrative Theory in the USSR," *Comparative Politics*, 18 (Jan. 1986), 193-210.

5842. "The Soviet Chemical Industry and the Gorbachev Reforms," *Chemical and Engineering News*, 66, no. 3 (18 Jan. 1987), 28ff.

5843. Spagat, Michael, "RSFSR Asserts Autonomy in Enterprise Law That Discards Soviet Ideology," *SEEL: Soviet and East European Law*, 2, no. 1 (Feb. 1991), 7ff.

5844. -----, "USSR Fundamental Principles of Denationalization and Privatization of Enterprises," *SEEL: Soviet and East European Law*, 2, no. 6 (Aug. 1991), 10-12.

5845. "Soviet Restructuring Yields New State and Industry Aviation Agencies," *Aviation Week & Space Technology*, 135, no. 19 (11 Nov. 1991), 21.

5846. "Soviets Plan Dramatic Chemical Sector Growth," *Business International*, 36, no. 34 (28 Aug. 1989), 264.

5847. Stokes, Bruce, "Soviet Oil Not a Salve," *National Journal*, 23, no. 46 (16 Nov. 1991), 2809-12.

5848. Thornton, Judith, "Chernobyl' and Soviet Energy," *Problems of Communism*, 35, no. 6 (Nov-Dec. 1986), 1-16.

5849. -----, "Soviet Electric Power After Chernobyl': Economic Consequences and Options," *Soviet Economy*, 2, no. 2 (Apr-June 1986), 131-79.

5850. Tiagunenko, A., "Big Things for Small Enterprises," *Problems of Economics*, 34, no. 12 (Apr. 1992), 65-77.

5851. Tomarchio, Jack Thomas, "New Hope for the High-Technology and Defense Industries: Eastern Europe as the Back Door into the EC Market," *Journal of European Business*, 2, no. 3 (Jan-Feb. 1991), 42-46.

5852. Toumanoff, Peter G., "An Investigation of Soviet Industrial Reform," *Soviet Union/ Union Sovietique*, 12, no. 2 (1985), 152-60.

5853. -----, "The Use of Production Functions to Investigate Soviet Industrial Reform," *Comparative Economic Studies*, 29, no. 3 (Fall 1987), 94-111.

5854. "Trouble in Barrels: Russia's Oil Industry," *Economist*, 321 (21 Dec. 1991), 84.

5855. Velocci, Anthony L., Jr., "Soviets, U.S. Aerospace Firms Explore Ventures to Privatize USSR Industries," *Aviation Week & Space Technology*, 135, no. 7 (19 Aug. 1991), 56-57.

5856. "Volga Dnepr, Heavy Lift Form Cargo Charter Joint Venture," *Aviation Week & Space Technology*, 135, no. 14 (7 Oct. 1991), 32.

5857. "Western Companies Aid Soviets in $10-Billion ATC Modernization," *Aviation Week & Space Technology*, 134, no. 13 (1 Apr. 1991), 46-47.

5858. Wilson, David C., "The Search for Profit in a USSR Refinery Leads to a Product Switch and Less Cost," *Petroleum Review*, 41, no. 489 (Oct. 1987), 22-23.

5859. -----, "Serious Implications in Oil Shortfall in the USSR," *Petroleum Review*, 40, no. 468 (Jan. 1986), 18-19.

5860. Yergin, Daniel, "The Next Oil Surprise," *New York Times Magazine* (2 Dec. 1990), 8ff.

5861. Zaslow, David, "Trucking in the Soviet Economy," *Soviet Geography*, 31, no. 3 (Mar. 1990), 173-94.

XXVI. Labor, Trade Unions, Strikes

BOOKS

5862. Alexeev, Michael B., and Cliffford V. Gaddy, *Trends in Wage and Income Distribution under Gorbachev: Analysis of New Soviet Data* (Bala Cynwyd, PA: WEFA Group, 1991).

5863. Arnot, Bob, *Controlling Soviet Labour: Experimental Change from Brezhnev to Gorbachev* (Armonk, NY: M. E. Sharpe, 1988).

5864. Connor, Walter D., *The Accidental Proletariat: Workers, Politics and Crisis in Gorbachev's Russia* (Princeton: Princeton University Press, 1991).

5865. Cook, Linda, *The Soviet Social Contract and Why It Failed: Welfare Policy and Worker Politics from Brezhnev to Yeltsin* (Cambridge, MA: Harvard University Press, 1993).

5866. Filtzer, Donald, *Soviet Workers and the Collapse of Perestroika: The Soviet Labour Process and Gorbachev's Reforms, 1985-1991* (New York: Cambridge University Press, 1994).

5867. Friedgut, Theodore H., and Lewis H. Siegelbaum, *The Soviet Miners' Strike, July 1989: Perestroika from Below*, The Carl Beck Papers in Russian and East European Studies, no. 804 (Pittsburgh: University of Pittsburgh Center for Russian and East European Studies, 1990).

5868. Gaddy, Clifford G., *The Labor Market and the Second Economy in the Soviet Union* (Bala Cynwyd, PA: WEFA Group, 1991).

5869. Grancelli, Bruno, *Soviet Management and Labor Relations* (Winchester, MA: Allen & Unwin, 1988).

5870. Jones, Anthony, ed., *Professions and the State: Expertise and Autonomy in the Soviet Union and Eastern Europe* (Philadelphia: Temple University Press, 1991).

5871. Keremetsky, Jacob, and John Logue, *Perestroika: Privatization and Worker Ownership in the USSR* (Kent, OH: Kent Popular Press, 1991).

5872. Malle, Silvana, *Employment Planning in the Soviet Union: Continuity and Change* (New York: St. Martin's Press, 1990).

5873. Mandel, David, *Perestroika and the Soviet People: Rebirth of the Labour Movement* (Montreal: Black Rose, 1991).

5874. Milibank, Ralph, Leo Panitch and John Saville, eds., *Socialist Register 1989* (London: Merlin Press, 1989), 194-221.

5875. Oxenstierna, Susanne, *From Labour Shortage to Unemployment? The Soviet Labour Market in the 1980s* (Stockholm: Gotab, distributed by Almqvist and Wicksell International, 1990).

5876. Porket, J. L., *Work, Employment and Unemployment in the Soviet Union* (New York: St. Martin's Press, 1989).

5877. Silverman, Bertram, Robert Vogt and Murray Yanowitch, eds., *Double Shift: Transforming Work in Postsocialist and Postindustrial Societies: A U.S.-Post Soviet Dialogue* (Armonk, NY: M. E. Sharpe, 1992).

5878. Standing, Guy, ed., *In Search of Flexibility: The New Soviet Labour Market* (Geneva: International Labour Office, 1991).

5879. Teague, Elizabeth, *Solidarity and the Soviet Workers* (London: Croom Helm, 1988).

ARTICLES

5880. Aganbegyan, Abel, "What Perestroika Means for Soviet Enterprises," *International Labour Review*, 128, no. 1 (1989), 85-101.

5881. "Alternative Trade Unions: Possibilities and Reality," *Soviet Sociology*, 30, no. 1 (Jan-Feb. 1991), 54-84.

5882. Antosenkov, E. G., "Current Employment Problems in the Soviet Economy and Means of Resolving Them," *Problems of Economics*, 34, no. 9 (Jan. 1992), 15-28.

5883. Ashwin, Sarah, "The 1991 Miners' Strike: New Departures in the Independent Workers' Movement," *Report on the USSR*, 3, no. 33 (16 Aug. 1991), 1-7.

5884. Bestuzhev-Lada, Igor, "A Soviet Perspective: Unemployment without Unemployed?" *Contemporary Review*, 258, no. 1505 (Jan. 1991), 281-84.

5885. Block, K. P., "The Legal Status of Strikes in the U.S.S.R.," *Comparative Labor Law Journal*, 12 (Winter 1991), 133-50.

5886. Bocharov, Gennadii, "Working While They Strike," *Soviet Law and Government*, 28, no. 4 (Spring 1990), 93-94.

5887. Bova, Russell, "Informal Activity and the Soviet Working Class," *Nationalities Papers*, 28, no. 2 (Fall 1990), 42-49.

5888. -----, "On *Perestroyka*: The Role of Workplace Participation," *Problems of Communism*, 36, no. 4 (July-Aug. 1987), 76-86.

5889. Brand, Horst, "*Perestroika* and Its Impact on the Soviet Labor Market," *Monthly Labor Review*, 114, no. 12 (Dec. 1991), 38-45.

5890. Britvin, V. G., "Strikes at Enterprises from the Standpoint of Working People," *Soviet Sociology*, 30, no. 3 (May-June 1991), 49-58.

5891. Burawoy, Michael, and Pavel Krotov, "The Soviet Transition from Socialism to Capitalism: Worker Control and Economic Bargaining in the Wood Industry," *American Sociological Review*, 57, no. 1 (Feb. 1992), 16-38.

5892. Burzynska, Grazyna, "The Kuzbas Miners Seize Their Future: Interview with Alojzy Pietrzyk," *Uncaptive Minds*, 4, no. 3 (Fall 1991), 63-66.

5893. Chapman, Janet G., "Gorbachev's Wage Reform," *Soviet Economy*, 4, no. 4 (Oct-Dec. 1988), 338-65.

5894. Cook, Linda J., "Brezhnev's `Social Contract' and Gorbachev's Reforms," *Soviet Studies*, 44, no. 1 (Jan. 1992), 37-56.

5895. -----, "Lessons of the Soviet Coal Miners' Strike of Summer 1989," *Harriman Institute Forum*, 4, no. 3 (Mar. 1991).

5896. Corneo, Giacomo G., "Job Rights and Labor Productivity in a Soviet-Type Economy," *Journal of Comparative Economics*, 17, no. 1 (Mar. 1993), 113-28.

5897. Crow, Suzanne, "Importing and Exporting Labor in the Soviet Union," *Report on the USSR*, 2, no. 28 (13 July 1990), 8-10.

5898. Egorov, Vladislav, "The Reform of Soviet Labor Legislation: Problems and Prospects," *Columbia Journal of Transnational Law*, 28, no. 1 (Spring 1990), 263-75.

5899. "Et Tu, Minsk?" *Economist*, 319 (20 Apr. 1991), 49-50.

5900. "An Exchange on Unemployment in Central Asia," *Journal of Soviet Nationalities*, 1, no. 2 (Summer 1990), 127-29.

5901. Friedgut, Theodore, and Lewis Siegelbaum, "Perestroika from Below: The Soviet Miners' Strike and Its Aftermath," *New Left Review*, no. 181 (May-June 1990), 5-32.

5902. Gaddy, Clifford, "The Soviet Miners' Strike," *Brookings Review*, 9, no. 3 (Summer 1991), 54.

5903. Gagnon, V. P., Jr., "Gorbachev and the Collective Contract Brigade," *Soviet Studies*, 39, no. 1 (Jan. 1987), 1-23.

5904. Gerchikov, V. I., "The Human Factor and Industrial Democracy," *Soviet Sociology*, 29, no. 2 (Mar-Apr. 1990), 41-61.

5905. -----, "New Social Problems of Enterprises," *Problems of Economics*, 34, no. 12 (Apr. 1992), 21-29.

5906. Gimpel'son, V. E., and V. S. Magun, "Waiting for Change: Workers' Views on the Situation at Industrial Enterprises," *Soviet Sociology*, 29, no. 6 (Nov-Dec. 1990), 6-27.

5907. Girnius, Saulius, "Lithuania's Union of Workers," *Report on the USSR*, 3, no. 17 (26 Apr. 1991), 26-28.

5908. "Glasnost and Unemployment: The Labour Pains of Perestroika," *Economist*, 305 (26 Dec. 1987), 15-19.

5909. Hauslohner, Peter, "Democratization `From the Middle Out': Soviet Trade Unions and Perestroika," *Harriman Institute Forum*, 1, no. 10 (Oct. 1988).

5910. -----, "Gorbachev's Social Contract," *Soviet Economy*, 3, no. 1 (Jan-Mar. 1987), 54-89.

5911. Hausmaninger, H., "Soviet Parasites-Evading the Constitutional Duty to Work," *Texas International Law Journal*, 21 (Summer 1986), 425-40.

5912. Jacobs, Margot, "The Hard Life of Soviet Miners," *Report on the USSR*, 2, no. 32 (10 Aug. 1990), 10-12.

5913. Kerr, Richard A., "Hunger Strike at Kamchatka Institute," *Science*, 254 (8 Nov. 1991), 793.

5914. Kiss, Ilona, "The Coal Miners: Spearhead of the Soviet Working Class," *Uncaptive Minds*, 3, no. 4 (Aug-Oct. 1990), 42-44.

5915. Klebnikov, P., "Good-bye, Gorbachev?" *Forbes*, 147 (15 Apr. 1991), 40-41.

5916. Koenker, Diane P., "Strike's Back: Worker Power in the `Workers' State'," *New Republic* (23 Oct. 1989), 14-16.

5917. Komisar, Lucy, "Soviet Workers Organize," *Progressive*, 54, no. 1 (Jan. 1990), 14.

5918. Kondracke, Morton, "Life in Hell," *New Republic* (24 June 1991), 20.

5919. Kosaev, A., "The Current Labor Market in the USSR: Problems of Equilibrium," *Problems of Economics*, 35, no. 1 (May 1992), 38-46.

5920. Kostakov, Vladimir, "Labor Problems in Light of Perestroika," *Soviet Economy*, 4, no. 1 (Jan-Mar. 1988), 95-101.

5921. Kotliar, A., "Current Employment Problems," *Problems of Economic Transition*, 35, no. 2 (June 1992), 30-45.

5922. Kravchenko, A. I., chairman, "Alternative Trade Unions: Possibilities and Realities (An Editorial Roundtable Discussion)," *Soviet Review*, 32, no. 2 (Mar-Apr. 1991), 21-51.

5923. Kubas', G. V., "Workers' Committees in the Kuzbass," *Soviet Sociology*, 30, no. 3 (May-June 1991), 59-67.

5924. Light, Margot, "Perestroika Isn't Working: The Miners' Strike in Siberia Shows That Gorbachev's Reform Programme Is Failing," *New Statesman and Society*, 2 (28 July 1989), 16-17.

5925. Logue, John, and Dan Bell, "Worker Ownership in Russia," *Dissent*, 39, no. 2 (Spring 1992), 199-204.

5926. MacShane, Denis, "Statist Unions Wither Away," *Nation*, 251 (26 Nov. 1990), 646-47.

5927. Mal'tseva, L. L., and O. N. Puliaeva, "What Led to the Strike?" *Soviet Sociology*, 30, no. 3 (May-June 1991), 41-48.

5928. Mamutov, V. K., "The Miners' Strike and Improving Economic Legislation," *Soviet Law and Government*, 30, no. 1 (Summer 1991), 80-92.

5929. Mandel, David, "Perestroika and the Working Class," *Against the Current* (May-June 1989), 22-31.

5930. Manevich, E., "Wages Under Conditions of a Market Economy," *Problems of Economics*, 34, no. 12 (Apr. 1992), 6-20.

5931. Marcus, N., "What's In It For Me, Comrade?" *Mother Jones*, 14 (Oct. 1988), 26ff.

5932. Marples, David, "The Background of the Coal Strike on July 11," *Report on the USSR*, 2, no. 30 (27 July 1990), 15-17.

5933. -----. "No Soap, Say Striking Soviet Miners," *Bulletin of the Atomic Scientists*, 45, no. 10 (1989), 38-40.

5934. Mihalisko, Kathleen, "Workers and Soviet Power: Notes from Minsk," *Report on the USSR*, 3, no. 27 (5 July 1991), 15-21.

5935. -----, "The Soviet Labor Movement: The Coalminers' Strike of 1989," *Politics & Society*, 18, no. 3 (Sept. 1990), 381-404.

5936. Moses, Joel C., "Consensus and Conflict in Soviet Labor Policy: The Reformist Alternative," *Soviet Union/Union Sovietique*, 13, no. 3 (1986), 301-47.

5937. "Nothing to Eat But His Words: Mikhail Gorbachev," *Economist*, 313 (7 Oct. 1989), 56ff.

5938. Ollman, Bertell, "The Regency of the Proletariat in Crisis: A Job for Perestroika," *PS*, 24 (Sept. 1991), 456-60.

5939. Panitch, Leo, and Sam Gindin, "Soviet Workers: A New Beginning?" *Monthly Review*, 42, no. 11 (Apr. 1991), 17-35.

5940. Penn, Dan, "Trade Unions' Rights Widened in USSR Law," *SEEL: Soviet and East European Law*, 2, no. 32 (Mar. 1991), 6ff.

5941. Peterson, D. J., "New Data Published on Employment and Unemployment in the USSR," *Report on the USSR*, 2, no. 1 (5 Jan. 1990), 3-5.

5942. Plokker, Karin, "The Development of Individual and Cooperative Labour Activity in the Soviet Union," *Soviet Studies*, 42, no. 3 (July 1990), 403-28.

5943. Rakitskii, B., "Specific Historical Peculiarities of the Formation of a Labor Market in the USSR," *Problems of Economics*, 35, no. 1 (May 1992), 16-37.

5944. Rudyk, E., "The Western Experience of Industrial Democracy and Its Significance for the USSR," *Problems of Economics*, 34, no. 9 (Jan. 1992), 37-47.

5945. Rutland, Peter, "Labor Unrest and Movements in 1989 and 1990," *Soviet Economy*, 6, no. 4 (Oct-Dec. 1990), 345-84.

5946. Shkira, A. D., "The Employment Problem in the USSR During the Transition to a Market Economy," *Problems of Economics*, 34, no. 9 (Jan. 1992), 29-36.

5947. Shlapentokh, Vladimir, "Workers' Involvement in the Soviet Union: From Lenin to Gorbachev," *Work and Occupations: An International Sociological Journal*, 15, no. 4 (Nov. 1988), 449-67.

5948. Shokhin, A., "The Labor Market in the USSR in the Transition Period," *Problems of Economics*, 35, no. 1 (May 1992), 5-15.

5949. Siegelbaum, Lewis H., "Behind the Soviet Miners' Strike: `We Haven't Seen *Perestroika*'," *Nation* (23 Oct. 1989), 451ff.

5950. -----, "Labor Pains in the USSR," *Nation*, 252 (27 May 1991), 693-94.

5951. Sikorski, Radek, "Notes from Underground," *National Review*, 43 (29 Apr. 1991), 32-33.

5952. "The Soviet Union's Wasted Workers," *Economist*, 319 (15 June 1991), 63.

5953. "Strikes in the USSR: A New Social Reality (A Roundtable Discussion)," *Soviet Sociology*, 29, no. 2 (Mar-Apr. 1990), 74-92.

5954. Sziraczki, Gyorgy, "Employment Policy and Labour Market in Transition: From Labour Shortage to Unemployment," *Soviet Studies*, 42, no. 4 (Oct. 1990), 701-22.

5955. Teague, Elizabeth, "Perestroika and the Soviet Worker," *Government and Opposition*, 25, no. 2 (Spring 1990), 191-211.

5956. -----, "Soviet Workers Find a Voice," *Report on the USSR*, 2, no. 28 (13 July 1990), 13-17.

5957. -----, "Tackling the Problem of Unemployment," *Report on the USSR*, 3, no. 45 (8 Nov. 1991), 1-7.

5958. -----, "Workers' Reactions to *Perestroika* and *Glasnost*," *Journal of Communist Studies*, 9, no. 1 (Mar. 1993), 163-72.

5959. -----, "Worker Unrest in 1989," *Report on the USSR*, 2, no. 4 (26 Jan, 1990), 12-14.

5960. -----, and Philip Hanson, "Most Soviet Strikes Politically Motivated," *Report on the USSR*, 2, no. 34 (24 Aug. 1990), 1-2.

5961. Temkina, Anna A., "The Workers' Movement in Leningrad, 1980-1991," *Soviet Studies*, 44, no. 2 (1992), 209-36.

5962. Thorne, Ludmilla, "What Soviet Strikers Want," *Freedom at Issue*, no. 113 (Mar-Apr. 1990), 25-29.

5963. Tidmarsh, Kyril, "Russia's Work Ethic," *Foreign Affairs*, 72, no. 2 (Spring 1993), 67-77.

5964. "Trade Unions in Post-Communist Society: The USSR Learns from Eastern Europe's Experience," *Report on the USSR*, 3, no. 41 (11 Oct. 1991), 16-22.

5965. "Undermined," *Economist*, 318 (30 Mar. 1991), 45.

5966. Vaghin, M., "The Working Man Coming Into His Own," *World Marxist Review*, 32, no. 1 (Jan. 1989), 10-11.

5967. Vasil'ev, Andrei, and Maksim Krans, "The Miners' Alternative: A Few Questions for Reflection," *Soviet Law and Government*, 30, no. 2 (Fall 1991), 45-61.

5968. Voronitsyn, Sergei, "The Soviet Working Class-The Silent Majority?" *Report on the USSR*, 1, no. 28 (14 July 1989), 8-9.

5969. Werth, Nicholas, "In the Years of Perestroika: Workers' Actions, Workers' Politics in the USSR," *Dissent*, 39, no. 4 (Fall 1992), 498-510.

5970. "The Workers Rattle Their Chains," *Economist*, 312 (22 July 1989), 35-36.

5971. Yanaev, Gennadi I., "Soviet Restructuring: The Position and Role of the Trade Unions," *International Labour Review*, 126, no. 6 (Nov-Dec. 1987), 703-13.

5972. Zaslavskaia, T. I., and V. L. Kosmarskii, "Phenomena of the Labor Market and Public Opinion: Some Features of the Current Phase," *Problems of Economics*, 34, no. 9 (Jan. 1992), 6-14.

XXVII. Law

BOOKS

5973. Barry, Donald D., et al., eds., *Law and the Gorbachev Era: Essays in Honor of Dietrich Andre Loeber* (Norwell, MA: Kluwer Academic Publishers, 1988).

5974. -----, ed., *Toward the "Rule of Law" in Russia? Political and Legal Reform in the Transition Period* (Armonk, NY: M. E. Sharpe, 1992).

5975. Block, Kevin, *Depoliticizing Ownership: An Examination of the Property Reform Debate and the New Law on Ownership in the USSR* (Bala Cynwyd, PA: WEFA Group, 1991).

5976. Boguslavskii, A. M., *Private International Law: The Soviet Approach* (Boston: Martinus Nijhoff, 1988).

5977. Booth, Ken, *Law, Force and Diplomacy at Sea* (London: Allen & Unwin, 1985).

5978. Braginsky, M., *The Soviet State as a Subject of Civil Law*

(Moscow: Foreign Languages Publishing House, 1988).

5979. Busuttil, James J., *Toward the Rule of Law: Soviet Legal Reform and Human Rights under Perestroika* (New York: Helsinki Watch Committee, 1989).

5980. Butler, William E., *Arbitration in the Soviet Union* (New York: Oceana Publications, 1989).

5981. -----, *Perestroika and International Law* (Boston: M. Nijhoff, 1990).

5982. -----, *Soviet Law*, 2nd ed. (London: Butterworth & Co., Ltd., 1988).

5983. -----, ed., *Perestroika and the Rule of Law: Anglo-American and Soviet Perspectives* (London: Tauris, 1991).

5984. Carty, Anthony, and Gennady Danilenko, eds., *Perestroika and International Law: Current Anglo-Soviet Approaches to International Law* (Edinburgh: Edinburgh University Press, 1990).

5985. Feldbrugge, F. J. M., *The Emancipation of Soviet Law* (Dordrecht: Martinus Nijhoff, distributed by Kluwer Academic Publishers Group, 1994).

5986. Ginsburgs, George, *et al.*, eds., *Soviet Administrative Law: Theory and Policy* (Boston: Martinus Nijhoff, distributed by Kluwer Academic Publishers, 1989).

5987. Goldman, Stuart D., *The New Soviet Legislature* (Washington, DC: Library of Congress, Congressional Research Service, 1990).

5988. Grzybowski, Kazimierz, *Soviet International Law and World Economic Order* (Durham, NC: Duke University Press, 1987).

5989. Huskey, Eugene, ed., *Executive Power and Soviet Politics: The Rise and Decline of the Soviet State* (Armonk, NY: M. E. Sharpe, 1992).

5990. Ioffe, Olimpiad S., and Peter B. Maggs, *The Soviet Economic System: A Legal Analysis* (Boulder, CO: Westview Press, 1987).

5991. Kavass, Igor I., *Gorbachev's Law: A Bibliographic Survey of English Writings on Soviet Legal Developments, 1987-1990* (Buffalo: William S. Hein & Co., 1991).

5992. Kim, Julie, *USSR Supreme Soviet: Major Legislation* (Washington, DC: Library of Congress, Congressional Research Service, 1990).

5993. Matthews, Mervyn, ed., *Party, State and Citizen in the Soviet Union: A Collection of Documents* (Armonk, NY: M. E. Sharpe, 1989).

5994. Rand, Robert, *Comrade Lawyer: Inside Soviet Justice in an Era of Reform* (Boulder, CO: Westview Press, 1991).

5995. Sadikov, O. N., ed., *Soviet Civil Law* (Armonk, NY: M. E. Sharpe, 1988).

5996. Schmidt, Albert J., ed., *The Impact of Perestroika on Soviet Law* (Norwell, MA: Kluwer Academic, 1990).

5997. Sharlet, Robert, *Soviet Constitutional Crisis: From De-Stalinization to Disintegration* (Armonk, NY: M. E. Sharpe, 1992).

5998. Stephan, Paul B., III, *Soviet Economic Law: The Paradox of Perestroyka*, The Carl Beck Papers in Russian and East European Studies, no. 805 (Pittsburgh: University of Pittsburgh Center for Russian and East European Studies, 1990).

5999. Thornburgh, Dick, *The Rule of Law in the Soviet Union: A Necessary Framework for Democratic Reform* (Washington, DC: Heritage Foundation, 1990).

ARTICLES

6000. "Agora: New Thinking by Soviet Scholars," *American Journal of International Law*, 83, no. 3 (July 1989), 494-518.

6001. Arzt, Donna E., "The New Soviet Emigration Law Revisited: Implementation and Compliance with Other Laws," *Soviet Jewish Affairs*, 18, no. 1 (Spring 1988), 17-28.

6002. Aug, V. J., Jr., "Mission to Moscow: Bringing the Rule of Law to the Russian People," *Federal Bar News and Journal*, 39 (Nov-Dec. 1992), 572-78.

6003. Bazyler, M. J., "Soviet Family Law," *University of Kansas Law Review*, 39 (Fall 1990), 125-74.

6004. Belousovitch, Igor N., "The New Soviet Parliament: Process, Procedures, and Legislative Priority," *Cornell International Law Journal*, 23, no. 2 (1990), 275-86.

6005. "Berne-ing the Soviet Copyright Codes: Will the U.S.S.R. Alter Its Copyright Laws to Comply with the Berne Convention?" *Dickinson Journal of International Law*, 8 (Spring 1990), 395-414.

6006. Boguslavskii, M. M., "The Legal Status of Free Economic Zones in the USSR," *Soviet Law and Government*, 29, no. 4 (Spring 1991), 78-91.

6007. Boiter, Albert, "Drafting a Freedom of Conscience Law," *Columbia Journal of Transnational Law*, 28, no. 1 (Spring 1990), 157-87.

6008. Bregman, Randy, and Dorothy C. Lawrence, "New Developments in Soviet Property Law," *Columbia Journal of Transnational Law*, 28, no. 1 (Spring 1990), 189-206.

6009. Brovkin, Vladimir N., "The Politics of Constitutional Reform: The New Power Structure and the Role of the Party," *Cornell International Law Journal*, 23, no. 2 (1990), 323-40.

6010. Brownfield, Allan C., "The Daniloff Case: A Timely Reminder of the Nature of the Soviet System," *World & I*, 1, no. 11 (Nov. 1986), 134-37.

6011. Brzezinski, Mark F., "Toward `Constitutionalism' in Russia: The Russian Constitutional Court," *International and Comparative Law Quarterly*, 42, no. 3 (July 1993), 673-89.

6012. Bungs, Dzintra, "New USSR Minister of Internal Affairs,"

Report on the USSR, 2, no. 50 (14 Dec. 1990), 8-9.

6013. Burgess, Geoff, and Sean Garrison, "RSFSR Draft Law on Commodities Markets and Stock Exchanges," *SEEL: Soviet and East European Law*, 1, no. 8 (Oct. 1990), 9-10.

6014. Burrage, Michael, "*Advokatura*: In Search of Professionalism and Pluralism in Moscow and Leningrad," *Law and Social Inquiry*, 15, no. 3 (1990), 433-78.

6015. Butler, William E., "International Law, Foreign Policy, and the Gorbachev Style," *Journal of International Affairs*, 42 (Spring 1989), 363-75.

6016. -----, "Legal Reform in the Soviet Union," *Harriman Institute Forum*, 1, no. 9 (Sept. 1988), 1-8.

6017. -----, "Soviet Union: The Transition to the Gorbachev Era," *Journal of Family Law*, 25 (1986-87), 237-43.

6018. Cameron, George D., III, "A Comparison of U.S. and Soviet Laws on the Sale of Goods," *Journal of Social, Political and Economic Studies*, 11, no. 2 (Summer 1986), 237-51.

6019. Coppieters, Bruno, "Conscientious Objection Policies and the Soviet National Ethos," *Journal of Communist Studies*, 8, no. 4 (Dec. 1992), 186-209.

6020. "Crisis in the USSR: Are the Constitutional and Legislative Changes Enough? Roundtable Discussion," *Cornell International Law Journal*, 23, no. 2 (1990), 377-98.

6021. "Czech Law Privatizes Law Practice," *SEEL: Soviet and East European Law*, 1, no. 5 (June-July 1990), 10.

6022. Denber, Rachel, "Soviet Judges Guaranteed Independence," *SEEL: Soviet and East European Law*, 1, no. 1 (Feb. 1990), 1ff.

6023. De Sanctis, Sergio, "Legal and Criminal Law Reform: Another Failure of *Perestroika?*" *Journal of Communist Studies*, 9, no. 1 (Mar. 1993), 150-62.

6024. Ebke, Werner F., "Legal Implications of Germany's Unification," *International Lawyer*, 24, no. 4 (Winter 1990), 1130-32.

6025. Ericson, Richard E., "New Enterprise Law," *SEEL: Soviet and East European Law*, 1, no. 6 (Aug. 1990), 1ff.

6026. "Fear: Confessions of a Well-Known Legal Expert Who Has Criticized the Draft Law on the KGB," *Soviet Law and Government*, 30, no. 2 (Fall 1991), 88ff.

6027. Feldbrugge, F. J. M., "The New Soviet Law on Emigration," *Soviet Jewish Affairs*, 17, no. 1 (Spring 1987), 9-24.

6028. Feinberg, G., "Restructuring Justice in the Shadow of the Kremlin: A Journey from Rhetoric to Reason," *Judicature*, 72 (Apr-May 1989), 348-58.

6029. Feinrider, Martin, "The Strategic Defense Initiative and International Law," *Fletcher Forum*, 10, no. 1 (Winter 1986), 19-32.

6030. Feofanov, Iurii, "A Return to Origins: Reflections on Power and Law," *Soviet Law and Government*, 29, no. 3 (Winter 1990-91), 15-52.

6031. Fleishman, Lana C., "The Empire Strikes Back: The Influence of the United States Motion Picture Industry on Russian Copyright Law," *Cornell International Law Journal*, 26, no. 1 (1993), 189-238.

6032. Fletcher, G. P., "Searching for the Rule of Law in the Wake of Communism," *Brigham Young University Law Review* (1992), 145-64.

6033. Foster, F. H., "Procedure as a Guarantee of Democracy: The Legacy of the Perestroika Parliament," *Vanderbilt Journal of Transnational Law*, 26, no. 1 (Apr. 1993), 1-109.

6034. Frenkel, William, "RSFSR Banking Legislation Could Provoke Conflict with USSR," *SEEL: Soviet and East European Law*, 2, no. 3 (Apr-May 1991), 7-8.

6035. -----, "Soviet Legislation Sanctions Restructuring of Banking," *SEEL: Soviet and East European Law*, 2, no. 1 (Feb. 1991), 5ff.

6036. -----, "USSR and RSFSR Company Laws: A Comparison," *SEEL: Soviet and East European Law*, 2, no. 2 (Mar. 1991), 10.

6037. Gardner, Anthony, "The Draft Soviet Stock Exchange Law," *SEEL: Soviet and East European Law*, 2, no. 8 (Oct. 1991), 4ff.

6038. Ginsburgs, George, "Extradition in the USSR's Treaties on Legal Assistance with Non-'Socialist' States," *Canadian Yearbook of International Law*, no. 29 (1991), 92-141.

6039. -----, "Soviet Citizenship Law Aims to Strengthen Federal Union," *SEEL: Soviet and East European Law*, 1, no. 6 (Aug. 1990), 10.

6040. "The Glasnost Track: Are You Ready, Comrade Associate?" *Human Rights*, 16 (Spring 1989), 28-30.

6041. Glukhovsky, Mikhail, "Is Russia Losing the Legal Battle?" *Delovie Lyudi*, no. 40 (Dec. 1993), 18-19.

6042. Goble, Paul, "Draconian State of Emergency Law," *Report on the USSR*, 2, no. 18 (4 May 1990), 8-9.

6043. -----, "Federalism and Human Rights in the Soviet Union," *Cornell International Law Journal*, 23, no. 2 (1990), 399ff.

6044. Goldberg, S. B., "A More Perfect Union," *American Bar Association Journal*, 76 (Oct. 1990), 58ff.; (Nov. 1990), 70-75; (Dec. 1990), 70-74.

6045. Gorbachev, Mikhail S., "The Rule of Law," *Stanford Journal of International Law*, 28 (Spring 1992), 477-84.

6046. Grazin, Igor, "The Problems of Federalism in the Former Soviet Union: The Parallels with Pre-Civil War America," *Journal of Legislation*, 18, no. 1 (1992), 69-86.

6047. -----, "The Rule of Law, But of Which Law? The Natural and Positive Law in Post-Communist Transformations," *John Marshall Law Review*, 26 (Spring 1993), 719-37.

6048. Griffin, Andrew, "Supreme Soviet Slaps New Restrictions on Cooperatives," *SEEL: Soviet and East European Law*, 1, no. 1 (Feb. 1990), 1ff.

6049. -----, "USSR Committee on Constitutional Oversight Issues Its First Opinions," *SEEL: Soviet and East European Law*, 1, no. 9 (Nov. 1990), 9.

6050. -----, and Brenda Horrigan, "USSR Law Sets out Conditions for Labor Strikes," *SEEL: Soviet and East European Law*, 1, no. 1 (Feb. 1990), 3ff.

6051. Hanson, Philip, "Reinventing the Law of Contract," *Report on the USSR*, 3, no. 30 (26 July 1991), 12-14.

6052. Hartwig, M., "The Institutionalization of the Rule of Law: The Establishment of Constitutional Courts in the Eastern European Countries," *American University Journal of International Law and Policy*, 7 (Spring 1992), 449-70.

6053. Hausmaninger, Herbert, "The Committee of Constitutional Supervision of the USSR," *Cornell International Law Journal*, 23, no. 2 (1990), 287-322.

6054. -----, "Soviet Parasites-Evading the Constitutional Duty to Work," *Texas International Law Journal*, 21, no. 3 (Summer 1986), 425-40.

6055. Hazard, John N., "Gorbachev's Attack on Stalin's Etatisation of Ownership," *Columbia Journal of Transnational Law*, 28, no. 1 (Spring 1990), 207-23.

6056. -----, "Presidential Decree Forces USSR Local Authorities to Conclude State Contracts," *SEEL: Soviet and East European Law*, 1, no. 8 (Oct. 1990), 6.

6057. -----, "The Soviet Legislative Process," *SEEL: Soviet and East European Law*, 1, no. 5 (June-July 1990), 6.

6058. Hober, Kaj, "The Russian Law on Foreign Investments," *SEEL: Soviet and East European Law*, 2, no. 7 (Sept. 1991), 5-8.

6059. -----, "Soviet Company Law Reform, Quo Vadis?" *SEEL: Soviet and East European Law*, 1, no. 7 (Sept. 1990), 6ff.

6060. Holland, Mary, "Legal Reform in the Soviet Union," *Columbia Journal of Transnational Law*, 28, no. 1 (Spring 1990), 1-2.

6061. -----, "Overview of the `Fundamentals of Civil Law of the USSR and the Republics,'1991," *SEEL: Soviet and East European Law*, 2, no. 6 (Aug. 1991), 4-5.

6062. Huskey, Eugene, "Between Citizen and State: The Soviet Bar (Advokatura) Under Gorbachev," *Columbia Journal of Transnational Law*, 28, no. 1 (Spring 1990), 95-116.

6063. -----. "Government Rulemaking as a Brake on Perestroika," *Law and Social Inquiry*, 15, no. 3 (1990), 419-32.

6064. -----, "The Politics of the Soviet Criminal Process: Expanding the Right to Counsel in Pre-Trial Proceedings," *American Journal of Comparative Law*, 34, no. 1 (Winter 1986), 93-112.

6065. Iakovlev, Aleksandr, "Constitutional Socialist Democracy: Dream or Reality?" *Columbia Journal of Transnational Law*, 28,

no. 1 (Spring 1990), 117-32.

6066. "The Jackson-Vanik Amendment to the Trade Act of 1974: Soviet Progress on Emigration Reform Is Insufficient to Merit a Waiver," *Georgetown Immigration Law Journal*, 4 (Fall 1990), 639-79.

6067. Jorgensen-Dahl, Arnfinn, "The Soviet-Norwegian Maritime Disputes in the Arctic: Law and Politics," *Ocean Development and International Law*, 21, no. 4 (1990), 411-30.

6068. Juviler, Peter, "Guaranteeing Human Rights in the Soviet Context," *Columbia Journal of Transnational Law*, 28, no. 1 (Spring 1990), 133-55.

6069. Kampelman, Max M., "The Rule of Law and Free Elections," *World Affairs*, 153, no. 1 (Summer 1990), 13-15.

6070. -----, "The Rule of Law in the Soviet Union," *Freedom at Issue*, no. 111 (Nov-Dec. 1989), 23-26.

6071. Kartashkin, V. A., "Comments from a Soviet Perspective," *Cornell International Law Journal*, 24 (1991), 517-20.

6072. -----, "Human Rights and the Emergence of the State of the Rule of Law in the USSR," *Emory Law Journal*, 40 (Summer 1991), 889-902.

6073. Kempton, Murray, "Soviet Lawyers in New York," *New York Review of Books*, 37 (26 Apr. 1990), 60.

6074. Khazova, O., "USSR: Some Problems of Soviet Family Law," *Journal of Family Law*, 29 (1990-91), 463-70.

6075. Kitchin, William, "The Implications for Judicial Review in the Current Legal Reforms in the Soviet Union," *Policy Studies Journal*, 19, no. 1 (Fall 1990), 96-105.

6076. Klishin, Alexei, "Economic Reform and Contract Law in the USSR," *Columbia Journal of Transnational Law*, 28, no. 1 (Spring 1990), 253-62.

6077. Knight, Amy, "The Future of the KGB," *Problems of Communism*, 39, no. 6 (Nov-Dec. 1990), 20-33.

6078. Knop, Karen, "All Power to the Soviets?" *SEEL: Soviet and East European Law*, 1, no. 4 (May 1990), 8ff.

6079. -----, "Committee Created to Rule on Constitutionality of Laws in the USSR," *SEEL: Soviet and East European Law*, 1, no. 3 (Apr. 1990), 4.

6080. -----, "The USSR Committee on Constitutional Oversight and the War of Laws," *SEEL: Soviet and East European Law*, 2, no. 3 (Apr-May 1991), 1ff.

6081. Kondracke, Morton M., "Gulag? What Gulag? Moscow's Human Rights Record," *New Republic* (13 Feb. 1989), 9-12.

6082. Kroll, Heidi, "Property Rights and the Soviet Enterprise: Evidence from the Law of Contract," *Journal of Comparative Economics*, 13, no. 1 (Mar. 1989), 115-33.

6083. -----, "Reform and Damages for Breach of Contract in the Soviet Economy," *Soviet Economy*, 5, no. 3 (July-Sept. 1989), 276-97.

6084. Kudryavtsev, Vladimir N., "Towards a Socialist Rule-of-Law State," *Perestroika Annual*, 1 (1988), 109-25.

6085. Kushen, Robert, "The `Ostashvili' Case: Has the Rule of Law Come to the USSR?" *SEEL: Soviet and East European Law*, 1, no. 9 (Nov. 1990), 5ff.

6086. ——, "Soviet Judicial Review of Administrative Action," *SEEL: Soviet and East European Law*, 1, no. 2 (Mar. 1990), 10.

6087. ——, "Soviet Law Sets Out Procedure for Republic Secession," *SEEL: Soviet and East European Law*, 1, no. 4 (May 1990), 9ff.

6088. Lampert, Nicholas, "Criminal Justice and Legal Reform in the Soviet Union," *Soviet Union/Union Sovietique*, 15, no. 1 (1988), 1-29.

6089. Lawrence, W. H., and J. H. Minan, "The Soviet Legal System: Some Personal Impressions of a Trial," *Journal of the Kansas Bar Association*, 58 (Feb. 1989), 31-36.

6090. Lazarev, B. M., "The President of the USSR," *Soviet Law and Government*, 30, no. 1 (Summer 1991), 7-26.

6091. Lee, J., "The Evolution of Cooperative Legislation: A Case Study of Reform in the Soviet Union," *Stanford Journal of International Law*, 27 (Fall 1990), 155-87.

6092. "Legal and Constitutional Change in Russia and the Soviet Union" (Special Issue), *Coexistence*, 30, no. 1 (Mar. 1993), 1-85.

6093. "Legal Reform in the Soviet Union," *Columbia Journal of Transnational Law*, 28 (Spring 1990), 1-300.

6094. Levine, Herbert S., "The Soviet Economy: In Search of Reform," in *Global Security: A Review of Strategic and Economic Issues*, ed. by Barry M. Blechman and Edward N. Luttwak (Boulder, CO: Westview Press, 1987).

6095. Levitsky, Serge L., "Adjusting Law to the Changing Focus of *Perestroika*," *Law and Social Inquiry*, 15, no. 3 (1990), 535-51.

6096. ——, "The Restructuring of *Perestroika*: Pragmatism and Ideology (The Preamble to the Soviet Constitution of 1977 Revisited)," *Cornell International Law Journal*, 23, no. 2 (1990), 227-74.

6097. Lewame, Stephen, "Legal Aspects of Monetary Policy in the Former Soviet Union," *Europe-Asia Studies*, 45, no. 2 (1993), 193-210.

6098. Lipson, Leon, "Piety and Revision: How Will the Mandarins Survive Under the Rule of Law?" *Cornell International Law Journal*, 23, no. 2 (1990), 191-204.

6099. Litman, Gary V., "Reinventing a Law on Inventions: International Aspects of the New Russian Patent Law," *George Washington Journal of International Law and Economics*, 25, no. 1 (1991), 171-226.

6100. Loeber, Dietrich, "Legal Issues Raised by the Dissolution of the USSR," *SEEL: Soviet and East European Law*, 2, no. 9 (Nov-Dec. 1991), 3.

6101. Lomako, Sergei, "Legal Framework for Oil and Gas Development in the USSR," *SEEL: Soviet and East European Law*, 2, no. 3 (Apr-May 1991), 8-9.

6102. Luchterhandt, Otto, "The Human Right of Freedom of Religion and Soviet Law," *Occasional Papers on Religion in Eastern Europe*, 6, no. 2 (Apr. 1986), 79-94.

6103. Ludwikowski, Rett R., "Constitution Making in the Countries of Former Soviet Dominance: Current Development," *Georgia Journal of International and Comparative Law*, 23, no. 2 (1993), 155-268.

6104. Maggs, Peter B., "Choice of Law," *SEEL: Soviet and East European Law*, 2, no. 6 (Aug. 1991), 7-9.

6105. ——, "Constitutional Implications of Changes in Property Rights in the USSR," *Cornell International Law Journal*, 23, no. 2 (1990), 363-76.

6106. ——, "Enforcing the Bill of Rights in the Twilight of the Soviet Union," *University of Illinois Law Review* (1991), 1049-63.

6107. ——, "Intellectual Property," *SEEL: Soviet and East European Law*, 2, no. 6 (Aug. 1991), 6-7.

6108. ——, "Post-Soviet Law: The Case of Intellectual Property Law," *Harriman Institute Forum*, 5, no. 3 (Nov. 1991), 1-9.

6109. ——, "The Restructuring of the Soviet Law of Inventions," *Columbia Journal of Transnational Law*, 28, no. 1 (Spring 1990), 277-89.

6110. ——, "Second Soviet Draft Law on Inventions Published," *SEEL: Soviet and East European Law*, 1, no. 5 (June-July 1990), 7ff.

6111. Magraw, Daniel B., and Theresa Ketler, "Law Relating to Outer Space: A Bibliography, Part II," *International Lawyer*, 20, no. 1 (Winter 1986), 399-421.

6112. Mamiosa, I. E., "The Draft of a New Soviet Patent Law," *European Intellectual Property Review*, 12 (Jan. 1990), 21-27.

6113. Mann, Dawn, "Supreme Soviet Adopts Laws on the Status of People's Deputies," *Report on the USSR*, 2, no. 39 (28 Sept. 1990), 1-4.

6114. ——, "The USSR Constitution: The Electoral System," *Report on the USSR*, 2, no. 5 (2 Feb. 1990), 10-13.

6115. Markovits, Inga, "Law and Glasnost: Some Thoughts About the Future of Judicial Review under Socialism," *Law and Society Review*, 23, no. 3 (1989), 399-447.

6116. "Marxism and the Rule of Law," *Law and Social Inquiry*, 15 (Fall 1990), 633-730.

6117. Matiaszek, Petro, "International Legal Aspects of Ukraine's Claim to the Soviet Nuclear Legacy," *Ukrainian Quarterly*, 49, no. 3 (Fall 1993), 252-93.

6118. Matlock, Jack, "Recent Changes in the `Soviet Union'," *John Marshall Law Review*, 25 (Winter 1992), 295-308.

6119. McWhinney, E., "Contemporary Soviet General Theory of International Law: Reflections on the Tunkin Era," *Canadian Yearbook of International Law*, 25 (1987), 187-217.

6120. -----, "The `New Thinking' in Soviet International Law: Soviet Doctrines and Practice in the Post-Tunkin Era," *Canadian Yearbook of International Law*, 28 (1990), 309-37.

6121. Meerovich, Aleksandr, "Soviet Draft Law on Public Associations Makes Slow Progress," *Report on the USSR*, 2, no. 28 (13 July 1990), 6-8.

6122. Meyer, H. N., "Global Law: The Legacy of Gorbachev," *Human Rights*, 19 (Spring 1992), 7.

6123. Mullerson, Rein, "The Continuity and Succession of States by Reference to the Former USSR and Yugoslavia," *International and Comparative Law Quarterly*, 42, no. 3 (July 1993), 473-93.

6124. Murphy, Michael, "The Russian Anti-Monopoly Law," *SEEL: Soviet and East European Law*, 2, no. 7 (Sept. 1991), 8-11.

6125. "National Law and the Courts: Soviet Union Accepts Jurisdiction of the International Court of Justice," *Human Rights Internet Reporter*, 13, no. 1 (Spring 1989), 70.

6126. Neier, Aryeh, "What Should Be Done about the Guilty?" *New York Review of Books*, 37 (1 Feb. 1990), 32-35.

6127. Newcity, Michael, "Amendments to 1990 Soviet Tax Law Drastically Reduce Tax Rates," *SEEL: Soviet and East European Law*, 2, no. 5 (July 1991), 10.

6128. -----, "New Law Overhauls Soviet Income Tax System," *SEEL: Soviet and East European Law*, 1, no. 5 (June-July 1990), 1-2.

6129. -----, "Perestroika, Private Enterprise and Soviet Tax Policy," *Columbia Journal of Transnational Law*, 28, no. 1 (Spring 1990), 225-52.

6130. -----, "USSR Enterprise Law Attempts to Unify Tax System," *SEEL: Soviet and East European Law*, 1, no. 6 (Aug. 1990), 3ff.

6131. -----, "USSR Tax Decree Seeks to Alleviate Effects of Higher Prices," *SEEL: Soviet and East European Law*, 2, no. 4 (June 1991), 7ff.

6132. "Note: The Doctrine of Separability in Soviet Arbitration Law: An Analysis of Sojuznefteksport v. JOC Oil Co.," *Columbia Journal of Transnational Law*, 28, no. 1 (Spring 1990), 301-28.

6133. Oda, H., "Judicial Review of Administration in the USSR," *Public Law* (Spring 1989), 111-30.

6134. Orland, L., "Soviet Justice in the Gorbachev Era: The 1988 Draft Fundamental Principles of Criminal Legislation," *Connecticut Journal of International Law*, 4 (Winter 1989), 513-76.

6135. Patterson, Carol, "Putting the Laws into Practice," *SEEL: Soviet and East European Law*, 2, no. 2 (Mar. 1991), 10-11.

6136. Pavluk, Jonathan, "The New Soviet Presidency," *SEEL: Soviet and East European Law*, 1, no. 3 (Apr. 1990), 5.

6137. Pechota, Vratislav, ed., "Developments in Foreign and Comparative Law," *Columbia Journal of Transnational Law*, 25, no. 2 (Summer 1987), 483-507, esp. 501-04.

6138. -----, "Soviet Company Law in the Making," *SEEL: Soviet and East European Law*, 1, no. 4 (May 1990), 5.

6139. -----, "The Soviet Union in Transition: Constitutional Developments," *SEEL: Soviet and East Europrean Law*, 2, no. 7 (Sept. 1991), 1-2.

6140. -----, "USSR Creates High Arbitration Court and Arbitral Procedures," *SEEL: Soviet and East European Law*, 2, no. 4 (June 1991), 6-7.

6141. Penn, Dan, "Laws on Religious and Public Organizations to Enhance Citizens' Rights in USSR," *SEEL: Soviet and East European Law*, 1, no. 9 (Nov. 1990), 10-11.

6142. -----, "USSR Emigration Law Enhances Freedom of Movement, Despite Continuing Restrictions," *SEEL: Soviet and East European Law*, 2, no. 5 (July 1991), 7-8.

6143. "Perestroika in Soviet Legal Institutions: A Symposium," *Law and Social Inquiry*, 15 (Summer 1990), 419-551.

6144. "Perspectives on the Legal Perestroika: Soviet Constitutional and Legislative Change. A Symposium," *Cornell International Law Journal*, 23 (1990), 187-404.

6145. Petrukhin, I. L., "Justice and Legality," *Soviet Law and Government*, 27, no. 3 (Winter 1988-89), 19-30.

6146. Pipko, S., and R. Pipko, "Inside the Soviet Bar: A View from the Outside," *International Lawyer*, 21 (Summer 1987), 853-72.

6147. Prins, C., "The New Civil Code of the Soviet Union: Major Changes in the Field of Intellectual Property Rights," *European Intellectual Property Review*, 13 (Oct. 1991), 388-91.

6148. Quigley, John, "Law Reform and the Soviet Courts," *Columbia Journal of Transnational Law*, 28, no. 1 (Spring 1990), 59-75.

6149. -----, "The New Soviet Law on Appeals: Glasnost in the Soviet Courts," *International and Comparative Law Quarterly*, 37 (Spring 1987), 172-77.

6150. -----, "Perestroika and International Law," *American Journal of International Law*, 82, no. 4 (Oct. 1988), 788-97.

6151. -----, "The Soviet `New Thinking' in International Law: An Opening to End the Cold War?" *Wisconsin International Law Journal*, 8 (Fall 1989), 97-122.

6152. -----, "The Soviet Presidency," *American Journal of Comparative Law*, 39, no. 1 (Winter 1991), 67-94.

6153. -----, "The Soviet Union As a State Under the Rule of Law: An Overview," *Cornell International Law Journal*, 23, no. 2 (1990), 205-26.

6154. Reisman, Michael W., "International Law after the Cold War," *American Journal of International Law*, 84, no. 4 (Oct. 1990), 859-66.

6155. "Release of Political Prisoners in the USSR," *Human Rights Internet Reporter*, 11, no. 5-6 (Winter-Spring 1987), 57.

6156. Reynolds, Sarah, "Ownership and Property," *SEEL: Soviet and East European Law*, 2, no. 6 (Aug. 1991), 5-6.

6157. -----, "RSFSR Law Overhauls Old Regime of Property Rights, Leaves Ambiguities," *SEEL: Soviet and East European Law*, 2, no. 2 (Mar. 1991), 9ff.

6158. Ruebner, R., "Public Demonstrations and the Rule of Law in the Age of Glasnost and Perestroika," *American University Journal of International Law and Policy*, 5 (Fall 1989), 13-71.

6159. Rumyantsev, Oleg, "Russia's New Constitution," *Journal of Democracy*, 2, no. 2 (Spring 1991), 35-46.

6160. Samuelian, T. J., "Cultural Ecology and Gorbachev's Restructured Union," *Harvard International Law Journal*, 32 (Winter 1991), 159-200.

6161. Schmidt, A. J., "Law and Perestroika," *University of Bridgeport Law Review*, 9 (1988), 295-323.

6162. Schneider, R. C., "Developments in Soviet Property Law," *Fordham International Law Journal*, 13 (1989-90), 446-80.

6163. Schumaker, Kathy, "Religious and Public Organizations to Gain New Status," *SEEL: Soviet and East European Law*, 1, no. 6 (Aug. 1990), 9.

6164. Sharlet, Robert, "Party and Public Ideals in Conflict: Constitutionalism and Civil Rights in the USSR," *Cornell International Law Journal*, 23, no. 2 (1990), 341-62.

6165. -----, "Soviet Law and the Daniloff Case," *Bulletin of the Atomic Scientists*, 42, no. 10 (Dec. 1986), 14-18.

6166. -----, "Soviet Legal Reform in Historical Context," *Columbia Journal of Transnational Law*, 28, no. 1 (Spring 1990), 5-17.

6167. Sheehy, Ann, "Supreme Soviet Adopts Law on Mechanics of Secession," *Report on the USSR*, 2, no. 17 (27 Apr. 1990), 2-5.

6168. -----, "*Perestroika* and Legal Reform," *AAASS Newsletter*, 29, no. 2 (Mar. 1989), 1.

6169. -----, "Soviet Courts as Vehicles for Political Maneuver, *Soviet Union/Union Sovietique*, 13, no. 2 (1986), 163-86.

6170. Shaw, Denis J. B., "New Law to Streamline Moscow's Administration?" *Soviet Geography*, 32, no. 3 (Mar. 1991), 197-98.

6171. Sheremet, Konstantin, "Law and Social Change in the USSR of the 1990s," *Society*, 27, no. 4 (May-June 1990), 90-97.

6172. Simmons, Rebecca J., "Soviet Union Emigration Law May Lead to Improved Trade Relations," *SEEL: Soviet and East European Law*, 1, no. 3 (Apr. 1990), 8.

6173. Slobogin, C., "The Soviet Legal System," *Florida Business Journal*, 63 (July-Aug. 1989), 31-33.

6174. Smith, Gordon B., "The Procuracy, Citizens' Rights and Legal Reform," *Columbia Journal of Transnational Law*, 28, no. 1 (Spring 1990), 77-93.

6175. Smith, Polina, "Amendments Further Regulate But Open New Opportunities for Soviet Cooperative Activity," *SEEL: Soviet and East European Law*, 1, no. 7 (Sept. 1990), 7ff.

6176. -----, "USSR Supreme Soviet Enacts Land Law," *SEEL: Soviet and East European Law*, 1, no. 3 (Apr. 1990), 1ff.

6177. Sobchak, A. A., "The New Soviet Union: Challenges in the Development of a Law-Abiding State," *Stetson Law Review*, 20 (Fall 1990), 211-16.

6178. Solomon, Peter H., Jr., "The Role of Defence Counsel in the USSR: The Politics of Judicial Reform under Gorbachev," *Criminal Law Quarterly*, 31 (Dec. 1988), 76-93.

6179. -----, "The U.S.S.R. Supreme Court: History, Role and Future Prospects," *American Journal of Comparative Law*, 38, no. 1 (Winter 1990), 127-42.

6180. Soubbotin, Nikolai A., "Law on Ownership Shapes New Property Rights," *SEEL: Soviet and East European Law*, 1, no. 3 (Apr. 1990), 1ff.

6181. "Soviet Due Process Norms Strengthened," *SEEL: Soviet and East European Law*, 2, no. 1 (Mar. 1990), 6ff.

6182. "Soviet Inheritance Law: Ideological Consistency or a Retreat to the West?" *Gonzaga Law Review*, 23 (1987-88), 593-619.

6183. Spaethe, S. M., "The Deregulation of Transportation and Natural Gas Production in the United States and Its Relevance to the Soviet Union and Eastern Europe in the 1990s," *University of Bridgeport Law Review*, 12 (1991), 43-95.

6184. Spagat, Michael, "Council of Ministers Regulations on Small Enterprises Typifies Soviets' Poor Understanding of Markets," *SEEL: Soviet and East European Law*, 1, no. 7 (Sept. 1990), 8-9.

6185. Speake, J. G., "The Soviet Experiment: The Perspective of an Alabama Lawyer," *Alabama Lawyer*, 52 (Mar. 1991), 106-08.

6186. "The Status of People's Deputies in the USSR: Law of the Union of Soviet Socialist Republics," *Soviet Law and Government*, 30, no. 1 (Summer 1991), 27-49.

6187. Stephan, Paul B., III, "Glasnost and the Soviet System of Justice" (Review Article), *Law and Society Review*, 21, no. 5 (1988), 837-38.

6188. -----, "*Perestroyka* and Property: The Law of Ownership in the Post-Socialist Soviet Union," *American Journal of Comparative Law*, 39, no. 1 (Winter 1991), 35-66.

6189. "Strengthening the Legal Basis of Perestroika: The U.S.S.R. Draft Laws on Inventive Activity," *Santa Clara Computer and High Technology Law Journal*, 7 (Dec. 1991), 321-56.

6190. "Symposium: State Succession in the Former Soviet Union and in Eastern Europe," *Virginia Journal of International Law*,

33, no. 2 (Winter 1993), 253-350.

6191. Teague, Elizabeth, "Constitutional Watchdog Suspends Presidential Decree," *Report on the USSR*, 2, no. 42 (19 Oct. 1990), 9-11.

6192. -----, "Executive Presidency Approved," *Report on the USSR*, 2, no. 10 (9 Mar. 1990), 14-17.

6193. -----, "The Powers of the Soviet Presidency," *Report on the USSR*, 2, no. 12 (23 Mar. 1990), 4-7.

6194. Thornburgh, Richard, "The Rule of Law in the Soviet Union," *Vital Speeches of the Day*, 56 (15 Aug. 1990), 648-51.

6195. -----, "Soviets Need Rule of Law for Democracy," *World & I*, 5 (Dec. 1990), 129-35.

6196. -----, "The Soviet Union and the Rule of Law," *Foreign Affairs*, 69, no. 2 (Spring 1990), 13-27.

6197. Thorson, Carla, "RSFSR Forms Constitutional Court," *Report on the USSR*, 3, no. 51-52 (20 Dec. 1991), 13-16.

6198. Timmermans, W. A., "The New Statute on the Arbitration Court at the USSR Chamber of Commerce and Industry (14 December 1987)," *Journal of International Arbitration*, 5 (Spring 1988), 97-102.

6199. Tolz, Vera, "The Law on Public Associations: Legalization of the Multiparty System," *Report on the USSR*, 2, no. 46 (16 Nov. 1990), 1-3.

6200. Tracy, L. M., "Prospects for an Independent Judiciary: The Russian Constitutional Court and the CPSU," *Akron Law Review*, 26 (Winter-Spring 1993), 581-608.

6201. Troitskii, N. A., "The Trial of March 1, 1987," *Soviet Law and Government*, 27, no. 4 (Spring 1989), 87-99.

6202. Varga, C., "Transformation to Rule of Law from No-Law: Societal Contexture of the Democratic Transition in Central and Eastern Europe," *Connecticut Journal of International Law*, 8 (Spring 1993), 487-505.

6203. Vause, W. G., "The Coming End of Perestroika's Golden Age of Law Reform?" *Stetson Law Review*, 20 (Fall 1990), 201-09.

6204. Vereshchetin, V. S., and R. A. Mullerson, "International Law in an Interdependent World," *Columbia Journal of Transnational Law*, 28, no. 1 (Spring 1990), 291-300.

6205. Viechtbauer, Volker, "Arbitration in Russia," *Stanford Journal of International Law*, 29 (Summer 1992), 355ff.

6206. Vlasihin, V. A., "Towards a Bill of Rights for Russia: Progress and Roadblocks," *Nova Law Review*, 17 (Spring 1993), 1201-12.

6207. "What Should a Law-Governed State Be?" *Soviet Law and Government*, 28, no. 1 (Summer 1989), 51-65.

6208. Wiley, Buck, "Russian Membership in the IMF: A Look at the Problems, Past and Present," *Georgia Journal of International and Comparative Law*, 22, no. 2 (1992), 469-85.

6209. "Will the Soviet Union and the People's Republic of China Follow the United States' Adherence to the Berne Convention?" *Boston College International and Comparative Law Review*, 13, no. 1 (Winter 1990), 207-35.

6210. Wishnevsky, Julia, "The `Law-Based State': Soviet Style," *Report on the USSR*, 3, no. 10 (8 Mar. 1991), 1-4.

6211. Yakovlev, A. M., "Transforming the Soviet Union into a Rule of Law Democracy: A Report from the Front Lines," *Record of the Association of the Bar of the City of New York*, 46 (Mar. 1991), 129-48.

6212. Yassman, Victor, "Law on the KGB Published," *Report on the USSR*, 3, no. 31 (2 Aug. 1991), 12-18.

6213. Zabigailo, V. K., "Perestroika, Glasnost and Law Reform in the Soviet Union Today," *Dalhousie Law Journal*, 12 (Apr. 1989), 165-75.

XXVIII. Literature

BOOKS

6214. Brown, Deming, *The Last Years of Soviet Russian Literature: Prose Fiction 1975-1991* (Cambridge: Cambridge University Press, 1993).

6215. Chances, Ellen, *Andrei Bitov: Ecology and Inspiration* (New York: Cambridge University Press, 1993).

6216. Chukhontsev, Oleg, ed., *Dissonant Voices: The New Russian Fiction* (London: Harvill, 1991).

6217. Decter, Jacqueline, ed., and Sergei Zalygin, comp., *The New Soviet Fiction: Sixteen Short Stories* (New York: Abbeville Press, 1990).

6218. Garrard, John, and Carol Garrard, *Inside the Soviet Writers' Union* (New York: Free Press, 1990).

6219. Goscilo, Helena, and Byron Lindsey, eds., *Glasnost: An Anthology of Russian Literature under Gorbachev* (Ann Arbor: Ardis, 1990).

6220. Grossman, Vasilii S., *Forever Flowing* (New York: Perennial Library, 1986).

6221. -----, *Life and Fate: A Novel* (New York: Harper & Row, 1986).

6222. Hawkesworth, Celia, ed., *Literature and Politics in Eastern Europe* (London: Macmillan, 1992).

6223. Kuraev, Mikhail, *Night Patrol and Other Stories*, trans. by Margaret O. Thompson (Durham, NC: Duke University Press, 1994).

6224. Magnusson, Marta-Lisa, *The Louisiana Conference on Literature and Perestroika, 2-4 March 1988* (Esbjerg: South Jutland University Press, 1989).

6225. Parthe, Kathleen, *The Radiant Past: Russian Village Prose from Ovechkin to Rasputin* (Princeton: Princeton University Press, 1992).

6226. -----, *Time Backward! Memory and the Past in Soviet Russian Village Prose* (Washington, DC: Kennnan Institute for Advanced Russian Studies, Occasional Paper no. 224, 1987).

6227. Pavlyshyn, Marko, ed., *Glasnost' in Context: On the Recurrence of Liberalizations in Central and Eastern European Literatures and Cultures* (New York: Berg, distributed by St. Martin's Press, 1990).

6228. Rasputin, Valentin, *Live and Remember* (Evanston, IL: Northwestern University Press, 1992).

6229. -----, *Siberia on Fire: Stories and Essays* (DeKalb, IL: Northern Illinois University Press, 1989).

6230. Rybakov, Anatolii N., *Children of the Arbat* (Boston: Little Brown, 1988).

6231. Reid, J. H., *Writing Without Taboos: The New East German Literature* (New York: distributed by St. Martin's Press, 1990).

6232. Scriven, Michael, and Dennis Tate, *European Socialist Realism* (Oxford: Berg, 1988).

6233. Shneidman, N. N., *Soviet Literature in the 1980s: Decade of Transition* (Toronto: University of Toronto Press, 1989).

6234. Thompson, Ewa M., ed., *The Search for Self-Definition in Russian Literature* (Houston: Rice University Press, 1991).

6235. Tokareva, Viktoriia S., *The Talisman and Other Tales* (London: Picador, 1993).

6236. Voznesenskaia, Iulia Nikolaevna, *The Star Chernobyl* (London: Quartet Books, 1987).

6237. Zalygin, Sergei, comp., *The New Soviet Fiction: Sixteen Short Stories* (New York: Abbeville Press, 1989).

ARTICLES

6238. "Abbeville Announces Joint Publishing Program with the Soviets," *Publishers Weekly*, 232 (4 Sept. 1987), 24.

6239. Aitmatov, Chinghiz, *et al.*, "Perestroika and Soviet Literature," *Soviet Literature*, no. 9 (1987), 144-50.

6240. Alt, Noamy, "Is There a Cultural Thaw? *Index on Censorship*, 15 (Sept. 1986), 11-13.

6241. Amiel, B., "Two Visions of *Perestroika*," *Maclean's*, 101 (25 July 1988), 5.

6242. Bailey, B., "Reading by Fiat in the Soviet Union," *USA Today*, 115 (Nov. 1986), 23-25.

6243. Barratt, Andrew, and Edith W. Clowes, "Gor'ky, *Glasnost'* and *Perestroika*: The Death of a Cultural Superhero?" *Soviet Studies*, 43, no. 6 (1991), 1123-42.

6244. Barta, Peter I., "The Author, the Cultural Tradition and Glasnost: An Interview with Tatyana Tolstaya," *Russian Language Journal*, 44, no. 147-49 (Winter-Fall, 1990), 265-84.

6245. Beneduce, Ann, "New Role for VAAP: New Kind of Children's Book Publishing," *Publishers Weekly*, 238, no. 31 (19

July 1991), 13.

6246. Carsten, Svetlana, "The Writer in Society: Current Polemics Among Soviet Literary Critics," *Scottish Slavonic Review*, 17 (Autumn 1991), 61-85.

6247. Chuprinin, Sergei, "A Normal Pace: Russian Literature Since *Perestroika*," *Russian Studies in Literature*, 29, no. 1 (Winter 1992-93), 62-88.

6248. Colfin, B., "Freedom of Expression and the Exploitation of Creative Rights: The Struggle for Expression by Dissident Authors," *European Intellectual Property Review*, 9 (Jan. 1987), 18-24.

6249. Conquest, Robert, "At the Rebirth of St. Petersburg" (Poem), *American Spectator*, 24, no. 12 (Dec. 1991), 20.

6250. "Current Problems in the Study of the History of Russian Soviet Literature," *Soviet Studies in Literature*, 28, no. 3 (Summer 1992), 5-28.

6251. Dedkov, Igor, "Literature and the New Thinking," *Social Sciences*, no. 4 (1988), 62-77.

6252. Deviatko, I. F., and S. S. Shvedov, "The Journal and Its Reader," *Soviet Studies in Literature*, 26, no. 4 (Fall 1990), 70-93.

6253. Diment, Galya, "Valentin Rasputin and Siberian Nationalism," *World Literature Today*, 67, no. 1 (Winter 1993), 69-74.

6254. Dunlop, John B., "Reactions in the USSR to Solzhenitsyn's *The Gulag Archipelago*," *Report on the USSR*, 2, no. 10 (9 Mar. 1990), 3-6.

6255. Epstein, Mikhail, "After the Future: On the New Consciousness in Literature," *South Atlantic Quarterly*, 90, no. 2 (Spring 1991), 409-44.

6256. Erofeev, Viktor, "A Farewell Feast for Soviet Literature," *Soviet Studies in Literature*, 26, no. 4 (Fall 1990), 10-18.

6257. Fanger, Donald, "The Two *Perestroikas*," *New Republic* (23 Oct. 1989), 26-30.

6258. Feldman, Gale, "The Russians ARE Coming: A Flurry of Publishing Activity on All Fronts," *Publishers Weekly*, 238, no. 40 (6 Sept. 1991), 66.

6259. Filipowicz, Halina, "Solidarity with Solidarity: Six Polish Plays," *Modern Drama*, 33, no. 1 (Mar. 1990), 106-19.

6260. "From the 1987 Plenum of the USSR Writers' Union," *Soviet Studies in Literature*, 25, no. 2 (Spring 1989), 79-87.

6261. "From the 1988 Plenum of the USSR Writers' Union," *Soviet Studies in Literature*, 25, no. 2 (Spring 1989), 88-113.

6262. Gass, William H., "East vs. West in Lithuania: Rising Tempers at a Writers' Meeting," *New York Times Book Review* (2 Feb. 1986), 3ff.

6263. Gilenson, Boris, "Byron in Russia," *Contemporary Review*, 253, no. 1472 (Sept. 1988), 155-58.

6264. Gillespie, David, "Apocalypse Now: Village Prose and the

Death of Russia," *Modern Language Review*, 87, no. 2 (Apr. 1992), 407-19.

6265. -----, "Art, Politics and Glasnost: The Eighth Soviet Writers' Congress and Soviet Literature 1986-7," in Michael Scriven and Dennis Tate, eds., *European Socialist Realism*, (Oxford: Berg, 1988), 149-70.

6266. -----, "Ironies and Legacies: Village Prose and Glasnost," *Forum for Modern Language Studies*, 27, no. 1 (Jan. 1991), 70-84.

6267. Gremitskikh, Yuri, "Perestroika and Information," *Soviet Literature*, no. 4 (1988), 122-26.

6268. Gurewich, David, "Glasnost Ho!" *New Criterion*, 7, no. 1 (Sept. 1988), 77-81.

6269. Heller, Leonid, "Perestrojka and Literature: Texts and Context," *Studies in Soviet Thought*, 40, no. 1-3 (Aug-Nov. 1990), 189-204.

6270. Hellie, Jean Laves, "Whither Russian Literature?" *Soviet Studies in Literature*, 26, no. 4 (Fall 1990), 3-9.

6271. Iovine, Micaela S., "Bulgarian Literature after the Revolution," *World Literature Today*, 65, no. 2 (Spring 1991), 253-56.

6272. Jackson, J. O., "Tales from a Time of Terror," *Time*, 129 (27 Apr. 1987), 45-46.

6273. Johnson, Kent, and Stephen Ashby, "Switching Languages: The New Soviet Poetry," *Michigan Quarterly Review*, 28, no. 4 (Fall 1989), 719-42.

6274. Jones, Stephen F., "National Conflict at the Eighth All-Union Writers' Congress," *Nationalities Papers*, 15, no. 1 (Spring 1987), 7-21.

6275. Karpov, V. V., "A Conversation with Stalin," *New Perspectives Quarterly*, 5 (Spring 1988), 51-53.

6276. Kaufman, Peter B., "Troubles Grow at Prague Book Fair; Warsaw Fair Studies West Publishers," *Publishers Weekly*, 238, no. 20 (3 May 1991), 14.

6277. -----, "What East Europe Needs," *Publishers Weekly*, 238, no. 27 (21 June 1991), S14-15.

6278. Kulakov, Vladislav, "What's Needed Is Lyricism: The Poetry of the `New Wave'," *Russian Social Science Review*, 35, no. 1 (Jan-Feb. 1994), 74-92.

6279. Kustanovich, Konstantin, "Erotic Glasnost: Sexuality in Recent Russian Literature," *World Literature Today*, 67 (Winter 1993), 136-44.

6280. Laird, Sally, "Soviet Literature-What Has Changed?" *Index on Censorship*, 16, no. 7 (July-Aug. 1987), 8-13.

6281. Laqueur, Walter, "Beyond Glasnost" (Review Article), *Commentary*, 84 (Oct. 1987), 63-65.

6282. Likhachev, D. S., "Russian Culture in the Modern World," *Russian Social Science Review*, 34, no. 1 (Jan-Feb. 1993), 70-81.

6283. Lubin, P., "A Literary Thaw," *New Republic* (1 Aug. 1988), 54-55.

6284. Markish, Simon, "A Russian Writer's Jewish Fate," *Commentary*, 81 (Apr. 1986), 39-47.

6285. Marsh, Rosalind, "The Death of Soviet Literature: Can Russian Literature Survive?" *Europe-Asia Studies*, 45, no. 1 (1993), 115-40.

6286. -----, "*Glasnost'* and Russian Literature," *Australian Slavonic and East European Studies*, 6, no. 2 (1992), 21-39.

6287. McDowell, E., "'Exodus' in Samizdat: Still Popular and Still Subversive," *New York Times Book Review*, 92 (26 Apr. 1987), 13.

6288. Mestrovic, Marta, "Perestroika and Picture Books," *Publishers Weekly*, 238, no. 10 (22 Feb. 1991), 128-31.

6289. Mitgang, H., "Jay Gatsby Meets the Russians," *Nation*, 243 (2-9 Aug. 1986), 75-76.

6290. Moroz, Valentyn, "Ukrainian Literary Industry Faces Uncertain Future," *Report on the USSR*, 3, no. 11 (15 Mar. 1991), 15-17.

6291. Murray, J., "The Last Word on Glasnost," *Times Higher Education Supplement*, 969 (31 May 1991), 17.

6292. Nepomnyashchy, Catherine Theimer, "Famine in Time of Feast: Soviet Literary Publishing under *Glasnost*," *Harriman Institute Forum*, 3, no. 3 (Mar. 1990), 1-8.

6293. Olcott, Anthony, "What Faith the God-Contemporary? Chingiz Aitmatov's *Plakha*," *Slavic Review*, 49, no. 2 (Summer 1990), 213-26.

6294. Peterson, Nadya, "Science Fiction and Fantasy: A Prelude to the Literature of *Glasnost'*," *Slavic Review*, 48, no. 2 (Summer 1989), 254-68.

6295. Pittman, Riita H., "*Perestroika* and Soviet Cultural Policies: The Case of the Major Literary Journals," *Soviet Studies*, 42, no. 1 (Jan. 1990), 111-32.

6296. -----, "Writers and Politics in the Gorbachev Era," *Soviet Studies*, 44, no. 4 (1992), 665-86.

6297. Plante, David, "Under Eastern Eyes: What America Meant to the Writers of Russia," *New York Times Book Review* (27 Feb. 1994), 3ff.

6298. "Politics and Literature under Gorbachev: Speeches Before the USSR Writers' Congress," *Orbis*, 30, no. 3 (Fall 1986), 543-69.

6299. Polivanov, Mikhail, "The *Glasnost'* Papers: What the Soviets Are Saying About the Writers They Are Resurrecting," *New Republic* (20 Feb. 1989), 28-37.

6300. Pulkhritudova, Elizaveta, "Popular Fiction as Journalism," *Journal of Communication*, 41, no. 2 (Spring 1991), 92-101.

6301. "Recent Reports 1990: Current Changes in Soviet Literature" (Special Issue), *Soviet Studies in Literature*, 26, no. 4 (Fall 1990), 3-93.

6302. Reed, S. K., "Tearing a Veil from History: Anatoli Rybakov Tries to Exorcise the Monstrous Spirit of Stalin," *People Weekly*, 29 (27 June 1988), 73-74.

6303. Reeve, F. D., "Vanka-Vstanka among the Bears: A Literary Letter from Moscow," *Sewanee Review*, 99, no. 2 (328-35).

6304. Remnick, David, "Chaplygin Street Blues," *New York Review of Books*, 38 (25 Apr. 1991), 3-4.

6305. -----, "The Exile Returns," *New Yorker* (14 Feb. 1994), 64ff.

6306. -----, "Invitation to a Beheading," *New York Review of Books*, 39 (5 Nov. 1992), 12ff.

6307. -----, "Native Son," *New York Review of Books*, 38 (14 Feb. 1991), 6-10.

6308. "The Return of Abram Tertz: Siniavskii's Reception in Gorbachev's Russia" (Special Issue), *Studies in Soviet Literature*, 28, no. 1 (Winter 1991), 2-98.

6309. Reuter, Madalynne, "Britannica and the Soviets to Publish Russian-Language Encyclopedia," *Publishers Weekly*, 238, no. 2 (11 Jan. 1991), 10.

6310. "Revisions in Soviet Literary History" (Special Issue), *Studies in Soviet Literature*, 28, no. 3 (Summer 1992), 3-95.

6311. Rich, Elizabeth, "Russian Writers, Critics and Publishers on Perestroika and Its Influence on Soviet Literature," *Soviet Literature*, no. 1 (1990), 149-57.

6312. Rubinshtein, Natalya, "Glasnost Bestseller," *Index on Censorship*, 17, no. 9 (Oct. 1988), 18-19.

6313. Rumens, Carol, "Fish Out of Water: Poets in Perestroika," *New Statesman and Society*, 3 (19 Jan. 1990), 34-35.

6314. -----, "Unthawed Ice," *Poetry Review*, 77, no. 3 (Autumn 1987), 11-12.

6315. "Russian Literature: New Directions" (Special Issue), *Soviet Studies in Literature*, 28, no. 4 (Fall 1992), 3-85.

6316. "Russia's Rediscovery of Solzhenitsyn" (Special Issue), *Soviet Studies in Literature*, 27, no. 2 (Spring 1991), 2-96.

6317. Scammell, Michael, "To the Finland Station?" *New Republic* (19 Nov. 1990), 18-23.

6318. Schultze, Sydney, "The Moral Dimension of Rybakov's *Deti Arbata*," *Russian Language Journal*, 47, no. 156-58 (Winter-Spring-Fall 1993), 147-55.

6319. Seton-Watson, Mary, "Soviet Literature under Gorbachev," *Washington Quarterly*, 11, no. 2 (Spring 1988), 157-68.

6320. "Siberian `Zharki': The Establishment of a Cooperative Publishing House," *Soviet Law and Government*, 27, no. 1 (Summer 1988), 97-99.

6321. Sidorov, Evgeni, "The Wind of Change," *Soviet Literature*, no. 1 (1988), 113-16.

6322. Silenieks, Juris, "Decolonization and Renewal of Latvian Letters," *World Literature Today*, 65, no. 2 (Spring 1991), 221-25.

6323. Simecka, Milan, "Newspeak and Glasnost," *Times Literary Supplement*, no. 4475 (6-12 Jan. 1989), 10.

6324. Simon, John, "Speaking Around Literature," *New Leader*, 69 (11-25 Aug. 1986), 14-16.

6325. "A Soviet Poet's Praise for Freedom," *World Press Review*, 34 (June 1987), 61.

6326. Stevens, Norman, "Russian Libraries in Transition: An Anthology of Glasnost Literature" (Review Article), *Wilson Library Bulletin*, 67, no. 4 (Dec. 1992), 92-93.

6327. Stites, Richard, "*Glasnost* for Soviet Science Fiction," *Futurist*, 25 (Mar-Apr. 1991), 49-50.

6328. Stover, L. T., and R. Karr, "Glasnost in the Classroom: Likhanov's *Shadows Around the Sun*," *English Journal*, 79 (Dec. 1990), 47-53.

6329. Tall, Emily, "Behind the Scenes: How *Ulysses* Was Finally Published in the Soviet Union," *Slavic Review*, 49, no. 2 (Summer 1990), 183-99.

6330. Thatcher, Ian D., "Soviet Writings on Leon Trotsky: An Update," *Coexistence*, 29, no. 1 (Mar. 1992), 73ff.

6331. "Thirty Years Late: Critical Responses to the Soviet Publication of *Doctor Zhivago*" (Special Issue), *Soviet Studies in Literature*, 26, no. 3 (Summer 1990), 1-99.

6332. Tokmakoff, George, "P. A. Stolypin in Solzhenitsyn's *Krasnoe koleso*: A Historian's View," in Arnold McMillin, ed., *Aspects of Modern Russian and Czech Literature* (Columbus, OH: Slavica, 1989), 150-58.

6333. Tolstaya, Tatyana, "Is There Hope for Pushkin's Children?" *Wilson Quarterly*, 16, no. 2 (Winter 1992), 121-29.

6334. Tolz, Vera, and Elizabeth Teague, "Prokhanov Warns of Collapse of Soviet Empire," *Report on the USSR*, 2, no. 6 (9 Feb. 1990), 1-3.

6335. Utley, A., "Soaps Score over Solzhenitsyn," *Times Higher Education Supplement*, 1061 (5 Mar. 1993).

6336. "Vasili Belov: Speech at the Second Congress of the USSR People's Deputies," *Soviet Literature*, no. 11 (1990), 155-60.

6337. Venclova, T., "Ethnic Identity and the Nationality Issue in Contemporary Soviet Literature," *Studies in Comparative Communism*, 21 (Autumn-Winter 1988), 319-29.

6338. Voznesenskii, Andrei, "Revolution by Culture: A Poet's View of *Glasnost*," *Nation*, 244 (13 June 1987), 810-12.

6339. Walker, Martin, "The Sons of the Elite," in his *The Waking Giant: Gorbachev's Russia* (New York: Pantheon Books, 1986), 188-205.

6340. Weiss, Sydna Stern, "From Hiroshima to Chernobyl: Literary Warnings in the Nuclear Age," *Papers on Language & Literature*, 26, no. 1 (Winter 1990), 90-111.

6341. Whitney, Craig R., *"Glasnost'* Writing: So Where's the Golden Age?" *New York Times Book Review* (19 Mar. 1989), 941ff.

6342. Woodward, James B., "Chingiz Aitmatov's Second Novel," *Slavonic and East European Review*, 69, no. 2 (Apr. 1991), 201-20.

6343. Yerofeyev, V., "Turning the Page in the Soviet Union," *World Press Review*, 38 (Jan. 1991), 74.

6344. Yevtushenko, Yevgeny A., "A Poet's View of *Glasnost*," Time, 129 (9 Feb. 1987), 32-33.

6345. Yurke, A. F. "Copyright Issues Concerning the Publication of Samizdat Literature in the United States," *Columbia-VLA Journal of Law and the Arts*, 11 (Spring 1987), 449-70.

6346. Zdanys, Jonas, "Voices from the Other Europe," *Yale Review*, 79, no. 3 (Spring 1990), 467-82.

6347. Ziolkowski, Margaret, *"Glasnost'* in Soviet Literature; An Introduction to Two Stories," *Michigan Quarterly Review*, 28, no. 4 (Fall 1989), 639-47.

XXIX. Media, Publishing, Public Opinion

BOOKS

6348. Bassow, Whitman, *The Soviet Correspondents: Reporting on Russia from the Revolution to Glasnost'* (New York: Paragon House, 1989).

6349. Billington, James H., *The Electronic Erosion of Democracy* (Urbana: University of Illinois Library, 1990).

6350. Bittman, Ladislav, ed., *The New Image-Makers: Soviet Propaganda and Disinformation Today* (Washington, DC: Pergamon-Brassey's International Defense Publications, 1988).

6351. Center for Democracy in the USSR, *Soviet Events of 1989 and 1990 as Reported by the Express Chronicle* (New York, 1991).

6352. Cerf, Christopher, and Marina Albee, eds., *Small Fires: Letters from the Soviet People to Ogonyok Magazine, 1987-1990* (New York: Summit Books, 1990).

6353. Dizard, Wilson P., and S. Blake Swensrud, *Gorbachev's Information Revolution: Controlling Glasnost in a New Electronic Age* (Boulder, CO: Westview Press, 1987).

6354. Gerol, Ilya, and Geoffrey Molyneaux, *The Manipulators: Inside the Soviet Media Empire* (Toronto: Stoddart, 1988).

6355. Graffy, Julian, and Geoffrey A. Hosking, eds., *Culture and the Media in the USSR Today* (New York: St. Martin's Press, 1989).

6356. Hester, Al, and L. Earle Reybold, eds., *Revolution for Freedom: The Mass Media in Eastern and Central Europe* (Athens, GA: James W. Cox Jr. Center for International Mass Communication Training and Research, 1991).

6357. Korotich, Vitaly, ed., *The New Soviet Journalism: The Best of the Soviet Weekly Ogonyok* (Boston: Beacon Press, 1990).

6358. Lowry, Montecue J., *Glasnost': Deception, Desperation, Dialectics* (New York: Peter Lang Publishing, 1991).

6359. McKay, Ron, ed., *Letters to Gorbachev: Life in Russia through the Postbag of Argumenty i Fakty* (London: Michael Joseph, 1991).

6360. McNair, Brian, *Glasnost, Perestroika and the Soviet Media* (London: Routledge, 1991).

6361. Mickiewicz, Ellen, *Split Signals: Television and Politics in the Soviet Union* (New York: Oxford University Press, 1988).

6362. Miller, Arthur H., William M. Resinger and Vicki L. Hesli, eds., *Public Opinion and Regime Change: The New Politics of Post-Soviet Societies* (Boulder, CO: Westview Press, 1993).

6363. Murray, John, *The Russian Press from Brezhnev to Yeltsin: Behind the Paper Curtain* (Brookfield, VT: Edward Elgar, 1994).

6364. Oberg, James E., *Uncovering Soviet Disasters: Exploring the Limits of Glasnost* (New York: Random House, 1988).

6365. Remington, Thomas, *The Truth of Authority: Ideology and Communication in the Soviet Union* (Pittsburgh: University of Pittsburgh Press, 1989).

6366. Riordan, Jim, and Sue Bridger, trans. and eds., *Dear Comrade Editor: Letters to the Soviet Press under Perestroika* (Bloomington: Indiana University Press, 1992).

6367. Romerstein, Herbert, *Soviet Active Measures and Propaganda: "New Thinking" and Influence Activities in the Gorbachev Era* (Toronto: Mackenzie Institute for the Study of Terrorism, Revolution and Propaganda, 1989).

6368. Roxburgh, Angus, *Pravda: Inside the Soviet News Machine* (London: Victor Gollancz, 1987).

6369. Siefert, Marsha, ed., *Mass Culture and Perestroika in the Soviet Union* (New York: Oxford University Press, 1991).

6370. Tarasulo, Isaac J., *Gorbachev and Glasnost: Viewpoints from the Soviet Press* (Wilmington, DE: Scholarly Resources, 1989).

6371. -----, *Perils of Perestroika: Viewpoints from the Soviet Press* (Wilmington, DE: Scholarly Resources, 1992).

6372. Trager, Oliver, ed., *Gorbachev's Glasnost': Red Star Rising* (New York: Facts on File, 1989).

6373. Tsypkin, Mikhail, *Gorbachev's "Glasnost": Another Potemkin Village?* (Washington, DC: Heritage Foundation, 1987).

6374. US Central Intelligence Agency. Directorate of Intelligence. *The USSR Confronts the Information Revolution: A Conference Report* (Washington, DC: CIA, 1987).

6375. US Commission on Security and Cooperation in Europe. *The London Information Forum of the Conference on Security and Cooperation in Europe: Compilation of Speeches* (Washington, DC: US Government Printing Office, 1989).

6376. US Congress. House. Committee on Foreign Affairs. Subcommittee on International Operations. *United States Public*

Diplomacy in Eastern Europe and the Soviet Union: Hearing before the Subcommittee on International Operations of the Committee on Foreign Affairs, House of Representatives. 102nd Congress, 1st Session, 30 July 1991 (Washington, DC: Government Printing Office, 1991).

6377. Wilhelm, Donald, *Global Communications and Political Power* (New Brunswick, NJ: Transaction, 1990).

ARTICLES

6378. Aage, Hans, "Popular Attitudes and Perestroika," *Soviet Studies*, 43, no. 1 (1991), 3-25.

6379. Agopsowicz, Monika, "The Ukrainian Piedmont: Interview with Vyacheslav Chornovil," *Uncaptive Minds*, 4, no. 1 (Spring 1991), 17-18.

6380. Andreev, Nikolai, "After the Election: Comments of a Public-Affairs Journalist," *Soviet Law and Government*, 27, no. 2 (Fall 1988), 100ff.

6381. Androunas, Elena, "The Struggle for Control Over Soviet Television," *Journal of Communication*, 41, no. 2 (Spring 1991), 185-200.

6382. Aumente, Jerome, "Growing a Free Press: The Struggle in Eastern Europe," *Washington Journalism Review*, 13, no. 3 (Apr. 1991), 38-42.

6383. Beneduce, Ann, "New Role for VAAP, New Kind of Children's Book Publishing," *Publishers Weekly*, 238, no. 31 (19 July 1991), 13.

6384. Bennett, James R., "Soviet Scholars Look at U.S. Media" Review Article), *Journal of Communication*, 36, no. 1 (Winter 1986), 126-32.

6385. Berman, Harold J., "Political and Legal Control of Freedom of Expression in the Soviet Union," *Soviet Union/Union Sovietique*, 15, nos. 2-3 (1988), 263-72.

6386. Boccardi, Louis, "The Soviet Union: A Tempered Darkness," *Quill*, 79, no. 1 (Jan-Feb. 1991), 36-37.

6387. Borin, Iurii, and Mikhail Fedotov, "The Right to Information," *Soviet Law and Government*, 27, no. 3 (Winter 1988-89), 44-49.

6388. "Born of Glasnost: Publication of CC CPSU News Resumed," *World Marxist Review*, 32 (Apr. 1989), 60.

6389. Brancaccio, David A., "Disarming the Press," *Psychology Today*, 22 (June 1988), 40-42.

6390. Branson, L., "Glasnost in Print," *World Press Review*, 34 (Aug. 1987), 34-35.

6391. Brown, Clarence, "Untruth," *New Republic* (1 Apr. 1991), 16-17.

6392. Brym, Robert J., "*Perestroika*, Public Opinion, and Pamyat," *Soviet Jewish Affairs*, 19, no. 3 (1989), 23-32.

6393. Bubnicki, Rafal, "Dictators Do Not Like Photo-journalists:

An Interview with Tomasz Kizny," *Uncaptive Minds*, 3, no. 2 (Mar-Apr. 1990), 10-11.

6394. Campbell, Kurt M., "The Soviets Go Galluping," *National Interest*, no. 16 (Summer 1989), 110-13.

6395. Carlson, Richard W., "No More Static: People in Glasnost Houses Shouldn't Jam Broadcasts," *Policy Review*, no. 43 (Winter 1988), 80-83.

6396. Charles, Dan, "Time Runs Out for Magazine with a Mission" [*Znanie-Sila*], *New Scientist*, 135, no. 1835 (22 Aug. 1992), 8.

6397. Chetverikov, Nikolai N., "A Secret No Longer: The Mass Media at the New Stage of *Perestroika*," *Perestroika Annual*, 2 (1989), 123-37.

6398. Chorbajian, Levon, "For the Masses: Television in the Armenian S.S.R.," *Armenian Review*, 42, no. 3 (Autumn 1989), 37-52.

6399. Dejevsky, Mary, "The Desperate Search for a Western Fairy-Godmother," *IPI Report*, 41, no. 4 (Apr. 1992), 12-13.

6400. Downing, John, "Perestroika, Glasnost, and Soviet Media," *Journal of Communication*, 42, no. 2 (Spring 1992), 153-62.

6401. Dufresne, Marcel, "A Soviet Press Code," *Washington Journalism Review*, 12, no. 6 (July-Aug. 1990), 28-30.

6402. Dukess, Karen, "Moscow Rules: Checkbook Journalism, Soviet Style," *Columbia Journalism Review*, 30, no. 2 (July-Aug. 1991), 14.

6403. "Editor Has the Write Stuff," *Glasnost*, 2, no. 4, issues no. 26-27 (Sept.-Oct. 1989), 32-39.

6404. Engelbrekt, Kjell, "The Media Adjust to Their New Environment," *Report on Eastern Europe*, 2, no. 23 (7 June 1991), 6-10.

6405. Fedotov, Mikhail A., "Toward Conceptualization of the Law on the Press and Information," *Soviet Law and Government*, 27, no. 1 (Summer 1988), 6-21.

6406. -----, and Dimitrii V. Luchkin, "The Journalist in the Courtroom," *Soviet Law and Government*, 27, no. 4 (Spring 1989), 79-86.

6407. Fields, Howard, "East Europe Treats U.S. Copyright Holders Unfairly," *Publishers Weekly*, 238, no. 2 (11 Jan. 1991), 12.

6408. -----, "Soviet Publishers and Retailers to Attend ABA," *Publishers Weekly*, 237, no. 121 (16 Mar. 1990), 11.

6409. -----, "USIA's New Role in East Europe: Books Are Crucial," *Publisher's Weekly*, 237, no. 15 (13 Apr. 1990), 18.

6410. "First Issue of Glasnost Information Bulletin and the Press Club Glasnost," *Human Rights Internet Reporter*, 12, no. 1 (Fall 1987), 40-41.

6411. Fossedal, Gregory A., "Tuning in to *Glasnost'*: America's Radio Voices," in *The Democratic Imperative: Exporting the*

American Revolution (New York: Basic Books, 1989), 88-114.

6412. Franklin, Lynn C., "Back to Moscow," *Publishers Weekly*, 237, no. 20 (18 May 1990), 34-35.

6413. "Freedom of Expression in the Soviet Media: Special Soviet Issue," *Loyola of Los Angeles Entertainment Law Journal*, 11 (1991), 269-351.

6414. Friedman, Sharon M., Carole M. Gorney and Brenda P. Egolf, "Reporting on Radiation: A Content Analysis of Chernobyl Coverage," *Journal of Communications*, 37, no. 3 (Summer 1987), 58-79.

6415. Garbus, Martin, "New Magazine in Moscow" ['*Glasnost*'], *New York Review of Books*, 34 (13 Aug. 1987), 49.

6416. Gardner, Anthony, "Interview-Vitalii Korotich: The Media under Gorbachev," *Journal of International Affairs*, 42 (Spring 1988), 357-62.

6417. Gaunt, Philip, "Developments in Soviet Journalism," *Journalism Quarterly*, 64, no. 2-3 (Summer 1987), 526-32.

6418. Girnius, Saulius, "Controversy over Free Press in Lithuania," *Report on the USSR*, 3, no. 51-52 (20 Dec. 1991), 20-23.

6419. Gitlin, Todd, "A Tale of Two Moral Prisms," *Tikkun*, 6, no. 2 (Mar-Apr. 1991), 33ff.

6420. "Glasnost and Perestroika," *Sputnik: Digest of the Soviet Press* (regular monthly feature from Jan. 1988).

6421. "*Glasnost* Gives a Journalism Lesson," *U.S. News & World Report*, 104 (11 Jan. 1988), 9.

6422. "Glasnost, R.I.P.," *Harper's*, 282 (Apr. 1991), 22ff.

6423. Goban-Klas, Tomasz, "Making Media Policy in Poland," *Journal of Communication*, 40, no. 1 (Winter 1990), 50-54.

6424. Godson, R., "Soviet Manipulation of the Media," *Vital Speeches of the Day*, 51 (15 Apr. 1985), 406-10.

6425. "Gorbachev Seeks Crackdown on Free Press," *Editor and Publisher*, 124, no. 4 (26 Jan. 1991), 14.

6426. Grey, Robert D., Lauri A. Jennisch and Alanna S. Tyler, "Soviet Public Opinion and the Gorbachev Reforms," *Slavic Review*, 49, no. 2 (Summer 1990), 261-71.

6427. Gross, Natalie, "Glasnost': Roots and Practice," *Problems of Communism*, 36, no. 5 (Nov-Dec. 1987), 69-80.

6428. Gross, Peter, "Censorship without Censors: Restricting the Free Press in Romania," *Orbis*, 35, no. 3 (Summer 1991), 365-76.

6429. Gruliow, Leo, "The *Current Digest*: Pravda-Watching from Stalin to Gorbachev," *AAASS Newsletter*, 25, no. 4 (Sept. 1985), 1-2.

6430. Grushin, B. A., "Public Opinion in the System of Management," *Soviet Sociology*, 28, no. 4 (July-Aug. 1989), 72-80.

6431. Gubar', O. M., V. N. Zybtsev and A. N. Saunin, "Public Opinion in the Preelection Campaign," *Soviet Sociology*, 30, no. 2 (Mar-Apr. 1991), 81-87.

6432. Hardy, J. E., and K. Monagle, "Breaking From the Past," *Scholastic Update*, 124 (6 Dec. 1991), 8-10.

6433. Hayden, Robert M., "Politics and the Media," *Report on Eastern Europe*, 2, no. 49 (6 Dec. 1991), 17-26.

6434. Hill, Ronald J., "Glasnost: Communications and the Communist System," *Contemporary Review*, 251, no. 1461 (Oct. 1987), 173-78.

6435. Holtz, J., "Gorbachev Studies the Master," *World Press Review*, 33 (Sept. 1986), 61.

6436. Horvat, Janos, "The East European Journalist," *Journal of International Affairs*, 45 (Summer 1991), 191-200.

6437. Iadov, V., "The Sociology of *Perestroika* and the *Perestroika* of Sociology," *Soviet Sociology*, 29, no. 3 (May-June 1990), 22-28.

6438. Ivanov, M. K., "What Should Be the Nature of the Law on the Press and Information," *Soviet Law and Government*, 27, no. 1 (Summer 1988), 22-25.

6439. Jensen, Linda, "The Press and Power in the Russian Federation," *Journal of International Affairs*, 47 (Summer 1993), 97-126.

6440. Johnson, Owen V., "Half Slave - Half Free: The Crisis of the Russian and East European Press," *AAASS Newsletter*, 33, no. 2 (Mar. 1993), 1ff.

6441. Kaszubski, Marek, "Telecommunications Law Opens Polish Air Waves," *SEEL: Soviet and East European Law*, 1, no. 10 (Jan. 1991), 4ff.

6442. Kaufman, Peter B., "Polish Publishing Goes to Market," *Nation*, 252, (20 May 1991), 650ff.

6443. Kimmage, Dennis, "Glasnost and Soviet Libraries," *American Libraries*, Part 1: 18 (July-Aug. 1988), 570-72; Part 2: 18 (Sept. 1988), 652-56.

6444. Klose, Kevin, "Reporting from Moscow: Fiction and Secrets," *Bulletin of the Atomic Scientists*, 42, no. 10 (Dec. 1986), 22-23.

6445. Kniazkov, M., "Hack in the USSR," *Washington Monthly*, 23 (June 1991), 16-23.

6446. Kobak, F., "Is There an Accounting Textbook Market in the New Soviet Union?" *Publishers Weekly*, 238 (20 Sept. 1991), 43-44.

6447. Kolesnik, Svetlana, "Advertising and Cultural Politics," *Journal of Communication*, 41, no. 2 (Spring 1991), 46-54.

6448. Kondracke, Morton, "Fine Tuning," *New Republic* (28 May 1990), 10-11.

6449. Kondrashov, Stanislav, "Out of the Darkness of Ignorance: Glimmers of *Glasnost'* in the Kingdom of Military Secrets," *Soviet Law and Government*, 29, no. 4 (Spring 1991), 21-77.

6450. Koppel, Ted, "'Guest Reporter' in Kiev," *Progressive*, 55, no. 3 (Mar. 1991), 43.

6451. Korobeinikov, Valery, "Opinion Polls in the Soviet Union: Perestroika and the Public," *European Research*, 16 (Aug. 1988), 160-62.

6452. Korzun, Sergei, "The Role of Radio," *Report on the USSR*, 3, no. 43 (25 Oct. 1991), 3-4.

6453. Kroulik, Barbara, and Peter Martin, "Recent Developments in the Media: Czechoslovakia Media Law," *Report on Eastern Europe*, 2, no. 16 (19 Apr. 1991), 19-20.

6454. Krug, Peter, "The Abandonment of the State Radio-Television Monopoly in the Soviet Union: A First Step toward Broadcasting Pluralism?" *Wisconsin International Law Journal*, 9, no. 2 (Spring 1991), 377-412.

6455. Kusin, Vladimir V., "Media in Transition," *Report on Eastern Europe*, 2, no. 18 (3 May 1991), 5-19.

6456. Lampert, Nick, "The *Anonimka* Under Perestroika: A Note," *Soviet Studies*, 41, no. 1 (Jan. 1989), 67-87.

6457. Lance, N., "New Game in Moscow: A TV Crew Tests Glasnost," *WJR*, 10 (Sept. 1988), 38-40.

6458. Laptev, Ivan D., "Glasnost Increases Soviet Newspaper Readership," *Editor and Publisher*, 121 (4 June 1988), 11-12.

6459. Lasorsa, Dominic L., "Real and Perceived Effects of `Amerika'," *Journalism Quarterly*, 66, no. 2 (Summer 1989), 373ff.

6460. Lawton, Anna, "Sex, Violence, and Videotape in the USSR," *World & I*, 6, no. 2 (Feb. 1991), 182-87.

6461. Leinwoll, S., "Jamming: The End of an Era?" *Radio-Electronics*, 60 (June 1989), 75-77.

6462. -----, "The Soviet Jamming System and the Future of Jamming," *Radio-Electronics*, 60 (Oct. 1989), 78-79.

6463. Lottman, Herbert R., "Benign Neglect in Eastern Europe," *Publishers Weekly*, 238, no. 18 (19 Apr. 1991), S13.

6464. Manaev, Oleg T., "A Dissenting Audience: Changing Criteria of Effectiveness of the Mass Media in the Process of Society's Democratization," *Soviet Sociology*, 30, no. 3 (May-June 1991), 23-40.

6465. -----, "The Influence of Western Radio on the Democratization of Soviet Youth," *Journal of Communication*, 41, no. 2 (Spring 1991), 72-91.

6466. Manoff, R. K., "Reinventing Politics in the Soviet Press," *Progressive*, 51, no. 5 (May 1987), 18.

6467. Mason, David S., and Svetlana Sydorenko, "*Perestroyka*, Social Justice and Soviet Public Opinion," *Problems of Communism*, 39, no. 6 (Nov-Dec. 1990), 34-43.

6468. Massing, M., "How Free Is the Soviet Press?" *New York Review of Books*, 36 (28 Sept. 1989), 55-58.

6469. McNair, Brian, "Glasnost and Restructuring in the Soviet Media," *Media, Culture and Society*, 11 (July 1989), 327-49.

6470. -----, "Television in a Post-Soviet Union," *Screen*, 33, no. 3 (Autumn 1992), 300-20.

6471. McReynolds, Louise, "St. Petersburg's `Boulevard' Press and the Process of Urbanization," *Journal of Urban History*, 18, no. 2 (Feb. 1992), 123-40.

6472. Mickiewicz, Ellen, "Mass Culture, Change, and Mobilization: The Media Revolution," *Soviet Union/Union Sovietique*, 15, no. 2-3 (1988), 187-200.

6473. -----, "Soviet Viewers Are Seeing More, Including News of the US," *AAASS Newsletter*, 27, no. 3 (May 1987), 1ff.

6474. -----, "Understanding the World: the Cognitive Grid of Soviet Television News," in Thomas F. Remington, ed., *Politics and the Soviet System: Essays in Honor of Frederick Barghoorn* (New York: St. Martin's Press, 1989), 12-28.

6475. -----, and Dawn Plumb Jamison, "Ethnicity and Soviet Television," *Journal of Communication*, 41, no. 2 (Spring 1991), 150-61.

6476. Mihajlov, Mihajlo, "A Talk with the Editor of `Ogonyok': Spectator and Participant," *New Leader* (20 Feb. 1989), 10-16.

6477. Milligan, Ron, "Soviet Journalists Discuss Glasnost," *Editor and Publisher*, 121 (11 June 1988), 54-56.

6478. Mitkova, Tatyana, and Pyotr Reshetov, "Glasnost, R.I.P." *Harper's*, 282, no. 1691 (Apr. 1991), 22ff.

6479. "Monday Memo: `It's Creating a Brand-New Marketplace'" [Cable Television], *Broadcasting*, 121, no. 20 (11 Nov. 1991), 95.

6480. Moore, Patrick, "War Comes to the Airwaves," *Report on Eastern Europe*, 2, no. 39 (27 Sept. 1991), 34-37.

6481. Morton, John, "The Business of Journalism: Power of the Press in Russia and the U.S.," *Washington Journalism Review*, 13, no. 8 (Oct. 1991), 54-55.

6482. "Moscow Bookstore, with Sales of $250,000, Starts Second Year," *Publishers Weekly*, 236 (8 Dec. 1989), 9.

6483. Muratov, Sergei Aleksandrovich, "Soviet Television and the Structure of Broadcasting Authority," *Journal of Communication*, 41, no. 2 (Spring 1991), 172-84.

6484. Naylor, Thomas H., "Gorbachev's Public Relations Strategy," *Communication World*, 5 (May 1988), 20-23.

6485. O'Clery, Conor, "Hold the Presses," *New Republic* (1 Apr. 1991), 15-18.

6486. Oltay, Edith, "Book Publishing and Distribution: The Struggle to Survive," *Report on Eastern Europe*, 2, no. 45 (8 Nov. 1991), 11-14.

6487. Pearson, Tony, "Soviet Television in Transition," *Coexistence*, 29, no. 2 (June 1992), 227ff.

6488. Peroomian, Rubina, "Perestroika Hits Publishing," *Ararat*, 32, no. 126 (Spring 1991), 50-51.

6489. Pipes, Daniel, "The Poll Gorbachev Hated," *Orbis*, 34, no. 1 (Winter 1990), 107-08.

6490. "Public Opinion Polls in the USSR," *Perestroika Annual*, 2 (1989), 291-94.

6491. Reid, C., "Oman is Optimistic on Copyright Protection in China and Russia," *Publishers Weekly*, 232 (4 Dec. 1987), 14.

6492. Remington, Thomas F., "Gorbachev and the Strategy of Glasnost'," in his *Politics and the Soviet System: Essays in Honor of Frederick Barghoorn* (New York: St. Martin's Press, 1989), 56-82.

6493. Remnick, David, "Chaplygin Street Blues," *New York Review of Books*, 38 (25 Apr. 1991), 3-4.

6494. Rich, Vera, "Russia: Future of Medical Newspaper," *Lancet*, 341, no. 8850 (10 Apr. 1993), 950.

6495. Rubanov, V., "From the `Cult of Secrecy' to the Information Culture," *Soviet Law and Government*, 28, no. 1 (Summer 1989), 6-23.

6496. Rubin, David M., "How the News Media Reported on Three Mile Island and Chernobyl," *Journal of Communications*, 37, no. 3 (Summer 1987), 42-57.

6497. Rubinstein, Alvin Z., "The USSR in Turmoil: Views from the Right, Center, and Left," *Orbis*, 35, no. 2 (Spring 1991), 267-84.

6498. Rudenko, M., "On the Brink of an Information Abyss," *Soviet Law and Government*, 28, no. 4 (Spring 1990), 91-92.

6499. Runnion, Norman, "A Productive Exchange," *Editor and Publisher*, 121 (6 Aug. 1988), 12-15.

6500. "Samizdat in Moscow," *Glasnost*, 2, no. 5, issues no. 28-29 (Jan-Mar. 1990), 14-21.

6501. Sanoff, A. P., "Mikhail Gorbachev, Author," *U.S. News & World Report*, 103 (12 Oct. 1987), 73.

6502. Savchenko, Alexei, "The Truth and Nothing But...," *World & I*, 6, no. 8 (Aug. 1991), 533-36.

6503. Schillinger, Elisabeth, "Two Moscow Dailies: Content Changes and *Glasnost'*," *Journalism Quarterly*, 66, no. 4 (Winter 1989), 828-35.

6504. -----, and Catherine Porter, "Glasnost and the Transformation of *Moscow News*," *Journal of Communication*, 41, no. 2 (Spring 1991), 125-49.

6505. Schneider, William, "Political Pulse," *National Journal*, 22, no. 23 (9 June 1990), 1438.

6506. Shatzkin, Leonard, "Plus ca Change ...," *Publishers Weekly*, 238, no. 9 (15 Feb. 1991), S5-8.

6507. Sheikh, Ali T., "Not the Whole Truth: Soviet and Western Media Coverage of the Afghan Conflict," *Conflict Quarterly*, 10, no. 4 (Fall 1990), 73-92.

6508. Simpson, John, "Did TV Undo an Empire?" *World Monitor*, 3, no. 3 (Mar. 1990), 28-30.

6509. Skedgell, M., "Russian Bookstores Slow to Change," *Publishers Weekly*, 234 (8 Apr. 1988), 21-22.

6510. Slowik, George W., Jr., "Fourth U.S.-Soviet Book Talks `Most Productive' Yet," *Publishers Weekly*, 237, no. 47 (23 Nov. 1990), 10.

6511. "Soviet Presswatch," *American Spectator* (a regular department produced between Fall 1990 and Jan. 1992).

6512. "Soviet TV: Now You See It, Now You Don't," *AAASS Newsletter*, 31, no. 3 (May 1991), 5-6.

6513. Stefanescu, Crisula, "An Overview of Radio Broadcasting," *Report on Eastern Europe*, 2, no. 31 (2 Aug. 1991), 35-39.

6514. -----, "Publishing Industry Faces Economic Problems," *Report on Eastern Europe*, 2, no. 34 (23 Aug. 1991), 22-26.

6515. Strelyanyi, Anatolii, "Soviet Journalists Debate the Future," *Report on the USSR*, 2, no. 50 (14 Dec. 1990), 10-11.

6516. Sussman, Leonard R., "The New Press Law of the USSR," *Freedom at Issue*, no. 116 (Sept-Oct. 1990), 34-36.

6517. -----, "Shock Waves of a Freer Press," *Freedom at Issue*, no. 112 (Jan-Feb. 1990), 56-63.

6518. -----, and Mark J. Sussman, "The Birth of *Glasnost'*," *Freedom at Issue*, no. 98 (Sept-Oct. 1987), 17-20.

6519. Taubman, Philip, "The Perils of Reporting from Moscow," *New York Times Magazine* (21 Sept. 1986), 59ff.

6520. -----, "The USSR and the Press," *Current*, 291 (Mar-Apr. 1987), 28-33.

6521. Teague, Elizabeth, "Airbrushing in These Days of Glasnost," *Report on the USSR*, 2, no. 45 (9 Nov. 1990), 11-14.

6522. Tismaneanu, Vladimir, "Eastern Europe: The Story the Media Missed," *Bulletin of the Atomic Scientists*, 46, no. 2 (Mar. 1990), 17-21.

6523. Tolz, Vera, "Adoption of the Press Law: A New Situation for the Soviet Media?" *Report on the USSR*, 2, no. 27 (6 July 1990), 9-11.

6524. -----, "Alternative Press in the USSR," *Report on the USSR*, 3, no. 21 (24 May 1991), 6-11.

6525. -----, "Central Media Wage Propaganda Campaign Against Lithuania," *Report on the USSR*, 2, no. 15 (13 Apr. 1990), 1-3.

6526. -----, "The Impact of the New Press Law: A Preliminary Assessment," *Report on the USSR*, 2, no. 45 (9 Nov. 1990), 4-7.

6527. -----, "The New Role of the Media and Public Opinion under Mikhail Gorbachev," *Journal of Communist Studies*, 9, no. 1 (Mar. 1993), 192-212.

6528. -----, "Recent Attempts to Curb *Glasnost'*," *Report on the USSR*, 3, no. 9 (1 Mar. 1991), 1-6.

6529. -----, "The Traditional Press," *Report on the USSR*, 3, no. 43 (25 Oct. 1991), 4-5.

6530. "Towards a Free Press," *Soviet Analyst*, 17 (1 June 1988), 6.

6531. Urban, George R., "Radio Freeing Europe," *National*

Review, 42 (25 June 1990), 40-43.

6532. Urban, Michael E., "The Russian Free Press in the Transition to a Post-Communist Society," *Journal of Communist Studies*, 9, no. 2 (June 1993), 20-40.

6533. "US-USSR Commission on TV," *AAASS Newsletter*, 30, no. 5 (Nov. 1990), 6.

6534. Vamos, Miklos, "Eastern Europe's New Press Lords," *Nation*, 253 (30 Sept. 1991), 368ff.

6535. Vartanov, Anri, "Television as Spectacle and Myth," *Journal of Communication*, 41, no. 2 (Spring 1991), 162-71.

6536. Voinovich, Vladimir, "Where Glasnost Has Its Limits," *New York Times Magazine* (19 July 1987), 30-31.

6537. Volos, Vadim, "The Media Revolution in Leningrad," *Freedom Review*, 22, no. 3 (May-June 1991), 34-37.

6538. Walker, Martin, "Geraldoski," *New Republic* (26 Aug. 1991), 16-17.

6539. -----, "Soviet Free Press: Can It Survive the Free Market?" *Nation*, 253 (25 Nov. 1991), 664-67.

6540. Watters, Kathleen, "Central Asia and the Central Press: A Study in News Coverage," *Journal of Soviet Nationalities*, 1, no. 2 (Summer 1990), 99-121.

6541. Wedgwood-Benn, David, "Gorbachev, the Media and Liberalisation," *World Today*, 42, no. 4 (Apr. 1986), 57-58.

6542. Weinberg, Steven, "Soviet Journalists: Starting to Dig," *Bulletin of the Atomic Scientists*, 47, no. 6 (July-Aug. 1991), 22-25.

6543. -----, "Summer of Muck," *Mother Jones*, 16 (July-Aug. 1991), 20-23.

6544. "When All the News No Longer Fits," *Glasnost*, 2, no. 2, issues no. 21-23 (Mar-May 1989), 4-7.

6545. White, Stephen, and Olga Kryshtanovskaya, "Public Attitudes to the KGB: A Research Note," *Europe-Asia Studies*, 45, no. 1 (1993), 169ff.

6546. Wishnevsky, Julia, "Press Law Makes Trouble for Writers' Unions," *Report on the USSR*, 2, no. 36 (2 Sept. 1990), 19-22.

6547. -----, "The Purge of TSN: A Ban on Information," *Report on the USSR*, 3, no. 14 (5 Apr. 1991), 4-9.

6548. -----, "A Rare Insight into Soviet Censorship," *Report on the USSR*, 2, no. 36 (7 Sept. 1990), 5-7.

6549. Woll, Josephine, "Fruits of *Glasnost*: A Sampling from the Soviet Press," *Dissent*, 36, no. 1 (Winter 1989), 25-38.

6550. Yasmann, Viktor, "Can *Glasnost'* Be Reversed?" *Report on the USSR*, 3, no. 5 (1 Feb. 1991), 26-29.

6551. -----, "Soviet Television after Glasnost," *Report on the USSR*, 2, no. 45 (9 Nov. 1990), 7-11.

6552. Young, Cathy, "Soviet Presswatch: Growing Pains," *American Spectator*, 24, no. 9 (Sept. 1991), 29-30.

6553. -----, "Soviet Presswatch: Mr. Personality," *American Spectator*, 24, no. 6 (June 1991), 27-28.

6554. -----, "Soviet Presswatch: Solidarity with Saddam," *American Spectator*, 24, no. 2 (Feb. 1991), 31-32.

6555. -----, "Soviet Presswatch: Taking Care of Business," *American Spectator*, 24, no. 3 (Mar. 1991), 29-30.

6556. Young, Marilyn J., and Michael K. Launer, "Redefining Glasnost in the Soviet Media: The Recontextualization of Chernobyl," *Journal of Communication*, 41, no. 2 (Spring 1991), 102-24.

6557. Zagalsky, Leonid, "Soviet Journalists: We Can Talk, But the Line Is Busy," *Bulletin of the Atomic Scientists*, 47, no. 6 (July-Aug. 1991), 26-30.

6558. Zakharov, Igor, "The New Press," *Report on the USSR*, 3, no. 43 (25 Oct. 1991), 1-2.

6559. Zanga, Louis, "The State of the Press," *Report on Eastern Europe*, 2, no. 45 (8 Nov. 1991), 1-3.

6560. Zaraev, Mikhail, "Rip Van Winkle Meets the Soviet Union," *World Monitor*, 4, no. 4 (Apr. 1991), 16ff.

6561. Zaslavskaia, T., "Living with One's Eyes Open," *Soviet Sociology*, 29, no. 3 (May-June 1990), 7-21.

6562. Zilper, Nadia, "The Consequences of Glasnost," *Library Journal*, 116, no. 9 (15 May 1991), 44-49.

XXX. Military Affairs and Military Doctrine
BOOKS

6563. Armstrong, G. P., *Reasonable Sufficiency: The New Soviet Military Doctrine* (Ottawa: Department of National Defence, Operational Research and Analysis Establishment, 1989).

6564. Becker, Abraham S., *Ogarkov's Complaint and Gorbachev's Dilemma: The Soviet Defense Budget and Party-Military Conflict* (Santa Monica, CA: RAND, 1987).

6565. Blank, Stephen J., and Jacob W. Kipp, *The Soviet Military and the Future* (Westport, CT: Greenwood Press, 1992).

6566. Bluth, Christopher, *New Thinking in Soviet Military Policy* (New York: Council on Foreign Relations Press, 1990).

6567. Bowman, Steven R., *NATO-Warsaw Pact Ground and Air Conventional Force Estimates: A Primer* (Washington, DC: Library of Congress, Congressional Research Service, 1990).

6568. Catudal, Honore M., *Soviet Nuclear Strategy from Stalin to Gorbachev: A Revolution in Soviet Military and Political Thinking* (Atlantic Highlands, NJ: Humanities Press International, 1989).

6569. Cohen, Richard, *Superpowers in Economic Decline: U.S. Strategy for the Transcentury Era* (Bristol, PA: Crane Russak, 1990).

6570. Colton, Timothy, and Thane Gustafson, eds., *Soldiers and the Soviet State: Civil-Military Relations from Brezhnev to*

Gorbachev (Princeton: Princeton University Press, 1990).

6571. Cooper, Leo, *The Political Economy of Soviet Military Power* (Basingstoke and London: Macmillan Press, 1989).

6572. Corcoran, Edward A., *Perestroika and the Soviet Military: Implications for U.S. Policy* (Washington, DC: Cato Institute, 1990).

6573. Currie, Kenneth, *Soviet Military Politics: Contemporary Issues* (New York: Paragon House, 1992).

6574. Douglass, Joseph D., Jr., and Neil C. Livingstone, *America the Vulnerable: The Threat of Chemical and Biological Warfare* (Lexington, MA: Lexington Books, 1987).

6575. Eyal, Jonathan, ed., *The Warsaw Pact and the Balkans: Moscow's Southern Flank* (New York: St. Martin's Press, 1989).

6576. Fitzgerald, Mary C., *The Soviet Military on SDI* (Alexandria, VA: Center for Naval Analyses, 1987).

6577. Flynn, Gregory, ed., *Soviet Military Doctrine and Western Policy* (New York: Routledge & Kegan Paul, 1989).

6578. Frank, William C., and Philip S. Gillette, eds., *Soviet Military Doctrine from Lenin to Gorbachev, 1915-1991* (Westport, CT: Greenwood Publishing Group, 1992).

6579. Furtado, Francis J., *U.S. and Soviet Land-Attack SLCM Programs: Implications for Strategic Stability* (Ottawa: Operational Research and Analysis Establishment, 1990).

6580. Garthoff, Raymond, *Deterrence and the Revolution in Soviet Military Doctrine* (Washington, DC: Brookings Institution, 1992).

6581. Goldberg, Andrew C., *New Developments in Soviet Military Strategy* (Washington, DC: Center for Strategic and International Studies, 1987).

6582. Green, William C., and Theodore Karasik, eds., *Gorbachev and His Generals: The Reform of Soviet Military Doctrine* (Boulder, CO: Westview Press, 1990).

6583. Hall, Robert, *Soviet Military Art in a Time of Change: Command and Control of the Future Battlefield* (Washington, DC: Brassey's, 1991).

6584. Herspring, Dale R., *The Soviet High Command 1967-1989: Personalities and Policies* (Princeton: Princeton University Press, 1990).

6585. Holden, Gerard, *Soviet Military Reform: Conventional Disarmament and the Crisis of Militarised Socialism* (London: Pluto Press, with the Transnational Institute, distributed in the USA by Paul & Co., 1991).

6586. Holoboff, Elaine M., *The Soviet Response to Star Wars: Past, Present and Future* (York: York Centre for International and Strategic Studies, 1987).

6587. Jacobsen, Carl G., ed., *The Soviet Defence Enigma: Estimating Costs and Burden* (Oxford: Oxford University Press, 1987).

6588. -----, *Strategic Power: USA/USSR* (New York: St. Martin's Press, 1990).

6589. Johnson, Nicholas L., *Soviet Military Strategy in Space* (London: Jane's Publications, Inc., 1987).

6590. Kagan, Boris, *Soviet ABM Early Warning System: Satellite-Based Project M* (Falls Church, VA: Delphic Associates, 1991).

6591. Krause, Joachim, and Charles K. Mallory, *Chemical Weapons in Soviet Military Doctrine: Military and Historical Experience, 1915-1991* (Boulder, CO: Westview Press, 1992).

6592. Lambeth, Benjamin S., *Is Soviet Defense Becoming Civilianised?* (Santa Monica, CA: RAND, 1990).

6593. Langdon, Frank C., and Douglas A. Ross, eds., *Superpower Maritime Strategy in the Pacific* (New York: Routledge, 1990).

6594. Leebaert, Derek, and Timothy Dickinson, eds., *Soviet Stategy and the New Military Thinking* (Cambridge: Cambridge University Press, 1992).

6595. Macgregor, Douglas A., *The Soviet-East German Military Alliance* (New York: Cambridge University Press, 1989).

6596. MccGwire, Michael, *Military Objectives in Soviet Foreign Policy* (Washington, DC: Brookings Institution, 1987).

6597. Olkhovsky, Paul, *After Afghanistan: Two Opposing Views on the Soviet Military* (Alexandria, VA: Center for Naval Analyses, 1991).

6598. Pay, John, and Geoffrey Till, eds., *East-West Relations in the 1990s: The Naval Dimension* (New York: St. Martin's Press, 1990).

6599. Perkins, Ray, Jr., *The ABCs of the Soviet-American Nuclear Arms Race* (Pacific Grove, CA: Brooks-Cole, 1991).

6600. Popper, Steven W., *The Economic Cost of Soviet Military Manpower Requirements* (Santa Monica, CA: RAND, 1989).

6601. Porter, Bruce D., *Red Armies in Crisis* (Washington, DC: Center for Strategic and International Studies, 1991).

6602. Ranft, Bryan, and Geoffrey Till, *The Sea in Soviet Strategy*, 2nd ed. (Annapolis: Naval Institute Press, 1989).

6603. Rivkin, David B., Jr., *Changes in Soviet Military Thinking: How Do They Add Up?* (Washington, DC: Heritage Foundation, 1989).

6604. Rossignol, Michel, *NATO in a Changing World* (Ottawa: Library of Parliament, Research Branch, 1989).

6605. Rowen, Henry S., and Charles Wolf, Jr., eds., *The Impoverished Superpower: Perestroika and the Soviet Military Burden* (San Francisco: Institute for Contemporary Studies Press, 1990).

6606. Rumer, Eugene B., *The End of a Monolith: The Politics of Military Reform in the Soviet Armed Forces* (Santa Monica, CA: RAND, 1991).

6607. Scanlan, Michael D., *Conventional Armed Forces in Europe (CFE) Negotiations: Facts and Figures* (Washington, DC: Library of Congress, Congressional Research Service, 1990).

6608. Sherr, James, *Soviet Power: The Continuing Challenge* (New York: St. Martin's Press, 1987).

6609. Snow, Donald M., ed., *Soviet-American Security Relations in the 1990s* (Lexington, MA: Lexington Books, 1989).

6610. Stringer, Hugh, *Deterring Chemical Warfare: U.S. Policy Options for the 1990s* (Washington, DC: Pergamon-Brassey's International Defense Publications, 1986).

6611. Tanham, George K., and Alvin H. Bernstein, eds., *Military Basing and the U.S.-Soviet Military Balance in Southeast Asia* (New York: Crane Russak, 1989).

6612. US Congress. House. Committee on Armed Services. Defense Burdensharing Panel. *The Balance of Military Forces.* 100th Congress, 2nd Session, 1988, HASC 100-112.

6613. US Congress. House. Committee on Armed Services. Defense Policy Panel. *The Fading Threat: Soviet Conventional Military Power in Decline.* 101st Congress, 2nd Session (Washington, DC: Government Printing Office, 1990).

6614. US Congress. House. Committee on Armed Services. Defense Policy Panel. *General Secretary Mikhail Gorbachev and the Soviet Military: Assessing His Impact and the Potential for Future Changes.* 100th Congress, 2nd Session, 13 Sept. 1988 (Washington, DC: Government Printing Office, 1988).

6615. US Congress. House. Committee on Armed Services. Defense Policy Panel. *Gorbachev's Force Reductions and the Restructuring of Soviet Forces.* 101st Congress, 1st Session (Washington, DC: Government Printing Office, 1989).

6616. US Congress. House. Committee on Armed Services. Defense Policy Panel. *The Impact of Gorbachev's Reform Movement on the Soviet Military.* 100th Congress, 2nd Session (Washington, DC: Government Printing Office, 1988).

6617. US Congress. House. Committee on Armed Services. Defense Policy Panel. *Soviet Mobilization Readiness and the U.S. Defense Program,* 100th Congress, 2nd Session, 1988, HASC 100-86.

6618. US Congress. Senate. Committee on Foreign Relations. *The Future of NATO.* 101st Congress, 2nd Session (Washington, DC: Government Printing Office, 1990).

6619. US Department of Defense. *Soviet Military Power* (Washington, DC: Government Printing Office, annually).

6620. Voas, Jeanette, *Preventing Afghanistans: Reform in Soviet Policymaking on Military Intervention Abroad* (Alexandria, VA: Center for Naval Analyses, 1990).

6621. Wardak, Ghulam D., comp., *The Voroshilov Lectures: Material from the Soviet General Staff,* vol. 1: *Issues of Soviet Military Strategy* (Washington, DC: National Defense University Press, Government Printing Office, 1989).

6622. Watson, Bruce W., and Susan M. Watson, eds., *The Soviet Naval Threat to Europe: Military and Political Dimensions* (Boulder, CO: Westview Press, 1989).

6623. Weinberger, Caspar, *Soviet Military Power 1986* (Washington, DC: US Department of Defense, Government Printing Office, 1986).

6624. Zamascikov, Sergei, *Gorbachev and the Soviet Military* (Santa Monica, CA: RAND, 1988).

6625. Zisk, Kimberly Marten, *Engaging the Enemy: Organization Theory and Soviet Military Innovation* (Princeton: Princeton University Press, 1993).

ARTICLES

6626. Adragna, Steven P., "A New Soviet Military? Doctrine and Strategy," *Orbis,* 33, no. 2 (Spring 1989), 165-79.

6627. Alan, Ray, "Can NATO Survive Gorbachev?" *New Leader,* 73, no. 6 (16 Apr. 1990), 5-6.

6628. Arbatov, Georgii, "The Army for the Country or the Country for the Army?" *Soviet Law and Government,* 30, no. 3 (Winter 1991-92), 28-33.

6629. Arkin, William H., Joshua Handler and Hans Kristensen, "Soviets Disarm Navy, Mysteriously," *Bulletin of the Atomic Scientists,* 46, no. 4 (May 1990), 7ff.

6630. Armstrong, G. P., "Reasonable Sufficiency: The New Soviet Military Doctrine," *Canadian Defence Quarterly,* 19, no. 2 (Autumn 1989), 22-26.

6631. Arnett, Robert, "Can Civilians Control the Military?" *Orbis,* 38, no. 1 (Winter 1994), 41-57.

6632. -----, and Mary FitzGerald, "A Volunteer Red Army?" *Orbis,* 34, no. 3 (Summer 1990), 398-402.

6633. Atkeson, Edward B., "*Perestroika* and the Soviet Armed Forces: Can Gorbachev Count on Their Loyalty?" *Army,* 39, no. 12 (Dec. 1989), 18ff.

6634. -----, "The Soviet Military: Post-Coup," *Army,* 41, no. 11 (Nov. 1991), 14-25.

6635. Aubin, Stephen P., "New Realities on the European Front," *Air Force Magazine,* 72, no. 4 (Apr. 1989), 70-74.

6636. Ball, Deborah Yarmike, "Ethnic Conflict, Unit Performance, and the Soviet Armed Forces," *Armed Forces and Society,* 20, no. 2 (Winter 1994), 239-58.

6637. Baucom, Donald R., "Hail to the Chiefs: The Untold History of Reagan's SDI Decision," *Policy Review,* no. 53 (Summer 1990), 66-73.

6638. Bell, Coral, "Why Russia Should Join NATO," *National Interest,* no. 22 (Winter 1990-91), 37-47.

6639. Blackwill, Robert D., and Jeffrey W. Legro, "Constraining Ground Force Exercises of NATO and the Warsaw Pact," *International Security,* 14, no. 3 (Winter 1989-90), 68-98.

6640. Bluth, Christoph, "The Evolution of Soviet Military Doctrine," *Survival,* 30, no. 2 (Mar-Apr. 1988), 149-61.

6641. Bova, Russell, "The Soviet Military and Economic Reform," *Soviet Studies,* 40, no. 3 (July 1988), 385-405.

6642. Brada, J. C., and R. L. Graves, "The Slowdown in Soviet Defense Expenditures," *Southern Economic Journal*, 54 (Apr. 1988), 969-84.

6643. Braun, Aurel, "Whither the Warsaw Pact in the Gorbachev Era?" *International Journal*, 43, no. 1 (Winter 1987-88), 63-105.

6644. Brement, Marshall, "Reflections on Soviet New Thinking on Security Questions," *Naval War College Review*, 42, no. 4 (Autumn 1989), 22-36.

6645. Briancon, Pierre, "Discontent in the Soviet Army," *World Press Review*, 37 (Sept. 1990), 47.

6646. Bridge, T. D., "Gorbachev Reforms: Soviet Army Views," *Army Quarterly and Defence Journal*, 117 (Apr. 1987), 188-93.

6647. Broad, William J., "The Secrets of Soviet Star Wars," *New York Times Magazine* (28 June 1987), 22ff.

6648. Brooks, Thomas A., "Gorshkov's Final Words: What Do They Mean? A Nuclear War-Fighting Treatise," *US Naval Institute Proceedings*, 115, no. 5 (May 1989), 136-38.

6649. -----, "The Soviet Navy in 1989: A U.S. View," *US Naval Institute Proceedings*, 116, no. 5 (May 1990), 235-38.

6650. Carter, Stephen, "Soviet Military Ideology," *Report on the USSR*, 3, no. 36 (6 Sept. 1991), 16-19.

6651. Cebrowski, Arthur K., "Gorshkov's Final Words: What Do They Mean? A Matter of Timing?" *US Naval Institute Proceedings*, 115, no. 5 (May 1989), 138ff.

6652. Chernoff, F., "Ending the Cold War: The Soviet Retreat and the US Military Buildup," *International Affairs*, 67 (Jan. 1991), 111-26.

6653. Cheung, T. M., "Holding the Line: Soviet Commander Reveals Details of Far East Cutbacks," *Far Eastern Economic Review*, 152 (27 June 1991), 23ff.

6654. Cigar, Norman, "The Navy's Battle of the Budget: Soviet Style," *Naval War College Review*, 63, no. 2 (Spring 1990), 6-30.

6655. -----, "The Soviet Navy in the Persian Gulf: Naval Diplomacy in a Combat Zone," *Naval War College Review*, 42, no. 2 (Spring 1989), 56-88.

6656. Cimbala, S. J., "U.S.-Soviet Command Reciprocity: Interdependence of Survivable Leadership," *Armed Forces and Society*, 13, no. 3 (Spring 1987), 353-69.

6657. Clarke, Douglas L., "Proposals for Troop Cuts in Central Europe," *Report on Eastern Europe*, 1, no. 7 (16 Feb. 1990), 38-39.

6658. -----, "Some Revelations about the Warsaw Pact," *Report on Eastern Europe*, 2, no. 18 (3 May 1991), 34-37.

6659. -----, "Soviet Military Reform: A Moving Target," *Report on the USSR*, 3, no. 47 (22 Nov. 1991), 14-19.

6660. -----, "USSR Reveals Arms Data," *Report on the USSR*, 2, no. 2 (12 Jan. 1990), 10-11.

6661. -----, "The Warsaw Pact's Finale," *Report on Eastern Europe*, 2, no. 29 (19 July 1991), 39-42.

6662. -----, "What Future for the Warsaw Pact?" *Report on Eastern Europe*, 1, no. 3 (19 Jan. 1990), 37-39.

6663. Codevilla, A. M., "Is There Still a Soviet Threat?" *Commentary*, 86 (Nov. 1988), 23-28.

6664. Colton, Timothy J., "The Military and Economic Reform: A Comment," *Soviet Economy*, 2, no. 3 (July-Sept. 1986), 228-32.

6665. Cooper, Julian, "Soviet Military Has a Finger in Every Pie," *Bulletin of the Atomic Scientists*, 46, no. 10 (Dec. 1990), 22-25.

6666. Courter, Jim, "The Gathering Storm: Are The Soviets Preparing for World War III?" *Policy Review*, no. 42 (Fall 1987), 2-9.

6667. Covault, Craig, "USSR Breakup Paralyzing Advanced Soviet Military, Space Development," *Aviation Week & Space Technology*, 135, no. 9 (2 Sept. 1991), 22-23.

6668. Covington, Stephen R., "NATO and Soviet Military Doctrine," *Washington Quarterly*, 12, no. 4 (Autumn 1989), 73-81.

6669. Crozier, Brian, "Will the Army Take Over?" *National Review*, 40 (9 Dec. 1988), 26ff.

6670. Cutshaw, Charles Q., "Behind Soviet Force Cuts, Ominous New Directions in Posture," *Army*, 39, no. 8 (Aug. 1989), 16ff.

6671. Danilenko, Ignat, "Perestroika: Challenge of the Times Accepted," *Soviet Military Review*, no. 11 (Nov. 1987), 10-12.

6672. Daskal, Steven E., "Estimating Soviet Defense Expenditures," *US Naval Institute Proceedings*, 115, no. 4 (Apr. 1989), 107-10.

6673. "The Day Glasnost Came to the Soviet Army," *Economist*, 311 (29 Apr. 1989), 39-40.

6674. Dobriansky, Paula J., and David B. Rivkin, Jr., "Does the Soviet Military Oppose Perestroika?" *Orbis*, 35, no. 2 (Spring 1991), 163-78.

6675. Doerner, W. R., "Questions about Doctrine," *Time*, 131 (28 Mar. 1988), 38.

6676. Donnelly, Christopher, "The Development of Soviet Military Policy in the 1990s," *RUSI Journal*, 135, no. 1 (Spring 1990), 21-25.

6677. -----, "Evolutionary Problems in the Former Soviet Armed Forces," *Survival*, 34, no. 3 (Autumn 1992), 28-42.

6678. Erickson, John, "Fallen from Grace: The New Russian Military," *World Policy Journal*, 10, no. 3 (Summer 1993), 19-26.

6679. Evangelista, Matthew, "Exploring the Soviet `Threat' to Europe," *Bulletin of the Atomic Scientists*, 43, no. 1 (Jan-Feb. 1987), 14ff.

6680. FitzGerald, Mary C., "Soviet Armed Forces after the Gulf

War: Demise of the Defensive Doctrine?" *Report on the USSR*, 3, no. 16 (19 Apr. 1991), 1-4.

6681. -----. "The Soviet Image of Future War: 'Through the Prism of the Persian Gulf'," *Comparative Strategy*, 10, no. 4 (Oct-Dec. 1991), 393-435.

6682. -----, "The Soviet Military and the New 'Technological Operation'," *Naval War College Review*, 44, no. 4 (Autumn 1991), 16-44.

6683. -----, "The Soviet Military on SDI," *Studies in Comparative Communism*, 19, no. 3-4 (Autumn-Winter 1986), 177-91.

6684. Foye, Stephen, "The Armed Forces: From Defending the Empire to Saving the Union," *Report on the USSR*, 3, no. 1 (4 Jan. 1991), 10-12.

6685. -----, "The Case for a Coup: Gorbachev or the Generals?" *Report on the USSR*, 3, no. 2 (11 Jan. 1991), 1-5.

6686. -----, "El'tsin Begins Housecleaning in the Defense Ministry," *Report on the USSR*, 3, no. 36 (6 Sept. 1991), 31-34.

6687. -----, "From Union to Commonwealth: Will the Armed Forces Go Along?" *Report on the USSR*, 3, no. 51-52 (20 Dec. 1991), 4-7.

6688. -----, "Gorbachev and His Generals," *Report on the USSR*, 2, no. 20 (18 May 1990), 15-16.

6689. -----, "Gorbachev and the Depoliticization of the Army," *Report on the USSR*, 2, no. 37 (14 Sept. 1990), 1-3.

6690. -----, "Gorbachev Boosts Military Reform," *Report on the USSR*, 2, no. 35 (31 Aug. 1990), 8-9.

6691. -----, "Gorbachev's Return to Reform: What Does It Mean for the Armed Forces?" *Report on the USSR*, 3, no. 28 (12 July 1991), 5-9.

6692. -----, "Gorbachev, the Army and the Union," *Report on the USSR*, 2, no. 49 (7 Dec. 1990), 1-3.

6693. -----, "The High Command Confronts 'New Political Thinking' at Home and Abroad," *Report on the USSR*, 3, no. 13 (29 Mar. 1991), 24-27.

6694. -----, "Lopatin on Party Control of the Armed Forces," *Report on the USSR*, 2, no. 37 (14 Sept, 1990), 3-5.

6695. -----, "Oversight Committee Rejects CPSU Control over Armed Forces," *Report on the USSR*, 3, no. 16 (19 Apr. 1991), 4-6.

6696. -----, "The Soviet High Command and the Politics of Military Reform," *Report on the USSR*, 3, no. 27 (5 July 1991), 9-14.

6697. -----, "The Soviet Officers Corps and Gorbachev's Crackdown," *Report on the USSR*, 3, no. 5 (1 Feb. 1991), 29-30.

6698. Friedberg, A. L., "The Assessment of Soviet Military Power: Review Essay," *International Security*, 12, no. 3 (Winter 1987-88), 190-202.

6699. Frost, H. E., "A Content Analysis of Recent Soviet Party-

Military Relations," *American Journal of Political Science*, 33 (Feb. 1989), 91-135.

6700. Fulghum, David A., "Third World Threat, Military Budget, Shape Early Concepts of MRF," *Aviation Week & Space Technology*, 135, no. 16 (21 Oct. 1991), 20-21.

6701. Gareyev, Makhmut, "The Revised Soviet Military Doctrine," *Bulletin of the Atomic Scientists*, 44 (Dec. 1988), 30-34.

6702. -----, "Soviet Armed Forces and Glasnost," *Soviet Military Review*, no. 3 (March 1989), 8-9.

6703. Gebhardt, James F., "Restructuring the Tactical Defense," *Military Review*, 70, no. 12 (Dec. 1990), 29-40.

6704. Glantz, David M., "Observing the Soviets: U.S. Army Attaches," *Journal of Military History*, 55, no. 2 (Apr. 1991), 153-84.

6705. Goldberg, Andrew C., "The Present Turbulence in Soviet Military Doctrine," *Washington Quarterly*, 11, no. 3 (Summer 1988), 159-70.

6706. "Gorbachev Takes on the Generals," *Economist*, 303 (6 June 1987), 47-48.

6707. Gorshenin, Aleksandr, "Perestroika Is As Perestroika Does," *Soviet Military Review*, no. 7 (July 1989), 8-9.

6708. Gorshkov, Sergei G., "Gorshkov's Final Words: What Do They Mean? Foreword," *US Naval Institute Proceedings*, 115, no. 5 (May 1989), 132ff.

6709. Goure, Leon, "The Soviet Strategic View," *Strategic Review*, 15, no. 1 (Winter 1987), 81-94.

6710. Greenwald, G. Jonathan, and Walter B. Slocombe, "The Economic Constraints on Soviet Military Power," *Washington Quarterly*, 10, no. 3 (Summer 1987), 117-32.

6711. Gross, Natalie, "Perestroika and Glasnost in the Soviet Armed Forces," *Parameters*, 18 (Sept. 1988), 68-75.

6712. -----, "Youth and the Army in the USSR in the 1980s," *Soviet Studies*, 42, no. 3 (July 1990), 481-98.

6713. Grove, Eric, "The Challenge of East-West Naval Dialogue," *US Naval Institute Proceedings*, 115, no. 9 (Sept. 1989), 113-15.

6714. Haberman, C., "Challenge in the Pacific," *New York Times Magazine* (7 Sept. 1986), 26ff.

6715. Hayward, Thomas B., and Ronald J. Hays, "The Pacific: Is It in the Interest of the West to Make *Perestroika* Work throughout the Pacific," *Sea Power*, 32, no. 1 (Jan., 1989), 44ff.

6716. Herspring, Dale R., "Marshal Akhromeyev and the Future of the Soviet Armed Forces," *Survival*, 28, no. 6 (Nov-Dec. 1986), 524-37.

6717. -----, "Nikolay Ogarkov and the Scientific-Technical Revolution in Soviet Military Affairs," *Comparative Strategy*, 6, no. 1 (Jan-Mar. 1987), 29-59.

6718. -----, "On *Perestroyka*: Gorbachev, Yazov and the Military," *Problems of Communism*, 36, no. 4 (July-Aug. 1987), 99-107.

6719. -----, "The Soviet Military in the Aftermath of the Twenty-seventh Party Congress," *Orbis*, 30, no. 2 (Summer 1986), 297-315.

6720. Hessman, James D., "Soviet Military Power: The *Glasnost'* Edition," *Sea Power*, 32, no. 11 (Nov. 1989), 37-38.

6721. Holloway, David, "State, Society and the Military under Gorbachev," *International Security*, 14, no. 3 (Winter 1989-90), 5-24.

6722. -----, "The Strategic Defense Initiative and the Soviet Union," *Daedalus*, 114, no. 3 (Summer 1985), 257-78.

6723. Holzman, Franklyn D., "Politics and Guesswork: CIA and DIA Estimates of Soviet Military Spending," *International Security*, 14, no. 2 (Fall 1989), 101-31.

6724. "How Russia's Marshals Could Burst Gorbachev's Bubble," *Economist*, 297 (30 Nov. 1985), 45-46.

6725. "International Agreements: Agreement on the Prevention of Dangerous Military Activities, June 12, 1989, United States-Union of Soviet Socialist Republics," *Harvard International Law Journal*, 31 (Winter 1990), 333-38.

6726. Jones, David R., "Gorbachev, the Military and Perestroika," *International Perspectives*, 17, no. 3 (1988), 10-12.

6727. -----, "The Two Faces of Soviet Military Power," *Current History*, 86, no. 522 (Oct. 1987), 313ff.

6728. Jones, Royal Maurice, "Gorbachev, Glasnost, and Perestroika: Their Impact on the Soviet Military," *Journal of Business and Economic Perspectives*, 15 (Spring 1989), 33-45.

6729. Kass, Ilana, and Fred Clark Boli, "The Soviet Military's Transcentury Agenda," *Comparative Strategy*, 9, no. 4 (Oct-Dec. 1990), 319-34.

6730. Kaw, M., "Predicting Soviet Military Intervention," *Journal of Conflict Resolution*, 33, no. 3 (Sept. 1989), 402-29.

6731. Kime, Steve F., "Gorshkov's Final Words: What Do They Mean? Introduction," *US Naval Institute Proceedings*, 115, no. 5 (May 1989), 132.

6732. -----, "War and Politics in the USSR," *Strategic Review*, 15, no. 4 (Fall 1987), 44-54.

6733. Kipp, Jacob W., "A Gde Zhe Ugroza? Soviet Military Doctrine in the Post-Cold War Era," *Military Review*, 70, no. 12 (Dec. 1990), 2-15.

6734. Kiser, John W., "How the Arms Race Really Helps Moscow," *Foreign Policy*, no. 60 (Fall 1985), 40-51.

6735. Kramer Mark, "The Armies of the Post-Soviet States," *Current History*, 91, no. 567 (Oct. 1992), 327-33.

6736. Krause, Keith, "Military Statecraft: Power and Influence in Soviet and American Arms Transfer Relationships," *International Studies Quarterly*, 35, no. 3 (Sept. 1991), 313-36.

6737. "Kremlin Shake-up Moves to Military," *U.S. News & World Report*, 99 (29 July 1985), 8.

6738. Kusin, Vladimir V., "Gorbachev Agrees to Warsaw Pact Meeting on Military Structures," *Report on Eastern Europe*, 2, no. 8 (22 Feb. 1991), 43-45.

6739. -----, "The Soviet Troops: Mission Abandoned," *Report on Eastern Europe*, 1, no. 36 (7 Sept. 1990), 37-38.

6740. -----, "Yet Another End for the Warsaw Pact," *Report on Eastern Europe*, 2, no. 11 (15 Mar. 1991), 34-35.

6741. Larrabee, F. Stephen, "Gorbachev and the Soviet Military," *Foreign Affairs*, 66, no. 5 (Summer 1988), 1002-26.

6742. Lepingwell, John W. R., "Soviet Strategic Air Defense and the Stealth Challenge," *International Security*, 14, no. 2 (Fall 1989), 64-100.

6743. -----, "Towards a Post-Soviet Army," *Orbis*, 36, no. 1 (Winter 1992), 87ff.

6744. Levchenko, Stanislav, "Inside the Soviet Army," *World & I* (Aug. 1990), 108-12.

6745. Livingston, Noyes B., III, "Blitzkrieg in Europe: Is It Still Possible?" *Military Review*, 66, no. 6 (June 1986), 26-38.

6746. Lobov, Vladimir N., General, "Military Reform: Objectives, Principles, Content," *Soviet Law and Government*, 30, no. 3 (Winter 1991-92), 52-65.

6747. Lopatin, V., "The Army and the Economy: Economic Aspects of Military Reform," *Problems of Economics*, 34, no. 3 (July 1991), 62-78.

6748. Lord, Carnes, "On the Future of Strategic Forces," *Parameters*, 16, no. 1 (Spring 1986), 24-32.

6749. Lucas, Michael, "SDI and Europe: Militarization or Common Security?" *World Policy Journal*, 3, no. 2 (Spring 1986), 219-49.

6750. Lushev, Petr, "Soviet and Warsaw Pact Goals and Developments," *RUSI Journal*, 134, no. 3 (Autumn 1989), 3-8.

6751. Mackintosh, Malcolm, "The Evolution of the Warsaw Pact," *RUSI Journal*, 134, no. 4 (Winter 1989), 16-22.

6752. -----, "The New Russian Revolution: The Military Dimension," *Conflict Studies*, no. 247 (Jan. 1992), 1-25.

6753. Mahoney, Shane E., "Defensive Doctrine: The Crisis in Soviet Military Thought," *Slavic Review*, 49, no. 3 (Fall 1990), 398-408.

6754. Mann, Paul, "CIA Sees Long-Term Pressures against Soviet Defense Budget," *Aviation Week & Space Technology* (1 May 1989), 30.

6755. -----, "Judging the Soviets in the Gulf: Are They As Weak As They Look?" *Aviation Week & Space Technology*, 133, no. 23 (3 Dec. 1990), 24.

6756. -----, "Reagan Rules Out Ending SDI Effort in Exchange for Soviet Missile Cuts," *Aviation Week & Space Technology* (30

Sept. 1985), 93ff.

6757. -----, "Soviet Economic Reform May Force Transformation of Entire Military," *Aviation Week & Space Technology*, 128 (2 May 1988), 19.

6758. -----, et al., "Reagan/Gorbachev Summit," *Aviation Week & Space Technology* (14 Dec. 1987), 18-24.

6759. Manthrope, William H. J., "The Soviet Navy in 1989: A Soviet View," *US Naval Institute Proceedings*, 116, no. 5 (May 1990), 232-34.

6760. -----, "The Soviet View," *U.S. Naval Institute Proceedings*, 117, no. 2 (1991), 103-04; 117, no. 5 (1991), 187-90; 117, no. 7 (1991), 103-04; 117, no. 9 (1991), 119-21.

6761. Mark, Hans, "War and Peace in Space," *Journal of International Affairs*, 39 (Summer 1985), 1-21.

6762. McCain, John, "A New Soviet Military? Weapons and Budgets," *Orbis*, 33, no. 2 (Spring 1989), 181-93.

6763. MccGwire, Michael, "Gorshkov's Navy," *US Naval Institute Proceedings*, 115, no. 8 (Aug. 1989), 44-51; no. 9 (Sept. 1989), 42-47.

6764. -----, "Update: Soviet Military Objectives," *World Policy Journal*, 4, no. 4 (Fall 1987), 723-31.

6765. McConnell, J. M., "Shifts in Soviet Views on the Proper Focus of Military Development," *World Politics*, 37 (Apr. 1985), 317-43.

6766. McMichael, Scott R., "Market Relations Threaten Combat-Readiness of Soviet Armed Forces," *Report on the USSR*, 3, no. 42 (18 Oct. 1991), 11-15.

6767. -----, "Military Reform Plan Begins to Take Shape," *Report on the USSR*, 3, no. 43 (25 Oct. 1991), 7-11.

6768. Michta, Andrew A., "The Northern Tier of the Warsaw Pact after 1989," *Journal of Social, Political and Economic Studies*, 15, no. 2 (Summer 1990), 157-73.

6769. Mordoff, Keith F., "NATO Disputes Warsaw Pact Claim of Conventional Parity," *Aviation Week & Space Technology* (6 Feb. 1989), 21-22.

6770. -----, "Perception of Declining Soviet Threat Erodes Support for NATO Modernization," *Aviation Week & Space Technology* (20 Mar. 1989), 84-85.

6771. Morrison, David C., "The Build-Down," *Atlantic Monthly*, 263, no. 6 (June 1989), 60-64.

6772. -----, "Loose Nukes," *National Journal*, 22, no. 9 (3 Mar. 1990), 536.

6773. -----, "SDI: The Living Dead," *National Journal*, 22, no. 47 (24 Nov. 1990), 2846-50.

6774. Morrocco, J. D., "Unilateral Soviet Military Cutbacks Put West on Political Defensive," *Aviation Week & Space Technology*, 129 (12 Dec. 1988), 38-39.

6775. Nagler, Jonathan, "Information, Attitude, and Elite Opinions on the Strategic Defense Initiative," *Social Science Quarterly*, 71, no. 3 (Sept. 1990), 531-42.

6776. Nelson, Ronald R., and Peter Schweizer, "A New Soviet Military? The Next Generation," *Orbis*, 33, no. 2 (Spring 1989), 195-207.

6777. Nihart, F. B., "U.S.-Soviet Armed Forces Exchange Visits," *US Naval Institute Procedings*, 115, no. 9 (Sept. 1989), 116.

6778. Odom, William E., "Can Gorbachev Reform the Soviet Military?" *U.S. News & World Report*, 107 (11 Sept. 1989), 43.

6779. -----, "Soviet Military Doctrine," *Foreign Affairs*, 67 (Winter 1988-89), 114-34.

6780. -----, "The Soviet Military in Transition," *Problems of Communism*, 39, no. 3 (May-June 1990), 51-71.

6781. O'Malley, William D., "The Receding Soviet Military Threat," *Military Review*, 71, no. 12 (Dec. 1991), 25-33.

6782. Panin, Vasily, "Soviet Navy Steering Towards Perestroika," *Soviet Military Review*, no. 7 (July 1989), 12-14.

6783. Partan, M., "Soviet Military Objectives" (Review Article), *International Security*, 12, no. 3 (Winter 1987-88), 203-14.

6784. Peel, Q., and S. Schofield, "The Army Holds the Key to the Future," *World Press Review*, 38 (5 Mar. 1991), 22.

6785. Perle, Richard N., "What the Soviet Army Fears," *U.S. News & World Report*, 111 (30 Sept. 1991), 61.

6786. Petersen, Charles C., "Soviet Military Objectives in the Arctic Theater," *Naval War College Review*, 40, no. 4 (Autumn 1987), 3-22.

6787. Petrie, W., "Military Activity in Space-Is There a Choice?" *Canadian Defence Quarterly*, 15, no. 3 (Winter 1985-86), 31-36.

6788. Pilat, Joseph F., and Paul C. White, "Technology and Strategy in a Changing World," *Washington Quarterly*, 13, no. 2 (Spring 1990), 79-91.

6789. Piotrowski, John L., "A Soviet Space Strategy," *Strategic Review*, 15, no. 4 (Fall 1987), 55-62.

6790. Plous, S., "Perceptual Illusions and Military Realities: Results from a Computer-Simulated Arms Race," *Journal of Conflict Resolution*, 31, no. 1 (Mar. 1987), 5-33.

6791. Polmar, Norman, "The Soviet Navy: A Friendly Assault on Norfolk," *US Naval Institute Proceedings*, 115, no. 11 (Nov. 1989), 136-39.

6792. Prescott, J. M., "Soviet Military Justice and the Challenge of Perestroika," *Military Law Review*, 123 (Winter 1989), 129-50.

6793. Prins, Gwyn, "Soviet Might and Western Blindness" (Review Article), *New Statesman*, 114 (24 July 1987), 15.

6794. Quinn-Judge, Sophie, "Budget Battle: Financial Crunch Puts Generals on the Defensive," *Far Eastern Economic Review*, 152 (30 June 1991), 30.

6795. -----, "Purely Defensive: Moscow Says Its Pacific Fleet Is

Coast-Bound," *Far Eastern Economic Review*, 142 (22 Dec. 1988), 30.

6796. -----, "Ship Out, Navy! Vladivostok's Civilians Would Like the Sailors Gone," *Far Eastern Economic Review*, 146 (16 Nov. 1989), 32.

6797. Rarh, Alexander, "Gorbachev Moves to Placate and Forestall Disgruntled Military Establishment," *Report on the USSR*, 2, no. 11 (16 Mar. 1990), 6-8.

6798. Reynolds, Dana D., "The Washington Papers: Gorbachev's Military Policy in the Third World," *Annals of the Academy of Political and Social Sciences*, 515 (May 1991), 179-80.

6799. Rice, Condoleezza, "Gorbachev and the Military: A Revolution in Security Policy, Too?" *Harriman Institute Forum*, 2, no. 4 (Apr. 1989), 1-8.

6800. -----, "The Soviet Military under Gorbachev," *Current History*, 85, no. 513 (Oct. 1986), 313ff.

6801. Rosefielde, Steven, "Assessing Soviet Reforms in the Defense Industry," *Global Affairs*, 4, no. 4 (Fall 1989), 57-73.

6802. -----, "Soviet Defence Spending: The Contribution of the New Accountancy," *Soviet Studies*, 42, no. 1 (Jan. 1990), 59-80.

6803. Rowny, Edward L., "The New Military Balance," *Freedom at Issue*, no. 114 (May-June 1990), 24-26.

6804. Ruhle, Hans, "Gorbachev's Star Wars," *Atlantic Community Quarterly*, 23, no. 4 (Winter 1985-86), 307-13.

6805. Sandrart, Hans-Henning von, "Defence of the Central Region and Canada's Contribution," *Canadian Defence Quarterly*, 18, no. 4 (Feb. 1989), 13ff.

6806. Schmitt, M. N., and J. E. Moody, "The Soviet Military Justice System," *Air Force Law Review*, 34 (1991), 1-108.

6807. Schweizer, Peter, "The Soviet Military Today: Going High-Tech," *Orbis*, 35, no. 2 (Spring 1991), 195-206.

6808. Scott, Harriet F., "Organization of the Soviet Armed Forces," *Air Force Magazine*, 72, no. 3 (Mar. 1989), 72.

6809. -----, "Top Leaders of the Soviet Armed Forces," *Air Force Magazine*, 70, no. 3 (Mar. 1987), 58.

6810. Scott, William F., "Moscow's Military-Industrial Complex," *Air Force Magazine*, 70, no. 3 (Mar. 1987), 46-51.

6811. -----, "The Soviets and Strategic Defense," *Air Force Magazine*, 69, no. 3 (Mar. 1986), 40-45.

6812. Seaquist, Larry, "Gorshkov's Final Words: What Do They Mean? Hull Down on the Red Horizon," *US Naval Institute Proceedings*, 115, no. 5 (May 1989), 141ff.

6813. Seliunin, Vasilii, "On the General's Bass Notes: From a Conversation with Russian Minister of Defense Pavel Grachev," *Russian Social Science Review*, 34, no. 4 (July-Aug. 1993), 16-23.

6814. Shanker, Thom, "The Soviet Empire Seeks a Course," *Air Force Magazine*, 72, no. 11 (Nov. 1989), 54-59.

6815. Sharpe, Richard, "The Soviet Navy: Will We Have the Forces with Which to Counter Soviet Naval Strategies?" *Sea Power*, 32, no. 1 (Jan. 1989), 28ff.

6816. Snow, Donald M., "Soviet Reform and the High Technology Imperative," *Parameters*, 20, no. 1 (Mar. 1990), 76-87.

6817. "Soviet Bloc Affairs," *International Defense Review* (regular feature in each issue).

6818. "The Soviet Empire: The Military," *U.S. News & World Report*, 106 (13 Mar. 1989), 18ff.

6819. "Soviet General Says Retaliation Considered if U.S. Pursues SDI," *Aviation Week & Space Technology*, 134, no. 14 (8 Apr. 1991), 21.

6820. "Soviet SDIphobia," *Scientific American*, 255 (Dec. 1986), 72ff.

6821. "Soviets May Not Copy Star Wars," *USA Today*, 116 (Aug. 1987), 15.

6822. "Soviet Strategic Forces," *Congressional Digest*, 65 (Oct. 1986), 232ff.

6823. Stares, Paul. "U.S. and Soviet Military Space Programs: A Comparative Assessment," *Daedalus*, 114, no. 2 (Spring 1986), 127-45.

6824. Steinberg, Dmitri, "Trends in Soviet Military Expenditure," *Soviet Studies*, 42, no. 4 (Oct. 190), 675-700.

6825. Strode, Rebecca, "The Soviet Armed Forces: Adaptation to Resource Scarcity," *Washington Quarterly*, 9, no. 2 (Spring 1986), 55-69.

6826. Stubbs, E., and R. Nimroody, "The Soviet Response to Star Wars," *Challenge*, 30 (Mar-Apr. 1987), 21-27.

6827. Sullivan, Eugene P., "The Soviet Navy and the Chernobyl Syndrome," *US Naval Institute Proceedings*, 116, no. 8 (Aug. 1990), 91-92.

6828. Summers, Harry G., Jr., "A Bankrupt Military Strategy," *Atlantic Monthly*, 263, no. 6 (June 1989), 34ff.

6829. Takeshita, Lloyd S., "The Strategic Defense Initiative and NATO," *Military Review*, 66, no. 4 (Apr. 1986), 31-37.

6830. Tedstrom, John, "*Glasnost'* and the Soviet Defense Budget," *Report on the USSR*, 3, no. 29 (19 July 1991), 6-14.

6831. Thies, Wallace J., "'The Demise' of NATO: A Post-mortem," *Parameters*, 20, no. 2 (June 1990), 17-30.

6832. Thomas, Timothy L., "The Reformist Military Deputies: Yeltsins in Fatigues?" *Military Review*, 70, no. 12 (Dec. 1990), 41-48.

6833. Trost, A. H., "The Soviet Navy Arms Control Offensive," *Vital Speeches of the Day*, 54 (1 May 1988), 421-24.

6834. "U.S. and Russian Military-Technical Policy," *Comparative Strategy*, 13, no. 1 (Jan-Mar. 1994), 1-112.

6835. Tsypkin, Mikhail, "The Soviet Military Today: Countering the West in New Ways," *Orbis*, 35, no. 2 (Spring 1991), 207-18.

6836. -----, "The Soviet Military: *Glasnost'* Against Secrecy," *Problems of Communism*, 40, no. 3 (May-June 1991), 51-66.

6837. -----, "Will the Soviet Navy Become a Volunteer Force?" *Report on the USSR*, 2, no. 5 (2 Feb. 1990), 5-7.

6838. Ulsamer, Edgar, "The Guns of Glasnost," *Air Force Magazine*, 70, no. 6 (June 1987), 84ff.

6839. Van Cleave, William R., "Soviet Military Policy: Continuity and Change," *Global Affairs*, 7, no. 1 (Winter 1992), 36-58.

6840. Vikulov, S., "The Military Economic Reform: Essence, Content, and Problems," *Problems of Economics*, 34, no. 3 (July 1991), 79-93.

6841. Volgyes, Ivan, "The Warsaw Pact: Changes in Structure and Function," *Armed Forces and Society*, 15, no. 4 (Summer 1989), 551-70.

6842. Weeks, Albert L., "Soviet Military Doctrine," *Global Affairs*, 3, no. 1 (Winter 1988), 170-87.

6843. Weitz, Richard, "The Evolving Soviet View of Regional Conflicts," *Report on the USSR*, 2, no. 42 (19 Oct. 1990), 4-9.

6844. Westwood, James T., "An Economic and Technological Assessment of the Soviet Navy," *RUSI Journal*, 134, no. 3 (Autumn 1989), 39-44.

6845. Wettig, G., "Changes in Soviet Military Doctrine?" *Atlantic Community Quarterly*, 26, no. 3-4 (Fall-Winter 1988), 275-83.

6846. "Why the Russians Aren't Coming," *Glasnost*, 3, no. 2 (Oct-Dec. 1990), 14-33.

6847. Wolfowitz, Paul, "Regional Conflicts: New Thinking, Old Policy?" *Parameters*, 20, no. 1 (Mar. 1990), 2-8.

6848. Woodard, Joseph K., "The Soviet Navy and Command of the Seas," *Global Affairs*, 4, no. 2 (Spring 1989), 36-48.

6849. Yatron, Gus, "NATO and the Democratic Transition in Eastern Europe," *Freedom Review*, 22, no. 2 (Mar-Apr. 1991), 11-14.

6850. Yazov, [Dmitrii], Army General, "On Soviet Military Doctrine," *RUSI Journal*, 134, no. 4 (Winter 1989), 1-4.

6851. Zeeman, Bert, "The Origins of NATO," *Bulletin of Bibliography*, 47, no. 4 (Dec. 1990), 209-17.

6852. Zhong, Yang, "Civil-Military Relations in Changing Communist Societies: A Comparative Study of China and the Soviet Union," *Studies in Comparative Communism*, 24, no. 1 (Mar. 1991), 77-102.

6853. Zisk, Kimberly Marten, "Soviet Academic Theories on International Conflict and Negotiation: A Research Note," *Journal of Conflict Resolution*, 34, no. 4 (Dec. 1990), 678-93.

XXXI. Nationalism and Separatism; Minorities
BOOKS

6854. Aron, Leon, *Gorbachev's Mounting Nationalities Crisis* (Washington, DC: Heritage Foundation, 1989).

6855. Azrael, Jeremy, *The Soviet "Nationality Front": Some Implications for U.S. Foreign and Security Policy* (Santa Monica, CA: RAND, 1991).

6856. Black, J. L., *Inter-Ethnic Conflict in the USSR, 1990-1991: An International Crisis in Waiting* (Ottawa: Department of National Defence, 1991).

6857. Bremmer, Ian A., and Norman M. Naimark, eds., *Soviet Nationalities Problems* (Stanford: Center for Russian and East European Studies, Stanford University, 1990).

6858. Buttino, Marco, ed., *In a Collapsing Empire: Underdevelopment, Ethnic Conflicts and Nationalisms in the Soviet Union* (Milan: Feltrinelli Editore Milano, 1992).

6859. Carrere d'Encausse, Helene, *The End of the Soviet Empire: The Triumph of Nations* (New York: Basic Books, 1993).

6860. Carter, Stephen K., *Russian Nationalism: Yesterday, Today and Tomorrow* (New York: St. Martin's Press, 1990).

6861. Conquest, Robert, ed., *The Last Empire: Nationality and the Soviet Future* (Stanford: Hoover Institution Press, 1986).

6862. Denber, Rachel, ed., *The Soviet Nationality Reader: The Disintegration in Context* (Boulder, CO: Westview Press, 1992).

6863. Diuk, Nadia, and Adrian Karatnycky, *The Hidden Nations: The People Challenge the Soviet Union* (New York: W. Morrow, 1990).

6864. -----, *New Nations Rising: The Fall of the Soviets and the Challenge of Independence* (New York: John Wiley and Sons, 1993).

6865. Eickelman, Dale F., ed., *Russia's Muslim Frontiers: Directions in Cross-Cultural Analysis* (Bloomington: Indiana University Press, 1993).

6866. Furtado, Charles F., Jr., and Andrea Chandler, eds., *Perestroika in the Soviet Republics* (Boulder, CO: Westview Press, 1992).

6867. Gleason, Gregory, *Federalism and Nationalism: The Struggle for Republican Rights in the USSR* (Boulder, CO: Westview Press, 1990).

6868. Hajda, Lubomyr, and Mark Beissinger, eds., *The Nationalities Factor in Soviet Politics and Society* (Boulder, CO: Westview Press, 1990).

6869. Huttenbach, Henry R., ed., *Soviet Nationality Policies: Ruling Ethnic Groups in the USSR* (New York: Mansell, 1990).

6870. Karklins, Rasma, *Ethnic Relations in the USSR: The Perspective from Below* (Boston: Allen & Unwin, 1986).

6871. -----, *Ethnopolitics and Transition to Democracy: The*

Collapse of the USSR and Latvia (Baltmore: Woodrow Wilson Center Press/Johns Hopkins University Press, 1994).

6872. Kux, Stephan, *Soviet Federalism: A Comparative Perspective* (Boulder, CO: Westview Press, 1990).

6873. Lallukka, Seppo, *The East Finnic Minorities in the Soviet Union: An Appraisal of the Erosive Trends* (Helsinki: Suomalainen Tiedeakatemia, 1990).

6874. Lapidus, Gail, and Victor Zaslavsky, eds., *From Union to Commonwealth: Nationalism and Separatism in the Soviet Republics* (Cambridge: Cambridge University Press, 1993).

6875. Mandelbaum, Michael, ed., *The Rise of Nations in the Soviet Union: American Foreign Policy and the Disintegration of the USSR* (New York: Council on Foreign Relations Press, 1991).

6876. McAuley, Alastair, *Soviet Federalism: Nationalism and Economic Decentralization* (New York: St. Martin's Press, 1991).

6877. Motyl, Alexander, ed., *The Post-Communist Nations: Perspectives on the Demise of the USSR* (New York: Columbia University Press, 1992.

6878. -----, *Sovietology, Rationality, and Nationality: Coming to Grips with Nationalism in the USSR* (New York: Columbia University Press, 1990).

6879. -----, *Will the Non-Russians Rebel? State, Ethnicity and Stability in the USSR* (Ithaca: Cornell University Press, 1987).

6880. Nahaylo, Bohdan, and Victor Swoboda, *Soviet Disunion: A History of the Nationalities Problem in the USSR* (New York: The Free Press, 1990).

6881. Olcott, Martha B., Lubomyr Hajda and Anthony Olcott, eds., *The Soviet Multinational State: Readings and Documents* (Armonk, NY: M. E. Sharpe, 1990).

6882. Ra'anan, Uri, ed., *The Soviet Empire: The Challenge of National and Democratic Movements* (Lexington, MA: Lexington Books, 1990).

6883. Radio Free Europe/Radio Liberty, *Glasnost' and Empire: National Aspirations in the USSR* (Washington, DC: RFE/RL, 1989).

6884. Rezun, Miron, ed., *Nationalism and the Breakup of an Empire: Russia and Its Periphery* (Westport, CT: Praeger, 1992).

6885. Rupesinghe, Kumar, Peter G. King and Olga Vorkunova, *Ethnicity and Conflict in a Post-Communist World* (New York: St. Martin's Press, 1992).

6886. Seay, Douglas, *Promoting the Peaceful Decolonization of the Soviet Union* (Washington, DC: Heritage Foundation, 1990).

6887. Smith, Graham, ed., *The Nationalities Question in the Soviet Union* (New York: Longman, 1990).

6888. *The Soviet Empire: Its Peoples Speak Out: The First Congress of People's Deputies, Moscow, 25 May to 10 June 1989* (New York: Harwood Academic, 1989).

6889. Suh, Dae-Sook, ed., *Koreans in the Soviet Union* (Honolulu: Center for Korean Studies and the Soviet Union in the Pacific-Asian Region Program, University of Hawaii, 1987).

6890. Szporluk, Roman, *Communism and Nationalism: Karl Marx versus Friedrich List* (New York: Oxford University Press, 1988).

6891. US Congress. Senate. Committee on Foreign Relations. Subcommittee on European Affairs. *Soviet Disunion: Creating a Nationalities Policy.* 101st Congress, 2nd Session (Washington, DC: Government Printing Office, 1990).

6892. US Department of State. Bureau of Intelligence and Research, *Soviet Nationalities Survey*, no. 9 (Washington, DC: US Department of State, 7 Nov. 1985).

ARTICLES

6893. Adams, R. M., "What Should Be Our Stance Toward the Newly Independent States That Once Composed the Monolithic USSR?" *Smithsonian*, 22 (Feb. 1992), 8.

6894. Alekseev, V. V., "Soviet Regional Problems: Causes and Effects," *Russian History/Histoire Russe*, 18, no. 1 (Spring 1991), 77-83.

6895. "Appeal of the Crimean Tatars to the U.N.," *Religion in Communist Dominated Areas*, 30, no. 3-4 (1991), 54-55.

6896. "Armenia-Azerbaijan-Belarus-Kazakhstan-Kyrgyz-stan-Moldova-Russia-Tajikistan-Turkmenistan-Uzbekistan- Ukraine: Agreements Establishing the Commonwealth of Independent States," *International Legal Materials*, 31, no. 1 (Jan. 1992), 138-54.

6897. Armstrong, John A., "Asessing the Soviet Nationalities Movements: A Critical Review," *Nationalities Papers*, 19, no. 1 (Spring 1991), 1-18.

6898. -----, "Contemporary Ethnicity: The Moral Dimension in Comparative Perspective," *Review of Politics*, 52, no. 2 (Spring 1990), 163-88.

6899. -----, "The Ethnic Scene in the Soviet Union: The View of the Dictatorship," *Journal of Soviet Nationalities*, 1, no. 1 (Spring 1990), 14-65.

6900. -----, "Nationalism in the Former Soviet Union," *Problems of Communism*, 41, no. 1-2 (Jan-Apr. 1992), 121-33.

6901. -----, "The Soviet Ethnic Scene: A Quarter Century Later," *Journal of Soviet Nationalities*, 1, no. 1 (Spring 1990), 66-75.

6902. -----, "Soviet Nations" (Review Article), *Problems of Communism*, 39, no. 4 (July-Aug. 1990), 78-83.

6903. Avineri, Shlomo, "The Return to History: Break-Up of the Soviet Union," *Brookings Review*, 10, no. 2 (Spring 1992), 30-33.

6904. Bahry, Donna, "Republican Economic Reforms," *Nationalities Papers*, 19, no. 1 (Spring 1991), 62-67.

6905. Beissinger, Mark R., "John Armstrong's Functionalism and Beyond: Approaches to the Study of Soviet Nationalities

Politics," *Journal of Soviet Nationalities*, 1, no. 1 (Spring 1990), 91-100.

6906. Bernstein, Alvin H., "Ethnicity and Imperial Break-up: Ancient and Modern," *SAIS Review*, 13, no. 1 (Winter-Spring 1993), 121-32.

6907. -----, "Insurgents against Moscow: The Reagan Doctrine Can Put Soviet Imperialism on the Defensive," *Policy Review*, no. 42 (Summer 1987), 26-29.

6908. Bilinsky, Yaroslav, "Nationality Policy in Gorbachev's First Year," *Orbis*, 30, no. 2 (Summer 1986), 331-42.

6909. Blase, John C., and Cynthia M. Smith, "Soviet Republics' Demand for Autonomy: The Need for Constitutional Reform and the Institution of Canadian-Style Judicial Review," *Journal of Legislation*, 17, no. 2 (1991), 237-60.

6910. Braithwaite, Jeanine D., "Income Distribution and Poverty in the Soviet Republics," *Journal of Soviet Nationalities*, 1, no. 3 (Fall 1990), 158-73.

6911. Brandt, Joseph C., "Economic Reform and the Soviet National Question," *Telos*, no. 84 (Summer (1990), 58-68.

6912. Bromlei, Julian V., "Ethnic Relations and *Perestroika*," *Perestroika Annual*, 2 (1989), 101-19.

6913. Brumberg, Abraham, "The Road to Minsk," *New York Review of Books*, 38 (30 Jan. 1992), 21-26.

6914. Brzezinski, Zbigniew, "The Breakup of the USSR," *World Monitor*, 3, no. 11 (Nov. 1990), 30-33.

6915. -----, "Post-Communist Nationalism," *Foreign Affairs*, 68, no. 5 (1990), 1-25.

6916. Bugromenko, V. N., "Social Justice and Inter-Nationality Relations: Territorial Aspects," *Soviet Geography*, 32, no. 8 (Oct. 1991), 572-75.

6917. Bukovsky, Vladimir, "The Ex-Soviet Union," *Commentary*, 93 (Feb. 1992), 8-10.

6918. Burg, Steven L., "Ethnic Refuseniks," *New Republic* (29 Aug. 1988), 10-11.

6919. -----, "Nationalism Redux: Through the Glass of the Post-Communist States Darkly," *Current History*, 92, no. 573 (Apr. 1993), 162-68.

6920. -----, "The Soviet Union's Nationalities Question," *Current History*, 88, no. 540 (Oct. 1989), 341ff.

6921. Butterfield, Jim, "The Vagaries of Political Change," *Nationalities Papers*, 28, no. 1 (Spring 1990), 6-9.

6922. Carrere d'Encausse, Helene, "Springtime of Nations," *New Republic* (21 Jan. 1991), 20-22.

6923. Chirovsky, Nicholas, "The Commonwealth of Independent States," *Ukrainian Quarterly*, 48, no. 4 (Winter 1992), 397-408.

6924. Clemens, Walter, "Foreign Policy Implications of Nationality Unrest," *Nationalities Papers*, 28, no. 1 (Spring 1990), 21-22.

6925. Cockburn, Patrick, "Dateline USSR: Ethnic Tremors," *Foreign Policy*, no. 74 (Spring 1989), 168-84.

6926. Cole, John P., "Republics of the Former USSR in the Context of a United Europe and New World Order," *Soviet Geography*, 32, no. 9 (Nov. 1991), 587-603.

6927. Crow, Suzanne, "Distorting the Image of Ethnic Unrest," *Report on the USSR*, 2, no. 13 (30 Mar. 1990), 17-19.

6928. "Death of an Empire," *National Review*, 43 (30 Dec. 1991), 13-14.

6929. Diuk, Nadia, and Adrian Karatnycky, "Nationalism: Part of the Solution," *Orbis*, 34, no. 4 (Fall 1990), 531-46.

6930. Dobriansky, Lev, "From Myths to Reality in Critical Period," *Ukrainian Quarterly*, 48, no. 3 (Fall 1992), 265-87.

6931. Doherty, Carroll J., "Soviet Republics in Spotlight as Hill Mulls U.S. Policy," *Congressional Quarterly Weekly Report*, 49 (24 Aug. 1991), 2322-23.

6932. Drobizheva, L. M., "The Role of the Intelligentsia in Developing National Consciousness among the Peoples of the USSR under Perestroika," *Ethnic and Racial Studies*, 14 (Jan. 1991), 87-99.

6933. Dunlop, John B., "Will the Soviet Union Survive Until the Year 2000?" *National Interest*, no. 18 (Winter 1989-90), 65-76.

6934. Dutter, Lee E., "Theoretical Perspectives on Ethnic Political Behavior in the Soviet Union," *Journal of Conflict Resolution*, 34, no. 2 (June 1990), 311-34.

6935. "End of an Empire," *U.S. News & World Report*, 111 (9 Sept. 1991), 20ff.

6936. Fallenbuchl, Zbigniew M., "Economic Nationalism in the Eastern Bloc Countries," *Canadian Review of Studies in Nationalism*, 16, no. 1-2 (1989), 153-68.

6937. "Forced Union," *New Republic* (8 Apr. 1991), 7-8.

6938. Foye, Stephen, "Gorbachev Denies Responsibility for Crackdown," *Report on the USSR*, 3, no. 4 (25 Jan. 1991), 1-3.

6939. Galuszka, Philip, "Can Gorbachev Control the Nationalism *Glasnost* Unleashed?" *Business Week* (28 Mar. 1988), 43.

6940. Gastor, Kristopher, "Ethnic Unrest Is the Quake Gorbachev Fears Most," *Business Week* (26 Dec. 1988), 86.

6941. -----, "Poles in the Soviet Union," *Report on the USSR*, 2, no. 52 (28 Dec. 1990), 10-16.

6942. Gellner, Ernest, "Ethnicity Unbound" (Review Article), *New Republic* (18 June 1990), 34-38.

6943. Germroth, David S., "The Soviet Republics and Nationalism," *Global Affairs*, 4, no. 2 (Spring 1989), 140-57.

6944. Gleason, Gregory, "Soviet Federalism and Republican Rights," *Columbia Journal of Transnational Law*, 28, no. 1 (Spring 1990), 19-40.

6945. Goble, Paul, "Ethnic Politics in the USSR," *Problems of*

Communism, 38, no. 4 (July-Aug. 1989), 1-14.

6946. -----, "Ethnic Politics in the USSR: Gorbachev and Glasnost," *Current* (Washington), 322 (May 1990), 30-40.

6947. -----, "Gorbachev, Secession and the Fate of Reform," *Report on the USSR*, 2, no. 17 (27 Apr. 1990), 1-2.

6948. -----, "Managing the Multinational USSR" (Review Article), *Problems of Communism*, 34, no. 4 (July-Aug. 1985), 79-83.

6949. Gonchar, Nikolai, "Back to the USSR?" *Delovie Lyudi*, no. 40 (Dec. 1993), 52-53.

6950. Gorbachev, Mikhail S., "Ethnic Relations and the Logic of Perestroika," *Political Affairs*, 68 (Dec. 1988), 10-16.

6951. -----, "The Importance of a Union," *Vital Speeches of the Day*, 57 (15 Sept. 1991), 17-22.

6952. -----, "The New Union Treaty," *Vital Speeches of the Day*, 57 (1 Sept. 1991), 676-77.

6953. "The Great Soviet Divorce," *World Today*, 48, no. 2 (Feb. 1992), 19-20.

6954. Gudkov, Leon, "The Disintegration of the USSR and Russians in the Republics," *Journal of Communist Studies*, 9, no. 1 (Mar. 1993), 75-90.

6955. Hajda, L., "The Nationalities Problem in the Soviet Union," *Current History*, 87 (Oct. 1988), 325ff.

6956. Harasymiw, Bohdan, "Ethnic Political Recruitment in the USSR," *Canadian Slavonic Papers*, 30, no. 2 (June 1988), 171-89.

6957. Harries, Owen, "Of Unstable Disposition," *National Interest*, no. 22 (Winter 1990-91), 100-05.

6958. Hawkins, Robert, "Greater Economic Autonomy for Soviet Republics," *SEEL: Soviet and East European Law*, 1, no. 5 (June-July 1990), 9.

6959. Hazard, John, "Accords of Minsk and Alma Ata," *SEEL: Soviet and East European Law*, 2, no. 9 (Nov-Dec. 1991), 1-2.

6960. -----, "The Vagaries of Political Change," *Nationalities Papers*, 19, no. 1 (Spring 1991) 19-23.

6961. Henze, Paul B., "The Last Empire," *Journal of Democracy*, 1, no. 2 (Spring 1990), 27-34.

6962. Hill, Ronald J., "Managing Ethnic Conflict," *Journal of Communist Studies*, 9, no. 1 (Mar. 1993), 57-74.

6963. Hoffman, George W., "Ethnic Conflict and Resurgent Nationalism," *AAASS Newsletter*, 30, no. 2 (Mar. 1990), 87-90.

6964. Howard, Michael, "The Springtime of Nations," *Foreign Affairs*, 69, no. 1 (1989-90), 17-32.

6965. Hughes, Michael, "The Never-Ending Story: Russian Nationalism, National Communism, and Opposition to Reform in the USSR and Russia," *Journal of Communist Studies*, 9, no. 2 (June 1993), 41-61.

6966. "Hunting for a Heritage: Post-Soviet Yakutiya," *World Today*, 48, no. 4 (Apr. 1992), 56-57.

6967. Huttenbach, Henry R., "Nationalism Shakes the USSR," *World & I* (Apr. 1990), 60-71.

6968. -----, "Sources of National Movements," *Nationalities Papers*, 28, no. 1 (Spring 1990), 49-52.

6969. -----, and Alexander Motyl, eds., "The Soviet Nationalities against Gorbachev," *Nationalities Papers*, 18, no. 1 (Spring 1990), 6-103.

6970. -----, and Judith Sedaitis, eds., "A Symposium on Social Movements in the USSR," *Nationalities Papers*, 18, no. 2 (Fall 1990), 5-75.

6971. Ivanov, V. N., "Interethnic Conflicts: The Sociopsychological Aspect," *Russian Social Science Review*, 34, no. 4 (July-Aug. 1993), 24-36.

6972. Jackson, William D., "Russia after the Crisis: Imperial Temptations-Ethnics Abroad," *Orbis*, 38, no. 1 (Winter 1994), 17ff.

6973. Juviler, Peter, "Getting to `Yes' on Self-Determination," *Nationalities Papers*, 19, no. 1 (Spring 1991), 32-36.

6974. Kagedan, Allen, "Nationalism, Language, and Culture," *Nationalities Papers*, 19, no. 1 (Spring 1991), 59-62.

6975. Karklins, R., "Perestroika and Ethnopolitics in the USSR," *PS*, 21 (June 1989), 208-14.

6976. Kavass, Igor, "Draft Union Treaty Is Gorbachev's Dream of a Federation," *SEEL: Soviet and East European Law*, 1, no. 10 (Jan. 1991), 1ff.

6977. Kaza, Juris, "Confronting the Russian Bear," *National Review*, 42 (30 Apr. 1990), 31-34.

6978. Khazanov, A. M., "The Current Ethnic Situation in the USSR: Perennial Problems in the Period of `Restructuring'," *Nationalities Papers*, 16, no. 2 (Fall 1988), 147-70.

6979. Kirkwood, Michael, "*Glasnost'*, `The National Question' and Soviet Language Policy," *Soviet Studies*, 43, no. 1 (1991), 61-82.

6980. Knight, R., "Squaring Off Over the Future of a Single Soviet Union," *U.S. News & World Report*, 110 (24 June 1991), 46.

6981. Kolack, Shirley, "Ethnic Minorities in the Soviet Union: The Unfinished Revolution," *Journal of Ethnic Studies*, 13, no. 2 (Summer 1985), 125-32.

6982. Kolosov, V. A., "The Geography of Elections of USSR People's Deputies by National-Territorial Districts and the Nationalities Issue," *Soviet Geography*, 31, no. 10 (Dec. 1990), 753-66.

6983. Kortunov, Andrei, "Relations between Former Soviet Republics," *Society*, 30, no. 3 (Mar-Apr. 1993), 36-48.

6984. Krupnik, I. I., "Multinational Society: The Status of

Nationality Relations in the USSR and the Tasks of Science," *Soviet Review*, 31, no. 2 (Mar-Apr. 1990), 3-15.

6985. Kux, Stephan, "Soviet Federalism," *Problems of Communism*, 39, no. 2 (Mar-Apr. 1990), 1-20.

6986. Laitin, David D., "The Four Nationality Games and Soviet Politics," *Journal of Soviet Nationalities*, 2, no. 1 (Spring 1991), 1-37.

6987. -----, "Nationality Problems" (Review Article), *Russian History*, 17, no. 4 (Winter 1990), 437-41.

6988. -----, "The National Uprisings in the Soviet Union" (Review Article), *World Politics*, 44, no. 1 (Oct. 1991), 139ff.

6989. Lapidus, Gail W., "Gorbachev and the `National' Question: Restructuring the Soviet Federation," *Soviet Economy*, 5, no. 3 (July-Sept. 1989), 201-50.

6990. -----, "Gorbachev's Nationalities Problem," *Foreign Affairs*, 67, no. 1 (Fall 1989), 92-107.

6991. -----, "Gorbachev's Problem: The U.S.S.R. and Its Nationalities," *Current* (Washington), 319 (Jan. 1990), 27-34.

6992. "Let the Peoples Go," *New Republic* (21 Jan. 1991), 7-9.

6993. Lewin, Moshe, "Russia: Nationalism and Economy," *Dissent*, 39, no. 2 (Spring 1992), 172-75.

6994. Lewis, W. H., "Gorbachev and Ethnic Coexistence," *Comparative Strategy*, 8, no. 4 (Oct-Dec. 1989), 399-410.

6995. Lieven, Dominic, "Gorbachev and the Nationalities," *Conflict Studies*, no. 216 (Nov. 1988), 1-31.

6996. -----, "The Soviet Crisis," *Conflict Studies*, no. 241 (May 1991), 1-27.

6997. Lloyd, J., "The Last Emperor: Gorbachev Must Preside Over the End of the Empire He Now Rules," *New Statesman and Society*, 3 (22 June 1990), 22-23.

6998. Lourie, Richard, "Does the Soviet Union Exist?" *Dissent*, 37, no. 2 (Spring 1990), 262ff.

6999. Lukic, Reneo, "Twilight of the Federations in East Central Europe and the Soviet Union," *Journal of International Affairs*, 45 (Winter 1992), 575-98.

7000. McDonald, H., "Tremors in Tartary: Islamic Republics Assert Identity As Moscow Falters," *Far Eastern Economic Review*, 148 (24 May 1990), 27-28.

7001. Medvedev, Roy, "Ethnic Conflict and Gorbachev's Reforms," *Dissent*, 35, no. 3 (Summer 1988), 269-71.

7002. Meissner, Boris, "The Transformation of the Soviet Union," *Aussenpolitik*, 43, no. 1 (1992), 54-61.

7003. Mickiewicz, Ellen, "Ethnicity and Support: Findings from a Soviet-American Public Opinion Poll," *Journal of Soviet Nationalities*, 1, no. 1 (Spring 1990), 140-47.

7004. Mitchneck, Beth, "Territoriality and Regional Economic Autonomy in the USSR," *Studies in Comparative Communism*,

24, no. 2 (June 1991), 218-24.

7005. Motyl, Alexander J., "The Demise of Soviet Language," *Nationalities Papers*, 28, no. 1 (Spring 1990), 14-16.

7006. -----, "Empire or Stability?" *World Policy Journal*, 8, no. 3 (Summer 1991), 499-524.

7007. -----, "Identity Crisis in the Soviet West," *Bulletin of the Atomic Scientists*, 45, no. 2 (Mar. 1989), 21-24.

7008. Muray, Leo, "The Soviet Inheritance," *Contemporary Review*, 260, no. 1515 (Apr. 1992), 190-94.

7009. "Nationalities Up-date: USSR: Estonia, Lithuania, Tadjikistan," *Nationalities Papers*, 16, no. 2 (Fall 1988), 272-89.

7010. Olcott, Martha B., "Moscow's Troublesome Muslim Minority," *Washington Quarterly*, 9, no. 2 (Spring 1986), 73-83.

7011. -----, "The Slide into Disunion," *Current History*, 90, no. 558 (Oct. 1991), 338-46.

7012. -----, "The Soviet (Dis)Union," *Foreign Policy*, no. 82 (Spring 1991), 118-36.

7013. -----, "Youth and Nationality in the USSR," *Journal of Soviet Nationalities*, 1, no. 1 (Spring 1990), 128-39.

7014. Otorbayev, K., and K. Nanayev, "Social Injustice and Inter-Nationality Relationships in the USSR," *Soviet Geography*, 32, no. 8 (Oct. 1991), 542-44.

7015. Ozerov, Michael, "Is a Commonwealth of Nations Possible in the USSR?" *Round Table*, no. 321 (Jan. 1992), 19-22.

7016. Ozornoy, Gennady I., "Some Issues of Regional Inequality in the USSR under Gorbachev," *Regional Studies*, 25 (Oct. 1991), 381-93.

7017. "Panel on Nationalism in the USSR: Environmental and Territorial Aspects," *Soviet Geography*, 30, no. 6 (June 1989), 441-509.

7018. Perkovich, George, "Window of Opportunity: Why We Need a New Soviet Policy," *Present Tense*, 16, no. 4 (May-June 1989), 12-17.

7019. Petro, Nikolai N., "The Project of the Century: A Case Study of Russian Nationalist Dissent," *Studies in Comparative Communism*, 20, no. 3-4 (1987), 235-52.

7020. Pipes, Richard, "The `Glasnost Test': Gorbachev's Push Comes to Shove," *New Republic* (2 Feb. 1987), 16-17.

7021. -----, "Russia's Shuddering Empire: The Prospects for Soviet Disunion," *New Republic* (6 Nov. 1989), 52-55.

7022. Pustogarov, Vladimir, "What Erosion of the Union Means Internationally," *International Affairs* (Moscow), no. 1 (1992), 66-72.

7023. Rakowska-Harmstone, Teresa, "Brotherhood in Arms: The Ethnic Factor in the Soviet Armed Forces," in N. F. Dreisziger, ed., *Ethnic Armies: Polyethnic Armed Forces from the Time of the Habsburgs to the Age of the Superpowers* (Waterloo, Ontario: Wilfrid Laurier University Press, 1990), 123-57.

7024. -----, "Chickens Coming Home to Roost: A Perspective on Soviet Ethnic Relations," *Journal of International Affairs*, 45 (Winter 1992), 519-48.

7025. Reddaway, Peter, "Empire on the Brink," *New York Review of Books*, 38 (31 Jan. 1991), 7-9.

7026. "Refugees and Citizens: The Case of the Volga Germans," *World Today*, 48, no. 3 (Mar. 1992), 41-43.

7027. Rich, Vera, "The Great Soviet Divorce," *World Today*, 48, no. 2 (Feb. 1992), 19-20.

7028. -----, "Soviet Union: Speaking in Tongues," *World Today*, 43, no. 10 (Oct. 1987), 170-72.

7029. Roeder, Philip G., "Soviet Federalism and Ethnic Mobilization," *World Politics*, 43, no. 2 (Jan. 1991), 196-232.

7030. Rupnik, Jacques, "The Empire Breaks Up: Gorbachev's Nationality Crisis," *New Republic* (20 Feb. 1989), 20-24.

7031. Rywkin, Michael, "The Struggle for Political Sovereignty," *Nationalities Papers*, 19, no. 1 (Spring 1991), 78-79.

7032. Sacks, Michael Paul, "Ethnicity and Class in the USSR," *Nationalities Papers*, 28, no. 1 (Spring 1990), 57-58.

7033. Safran, William, "Language, Ideology, and State Building: A Comparison of Policies in France, Israel, and the Soviet Union," *International Political Science Review*, 13, no. 4 (1992), 397-414.

7034. Salitan, Laurie P., "The Dynamics of Emigration and Nationality in the Soviet Union," *Harriman Institute Forum*, 2, no. 2 (Feb. 1989), 1-8.

7035. -----, "Human Rights and the Republics," *Nationalities Papers*, 28, no. 1 (Spring 1990), 17-20.

7036. Samuelian, Thomas J., "Cultural Ecology and Gorbachev's Restructured Union," *Harvard International Law Journal*, 32, no. 1 (Winter 1991), 159-200.

7037. Schiffer, Jonathan R., "Soviet Territorial Pricing and Emerging Republican Politics," *Journal of Soviet Nationalities*, 1, no. 3 (Fall 1990), 67-111.

7038. Schoenfeld, Gabriel, "The End," *New Republic* (21 Jan. 1991), 23-25.

7039. "Secession: State Practice and International Law after the Dissolution of the Soviet Union and Yugoslavia," *Duke Journal of Comparative and International Law*, 3 (Spring 1993), 299-349.

7040. Seytmuratova, Ayshe, "New Legislation Concerning the Crimean Tatar People," *Religion in Communist Dominated Areas*, 30, no. 3-4 (1991), 52-54.

7041. -----, "The Platform of the CPSU on Nationalities Policy and the Problem of the Crimean Tatars," *Religion in Communist Dominated Areas*, 28, no. 3 (Summer 1989), 91-93.

7042. Shanin, Teodor, "Ethnicity in the Soviet Union: Analytical Perception and Political Strategies," *Comparative Studies in Society and History*, 31, no. 3 (July 1989), 409-24.

7043. Sheehy, Ann, "Dates of Elections to Supreme Soviets and Local Soviets in Union Republics," *Report on the USSR*, 2, no. 1 (5 Jan. 1990), 16-17.

7044. -----, "Fact Sheet on Declarations of Sovereignty," *Report on the USSR*, 2, no. 45 (9 Nov. 1990), 23-25.

7045. -----, "Moves to Draw Up New Union Treaty," *Report on the USSR*, 2, no. 27 (6 July 1990), 14-17.

7046. -----, "Power Passes to the Republics," *Report on the USSR*, 3, no. 37 (13 Sept. 1991), 1-3.

7047. -----, "Solzhenitsyn's Concept of a Future `Russian Union': The Nationalities Angle," *Report on the USSR*, 2, no. 40 (5 Oct. 1990), 15-16.

7048. Shtromas, Alexander, "The Building of a Multi-National `Socialist Federation': Success and Failures," *Canadian Review of Studies in Nationalism*, 13, no. 1 (Spring 1986), 79-97.

7049. Sinyavsky, Andrei, "Russophobia," *Partisan Review*, 57, no. 3 (1990), 339-44.

7050. Skalnik, Peter, "Soviet *Etnografiia* and the National(ities) Question," *Cahiers du Monde russe et sovietique*, 31, nos. 2-3 (Apr-Sept. 1990), 183-92.

7051. Slider, Darrell, "The First `National' Referendum and the Referenda in the Republics," *Journal of Soviet Nationalities*, 2, no. 1 (Spring 1991).

7052. Smith, Graham, "Gorbachev's Greatest Challenge: Perestroika and the National Question," *Political Geography Quarterly*, 8, no. 1 (1989), 7-20.

7053. Snyder, Jack, "Nationalism and the Crisis of the Post-Soviet State," *Daedalus*, 35, no. 1 (Spring 1993), 5-26.

7054. Socor, Vladimir, "Political Forces of Six Republics Set Up Coordinating Mechanism," *Report on the USSR*, 3, no. 23 (7 June 1991), 18-20.

7055. Solchanyk, Roman, "The Draft Union Treaty and the `Big Five'," *Report on the USSR*, 3, no. 18 (3 May 1991), 16-18.

7056. -----, "The Gorbachev-El'tsin Pact and the New Union Treaty," *Report on the USSR*, 3, no. 19 (10 May 1991), 1-3.

7057. "Soviet Crackup," *Newsweek*, 118 (9 Sept. 1991), 18ff.

7058. "The Soviet Empire," *Time*, 135 (12 Mar. 1990), 26ff.

7059. "The Soviet Republics: A Time for Independence," *World & I* (July 1990), 104-13.

7060. "Soviet Republics: Toward a Common Market," *World & I*, 6, no. 12 (Dec. 1991), 130-35.

7061. Starr, S. Frederick, "Soviet Nationalities in Crisis," *Journal of Soviet Nationalities*, 1, no. 1 (Spring 1990), 76-90.

7062. Steel, Ronald, "Pax Sovietica," *New Republic* (21 Jan. 1991), 17ff.

7063. Suny, Ronald G., "A Delicate Balance: The Nationality Question," *Nation* (13 June 1987), 808-10.

7064. -----, "A Second Look at Sovietology and the National Question," *AAASS Newsletter*, 33, no. 3 (May 1993), 1-2.

7065. Susokolov, A. A., "Ethnic Groups Confront a Choice," *Soviet Sociology*, 29, no. 2 (Mar-Apr. 1990), 74-92.

7066. Teague, Elizabeth, "Ethnic Tensions Remain Main Cause of Work Stoppages," *Report on the USSR*, 2, no. 41 (12 Oct. 1990), 21-22.

7067. Tishkov, Valerii A., "An Assembly of Nations or an All-Union Parliament?" *Journal of Soviet Nationalities*, 1, no. 1 (Spring 1990), 101-27.

7068. -----, "Ethnicity and Power in the Republics of the USSR," *Journal of Soviet Nationalities*, 1, no. 3 (Fall 1990), 33-66.

7069. Trimble, J., "The Soviet Agony over States' Rights," *U.S. News & World Report*, 106 (24 Apr. 1989), 34-35.

7070. Vujacic, Veljko, and Victor Zaslavsky, "The Causes of Disintegration in the USSR and Yugoslavia," *Telos*, no. 88 (Summer 1991), 120-40.

7071. Watson, R., "Breaking Up the Empire?" *Newsweek*, 115 (5 Feb. 1990), 28-30.

7072. -----, "Gorbachev's Civil War," *Newsweek*, 115 (29 Jan. 1990), 38-39.

7073. "When a Nation Breaks Apart," *Maclean's*, 104 (1 Apr. 1991), 26-33.

7074. Wilson-Smith, Anthony, "Rebel Republics," *Maclean's*, 101 (5 Dec. 1988), 32-33.

7075. Ziegler, C. E., "Nationalism, Religion and Equality Among Ethnic Minorities: Some Observations on the Soviet Case," *Journal of Ethnic Studies*, 13 (Summer 1985), 19-32.

A. Baltic Region

BOOKS

7076. *Baltic Futures Seminar* (Hackettstown, NJ: AABS, 1986).

7077. *The Baltic States: A Reference Book* (Tallinn, Riga, Vilnius: Estonia Encyclopedia Publishers, Latvia Encyclopedia Publishers, Lithuania Encyclopedia Publishers, 1991).

7078. Clemens, Walter C., Jr., *Baltic Independence and Russian Empire* (New York: St. Martin's Press, 1991).

7079. *Conference on Security and Cooperation in Europe Follow-up Meeting in Vienna, November 1986: Soviet Violations in the Implementation of the Final Act in Occupied Latvia* (Rockville, MD: World Federation of Free Latvians, 1986).

7080. Gerner, Kristian, and Stefan Hedlund, *The Baltic States and the End of the Soviet Empire* (London: Routledge, 1993).

7081. Kitching, Laurence, ed., *Regional Identity under Soviet Rule: The Case of the Baltic States*, 3 parts (Hackettstown, NJ: AABS, 1987).

7082. Lieven, Anatol, *The Baltic Revolution: Estonia, Latvia, Lithuania and the Path to Independence* (New Haven: Yale University Press, 1993).

7083. Loeber, Dietrich Andre, V. Stanley Vardys and Laurence P. A. Kitching, eds., *Regional Identity under Soviet Rule: The Case of the Baltic States* (Hackettstown, NJ: Institute for the Study of Law, Politics and Society of Socialist States, 1990).

7084. Oleszczuk, Thomas A., *Political Justice in the USSR: Dissent and Repression in Lithuania, 1969-1987* (Boulder, CO, distributed by Columbia University Press, 1988).

7085. Petersen, Nikolai, ed., *The Baltic States in International Politics* (Copenhagen: DJOF Publishing, 1993).

7086. Raun, Toivo, *Estonia and the Estonians*, 2nd ed. (Stanford: Hoover Institution Press, 1991).

7087. Seay, Douglas, *How America Can Help Baltic Independence* (Washington, DC: Heritage Foundation, 1990).

7088. Senn, Alfred E., *Crisis in Lithuania, January 1991* (Chicago: Akiraciai, 1991).

7089. -----, *Lithuania Awakening* (Berkeley: University of California Press, 1990).

7090. Taagepera, Rein, *Estonia: Return to Independence* (Boulder, CO: Westview Press, 1993).

7091. Tiusanen, Tauno, *The Baltic States: Small Countries in Transition* (Helsinki: Centre for Finnish Business and Policy Studies, 1993).

7092. Trapans, Jan Arveds, ed., *Toward Independence: The Baltic Popular Front Movements* (Boulder, CO: Westview Press, 1991).

7093. US Congress. Commission on Security and Cooperation in Europe. *Implementation of the Helsinki Accords: The Baltic Question, 19 Oct. 1989*, 101st Congress, 1st Session (Washington, DC: Government Printing Office, 1990).

7094. US Congress. Commission on Security and Cooperation in Europe. *Implementation of the Helsinki Accords: Hearing before the Commission on Security and Cooperation in Europe, One Hundred Second Congress, First Session, Soviet Crackdown in the Baltic States, January 17, 1991* (Washington, DC: Government Printing Office, 1991).

7095. US Congress. Commission on Security and Cooperation in Europe. *Implementation of the Helsinki Accords: Hearing before the Commission on Security and Cooperation in Europe, One Hundred Second Congress, First Session, Soviet Crackdown in the Baltic States, January 22, 1991* (Washington, DC: Government Printing Office, 1991).

7096. US Congress. Commission on Security and Cooperation in Europe. *Implementation of the Helsinki Accords: Hearing before the Commission on Security and Cooperation in Europe, One Hundred Second Congress, First Session, Baltic Leadership on Status of Independence Movements, May 7, 1991* (Washington, DC: Government Printing Office, 1991).

7097. US Congress. Commission on Security and Cooperation in Europe. *Implementation of the Helsinki Accords: Meeting with*

Prime Minister Kazimiera Prunskiene of Lithuania, May 3, 1990. 101st Congress, 2nd Session (Washington, DC: Government Printing Office, 1990).

7098. US Congress. Commission on Security and Cooperation in Europe. *Renewal and Challenge:: The Baltic States, 1988-1989.* 101st Congress, 1st Session (Washington, DC: Government Printing Office, 1990).

7099. US Congress. House. Committee on Foreign Affairs. Subcommittee on Europe and the Middle East. *Recent Developments in the Baltics: Hearing before the Subcommittee on Europe and the Middle East and on Human Rights and International Organizations of the Committee on Foreign Affairs, House of Representatives, One Hundred Second Congress, First Session, January 23, 1991* (Washington, DC: Government Printing Office, 1991).

ARTICLES

7100. "The Achievement of Independence in the Baltic States and Its Justifications," *Emory International Law Review*, 6 (Spring 1992), 253-91.

7101. Agopsowicz, Monika, "Democracy Without Parties: Interview with Riho Laanemae and Mart Nutt," *Uncaptive Minds*, 4, no. 2 (Summer 1991), 75-79.

7102. Allison, William C., "Self-Determination and Recent Developments in the Baltic States," *Denver Journal of International Law and Policy*, 19, no. 3 (Spring 1991), 625-40.

7103. "Back the Baltics," *New Republic* (23 Apr. 1990), 7-8.

7104. Bond, Andrew R., and Matthew J. Sagers, "Adoption of Law on Economic Autonomy for the Baltic Republics and the Example of Estonia," *Soviet Geography*, 31, no. 1 (Jan., 1990), 1-10.

7105. Budris, John, "Orchestrating Freedom," *World Monitor*, 4, no. 12 (Dec. 1991), 16ff.

7106. -----, "War of Nerves," *National Review*, 43 (18 Mar. 1991), 25-26.

7107. Bungs, Dzintra, "Baltic Notebook," *Report on the USSR*, 3, no. 2 (11 Jan. 1991), 19-22.

7108. -----, "The First Joint Session of the Baltic Parliaments," *Report on the USSR*, 2, no. 50 (14 Dec. 1990), 16-18.

7109. -----, "A Further Step Towards Latvian Independence," *Report on the USSR*, 2, no. 9 (2 Mar. 1990), 25.

7110. -----, "Latvia Adopts Guidelines for Citizenship," *Report on the USSR*, 3, no. 44 (1 Nov. 1991), 17-19.

7111. -----, "Latvia Demands Departure of `Black Berets'," *Report on the USSR*, 3, no. 24 (14 June 1991), 14-19.

7112. -----, "Latvia Reaffirms Its Independence," *Report on the USSR*, 3, no. 36 (6 Sept. 1991), 54-58.

7113. -----, "Political Realignments in Latvia after the Congress of the People's Front," *Report on the USSR*, 3, no. 51-52 (20

Dec. 1991), 17-20.

7114. "Bush, Gorbachev Able to Reach No Agreement on Baltics," *Congressional Quarterly Weekly Report*, 48 (5 June 1990), 1824-27.

7115. "The Catholic Church in Lithuania," *Religion in Communist Lands*, 17, no. 2 (Summer 1989), 169-76.

7116. "Chicken Vilnius," *New Republic* (16 Apr. 1990), 8-10.

7117. Clemens, Walter C., Jr., "The Baltic Way," *World Monitor*, 3, no. 5 (May 1990), 56-60.

7118. Cullen, Robert, "Lithuania: Independence or Nothing," *Atlantic*, 266 (July 1990), 24-31.

7119. Darski, Jozef, "Moscow's Game Plan Has Failed: Interview with Francoise Thom," *Uncaptive Minds*, 4, no. 1 (Spring 1991), 8-16.

7120. Diamond, Joseph M., "Lithuanian Secession-The Finnish Precedent," *Freedom at Issue*, no. 116 (Sept-Oct. 1990), 32-33.

7121. Dreifelds, Juris, "Latvian National Rebirth," *Problems of Communism*, 38, no. 4 (July-Aug. 1989), 77-94.

7122. Drew, Elizabeth, "Letter from Washington," *New Yorker* (14 May 1990), 94-104.

7123. "Election Program of Sajudis," *Lituanus*, 36, no. 2 (Summer 1990), 47-61.

7124. Felton, John, "Hill Stance on Lithuania," *Congressional Quarterly Weekly Report*, 48 (9 June 1990), 1777.

7125. -----, "Lithuanian Events Highlight U.S. Stake in Gorbachev," *Congressional Quarterly Weekly Report*, 48 (7 Apr. 1990), 1084-85.

7126. Fink, Johann, "The Forgotten Fourth Baltic State," *Freedom Review*, 22, no. 3 (May-June 1991), 32-33.

7127. Freibergs, Imants, "Being Part of the Most Memorable Events in Latvia," *AABS Newsletter*, 13, no. 1-2 (Mar-Apr. 1989), 8-9.

7128. Garton Ash, Timothy, "The Trial of Lithuania," *New York Review of Books*, 37 (26 Apr. 1990), 3-6.

7129. Ginsburgs, George, "The Citizenship of the Baltic States," *Journal of Baltic Studies*, 21, no. 1 (Spring 1990), 3-26.

7130. -----, "Lithuanian Citizenship Issues: The Temptations of `Purity'," *SEEL: Soviet and East European Law*, 2, no. 9 (Nov-Dec. 1991), 9-10.

7131. Girnius, Saulius, "Conflicts with Soviet Troops in Lithuania," *Report on the USSR*, 3, no. 20 (17 May 1991), 27-30.

7132. -----, "Foreign Investment in Lithuania," *Report on the USSR*, 3, no. 31 (2 Aug. 1991), 31-33.

7133. -----, "Gorbachev's Visit to Lithuania," *Report on the USSR*, 2, no. 4 (26 Jan. 1990), 4-7.

7134. -----, "Independence of Baltic States Accepted by World Community," *Report on USSR*, 3, no.39 (27 Sept. 1991), 26-28.

7135. -----, "The Lithuanian Citizenship Law," *Report on the USSR*, 3, no. 39 (27 Sept. 1991), 21.

7136. -----, "Lithuanian Economy under Moscow's Economic Blockade," *Report on the USSR*, 2, no. 26 (29 June 1990), 20-22.

7137. -----, "Lithuania: Struggle for Independence and Recognition," *Report on the USSR*, 3, no. 1 (4 Jan. 1991), 51-54.

7138. -----, "Lithuania's National Salvation Committee," *Report on the USSR*, 3, no. 4 (25 Jan. 1991), 6-8.

7139. -----, "United Baltic Front for Independence," *Report on the USSR*, 2, no. 21 (25 May 1990), 15-16.

7140. Glasgow, Eric, "The Baltic's Eastern Seaboard," *Contemporary Review*, 257, no.1495 (Aug. 1990), 62-65.

7141. Goble, Paul, and Toomas Ilves, "A Breakthrough towards Baltic Independence?" *Report on the USSR*, 2, no. 35 (31 Aug. 1990), 19-21.

7142. "Gorbachev's Tanks," *New Republic* (4 Feb. 1991), 8-11.

7143. Grava, Sigurd, "The Urban Heritage of the Soviet Regime: The Case of Riga, Latvia," *Journal of the American Planning Association*, 59, no. 1 (Winter 1993), 9-30.

7144. Greene, Pat Ryan, "Two Days in Vilnius-July 1990)," *Lituanus*, 37, no. 1 (Spring 1991), 15-19.

7145. Grigorievs, Alexei, "The Controversy over Citizenship in Latvia," *Uncaptive Minds*, 4, no. 4 (Winter 1991-92), 57-60.

7146. Gryazin, Igor, "Constitutional Development of Estonia in 1988," *Notre Dame Law Review*, 65, no. 2 (1990), 141-64.

7147. Gureckas, Algimantas P., "Lithuania's Boundaries and Territorial Claims Between Lithuania and Neighboring States," *New York Law School Journal of International and Comparative Law*, 12, no. 1-2 (1991), 107-50.

7148. Hanson, Philip, "An Economic Deal between Russia and the Baltic Republics?" *Report on the USSR*, 2, no. 4 (26 Jan. 1990), 9-12.

7149. -----, "Gorbachev in Lithuania: Economic Issues," *Report on the USSR*, 2, no. 4 (26 Jan. 1990), 7-8.

7150. -----, "How Vulnerable Is Lithuania to Economic Pressure," *Report on the USSR*, 2, no. 17 (27 Apr. 1990), 15-17.

7151. Harmon, Danute S., "Chronology of Seminal Events Preceeding the Declaration of Lithuania's Independence," *Lituanus*, 36, no. 2 (Summer 1990), 31-44.

7152. -----, "Lithuania: An Overview of the Struggle for National Survival," *Lituanus*, 36, no. 2 (Summer 1990), 15-29.

7153. Hilton, Ronald, "The UN and the Baltic States," *World Affairs Report*, 20, no. 3 (Apr-June 1990), 198.

7154. Hylton, Lori, "Past and Present Trade with the Baltics: The Issue of Granting MFN Status and Its Possible Implications," *International Economic Review* (Nov. 1991), 17-23.

7155. Ilves, Toomas, "Estonian Supreme Soviet Declares Continued De Jure Existence of Estonian Republic as an Occupied State," *Report on the USSR*, 2, no. 15 (13 Apr. 1990), 23-24.

7156. Jarve, Priit, "The Baltics of the Early 1990s: Between Democracy and Authoritarianism," *Politiikka*, 34, no. 4 (1992), 308-15.

7157. Kalnins, O., "Gorbo, Pugo, and a Captive Nation," *American Spectator*, 21, no. 10 (Oct. 1988), 32-33.

7158. Kavass, Igor I., and Andrew T. Griffin, "Baltic Autonomy Law: Too Little, Too Late," *SEEL: Soviet and East European Law*, 1, no. 2 (Mar. 1990), 1ff.

7159. Kaza, Juris, "Fighting for `Socialist Pluralism' in Latvia," *New Leader* (23 Jan. 1989), 12-13.

7160. -----, "Gorby's Pugo Stick," *American Spectator*, 24, no. 2 (Feb. 1991), 24.

7161. -----, "Latvian Social Democrats Return," *New Leader*, 73, no. 2 (22 Jan. 1990), 10-12.

7162. Kionka, Riina, "A New Level of Glasnost' in Estonia," *Report on the USSR*, 2, no. 1 (5 Jan. 1990), 22-24.

7163. -----, "Are the Baltic Laws Discriminatory?" *Report on the USSR*, 3, no. 15 (12 Apr. 1991), 21-24.

7164. -----, "Debate about New Constitution Sparks Old Rivalries in Estonia," *Report on the USSR*, 3, no. 50 (13 Dec. 1991), 20-24.

7165. -----, "Estonia: Economic Woes and Political Disputes," *Report on the USSR*, 3, no. 1 (4 Jan. 1991), 45-47.

7166. -----, "Estonia Says `Yes' to Independence," *Report on the USSR*, 3, no. 11 (15 Mar. 1991), 26-28.

7167. -----, "Hard Currency and High Politics in the Baltic Republics," *Report on the USSR*, 3, no. 27 (5 July 1991), 22-25.

7168. -----, "How Will Estonia Cope after the Union Treaty?" *Report on the USSR*, 3, no. 30 (26 July 1991), 27-29.

7169. -----, "Russia Recognizes Estonia's Independence," *Report on the USSR*, 3, no. 5 (1 Feb. 1991), 14-16.

7170. -----, "A Russian in Estonia Speaks Frankly about Non-Estonians," *Report on the USSR*, 2, no. 39 (28 Sept. 1990), 22-24.

7171. -----, "Testing the Baltic Waters," *Report on the USSR*, 3, no. 6 (8 Feb. 1991), 28-30.

7172. -----, "Who Should Become a Citizen of Estonia?" *Report on the USSR*, 3, no. 39 (27 Sept. 1991), 23-26.

7173. -----, Dzintra Bungs and Saulius Girnius, "Political Disputes in the Baltic," *Report on the USSR*, 2, no. 44 (2 Nov. 1990), 26-29.

7174. Kirch, M., and A. Kirch, "The National Process in Estonia Today," *Nationalities Papers*, 16, no. 2 (Fall 1988), 171-76.

7175. Krickus, Richard J., "Lithuania's Polish Question," *Report on the USSR,* 3, no. 48 (29 Nov. 1991), 20-23.

7176. -----, "Nationalism and Baltic Independence" (Review Article), *Problems of Communism,* 40, no. 6 (Nov-Dec. 1991), 135-40.

7177. Krivickas, Domas, "The Molotov-Ribbentrop Pact of 1939: Legal and Political Consequences," *Lituanus,* 35, no. 2 (Summer 1989), 5-35.

7178. Kropiwnicki, Aleksander, "Estonia Is Short of Cash," *Uncaptive Minds,* 3, no. 4 (Aug-Oct. 1990), 47-48.

7179. Kuntz, P., "A Baltic Balancing Act," *Congressional Quarterly Weekly Report,* 48 (24 Mar. 1990), 929.

7180. Laber, Jeri, "The Baltic Revolt," *New York Review of Books,* 38 (28 Mar. 1991), 60-64.

7181. Laur, Mall, and Riina Lohmus, comp., "Documents: The May 1989 Baltic Assembly," *Nationalities Papers,* 16, no. 2 (Fall 1988), 242-58.

7182. Lauristin, Marju, "Baltic Up-Date," *Nationalities Papers,* 28, no. 1 (Spring 1990), 63-64.

7183. Lerner, Michael, "Editorial: Lithuania and the New Nationalism," *Tikkun,* 5, no. 3 (1990), 9-11.

7184. "Liberty or Union?" *New Republic* (5 Feb. 1990), 7-9.

7185. "Lithuania Gets a Bearhug," *U.S. News & World Report,* 108 (22 Jan. 1990), 12.

7186. Mann, A., "Lithuanians Lift Their Heads," *New Leader,* 71 (12 Dec. 1988), 8-10.

7187. Martz, L., "Lithuania: `Looking for a Way Out'," *Newsweek,* 115 (9 Apr. 1990), 30.

7188. McCombs, Phil, "Lithuania's Dynamo for Democracy," *The Washington Post* (4 May 1990), D1.

7189. Meilunas, Egidijus, "No Other Choice: Interview with Vytautas Landsbergis," *Uncaptive Minds,* 4, no. 2 (Summer 1991), 19-32.

7190. -----, "A Short History of Liberty," *Uncaptive Minds,* 4, no. 3 (Fall 1991), 61-62.

7191. Meri, Lennart, "Estonia as a Civic Society: A Security Factor in the Baltic Sea Region and Europe," *Studia Diplomatica,* 45, no. 6 (1992), 3-8.

7192. Mihalisko, Kathleen, "`For Our Freedom and Yours': Support among Slavs for Baltic Independence," *Report on the USSR,* 2, no. 21 (25 May 1990), 17-19.

7193. Miljan, Toivo, "*Perestroika*: An Interim Review of Its Objectives, Programs and Prospects," *Journal of Baltic Studies,* 20, no. 2 (Summer 1989), 109-26.

7194. -----, "Perestroika in the Baltic Republics," *Behind the Headlines,* 47, no. 3 (1990), 1-19.

7195. -----, "To Modernize the Baltic Mind-Set," *AABS Newsletter,* 13, no. 3 (Aug. 1989), 4-8.

7196. -----, "The Proposal to Establish Economic Autonomy in Estonia," *Journal of Baltic Studies,* 20, no. 2 (Summer 1989), 149-64.

7197. "Moscow's Financial War with the Baltics," *SEEL: Soviet and East European Law,* 1, no. 3 (Apr. 1990), 3.

7198. Moss, James, "Recent Developments in the Latvian Lutheran Church," *Religion in Communist Dominated Areas,* 27, no. 3 (Summer 1988), 76-77.

7199. Muiznieks, Nils R., "The Daugavpils Hydro Station and `Glasnost' in Latvia," *Journal of Baltic Studies,* 18, no. 1 (Spring 1987), 63-70.

7200. -----, "The Emerging Baltic Foreign Policy Establishments," *Report on the USSR,* 2, no. 35 (31 Aug. 1990), 17-19.

7201. -----, "The Evolution of Baltic Cooperation," *Report on the USSR,* 2, no. 26 (6 July 1990), 18-20.

7202. "No More Games: An Interview with Egidijus Meilunas," *Uncaptive Minds,* 3, no. 3 (May-July 1991), 35-37.

7203. Norgaard, Ole, "The Political Economy of Transition in Post-Socialist Systems: The Case of the Baltic States," *Scandinavian Political Studies,* 15, no. 1 (1992), 41-60.

7204. "Occupying Lithuania," *National Review,* 42 (16 Apr. 1990), 11-12.

7205. O'Clery, Conor, "Riga Mortis: The Latvians Fight Back," *New Republic* (11 Feb. 1991), 9-11.

7206. Olcott, Martha Brill, "The Lithuanian Crisis," *Foreign Affairs,* 69, no. 3 (Summer 1990), 30-46.

7207. "Order Banning the Books by Tomas Venclova," *Lituanus,* 33, no. 4 (Winter 1987), 87-88.

7208. Palm, Thomas, "Perestroika in Estonia: The Cooperatives," *Journal of Baltic Studies,* 20, no. 2 (Summer 1989), 127-48.

7209. Park, Andrus, "Ethnicity and Independence: The Case of Estonia in Comparative Perspective," *Europe-Asia Studies,* 46, no. 1 (1994), 69-88.

7210. -----, "Global Security and Soviet Nationalities," *Washington Quarterly,* 13, no. 2 (Spring 1990), 37-47.

7211. Plakans, Andrejs, "The Latvians and Their Neighbors," *Lituanus,* 37, no. 2 (Summer 1991), 65-77.

7212. -----, "Latvia's Return to Independence," *Journal of Baltic Studies,* 22, no. 3 (Fall 1991), 259-66.

7213. -----, "The Return of the Past: Baltic-Area Nationalism of the Perestroika Period," *Armenian Review,* 43, no. 2-3 (Summer 1990), 109-26.

7214. Prunskiene, K., "On Economic Independence of the Baltic Republics," *Problems of Economics,* 33, no. 5 (Sept. 1990), 71-83.

7215. Racanska, Luba, "Ethnonationalism in the Soviet Union: The Case of the Baltic States," *Journal of Political Science,* 19 (1991), 109-20.

7216. Raun, Toivo, "The Re-establishment of Estonian Independence," *Journal of Baltic Studies*, 22, no. 3 (Fall 1991), 251-58.

7217. -----, and Andrejs Plakans, "The Estonian and Latvian National Movements: An Assessment of Miroslav Hoch's Model," *Journal of Baltic Studies*, 21, no. 2 (Summer 1990), 131-44.

7218. Reagan, Ronald, "Lithuanian Independence Day," *US Department of State Bulletin*, 88 (May 1988), 46.

7219. Roche, John P., "Lithuania: Death on the Installment Plan," *National Review*, 42 (30 Apr. 1990), 32-33.

7220. Rostow, Eugene V., "Now, About Those Baltic Republics," *New Leader* (30 Oct. 1989), 8-9.

7221. Rudrakumaran, V., "The Legitimacy of Lithuania's Claim for Secession," *Boston University International Law Journal*, 10 (Spring 1992), 33-60.

7222. Ruus, Jurij, and Vygaudas Usackas, "The Transition to Polyarchy in Lithuania and Estonia," *Journal of Baltic Studies*, 22, no. 1 (Spring 1991), 77-86.

7223. Sapiets, Marite, "The Baltic Churches and the National Revival," *Religion in Communist Lands*, 18, no. 2 (Summer 1990), 155-68.

7224. Senn, Alfred Erich, "Lithuania's Path to Independence," *Journal of Baltic Studies*, 2, no. 3 (Fall 1991), 245-50.

7225. -----, "A New Lithuania," *AABS Newsletter*, 13, no. 1-2 (Mar-Apr. 1989), 15-16.

7226. -----, "Perestroika and Lithuanian Basketball," *Journal of Sports History*, 17, no. 1 (Spring 1990), 56-61.

7227. -----, "The Political Culture of Independent Lithuania: A Review Essay," *Journal of Baltic Studies*, 23, no. 3 (Fall 1992), 307-16.

7228. -----, "Toward Lithuanian Independence: Algirdas Brazauskas and the CPL," *Problems of Communism*, 39, no. 2 (Mar-Apr. 1990), 21-28.

7229. Sheehy, Ann, "Tug of War over Baltic Economic Autonomy," *Report on the USSR*, 2, no. 4 (26 Jan. 1990), 8.

7230. Shtromas, Aleksandras, "How Political Are the Social Movements in the Baltic Republics?" *Nationalities Papers*, 28, no. 2 (Fall 1990), 15-21.

7231. Singer, Daniel, "Death in Vilnius," *Nation*, 252 (4 Feb. 1991), 130.

7232. Spitz, Douglas, "The World Looks at the Baltics: South Indian Perspectives, Spring 1991," *Journal of Baltic Studies*, 22, no. 2 (Summer 1991), 183-86.

7233. Stanfield, Rochelle L., "Moscow's Ominous Sideshow," *National Journal*, 23, no. 3 (19 Jan. 1991), 168.

7234. Starr, S. Frederick, "Calling Estonia," *World Monitor*, 4, no. 5 (May 1991), 54-55.

7235. Suny, Ronald Grigor, "Test in Lithuania," *Nation*, 250 (23 Apr. 1990), 549.

7236. Supreme Council of the Republic of Lithuania, "Act on the Restoration of the Lithuanian State," *Lituanus*, 36, no. 2 (Summer 1990), 11.

7237. -----, "Address of the Supreme Council of the Republic of Lithuania to the Nations of the World," *Lituanus*, 36, no. 2 (Summer 1990), 12.

7238. Taagepera, Rein, "Building Democracy in Estonia," *PS*, 24, no. 3 (Sept. 1991), 478-81.

7239. -----, "The Ecological and Political Problems of Phosphorite Mining in Estonia," *Journal of Baltic Studies*, 20, no. 2 (Summer 1989), 165-74.

7240. -----, "Estonia in September 1988: Stalinists, Centrists and Restorationists," *Journal of Baltic Studies*, 20, no. 2 (Summer 1989), 175-95.

7241. -----, "A Note on the 1989 Elections in Estonia," *Soviet Studies*, 42, no. 2 (Apr. 1990), 329-40.

7242. -----, "A Proposal: Complete Self-Management for the Entire Estonian SSR," *AABS Newsletter*, 11, no. 3 (Nov. 1987), 6-7.

7243. -----, "Yuletide in Estonia, 1988," *AABS Newsletter*, 13, no. 1-2 (Mar-Apr. 1989), 16-17.

7244. Tavitian, I., "Rebuilding Armenia: Glasnost versus Perestroika," *Contemporary Review*, 256, no. 1490 (Mar. 1990), 137-39.

7245. Tedstrom, John, "Baltic Independence: The Economic Dimension," *Report on the USSR*, 3, no. 6 (8 Feb. 1991), 22-28.

7246. Terry, J. P., "Lithuanian Independence and International Law: A Retrospective Examination," *Naval Law Review*, 40 (1992), 133-41.

7247. "The Texts of Independence," *Uncaptive Minds*, 3, no. 3 (May-July 1990), 39-41.

7248. Trapans, Jan Arveds, "Documentation: Averting Moscow's Baltic Coup," *Orbis*, 35, no. 3 (Summer 1991), 427-40.

7249. -----, "Latvian Supreme Council Faces Split over Citizenship Law," *Report on the USSR*, 3, no. 39 (27 Sept. 1991), 22-23.

7250. Uibopuu, Henn-Juri, "Dealing with the Minorities: A Baltic Perspective," *World Today*, 48, no. 6 (June 1992), 108ff.

7251. Ulam, Adam B., "The Fatal Shore," *New Republic* (4 Feb. 1991), 23-24.

7252. US Department of Commerce, "Trade Watch: Baltic Nations," *Business America*, 112, no. 19 (23 Sept. 1991), ii.

7253. -----, "Trade Watch: OPIC Coverage for Baltics," *Business America*, 112, no. 18 (6 Sept. 1991), ii.

7254. "U. S. Recognizes Lithuania," *Lituanus*, 37, no. 4 (Winter 1991), 5-10.

7255. Vainu, Herbert, "Finland and the Baltic States in Global Politics," *Yearbook of Finnish Foreign Policy* (1991), 41-45.

7256. Valiunas, Algis, "Homage to Lithuania," *American Spectator*, 23, no. 7 (July 1990), 20-26.

7257. Vardys, V. Stanley, "Lithuanian National Politics," *Problems of Communism*, 38, no. 4 (July-Aug. 1989), 53-76.

7258. Venclova, Tomas, "Lithuania: The Opening and the Hand of the Past," *Salmagundi*, no. 90-91 (Spring-Summer 1991), 1-11.

7259. Vesilind, Pritt J., and Larry C. Price, "The Baltic Nations," *National Geographic*, 178, no. 5 (Nov. 1990), 2-37.

7260. Vetik, Raivo, "Ethnic Conflict and Accommodation in Post-Communist Estonia," *Journal of Peace Research*, 30, no. 3 (Aug. 1993), 271-80.

7261. Vikis-Freibergs, Vaira, "Riga, September 1988," *AABS Newsletter*, 13, no. 1-2 (Mar-Apr. 1989), 7-8.

7262. Viksnins, George J., "Latvia's Economic Sovereignty," *AABS Newsletter*, 13, no. 3 (Aug. 1989), 15-16.

7263. "Villains of Vilnius," *New Republic* (4 May 1990), 7-8.

7264. Webb, William T., "The International Legal Aspects of the Lithuanian Secession," *Journal of Legislation*, 17, no. 2 (1991), 309ff.

7265. Willeke, Audrone, "Visit to Vilnius, Lithuania, June 1988," *AABS Newsletter*, 13, no. 1-2 (Mar-Apr. 1989), 17-18.

7266. Yasmann, Viktor, "Role of KGB in Lithuanian Crisis," *Report on the USSR*, 2, no. 25 (22 June 1990), 22-24.

B. Byelorussia and Ukraine
BOOKS

7267. Armstrong, John A., *Ukrainian Nationalism*, 3rd ed. (Englewood, CO: Ukrainian Academic Press, 1990).

7268. Bahry, Romana M., ed., *Echoes of Glasnost in Soviet Ukraine* (North York, Ontario: Captus University Publications, 1990).

7269. Horyn, Mikhailo, *Building an Independent and Democratic Ukraine* (Washington, DC: Heritage Foundation, 1990).

7270. Kolasky, John, *Ukraine and the Subjugated Nations: Their Struggle for National Liberation: Selected Writings and Speeches* (New York: Philosophical Library, 1989).

7271. Koropeckyj, I. S., *Development in the Shadow: Studies in Ukrainian Economics* (Edmonton: Canadian Institute of Ukrainian Studies Press, University of Alberta, 1990).

7272. Krawchenko, Bohdan, ed., *Ukrainian Past, Ukrainian Present* (London: Macmillan, 1993).

7273. Kuzio, Taras, and Andrew Wilson, *Ukraine: Perestroika to Independence* (New York: St. Martin's Press, 1992).

7274. Little, David, *Ukraine: The Legacy of Intolerance* (Washington, DC: U.S. Institute of Peace, 1991).

7275. Marples, David R., *Ukraine under Perestroika: Ecology, Economics, and the Workers' Revolt* (New York: St. Martin's Press, 1991).

7276. Pavlychko, Solomea, *Letters from Kiev* (New York: St. Martin's Press, with the Canadian Institute of Ukrainian Studies, University of Alberta, 1992).

7277. -----, *Ukraine: The Road to Independence* (New York: St. Martin's Press, 1992).

7278. Solchanyk, Roman, *Ukraine: The Road to Independence* (New York: St. Martin's Press, 1994).

7279. -----, ed., *Ukraine from Chernobyl to Sovereignty: A Collection of Interviews* (New York: St. Martin's Press, 1992).

7280. Stets'ko, Yaroslav, *Ukraine and the Subjugated Nations: Their Struggle for National Liberation: Selected Writings and Speeches* (New York: Philosophical Library, 1989).

7281. Wynar, Bohdan S., *Ukraine: A Bibliographic Guide to the English Language Publications* (Littleton, CO: Ukrainian Academic Press, a Division of Libraries Unlimited, 1990).

7282. Zaprudnik, Jan, *Belarus: At a Crossroads in History* (Boulder, CO: Westview Press, 1993).

ARTICLES

7283. Arel, Dominique, "The Parliamentary Blocs in the Ukrainian Supreme Soviet: Who and What Do They Represent?" *Journal of Soviet Nationalities*, 1, no. 4 (Winter 1990-91), 108-54.

7284. Beissinger, M., "Ethnicity, the Personnel Weapon, and Neo-Imperial Integration: Ukrainian and RSFSR Provincial Party Officials Compared," *Studies in Comparative Communism*, 21 (Spring 1988), 71-85.

7285. Blank, Stephen J., "Russia, Ukraine, and the Future of the CIS," *World & I*, 7, no. 10 (Oct. 1992), 589-609.

7286. Blodgett, Michael D., "Ukraine and the Eastern Mediterranean: The Keys to the Defense of the Persian Gulf," *Ukrainian Quarterly*, 42, no. 3-4 (Fall-Winter 1986), 260-63.

7287. Burg, Steven L., "The European Republics of the Soviet Union," *Current History*, 89, no. 549 (Oct. 1990), 321ff.

7288. "The Case of Captive Nations," *Ukrainian Quarterly*, 46, no. 2 (Summer 1990), 125-27.

7289. Chalupa, Iryna, "Unrest in Ukraine," *Ukrainian Review*, 36, no. 3 (1988), 55-60.

7290. "The Citadel of Communism: Interview with Vintsuk Vyachorka," *Uncaptive Minds*, 4, no. 3 (Fall 1991), 39-52.

7291. Dienes, Leslie, "*Perestroyka* and the Slavic Regions," *Soviet Economy*, 5, no. 3 (July-Sept. 1989), 251-75.

7292. Diuk, Nadia, and Adrian Karatnycky, "Ukraine: Europe's New Nation," *World & I*, 7, no. 3 (Mar. 1992), 96-101.

7293. Gow, James, "Independent Ukraine: The Politics of Security," *International Relations*, 11, no. 3 (Dec. 1992), 253-68.

7294. Grishchenko, Dmitri, Andrei Vasilenko and Sergei Osika, "Ukraine Asserts Independence in Foreign Economic Activity,"

SEEL: Soviet and East European Law, 2, no. 8 (Oct. 1991), 1ff.

7295. Hunczak, Taras, "Ukraine: A Quiet Revolution," *World & I* (June 1990), 102-11.

7296. Iwanow, Mikolaj, "The Politics of *Perestroika* in the USSR and Byelorussian Nationalism," *Ukrainian Quarterly*, 48, no. 2 (Summer 1992), 185-98.

7297. Kachmarsky, Eugene, "Ukrainian Independence: The People's Movement," *Ukrainian Quarterly*, 39, no. 2 (1991), 26-28.

7298. Karatnycky, Adrian, "Rukh Awakening," *New Republic* (17 Dec. 1990), 16-18.

7299. -----, "The Ukrainian Factor," *Foreign Affairs*, 71, no. 3 (Summer 1992), 90-107.

7300. Kolsto, Pal, and Andrei Edemsky, with Natalya Kalashnikova, "The Dniester Conflict: Between Irredentism and Separatism," *Europe-Asia Studies*, 45, no. 6 (1993), 973-1000.

7301. Korotich, Vitaly, "The Ukraine Rising," *Foreign Policy*, no. 85 (Winter 1991-92), 73-82.

7302. Lapychak, Chrystyna, "Ukraine's Troubled Rebirth," *Current History*, 92, no. 576 (Oct. 1993), 337-41.

7303. Macieja, Dorota, "Where Communism Is Dying of Radiation Sickness," *Uncaptive Minds*, 3, no. 4 (Aug-Oct. 1990), 45-46.

7304. Magocsi, Paul Robert, "The Revolution of 1989," *Carpatho-Rusyn American*, 12, no. 4 (1989), 5-9.

7305. -----, "Revolution of 1989 Update," *Carpatho-Rusyn American*, 13, no. 1 (1990), 7-9; no. 2, 4-6; no. 3, 9.

7306. Marples, David, "The Case for Ukrainian Sovereignty," *Report on the USSR*, 2, no. 45 (9 Nov. 1990), 25-28.

7307. -----, "Glasnost and Ecology in Ukraine," *Soviet Analyst*, 17 (17 Aug. 1988), 3-5.

7308. -----, "The Prospects for an Independent Ukraine," *Report on the USSR*, 2, no. 15 (13 Apr. 1990), 17-18.

7309. -----, "A Sociological Survey of `Rukh'," *Report on the USSR*, 2, no. 2 (12 Jan. 1990), 18-20.

7310. -----, "Ukraine's Economic Prospects," *Report on the USSR*, 3, no. 40 (4 Oct. 1991), 14-16.

7311. -----, "The Ukrainian Election Campaign: The Opposition," *Report on the USSR*, 2, no. 10 (9 Mar. 1990), 17-18.

7312. Mearsheimer, John J., "The Case for a Ukrainian Nuclear Deterrent," *Foreign Affairs*, 72, no. 3 (Summer 1993), 50-66; Discussion, 67-80.

7313. Mihalisko, Kathleen, "Belorussia as a Sovereign State: An Interview with Henadz' Hrushavy," *Report on the USSR*, 2, no. 35 (31 Aug. 1990), 11-16.

7314. -----, "Belorussia: Tug-of-War between the Ruling Party and Its Challengers," *Report on the USSR*, 3, no. 1 (4 Jan. 1991), 20-22.

7315. -----, "The End of the Empire: Toward National Democracies; Belorussia: Malaise in the Soviet Union's `Model' Republic," *Armenian Review*, 43, no. 2-3 (Summer 1990), 81-108.

7316. -----, "Laying the Foundation for the Armed Forces of Ukraine," *Report on the USSR*, 3, no. 45 (8 Nov. 1991), 19-22.

7317. -----, "Stanislau Shushkevich and the `Republic of Belarus'," *Report on the USSR*, 3, no. 41 (11 Oct. 1991), 27-29.

7318. -----, "Ukraine Bows Out of Union Treaty in Midst of Political Crisis," *Report on the USSR*, 2, no. 43 (26 Oct. 1990), 17-19.

7319. -----, "Ukraine's Declaration of Sovereignty," *Report on the USSR*, 2, no. 30 (27 July 1990), 17-19.

7320. -----, "The Workers' Rebellion in Belorussia," *Report on the USSR*, 3, no. 17 (26 Apr. 1991), 21-25.

7321. Miller, Arthur H., William M. Resinger and Vicki L. Hesli, "Public Support for New Political Institutions in Russia, the Ukraine and Belorussia," *Journal of Soviet Nationalities*, 1, no. 4 (Winter 1990-91), 82-107.

7322. Miller, Steven E., "The Case Against the Ukrainian Nuclear Deterrent," *Foreign Affairs*, 72, no. 3 (Summer 1993), 67-80.

7323. Minakova, Lydia, and Joseph Ravitch, "Belarus Moves Towards Ownership of Land," *SEEL: Soviet and East European Law*, 2, no. 8 (Oct. 1991), 7.

7324. Moroz, Valentyn, "Ukrainian Gold: Its Political and Economic Implications," *Report on the USSR*, 3, no. 11 (15 Mar. 1991), 13-15.

7325. Mozur, Joseph, "Vasil' Bykau: Exhuming the Belorussian Past," *World Literature Today*, 64, no. 2 (Spring 1990), 251-58.

7326. "A New Slavic State? No Thanks!" *Ukrainian Quarterly*, 46, no. 4 (Winter 1990), 435-36.

7327. Palmer, M. S. R., "Privatization in Ukraine: Economics, Law and Politics," *Yale Journal of International Law*, 16, no. 3 (Summer 1991), 453-517.

7328. Paniotto, Vladimir, "The Ukrainian Movement for *Perestroika*-'Rukh': A Sociological Survey," *Soviet Studies*, 43, no. 1 (1991), 177-81.

7329. Popadiuk, Roman, "Ukraine: Challenges for a Former Soviet Republic," *Presidential Studies Quarterly*, 23, no. 2 (Spring 1993), 229-34.

7330. Roskies, David G., "There Go Our Little Jews," *Commentary*, 89 (Apr. 1990), 49-53.

7331. "*Rukh* Moves On, But Where To?" *Ukrainian Quarterly*, 46, no. 1 (Spring 1990), 5-8.

7332. Schneider, Eberhard, "The New Political Forces in Russia,

Ukraine, and Belorussia," *Report on the USSR*, 3, no. 50 (13 Dec. 1991), 10-18.

7333. Sikorski, Radek, "Too Many Communists," *National Review*, 42 (30 Apr. 1990), 20-22.

7334. -----, "Why Ukraine Must Be Independent," *National Review*, 42 (5 Nov. 1990), 74-77.

7335. Simon, Gerhard, "The Ukraine and the End of the Soviet Union," *Aussenpolitik*, 43, no. 1 (1992), 62-71.

7336. Solchanyk, Roman, "Chernobyl: The Political Fallout in Ukraine," *Journal of Ukrainian Studies*, 11, no. 1 (Summer 1986), 20-34.

7337. -----, "Roman Szporluk and Valerii Tishkov Talk About the National Question," *Report on the USSR*, 2, no. 22 (1 June 1990), 19-24.

7338. -----, "Solzhenitsyn and the Russian `Ukrainian Complex'," *Report on the USSR*, 2, no. 40 (5 Oct. 1990), 20-22.

7339. -----, "Ukraine and Russia: Before and After the Coup," *Report on the USSR*, 3, no. 39 (27 Sept. 1991), 13-17.

7340. -----, "Ukraine, the (Former) Center, Russia, and `Russia'," *Studies in Comparative Communism*, 25, no. 1 (1992), 31-42.

7341. -----, "Ukraine, the Kremlin, and the Russian White House," *Report on the USSR*, 3, no. 44 (1 Nov. 1991), 13-16.

7342. -----, "Ukrainian Party Congress Supports State Sovereignty," *Report on the USSR*, 2, no. 29 (20 July 1990), 21-22.

7343. Sorokowski, Andrew, "The Current Religious Situation in the Ukraine," *Religion in Communist Dominated Areas*, 27, no. 2 (Spring 1988), 46-47.

7344. -----, "National Discrimination in Ukraine," *Ukrainian Quarterly*, 41, no. 3-4 (Fall-Winter 1985), 184-95.

7345. Stankiewicz, Walter, "Belorussian Popular Front Announces Its Electoral Platform," *Report on the USSR*, 2, no. 2 (12 Jan. 1990), 20-23.

7346. -----, "The Events behind Belorussia's Independence Declaration," *Report on the USSR*, 3, no. 38 (20 Sept. 1991), 24-26.

7347. Sysyn, Frank, "The Reemergence of the Ukrainian Nation and Cossack Mythology," *Social Research*, 58, no. 4 (Winter 1991), 845-64.

7348. Tedstrom, John, "The Economic Costs and Benefits of Independence for Ukraine," *Report on the USSR*, 2, no. 49 (7 Dec. 1990), 11-17.

7349. Tkachenko, Sergei I., "The Perestroika of Language Policy in Ukraine," in Kurt E. Muller, ed., *Language as Barrier and Bridge* (Lanham, MD: University Press of America, 1992), 67-71.

7350. "Your Pace or Mine?" *Economist*, 319 (22 June 1991), 50.

7351. Zaprudnik, Jan, "Belorussian Reawakening," *Problems of Communism*, 38, no. 4 (July-Aug. 1989), 36-52.

7352. Zlenko, Anatoly, "Ukrainian Security and the Nuclear Dilemma," *NATO Review*, 41, no. 4 (Aug. 1993), 11-14.

C. Caucasus

BOOKS

7353. Henze, Paul B., *The Transcaucasus in Transition* (Santa Monica, CA: RAND, 1991).

7354. Libaridian, Gerald J., ed., *Armenia at the Crossroads: Democracy and Nationhood in the Post-Soviet Era: Essays, Interviews and Speeches by the Leaders of the National Democratic Movement in Armenia* (Watertown, MA: Blue Crane, 1991).

7355. Melikian, Richard G., *The Armenian Answer to the Armenian Question* (Phoenix: Best Western Press, 1986).

7356. Nersessian, Vrej Nerses, comp., *Armenia: World Bibliographical Series*, vol. 163 (Oxford: Clio Press, 1993).

7357. Suny, Ronald Grigor, *Looking toward Ararat: Armenia in Modern History* (Bloomington: Indiana University Press, 1993).

7358. Swietochowski, Tadeusz, *Soviet Azerbaijan Today: The Problems of Group Identity* (Washington, DC: Woodrow Wilson International Center for Scholars, Kennan Institute, 1986).

ARTICLES

7359. Aaron, David, "An Open Letter on Anti-Armenian Pogroms in the Soviet Union," *New York Review of Books*, 37 (27 Sept. 1990), 66.

7360. Abele, Daniel, "Recent Developments in Soviet Georgia," *AAASS Newsletter*, 31, no. 2 (Mar. 1991), 1-2.

7361. Abrahamian, Levon H., "The Karabagh Movement As Viewed by an Anthropologist," *Armenian Review*, 43, no. 2-3 (Summer 1990), 67-80.

7362. Agopsowicz, Monika, and Manana Chyb, "Ethnic Diversity-Weakness or Wealth?" *Uncaptive Minds*, 3, no. 2 (Mar-Apr. 1990), 39-41.

7363. Allison, Lincoln, Alexander Kukhianidze and Malkhaz Matsaberidze, "The Georgian Election of 1992," *Electoral Studies*, 12, no. 2 (June 1993), 174-79.

7364. Ananicz, Andrzej, "The Country Without Friends [Azerbaidzhan]: Interview with Tadeusz Swietochowski," *Uncaptive Minds*, 4, no. 1 (Spring 1991), 2-7.

7365. "Azerbaijan and the Neighbors," *World Today*, 48, no. 1 (Jan. 1992), 1.

7366. Bonner, Elena, "The Shame of Armenia," *New York Review of Books*, 37 (11 Oct. 1990), 39-40.

7367. Christensen, Julie, "Tengiz Abuladze's *Repentance* and the Georgian National Cause," *Slavic Review*, 50, no. 1 (Spring 1991), 163-75.

7368. Clemens, Walter C., Jr., "Why Gorbachev Has Georgia On His Mind," *World Monitor*, 3, no. 9 (Sept. 1990), 52-58.

7369. Cullen, Robert, "Roots," *New Yorker* (15 Apr. 1991), 55ff.

7370. Daniloff, Ruth, "Defender of Dagestan: A Legendary Hero Embodies a Nation's Quest for Freedom," *World & I*, 7, no. 1 (Jan. 1992), 664-79.

7371. Darski, Jozef, "My Word," *Uncaptive Minds*, 3, no. 2 (Mar-Apr. 1990), 45ff.

7372. Deats, R. L., "Agony and Hope in Armenia," *Christian Century*, 106 (25 Jan. 1989), 81-82.

7373. Derrick, Jonathan, "Feud Across the Caucasus," *World & I* (Aug. 1990), 113-19.

7374. Dudwick, Nora, "The Karabagh Movement: An Old Scenario Gets Rewritten," *Armenian Review*, 42, no. 3 (Autumn 1989), 63-70.

7375. "The Empire Strikes Back," *Glasnost*, 3, no. 1 (July-Sept. 1990), 28-39.

7376. Fraser, Niall M., *et al.*, "A Conflict Analysis of the Armenian-Azerbaijani Dispute," *Journal of Conflict Resolution*, 34, no. 4 (Dec. 1990), 652-77.

7377. Fuller, Elizabeth, "The All-Union Referendum in the Transcaucasus," *Report on the USSR*, 3, no. 13 (29 Mar. 1991), 3-5.

7378. -----, "Armenia-From Apathy to Violence," *Report on the USSR*, 2, no. 23 (8 June 1990), 19-20.

7379. -----, "Armenia Votes Overwhelmingly for Secession," *Report on the USSR*, 3, no. 39 (27 Sept. 1991), 18-20.

7380. -----, "Azerbaijani Exodus from Georgia Imminent?" *Report on the USSR*, 3, no. 7 (15 Feb. 1991), 17-18.

7381. -----, "The Challenges to Armenia's Non-Communist Government," *Report on the USSR*, 3, no. 18 (3 May 1991), 19-24.

7382. -----, "El'tsin Brokers Agreement on Nagorno-Karabakh," *Report on the USSR*, 3, no. 40 (4 Oct. 1991), 16-18.

7383. -----, "Gamsakhurdia's First 100 Days," *Report on the USSR*, 3, no. 10 (8 Mar. 1991), 10-13.

7384. -----, "Georgia Declares Independence," *Report on the USSR*, 3, no. 16 (19 Apr. 1991), 11-12.

7385. -----, "Georgia Edges Toward Secession," *Report on the USSR*, 2, no. 22 (1 June 1990), 14-18.

7386. -----, "Georgia Since Independence: Plus Ca Change...," *Current History*, 92, no. 576 (Oct. 1993), 542-47.

7387. -----, "Georgian Parliament Votes to Abolish Ossetian Autonomy," *Report on the USSR*, 2, no. 51 (21 Dec. 1990), 8-9.

7388. -----, "Georgian Prosecutor Accused of Inciting Interethnic Hatred," *Report on the USSR*, 2, no. 17 (27 Apr. 1990), 12-14.

7389. -----, "Georgia's Adzhar Crisis," *Report on the USSR*, 3, no. 32 (9 Aug. 1991), 8-13.

7390. -----, "Gorbachev's Dilemma in Azerbaijan," *Report on the USSR*, 2, no. 5 (2 Feb. 1990), 14-16.

7391. -----, "Mediators for Transcaucasia's Conflicts," *World Today*, 49, no. 5 (May 1993), 89-92.

7392. -----, "South Ossetia: Analysis of a Permanent Problem," *Report on the USSR*, 3, no. 7 (15 Feb. 1991), 20-22.

7393. -----, "The Transcaucasian Republics Equivocate," *Report on the USSR*, 3, no. 36 (6 Sept. 1991), 40-42.

7394. -----, "Transcaucasus: Democratization Threatened by Interethnic Violence," *Report on the USSR*, 3, no. 1 (4 Jan. 1991), 41-44.

7395. -----, "What Lies Behind the Current Armenian-Azerbaijani Tensions?" *Report on the USSR*, 3, no. 21 (24 May 1991), 12-15.

7396. Gachechiladze, Revaz, with Michael J. Bradshaw, "Civil Unrest and Net Migration Balance in Tbilisi," *Post-Soviet Geography*, 34, no. 8 (Oct. 1993), 541-42.

7397. Gudava, Tengiz, "*Glasnost* and *Perestroika* in the USSR and Its Satellites: Myth and Reality," *Religion in Communist Dominated Areas*, 27, no. 3 (Summer 1988), 78-79.

7398. "Holy War," *New Republic* (12 Feb. 1990), 11.

7399. Horowitz, Irving Louis, "The Armenian Nation: Old Issues, New Realities," *Freedom Review*, 22, no. 5 (Sept-Oct. 1991), 25-26.

7400. Husarka, A., "Burned-Out," *New Republic* (24 Jan. 1994), 11-12.

7401. -----, "Tinder Box," *New Republic* (7 Feb. 1994), 16-17.

7402. Huttenbach, Henry R., "In Support of Nagorno-Karabakh: Social Components of the Armenian Nationalist Movement," *Nationalities Papers*, 28, no. 2 (Fall 1990), 5-14.

7403. "Instability Curve: Azerbaijani-Armenian Conflict," *Soviet Literature*, no. 9 (1990), 159-75.

7404. Jones, Stephen F., "Glasnost, Perestroika and the Georgian Soviet Socialist Republic," *Armenian Review*, 43, no. 2-3 (Summer 1990), 127-52.

7405. Kempton, M., "Gorbachev in Armenia," *New York Review of Books*, 35 (19 Jan. 1989), 58.

7406. Klebnikov, Peter, "Ethnic Troubles in Georgia," *World & I*, 7, no. 1 (Jan. 1992), 196-201.

7407. Langfur, H., "Gorbachev Through Georgian Eyes," *New Leader*, 71 (3-17 Oct. 1988), 8-11.

7408. Lloyd, J., "From the Rubble," *National Review*, 41 (27 Jan. 1989), 43ff.

7409. Mackenzie, Kenneth, "Azerbaijan and the Neighbours," *World Today*, 48, no. 1 (Jan. 1992), 1-2.

7410. Mikaelian, Vardges, and Lendrush Khurshudian, "Several Issues Concerning the History of Mountainous Karabagh," *Armenian Review*, 43, no. 2-3 (Summer 1990), 51-65.

7411. Montefiore, Simon Sebag, "Eduard Shevardnadze," *New*

York Times Magazine (26 Dec. 1993), 16-19.

7412. Mouradian, Claire, "The Mountainous Karabagh Question: An Inter-Ethnic Conflict or Decolonization Crisis?" *Armenian Review*, 43, no. 2-3 (Summer 1990), 1-34.

7413. "Mr. Gorbachev's Crisis," *National Review*, 42 (19 Feb. 1990), 12-15.

7414. "Nagorno-Karabakh: Challenge to Glasnost," *Soviet Analyst*, 17 (6 Apr. 1988), 1-4.

7415. "Nightmare of the Generals," *Time*, 134 (18 Sept. 1989), 48.

7416. Norman, C., "U.S. Physicians Probe Deaths in Soviet Georgia," *Science*, 244 (9 June 1989), 1133.

7417. O'Clery, Conor, "Azerbaijan Postcard: Pajama Game," *New Republic* (10 June 1991), 12-13.

7418. "Programme of the National Party of Georgia," *Religion in Communist Lands*, 17, no. 4 (Winter 1989), 340-42.

7419. Rosen, Roger, "Perestroika in Soviet Georgia," *Publishers Weekly*, 237, no. 20 (18 May 1990), 30-34.

7420. Rybarczyk, Sebastian, "The Roots of the Civil War: Two Views: Interview with Nodar Gabashvili and Vakhtangi Talakhadze," *Uncaptive Minds*, 4, no. 4 (Winter 1991-92), 81-92.

7421. Saroyan, Mark, "Beyond the Nation-State: Culture and Ethnic Politics in Soviet Transcaucasia," *Soviet Union/Union Sovietique*, 15, no. 2-3 (1988), 219-44.

7422. -----, "'The Karabakh Syndrome' and Azerbaijani Politics," *Problems of Communism*, 39, no. 5 (Sept-Oct. 1990), 14-29.

7423. -----, "Trouble in the Transcaucasus," *Bulletin of the Atomic Scientists*, 45, no. 2 (Mar. 1989), 16ff.

7424. Sheehy, Ann, "Armenia Invokes Law on Mechanics of Secession," *Report on the USSR*, 3, no. 11 (15 Mar. 1991), 21.

7425. Shevardnadze, Eduard, "Georgia's Security Outlook," *NATO Review*, 41, no. 4 (Aug. 1993), 7-10.

7426. Slider, Darrell, "The Politics of Georgia's Independence," *Problems of Communism*, 40, no. 6 (Nov-Dec. 1991), 63-79.

7427. Soldatova, G. U., "The Former Checheno-Ingushetia: Interethnic Relations and Ethnic Conflicts," *Russian Social Science Review*, 34, no. 6 (Nov-Dec. 1993), 52-72.

7428. "Soviet Transcaucasus: A Mess on a Map," *Economist*, 320 (28 Sept. 1991), 56.

7429. Swietochowski, Tadeusz, "Azerbaijan: Between Ethnic Conflict and Irredentism," *Armenian Review*, 43, no. 2-3 (Summer 1990), 35-49.

7430. Tedstrom, John, "Armenia: An Energy Profile," *Report on the USSR*, 3, no. 8 (22 Feb. 1991), 18-20.

7431. "A Test for Perestroika," *Nation*, 246 (12 Mar. 1988), 325.

7432. Thom, Francoise, "The War Against the Azeri Popular Front: An Interview with Tofik Gasymov," *Uncaptive Minds*, 3,

no. 5 (Nov-Dec. 1990), 12-16.

7433. "Tragedy in the Transcaucasus," *Glasnost*, 2, no. 2, issues no. 16-18 (Jan. 1989), 6-33; issues no. 21-23 (Mar-May 1989), 51-56.

7434. Walker, Christopher J., "Between Turkey and Russia: Armenia's Predicament," *World Today*, 44, nos. 8-9 (Aug-Sept. 1988), 140-44.

7435. Wilson-Smith, Anthony, "Fires of Nationalism," *Maclean's*, 102 (30 Oct. 1989), 43ff.

7436. Wishnevsky, Julia, "Shevardnadze Said to Have Threatened to Resign in Dispute over Tbilisi Commission," *Report on the USSR*, 2, no. 5 (2 Feb. 1990), 1-3.

D. Central Asia

BOOKS

7437. Akiner, Shirin, ed., *Cultural Change and Continuity in Central Asia* (New York: Kegan Paul with the Central Asia Research Forum, School of Oriental and African Studies, London, distributed by Routledge, Chapman and Hall, 1991).

7438. Alexiev, Alexander R., *Gorbachev's Muslim Dilemma* (Santa Monica, CA: RAND, 1987).

7439. Allworth, Edward A., *The Modern Uzbeks: From the Fourteenth Century to the Present: A Cultural History* (Stanford: Stanford University Press, 1990).

7440. Aron, Leon, *Gorbachev's Central Asian Time Bomb Is Ticking* (Washington, DC: Heritage Foundation, 1990).

7441. Atkin, Muriel, *The Subtlest Battle: Islam in Soviet Tajikistan* (Philadelphia: Foreign Policy Research Institute, 1988).

7442. Banuazizi, Ali, and Myron Weiner, ed., *The New Geopolitics of Central Asia* (New York: St. Martin's Press, 1994).

7443. Critchlow, James, *Nationalism in Uzbekistan: A Soviet Republic's Road to Sovereignty* (Boulder, CO: Westview Press, 1991).

7444. Eickelman, Dale F. (ed.), *Russia's Muslim Frontiers* (Bloomington: Indiana University Press, 1993).

7445. Frierman, William, ed., *Soviet Central Asia: The Failed Transformation* (Boulder, CO: Westview Press, 1991).

7446. Gross, Jo-Ann, ed., *Muslims in Central Asia: Expressions of Identity and Change* (Durham, NC: Duke University Press, 1992).

7447. Hostler, Charles Warren, *The Turks of Central Asia* (Westport, CT: Praeger, 1993).

7448. Human Rights Watch, *Conflict in the Soviet Union: Tadzhikistan* (New York: Helsinki Watch Committee, 1991).

7449. Hyman, Anthony, *Political Change in Post-Soviet Central Asia* (London: Royal Institute of International Affairs, 1994).

7450. Imart, Guy, *From "Roots" to "Great Expectations": Kirghizia and Kazakhstan Between the Devil and the Deep-Green*

Sea (Bloomington: Indiana University, Research Institute for Inner Asian Studies, 1990).

7451. Lewis, Robert A., ed., *Geographic Perspectives on Soviet Central Asia* (New York: Routledge, 1992).

7452. Paksoy, H. B., ed., *Central Asia Reader: The Rediscovery of History* (Armonk, NY: M. E. Sharpe, 1993).

7453. Poliakov, Sergei P., *Everyday Islam: Religion and Tradition in Rural Central Asia* (Armonk, NY: M. E. Sharpe, 1992).

7454. Rumer, Boris Z., *Soviet Central Asia: "A Tragic Experiment"* (Boston: Unwin Hyman, 1989).

7455. Rywkin, Michael, *Moscow's Muslim Challenge: Soviet Central Asia*, rev. ed. (Armonk, NY: M. E. Sharpe, 1990).

ARTICLES

7456. Ahmed, Mutahir, "Prospects of Fundamentalism in Central Asia," *Pakistan Horizon*, 45, no. 3 (July 1992), 71-82.

7457. Aitmatov, C., "The Influence of Information Technology on the Economic and Cultural Life of Soviet Central Asia," *Impact of Science on Society*, no. 146 (1987), 183-87.

7458. Akchurin, Marat, "Soviet Muslims: Seeking Reform, Not Revolution," *World & I*, 6, no. 10 (Oct. 1991), 86-93.

7459. Asalan, Yasin, "Muslim Support for Baltic Independence," *Report on the USSR*, 2, no. 21 (25 May 1990), 16.

7460. Atkin, Muriel, "The Survival of Islam in Soviet Tajikistan," *Middle East Journal*, 43, no. 4 (Autumn 1989), 605-18.

7461. Bohr, Annette, "Turkmenistan under Perestroika: An Overview," *Report on the USSR*, 2, no. 12 (23 Mar. 1990), 20-30.

7462. Bremmer, I., "Minority Rules," *New Republic* (11 Apr. 1994), 26.

7463. Brown, Bess, "The All-Union Referendum in Central Asia," *Report on the USSR*, 3, no. 13 (29 Mar. 1991), 1-3.

7464. -----, "Alma-Ata Commission of Inquiry Publishes Report," *Report on the USSR*, 2, no. 42 (19 Oct. 1990), 20-21.

7465. -----, "The Alma-Ata Events of 1986 Reexamined," *Report on the USSR*, 2, no. 9 Feb. 1990), 25-27.

7466. -----, "Central Asia and the East Asian Model," *Report on the USSR*, 3, no. 6 (8 Feb. 1991), 18-19.

7467. -----, "Democratization in Turkmenistan," *Report on the USSR*, 2, no. 22 (1 June 1990), 13-14.

7468. -----, "Ethnic Unrest Claims More Lives in Fergana Valley," *Report on the USSR*, 2, no. 24 (15 June 1990), 16-18.

7469. -----, "The Fall of Masaliev: Kyrgyzstan's `Silk Revolution' Advances," *Report on the USSR*, 3, no. 16 (19 Apr. 1991), 12-15.

7470. -----, "The Islamic Renaissance Party in Central Asia," *Report on the USSR*, 3, no. 19 (10 May 1991), 12-14.

7471. -----, "Kazakhs Protest against Solzhenitsyn's Proposal for "A New Russia'," *Report on the USSR*, 2, no. 40 (5 Oct. 1990), 19-20.

7472. -----, "Kazakhstan: Interethnic Tensions, Unsolved Economic Problems," *Report on the USSR*, 3, no. 1 (4 Jan. 1991), 29-30.

7473. -----, "Kazakhstan's Economic Reform Program," *Report on the USSR*, 3, no. 24 (14 June 1991), 24-26.

7474. -----, "Liberalization Reaches Kirgizia: Profile of the New President," *Report on the USSR*, 2, no. 48 (30 Nov. 1990), 17-20.

7475. -----, "Nazarbaev Turns Strike Threat to Kazakhstan's Advantage," *Report on the USSR*, 3, no. 32 (9 Aug. 1991), 13-15.

7476. -----, "The Role of Public Groups in Perestroika in Central Asia," *Report on the USSR*, 2, no. 4 (26 Jan. 1990), 20-25.

7477. -----, "Setback for Conservatives in Tajikistan," *Report on the USSR*, 3, no. 40 (4 Oct. 1991), 18-21.

7478. -----, "Tajikistan: Ten Months after the Dushanbe Riots," *Report on the USSR*, 3, no. 1 (4 Jan. 1991), 32-34.

7479. -----, "Unrest in Tajikistan," *Report on the USSR*, 2, no. 8 (23 Feb. 1990), 28-31.

7480. Broxup, Marie, "Comrade Muslims," *Wilson Quarterly*, 16, no. 4 (Summer 1992), 39-47.

7481. -----, "Islam in Central Asia since Gorbachev," *Asian Affairs*, 18 (Oct. 1987), 283-93.

7482. Canfield, Robert L., "Restructuring in Greater Central Asia: Changing Political Configurations," *Asian Survey*, 32, no. 10 (Oct. 1992), 875-87.

7483. Carlson, Charles, "Kirgizia: Political Stagnation Gives Way to Democratic Impulses," *Report on the USSR*, 3, no. 1 (4 Jan. 1991), 31-32.

7484. Carver, Jeremy P., and Greg Englefield, "Oil and Gas Pipelines from Central Asia: A New Approach," *World Today*, 50, no. 6 (June 1994), 102-03.

7485. Chmielowska, Jadwiga, "The National Movements in Central Asia: Interview with Abdurrakhim Pulatov, Muhamad Nurdymurad, Sobyetkazy Akatayev and Zhypar Zheksheyev," *Uncaptive Minds*, 4, no. 3 (Fall 1991), 67-72.

7486. Critchlow, James, "Central Asia: The Shape of Things to Come," *Journal of Soviet Nationalities*, 1, no. 2 (Summer 1990), 122-26.

7487. -----, "Further Repercussions of `The Uzbek Affairs'," *Report on the USSR*, 2, no. 18 (4 May 1990), 20-22.

7488. -----, "Religious-Nationalist Dissent in the Turkestan Communist Party: An Old Document Surfaces," *Report on the USSR*, 2, no. 3 (19 Jan. 1990), 19-21.

7489. -----, "Tajik Scholar Describes a Source of Ethnic Discontent," *Report on the USSR*, 2, no. 8 (23 Feb. 1990), 19-20.

7490. -----, "Will Soviet Central Asia Become a Greater Uzbekistan?" *Report on the USSR*, 2, no. 37 (14 Sept. 1990), 17-

19.

7491. Doroszewska, Urszula, "The Tatars Against the Empire: An Interview with Rafael Fardiievich," *Uncaptive Minds*, 3, no. 5 (Nov-Dec. 1990), 9-11.

7492. Freidin, Gregory, "After the Stand-Off," *Uncaptive Minds*, 4, no. 4 (Winter 1991-92), 93-95.

7493. -----, "Coup II," *New Republic* (14 Oct. 1991), 14-16.

7494. Fuller, Graham E., "The Emergence of Central Asia," *Foreign Policy*, no. 78 (Spring 1990), 49-67.

7495. "The Future of Central Asia," *Pakistan Horizon*, 45, no. 3 (July 1992), 7-22.

7496. Gleason, Gregory, "Fealty and Loyalty: Informal Authority Structures in Soviet Asia," *Soviet Studies*, 43, no. 4 (Dec. 1991), 613-28.

7497. -----, "Marketization and Migration: The Politics of Cotton in Central Asia," *Journal of Soviet Nationalities*, 1, no. 2 (Summer 1990), 66-98.

7498. -----, "The Political Economy of Dependency under Socialism: The Asian Republics in the USSR," *Studies in Comparative Communism*, 24, no. 4 (1991), 335-54.

7499. Goble, Paul, "Central Asians Form Political Bloc," *Report on the USSR*, 2, no. 28 (13 July 1990), 18-20.

7500. -----, "Islamic `Explosion' Possible in Central Asia," *Report on the USSR*, 2, no. 7 (16 Feb. 1990), 22-23.

7501. Harrison, Selig S., "Nationalism in Asia," *World & I*, 6, no. 7 (July 1991), 542-57.

7502. Hilf, Rudolf, "The Rise of Islam in the Wake of Perestrojka," *Plural Societies*, 21, no. 1-2 (June 1991), 67-74.

7503. -----, "Nationalist Movements in Soviet Asia," *Current History*, 89, no. 549 (Oct. 1990), 325ff.

7504. Hunter, Shireen T., "Nationalist Movements in Soviet Asia," *Current History*, 89, no. 549 (Oct. 1990), 325ff.

7505. Hyman, Anthony, "Moving Out of Moscow's Orbit: The Outlook for Central Asia," *International Affairs*, 69, no. 2 (Apr. 1993), 289-304.

7506. Imart, Guy G., "Kirgizia-Kazakhstan: A Hinge or a Fault Line?" *Problems of Communism*, 39, no. 5 (Sept-Oct. 1990), 1-13.

7507. "Islam and Nationalist Unrest in Soviet Central Asia," *Religion in Communist Lands*, 17, no. 3 (Autumn 1989), 264-66.

7508. Jackson, James O., "What Really Happened in Alma-Ata: A Visit to the Scene of Last Year's Minority Riots in Kazakhstan," *Time*, 129 (2 Mar. 1987), 25.

7509. "The Kazakhstan Revolt: Candor or Crackdown?" *Newsweek*, 108 (29 Dec. 1986), 24-25.

7510. Laber, Jeri, "Stalin's Dumping Ground," *New York Review of Books*, 37 (11 Oct. 1990), 50-53.

7511. Lubin, Nancy, "Uzbekistan: The Challenges Ahead," *Middle East Journal*, 43, no. 4 (Autumn 1989), 619-34.

7512. Melvin, Neil, "Russia and the Ethno-Politics of Kazakhstan," *World Today*, 49, no. 11 (Nov. 1993), 208-09.

7513. Mirsky, George I., "Central Asia's Emergence," *Current History*, 91, no. 567 (Oct. 1992), 334-38.

7514. Motyl, Alexander J., "Meanwhile, Back in the Kazakh SSR," *New Leader* (9-23 Feb. 1987), 9.

7515. Naby, Eden, "Tajiks Reemphasize Iranian Heritage as Ethnic Pressures Mount in Central Asia," *Report on the USSR*, 2, no. 7 (16 Feb. 1990), 20-22.

7516. Oezgen, Abdulhakim, "Chingiz Aitmatov's Appeal to the Kirgiz and Uzbek Peoples," *Report on the USSR*, 2, no. 24 (15 June 1990), 18-19.

7517. Olcott, Martha B., "Central Asia's Catapult to Independence," *Foreign Affairs*, 71, no. 1 (Summer 1992), 108-30.

7518. -----, "Central Asia's Post-Empire Politics," *Orbis*, 36, no. 2 (Spring 1992), 253-68.

7519. -----, and William Fierman, "The Challenge of Integration: Soviet Nationality Policy and the Muslim Conscript," *Soviet Union/Union Sovietique*, 14, no. 1 (1987), 65-101.

7520. Pipes, Richard, "The `Glasnost' Test," *New Republic* (2 Feb. 1987), 16-17.

7521. Puzanov, O., "Quiet Tensions," *Bulletin of the Atomic Scientists*, 49 (Oct. 1994), 30ff.

7522. Rashid, A., "Point of Conflict: Russia and Islamic Militants in Tajik Proxy War," *Far Eastern Economic Review*, 156 (3 June 1993), 24-25.

7523. Riva, Joseph P., Jr., "Large Oil Reserve Awaits Exploitation in Former Soviet Union's Muslim Republics," *Oil and Gas Journal*, 91 (4 Jan. 1993), 56-59.

7524. Robins, Philip, "Between Sentiment and Self-Interest: Turkey's Policy toward Azerbaijan and the Central Asian States," *Middle East Journal*, 47, no. 4 (Autumn 1993), 593-610.

7525. Ro'i, Yaacov, "The Islamic Influence on Nationalism in Soviet Central Asia," *Problems of Communism*, 39, no. 4 (July-Aug. 1990), 49-64.

7526. -----, "The Soviet and Russian Context of the Development of Nationalism in Soviet Central Asia," *Cahiers du Monde russe and sovietique*, 32, no. 1 (1991), 123-42.

7527. Rorlich, Azade-Ayse, "`Adilet'-The Kazakh Chapter of `Memorial'," *Report on the USSR*, 2, no. 4 (26 Jan. 1990), 27-28.

7528. Rubin, Barnett R., "The Fragmentation of Tajikistan," *Survival*, 35, no. 4 (Winter 1993-94), 71-91.

7529. Rumer, Boris Z., "The Gathering Storm in Central Asia," *Orbis*, 37, no. 1 (Winter 1993), 89-105.

7530. Rupert, James, "Dateline Tashkent: Post-Soviet Central Asia," *Foreign Policy* (Summer 1992), 175-95.

7531. Schafer, Daniel E., "Cultural Survival in Soviet Society: The Case of the Volga Tatars," *Armenian Review*, 43, no. 2-3 (Summer 1990), 195-216.

7532. Watters, Kathleen, "The Current Family Planning Debate in Soviet Central Asia," *Central Asian Survey*, 9, no. 1 (1990), 75-86.

7533. Wolf, Markus, and Alexander Frank, "No Future for the Ethnic Germans in Kazakhstan?" *Aussenpolitik*, 44, no. 2 (1993), 153-62.

E. Jews in the USSR

BOOKS

7534. Brym, Robert J., with Rozalina Ryvkina, *Between East and West: The Jews of Moscow, Kiev, and Minsk* (New York: New York University Press, 1994).

7535. Drachman, Edward, *Challenging the Kremlin: The Soviet Jewish Movement for Freedom, 1967-1990* (New York: Paragon House, 1991).

7536. Freedman, Robert O., ed., *Soviet Jewry in the 1980's: The Politics of Emigration and the Dynamics of Resettlement* (Durham, NC: Duke University Press, 1989), 51-57.

7537. Sanford, Margery, and Adele E. Sandberg, *Mr. Gorbachev, Let My People Go* (Miami: South Florida Conference on Soviet Jewry, 1986).

7538. US Commission on Security and Cooperation in Europe. *Implementation of the Helsinki Accords: Soviet Jewry Struggle* (Washington, DC: Government Printing Office, 1989).

7539. US Congress. Commission on Security and Cooperation in Europe. *Implementation of the Helsinki Accords: Status Report on Soviet Jewry, March 7, 1990.* 101st Congress, 2nd Session (Washington, DC: Government Printing Office, 1990).

7540. US Congress. House. Committee on Foreign Affairs. *Appeal for the Release of Soviet Jewry.* Hearing and Markup. 99th Congress, 24 July 1985 (Washington, DC: Government Printing Office, 1985).

7541. Wiesel, Elie, *The Jews of Silence: A Personal Report on Soviet Jewry*, trans. by Neal Kozodoy (New York: Schocken, 1987).

ARTICLES

7542. Anderson, H., "Gorbachev and the Jews," *Newsweek*, 109 (13 Apr. 1987), 34-35.

7543. Arzt, Donna E., "Paternalism in the Human Rights Movement: The Case of Soviet Jewry," *Human Rights Internet Reporter*, 11, no. 5-6 (Winter-Spring 1987), 10-12.

7544. "Between Issues," *New Leader*, 74, no. 11 (7-21 Oct. 1991), 2.

7545. Brym, Robert J., "'Perestroyka,' Public Opinion and 'Pamyat'," *Soviet Jewish Affairs*, 19, no. 3 (1989), 23-32.

7546. Buruma, Ian, "Anti-Semitism and the New Europe," *Harper's*, 281, no. 1683 (Aug. 1990), 26-28.

7547. Charles, K., "The Limits of Tolerance," *Maclean's*, 98 (25 Nov. 1985), 32-33.

7548. Chlenov, Michael, "The Soviet Jewish Future," *Midstream*, 36, no. 4 (May 1990), 3-6.

7549. Clifton, Tony, "A Troublesome Exodus: President Bush Says Nyet So Fast to Soviet Jews," *Newsweek*, 114 (25 Sept. 1989), 51-52.

7550. Cotler, Irvin, "Soviet Jewry, Human Rights, and the Rule of Law: A Pre- and Post-Glasnost Case Study," *Touro Journal of Transnational Law*, 2, no. 1 (Spring 1991), 107-51.

7551. Cullen, Robert H., "Soviet Jewry," *Foreign Affairs*, 65, no. 2 (Winter 1986-87), 252-66.

7552. Drinan, Robert F., SJ, "New Crisis for Soviet Jews," *Christian Century*, 107, no. 10 (21-28 Mar. 1990), 294-95.

7553. "Evicted: A Russian Jew's Story (Again)," *Harper's*, 282, no. 1693 (June 1991), 17-19; reprinted from *Tikkun* (Mar-Apr. 1991).

7554. Fain, Benjamin, and Jane Gerber, "Soviet Jewry in the Age of *Glasnost*: Toward a Recovery of Jewish Culture," *Congress Monthly*, 56, no. 4 (May-June 1989), 10-12.

7555. Fenson, Melvin, "Soviet Jews, Staying & Going," *Congress Monthly*, 57, no. 2 (Feb. 1990), 2.

7556. Friedberg, Maurice, "The Euphoria of Glasnost and Jewish Fears," *Midstream*, 36, no. 3 (Apr. 1990), 3-8.

7557. Garrard, John, "The Challenge of Glasnost: *Ogonek's* Handling of Russian Antisemitism," *Nationalities Papers*, 19, no. 2 (Fall 1991), 228-50.

7558. Gibson, James L., and Raymond M. Duch, "Anti-Semitic Attitudes of the Mass Public: Estimates and Explanations Based on a Survey of the Moscow Oblast," *Public Opinion Quarterly*, 56, no. 1 (Spring 1992), 1-28.

7559. -----, "Attitudes Toward Jews and the Soviet Political Culture," *Journal of Soviet Nationalities*, 2, no. 1 (Spring 1991), 77-117.

7560. Gidwitz, Betsy, "Contemporary Anti-Semitism in the USSR," *Russia*, no. 11 (1985), 19-25.

7561. Gitelman, Zvi, "Glasnost, Perestroika and Antisemitism," *Foreign Affairs*, 70, no. 2 (Spring 1991), 141-59.

7562. Goldansky, Vitalii I., "On `Special Dangers' of Perestroika to Soviet Jews," *Physics Today*, 43, no. 3 (Mar. 1990).

7563. Goldfarb, A., "Testing *Glasnost*: An Exile Visits His Homeland," *New York Times Magazine* (6 Dec. 1987), 46ff.

7564. Goldman, Karia, "Pogroms and Perestroika," *World Monitor*, 3, no. 5 (May 1990), 12ff.

7565. Goldman, Philip, "*Perestroika*: End or Beginning of Soviet Federalism?" *Telos*, no. 84 (Summer 1990), 69-87.

7566. Goodwin, Irwin, "The Paradox of Perestroika: Ethnic Turmoil and Anti-Semitism," *Physics Today*, 43, no. 3 (Mar. 1990).

7567. Gordon, Murray, "Communism's Collapse: The Impact on Jewish Communities," *Midstream*, 36, no. 3 (Apr. 1990), 9-13.

7568. Greenbaum, Avraham, "The Status of Hebrew in Soviet Russia from the Revolution to the Gorbachev Thaw," in Lewis Gilbert, ed., *Hebrew in Ashkenaz: A Language in Exile* (New York: Oxford University Press, 1993), 242-48.

7569. Gruntman, M. A., "Soviet Anti-Semitism In *Perestroika*'s Wake," *Physics Today*, 43, part 1 (Aug. 1990), 15ff.

7570. Hareven, Gail, "From Russia with Luggage," *Tikkun*, 6, no. 2 (Mar-Apr. 1991), 39ff.

7571. -----, "Glasnost in the Promised Land," *Tikkun*, 6, no. 4 (July-Aug. 1991), 16ff.

7572. Harris, David A., "Crisis in Soviet Jewry," *Midstream*, 32, no. 3 (Mar. 1986), 6-8.

7573. Hertzberg, Arthur, "Glasnost and the Jews," *New York Review of Books* (17 Oct. 1987), 20-23.

7574. Idinopulos, Thomas A., "Vanishing Jews and Visible Christians in Gorbachev's Soviet Union," *Christian Century*, 105, no. 31 (26 Oct. 1988), 950-53.

7575. "I'm Not Fleeing, I'm Being Evicted," *Tikkun*, 6, no. 2 (Mar-Apr. 1991), 37ff.

7576. Irwin, Zachary T., "Soviet Jewry and the Diplomacy of Detente," *Religion in Communist Dominated Areas*, 27, no. 3 (Summer 1988), 68-71.

7577. Kagedan, Allan, "Gorbachev and the Jews," *Commentary*, 81 (May 1986), 47-50.

7578. -----, "The Soviet `No-Exit' Policy: Gorbachev and the Jews," *Current*, 285 (Sept. 1986), 36-40.

7579. Karavansky, Sviatoslav, "What Ruins Jewish-Ukrainian Relations," *Ukrainian Quarterly*, 42, no. 1-2 (Spring-Summer 1986), 81-86.

7580. Kassow, Samuel D., "Should Soviet Jews Leave?" *Tikkun*, 5, no. 5 (1990), 27-36.

7581. Klier, John D., "Pamyat and the Jewish Menace: Remembrance of Things Past," *Nationalities Papers*, 19, no. 2 (Fall 1991), 214-27.

7582. Kogan, J., "The Plight of Jewish Scientists," *Midstream*, 33, no. 2 (Feb. 1987), 37-38.

7583. Korey, William, "The Current Plight of Soviet Jewry," *Midstream*, 32, no. 9 (Nov. 1986), 8-11.

7584. -----, "Soviet Jewry: What's To Be Done?" *Present Tense*, 14, no. 2 (Jan-Feb. 1987), 24.

7585. Kornblatt, M., "A Tradition of Hatred," *Scholastic Update*, 123 (7 Dec. 1990), 14.

7586. Leibler, Isi J., "Soviet Jewry: A Turning Point?" *Midstream*, 33, no. 2 (Feb. 1987), 29-32.

7587. Levin, Nora, "Will `Glasnost' Reach the Jews? Gorbachev and Soviet Anti-Semitism," *Commonweal*, 114 (23 Oct. 1987), 596-99.

7588. -----, "The Yiddish Factor," *Present Tense*, 14, no. 4 (May-June 1987), 41-44.

7589. Paramonov, Boris, "The Culture of Soviet Anti-Semitism," *Partisan Review*, 57, no. 2 (Spring 1990), 193-201.

7590. Pearson, John, "Gorbachev Opens the Border for Jews-with Good Reason," *Business Week* (20 Apr. 1987), 28.

7591. Pilon, R., "The Systematic Repression of Soviet Jews," *Department of State Bulletin*, 86 (Dec. 1986), 67-70.

7592. Quigley, John, "Soviet Immigration to the West Bank: Is It Legal?" *Georgia Journal of International and Comparative Law*, 21 (Fall 1991), 387-413.

7593. Reznik, Semyon E., "Soviet Jews in the Glasnost Era," *Society*, 28, no. 4 (May-June 1991), 73-83.

7594. Rosen, Stephen, "The Soviet Brain Drain Is Our Brain Gain: A Career Transition Program for Emigre Scientists and Engineers," *Journal of Jewish Communal Service*, 68, no. 2 (Winter 1991-92), 183-91.

7595. Rosenfeld, Barbara B., "Soviet Jewry at the Crossroads: Is the Jewish Experience in Russia Coming to an End?" *Present Tense*, 16, no. 6 (Sept-Oct. 1989), 24-31.

7596. Ross, Jeffrey A., "Declaration of the Secretariat of the Soviet Public Anti-Zionist Committee: RCDA Comment," *Religion in Communist Dominated Areas*, 29, no. 1 (Winter 1990), 11-16.

7597. -----, "Soviet Union and the Jews: Perestroika, Policy, and Promise and Peril," *Religion in Communist Dominated Areas*, 28, no. 4 (Fall 1989), 108ff.

7598. Ruby, W., "Among the Refuseniks," *World Press Review*, 34 (Sept. 1987), 56.

7599. Smith, William E., "Sounds of Freedom: Moscow Releases Some Dissidents, But Cracks Down on Refuseniks," *Time*, 129 (23 Feb. 1987), 52-53.

7600. Snitow, Alan, "Soviet Prospects, Jewish Fears," *Tikkun*, 5, no. 4 (1990), 15ff.

7601. "Soviet Jews under Soviet Law: A Practical Guide," *Loyola of Los Angeles International and Comparative Law Journal*, 9 (1987), 711-50.

7602. Spier, Howard, "Soviet Anti-Semitism Unchained: The Rise of the Historical and Patriotic Organization, Pamyat," in Robert O. Freedman, ed., *Soviet Jewry in the 1980's: The Politics of Emigration and the Dynamics of Resettlement* (Durham, NC: Duke University Press, 51-57.

7603. Tumarkin, Nina, "The Soviet Union: Russians against

Jews," *Atlantic*, 266 (Oct. 1990), 32-45.

7604. Walsh, John, "Some Refuseniks See No Glasnost," *Science*, 237 (24 July 1987), 356-57.

7605. Weinberg, Henry H., "Soviet Jewry: New Tragic Dilemmas," *Midstream*, 37, no. 7 (Oct. 1991), 15-17.

7606. Weiss, Avraham, "Public Protest and Soviet Jewry," *Midstream*, 33, no. 2 (Feb. 1987), 25-28.

7607. Wistrich, Robert S., "Gorbachev's Russia: The Jews, Too, Have a Stake in *Glasnost'* and *Perestroika*," *Present Tense*, 16, no. 2 (Jan-Feb. 1989), 20-24.

7608. Wotzman, Herbert M., "Israel Expects 40,000 Immigrant Students from USSR Over Next 4 Years," *Chronicle of Higher Education*, 37, no. 8 (24 Oct. 1990), A35ff.

7609. Zipperstein, Steven J., "Old Ghosts: Pogroms in the Jewish Mind," *Tikkun*, 6, no. 3 (May-June 1991), 49ff.

F. Moldavia (Moldova)

BOOKS

7610. Dima, Nicholas, *From Moldavia to Moldova: The Soviet-Romanian Territorial Dispute* (Boulder, CO: East European Monographs, distributed by Columbia University Press, 1991).

ARTICLES

7611. Berkin, George, "Secession Blues," *National Review*, 43 (9 Sept. 1991), 22-23.

7612. Cioranescu, George, "The Moldavian Clan in the Kremlin Power Struggle," *Journal of the American Romanian Academy of Arts and Sciences*, no. 12 (1989), 160-69.

7613. Crowther, William, "Ethnicity and Participation in the Communist Party of Moldavia," *Journal of Soviet Nationalities*, 1, no. 1 (Spring 1990), 148-49.

7614. -----, "The Politics of Ethno-National Mobilization: Nationalism and Reform in Soviet Moldavia," *Russian Review*, 50, no. 2 (Apr. 1991), 183-202.

7615. Dima, Nicholas, "Recent Ethno-Demographic Changes in Soviet Moldavia," *East European Quarterly*, 25, no. 2 (Summer 1991), 167-73.

7616. -----, "The Soviet Political Upheaval of the 1980s: The Case of Moldavia," *Journal of Social, Political and Economic Studies*, 16, no. 1 (Spring 1991), 39-58.

7617. Doerner, William R., "The Language of Unrest," *Time*, 134 (11 Sept. 1989), 40.

7618. Gabanyi, Anneli Ute, "Moldova Between Russia, Romania and Ukraine," *Aussenpolitik*, 44, no. 1 (1993), 98ff.

7619. Gray, Malcolm, "Militant Moldova: Ethnic Unrest Unsettles Another Republic," *Maclean's*, 103 (12 Nov. 1990), 34.

7620. Gritsiuk, Grigorii, "Privatization: Reality and the Mirage of the Market," *Russian Social Science Review*, 34, no. 2 (Mar-Apr.

1993), 24-40.

7621. King, Charles, "Moldova and the New Bessarabian Questions," *World Today*, 49, no. 7 (July 1993), 135-38.

7622. Livezeanu, Irina, "Moldavia, 1917-1990: Nationalism and Internationalism Then and Now," *Armenian Review*, 43, no. 2-3 (Summer 1990), 153-93.

7623. Melvin, Neil, "Moldova Looks Back to the Future," *World Today*, 50, no. 6 (June 1994), 102-03.

7624. Perrins, Michael, "Moldova and the Trans-Dniestr Region: The Anatomy of Conflict," Brilrigg Paper no. 13, CDISS, Lancaster University (Sept. 1992).

7625. Socor, Vladimir, "Gagauz in Moldavia Demand Separate Republic," *Report on the USSR*, 2, no. 36 (7 Sept. 1990), 8-13.

7626. -----, "Gorbachev and Moldavia," *Report on the USSR*, 2, no. 51 (21 Dec. 1990), 11-14.

7627. -----, "Moldavia: Political Power Passes to Democratic Forces," *Report on the USSR*, 3, no. 1 (4 Jan. 1991), 24-28.

7628. -----, "Moldavia Resists Pressure and Boycotts Union Referendum," *Report on the USSR*, 3, no. 13 (29 Mar. 1991), 9-14.

7629. -----, "Moldavian Land between Romania and Ukraine: The Historical and Political Geography," *Report on the USSR*, 2, no. 46 (16 Nov. 1990), 16-18.

7630. -----, "Moldavian Parliament Endorses Confederation," *Report on the USSR*, 3, no. 9 (1 Mar. 1991), 18-20.

7631. -----, "Moldavian President Breaks New Ground in Romania," *Report on the USSR*, 3, no. 8 (22 Feb. 1991), 20-23.

7632. -----, "Moldavians Reject Union Treaty," *Report on the USSR*, 3, no. 2 (11 Jan. 1991), 12-14.

7633. Stephen, C., "Blood and Honour," *New Statesman and Society* (17 July 1992), 15-16.

7634. "Trouble, Trouble, Trouble," *Economist*, 312 (2 Sept. 1989), 48-49.

7635. US Department of Commerce, "Trade Watch: Ukraine and Moldavia/ Community Treaty," *Business America*, 112, no. 23 (18 Nov. 1991), ii.

7636. Wilson-Smith, Anthony, "'Happy' Moldavia," *Maclean's*, 102 (13 Nov. 1989), 32ff.

G. Russian Republic

BOOKS

7637. Carter, Stephen K., *Russian Nationalism: Yesterday, Today, Tomorrow* (New York: St. Martin's Press, 1990).

7638. Henze, Paul B., *Ethnic Dynamics and Dilemmas of the Russian Republic* (Santa Monica, CA: RAND, 1991).

7639. Lyonhardt, Lawrence, and John Howells, *Russians and Others: Conversations with Twelve Soviet Citizens About Change*

(Jefferson, NC: McFarland & Co., 1991).

7640. Parland, Thomas, *The Rejection in Russia of Totalitarian Socialism and Liberal Democracy: A Study of the Russian New Right* (Helsinki: Societas Scientiarum Fennica, 1993).

7641. Shlapentokh, Vladimir, Munir Sendich and Emil Payin, eds., *The New Russian Diaspora: Russian Minorities in the Former Soviet Republics* (Armonk, NY: M. E. Sharpe, 1990).

ARTICLES

7642. Arutiunian, Yuri, "Changing Values of Russians from Brezhnev to Gorbachev," *Journal of Soviet Nationalities*, 2, no. 2 (Summer 1991), 1-34.

7643. "Border Changes Are a Possibility, Says Russia," *World & I*, 7, no. 10 (Oct. 1992), 606-09.

7644. Bremmer, Ian, "The Politics of Ethnicity: Russians in the New Ukraine," *Europe-Asia Studies*, 46, no. 2 (1994), 261-83.

7645. Carlson, Charles, "Cheremis Jump on Sovereignty Bandwagon," *Report on the USSR*, 2, no. 45 (9 Nov. 1990), 21-23.

7646. Confino, Michael, "Solzhenitsyn, the West and the New Russian Nationalism," *Journal of Contemporary History*, 26, no. 3-4 (Sept. 1991), 611-36.

7647. Dienes, Leslie, "Siberia: *Perestroyka* and Economic Development," *Soviet Geography*, 32, no. 7 (Sept. 1991), 445-57.

7648. Dunlop, John B., "Ethnic Russians on Possible Breakup of the Soviet Union," *Report on the USSR*, 2, no. 9 (2 Mar. 1990), 16-18.

7649. ------, "Monarchist Sentiment in Present-Day Russia," *Report on the USSR*, 3, no. 31 (2 Aug. 1991), 27-30.

7650. ------, "Pamiat' as a Social Movement," *Nationalities Papers*, 28, no. 2 (Fall 1990), 22-27.

7651. ------, "The Return of Russian Nationalism," *Journal of Democracy*, 1, no. 3 (Summer 1990), 114-22.

7652. ------, "Russian Nationalism Today: Organizations and Programs," *Nationalities Papers*, 19, no. 2 (Fall 1991), 146-66.

7653. Ericson, Edward E., Jr., "Solzhenitsyn and the Rebuilding of Russia," *Intercollegiate Review*, 27, no. 2 (Spring 1992), 11-18.

7654. "From Russia with Hate," *Glasnost*, 3, no. 1 (July-Sept. 1990), 40-47.

7655. Garrard, John, "A Pamyat Manifesto: Introductory Note and Translation," *Nationality Papers*, 19, no. 2 (Fall 1991), 134-45.

7656. Greenfeld, Liah, "The Closing of the Russian Mind," *New Republic* (6 Feb. 1990), 30-34.

7657. Harris, Chauncy D., "Ethnic Tensions in Areas of the Russian Diaspora," *Post-Soviet Geography*, 34, no. 4 (Apr. 1993), 233-38.

7658. ------, "The New Russian Minorities: A Statistical Over-view," *Post-Soviet Geography*, 34, no. 1 (Jan. 1993), 1-28.

7659. Henze, Paul B., "Ethnic Dynamics and Dilemmas of the Russian Republic," *Studies in Conflict and Terrorism*, 17, no. 1 (Jan-Mar. 1994), 61-86.

7660. Hosking, Geoffrey, "The Russian National Revival," *Report on the USSR*, 3, no. 44 (1 Nov. 1991), 5-8.

7661. Hyman, Anthony, "Russians Outside Russia," *World Today*, 49, no. 11 (Nov. 1993), 205-07.

7662. Keller, Bill, "Russian Nationalists: Yearning for an Iron Hand," *New York Review of Books* (28 Jan. 1990), 18-20ff.

7663. Kolsto, Pal, "The New Russian Diaspora: Minority Protection in the Soviet Successor States," *Journal of Peace Research*, 30, no. 2 (May 1993), 197-218.

7664. Krasnov, Vladislav, "Pamyat: A Force for Change?" *Nationalities Papers*, 19, no. 2 (Fall 1991), 167-82.

7665. Kuzio, Taras, "Russia-Crimea-Ukraine," *Conflict Studies*, no. 275 (Jan. 1994), 1-35.

7666. Laqueur, Walter, "From Russia with Hate," *New Republic* (5 Feb. 1990), 21-25.

7667. Magdziak-Miszewska, Agnieszka, "Russian Politics from Left to Right," *Uncaptive Minds*, 4, no. 2 (Summer 1991), 57-66.

7668. Malik, Hafeez, "Tatarstan: A Kremlin of Islam in the Russian Federation," *Journal of South Asian and Middle Eastern Studies*, 17, no. 1 (Fall 1993), 1-27.

7669. "Manifesto of the National Patriotic Front Pamiat'," *Central Asia and Caucasus Chronicle* (London), 8, no. 3 (July 1989), 14-15.

7670. McMullen, Ronald K., "Ethnic Conflict in Russia: Implications for the United States," *Studies in Conflict and Terrorism*, 16, no. 3 (July-Sept. 1993), 201-18.

7671. Midford, Paul, "Pamyat's Political Platform: Myths and Realities," *Nationalities Papers*, 19, no. 2 (Fall 1991), 183-213.

7672. Newcity, Michael, "RSFSR Asserts Autonomy in Tax Law," *SEEL: Soviet and East European Law*, 2, no. 1 (Feb. 1991), 6ff.

7673. Otto, Robert, "Contemporary Russian Nationalism" (Review Article), *Problems of Communism*, 39, no. 6 (Nov-Dec. 1990), 96-105.

7674. Petro, Nicolai N., "The Emerging Russian Consensus," *World & I* (Oct. 1990), 118-25.

7675. ------, "New Political Thinking and Russian Patriotism: The Dichotomy of Perestroika," *Comparative Strategy*, 9, no. 4 (Oct-Dec. 1990), 351-70.

7676. ------, "Rediscovering Russia," *Orbis*, 34, no. 1 (Winter 1990), 33-50.

7677. ------, "Toward a New Russian Federation," *Wilson Quarterly*, 14, no. 1 (Spring 1990), 114-22.

7678. Piskotin, M., and Iu. Zviagin, "Establishing Russian Statehood," *Russian Social Science Review*, 34, no. 4 (July-Aug. 1993), 3-15.

7679. Porter, Bruce D., "The Coming Resurgence of Russia," *National Interest*, no. 23 (Spring 1991), 14-23.

7680. Pospielovsky, Dimitry, "Russian Nationalism: An Update," *Report on the USSR*, 2, no. 6 (9 Feb. 1990), 8-17.

7681. Quinn-Judge, Paul, "Flying Circus," *New Republic* (11 Nov. 1991), 20-21.

7682. Rahr, Alexander, "The Russian Triangle: Gorbachev-El'tsin-Polozkov," *Report on the USSR*, 2, no. 27 (6 July 1990), 4-6.

7683. Rorlich, Azade-Ayse, "Political Radicalization in the Tatar ASSR: The Mothers' Council," *Report on the USSR*, 2, no. 20 (18 May 1990), 13-14.

7684. Ross, Jeffrey A., "*Pamyat*, the Soviet Regime, and *Glasnost*," *Religion in Communist Dominated Areas*, 27, no. 3 (Summer 1988), 72-74.

7685. Rowley, David G., "Russian Nationalism and the Cold War" (Review Article), *American Historical Review*, 99, no. 1 (February 1994), 155-71.

7686. "Russia: One Year after the Coup" (Special Report), *World & I*, 7, no. 8 (Aug. 1992), 22-57.

7687. "Russians Abroad: Pawns or Knights?" *Economist*, 328 (10 July 1993), 39-41.

7688. Sheehy, Ann, "Gorbachev Proposes Commission to Examine Ingush Demands," *Report on the USSR*, 2, no. 12 (23 Mar. 1989), 17-19.

7689. -----, "Power Struggle in Checheno-Ingushetia," *Report on the USSR*, 3, no. 46 (15 Nov. 1991), 20-26.

7690. -----, "Russians Are the Target of Interethnic Violence in Tuva," *Report on the USSR*, 2, no. 37 (14 Sept. 1990), 13-17.

7691. Silverman, S., "Russians May Soon Be a Minority," *Scholastic Update*, 118 (7 Mar. 1986), 6.

7692. Simes, Dimitri, "Russia Reborn," *Foreign Policy*, no. 85 (Winter 1991-92), 41-62.

7693. Sinyavsky, Andrey, "Russian Nationalism," *Massachusetts Review*, 31, no. 1-2 (Winter 1990), 475-94.

7694. Specter, Michael, "`The Great Russia Will Live Again'," *New York Times Magazine* (19 June 1994), 26ff.

7695. Stavrou, Nikolaos A., "The Russian Republic: In Search of Global Status," *World & I*, 7, no. 4 (Apr. 1992), 78ff.

7696. Szajkowski, Bogdan, "Will Russia Disintegrate into Bantustans?" *World Today*, 49, no. 8-9 (Aug-Sept. 1993), 172-75.

7697. Teague, Elizabeth, and Vera Tolz, "Moves to Create a Russian Communist Party," *Report on the USSR*, 2, no. 19 (11 May 1990), 1-3.

7698. Tolz, Vera, "Democrats Start Their Own Discussion of Russian National Problems," *Report on the USSR*, 2, no. 13 (30 Mar. 1990), 1-3.

7699. Wishnevsky, Julia, "Conflict Between State and `Memorial' Society," *Report on the USSR*, 1, no. 3 (20 Jan. 1989), 8-9.

7700. -----, "The Origins of Pamyat," *Survey*, 30, no. 3 (Oct. 1988), 79-91.

7701. -----, "Patriots Urge Annulment of RSFSR Elections," *Report on the USSR*, 2, no. 14 (6 Apr. 1990), 18-21.

7702. -----, "The Two Sides of the Barricades in Russian Politics Today," *Report on the USSR*, 2, no. 34 (24 Aug. 1990), 16-18.

7703. Wolfe, Dan, "In the RSFSR Supreme Soviet," *SEEL: Soviet and East European Law*, 1, no. 7 (Sept. 1990), 9.

XXXII. Religion

BOOKS

7704. Anderson, John, *Religion and the Soviet State: A Report on Religious Repression in the U.S.S.R. on the Occasion of the Christian Millennium*, ed. by Anna Tapay (Washington, DC: Puebla Institute, 1988).

7705. Andrijisyn, Joseph, ed., *Millennium of Christianity in Ukraine: A Symposium* (Ottawa: Saint Paul University, 1987).

7706. Bailey, J. Martin, *The Spring of Nations: Churches in the Rebirth of Eastern Europe* (New York: Friendship Press, 1991).

7707. Bourdeaux, Michael, *Gorbachev, Glasnost and the Gospel: The Gospel's Triumph over Communism* (Minneapolis: Bethany House, 1991).

7708. Broun, Janice, *Conscience and Captivity: Religion in Eastern Europe* (Washington, DC: Ethics and Public Policy Center, 1988).

7709. Bultman, Bud, *Revolution by Candlelight: The Real Story Behind the Changes in Eastern Europe* (Portland, OR: Multnomah Press, 1991).

7710. Chadwick, Owen, *The Christian Church in the Cold War* (New York: Viking, 1992).

7711. Dunn, Dennis J., ed., *Religion & Nationalism in Eastern Europe & the Soviet Union* (Boulder, CO: Westview Press, 1987).

7712. Eliason, Lynn R., *Perestroika of the Russian Soul: Religious Renaissance in the Soviet Union* (Jefferson, NC: McFarland & Co., 1991).

7713. Elliott, Mark, and Scott Lingenfelter, eds., *Ethics in the Russian Marketplace: An Anthology* (Wheaton, IL: Institute for East-West Christian Studies, 1992).

7714. Forest, James H., *Pilgrim to the Russian Church: An American Journalist Encounters a Vibrant Religious Faith in the Soviet Union* (New York: Crossroads, 1988).

7715. -----, *Religion in the New Russia: The Impact of Perestroi-*

ka on the Varieties of Religious Life (New York: Crossroad, 1990).

7716. Gerus, Oleh W., and Alexander Baran, eds., *Millennium of Christianity in Ukraine 988-1988* (Winnipeg: Ukrainian Academy of Arts and Sciences in Canada, 1989).

7717. Geyer, Alan, *Christianity & the Superpowers: Religion, Politics and History in US-USSR Relations* (Nashville: Abingdon Press, 1990).

7718. Hanson, Eric O., *The Catholic Church in World Politics* (Princeton: Princeton University Press, 1987).

7719. Hill, Kent R., *The Puzzle of the Russian Church: An Inside Look at Christianity and Glasnost'*, 2nd rev. ed. (Portland, OR: Multnomah Press, 1991).

7720. -----, *The Soviet Union on the Brink: An Inside Look at Christianity and Glasnost*, 2nd rev. ed. (Portland, OR: Multnomah Press, with the Institute on Religion and Democracy, 1991).

7721. -----, *Turbulent Times for the Soviet Church* (Portland, OR: Multnomah Press, with the Institute for Religion and Democracy, 1991).

7722. Hosking, Geoffrey, ed., *Church, Nation and State in Russia and Ukraine* (New York: St. Martin's Press, 1991).

7723. House, Francis, *Millennium of Faith: Christianity in Russia, AD 988-1988* (Crestwood, NY: St. Vladimir's Seminary Press, 1988).

7724. Lobachev, Valery, and Vladimir Pravotorov, *A Millennium of Russian Orthodoxy* (Moscow: Novosti Press Agency Publishing House, 1988).

7725. Parsons, Howard L., *Christianity Today in the USSR* (New York: International Publishers, 1987).

7726. Petro, Nicolai N., *Christianity and Russian Culture in Soviet Society* (Boulder, CO: Westview Press, 1990).

7727. Pospielovsky, Dimitri V., *Some Observations on Russian Self-Awareness and the Orthodox Church in the Era of Gorbachev* (Cologne: Bundesinstitut fuer Ostwissenschaftliche und Internationale Studien, 1989).

7728. Ramet, Pedro, *Christianity Under Stress*, vol. 1: *Eastern Christianity and Politics in the Twentieth Century*; vol. 2: *Catholicism and Politics in Communist Societies* (Durham, NC: Duke University Press, 1988-1990).

7729. -----, ed., *Cross and Commissar: The Politics of Religion in Eastern Europe and the USSR* (Bloomington: Indiana University Press, 1987).

7730. -----, ed., *Religion and Nationalism in Soviet and East European Politics* (Durham, NC: Duke University Press, 1989).

7731. Ramet, Sabrina Petra, *Religious Policy in the Soviet Union* (New York: Cambridge University Press, 1993).

7732. -----, ed., *Protestantism and Politics in Eastern Europe and Russia: The Communist and Post-Communist Eras* (Durham, NC: Duke University Press, 1993).

7733. Shirley, Eugene B., Jr., and Michael Rowe, eds., *Candle in the Wind: Religion in the Soviet Union* (Washington, DC: Ethics and Public Policy Center, 1989).

7734. Steeves, Paul, *Keeping the Faiths: Religion and Ideology in the Soviet Union* (New York: Holmes & Meier, 1989).

7735. -----, ed., *The Modern Encyclopedia of Religions in Russia and the Soviet Union* (Gulf Breeze, FL: Academic International Press, 1988 and continuing).

7736. Troyanovsky, Igor, *Religion in the Soviet Republics: A Guide to Christianity, Judaism, Islam, Buddhism and Other Religions* (San Francisco: Harper, 1991).

7737. Van Rossum, Jacob, "*Perestroika* on Religion Is Just Warmed-Over Leninism," *Religion in Communist Dominated Areas*, 27, no. 2 (Spring 1988), 37-39.

7738. Webster, Alexander F. C., *The Price of Prophecy: Orthodox Churches on Peace, Freedom, and Security* (Lanham, MD: University Press of America, for the Ethics and Public Policy Center, 1993).

7739. Weigel, George, *The Final Revolution: The Resistance Church and the Collapse of Communism* (New York: Oxford University Press, 1992).

7740. Weisman, Erik, *Expenditures for Religious Services by the Soviet Population* (Bala Cynwyd, PA: WEFA Group, 1991).

7741. Zimkewych, Osyp, and Andrew Sorokowski, eds., *A Thousand Years of Christianity in Ukraine: An Encyclopedic Chronology* (New York: Smoloskyp Publishers and the National Committee to Commemorate the Millennium of Christianity in Ukraine, 1988).

ARTICLES

7742. Achil'diyev, Igor, "Interview with Konstantin Kharchev," *Religion in Communist Dominated Areas*, 26, no. 4 (Fall 1987), 115-20.

7743. "Advent Meditation from PBS," *America*, 155 (6 Dec. 1986), 353-54.

7744. "Afterthoughts: Four Humanist Leaders Appraise Soviet Atheism," *Humanist*, 47 (Jan-Feb. 1987), 16ff.

7745. Aitmatov, Chingiz, "The Age of Repentance," *Encounter*, 72 (Apr. 1989), 71-73.

7746. Alexiy, Metropolitan, "Looking Back after the Millennium," *Perestroika Annual*, 1 (1988), 309-28.

7747. Ambrose, Elizabeth, "The Reemergence of Eastern-Rite Catholicism in Belorussia," *Report on the USSR*, 2, no. 42 (19 Oct. 1990), 21-23.

7748. Antic, Oxana, "Alternative Military Service for Religious Believers," *Report on the USSR*, 2, no. 22 (1 June 1990), 7-8.

7749. -----, "Conditions Improve for Old Believers, Dukhobors, Molokans and Mennonites," *Report on the USSR*, 3, no. 25 (21 June 1991), 8-10.

7750. -----, "Draft Law on Freedom of Conscience Criticized," *Report on the USSR*, 2, no. 39 (28 Sept. 1990), 13-14.

7751. -----, "Moral Crisis in the USSR and the Role of the Russian Orthodox Church," *Report on the USSR*, 2, no. 52 (28 Dec. 1990), 6-8.

7752. -----, "The New Law on Religion," *Report on the USSR*, 2, no. 47 (23 Nov. 1990), 9-10.

7753. -----, "New Structures for the Catholic Church in the USSR," *Report on the USSR*, 3, no. 21 (24 May 1991), 16-19.

7754. -----, "Relics of Seraphim of Sarotov Returned to Church," *Report on the USSR*, 3, no. 10 (8 Mar. 1991), 5.

7755. -----, "Revival of Buddhism in the Soviet Union," *Report on the USSR*, 3, no. 39 (Sept. 1991), 10-12.

7756. -----, "The Russian Orthodox Church and Islam," *Report on the USSR*, 2, no. 18 (4 May 1990), 10-11.

7757. -----, "Series of Assaults on Russian Orthodox Priests," *Report on the USSR*, 3, no.8 (22 Feb. 1991), 3-4.

7758. -----, "Smaller Religious Denominations Flourish in New Conditions," *Report on the USSR*, 3, no. 7 (15 Feb. 1991), 10-12.

7759. -----, "Welfare and Charity Programs of Soviet Religious Organizations, 1989-90," *Report on the USSR*, 2, no. 48 (30 Nov. 1990), 8-10.

7760. Bain, Daniel E., "Iron Curtain/Steel Cross: The Politics of East European Religious Nationalism" (Review Article), *East European Quarterly*, 24, no. 1 (Spring 1990), 113-24.

7761. Baran, Alexander, "The Ukrainian Catholic Church Today," *Diakonia*, 23, no. 3 (1990), 175-83.

7762. Bell, Helen, and Jane Ellis, "The Millennium Celebrations of 1988 in the USSR," *Religion in Communist Lands*, 16, no. 4 (Winter 1988), 308-11.

7763. Berman, Harold J., "Christianity and Democracy in the Soviet Union," *Emory International Law Review*, 6 (Spring 1992), 23-34.

7764. "Bibles for the East: A Word of Warning," *Religion in Communist Dominated Areas*, 30, no. 3-4 (1991), 48.

7765. "Bibles in the Soviet Union," *Religion in Communist Lands*, 17, no. 3 (Autumn 1989), 257-63.

7766. Bociurkiw, Bohdan R., "The Formulation of Religious Policy in the Soviet Union," *Journal of Church and State*, 28, no. 3 (Autumn 1986), 423-38.

7767. -----, "The Ukrainian Catholic Church in the USSR under Gorbachev," *Problems of Communism*, 39, no. 6 (Nov-Dec. 1990), 1-19.

7768. Boiter, Albert, "How Secure Are the New Freedoms of Church and Religion in the USSR Today?" *Religion in Communist Dominated Areas*, 29, no. 3-4 (Summer-Fall 1990), 78-79.

7769. -----, "Law and Religion in the Soviet Union," *American Journal of Comparative Law*, 35, no. 1 (Winter 1987), 97-126.

7770. Broun, Janice, "Lithuania: Land of the Unquenchable Wick," *Commonweal* (23 Oct. 1987), 594-95.

7771. -----, "Religious Freedom in the Soviet Union and Eastern Europe," *Freedom Review*, 22, no. 2 (Mar-Apr. 1991), 30-34.

7772. -----, "Still Waiting for the Millennium: The Churches and Soviet `Glasnost'," *Commonweal* (23 Oct. 1987), 592-95.

7773. Brown, Bess, "Religion and Nationalism in Soviet Central Asia," *Report on the USSR*, 2, no. 29 (20 July 1990), 25-27.

7774. Brown, J. A., "No *Glasnost* Yet for Religion in Bulgaria," *Christian Century*, 106 (29 Nov. 1989), 1124-25.

7775. Broxup, Marie, "Islam in Dagestan under Gorbachev," *Religion in Communist Lands*, 18, no. 3 (Autumn 1990), 212-25.

7776. Bruun, Kirsten, "The Dispute Over the Red Church in Ivanovo: Changing Relations Between Party, State and Society as Rooted in Religious Policy in a Russian Provincial Region, 1984-1989," *Soviet and Post-Soviet Review*, 21, no. 1 (1994), forthcoming.

7777. Calian, Carnegie, "Religious Revival among the Communists," *Ararat*, 32, no. 127 (Summer 1991), 58-60.

7778. Chirovsky, Nicholas L., "The Church: Defender of Ukrainian National Identity," *Ukrainian Quarterly*, 46, no. 1 (Spring 1990), 45-58.

7779. -----, "The Significance of the Millennium of Ukrainian Christianity," *Ukrainian Quarterly*, 47, no. 1 (Spring 1991), 9-22.

7780. "The Church Is Risen Indeed," *Economist*, 307 (2 Apr. 1988), 17-19.

7781. "Clergy Protests to Gorbachev about Massive Discrimination," *Lituanus*, 33, no. 4 (Winter 1987), 89-91.

7782. Codevilla, Giovanni, "Commentary on the New Soviet Law on Freedom of Conscience and Religious Organisations," *Religion in Communist Lands*, 19, nos. 1-2 (Summer 1991), 119ff.

7783. Colson, C. W., "How Open Shall Be to *Glasnost*?" *Christianity Today*, 33 (12 May 1989), 72.

7784. Critchlow, James, "Islam in Public Life: Can This Be `Soviet' Uzbekistan?" *Report on the USSR*, 2, no. 11 (16 Mar. 1990), 23-25.

7785. -----, "Islam in Soviet Central Asia: Renaissance or Revolution?" *Religion in Communist Lands*, 18, no. 3 (Autumn 1990), 196-211.

7786. D'Agostino, A., "*Glasnost* and Religion: Some Reflections after a Journey to Russia," *America*, 158 (2-9 Jan. 1988), 12ff.

7787. Dahm, Helmut, "The Problem of Atheism in Recent Soviet Publications," *Studies in Soviet Thought*, 41, no. 2 (Mar. 1991), 85-126.

7788. Daniel, W., "Religion and Science: The Evolution of Soviet Debate," *Christian Century*, 109 (29 Jan. 1992), 98-100.

7789. Davies, Richard T., "Gorbachevism and Religious Freedom in the Soviet Union," *Religion in Communist Dominated Areas*, 27, no. 1 (Winter 1988), 2-4.

7790. -----, "The Millennium: The Russian Orthodox Church on the Threshold of Its Second Millennium," *Religion in Communist Dominated Areas*, 27, no. 4 (Fall 1988), 99-100.

7791. -----, "Orphans of Perestroika," *Religion in Communist Dominated Areas*, 29, no. 1 (Winter 1990), 4-5.

7792. Derwinski, E. J., and R. Schifter, "Religious Persecution in the Soviet Union," *Department of State Bulletin*, 86 (Nov. 1986), 77-83.

7793. Devlet, N., "Islamic Revival in the Volga-Ural Region," *Cahiers du Monde russe et sovietique*, 32, no. 1 (1991), 107-16.

7794. Deyneka, Anita, and Peter Deyneka, Jr., "The Church under Gorbachev," *Christianity Today*, 30 (Dec. 1986), 26-31.

7795. "Documents: *Perestroika* and Freedom of Conscience," *Religion in Communist Lands*, 17, no. 3 (Autumn 1989), 269-74.

7796. "The Doomed People of Turkmemia," *Religion in Communist Dominated Areas*, 29, no. 2 (Spring 1990), 53.

7797. Dunlop, John B., "Gorbachev and Russian Orthodoxy," *Problems of Communism*, 38, no. 4 (July-Aug. 1989), 96-116.

7798. -----, "'Kharchev Affair' Sheds New Light on Severe Controls on Religion in the USSR," *Report on the USSR*, 2, no. 8 (23 Feb. 1990), 6-9.

7799. -----, "The Moscow Patriarchate on the Eve of the Thousandth Anniversary of the Baptism of Russia," *Orthodox Life*, 38, no. 1 (Jan-Feb. 1988), 32-49.

7800. Elliott, Mark, "Bibles East, Letters West: Religious *Glasnost* and the Availability of Scriptures in the Soviet Union," *Occasional Papers on Religion in Eastern Europe*, 9, no. 6 (Nov. 1989), 27-32.

7801. -----, "Increasing Options for Theological Training in East Central Europe and the Soviet Successor States," *East-West Church and Ministry Report*, 1 (Winter 1993), 10.

7802. -----, "New Opportunities, New Demands in the Old Red Empire," *Evangelical Missions Quarterly*, 28 (Jan. 1992), 32-39.

7803. Ellis, Jane, "The Millennium Celebrations of 1988 in the USSR," *Religion in Communist Lands*, 16, no. 4 (Winter 1988), 308-11.

7804. -----, "New Soviet Thinking on Religion," *Religion in Communist Lands*, 17, no. 2 (Summer 1989), 100-11.

7805. Emerson, Caryl, "And the Demons Entered into the Swine: The Russian Intelligentsia and Post-Soviet Religious Thought," *Journal of the Association for Religion and Intellectual Life*, 43, no. 2 (Summer 1993), 184-203.

7806. Feodosi, Archbishop, "In Defence of the Kiev-Caves Lavra: An Appeal by Archbishop Feodosi of Astrakhan and Yenotayevka. To: The General Secretary of the CC CPSU, Mikhail Sergeyevich Gorbachev," *Orthodox Life*, 38, no. 1 (Jan-Feb. 1988), 13-15.

7807. Fierman, William, "Religion and Nationalism in Soviet Central Asia," *Problems of Communism*, 38, no. 4 (July-Aug. 1989), 123-27.

7808. Forest, Jim, "Mark Smirnoff: Priest-Journalist in Moscow," *Christianity and Crisis*, 50 (28 May 1990), 172-74.

7809. -----, "Religious Openings in the U.S.S.R.," *Christian Century*, 106, no. 27 (27 Sept. 1989), 848-50.

7810. -----, "Reviving Religion in the U.S.S.R.," *Christian Century*, 107, no. 10 (10 Oct. 1990), 905-08.

7811. -----, "Russia's Tenacious Old Believers," *Christian Century*, 106, no. 36 (29 Nov. 1989), 1121-23.

7812. Franklin, Simon, "988-1988: Uses and Abuses of the Millennium," *World Today*, 44, no. 4 (Apr. 1988), 65-68.

7813. Fronta, Mlada, "From an Interview with Chairman Kharchev," *Religion in Communist Dominated Areas*, 27, no. 3 (Summer 1988), 75ff.

7814. Goble, Paul, "Soviet Myths about Religion Crumble," *Report on the USSR*, 2, no. 10 (9 Mar. 1990), 8-9.

7815. "Gorbachev: Hopes and Fears," *Religion in Communist Lands*, 15, no. 3 (Winter 1987), 320-22.

7816. Grigorieff, Dimitry, "The Millennium of the Baptism of Rus'," *Religion in Communist Dominated Areas*, 27, no. 4 (Fall 1988), 101-05.

7817. Gudziak, Boris, "Four Publications Commemorate the Millennium of Christianity in Rus'-Ukraine" (Review Article), *Harvard Ukrainian Studies*, 15, no. 1-2 (June 1991), 177-91.

7818. Guetta, Bernard, "Mass for Glasnost," *World Press Review*, 35 (Sept. 1988), 56-57.

7819. Hanson, Eric O., "Catholicism and Soviet-American Competition in the Third World," in Eric O. Hanson, *The Catholic Church in World Politics* (Princeton: Princeton University Press, 1987).

7820. Haughey, J. C., "The Spirituality of *Perestroika*," *America*, 158 (23 Apr. 1988), 426-28.

7821. Heim, David, "Some Ironies of Communist History," *Christian Century*, 106, no. 36 (29 Nov. 1989), 1107-08.

7822. -----, "Without Czar or Commissar: Church and Nation in Russia," *Christian Century*, 107, no. 28 (10 Oct. 1990), 908-11.

7823. Henry, Catherine P., "Registration of Churches in the Soviet Union," *Religion in Communist Dominated Areas*, 26, no. 1 (Winter 1987), 13-22.

7824. Herlihy, Michael, "Gorbachev, Glasnost and God: New Thinking about Religion?" *America*, 158 (9 Jan. 1988), 175-203.

7825. Hetmanek, Allen, "Islamic Revival in the USSR," *Religion in Communist Dominated Areas*, 26, no. 3 (Summer 1987), 83ff.

7826. Hill, Kent R., "In Search of a Soul: The Fate of Religion under Glasnost," *Freedom Review*, 22, no. 4 (July-Aug. 1991), 52-54.

7827. -----, "The Summit, *Glasnost* and Religion," *Christian Century*, 105 (6-13 Jan. 1988), 6-7.

7828. Huttenbach, Henry, "Managing a Federation of Multiethnic Republics," *Nationalities Papers*, 19, no. 1 (Spring 1991), 26-32.

7829. Irwin, Zachary T., "Moscow and the Vatican," *Religion in Communist Dominated Areas*, 29, no. 2 (Spring 1990), 38-42.

7830. Janz, Denis R., "The Spiritual Crisis of the Russian People," *Christian Century*, 108, no. 25 (4 Sept. 1991), 796-97.

7831. Jones, P. M., "Why Religion Is Out in the Soviet Union," *Scholastic Review*, 117 (1 Mar. 1985), 21.

7832. Jones, S. F., "Soviet Religious Policy and the Georgian Orthodox Church: From Khrushchev to Gorbachev," *Religion in Communist Lands*, 17, no. 4 (Winter 1989), 292-312.

7833. Kazachkov, Mikhail P., "Open Christianity," *Religion in Communist Dominated Areas*, 30, no. 2 (1991), 30-31.

7834. -----, "Spiritual Marshall Plan for Russia," *Religion in Communist Dominated Areas*, 30, no. 3-4 (1991), 44-48.

7835. Keenan, Edward L., "The Millennium of the Baptism of Rus' and Russian Self-Awareness," *Harriman Institute Forum*, 1, no. 7 (July 1988), 1-7.

7836. Kharchev, K., "USSR: The Current Situation of Church and State Relations," *Religion in Communist Dominated Areas*, 27, no. 2 (Spring 1988), 36.

7837. K. L., "Optina Monastery Today," *Orthodox Life*, 38, no. 2 (Mar-Apr. 1988), 10.

7838. Kojevnikov, Alyona, "Religious Renaissance in the Russian Orthodox Church: Fact or Fiction?" *Journal of Church and State*, 28, no. 3 (Autumn 1986), 459-74.

7839. Krakhmalnikova, Zoya, "Orthodox Christians Must Still Carry a Soviet Cross," *Glasnost*, 2, no. 5 (Jan-Mar. 1990), 24-28.

7840. Kuehnelt-Leddihn, E. von, "Gorbachev Facing Faith and Nationality," *National Review*, 39 (27 Mar. 1987), 48.

7841. Kulakov, Mikhail P., "An Open Door," *Perestroika Annual*, 2 (1989), 213-28.

7842. "'Learning from the Past': Historical Monuments in the USSR," *Religion in Communist Lands*, 15, no. 2 (Summer 21987), 206-08.

7843. "Legal Changes for Russian Orthodox Church?" *Religion in Communist Lands*, 15, no. 3 (Winter 1987), 318-19.

7844. "Letter to Gorbachev by Gleb Yakunin and Others, Aug. 12, 1987. Reply by USSR Ministry of Justice, Sept. 9, 1987," *Occasional Papers on Religion in Eastern Europe*, 8, no. 4 (Aug. 1988), 19-23.

7845. "Letter to Mikhail Gorbachev by Russian Orthodox Clergymen and Laymen," *Religion in Communist Dominated Areas*, 26, no. 3 (Summer 1987), 76-77.

7846. Luchs, K., "How Will the New Soviet Leader Affect the Plight of Christians in the USSR," *Christianity Today*, 29 (5 Apr. 1985), 43-44.

7847. Maas, Peter, "Moonskies," *New Republic* (19 Nov. 1990), 7-10.

7848. Magocsi, Paul Robert, "The Year of the Millennium," *PMC: Practice of Ministry in Canada*, 5, no. 1 (1988), 17-18.

7849. Malik, Hafeez, "Editorial: Islam in Russia," *Journal of South Asian and Middle Eastern Studies*, 15, no. 1 (Fall 1991), iii-iv.

7850. Martin, Peter, "The New Law on Freedom of Religion and the Churches," *Report on Eastern Europe*, 2, no. 36 (6 Sept. 1991), 16-21.

7851. Marty, Martin E., "Gorbachev on Morality and Natural Religion," *Christian Century*, 109, no. 18 (20 May 1992), 532-33.

7852. Masani, P. R., "The Untenability of *Glasnost'* without *Tchestnost'*," *Occasional Papers on Religion in Eastern Europe*, 9, no. 3 (June 1989), 29-42.

7853. Melnick, A. James, "Discussion: `Scientific Atheism' in the Era of Perestrojka," *Studies in Soviet Thought*, 40, no. 1-3 (Aug-Nov. 1990), 223-29.

7854. Metlif, I. V., "Religion in School: Experience of a Study of the Problem," *Russian Social Science Review*, 33, no. 4 (July-Aug. 1992), 64-78.

7855. Mihalisko, Kathleen, "The Ukrainian Catholics and the Russian Orthodox Church: The Unfolding Conflict in Western Ukraine," *Report on the USSR*, 2, no. 1 (5 Jan. 1990), 12-15.

7856. Mojzes, Paul, "On a Roller Coaster: Religion and Perestroika," *Occasional Papers on Religion in Eastern Europe*, 8 no. 5 (Oct. 1988), 22-39.

7857. -----, "The Rehabilitation of Religion in the U.S.S.R. and Eastern Europe," *Christian Century*, 107, no. 1 (3-10 Jan. 1990), 15-18.

7858. Monsma, J. E., "*Glasnost* and Religion: Meeting in the Popular Arts," *Christian Century*, 105 (23-30 Mar. 1988), 10-13.

7859. Moore, Patrick, "The Islamic Community's Sense of Identity," *Report on Eastern Europe*, 2, no. 44 (1 Nov. 1991), 19-23.

7860. Moroziuk, Russel P., "Politics and Ecumenics of the Millennium of Christianity in Kyivan Rus," *Ukrainian Quarterly*, 45, no. 2 (1989), 120-32; no. 3, 318-31.

7861. Moss, James R., "Religion in the USSR: Theological Education 1988-1991," *Religion in Communist Dominated Areas*, 30, no. 2 (1991), 29.

7862. -----, "The Russian Orthodox Church 1988-90: The Episcopacy," *Religion in Communist Dominated Areas*, 29, no. 1 (Winter 1990), 9ff.

7863. -----, "The Russian Orthodox Church 1989-90: Monastic Life," *Religion in Communist Dominated Areas*, 29, no. 3-4 (Summer-Fall 1990), 94.

7864. -----, "The Russian Orthodox Church 1989-91: Parishes,"

Religion in Communist Dominated Areas, 30, no. 1 (1991), 9-11.

7865. Moss, Vladimir, "The Free Russian Orthodox Church," *Report on the USSR*, 3, no. 44 (1 Nov. 1991), 8-12.

7866. -----, "Russian Orthodoxy and the Future of the Soviet Union," *Report on the USSR*, 3, no. 24 (14 June 1991), 1-5.

7867. Muck, T. C., "Still the Evil Empire?" *Christianity Today*, 32 (15 July 1988), 14-15.

7868. Murphy, Francis X., "Aggiornamento to *Perestroika*: Vatican Ostpolitik," *America*, 162 (19 May 1990), 494-98.

7869. Nahaylo, Bohdan, "Moscow Manipulated the Millennium, but the Pope Has Many Divisions," *Forum*, no. 74 (Summer 1988), 62-64.

7870. Nakas, Victor A., "The Catholic Church in Lithuania before the Millennium," *Religion in Communist Dominated Areas*, 26, no. 3 (Summer 1987), 67-70.

7871. "A New Russian Revolution?" *America*, 151 (21 Nov. 1987), 371.

7872. Nezhny, Alexander, "The Optina Monastery Opens," *Religion in Communist Dominated Areas*, 26, no. 4 (Fall 1987), 121-23.

7873. Oden, T. C., "Moscow State Discovers Religion," *Christianity Today*, 35 (24 June 1991), 27-29.

7874. O'Malley, T. P., "Religious Liberties Long Denied," *America*, 161 (14 Oct. 1989), 229.

7875. O'Neil, Daniel J., "The Russian Church and Its Future," *International Journal of Social Economics*, 20, nos. 5-7 (1993), 126-41.

7876. Ordynsky, Eugenia, "The Persecution of the Russian Orthodox Church and the Rise of `Russian Nationalism'," *Russian-American Review* (Fall 1990), 1ff.

7877. Ostling, R. N., "No Longer Godless Communism," *Time*, 136 (15 Oct. 1990), 70-71.

7878. Pierard, Richard V., "Religion and the East German Revolution," *Journal of Church and State*, 32, no. 3 (Summer 1990), 501-09.

7879. Pomian, Krzysztof, "Religion and Politics in a Time of Glasnost," in Ronald J. Hill and Jan Zielonka, eds., *Restructuring Eastern Europe: Towards a New European Order* (Brookfield, VT: E. Elgar, 1990), 113-28.

7880. Pospielovsky, Dimitry V., "The Millennium: The Soviet State versus the Russian Orthodox Church, 1959-1988," *Religion in Communist Dominated Areas*, 27, no. 4 (Fall 1988), 105-13.

7881. -----, "Russian Nationalism and the Religious Revival," *Religion in Communist Lands*, 15, no. 3 (Winter 1987), 299ff.

7882. Potapov, Victor S., "The Religious Revival in the USSR on the Eve of the Millennium," *Religion in Communist Dominated Areas*, 26, no. 2 (Spring 1987), 36-41.

7883 Powell, David E., "The Revival of Religion," *Current History*, 90, no. 558 (Oct. 1991), 328-32.

7884. -----, "The Rise of Religion," *Current History*, 90, no. 558 (Oct. 1991), 328-32.

7885. "Prisoners of Conscience in Perm," *Religion in Communist Dominated Areas*, 28, no. 2 (Spring 1989), 36.

7886. "Prolonged Visits to the Soviet Gulag," *Whole Earth Review*, no. 54 (Spring 1987), 20-26.

7887. Ramet, Sabrina Petra, "The Catholic Church in Czechoslovakia, 1948-1991," *Studies in Comparative Communism*, 24, no. 4 (Dec. 1991), 377-94.

7888. -----, "The New Church-State Configuration in Eastern Europe," *East European Politics and Societies*, 5, no. 2 (Spring 1991), 247-67.

7889. "Religion and Atheism in the Soviet Union," *Humanist*, 47 (Jan-Feb. 1987), 5ff.

7890. "Returning to God," *Economist*, 313 (9 Dec. 1989), 50.

7891. Riley, Paul C., and Peter M. Anderson, "Ecumenical Events: Seattle-Leningrad `Sister Churches' Program," *Journal of Ecumenical Studies*, 25, no. 4 (Fall 1988), 692-93.

7892. Rorlich, Azade-Ayse, "Islam in Kirgizia: The Making of `Thinking Believers'," *Report on the USSR*, 2, no. 19 (11 May 1990), 21.

7893. Rossum, Jacob van, "Perestroika on Religion Is Just Warmed Over Leninism," *Religion in Communist Dominated Areas*, 27, no. 2 (Spring 1988), 37-39.

7894. Sawatsky, Walter, "After the Glasnost Revolution: Soviet Evangelicals and Western Missions," *International Bulletin of Missionary Research*, 16 (Apr. 1992), 54-60.

7895. -----, "Glasnost', Perestroika and Religion: What Role for Churches in Changing Soviet Society," *Occasional Papers on Religion in Eastern Europe*, 9, no. 2 (Apr. 1989), 1-19.

7896. -----, "Truth Telling in Eastern Europe: The Liberation and the Burden," *Journal of Church and State*, 33, no. 4 (Fall 1991), 701-29.

7897. Scherer, James A., "Interviews with Soviet Religious Officials and Dissidents," *Occasional Papers on Religion in Eastern Europe*, 9, no. 2 (1989), 20-34.

7898. Scholes, A., "The Church/State Puzzle in the Soviet Classroom," *Christianity Today*, 35 (25 Nov. 1991), 22-23.

7899. Sidey, K. H., "New Law Extends Religious Freedom," *Christianity Today*, 34 (5 Nov. 1990), 76-77.

7900. Solchanyk, Roman, "Restructuring Church-State Relations," *Soviet Analyst*, 17 (28 Sept. 1988), 4-6.

7901. Sorokowski, Andrew, "Background: Ukraine and the Millennium," *Forum*, no. 74 (Summer 1988), 60-61.

7902. "Soviet Baptists Engage in Perestroika," *Religion in Communist Lands*, 18, no. 2 (Summer 1990), 184-87.

7903. "Soviet Religious Changes," *Christian Century*, 105 (17-24 Aug. 1988), 729-30.

7904. "Soviet Religious Growth Continues," *National Catholic Register*, 66, no. 44 (4 Nov. 1990), 9.

7905. "The Soviet State and Religion-CPSU: Documents and Analysis," *Religion in Communist Dominated Areas*, 27, no. 1 (Winter 1988), 5-6.

7906. Steeves, Paul D., "Russia and Orthodoxy: Reasons for Hope-and Alarm," *Christianity and Crisis*, 51, no. 14 (7 Oct. 1991), 310-12.

7907. Swift, Mary Grace, "Orthodox Convents in the Soviet Union," *Diakonia*, 23, no. 2 (1990), 69-84.

7908. "Text of Law of USSR: `On Freedom of Conscience and Religious Organisations'," *Journal of Church and State*, 33, no. 1 (Winter 1991), 192-201.

7909. Thrower, James, "Some Reflections on Religion in the USSR," *Humanist*, 47 (Jan-Feb. 1987), 21-23.

7910. Troyanovsky, Igor, "Illegally Requisitioned Church Returned to Catholics in Klaipeda," *Religion in Communist Dominated Areas*, 26, no. 4 (Fall 1987), 124-25.

7911. "Ukrainian Catholics Bear Soviet Cross," *Glasnost*, 2, no. 6, issues no. 30-31 (Apr-May 1990), 34-35.

7912. VanElderen, Marlin, "WCC Takes Its Agenda to the Soviet Union," *Christian Century*, 106, no. 25 (30 Aug-6 Sept. 1989), 773-75.

7913. Wall, James M., "Waking Up at Last to Gorbachev's Strategy," *Christian Century*, 107, no. 6 (21 Feb. 1990), 171-72.

7914. Walters, Philip, "The Russian Orthodox Church and the Soviet State," *American Academy of Political and Social Science. Annals*, 483 (Jan. 1986), 135-45.

7915. "Will God Help Us? Interview with Patriarch Aleksei II by Oleg Moroz," *Soviet Law and Government*, 30, no. 2 (Fall 1991), 62-75.

7916. Wollemborg, Leo J., "John Paul II and Ukrainian Catholics," *Freedom at Issue*, no. 102 (May-June 1988), 28-30.

7917. Wood, James R., "Rising Expectations for Religious Rights in Eastern Europe," *Journal of Church and State*, 33, no. 1 (Winter 1991), 1-15.

7918. Zawerucha, Ihor, "The Situation of Roman Catholics in Belorussia," *Report on the USSR*, 2, no. 19 (11 May 1990), 19-20.

XXXIII. Security

BOOKS

7919. Adomeit, Hannes, ed., *The Gorbachev Challenge and European Security: A Report from the European Strategy Group* (Baden-Baden: Nomos Verlagsgesellschaft, 1988).

7920. Allbutt, Lisa, ed., *Perestroika, Glasnost and International Security: Papers Presented at the 1989 Political Science Students' Conference* (Winnipeg: University of Manitoba, 1989).

7921. Allison, Graham, and Gregory Treverton, eds., *Rethinking America's Security Beyond the Cold War to the New World Order* (New York: W. W. Norton, 1992).

7922. Becker, Abraham S., *Gorbachev's Program for Economic Modernization and Reform: Some Important Political-Military Implications* (Santa Monica, CA: RAND, 1987).

7923. Blacker, Coit D., *Hostage to Revolution: Gorbachev and Soviet Security Policy, 1985-1991* (New York: Council on Foreign Relations Press, 1993).

7924. Blank, Stephen, *Russia and the Baltic: Is There a Threat to European Security?* (Carlisle Barracks, PA: US Army War College, 1993).

7925. -----, *SDI and Defensive Doctrine: The Evolving Soviet Debate* (Washington, DC: Woodrow Wilson International Center for Scholars, 1990).

7926. Brown, N. C., *The Strategic Defense Initiative and European Security: A Conference Report* (Santa Monica, CA: RAND, 1986).

7927. Center for Security Policy, *An Alternative "National Strategy Review": Designing an Effective Policy for U.S.-Soviet Relations* (Washington, DC: Center for Security Policy, 1989).

7928. Cimbala, Stephen J., *Uncertainty and Control: Future Soviet and American Strategy* (New York: St. Martin's Press, 1990).

7929. -----, ed., *The Soviet Challenge in the 1990s* (New York: Praeger, 1989).

7930. CSIS Working Group on Presidential National Security Choices, *National Security Choices for the Next President* (Washington, DC: Center for Strategic and International Studies, 1988).

7931. Feshbach, Murray, ed., *National Security Issues of the USSR: Workshop After the 27th Party Congress of the USSR: NATO, Brussels, 6-7 November 1986* (Boston: Martinus Nijhoff Publishers, 1987).

7932. Friedberg, Maurice, and Heyward Isham, eds., *Soviet Security under Gorbachev: Current Trends and the Prospects for Reform* (Armonk, NJ: M. E. Sharpe, 1987).

7933. Gervasi, Tom, *The Myth of Soviet Military Supremacy* (New York: Harper & Row, 1986).

7934. Giscard d'Estaing, Valery, Yasuhiro Nakasone and Henry A. Kissinger, *East-West Relations: A Task Force Report to the Trilateral Commission* (New York: Trilateral Commission, 1989).

7935. Goodpaster, Andrew J., *Gorbachev and the Future of East-West Security: A Response for the Mid-Term* (Washington, DC: Atlantic Council of the U.S., 1989).

7936. Gottfried, Kurt, and Paul Bracken, eds., *Reforging European Security: From Confrontation to Cooperation* (Boulder, CO:

Westview Press, 1991).

7937. Griffiths, Franklyn, *The CSIS, Gorbachev, and Global Change: Canada's Internal Security and Intelligence Requirements in Transition* (Toronto: Centre for Russian and East European Studies, University of Toronto, 1990).

7938. Guertner, Gary L., *Deterrence and Defense in a Post-Nuclear World* (New York: St. Martin's Press, 1990).

7939. Heisbourg, Francois, ed., *The Strategic Implications of Change in the Soviet Union* (Basingstoke and London: Macmillan Press and the International Institute for Strategic Studies, 1990).

7940. Holder, Kate, Robert E. Hunter and Paavo Lipponen, eds., *Conference on Security and Cooperation in Europe: the Next Phase: New Security Arrangements in Europe* (Washington, DC: Center for Strategic and International Studies, 1991).

7941. Horelick, Arnold L., *The Future of the Soviet Union: What Is the Western Interest?* (Santa Monica, CA: RAND/UCLA Center for Soviet Studies, 1991).

7942. Hudson, George E., ed., *Soviet National Security Policy under Perestroika* (Boston: Unwin Hyman, 1990).

7943. Kaufmann, William W., *Glasnost, Perestroika and U.S. Defense Spending* (Washington, DC: Brookings Institution, 1990).

7944. Klare, Michael T., and Daniel C. Thomas, *World Security: Trends and Challenges at Century's End* (New York: St. Martin's Press, 1991).

7945. Lehne, Stefan, *The Vienna Meeting of the Conference on Security and Cooperation in Europe, 1986-1989: A Turning Point in East-West Relations* (Boulder, CO: Westview Press, 1991).

7946. Lowenthal, Mark M., *The New Soviet Legislature: Committee on Defense and State Security.* 101st Congress, 2nd Session, 11 Apr. 1990 (Washington, DC: Government Printing Office, 1990).

7947. Luongo, Kenneth N., and W. Thomas Wander, eds., *The Search for Security in Space* (Ithaca: Cornell University Press, 1989).

7948. MccGwire, Michael, *Perestroika and Soviet National Security Policy* (Washington, DC: Brookings Institution, 1991).

7949. Miller, Steven E., ed., *Conventional Forces and American Defense Policy: An International Security Reader* (Princeton: Princeton University Press, 1986).

7950. Myers, David, *New Soviet Thinking and U.S. Nuclear Policy* (Philadelphia: Temple University Press, 1990).

7951. Nation, R. Craig, *Black Earth, Red Star: A History of Soviet Security Policy, 1917-1991* (Ithaca: Cornell University Press, 1993).

7952. Nichols, Thomas M., *The Current Soviet Debate on National Security: A Survey of Possible Outcomes* (Washington, DC: Center for Strategic and International Studies, 1989).

7953. -----, *The Sacred Cause: Civil-Military Conflict over Soviet National Security, 1917-1992* (Ithaca: Cornell University Press,

1993).

7954. Parrott, Bruce, ed., *The Dynamics of Soviet Defense Policy* (Washington, DC: Wilson Center Press, 1990).

7955. Payne, Keith B., *Strategic Defense: "Star Wars" in Perspective* (Lanham, MD: Hamilton Press, 1986).

7956. Pfaltzgraff, Robert L., Jr., and Richard H. Shultz, Jr., *Ethnic Conflict and Regional Instability: Implications for U.S. Policy and Army Roles and Missions* (Washington, DC: US Government Printing Office, for the Strategic Studies Institute, US Army War College, 1994).

7957. Scalapino, Robert A., *et al.*, *Internal and External Security Issues in Asia* (Berkeley: University of California-Berkeley, Institute of East Asian Studies, 1986).

7958. Sherr, James, *Soviet Power, the Continuing Challenge*, 2nd ed. (New York: St. Martin's Press, 1991).

7959. Smoke, Richard, and Andre Kortunov, eds., *Mutual Security: A New Approach to Soviet-American Relations* (New York: St. Martin's Press, 1991).

7960. Stares, Paul B., *Space and National Security* (Washington, DC: Brookings Institution, 1987).

7961. Stephan, Paul B., III, and Boris M. Klimenko, eds., *International Law and International Security: Military and Political Dimensions: A U.S.-Soviet Dialogue* (Armonk, NY: M. E. Sharpe, 1991).

7962. Stoll, Richard J., *U.S. National Security Policy and the Soviet Union: Persistent Regularities and Extreme Contingencies* (Columbia, SC: University of South Carolina Press, 1990).

7963. Twining, David Thomas, *Strategic Surprise in the Age of Glasnost* (New Brunswick, NJ: Transaction Publishers, 1992).

7964. US Congress. House. Committee on Armed Services. *Soviet Views on National Security Issues in the 1990s.* 101st Congress, 1st Session, 1989, HASC 101-24.

7965. US Congress. Joint Economic Committee. Subcommittee on National Security Economics. *Allocation of Resources in the Soviet Union and China, 1987.* 100th Congress, 2nd Session (Washington, DC: Government Printing Office, 1989).

7966. US Congress. Senate. Committee on Armed Services. *Changes in the European Security Environment. Hearings.* 102nd Congress, 1st Session (Washington, DC: Government Printing Office, 1991).

7967. US Congress. Senate. Committee on Armed Services. *International Security Environment (Strategy).* 101st Congress, 1st Session, 1989, S Hrg 101-316.

7968. US Congress. Senate. Committee on Armed Services. *The New Europe: Security and Political Arrangements for the Post-Cold War World. Hearing.* 101st Congress, 2nd Session (Washington, DC: Government Printing Office, 1991).

7969. US Department of Defense. *The Soviet Space Challenge* (Washington, DC: Department of Defense, 1987).

7970. US Department of State. Bureau of Public Affairs. *Military Confidence- and Security-Building Measures in Europe: Strengthening Stability through Openness* (Washington, DC: US Dept. of State, 1989).

7971. Wohlforth, William Curti, *The Elusive Balance: Power and Perceptions during the Cold War* (Ithaca: Cornell University Press, 1993).

ARTICLES

7972. Adelman, Kenneth, "Is the Soviet Threat Over?" *Intercollegiate Review*, 25, no. 2 (Spring 1990), 3-12.

7973. "After the Cold War: New Defense Priorities," *Policy Review*, no. 53 (Summer 1990), 6-16.

7974. Arkin, William M., "Gorbachev Talks But Who Listens?" *Bulletin of the Atomic Scientists*, 45, no. 2 (Mar. 1989), 5-6.

7975. -----, "Of Drugs and Star Wars," *Bulletin of the Atomic Scientists*, 42, no. 2 (Feb. 1986), 4-5.

7976. -----, "Reagan's Security Legacy: The Buildup That Wasn't," *Bulletin of the Atomic Scientists*, 45, no. 1 (Jan-Feb. 1989), 6-10.

7977. Armacost, M. H., "U.S.-Soviet Relations: Testing Gorbachev's `New Thinking'," *Department of State Bulletin*, 87 (Sept. 1987), 36-41.

7978. Bagley, Worth H., "The Shifting Balance," *Global Affairs*, 3, no. 1 (Winter 1988), 41-51.

7979. Belonogov, Aleksandr M., "Soviet Peace-Keeping Proposals," *Survival*, 32, no. 3 (May-June 1990), 206-11.

7980. Bertram, Christoph, "Strategic Defense and the Western Alliance," *Daedalus*, 114, no. 3 (Summer 1985), 279-96.

7981. Bode, William R., "The Reagan Doctrine," *Strategic Review*, 14, no. 1 (Winter 1986), 21-29.

7982. Bodie, William C., "Anarchy and Cold War in Moscow's `Near Abroad'," *Strategic Review*, 21, no. 1 (Winter 1993), 40-53.

7983. -----, "Threats from the Former USSR," *Orbis*, 37, no. 4 (Fall 1993), 509-26.

7984. Bouscaren, Anthony T., "Strategic Defense: Why We Need the Shield," *Intercollegiate Review*, 22, no. 1 (Fall 1986), 13-18.

7985. Boutwell, Jeffrey, and F. A. Long, "The SDI and U.S. Security," *Daedalus*, 114, no. 3 (Summer 1985), 315-29.

7986. Buckley, Gary J., "Rethinking the Teaching of Security Policy in a Post-Cold War Era," *International Studies Notes*, 18, no. 3 (Fall 1993), 5-7.

7987. Buckley, William F., "Gorbachev Entertains," *National Review*, 42 (9 July 1990), 63.

7988. Chaban-Delmas, J., "Nuclear Disarmament and Security in the Current Crisis in International Relations," *Atlantic Community Quarterly*, 23, no. 4 (Fall 1985), 239-49.

7989. Chandler, Andrea, "The Iron Curtain and Gorbachev: Recent Changes in the Soviet System of Border Control," *Soviet Observer*, 1 (Apr. 1990), 4-6.

7990. "China Applauds U.S.-Soviet Summit," *Beijing Review*, 31 (20 June 1988), 10.

7991. Chirac, Jacques, "Soviet Change and Western Security," *Strategic Review*, 17, no. 1 (Winter 1989), 9-15.

7992. Clark, J., "Reykjavik: Beginning of the End of Reaganism!" *Dissent*, 34, no. 1 (Winter 1987), 13-16.

7993. Clark, Susan L., "Security Issues and the Eastern Slavic States," *World Today*, 49, no. 10 (Oct. 1993), 189-93.

7994. Clausen, Peter A., "The SDI Debate: A Critic's Perspective," *Fletcher Forum*, 10, no. 1 (Winter 1986), 33-37.

7995. Codevilla, Angelo M., "The Reagan Doctrine-(As Yet) A Declaratory Policy," *Strategic Review*, 14, no. 3 (Summer 1986), 17-26.

7996. Cohen, Sam, "Needed: *Perestroika* for U.S. National Security Policy," *Journal of Social, Political and Economic Studies*, 15, no. 2 (Summer 1990), 131-40.

7997. Correll, John T., "Alliances in Turmoil," *Air Force Magazine*, 72, no. 11 (Nov. 1989), 36-40.

7998. Covington, Stephen R., "NATO and Soviet Security Reform," *Washington Quarterly*, 14, no. 1 (Winter 1991), 39-50.

7999. Dalby, Simon, "Security, Modernity, Ecology: The Dilemmas of Post-Cold War Security," *Alternatives*, 17, no. 1 (Winter 1992), 95-134.

8000. Davis, Christopher Mark, "The Exceptional Soviet Case: Defense in an Autarkic System," *Daedalus*, 120, no. 4 (Fall 1991), 113-34.

8001. Deudney, Daniel, and G. John Ikenberry, "The International Sources of Soviet Change," *International Security*, 16, no. 3 (Winter 1991-92), 74-118.

8002. Epstein, Joshua M., "The 3:1 Rule, the Adaptive Dynamic Model, and the Future of Security Studies," *International Security*, 13, no. 4 (Spring 1989), 90-127.

8003. Evangelista, Matthew, "Economic Reform and Military Technology in Soviet Security Policy," *Harriman Institute Forum*, 2, no. 1 (Jan. 1989), 1-8.

8004. Feld, Werner J., "Toward a *European* Security and Defense Policy," *Military Review*, 71, no. 7 (July 1991), 14-25.

8005. Fitzgerald, Mary C., "The Dilemma in Moscow's Defensive Force Posture," *Arms Control Today*, 19 (Nov. 1989), 15-20.

8006. Flynn, Gregory, and David J. Scheffer, "Limited Collective Security," *Foreign Policy*, no. 80 (Fall 1990), 77-101.

8007. Fought, Stephen O., "SDI: A Policy Analysis," *Naval War College Review*, 38, no. 6 (Nov-Dec. 1985), 59-95.

8008. Foye, Stephen, "The Gulf War and the Soviet Defense Debate," *Report on the USSR*, 3, no. 11 (15 Mar. 1991), 1-3.

8009. -----, "Military Hard-Liner Condemns `New Thinking' in Security Policy," *Report on the USSR*, 2, no. 28 (13 July 1990), 4-6.

8010. Garrity, Patrick J., and Sharon K. Weiner, "U.S. Defense Strategy after the Cold War," *Washington Quarterly*, 15, no. 2 (Spring 1992), 57-80.

8011. Garthoff, Raymond L., "The Bush Administration's Policy toward the Soviet Union," *Current History*, 90 (Oct. 1991), 311-16.

8012. -----, "Changing Realities, Changing Perceptions: Deterrence and U.S. Security after the Cold War," *Brookings Review*, 8, no. 4 (Fall 1990), 13-20.

8013. Gasteyger, Curt, "New Dimensions of International Security," *Washington Quarterly*, 8, no. 1 (Winter 1985), 85-91.

8014. Glantz, David M., "Challenges of the Future: Developing Security Issues in the Post-Cold War Era," *Military Review*, 71, no. 12 (Dec. 1991), 2-9.

8015. Glaser, Charles L., "Nuclear Policy without an Adversary: U.S. Planning for the Post-Soviet Era," *International Security*, 16, no. 4 (Spring 1992), 34-78.

8016. Goetze, B. A., "Deterrence and Dialogue: NATO Strategy for `Perestroika'," *Canadian Defence Quarterly*, 18, no. 1 (1988), 56-66.

8017. Goldberg, Andrew C., "Soviet Imperial Decline and the Emerging Balance of Power," *Washington Quarterly*, 13, no. 1 (Winter 1990), 157-67.

8018. Goodpaster, Andrew J., "Challenges to Western Security: A Current Assessment," *Atlantic Community Quarterly*, 24, no. 4 (Winter 1986-87), 331.

8019. Goure, Daniel, "A New Soviet National Security Policy for the Twenty-First Century," *Strategic Review*, 17, no. 4 (Fall 1989), 36-46.

8020. Goure, Leon, "The Soviet Strategic View," *Strategic Review*, 14, no. 3 (Summer 1986), 89-103.

8021. Gray, Alfred M., "Planning for the Future: A Policy of Stability," *Strategic Review*, 19, no. 1 (Winter 1991), 9-16.

8022. Gray, Colin S., "The Maritime Strategy in U.S.-Soviet Strategic Relations," *Naval War College Review*, 42, no. 1 (Winter 1989), 7-18.

8023. -----, "Nuclear Strategy: What Is True, What Is False, What Is Arguable," *Comparative Strategy*, 9, no. 1 (Jan-Mar. 1990), 1-32.

8024. Gregorovich, Andrew, "Canadian Prime Minister in Kiev," *Forum*, no. 80 (Winter 1989), 3-7.

8025. Griffiths, Franklyn, "`New Thinking' in the Kremlin," *Bulletin of the Atomic Scientists*, 43, no. 3 (Apr. 1987), 20ff.

8026. Gutsenko, Konstantin, "The Right to a Defense: What It Entails and Where It Is Going," *Soviet Law and Government*, 30, no. 3 (Winter 1991-92), 78ff.

8027. Herrmann, Richard K., "Soviet Behavior in Regional Conflicts: Old Questions, New Strategies and Important Lessons," *World Politics*, 44, no. 3 (Apr. 1992), 432-65.

8028. Hiebert, Timothy H., "Reagan's Strategic Defense Initiative: The U.S. Presentation and the European Response," *Fletcher Forum*, 10, no. 1 (Winter 1986), 51-64.

8029. Holloway, David, "State, Society and the Military under Gorbachev," *International Security*, 14, no. 3 (Winter 1989), 5-24.

8030. Hooper, R. W., "Mikhail Gorbachev's Economic Restructuring and Soviet Defence Policy," *RUSI Journal*, 134, no. 2 (Summer 1989), 15-22.

8031. Hough, Jerry F., "Soviet Decision-Making on Defense," *Bulletin of the Atomic Scientists*, 41 (Aug. 1985), 84-88.

8032. Howard, Michael, "The Gorbachev Challenge: The Defense of the West," *Survival*, 30, no. 6 (Nov-Dec. 1988), 483-92.

8033. Hudson, George E., "The New Political Thinking and Soviet National Security Policy: What Difference Has It Made?" *Crossroads*, no. 28 (1989), 23-34.

8034. Janes, Robert W., "The Soviet Union and Northern Europe: New Thinking and old Security Constraints," *Annals of the American Academy of Political and Social Science*, no. 512 (Nov. 1990), 163-72.

8035. Jastrow, R., and J. Frelk, "Emasculating America's Deterrence: Only SDI Can Avert Disaster," *Policy Review*, no. 41 (Summer 1987), 30-36.

8036. Javetski, B., *et al.*, "Two Summits, One Question: Aid for Gorbachev," *Business Week* (9 July 1990), 28-29.

8037. "Joint Chiefs Chairman Counsels Long-Term Strategic View of Soviets," *Aviation Week & Space Technology*, 126 (15 June 1987), 117ff.

8038. Jones, David T., "NATO's Defense in the New Europe," *Foreign Service Journal*, 67, no. 4 (Apr. 1990), 28-31.

8039. Karaganov, Sergei A., "The Year of Europe: A Soviet View," *Survival*, 32, no. 2 (Mar-Apr. 1990), 121-28.

8040. Kass, Ilana, "The U.S.-Soviet Strategic Relationship," *Annals of the American Academy of Political and Social Science*, 516 (July 1991), 25-38.

8041. Katz, Mark N., "The Decline of Soviet Power," *Survival*, 32, no. 1 (Jan-Feb. 1990), 15-28.

8042. Kortunov, Sergei, "Toward a New Pattern of Strategic Relationship," *International Affairs* (Moscow), no. 10 (Oct. 1991), 18-29.

8043. Kozyrev, Andrei, "Russia, A Chance for Survival," *Foreign Affairs*, 71, no. 2 (Spring 1990), 1-16.

8044. Kunsman, Eric A., "The 1990s: A Decade of Transition to a New European Security Order," *Comparative Strategy*, 10, no. 3 (July-Sept. 1991), 273-85.

8045. Kusin, Vladimir V., "Security Concerns in Central Europe," *Report on Eastern Europe*, 2, no. 10 (8 Mar. 1991), 25-40.

8046. Lapidus, Gail W., and Alexander Dallin, "Reagan's Security Legacy: The Pacification of Ronald Reagan," *Bulletin of the Atomic Scientists*, 45, no. 1 (Jan-Feb. 1989), 14-17.

8047. Leighton, Marian, and Robert Rudney, "Non-Offensive Defense: Towards a Soviet-German Security Partnership?" *Orbis*, 35, no. 3 (Summer 1991), 377-94.

8048. Lepingwell, John W. R., "Soviet Strategic Air Defense and the Stealth Challenge," *International Security*, 14, no. 2 (Fall 1989), 64-100.

8049. Liska, George, "The Reagan Doctrine: Monroe and Dulles Reincarnate?" *SAIS Review*, 6, no. 2 (Summer-Fall 1986), 83-98.

8050. Lubkemeier, Eckhard, "The Political Upheaval in Europe and the Reform of NATO Strategy," *NATO Review*, 39, no. 3 (June 1991), 16-21.

8051. Lucas, Michael, "SDI and Europe: Militarization or Common Security?" *World Policy Journal*, 3, no. 2 (Spring 1986), 219-49.

8052. Martin, Laurence, "Dismantling Deterrence?" *Review of International Studies*, 17, no. 3 (July 1991), 215-24.

8053. Mazzocco, William, "*Perestroika* and International Security," *Global Affairs*, 3, no. 3 (Summer 1988), 120-27.

8054. McCarthy, James P., "Strengthening Security in Central and Eastern Europe: New Opportunities for NATO," *Strategic Review*, 21, no. 1 (Winter 1993), 54-60.

8055. MccGwire, Michael, "A Mutual Security Regime for Europe?" *International Affairs*, 64 (Summer 1988), 361-79.

8056. Mearsheimer, John J., "Assessing the Conventional Balance: The 3:1 Rule and Its Critics," *International Security*, 13, no. 4 (Spring 1989), 54-89.

8057. -----, "A Strategic Misstep: The Maritime Strategy and Deterrence in Europe," *International Security*, 11, no. 2 (Fall 1986), 3-57.

8058. Meehan, John F., III, "NATO and Alternative Strategies," *Parameters*, 16, no. 1 (Spring 1986), 14-23.

8059. Meyer, Stephen M., "The Sources and Prospects of Gorbachev's New Political Thinking on Security," *International Security*, 13, no. 2 (Fall 1988), 124-63.

8060. Montbrial, T. de, "Security Requires Caution," *Foreign Policy*, no. 71 (Summer 1988), 86-98.

8061. Munton, Don, "Superpowers and National Security," *Peace and Security*, 2, no. 4 (1987-88), 2-3.

8062. Nadkarni, Vidya, "Soviet Perceptions of the East-West Balance: From the `Balance of Power' to a `Balance of Interests'," *Comparative Strategy*, 10, no. 3 (July-Sept. 1991), 241-56.

8063. Nordlinger, E. A., "Prospects and Policies for Soviet-American Reconciliation," *Political Science Quarterly*, 103, no. 2 (Summer 1988), 197-222.

8064. Odom, William E., "Gorbachev's Strategy and Western Security: Illusions Versus Reality," *Washington Quarterly*, 13, no. 1 (Winter 1990), 145-55.

8065. Owen, H., and E. C. Meyer, "Central European Security," *Foreign Affairs*, 68, no. 3 (Summer 1989), 22-40.

8066. Park, Andrus, "Global Security, *Glasnost* and the Retreat Dividend," *Government and Opposition*, 26 (Winter 1991), 75-85.

8067. Parrott, Bruce, "Soviet National Security under Gorbachev," *Problems of Communism*, 37, no. 6 (Nov-Dec. 1988), 1-36.

8068. Patterson, Lee Ann, "A `Marshall Plan' for the Former Soviet Union?" *Arms Control*, 14, no. 2 (Aug. 1993), 181-97.

8069. Payne, Keith B., "The Deterrence Requirement for Defense," *Washington Quarterly*, 9, no. 1 (Winter 1986), 139-54.

8070. -----, Linda H. Vlahos and Willis A. Stanley, "Evolving Russian Views on Defense: An Opportunity for Cooperation," *Strategic Review*, 21, no. 1 (Winter 1993), 61ff.

8071. Pfaltzgraff, Robert L., Jr., "The Emerging Global Security Environment," *Annals of the American Academy of Political and Social Science*, no. 517 (Sept. 1991), 10-24.

8072. -----, Jacquelyn K. Davis and Charles M. Perry, "The Atlantic Alliance and European Security in the 1990s," *Cornell International Law Journal*, 23, no. 3 (1990), 467-510.

8073. Pignon, Dominique, "The Strategic Defense Initiative and Europe," *Telos*, no. 67 (Spring 1986), 45-56.

8074. Porter, Gareth, "Post-Cold War Global Environment and Security," *Fletcher Forum of World Affairs*, 14, no. 2 (Summer 1990), 332-44.

8075. Puschel, Karen, "Can Moscow Live with SDI?" *Survival*, 31, no. 1 (Jan-Feb. 1989), 34-51.

8076. Raldugin, N. V., "The Development of Legislation on Safeguarding the State Security of the USSR," *Soviet Law and Government*, 28, no. 4 (Spring 1990), 82-90.

8077. "Reagan Gives Press Conference in Moscow," *Congressional Quarterly Weekly Report*, 46 (4 June 1988), 1542-45.

8078. Rice, Condoleezza, "Is Gorbachev Changing the Rules of Defense Decision-Making?" *Journal of International Affairs*, 42 (Spring 1989), 377-97.

8079. Richardson, R. C., "Some Consequences of a Declining Soviet Threat," *Journal of Social, Political and Economic Studies*, 13, no. 3 (Fall 1988), 239-46.

8080. Riemann, Robert H., "The Challenges of *Glasnost* for Western Intelligence," *Parameters*, 20, no. 4 (Dec. 1990), 85-94.

8081. Risse-Kappen, Thomas, "Did `Peace through Strength' End the Cold War? Lessons from INF," *International Security*, 16, no. 1 (Summer 1991), 162ff.

8082. Rogers, Bernard W., "Arms Control and NATO Deterrence," *Global Affairs*, 3, no. 1 (Winter 1988), 23-40.

8083. Rogov, Sergei, "International Security and the Collapse of the Soviet Union," *Washington Quarterly*, 15, no. 2 (Spring 1992), 15-32.

8084. Rosefielde, Steven S., "Economic Foundations of Soviet National Security Policy," *Orbis*, 30, no. 2 (Summer 1986), 317-30.

8085. Rostow, Eugene V., "The Double Crisis in Europe: A Strategic Opportunity for the West," *Global Affairs*, 3, no. 3 (Summer 1988), 65-74.

8086. "Security for the New Germany in the New Europe: The View from Moscow and Mikhail Gorbachev," *World Affairs*, 152, no. 4 (Spring 1990), 232-33.

8087. Sempa, Francis P., "The Geopolitics of the Post-Cold War World," *Strategic Review*, 20, no. 1 (Winter 1992), 9-18.

8088. Shulman, Marshall D., "The Superpowers: Dance of the Dinosaurs," *Foreign Affairs*, 66, no. 3 (1988), 494-515.

8089. Sigal, Leon V., "Reagan's Security Legacy. Reagan's Radical Challenge," *Bulletin of the Atomic Scientists*, 45, no. 1 (Jan-Feb. 1989), 38-41.

8090. Smith, D. L., "Reagan's National Security Legacy: Model-Based Analyses of Recent Changes in American Policy Use," *Journal of Conflict Resolution*, 32, no. 4 (Dec. 1988), 595-625.

8091. Sneider, Richard L., "United States Security Interests," in James W. Morley, ed., *The Pacific Basin: New Challenges for the United States* (New York: Academy of Political Science and Columbia University's East Asian Institute and Center on Japanese Economy and Business, 1986).

8092. Snyder, Jack, "The Gorbachev Revolution: A Waning of Soviet Expansion?" *International Security*, 12, no. 3 (Winter 1987-88).

8093. Solomon, Richard H., "The Pacific Basin: Dilemmas and Choices for American Security," *Naval War College Review*, 40, no. 1 (Winter 1987), 36-43.

8094. Sorenson, Theodore C., "Rethinking National Security," *Foreign Affairs*, 69, no. 3 (Summer 1990), 1-18.

8095. Sorokin, Konstantin E., "The Nuclear Strategy Debate," *Orbis*, 38, no. 1 (Winter 1994), 19-40.

8096. Stromseth, Jane E., "The North Atlantic Treaty and European Security After the Cold War," *Cornell International Law Journal*, 24, no. 3 (1991), 479-502.

8097. Svec, Milan, "Reordering Western Security: Removing Gorbachev's Edge," *Foreign Policy*, no. 69 (Winter 1987-88), 148-65.

8098. Szajkowski, Bogdan, "The Demise of the Warsaw Pact and Its Aftermath," *Coexistence*, 29, no. 1 (Mar. 1992), 1-18.

8099. Towell, Pat, "Fundamental Shift in NATO Strategy: Shultz, Soviets Draw Nearer to Agreement on Euromissiles," *Congressional Quarterly Weekly Report*, 45 (18 Apr. 1987), 718-19.

8100. Townsend, James J., "The East-West Military Balance," in Barry M. Blechman and Edward N. Luttwak, eds., *Global Security: A Review of Strategic and Economic Issues* (Boulder, CO: Westview, 1987), 22-90.

8101. Treverton, Gregory F., "Elements of a New European Security Order," *Journal of International Affairs*, 45 (Summer 1991), 91-112.

8102. Trofimenko, H., "Pan-European Security: A Soviet Scholar's View," *Journal of International Affairs*, 45 (Summer 1991), 113-25.

8103. "Unfortunately, 1917 Did Happen: The Daring Mr Gorbachev Has Not Demolished the Hard Facts That Require Europe to Be Defended," *Economist*, 309 (17 Dec. 1988), 12-13.

8104. "US-Soviet Relations: Confrontation or Cooperation?" *World Marxist Review*, 31, no. 2 (Feb. 1988), 78-83.

8105. "A Visit from Gorbachev: Here's a Chance to Show Him Our Best," *People Weekly*, 25 (3 Mar. 1986), 52-55.

8106. Wagner, R. H., "Nuclear Deterrence, Counterforce Strategies, and the Incentive to Strike First," *American Political Science Review*, 85 (Spring 1991), 727-49.

8107. Wallop, M., "Offense-Defense Strategic Balance in the 1990s," *Vital Speeches of the Day*, 53 (1 Aug. 1987), 610-13.

8108. Warner, Edward L., III, "New Thinking and Old Realities in Soviet Defense Policy," *Survival*, 31, no. 1 (Jan-Feb. 1989), 13-33.

8109. Weeks, Albert L., "The Soviet Defense Council: The Kremlin's Top Economic, Military-Industrial and War-Fighting Organ," *Defense and Diplomacy*, 8 (May 1990), 42-47.

8110. Weinberger, Caspar W., "U.S. Defense Strategy," *Foreign Affairs*, 64, no. 4 (Spring 1986), 675-97.

8111. Weisburd, S., "Soviets Visit Nevada Nuclear Test Site," *Science News*, 133, no. 5 (30 Jan. 1988), 71.

8112. -----, "U.S., Soviets Sign Scientific Accord," *Science News*, 133, no. 4 (23 Jan. 1988), 55.

8113. Wishnick, Elizabeth, "Soviet Asian Collective Security Policy from Brezhnev to Gorbachev," *Journal of Northeast Asian Studies*, 7, no. 3 (Fall 1988), 3-28.

8114. Wright, Susan, "Reagan's Security Legacy: The Buildup That Was," *Bulletin of the Atomic Scientists*, 45, no. 1 (Jan-Feb. 1989), 52-56.

8115. Yazov, D., "The Soviet Proposal for European Security," *Bulletin of the Atomic Scientists*, 44 (Sept. 1988), 8-11.

8116. Zhurkin, V., S. Karaganov and A. Kortunov, "Challenges of Security, Old and New," *Soviet Law and Government*, 27, no. 4 (Spring 1989), 52-64.

8117. Zucconi, Mario, "Reagan's Security Legacy: A Crisis of Confidence," *Bulletin of the Atomic Scientists*, 45, no. 1 (Jan-Feb. 1989), 34-37.

XXXIV. Society, Human Rights, Youth

BOOKS

8118. Adelman, Deborah, *The "Children of Perestroika": Moscow Teenagers Talk About Their Lives and the Future* (Armonk, NY: M. E. Sharpe, 1991).

8119. -----, *The "Children of Perestroika" Come of Age: Young People of Moscow Talk About Life in the New Russia* (Armonk, NY: M. E. Sharpe, 1994).

8120. Alexeyeva, Ludmilla, and Catherine A. Fitzpatrick, *Nyeformaly: Civil Society in the USSR* (New York: Helsinki Watch Report, 1990).

8121. Bonet, Pilar, *Figures in a Red Landscape* (Baltimore: Johns Hopkins University Press, 1993).

8122. Bovin, Alexander, Gennady Lischkin and Andrei Nuikin, *Social Justice, Social Change* (Winchester, MA: Unwin Hyman, 1989).

8123. Buckley, Mary E. A., *Redefining Russian Society and Polity* (Boulder, CO: Westview Press, 1993).

8124. Bukowski, Charles, and J. Richard Walsh, eds., *Glasnost', Perestroika and the Socialist Community* (New York: Praeger, 1990).

8125. Chalidze, Valerii, and Richard Schifter, *Glasnost' and Social and Economic Rights* (New York: Freedom House, 1988).

8126. Cornia, Giovanni Andrea, and Sandor Sipos, eds., *Children and the Transition to the Market Economy: Safety Nets and Social Policies in Central and Eastern Europe* (Brookfield, VT: Avebury, 1991).

8127. Csapo, L., *The General Crisis of the Soviet Model of the Collectivist Society* (Bundoora: La Trobe University School of Economics, 1988).

8128. Deacon, Bob, and Julia Szalai, eds., *Social Policy in the New Eastern Europe: What Future for Socialist Welfare?* (Brookfield, VT: Avebury, 1990).

8129. Edelman, Robert, *Serious Fun: A History of Spectator Sports in the U.S.S.R.* (New York: Oxford University Press, 1993).

8130. Gorbachev, Mikhail S., *Glasnost: How Open?* (Lanham, MD: Freedom House, 1987).

8131. Herlemann, Horst, ed., *Quality of Life in the Soviet Union* (Boulder, CO: Westview Press, 1987).

8132. Hixson, Walter L., *Witness to Disintegration: Provincial Life in the Last Year of the USSR* (Hanover, NH: University Press of New England, 1993).

8133. Human Rights Watch, *Glasnost in Jeopardy: Human Rights in the USSR* (New York: Helsinki Watch Committee, 1991).

8134. -----, *Prison Conditions in the Soviet Union: A Report of Facilities in Russia and Azerbaidzhan* (New York: Human Rights Watch, 1991).

8135. -----, *"Punished Peoples" of the Soviet Union: The Continuing Legacy of Stalin's Deportations* (New York: Human Rights Watch, 1991).

8136. Jones, Anthony, Walter D. Connor and David E. Powell, eds., *Soviet Social Problems* (Boulder, CO: Westview Press, 1991).

8137. Joyce, Walter, ed., *Social Change and Social Issues in the Former USSR* (New York: St. Martin's Press, 1992).

8138. Juviler, Peter, and Bertram Gross, eds., with Vladimir Kartashkin and Elena Lukasheva, *Human Rights for the Twenty-First Century: Foundations for Responsible Hope* (Armonk, NY: M. E. Sharpe, 1993).

8139. Klugman, Jeffrey, *The New Soviet Elite: How They Think and What They Want* (New York: Praeger, 1989).

8140. Kon, Igor, and James Riordan, eds., *Sex and Russian Society* (Bloomington: Indiana University Press, 1993).

8141. Korey, William, *The Promises We Keep: Human Rights, the Helsinki Process and United States Foreign Policy* (New York: St. Martin's Press, 1993).

8142. Kotkin, Stephen, *Steeltown, USSR: Soviet Society in the Gorbachev Era* (Berkeley: University of California Press, 1991).

8143. Kukathas, Chandran, David Lovell and William Malley, eds., *Transition from Socialism: State and Civil Society in Gorbachev's USSR* (Melbourne: Longman Cheshire, 1991).

8144. Lane, David, *Soviet Society under Perestroika*, rev. ed. (New York: Routledge, 1992).

8145. Matthews, Mervyn, *Patterns of Deprivation in the Soviet Union under Brezhnev and Gorbachev* (Stanford: Hoover Institution Press, 1989).

8146. Miles, F. Mike, *Gorbachev's Reform: The Consumer Goods and Services Sector* (Washington, DC: Library of Congress, Congressional Research Service, 1987).

8147. Millar, James, and Sharon Wolchik, eds., *The Social Legacy of Communism* (New York: Cambridge University Press, 1994).

8148. Miller, R. F., ed., *The Development of Civil Society in Communist Systems* (Sydney: Allen & Unwin, 1992).

8149. Miller, William Green, ed., *Toward a More Civil Society? The USSR under Mikhail Sergeevich Gorbachev: An Assessment by the American Committee on U.S.-Soviet Relations* (New York: Ballinger, 1989).

8150. Naylor, Thomas H., *The Gorbachev Strategy: Opening the Closed Society* (Lexington, MA: Lexington Books, 1988).

8151. Novak, Michael, *Human Rights and the New Realism: Strategic Thinking in a New Age* (New York: Freedom House, 1986).

8152. -----, *Taking Glasnost' Seriously: Toward an Open Soviet Union* (Washington, DC: American Enterprise for Public Policy Research, 1988).

8153. Ra'anan, Uri, Keith Ames and Kate Martin, *Russian Pluralism: Now Irreversible?* (New York: St. Martin's Press, 1993).

8154. Rau, Zbigniew, ed., *The Reemergence of Civil Society in Eastern Europe and the Soviet Union* (Boulder, CO: Westview Press, 1991).

8155. Richards, Susan, *Epics of Everyday Life: Encounters in a Changing Russia* (New York: Penguin USA, 1991).

8156. Riordan, Jim, ed., *Soviet Social Reality in the Mirror of Glasnost* (New York: St. Martin's Press, 1992).

8157. Ruble, Blair A., *Leningrad: Shaping a Soviet City* (Berkeley: University of California Press, 1989).

8158. Ryan, Michael, comp. and trans., *Contemporary Soviet Society: A Statistical Handbook* (Brookfield, VT: Edward Elgar, 1990).

8159. -----, *Social Trends in Contemporary Russia: A Statistical Source-Book* (New York: St. Martin's Press, 1993).

8160. Sacks, Michael Paul, and Jerry G. Pankhurst, eds., *Understanding Soviet Society* (Boston: Unwin Hyman, 1988).

8161. Schifter, Richard, *The Reality about Human Rights in the USSR* (Washington, DC: US Department of State, Bureau of Public Affairs, 1987).

8162. Sedaitis, Judith, and Jim Butterfield, *Perestroika from Below: Social Movements in the Soviet Union* (Boulder, CO: Westview Press, 1991).

8163. Smith, Hedrick, *The New Russians*, rev. and updated 2nd ed. (New York: Random House, 1991).

8164. Timofeyev, Lev, ed., *The Anti-Communist Manifesto* (Bellevue, WA: Free Enterprise Press, 1990).

8165. Tismaneanu, Vladimir, ed., *In Search of Civil Society: Independent Peace Movements in the Soviet Bloc* (New York: Routledge, 1990).

8166. Toscano, Roberto, *Soviet Human Rights Policy and Perestroika* (Cambridge, MA: Harvard University Center for International Affairs, 1989).

8167. US Congress. Commission on Security and Cooperation in Europe. *Implementation of the Helsinki Accords: Changing United States Attitudes on Eastern Europe and the Soviet Union.* 100th Congress, 1st Session, 28 Oct. 1987 (Washington, DC: Government Printing Office, 1988).

8168. US Congress. Commission on Security and Cooperation in Europe. *Implementation of the Helsinki Accords: Hearing on East European Perestroika. United States and Soviet Foreign Policy Options.* 100th Congress, 2nd Session, 15 Mar. 1988 (Washington, DC: Government Printing Office, 1988).

8169. US Congress. Commission on Security and Cooperation in Europe. *Implementation of the Helsinki Accords: Human Rights and the CSCE Process in Eastern Europe; and Human Rights and the CSCE Process in the Soviet Union. Hearings.* 99th Congress, 27 Feb. 1986 (Washington, DC: Government Printing Office, 1986).

8170. US Congress. Commission on Security and Cooperation in Europe.*Implementation of the Helsinki Accords: The New and Improved Supreme Soviet and the Institutionalization of Human Rights Reform, 28 Nov. 1989.* 101st Congress, 1st Session (Washington, DC: Government Printing Office, 1990).

8171. US Congress. Commission on Security and Cooperation in Europe. *Implementation of the Helsinki Accords: Soviet and East European Emigration Policies. Hearing.* 99th Congress, 22 Apr. 1986 (Washington, DC: Government Printing Office, 1986).

8172. US Congress. Commission on Security and Cooperation in Europe. *Reform and Human Rights: The Gorbachev Record. Report, May 1988.* 100th Congress, 2nd Session (Washington, DC: Government Printing Office, 1988).

8173. US Congress. House. Committee on Foreign Affairs. Subcommittee on Human Rights and International Organizations. *U.S. Human Rights Policy Toward the Soviet Union: Pre-Summit Assessment and Update* (Washington, DC: Government Printing Office, 1988).

8174. Weaver, Kitty, *Bushels of Rubles: Soviet Youth in Transition* (Westport, CT: Praeger, 1993).

8175. Wilson, Andrew, and Nina Bachkatov, *Living with Glasnost: Youth and Society in a Changing Russia* (New York: Penguin, 1988).

8176. Yanowitch, Murray, *Controversies in Soviet Social Thought: Democratization, Social Justice, and the Erosion of Official Ideology* (Armonk, NY: M. E. Sharpe, 1991).

ARTICLES

8177. Bahry, Donna, "Society Transformed? Rethinking the Social Roots of Perestroika," *Slavic Review*, 52, no. 3 (Fall 1993), 512-54.

8178. Barist J., *et al.*, "Who May Leave: A Review of Soviet Practice Restricting Emigration on Grounds of Knowledge of `State Secrets' in Comparison with Standards of International Law and the Policies of Other States," *Hofstra Law Review*, 15 (Spring 1987), 381-442.

8179. Beissinger, Mark R., "Political Reform and Soviet Society," *Current History*, 87, no. 531 (Oct. 1988), 317ff.

8180. Bernstam, Mikhail S., "The Collapse of the Soviet Welfare State," *National Review*, 39 (6 Nov. 1987), 40-41.

8181. -----, "The Soviet Misery Index: The Collapse of the Soviet Welfare State," *National Review*, 39 (Nov. 1987), 40-41.

8182. Bonnell, Victoria E., "Moscow: A View from Below: Ordinary Life in the Gorbachev Time," *Dissent*, 36, no. 3 (Summer 1989), 311-17.

8183. Broun, Janice, "The Role of the Church in East Germany," *Freedom at Issue*, no. 114 (May-June 1990), 15-17.

8184. Brahams, Diana, "Human Rights-USSR: Yuri Massover," *Lancet*, 336, no. 8706 (7 July 1990), 43.

8185. Buckley, William F., "Trivial Pursuits," *National Review*, 38 (28 Mar. 1986), 70-71.

8186. Bull, C., "No *Glasnost* for Gays," *Utne Reader* (Jan-Feb. 1991), 99.

8187. Burbank, Jane, "Controversies over Stalinism: Searching for a Soviet Society," *Politics and Society*, 19, no. 3 (Sept. 1991), 325-40.

8188. Bushnell, John, "Soviet Hippies," *Harriman Institute Forum*, 3, no. 4 (Apr. 1990), 1-8.

8189. Butterfield, Jim, "State Response to Informal Groups," *Nationalities Papers*, 28, no. 2 (Fall 1990), 56-64.

8190. Chalidze, Valerii, "Perestroika, Socialism and the Constitution," *Annals of the American Academy of Political and Social Science*, no. 506 (Nov. 1989), 98-103.

8191. Chickering, A. Lawrence, "Life Without Marx," *National Interest*, no. 14 (Winter 1988-89), 112-16.

8192. Chotiner, Barbara A., "Soviet Society Under Gorbachev" (Review Article), *Russian Review*, 48, no. 3 (July 1988), 321-25.

8193. Connor, Walter D., "Social Policy under Gorbachev," *Problems of Communism*, 35, no. 4 (July-Aug. 1986), 31-46.

8194. Copeland, Emily A., "Perestroika and Human Rights: Steps in the Right Direction," *Fletcher Forum of World Affairs*, 15, no. 2 (Summer 1991), 101-19.

8195. Cracraft, James, "A Soviet Turning Point," *Bulletin of the Atomic Scientists*, 42, no. 2 (Feb. 1986), 8-12.

8196. Crighton, Elizabeth, and David S. Mason, "Solidarity and the Greens: The Rise of New Social Movements in East and West Europe," *Research in Social Movements, Conflicts and Change*, 9 (1986), 155-75.

8197. Cullen, Robert B., "Human Rights: A Millennial Year," *Harriman Institute Forum*, 1, no. 12 (Dec. 1988), 1-8.

8198. Damrosch, Lori F., "International Human Rights Law in Soviet and American Courts," *Yale Law Journal*, 100, no. 8 (June 1991), 2315-34.

8199. Davies, Richard T., "Editorial: On Holding a Human Rights Conference in Moscow in 1991," *Religion in Communist Dominated Areas*, 28, no. 1 (Winter 1989), 2-5.

8200. Dorf, Julie, "Revolution in Russia," *Frontiers* (13 Sept. 1991), 13.

8201. Evans, Alfred, Jr., and Carol Nechemias, "Changes in Soviet Rural Resettlement Policy," *Studies in Comparative Communism*, 23, no. 2 (Summer 1990), 125-48.

8202. Farer, Tom J., "Defending Human Rights in the Post-Reagan Era: Candor and Competence," *Virginia Journal of International Law*, 28, no. 4 (Summer 1988), 855-61.

8203. Fierman, William, and Martha Olcott, "Youth Culture in Crisis," *Soviet Union/Union Sovietique*, 15, no. 2-3 (1988), 245-62.

8204. "Final Resolution: 2nd International Human Rights Conference," *Religion in Communist Dominated Areas*, 29, no. 3-4 (Summer-Fall 1990), 122-23.

8205. Fish, Steven, "The Emergence of Independent Associations and the Transformation of Russian Political Society," *Journal of Communist Studies*, 7, no. 3 (Sept. 1991), 199-334.

8206. Forsythe, David P., "Human Rights in a Post-Cold War World," *Fletcher Forum of World Affairs*, 15, no. 2 (Summer 1991), 55-69.

8207. Frank, Peter, "Gorbachev's Dilemma: Social Justice or Political Instability?" *World Today*, 42, no. 6 (June 1986), 93-95.

8208. "The Glasnost Track," *Human Rights*, 15 (Spring 1989), 28-30.

8209. Goble, Paul, "Federalism and Human Rights in the Soviet Union," *Cornell University Law Journal*, 23, no. 2 (1990), 399-404.

8210. Gorbachev, Mikhail S., "Social and Economic Development," *Vital Speeches of the Day*, 51 (15 Apr. 1985), 386-88.

8211. Graham, Loren R., "Scientists, Human Rights and the Soviet Union," *Bulletin of the Atomic Scientists*, 42, no. 4 (Apr. 1986), 8-9.

8212. Gustafson, D. Mauritz, "Soviet Human Rights under Gorbachev: Old Wine in a New Bottle?" *Denver Journal of International Law and Policy*, 16, no. 1 (Fall 1987), 177-89.

8213. Hansen, Carol R., "Preserving Our Human Rights Leverage in the USSR," *Religion in Communist Dominated Areas*, 28, no. 4 (Fall 1989), 117ff; 29, no. 1 (Winter 1990), 13-16.

8214. Holden, Constance, "Emigres Express Caution on Soviet Human Rights," *Science*, 235 (13 Feb. 1987), 738-40.

8215. Iadov, V. A., "The Social Processes of Perestroika," *Russian Social Science Review*, 33, no. 2 (Mar-Apr. 1992), 27-49.

8216. Jacoby, Tamar, "The Reagan Turnaround on Human Rights," *Foreign Affairs*, 64, no. 5 (Summer 1986), 1066-86.

8217. Judge, A. J. N., "Gorbachev as Dramaturge: Lessons of Social Transformation for International Organizations," *Futures*, 24 (Sept. 1992), 689-700.

8218. Juviler, Peter, "Human Rights after Perestroika: Progress and Perils," *Harriman Institute Forum*, 4, no. 6 (June 1991), 1-10.

8219. -----, "The Soviet Declaration of Individual Rights: The Last Act of the Old Regime," *SEEL: Soviet and East European Law*, 2, no. 8 (Oct. 1991), 3-4.

8220. Kaplan, Cynthia S., "Rural Residents: Social Change and Evolving Perceptions," *Studies in Comparative Communism*, 23, no. 2 (Summer 1990), 149-60.

8221. Keller, B., "Russia's Restless Youth," *New York Times Magazine* (26 July 1987), 14ff.

8222. Khazova, O., "USSR: Recent Developments in Divorces and Its Consequences," *Journal of Family Law*, 30 (1991-92), 439-45.

8223. Korey, William, "Making Helsinki Matter," *New Leader*, 69 (11-25 Aug. 1986), 11-13.

8224. Kowalewski, D., "The USSR," in Jack Donnelly and Rhoda Howard, *International Handbook of Human Rights* (New York: Greenwood Press, 1987), 409-28.

8225. Kozyrev, Andrei, "Russia and Human Rights," *Slavic Review*, 51, no. 2 (Summer 1992), 286-93.

8226. Kut'ev, V., and Z. Maliuk, "The Renovation of Society and the Teacher's Political Culture," *Soviet Education*, 33, no. 8 (Aug. 1991), 6-34.

8227. Lambelet, D., "The Contradiction between Soviet and American Human Rights Doctrine: Reconciliation through Perestroika and Pragmatism," *Boston University International Law Journal*, 7 (Spring 1989), 61-83.

8228. Lubarsky, Cronid, "The Human Rights Movement and Perestroika," *Index on Censorship*, 17 (May 1988), 16-20.

8229. Ludlam, Janine, "Reform and the Redefinition of the Social Contract under Gorbachev" (Review Article), *World Politics*, 43, no. 2 (Jan. 1991), 284-312.

8230. Maggs, Peter B., "Enforcing the Bill of Rights in the Twilight of the Soviet Union," *University of Illinois Law Review* (1991), 1049-63.

8231. Matthews, M., "Panhandling in Moscow: Poverty in the Soviet Union," *Current*, 279 (Jan. 1986), 36-40.

8232. Medvedev, R., "Ideology and Politics in Soviet Society," *Soviet Law and Government*, 30, no. 2 (Fall 1991), 26-44.

8233. Meilunas, Egidijus, "Protecting Human Rights: A Full-Time Job: Interview with Viktor Kogan-Yasny," *Uncaptive Minds*, 4, no. 2 (Summer 1991), 53-55.

8234. Murray, V., "Sex after `Glasnost'," *World Press Review*, 38 (Nov. 1991), 55.

8235. Nagy, Andras, "`Social Choice' in Eastern Europe," *Journal of Comparative Economics*, 15, no. 2 (June 1991), 266-83.

8236. Neale, Walter C., "Society, State, and Market: A Polanyian View of Current Change and Turmoil in Eastern Europe," *Journal of Economic Issues*, 25, no. 2 (June 1991), 467-73.

8237. Nelson, Lynn D., Lilia V. Babaeva and Rufat G. Babaev, "Perspectives on Entrepreneurship and Privatization in Russia: Policy and Public Opinion," *Slavic Review*, 51, no. 2 (Summer 1992), 271-86.

8238. Newhouse, John, "A Reporter at Large: Socialism or Death," *New Yorker* (17 Apr. 1992), 52ff.

8239. Oliver, D., "`Perestroika' and Public Administration in the USSR," *Public Administration*, 66 (Winter 1988), 411-28.

8240. Parchomenko, Walter, "Waiting for Mikhail: Old Neglect, New Reprisals," *Commonweal*, 112 (12 July 1985), 390-91.

8241. Peterson, D. J., "Goskomstat Report on Social Conditions in 1989," *Report on the USSR*, 2, no. 6 (9 Feb. 1990), 4-6.

8242. "The Political Philosophy of *Perestroika*," *Perestroika Annual*, 1 (1988), 33-70.

8243. Pomar, Mark, "The Role of Informal Groups and Independent Associations in the Evolution of Civil Society in the Soviet Union," *Nationalities Papers*, 28, no. 2 (Fall 1990), 50-55.

8244. Popov, Gavril Kh., "*Perestroika* and the Managers," *Perestroika Annual*, 2 (1989), 161-77.

8245. Popov, Vladimir, "Soviet Economic Reforms; Possible Difficulties in the Application of Public Choice Theory," *Journal of Comparative Economics*, 15, no. 2 (June 1991), 304-24.

8246. Porket, J. L., "Socialism on the Retreat, But Not Dead," *Slavonic and East European Review*, 71, no. 1 (Jan. 1993), 133-36.

8247. Powell, David E., "Social Problems in Russia," *Current History*, 92, no. 576 (Oct. 1993), 325-30.

8248. Raiklin, Ernest, "The Social Significance of the Current Soviet Economic Programs," *Journal of Social, Political and Economic Studies*, 16, no. 1 (Spring 1991), 3-38.

8249. Rakitskaia, G. Ia., and B. V. Rakitskii, "Reflections on *Perestroika* as a Social Revolution," *Soviet Sociology*, 28, no. 5 (Sept-Oct. 1989), 37-66.

8250. Reagan, Ronald, "Our Human Rights Agenda with the Soviet Union," *Department of State Bulletin*, 88 (July 1988), 4-6.

8251. Reiner, Thomas A., "Land and Housing in the USSR During the Gorbachev Years," *Soviet Geography*, 32, no. 10 (Dec. 1991), 683-700.

8252. Riordan, Jim, "Playing to New Rules: Soviet Sport and *Perestroika*," *Soviet Studies*, 42, no. 1 (Jan. 1990), 133-46.

8253. Rose, Richard, and Christian Haerpfer, "Mass Response to Transformation in Post-Communist Societies," *Europe-Asia Studies*, 46, no. 1 (1994), 3-28.

8254. Rosenfeld, Stephen S., "The Guns of July," *Foreign Affairs*, 64, no. 4 (Spring 1986), 698-714.

8255. Ryan, J. Ruthven, "Human Rights in the USSR, 1987-1988," *Religion in Communist Dominated Areas*, 28, no. 1 (Winter 1989), 6-8.

8256. Rybakovskii, L. L., and N. V. Tarasova, "Migration Processes in the USSR: New Phenomena," *Soviet Sociology*, 30, no. 3 (May-June 1991), 6-22.

8257. Sadomskaya, Natalia, "The Emergence of Civil Society," *Nationalities Papers*, 19, no. 1 (Spring 1991), 76-78.

8258. Sagdeev, Roald Z., "Where Did We Lose Momentum?"

Perestroika Annual, 2 (1989), 183-94.

8259. Sanjian, Andrea Stevenson, "Social Problems, Political Issues: Marriage and Divorce in the USSR," *Soviet Studies*, 43, no. 4 (1991), 629-50.

8260. Scanlan, James P., "Reforms and Civil Society in the USSR," *Problems of Communism*, 37, no. 2 (Mar-Apr. 1988), 41-47.

8261. Schifter, R., "Human Rights, the Soviet Union, and the Helsinki Process," *Department of State Bulletin*, 87 (Apr. 1987), 42-48.

8262. -----, "The Reality about Human Rights in the U.S.S.R.," *Department of State Bulletin*, 87 (Apr. 1987), 38-41.

8263. -----, "U.S.-Soviet Quality of Life: A Comparison," *Department of State Bulletin*, 85 (Sept. 1985), 40-42.

8264. Schwartz, Herman, "Perilous Entropy," *Nation*, 253 (21 Oct. 1991), 469.

8265. Shipler, David K., "Dateline USSR: On the Human Rights Track," *Foreign Policy*, no. 75 (Summer 1989), 164-81.

8266. Shultz, George P., "Human Rights and Soviet-American Relations," *Department of State Bulletin*, 86 (Dec. 1986), 26-29.

8267. "Social Choice: Changes in Social Psychology As Reflected in Social and Political Discussions of 1989," *Soviet Sociology*, 29, no. 3 (May-June 1990), 37-56.

8268. Sokolova, E. S., and V. M. Likhacheva, "The *Perestroika* Generation: What Is It Like?" *Russian Education and Society*, 35 (Oct. 1993), 5-23.

8269. "The Soviet Empire: The Society," *U.S. News & World Report*, 106 (3 Apr. 1989), 34ff.

8270. "Soviet Human Rights under Gorbachev: Old Wine in a New Bottle?" *Denver Journal of International Law and Policy*, 16 (Fall 1987), 177-89.

8271. "Soviet Reforms," *World Press Review*, 34 (Feb. 1987), 18.

8272. Starr, S. Frederick, "Party Animals: Pluralism Comes to the U.S.S.R.," *New Republic* (26 June 1989), 18-21.

8273. -----, "Soviet Union: A Civil Society," *Foreign Policy*, no. 70 (Spring 1988), 26-41.

8274. Sweet, W., "Orlov Provides Perspectives on Gorbachev's Reforms," *Physics Today*, 40 (May 1987), 79-82.

8275. Sweezy, P. M., and H. Magdoff, "Perestroika and the Future of Socialism," *Monthly Review*, 41, no. 10 (Mar. 1990), 1-13; no. 11 (Apr. 1990), 1-17; Discussion: 42, no. 4 (Sept. 1990), 50-53.

8276. Tempest, Richard, "Soviet Youth Today," *World & I* (May 1990), 124-29.

8277. Tolz, Vera, "Informal Groups in the USSR," *Washington Quarterly*, 11, no. 2 (Spring 1988), 137-44.

8278. Ugolnik, Anthony, "Burdened with History," *Commonweal*, 117 (21 Dec. 1990), 751-55.

8279. Vanden Heuvel, Katrina, "Soviet Voices," *Nation* (30 Sept. 1991), 359-61.

8280. Vasin, M., "The Voice of the People: An Interview with V. A. Iadov," *Soviet Sociology*, 29, no. 3 (May-June 1990), 29-36.

8281. Walker, M., "Strains in the Welfare State," *World Press Review*, 34 (6 Oct. 1987), 24-26.

8282. Walters, Vernon A., "Anniversary of the Universal Declaration of Human Rights," *Religion in Communist Dominated Areas*, 27, no. 4 (Fall 1988), 122ff.

8283. White, Ann, "Charity, Self-Help and Politics in Russia, 1985-91," *Soviet Studies*, 45, no. 5 (1993), 787-810.

8284. Willerton, John P., and Lee Sigelman, "Public Opinion Research in the USSR: Opportunities and Pitfalls," *Journal of Communist Studies*, 7, no. 2 (June 1991), 217-34.

8285. Yaroshevski, Dov B., "Political Participation and Public Memory: The Memorial Movement in the USSR, 1987-1989," *History & Memory: Studies in Representation of the Past*, 2, no. 2 (Winter 1990), 5-31.

8286. Zaslavskaia, Tat'iana I., "On Social Structure: The Fundamental Question of Restructuring," *Soviet Sociology*, 28, no. 4 (July-Aug. 1989), 7-15.

8287. -----, "On the Strategy of Social Management," *Soviet Sociology*, 28, no. 4 (July-Aug. 1989), 16-23.

8288. -----, "Socioeconomic Aspects of *Perestroika*," *Soviet Economy*, 3, no. 4 (Oct-Dec. 1987), 313-31.

8289. -----, and Ia. Kapeliush, "Public Opinion about the Results of the Congress," *Soviet Law and Government*, 29, no. 3 (Winter 1990-91), 10-14.

8290. -----, *et al.*, "Friends or Foes? Social Forces Working For and Against *Perestroika*," *Perestroika Annual*, 1 (1988), 255-78.

8291. Zimmermann, W., "The Evolving Soviet Approach to Human Rights," *Department of State Bulletin*, 87 (June 1987), 67-69.

XXXV. Technology and Science; Technology Transfer
BOOKS

8292. Ailes, Catherine P., and Arthur E. Pardee, Jr., *Cooperation in Science and Technology: An Evaluation of the US-Soviet Agreement* (Boulder, CO: Westview, 1986).

8293. Balzer, Harley D., *Soviet Science on the Edge of Reform* (Boulder, CO: Westview Press, 1989).

8294. Barzdins, J., and D. Bjorner, eds., *Baltic Computer Science: Selected Papers* (New York: Springer-Verlag, 1991).

8295. Bengston, J., R. R. Cronin and R. B. Davidson, *Soviet Science as Viewed by Western Scientists* (San Diego: Science Applications International Corp., 1989).

8296. Bertsch, Gary K., ed., *Controlling East-West Trade and*

Technology Transfer: Power, Politics, and Policies (Durham, NC: Duke University Press, 1988).

8297. -----, Heinrich Vogel and Jan Zielonka, eds., *After the Revolutions: East-West Trade and Technology Transfer in the 1990s* (Boulder, CO: Westview Press, 1991).

8298. Donahue, Thomas M., Kathleen Kearney and David M. Abramson, eds., *Planetary Sciences: American and Soviet Research: Proceedings from the US-USSR Workshop on Planetary Sciences, January 2-6, 1989* (Washington, DC: National Academy Press, 1991).

8299. Feiman, Vladimir, Ninel Kogan and Alexander Prutkovsky, *Innovation in the Soviet Chemical Industry: Selected Papers with Analysis* (Falls Church, VA: Delphic Associates, 1987).

8300. Fortescue, Stephen, *The Communist Party and Soviet Science* (Baltimore: Johns Hopkins University Press, 1986).

8301. -----, *Science Policy in the Soviet Union* (New York: Routledge, 1990).

8302. Francis, Arthur, and Peter Grootings, eds., *New Technologies and Work: Capitalist and Socialist Perspectives* (New York: Routledge & Kegan Paul, 1989).

8303. Graham, Loren, *Science and the Soviet Social Order* (Cambridge, MA: Harvard University Press, 1990).

8304. -----, *Science in Russia and the Soviet Union: A Short History* (New York: Cambridge University Press, 1993).

8305. -----, ed., *The Ghost of the Executed Engineer: Technology and the Fall of the Soviet Union* (Cambridge: Harvard University Press, 1993).

8306. Hill, Malcolm R., *Soviet Advanced Manufacturing Technology and Western Export Controls* (Brookfield VT: Gower, 1991).

8307. -----, and Caroline M. Hay, *Trade, Industrial Co-operation and Technology Transfer: Continuity and Change in a New Era of East-West Relations* (Aldershot: Avebury, 1993).

8308. Kassel, Simon, *A New Force in the Soviet Computer Industry: The Reorganization of the USSR Academy of Sciences in the Computer Field* (Santa Monica, CA: RAND, 1986).

8309. -----, *Soviet Advanced Technologies in the Era of Restructuring* (Santa Monica: RAND, 1989).

8310. -----, *Soviet High-Technology Restructuring Drive: The MNTK Network* (Santa Monica, CA: RAND, 1987).

8311. Monkiewicz, Jan, and Jan Maciejewicz, *Technology Export from the Socialist Countries* (Boulder, CO: Westview, 1986).

8312. Negroponte, John D., *U.S.-Soviet Scientific Exchanges* (Washington, DC: US Department of State, Bureau of Public Affairs, 1987).

8313. O'Neill, Robert, ed., *New Technology and Western Security Policy* (Hamden, CT: Archon Books, 1985).

8314. Parrott, Bruce, ed., *Trade, Technology and Soviet-American Relations* (Bloomington: Indiana University Press, 1985).

8315. Popper, Steven W., *Eastern Europe as a Source of High-Technology Imports for Soviet Economic Modernization* (Santa Monica, CA: RAND, 1991).

8316. Rabin, Yakov M., *Science Between the Superpowers* (New York: Priority Press, 1988).

8317. Schweitzer, Glenn E., *Techno-Diplomacy: U.S.-Soviet Confrontations in Science and Technology* (New York: Plenum Press, 1989).

8318. Sinclair, Craig, ed., *The Status of Civil Science in Eastern Europe: Proceedings of the Symposium on Science in Eastern Europe, NATO Headquarters, Brussels, Belgium, September 28-30, 1988* (Boston: Kluwer Academic Publishers, 1989).

8319. Smith, Gordon, *Experimental Reproduction and R&D in the Soviet Union* (Washington, DC: Woodrow Wilson International Center for Scholars, Kennan Institute, 1986).

8320. Smith, Marcia S., *Space Commercialization Activities in the Soviet Union* (Washington, DC: Library of Congress, Congressional Research Service, 1990).

8321. Spring, Baker, *Controls Still Needed on High Technology Exports to the USSR* (Washington, DC: Heritage Foundation, 1990).

8322. Staar, Richard F., ed., *The Future Information Revolution in the U.S.S.R.* (New York: Crane Russak and Co., 1988).

8323. Umpleby, Stuart A., and Vadim N. Sadovsky, eds., *A Science of Goal Formulation: American and Soviet Discussions of Cybernetics and Systems Theory* (New York: Hemisphere, 1991).

8324. US Congress. House. Committee on Foreign Affairs. Subcommittee on Europe and the Middle East. *United States-Soviet Scientific Exchanges. Hearing. 99th Congress, 31 July 1986* (Washington, DC: Government Printing Office, 1986).

8325. US Congress. House. Committee on Science, Space and Technology. *National Academy of Sciences Report on International Technology Transfer: Hearing. 100th Congress* (Washington, DC: Government Printing Office, 1987).

8326. US Congress. House. Committee on Science, Space and Technology. Subcommittee on International Scientific Cooperation. *To Examine U.S.-Soviet Science and Technology Exchanges. Hearing. 100th Congress, 23 and 25 June 1987* (Washington, DC: Government Printing Office, 1987).

8327. US Congress. Joint Economic Committee. Subcommittee on Technology and National Security. *Allocation of Resources in the Soviet Union and China. Part 15, April 20, May 16, June 28, 1990: Hearings. 101st Congress, 2nd Session* (Washington, DC: Government Printing Office, 1991).

8328. US Congress. Senate. Committee on Governmental Affairs. Subcommittee on Energy, Nuclear Proliferation and Government Processes. *First Special Session and Thirtieth Regular Session of the General Conference of the International Atomic Energy Agency: Hearing. 99th Congress, 18 Nov. 1986* (Washington, DC: Government Printing Office, 1987).

8329. Warner, Gale, *The Invisible Threads: Independent Soviets Working for Global Awareness and Social Transformation* (Washington, DC: Seven Locks Press, 1991).

8330. Wellman, David A., *A Chip in the Curtain: Computer Technology in the Soviet Union* (Washington, DC: National Defense University, 1989).

8331. Wolcott, P., and S. E. Goodman, *Soviet High-Speed Computers: The New Generation* (Los Alamitos, CA: IEEE Comput. Soc. Press, 1990).

ARTICLES

8332. Adirim, I., "Current Development and Dissemination of Computer Technology in the Soviet Economy," *Soviet Studies*, 43, no. 4 (1991), 651-668.

8333. Agamirzian, Igor, "Computing in the U.S.S.R.," *Byte*, 16, no. 4 (1991), 120-29.

8334. Alam, Shahid, "Russia and Western Technology Control," *International Relations*, 11, no. 5 (Aug. 1993), 469ff.

8335. Alexander, C. P., "Playing Computer Catch-Up," *Time*, 125 (15 Apr. 1985), 84-85.

8336. Anderson, G. Christopher, "Gorbachev Leads Silicon Summit," *Nature*, 345, no. 6274 (31 May 1990), 377.

8337. "Assessing Soviet Technology," *World Press Review*, 33 (Aug. 1986), 31-33.

8338. Bahr, F. M., "Perspectives on East-West Relations in Economics and Information," *Information and Software Technology*, 32, no. 5 (June 1990), 330-36.

8339. Beam, A., "Russia Gropes for a Way to Enter the High-Tech Age," *Business Week* (11 Nov. 1985), 98ff.

8340. Beil, L., "USSR Official Attacks Soviet Science," *Science News*, 134 (23 July 1988), 53.

8341. Berry, M. J., "Perestroika and the Changing Nature of East-West Scientific Contacts," *Technology in Society*, 13, no. 1-2 (1991), 151-78.

8342. Birkenes, Robert M., "Telecommunications in the Soviet Union: The Role of Joint Ventures," *Report on the USSR*, 2, no. 32 (10 Aug. 1990), 5-8.

8343. "A Bold Agenda for Soviet Astrophysics," *Sky and Telescope*, 74 (Dec. 1987), 601.

8344. Brady, Rose, "Help Wanted, and Fast," *Business Week* (Special Issue) (15 June 1990), 128ff.

8345. Brooks, Harvey, "The Strategic Defense Initiative as Science Policy," *International Security*, 11, no. 2 (Fall 1986), 177-84.

8346. Brown, Harold, "Is SDI Technically Feasible?" *Foreign Affairs*, 64, no. 3 (Winter 986), 435-54.

8347. Brown, Peter G., "Initial Conditions," *Sciences*, 31, no. 6 (Nov-Dec. 1991), 2.

8348. Brucan, S., "The Strategic Imperative of Reform," *New Perspectives Quarterly*, 15 (Winter 1988-89), 18-23.

8349. Buchan, D., "Seeking Western Knowledge," *Word Press Review*, 33 (Apr. 1986), 46.

8350. Burke, Justin, "Exodus of Researchers Stirs Fears Over Fate of Science in the Former Soviet Union," *Chronicle of Higher Education*, 38, no. 26 (4 Mar. 1992), A41-42.

8351. Canby, Thomas Y., "Are the Soviets Ahead in Space?" *National Geographic*, 170, no. 4 (Oct. 1986), 420-59.

8352. "Can Soviet Science Be Rescued?" *Nature*, 354, no. 6352 (5 Dec. 1991), 339-40.

8353. Cave, Jane, "Political Reform and Scientific Freedom under Gorbachev," *Technology in Society*, 13, no. 1-2 (1991), 69-90.

8354. Chu, Julian J., "Building the Future on the Past: The Expansion of Soviet Space," *Harvard International Review*, 13, no. 1 (Fall 1990), 55-58.

8355. Cleverley, J. Michael, "The Problem of Technology Transfer Controls," *Global Affairs*, 4, no. 3 (Summer 1989), 109-28.

8356. Cooper, Julian M., "Technology in the Soviet Union," *Current History*, 85, no. 513 (Oct. 1986), 317ff.

8357. Covault, Craig, "NASA, Soviets Discuss Joint Environmental Missions," *Aviation Week & Space Technology*, 135, no. 14 (7 Oct. 1991), 68-69.

8358. -----, "Soviet Aerospace Shakeup Has Strategic Impact," *Aviation Week & Space Technology*, 135, no. 13 (30 Sept. 1991), 20.

8359. -----, "Soviet Collapse Damaging Space Program Infrastructure," *Aviation Week & Space Technology*, 135, no. 24-25 (16-23 Dec. 1991), 18-19.

8360. -----, "U.S.-Soviet Pact Backs New Joint Manned Space Flights," *Aviation Week & Space Technology*, 135, no. 5 (5 Aug. 1991), 18-19.

8361. Crawford, M., "Soviets Buy Robots," *Science*, 232 (13 June 1986), 1332.

8362. -----, "Soviets Pin Economic Hopes on Technology," *Science*, 238 (18 Dec. 1987), 1644.

8363. Crowe, Gregory D., "Science and Technology with a Human Face: Russian-American Perspectives," *Slavic Review*, 52, no. 2 (Summer 1993), 319-32.

8364. Dahl, Henry, "U.S. Restrictions on High Technology Transfer: Impact Abroad and Domestic Consequences," *Columbia Journal of Transnational Law*, 26, no. 1 (Spring 1987), 27-52.

8365. Daniloff, Nicholas, "Why Soviets Are Behind in Computer Technology," *U.S. News and World Report* (13 Aug. 1984), 37-38.

8366. David, Leonard, "Introduction: Special Issue: Science and Technology Policy During *Perestroika*," *Technology in Society*,

13, no. 1-2 (1991), 7-10.

8367. -----, "Murky Future for Mir 2," *Ad Astra*, 3 (Sept. 1991), 31.

8368. -----, "Used Space Program for Sale?" *Ad Astra*, 3 (Nov. 1991), 6-7.

8369. -----, and Paul Dufour, "The New Geopolitics of Science and Technology," *Technology in Science*, 13, no. 1-2 (1991), 179-88.

8370. Dickman, Steven, "A Lifetime of Struggle to Do Good Science," *Science*, 258 (2 Oct. 1992), 25.

8371. -----, "Soviet Science: A Struggle for Survival," *Science*, 254, no. 5039 (20 Dec. 1991), 1716-19.

8372. Dickson, David, "Glasnost: Soviet Computer Lag," *Science*, 241 (1988), 1034.

8373. -----, "Soviet Academy Attacked for Being Undemocratic," *Science*, 243 (10 Feb. 1989), 728-29.

8374. -----, "Soviet Science to Be Self-Directed," *Science*, 237 (31 July 1987), 482.

8375. -----, "USSR to Set Up Fund for Basic Research," *Science*, 242 (7 Oct. 1988), 33-35.

8376. Dizard, Wilson, "Mikhail Gorbachev's Computer Challenge," *Washington Quarterly*, 9, no. 2 (Spring 1986), 157-66.

8377. Dobozi, I., "Impact of Market Reforms on USSR Energy Consumption: Scenarios for the Next Decade," *Energy Policy*, 19, no. 4 (May 1991), 303-24.

8378. Eberhart, J., "U.S.-Soviet Space Pact Signed," *Science News*, 131 (25 Apr. 1987), 260.

8379. Eenmaa, I. V., "Networking Potentialities and Limitations: The Main Ways of Perestroika in the Work of Scientific and Technical Libraries at the Present Stage," *INSPEL: International Journal of Special Libraries*, 23, no. 3 (1989), 176-79.

8380. Efimov, V. A., "Aims for Accelerating Scientific and Technical Progress in Improving Quality of Steel Ingots and Billets," *Steel in the USSR*, 18, no. 4 (Apr. 1988), 145-47.

8381. Evangelista, Matthew, "How Technology Fuels the Arms Race," *Technology Review*, 91, no. 6 (July 1988), 42-49.

8382. Fedorowycz, Ihor, "Preventing the Transfer of Militarily Critical Technology to the Soviet Bloc: The Case for Strong National Security Export Controls," *Columbia Journal of Transnational Law*, 26, no. 1 (Spring 1987), 53-102.

8383. "Finland-USSR to Revive Mining on Kola Peninsula," *Engineering and Mining Journal*, 188, no. 1 (Jan. 1987), 14-15.

8384. Florini, Ann M., and William C. Potter, "Boon for Soviet Space Business," *Bulletin of the Atomic Scientists*, 46, no. 9 (Nov. 1990), 31.

8385. Frankel, Sherman, "Moscow Meeting: The *Glasnost* Menagerie," *Bulletin of the Atomic Scientists*, 43, no. 4 (May 1987), 8-12.

8386. Frenkel, W. G., "From Borscht to Bits: Transfer of Technology and Industrial Property to the Soviet Union," *DePaul Business Law Journal*, 4 (Fall-Winter 1991), 3-48.

8387. Galuszka, Peter, "Soviet Technology: The Soviet Union Missed Out on the Revolutions in Computers and Biotechnology; with Gorbachev Determined to Catch Up, How Much Should the West Help Out?" *Business Week* (7 Nov. 1988), 68ff.

8388. Gannes, S., "The Soviet Lag in High-Tech Defense," *Fortune*, 112 (25 Nov. 1985), 107ff.

8389. Gavaghan, Helen, "US Looks Forward to Soviet Space Sale," *New Scientist*, 31, no. 1787 (21 Sept. 1991), 17.

8390. Geipel, Gary L., "The Failure and Future of Information Technology Policies in Eastern Europe," *Technology in Society*, 13, no. 1-2 (1991), 207-28.

8391. -----, Tomasz A. Jarmoszko and Seymour E. Goodman, "The Information Technologies and East European Societies," *East European Politics and Societies*, 5, no. 3 (Fall 1991), 394-438.

8392. Gingras, Bernard A., "Experience with Canadian/Soviet Scientific Cooperation," in Craig Sinclair, ed., *The Status of Soviet Civil Science: Proceedings of the Symposium on Soviet Scientific Research, NATO Headquarters, Brussels, Belgium, September 24-26, 1986* (Dordrecht: Nijhoff, 1987), 279-83.

8393. Gollon, Peter J., "SDI Funds Costly for Scientists," *Bulletin of the Atomic Scientists*, 42, no. 1 (Jan. 1986), 24-27.

8394. Goodman, Elliot R., "Gorbachev Takes Charge: Prospects for Soviet Society," *Atlantic Community Quarterly*, 24, no. 4 (Winter 1986), 356-73.

8395. Goodman, Seymour E., and W. K. McHenry, "Computing in the USSR: Recent Progress and Policies," *Soviet Economy*, 2, no. 4 (Oct-Dec. 1986), 327-54.

8396. -----, "The Soviet Computer Industry: A Tale of Two Sectors," *Communications of the ACM*, 34, no. 6 (June 1991), 25-29.

8397. Goodman, Seymour E., *et al.*, "Export Control Reconsidered," *Issues in Science and Technology*, 6, no. 2 (Winter 1989), 58-62.

8398. Goodwin, I., "At New Kind of Summit, Gorbachev Seeks Greater R&D Collaborations," *Physics Today*, 43 (Oct. 1990), 57-59.

8399. -----, "'Political' Scientists: Gorbachev Picks Ossipyan for Presidential Council," *Physics Today*, 43 (May 1990), 67-68.

8400. Graham, Loren R., "Science and Technology," *Nation*, 244 (13 June 1987), 804-08.

8401. -----, "Science and Technology with a Human Face: A Goal of US-USSR Cooperation," *Technology in Society*, 13, no. 1-2 (1991), 11-22.

8402. Greeley, B. M., "Soviets Target U.S. Companies, Universities for New Technologies," *Aviation Week & Space Technology*,

123 (30 Sept. 1985), 86ff.

8403. Greenfield, Meg, "Gorbachev vs. the Computer Age," *Newsweek*, 106 (4 Nov. 1985), 84.

8404. Hanson, Philip, "Soviet Industrial Espionage," *Bulletin of the Atomic Scientists*, 43 (Apr. 1987), 25-29.

8405. Holden, Constance, "Soviets Launch Computer Literacy Drive," *Science*, 231 (1988), 109-110.

8406. Holloway, David, "Soviet Scientists Speak Out," *Bulletin of the Atomic Scientists*, 49, no. 4 (May 1993), 18-19.

8407. Hughes, Thomas P., "U.S. Support for Soviet Technology: A Lesson from History," *Current*, 315 (Sept. 1989), 18-26.

8408. Inman, Bobby Ray, "Balancing Competing Interests in Technology Transfer," *Columbia Journal of Transnational Law*, 26, no. 1 (Spring 1987), 3-8.

8409. "A Joint Soviet-American Research Park?" *Futurist*, 19 (Oct. 1985), 59.

8410. Josephson, Paul R., "The Crisis in Russian Physics," *American Scientist*, 81, no. 6 (Nov-Dec. 1993), 571-79.

8411. -----, "Scientists, the Public and the Party under Gorbachev," *Harriman Institute Forum*, 3, no. 5 (May 1990), 1-8.

8412. -----, "Soviet Scientists and the State: Politics, Ideology, and Fundamental Research from Stalin to Gorbachev," *Social Research*, 59, no. 3 (Fall 1992), 589-614.

8413. Juvonen, E., "Russia: A Future Great APL Power?" *APL Quote Quad*, 22, no. 2 (Dec. 1991), 1-2.

8414. Kanin, Yuri, "Russia Takes Over Academy" [of Sciences], *Nature*, 353, no. 6346 (24 Oct. 1991), 690.

8415. Kapitza, Sergei P., "The State of Soviet Science," *Scientific American*, 264, no. 6 (June 1991), 132.

8416. Kapstein, J., and C. Gaffney, "A Suspect in the High-Tech Leaks to Russia," *Business Week* (1 Apr. 1985), 48.

8417. Karpukhin, D., and L. Rzhanitsyna, "Wages in Science," *Problems of Economics*, 33, no. 12 (Apr. 1991), 77-83.

8418. Kiely, T., "Soviet Science for Sale," *Technology Review*, 93, no. 7 (Oct. 1990), 16ff.

8419. Kiser, John W., "Reverse Technology Flows," *Washington Quarterly*, 8, no. 1 (Winter 1985), 77-84.

8420. Kneen, Peter, "Soviet Science Policy under Gorbachev," *Soviet Studies*, 41, no. 1 (Jan. 1989), 67-87.

8421. Knorre, Helene, "In the Wake of the Coup," *Nature*, 353, no. 6343 (3 Oct. 1991), 374.

8422. Koenig, M. E. D., "Information Technology and Perestroika," *Information Services and Use*, 10, no. 5 (1990), 315-20.

8423. Kozlov, Leonard A., and Boris M. Shtoulberg, "Regional Science in the Former Soviet Union: History and New Directions," *International Regional Science Review*, 15, no. 3 (1993), 229-34.

8424. Krasnov, Mikhail, "Glasnost in Scientific Cooperation," *International Affairs* (Moscow), 7 (July 1988), 99-106.

8425. Kristiansen, M., *et al.*, "On the Road to Tomsk," *Physics Today*, 43 (June 1990), 36-42.

8426. Ksanfomality, Leonid V., "Survival before Science," *Bulletin of the Atomic Scientists*, 47, no. 10 (Dec. 1991), 20-24.

8427. Lakoff, Sanford, "Science Policy after the Cold War: Problems and Opportunities," *Technology in Society*, 13, no. 1-2 (1991), 23-38.

8428. Lane, Alex, "An American Programmer in Moscow," *Byte*, 16, no. 4 (1991), 123.

8429. Lapin, N. I., "Alienation, Early Socialism, Perestroika and Liberty," *Cybernetics and Systems*, 22, no. 4 (July-Aug. 1991), 481-97.

8430. Lathrop, D. L., "Perestroika and Its Implications for Computer Security in the USSR," *Computers and Security*, 9, no. 8 (Dec. 1990), 693-96.

8431. Lavoie, Louis, "The Limits of Soviet Technology," *Technology Review*, 88, no. 8 (Nov-Dec. 1985), 68-75.

8432. Lawson, Michael, and Hazel Bradford, "Immigration: Soviet Engineers Want In," *ENR: Engineering News Record*, 222, no. 10 (9 Mar. 1989), 19-20.

8433. Lenerovitz, Jeffrey M., "Engineers Use New Soviet Freedoms to Establish Private Companies," *Aviation Week & Space Technology*, 133, no. 15 (8 Oct. 1990), 43.

8434. -----, "Soviet Space Program Policy in Flux After Social and Economic Upheaval," *Aviation Week & Space Technology*, 133, no. 18 (29 Oct. 1990), 68ff.

8435. -----, "Soviet Space Program Reflects New Policies Initiated by Gorbachev," *Aviation Week & Space Technology* (18-25 Dec. 1989), 52ff.

8436. -----, "Soviets Look to West for New Technical, Commercial Alliances," *Aviation Week & Space Technology*, 133, no. 22 (26 Nov. 1990), 76.

8437. Levin, Alexei E., "New Draft Legislation on Science Policy in the USSR," *Report on the USSR*, 3, no. 22 (31 May 1991), 6-9.

8438. -----, "Organizational Changes in Soviet Science and Learning," *Report on the USSR*, 2, no. 49 (7 Dec. 1990), 3-5.

8439. -----, "Soviet Science Policy in the *Perestroika* Period: An Overview," *Report on the USSR* (26 May 1989).

8440. -----, "Soviet Science: Towards a Civil Society," *Report on the USSR*, 2, no. 44 (2 Nov. 1990), 14-19.

8441. Litvinov, A. V., "Legal Issues in the Protection of Computer Information," *Soviet Law and Government*, 27, no. 1 (Summer 1988), 86-96.

8442. Lubrano, Linda L., "National and International Politics in US-USSR Cooperation," *Social Studies of Science*, 11 (1987),

451-80.

8443. -----, "New Initiatives and Old Bureaucrats: The Future Challenges and the Past in Academic Science," *Technology in Society*, 13, no. 1-2 (1991), 91-108.

8444. Luke, Timothy J., "Technology and Soviet Foreign Trade: On the Political Economy of an Underdeveloped Superpower," *International Studies Quarterly*, 29 (Sept. 1985), 327-53.

8445. L'vov, D., "Scientific-Technical Progress and the Economics of the Transition Period," *Problems of Economic Transition*, 35, no. 2 (June 1992), 46-60.

8446. Madsen, W., "Computer Security, Perestroika Style: An Overview of Problems in the Eastern Bloc," *Computer Fraud & Security Bulletin* (Oct. 1990), 6-9.

8447. Marshak, Robert E., "Time for Sakharov's Global Dialogue," *Bulletin of the Atomic Scientists*, 43, no. 8 (Oct. 1987), 7-8.

8448. McDonald, K., "Soviet Science Leaders Speak with Unusual Candor About Research Progress," *Chronicle of Higher Education*, 34 (24 Feb. 1988), p. A1.

8449. Medvedev, Zhores, "The Death of Big Science in Russia," *Dissent*, 40, no. 4 (Fall 1993), 423-26.

8450. "Meetings in Minsk," *Engineering*, 229, no. 11 (Dec. 1989), 52.

8451. Monastersky, R., "Soviets to Allow Monitoring in USSR," *Science News*, 132, no. 1 (4 July 1987), 6.

8452. -----, "Soviets Visit U.S. for Mock Nuclear Blast," *Science News*, 133, no. 16 (16 Apr. 1988), 245.

8453. Nau, Henry R., "International Technology Transfer," *Washington Quarterly*, 8, no. 1 (Winter 1985), 57-64.

8454. Nikitin, S., "The Economic Mechanism of Scientific-Technical Progress under Market Conditions," *Problems of Economic Transition*, 35, no. 2 (June 1992), 61-76.

8455. Nikonov, Aleksandr A., "'The Responsibility of Science and for Science'," *Soviet Review*, 28, no. 2 (Mar-Apr. 1989), 39-53.

8456. Oberg, James E., "The Postcoup Blues: The Future of the Soviet Space Program Looks More Uncertain Than Ever," *Omni*, 14 (Nov. 1991), 22.

8457. -----, "PSST! Wanna Buy a Spaceship? Desperate for Cash, the Soviets Are Hocking Their Spare Spacecraft," *Omni*, 14 (Jan. 1992), 12.

8458. O'Keefe, Bernard J., "The SDI and American R&D," *International Security*, 11, no. 2 (Fall 1986), 190-92.

8459. Palca, J., "Soviet Reforms: Promises, Promises," *Science*, 247 (2 Mar. 1990), 1025.

8460. "Panel on Growth and Technology in Perestroika," *Soviet Economy*, 3, no. 4 (Oct-Dec. 1987), 332-52.

8461. Parnas, David L., "Why Star Wars Software Won't Work,"

Harper's, 272, no. 1630 (Mar. 1986), 17-18.

8462. Parsons, J. E., "The Future of East-West Industrial Cooperation," *Technology Review*, 91, no. 8 (Nov-Dec. 1988), 56-63.

8463. Penksa, Robert C., "Some Systemic Impediments to Technological Invention, Innovation and Diffusion in the Soviet Economy," *Comparative Strategy*, 9, no. 4 (Oct-Dec. 1990), 335-49.

8464. "*Perestroika*'s Changes Grip Soviet Aerospace Industry," *Aviation Week & Space Technology* (5 June 1989), 34-98.

8465. Pilon, Juliana Geran, "U.S.-Soviet Scientific Exchanges: A Case for Caution," *World & I* (Mar. 1990), 134-40.

8466. Prins, C., "Computer Technology and Perestroika: Why Not to Do Business with the Soviet Union?" *Computer Law and Practice*, 6, no. 1 (1989), 12-19.

8467. Prousis, T. C., "Research in the Soviet Union under *Glasnost*," *American Scholar*, 59 (Spring 1990), 265-71.

8468. Pytte, Alyson, "Revisiting Ban on High-Tech Trade," *Congressional Quarterly Weekly Report*, 47 (25 Feb. 1989), 402.

8469. Rabkin, Yakov M., "Scientific and Political Freedoms," *Technology in Society*, 13, no. 1-2 (1991), 53-68.

8470. "Raise the Level of Scientific Criticism," *Soviet Law and Government*, 27, no. 1 (Summer 1988), 71-85.

8471. Rassokhin, V. P., "Centralization and Freedom of Creativity in Science and Technology," *Soviet Law and Government*, 27, no. 1 (Summer 1988), 55-70.

8472. Revkin, Andrew C., "Supercomputers and the Soviets," *Technology Review*, 89, no. 6 (Aug-Sept. 1986), 68-74.

8473. Rich, Vera, "Industry Must Fund Science Vital for Soviet Recovery," *New Scientist*, 131, no. 1781 (10 Aug. 1991), 14.

8474. -----, "Soviet Republics Call for Common Science Forum," *New Scientist*, 131, no. 1788 (28 Sept. 1991), 17.

8475. -----, "Vandals Run Riot in Russia's Science Cities," *New Scientist*, 132, no. 1796 (23 Nov. 1991), 17.

8476. Roberg, Jeffrey L., and Roger E. Kanet, "The Scientific-Technological Revolution: Soviet Views, Yesterday and Today," *Soviet Union/Union Sovietique*, 17, no. 1-2 (1990), 95-112.

8477. Robinson, A. L., "*Glasnost* Comes to Soviet Physics," *Science*, 236 (8 May 1987), 671-72.

8478. Roederer, Juan G., "Let a Thousand Sakharovs Bloom," *Bulletin of the Atomic Scientists*, 47, no. 6 (July-Aug. 1991), 18-21.

8479. Ruan, Robert, "Engineering Services Mission Gets Warm Welcome," *Business America*, 112, no. 3 (11 Feb. 1991), 24.

8480. Sagdeev, Roald Z., "Russian Scientists Save American Secrets," *Bulletin of the Atomic Scientists*, 49, no. 4 (May 1993), 32-36.

8481. -----, "Science and Perestroika: A Long Way to Go," *Issues in Science and Technology*, 4, no 4 (Summer 1988), 48-52.

8482. Schaefer, Elizabeth, "Old Secrets on the Market," *Nature*, 349, no. 6306 (17 Jan. 1991), 186.

8483. Schweitzer, Glenn E., "The Future of Scientific Research in Eastern Europe," *Technology in Society*, 13, no. 1-2 (1991), 39-52.

8484. -----, "US-Soviet Scientific Cooperation: The Interacademy Program," *Technology in Society*, 14, no. 2 (1992), 173-86.

8485. "Selling Russian Science: Laser-for-Burger Swaps," *Economist*, 314 (3 Mar. 1990), 78ff.

8486. Seltzer, Richard, "NSF to Aid Scientists in Former Soviet Union," *Chemical and Engineering News*, 70, no. 14 (6 Apr. 1992), 5.

8487. Sharp, Margaret, "Technology-A Case for Catch-Up," *Technology in Society*, 13, no. 1-2 (1991), 189-206.

8488. Smith, R. J., "Summit Ends with Exchange Agreements," *Science*, 230 (6 Dec. 1985), 1142-43.

8489. -----, "U.S. Tops Soviets in Key Weapons Technology," *Science*, 231 (7 Mar. 1986), 1063-64.

8490. Snell, Paul, "Inquest on Soviet Computing," *New Scientist*, 128, no. 1746 (1990), 46-49.

8491. "Soviet Space Program Threatened by Budget Policy Changes," *Aviation Week & Space Technology*, 134, no. 11 (18 Mar. 1991), 153-54.

8492. "Soviets Pursue Computer Literacy," *USA Today*, 117 (June 1989), 14.

8493. Staar, Richard F., "The High-Tech Transfer Offensive of the Soviet Union," *Strategic Review*, 17, no. 2 (Spring 1989), 32-39.

8494. "State Department Denies License to Export Satellites to the Soviet Union," *Aviation Week & Space Technology* (27 July 1987), 59.

8495. Sternberg, Kristen, "Computing in the Other Europe," *Compute*, 13, no. 5 (May 1991), 30-32.

8496. Stokes, Bruce, "Monitoring U.S. Exports: Why Bother?" *National Journal*, 23, no. 41 (12 Oct. 1991), 2487-88.

8497. Stubbs, Eric, "Soviet Strategic Defense Technology," *Bulletin of the Atomic Scientists*, 43, no. 3 (Apr. 1987), 14-19.

8498. Sweet, W., "Minnesota Lures Top Theorists from Leading Soviet Institutes," *Physics Today*, 44 (Feb. 1991), 83-84.

8499. Symington, J. W., "Peace through Science?" *Atlantic Community Quarterly*, 23, no. 4 (Fall 1985), 285-95.

8500. Taubes, G., and G. Garelik, "Soviet Science: How Good Is It?" *Discover*, 7 (Aug. 1986), 36ff.

8501. "The Technology of Strategic Defense: Where We Stand and How Far We Can Go: An Interview with Professor Hans Bethe," *Fletcher Forum*, 10, no. 1 (Winter 1986), 8-17.

8502. "Technology to Russia: You Know This Could Be Lethal," *Economist*, 297 (19 Oct. 1985), 49-50.

8503. Tolz, Vera, "'Brain Drain'-The Main Problem of Soviet Science?" *Report on the USSR*, 3, no. 26 (28 June 1991), 21-25.

8504. -----, "Controversy Over the Russian Academy of Sciences Continues," *Report on the USSR*, 3, no. 3 (18 Jan. 1991), 17-20.

8505. "Trends: Soviet Science for Sale," *Technology Review*, 93, no. 7 (Oct. 1990), 16.

8506. Vershik, A. M., "To Guard the Future of Soviet Mathematics," *Mathematical Intelligencer*, 14, no. 1 (Winter 1992), 12-15.

8507. Waldrop, M. M., "A New U.S.-Soviet Manned Space Mission?" *Science*, 227 (25 Jan. 1985), 394-95.

8508. -----, "Soviet Space Science Opens to the West," *Science*, 236 (12 June 1987), 1427-31.

8509. "We Should Elevate Computerization to Superproject Status," *Business Week* (11 Nov. 1985), 102.

8510. "White House Assesses Reports of Soviet ASAT Laser Facilities," *Aviation Week & Space Technology*, 125 (15 Sept. 1986), 21.

8511. Wieczynski, Joseph L., "Lenin Library to Automate with Virginia Tech Software," *AAASS Newsletter*, 30, no. 1 (Jan. 1990), 24.

8512. Winner, Langdon, "The Culture of Technology," *Technology Review*, 93, no. 2 (Feb-Mar. 1990), 70.

8513. -----, "*Glasnost* and Engineering," *Technology Review*, 93, no. 2 (Feb-Mar. 1990), 70.

8514. Wright, Richard, "Down the Drain," *New Republic* (28 Oct. 1991), 23.

8515. -----. "The Experiment That Failed," *New Republic* (28 Oct. 1991), 20-25.

8516. Zafran, R., and E. Etkina, "Astronomy in Moscow High Schools: Restructuring for Better Learning," *Physics Education*, 27, no. 6 (Nov. 1992), 306-09.

XXXVI. Women's Issues and Women's Studies

BOOKS

8517. Atwood, Lynne, *The New Soviet Man and Woman: Sex Role Socialization in the USSR* (Bloomington: Indiana University Press, 1991).

8518. -----, ed., *Red Women on the Silver Screen: Soviet Women and Cinema from the Beginning to the End of the Communist Era* (London: Pandora Press, 1993).

8519. Browning, G. K., *Women and Politics in the USSR* (Sussex: Wheatsheaf Books, 1987).

8520. Buckley, Mary, ed., *Perestroika and Soviet Women* (New York: Cambridge University Press, 1992).

8521. ------, *Women and Ideology in the Soviet Union* (Ann Arbor: University of Michigan Press, 1989).

8522. Clements, Barbara, Barbara Engle and Christine Worobec, eds., *Russia's Women: Accommodation, Resistance, Transformation* (Berkeley: University of California Press, 1991).

8523. Corrin, Chris, ed., *Superwomen and the Double Burden: Women's Experience of Change in Central and Eastern Europe and the Former Soviet Union* (Toronto: Second Story Press, 1992).

8524. Edmondson, Linda, *Women and Society in Russia and the Soviet Union* (New York: Cambridge University Press, 1992).

8525. Einhorn, Barbara, *Cinderella Goes to Market: Gender and the Women's Movement in East Central Europe* (London: Verso, 1993).

8526. Funk, Nanette, and Magda Mueller, eds., *Gender Politics and Post-Communism: Reflections from Eastern Europe and the Former Soviet Union* (New York: Routledge, 1993).

8527. Goscilo, Helena, ed., *Balancing Acts: Contemporary Stories by Russian Women* (Bloomington: Indiana University Press, 1989).

8528. ------, *Fruits of Her Plume: Essays on Contemporary Russian Women's Culture* (Armonk, NY: M. E. Sharpe, 1993).

8529. ------, ed., *Russian and Polish Women's Fiction* (Knoxville: University of Tennessee Press, 1985).

8530. Gray, Francine du Plessix, *Soviet Women: Walking the Tightrope* (New York: Anchor Books, 1990).

8531. Heitlinger, Alena, *Reproduction, Medicine, and the Socialist State* (London: Macmillan, 1986).

8532. Holland, Barbara, *Soviet Sisterhood* (Bloomington: Indiana University Press, 1985).

8533. Hyer, Janet, *Women in Russia and the Soviet Union: A Bibliography* (Ottawa: Carleton University, 1988).

8534. Iggers, Wilma, *Women of Prague: Four Worlds in One City* (Oxford: Berg, 1993).

8535. Jaworski, Rudolf, ed., *Women in Polish Society* (New York: Columbia University Press, 1992).

8536. Ledkovsky, Marina, comp., *Russia According to Women: Literary Anthology* (Tenafly, NJ: Ermitazh, 1991).

8537. ------, Charlotte Rosenthal and Mary Zirin, eds., *Dictionary of Russian Women Writers* (Westport, CT: Greenwood Press, 1994).

8538. Mamonova, Tatiana, *Russian Women's Studies: Essays on Sexism in Soviet Culture* (New York: Pergamon Press, 1989).

8539. ------, with Chandra Niles Folsom, *Women's Glasnost vs. Naglost: Stopping Russian Backlash* (New York: Praeger, 1993).

8540. McLaughlin, Sigrid, ed. and trans., *The Image of Women in Contemporary Soviet Fiction: Selected Stories from the USSR* (New York: St. Martin's Press, 1989).

8541. Millinship, William, *Front Line: Women of the New Russia* (London: Methuen, 1993).

8542. Moghadam, Valentine M., *Gender and Restructuring: Perestroika, the 1989 Revolutions, and Women* (Helsinki: World Institute for Development Economics Institute; Wider Publications, 1990).

8543. Nelson, Barbara, and Najma Chowdhury, eds., *Women and Politics Worldwide* (New Haven: Yale University Press, 1992).

8544. Nemec Ignashev, Diane, and Sarah Krive, *Women and Writing in Russia and the USSR: A Bibliography of English-Language Sources* (New York: Garland, 1992).

8545. Phillips, Anne, *Feminism and Equality* (Amherst: University of Massachusetts, 1987).

8546. Rai, Shirin, Annie Phizacklea and Hilary Pilkington, *Women in the Face of Change: Soviet Union, Eastern Europe and China* (New York: Routledge, 1992).

8547. Rueschemeyer, Marilyn, ed., *Women in the Politics of Post-Communist Eastern Europe* (Armonk, NY: M. E. Sharpe, 1993).

8548. Ruthchild, Rochelle Ginsburg, *Women in Russia and the Soviet Union: An Annotated Bibliography* (New York: G. K. Hall & Co., 1994).

8549. Wolchik, Sharon L., and Alfred G. Meyer, eds., *Women, State, and Party in Eastern Europe* (Durham, NC: Duke University Press, 1985).

8550. Zirin, Mary F., comp., *Women, Gender and Family in the Soviet Successor States and Central/East Europe: Bibliography* (Altadena, CA: Association for Women in Slavic Studies, 1994).

ARTICLES

8551. Adamik, Maria, "Hungary: A Loss of Rights?" *Feminist Review*, 39 (Winter 1991), 166-70.

8552. Ananieva, Nora, and Evka Razvigorova, "Women in State Administration in the People's Republic of Bulgaria," *Women & Politics*, 11, no. 4 (1991), 31-40.

8553. Ashwin, Sarah, "Development of Feminism in the *Perestroika* Era," *Report on the USSR*, 3, no. 35 (30 Aug. 1991), 21-25.

8554. Azhgikhina, Nadezhda, Galya Sharol and Rochelle Ruthchild, "Believing the Impossible," *Women's Review of Books*, 10, no. 10-11 (July 1993), 4-5.

8555. Bazyler, M. J., "The Rights of Women in the Soviet Union," *Whittier Law Review*, 9 (1987), 423-30.

8556. "Bibliographies: Central-Eastern Europe and the Soviet Union," *Journal of Women's History*, 3, no. 1 (Spring 1991), 166-75.

8557. Boldyreva, Tat'iana, "You Won't Stop the Revolutionary Horse in His Tracks," *Soviet Sociology*, 28, no. 5 (Sept-Oct. 1989), 102-18.

8558. Bridger, Susan, "Rural Women and *Glasnost*," in *Bradford Occasional Papers: Essays in Language, Literature and Area Studies*, 9 (1988), 103-16.

8559. -----, "Women and the Farming Campaigns of Perestroika," in Marianne Liljestrom et al., eds., *Gender Restructuring in Russian Studies: Conference Papers, Helsinki, August 1992* (Tampere: University of Tampere, 1993), 29-38.

8560. Butler, W. E., "USSR: Divorce in Soviet Courts," *Journal of Family Law*, 27 (1988-89), 315-20.

8561. Carnaghan, Ellen, and Donna Bahry, "Political Attitudes and the Gender Gap in the USSR," *Comparative Politics*, 22, no. 4 (July 1990), 379-400.

8562. Clayton, Elizabeth, and James R. Millar, "Education, Job Experience and the Gap Between Male and Female Wages in the Soviet Union," *Comparative Economic Studies*, 33, no. 1 (Spring 1991), 5-22.

8563. Denich, Better, "Paradoxes of Gender and Policy in Eastern Europe: A Discussant's Comment," *East European Quarterly*, 23, no. 4 (1990), 499-507.

8564. DeSilva, Lalith, "Women's Emancipation under Communism: A Re-evaluation," *East European Quarterly*, 27, no. 3 (Fall 1993), 301-15.

8565. Drakulich, S., "Wanted: A Nude *Glasnost*," *Nation*, 244 (20 June 1987), 846-48.

8566. Engel, Barbara Alpern, "An Interview with Olga Lipovskaia," *Frontiers*, 10, no. 3 (1989), 6-11.

8567. -----, "Women in Russia and the Soviet Union" (Review Article), *Signs: Journal of Women in Culture and Society*, 12, no. 4 (Summer 1987), 781-96.

8568. Fein, E. B., "Moscow Yuppies? Nyet Quite," *Mademoiselle*, 95 (Oct. 1989), 222ff.

8569. Feminist Network of Hungary, "Declaration of Intent," *Feminist Review*, 39 (Winter 1991), 171-73.

8570. Ferree, Myra Marx, "Between Two Worlds: German Feminist Approaches to Working-Class Women and Work," in Joyce McCarl Nielson, ed., *Feminist Research Methods: Exemplary Readings in Social Sciences* (Boulder, CO: Westview Press, 1990), 174-93.

8571. "Francine Gray, Who Interviewed Soviet Women from Siberia to Georgia, Tells Susan Jacoby of the Anger, Ironies, and Paradoxes in Their Voices," *Vogue*, 180, no. 3 (Mar. 1990), 319-21.

8572. Freeman, P., "After the Coronation, Moscow's First Beauty Queen Finds That Envy Takes the Glamour Out of *Glasnost*," *People Weekly*, 30 (12 Sept. 1988), 120-21.

8573. Galey, Margaret E., "International Enforcement of Women's Rights," *Human Rights Quarterly*, 6, no. 4 (Nov. 1985), 463-90.

8574. "Gender Contradictions/Gender Transformations: Cases from Eastern Europe" (Special Issue), *East European Quarterly*, 23, no. 4 (Winter 1989), 385-522.

8575. Goscilo, Helena, "Coming a Long Way, Baby: A Quarter-Century of Russian Women's Fiction," *Harriman Institute Forum*, 6, no. 1 (Sept. 1992).

8576. Gray, Francine du Plessix, "Reflections: Soviet Women," *New Yorker* (19 Feb. 1990), 48ff.

8577. Gruzdeva, Elena B., and E. S. Chertikhina, "The Occupational Status and Wages of Women in the USSR," *Soviet Review*, 29, no. 1 (Spring 1988), 55-69.

8578. Gruzdeva, Elena, Liudmilla Rzhanitsyna and Zoia Khotkina, "Women in the Labor Market," *Problems of Economic Transition*, 35, no. 10 (Feb. 1993), 45-55.

8579. Harsanyi, Doina Pasca, "Romania's Women," *Journal of Women's History*, 5, no. 3 (Winter 1994), 30-54.

8580. Heidt, B., "The Burden of Caring," *Nation*, 244 (13 June 1987), 820-24.

8581. Helle, Horst J., "Women in Germany," *World & I*, 6, no. 4 (Apr. 1991), 482-99.

8582. Hyer, Janet, trans., "Women Tell Their Story: Letters to the Editor from *Rabotnitsa* and *Krest'ianka*," *Canadian Woman's Studies/Les Cahiers de la Femme*, 10, no. 4 (1989), 15-16.

8583. Jacoby, Susan, "Soviet Women: What Does Political Change Mean for Them?" *Glamour*, 87 (May 1989), 268ff.

8584. Jankowska, Hanna, "Abortion, Church and Politics in Poland," *Feminist Review*, 39 (Winter 1991), 174-81.

8585. Kain, Philip J., "Modern Feminism and Marx," *Studies in Soviet Thought*, 44, no. 3 (Nov. 1992), 159ff.

8586. Kerriker, Alexandra Heidi, "Soviet Women and Glasnost: Vistas from Fiction and Film," *West Virginia University Philological Papers*, 38 (1992), 246-57.

8587. Kiss, Yudit, "The Second `No': Women in Hungary," *Feminist Review*, 39 (Winter 1991), 49-57.

8588. Kligman, Gail, "Gendering the Postsocialist Transition: Women in Eastern Europe," *AAASS Newsletter*, 34, no. 2 (Mar. 1994), 3.

8589. Komarov, Evgenii Ivanovich, "The Woman Manager," *Soviet Education*, 33, no. 11 (Nov. 1991), 56-81.

8590. Kustanovich, Konstantin, "Erotic Glasnost: Sexuality in Recent Russian Literature," *World Literature Today*, 67, no. 1 (Winter 1993), 136-44.

8591. Lampland, Martha, "Unthinkable Subjects: Women and Labour in Socialist Hungary," *East European Quarterly*, 23 (Jan. 1990), 388-96.

8592. "The Law of Abortion in the Union of Soviet Socialist Republics and the People's Republic of China: Women's Rights in Two Socialist Countries," *Stanford Law Review* (Apr. 1988), 1027-117.

8593. Lemke, Christiane, "Beyond the Ideological Stalemate: Women and Politics in the FRG and the GDR in Comparison," *German Studies Review* (1990), 87-98.

8594. Lentini, Peter, "A Note on Women in the CPSU Central Committee, 1990," *Europe-Asia Studies*, 45, no. 4 (1993), 729-36.

8595. Leven, Bozena, "The Welfare Effects on Women of Poland's Economic Reforms," *Journal of Economic Issues*, 25, no. 2 (June 1991), 581-88.

8596. Levinson, R. B., "The Meaning of Sexual Equality: A Comparison of the American and Soviet Definitions," *New York Law School Journal of International and Comparative Law*, 10 (1989), 151-82.

8597. "The Lila Manifesto," *Feminist Studies*, 16, no. 3 (1990), 621-34.

8598. Mamonova, Tatyana, "Perestroika, Pornography, and Prostitution," *MS.*, 2, no. 2 (Sept-Oct. 1991), 12.

8599. Mandel, David, "Perestroika and Women Workers," *Canadian Woman's Studies/Les Cahiers de la Femme*, 10, no. 4 (1989), 20-22.

8600. Marsh, Rosalind, "Olga Lipovskaya and Women's Issues in Russia," *Rusistika*, 5 (June 1992), 16-21.

8601. Marshall, Bonnie, "Images of Women in Soviet Jokes and Anecdotes," *Journal of Popular Culture*, 26, no. 2 (Fall 1992), 117-25.

8602. Mason, M. S., "The New Women in the Movies," *World Monitor*, 4, no. 2 (Feb. 1991), 66-68.

8603. McCuaig, Kerry, "Effects of Perestroika and Glasnost on Women," *Canadian Woman's Studies/Les Cahiers de la Femme*, 10, no. 4 (1989), 11-14.

8604. McLaughlin, Sigrid, "Women Writers of the Soviet Union" (Review Article), *Slavic Review*, 50, no. 3 (Fall 1991), 683-85.

8605. "Misery in the Maternity Wards," *Economist*, 314 (15 Jan. 1990), 52.

8606. Molyneux, M., "The `Woman Question' in the Age of Perestroika," *New Left Review*, no. 183 (1990), 23-49.

8607. Much, Rita, "Feminist Theater in the Soviet Union," *New Theatre Quarterly*, 7, no. 27 (Aug. 1991), 284-86.

8608. Murziya, A., "It Was the Women...," *Ms.*, 2 (Nov-Dec. 1991), 14-15.

8609. Nechemias, Carol, "Democratization and Women's Access to Legislative Seats: The Soviet Case, 1989-91," *Women and Politics*, 13 (1993).

8610. Nicolaescu, Madalina, "Post-Communist Transitions: Romanian Women's Responses to Changes in the System of Power," *Journal of Women's History*, 5, no. 3 (Winter 1994), 117-28.

8611. Noonan, Norma, "Marxism and Feminism in the USSR: Irreconcilable Differences?" *Women and Politics*, 8, no. 1 (1988), 31-50.

8612. -----, "Two Solutions to the Zhenskii Vopros," *Women & Politics*, 11, no. 3 (1991), 77-100.

8613. Novikova, E. E., O. L. Milova and E. V. Zaliubovskaia, "Modern Women at Work and at Home: A Sociopsychological Study," *Soviet Sociology*, 28, no. 5 (Sept-Oct. 1989), 89-101.

8614. Nowicka, Wanda, "Two Steps Back: Poland's New Abortion Law," *Journal of Women's History*, 5, no. 3 (Winter 1994), 150-55.

8615. Pakszys, Elzbieta, and Dorota Mazurczak, "From Totalitarianism to Democracy in Poland: Women's Issues in the Sociopolitical Transition of 1989-1993," *Journal of Women's History*, 5, no. 3 (Winter 1994), 144-50.

8616. Patrushev, V. D., "Past and Future Changes in Soviet Workers' Time-Budget," *International Social Science Journal*, 38, no. 1 (1986), 77-88.

8617. Pearson, Landon, "Sex Role Education in the USSR," *Canadian Woman's Studies/Les Cahiers de la Femme*, 10, no. 4 (1989), 93-95.

8618. Pearson, Ruth, "Questioning Perestroika: A Socialist-Feminist Interrogation," *Feminist Review*, no. 39 (Autumn 1991), 91-96.

8619. Penn, Shana, "The National Secret," *Journal of Women's History*, 5, no. 3 (Winter 1994), 55-69.

8620. Perevedentsev, V. I., "Women in a Changing World," *Soviet Studies in Literature*, 25, no. 4 (Fall 1989), 48-86.

8621. "Problems of Working Women: Equality and Opportunity: The Idea and Its Realization" (Editorial), *Soviet Sociology*, 28, no. 5 (Sept-Oct. 1989), 87-88.

8622. Reiter, Ester, and Meg Luxton, "Overemancipation? Liberation? Soviet Women in the Gorbachev Period," *Studies in Political Economy* (Spring 1991), 53-73.

8623. -----, "Soviet Women: A Canadian View," *Canadian Woman's Studies/Les Cahiers de la Femme*, 10, no. 4 (1989), 27-30.

8624. Rich, Vera, "Abortion and Contraception," *Lancet*, no. 8673 (18 Nov. 1989), 1208.

8625. Rimashevskaia, Natal'ia, "Changes in Social Policy and Labor Legislation: The Gender Aspect," *Russian Social Science Review*, 33, no. 6 (Nov-Dec. 1992), 49-58.

8626. -----, "Current Problems of the Status of Women," *Soviet Sociology*, 27, no. 1 (1988), 58-71.

8627. Robertson, Ann, "Women in Post-Communist Central and Eastern Europe," *News in Brief: International Research & Exchanges Board*, 4, no. 6 (Nov-Dec. 1993), 3-4.

8628. Rorlich, Azade-Ayse, "Role of Tatar Women in Restoration of Islamic Values," *Report on the USSR*, 2, no. 11 (16 Mar. 1990), 22-23.

8629. Rosen, Ruth, "A Letter to Irina Siklova: On Feminism and Gender Democracy," *Dissent*, 38, no. 4 (Fall 1991), 531-37.

8630. -----, "Male Democracies, Female Dissidents," *Tikkun*, 5, no. 6 (1990), 11ff.

8631. Rosenberg, Dorothy J., "Learning to Say `I' Instead of `We': Recent Works on Women in the Former GDR" (Review Article), *Women in German Yearbook*, no. 7 (1991), 161-68.

8632. -----, "Shock Therapy: GDR Women in Transition from Socialist Welfare State to a Capitalist Market Economy," *Signs*, 17, no. 1 (1991), 129-52.

8633. Rosenberg, Karen, "Looking for Spring," *Women's Review of Books*, 7, no. 10-11 (July 1990), 6-7.

8634. Rudder, Catherine E., "Soviets Sanction Gender Studies," *PS*, 23, no. 4 (Dec. 1990), 673-74.

8635. Rule, W., "Political Dialogue with Some Women Leaders in Moscow and Leningrad," *PS*, 25 (10 June 1992), 308-10.

8636. Ruthchild, Rochelle, "A Turn toward the Future," *Women's Review of Books*, 7, no. 10-11 (July 1990), 7-9.

8637. Schillinger, L., "Devushki!" *New Republic* (9 Aug. 1993), 9-10.

8638. Scholz, Hannelore, "East-West Women's Culture in Transition: Are East German Women the Losers of Reunification?" *Journal of Women's History*, 5, no. 3 (Winter 1994), 108-16.

8639. Shcheglova, Evgeniia, "In Her Own Circle: Polemical Remarks about `Women's Prose'," *Russian Social Science Review*, 33, no. 6 (Nov-Dec. 1992), 59-84.

8640. Shreeves, Rosamund, "Mothers Against the Draft: Women's Activism in the USSR," *Report on the USSR*, 2, no. 38 (21 Sept. 1990), 3-8.

8641. -----, "Sexual Revolution or Sexploitation?" *Report on the USSR*, 2, no. 31 (3 Aug. 1990), 4-8.

8642. Siemienska, Renata, "Women and Social Movements in Poland," *Women and Politics*, 6, no. 4 (1986), 5-35.

8643. -----, "Women in the Period of Systemic Change in Poland," *Journal of Women's History*, 5, no. 3 (Winter 1994), 70-90.

8644. -----, "Women Managers in Poland: In Transition from Communism to Democracy," in Nancy J. Adler and Dafna N. Izraeli, eds., *Competitive Frontiers: Women Managers in a Global Economy* (Cambridge: Blackwell, 1993), 246-65.

8645. Simpson, Peggy, "No Liberation for Women: Eastern Europe Turns Back the Clock," *Progressive*, 55, no. 2 (Feb. 1991), 20-24.

8646. "Skirted Issues: The Discreteness and Indiscretions of Russian Women's Prose" (Special Issue), *Soviet Studies in Literature*, 28, no. 2 (Spring 1992), 3-98.

8647. Slesinski, Robert, "An Eastern Perspective on Feminism," *Diakonia*, 23, no. 2 (1990), 85-94.

8648. Smolowe, J., "Heroines of Soviet Labor," *Time*, 131 (6 June 1988), 28ff.

8649. "Soviet Divorce Laws and the Role of the Russian Family," *BYU Law Review*, (1986), 821-33.

8650. "The Soviet Union: Feminist Manifesto: `Democracy Without Women Is No Democracy': A Founding Document," *Feminist Review*, no. 39 (Winter-Autumn 1991), 127-32.

8651. Streitmatter, Rodger, "American-Soviet Women Journalists," *Editor and Publisher*, 124, no. 31 (3 Aug. 1991), 48.

8652. Szalai, Julia, "Some Aspects of the Changing Situation of Women in Hungary," *Signs: Journal of Women in Culture and Society*, 17, no. 1 (Autumn 1991), 152-70.

8653. Tarasiewicz, Malgorzata, "Women in Poland: Choices to Be Made," *Feminist Review*, 39 (Winter 1991), 182-86.

8654. Todorova, Maria, "Historical Tradition and Transformation in Bulgaria: Women's Issues or Feminist Issues?" *Journal of Women's History*, 5, no. 3 (Winter 1994), 129-43.

8655. Troy, C., "Moscow's Women," *MS.*, 16 (Apr. 1988), 54-63.

8656. Tupitsyn, Margarita, "Unveiling Feminism: Women's Art in the Soviet Union," *Arts Magazine*, 65, no. 4 (Dec. 1990), 63-67.

8657. Voronina, Ol'ga, "Restructuring the Woman Question: Prostitution and Perestroika," *Feminist Review*, 33 (Autumn 1989), 3-19.

8658. -----, "Sex and Semiotic Confusion: Report from Moscow," *Australian Feminist Studies*, 12 (1990), 1-14.

8659. -----, "Soviet Patriarchy: Past and Present," *Hypatia*, 8, no. 4 (Fall 1993), 97-112.

8660. -----, "Women in a `Man's Society'," *Soviet Sociology*, 28, no. 2 (Mar-Apr. 1989), 66-79.

8661. Wagner, Elizabeth, "Equal Time," *U.S. News & World Report*, 111 (9 Sept. 1991), 16.

8662. Waters, Elizabeth, "Restructuring the `Woman Question': Perestroika and Prostitution," *Feminist Review*, no. 33 (Autumn 1989), 3-19.

8663. Watson, Peggy, "Gender Relations, Education and Social Change in Poland," *Gender and Education*, 4, no. 1-2 (1992), 127-47.

8664. Winkler, Karen J., "Opening a Window on Life in Soviet Labor Camps," *Chronicle of Higher Education*, 38, no. 10 (30 Oct. 1991), A8ff.

8665. Wolchik, Sharon L., "International Trends in Central and Eastern Europe: Women in Transition in the Czech and Slovak Republics: The First Three Years," *Journal of Women's History*, 5, no. 3 (Winter 1994), 100-07.

8666. -----, "Women and Politics-Central and Eastern Europe," in Valentine M. Moghadam, ed., *Wider Research for Action:*

Privatization, Democratization, and Women in East-Central Europe and the Soviet Union (New York: World Institute for Development Research of the United Nations University, 1993).

8667. -----, "Women and Work in Communist and Post-Communist Central and Eastern Europe," in Hilda Kahne and Janet Giele, eds., *Women's Work and Women's Lives in Modernizing and Industrial Countries* (Boulder, CO: Westview Press, 1991).

8668. -----, "Women in Eastern Europe," *World & I*, 6, no. 9 (Sept. 1991), 556-67.

8669. "Women's View," *Glas: New Russian Writing*, no. 3 (1992), 1-240.

8670. Yulina, Nina S., John Ryder and Kathryn Russell, "Women and Patriarchy," *Women's Studies International Forum*, 16, no. 1 (Jan-Feb. 1993), 57-63.

8671. Zhuk, Olga, "The Development of a Russian Lesbian Identity," *Tema International*, 2 (Autumn 1991), 8-11.

8672. Zielinska, Eleonora, and Jolanta Plakwicz, "Strengthening Human Rights for Women and Men in Matters Relating to Sexual Behavior and Reproduction," *Journal of Women's History*, 5, no. 3 (Winter 1994), 91-99.

8673. Zirin, Mary F., "Perestroika for Women?" *AAASS Newsletter*, 32, no. 2 (Mar. 1992), 3.

Index of Authors

(Citations are to item numbers, not to pages)

Burawoy, Michael 2388, 5761, 5788, 5891

Burbank, Jane 8187

Burchfield, Lisa 3407

Burck, Gordon M. 1532

Burg, Steven L. 6918-20, 7287

Burgess, Geoff 6013

Burke, James F. 3552, 4336

Burke, Justin 8350

Burks, R. V. 2692

Burlatsky, Fyodor M. 1123, 4847, 5624-25

Burman, R. 4085

Burns, Richard Dean 1792

Burns, W. F. 1928

Burrage, Michael 6014

Burt, Jeffrey A. 888

Buruma, Ian 7546

Burzynska, Grazyna 5892

Bush, George 409, 773, 4387, 4526-28, 5192

Bush, Keith 889, 2566

Bushnell, John 502, 553, 5626, 8188

Bustamante, Fernando 4086

Busuttil, James J. 5979

Buszynski, Leszek 3707-08, 3753-54, 4009

Butler, William E. 1450, 3553, 5980-83, 6015-17, 8560

Butson, Thomas G. 721

Butterfield, Jim 410, 6921, 8162, 8189

Buttino, Marco 6858

Byrnes, Robert F. 5194, 5627

Byzov, L. G. 5195

Caccavo, K. R. 891

Calabresi, Massimo 1289

Caldwell, Dan 1793

Caldwell, Lawrence T. 1930, 4531-32

Calian, Carnegie 7777

Calinescu, Matei 2389

Calingaert, Daniel 1794

Calvo, Michael A. 1814

Cameron, George D., III 6018

Campbell, Adrian 5196

Campbell, Kurt M. 1795, 3638, 3654, 4298, 4533-34, 5628, 6394

Campbell, Robert W. 1533, 2567-68

Campeanu, Pavel 1589, 2390

Canan, James W. 5197

Canby, Thomas Y. 8351

Canfield, Robert 236, 7482

Cantor, David J. 5762

Cappelli, Ottorino 1639, 5198

Cardani, Angelo M. 2694

Carey, Sarah 825, 892-94

Carlson, Charles 7483, 7645

Carlson, Richard W. 6395

Carlton, David 1796

Carlucci, Frank 4535

Carnaghan, Ellen 8561

Carnesale, Albert 1931

Carney, James 1451

Carpenter, Russell H., Jr. 895

Carr, Bob 1958

Carrere d'Encausse, Helene 6859, 6922

Carrington, Samantha 2695

Carsten, Svetlana 6246

Carter, April 1797

Carter, Stephen 6650, 6860, 7637

Carty, Anthony 5984

Carver, Jeremy P. 7484

Carvounis, Brinda C. 826

Carvounis, Chris C. 826

Casey, Francis M. 4337

Castaneda, Jorge G. 4087

Castoriadis, Cornelius 4849-50

Castro, J. 896

Catudal, Honore M. 6568

Cave, Jane 8353

Cebrowski, Arthur K. 6651

Cekuolis, Algimantas 1641

Cerf, Christopher 6352

Chaban-Delmas, J. 7988

Chadda, Maya 3975

Chadwick, Owen 7710

Chafetz, Glenn R. 2263

Chalidze, Francheska 3120, 5199

Chalidze, Valerii 8125, 8190

Chalupa, Iryna 7289

Chances, Ellen 6215

Chanda, Nayan 266-68, 3755-56, 3890

Chandler, Alfred D., Jr. 5789

Chandler, Andrea 7989

Chang, Gordon H. 3875

Chanis, J. A. 3410

Channon, John 411

Chapman, Janet G. 5893

Charles, Daniel 1933, 6396

Charles, K. 7547

Chayes, Abram 1934

Chayes, Antonia H. 1934

Checkel, Jeff 3554

Chengcai, Wan 1124

Chengjun, Zhu 1534

Chenoweth, Eric 1642

Cheow, Eric T. C. 3757

Chernoff, Fred 1935, 6652

Chernyayev, A. 1290

Chetverikov, Nikolai N. 554, 6397

Cheung, Tai Ming 1291, 3758-59, 6653

Chickering, A. Lawrence 8191

Chiesa, Giulietto 1125, 1590-91, 4790, 4965

Childs, David 2391-92

Chirac, Jacques 7991

Chirot, Daniel 2264, 2393

Chirovsky, Nicholas L. 6923, 7778-79

Chlenov, Michael 7548

Chmielowska, Jadwiga 7485

Choldin, Marianna Tax 503

Chorbajian, Levon 6398

Chotiner, Barbara Ann 412, 1126, 8192

Chowdhury, Najma 8543
Christensen, Julie 7367
Christensen, Peter G. 555
Christopher, Ian 4192
Christopher, M. 413
Chtiguel, Olga F. 556-57
Chu, Julian J. 8354
Chu, Wellington 3892
Chua-Eoan, H. G. 775
Chubais, Igor 1644
Chufrin, Gennady 3760-61
Chukhontsev, Oleg 6216
Chung, Yung Il 3709
Chuprinin, Sergei 6247
Chyb, Manana 7362
Cigar, Norman 4193-94, 6654-55
Cimbala, Stephen J. 1798, 6656, 7928-29
Cioranescu, George 1127, 7612
Cipkowski, Peter 2265
Cirincione, Joseph 4059
Clark, Andrew 558, 2696
Clark, Douglas L. 4195
Clark, John 2266, 2697, 7992
Clark, Mark T. 3555
Clark, Michael T. 4388
Clark, Susan L. 137, 4009-10, 4428, 7993
Clark, Terry D. 1645
Clark, William A. 1128, 1429, 1452
Clarke, Christopher F. 897
Clarke, Douglas L. 1936-39, 2394-96, 6657-62
Clarke, Michael 4536
Clarke, Simon 5790
Claudon, Michael P. 358, 414, 822, 827, 1521, 3345
Clausen, Peter A. 7994
Clem, Ralph S. 5200
Clemens, Walter C., Jr. 3556-57, 4339, 4753, 6924, 7078, 7117, 7368
Clements, Barbara 8522
Cleverley, J. Michael 8355
Clifford, Mark 3762
Clifton, Tony 7549
Cline, Ray 3710
Clines, Francis X. 3126
Cloud, D. S. 3411-12
Clough, Michael 3639
Clowes, Edith W. 6243
Clute, R. E. 3655
Cochran, Thomas 3128
Cochrane, Nancy J. 359
Cockburn, Alexander 1129, 1292-93, 4537, 4754
Cockburn, Patrick 4389, 5201, 6925
Codevilla, Angelo M. 6663, 7995
Codevilla, Giovanni 7782
Codrescu, Andrei 2267
Coffey, Joseph I. 1799
Coffman, Richard W. 416
Cogan, Charles G. 269
Cohen, Eve C. 1847

Cohen, Lenard J. 4390
Cohen, Mitchell 2397
Cohen, Richard 6569
Cohen, S. T. 1879
Cohen, Sam 7996
Cohen, Stephen F. 4391, 4538, 4755, 4851-52, 5202, 5629
Cohen, Warren I. 4392
Cohn, Stanley H. 1535
Coker, Christopher 3640, 3656
Colbert, James G. 1130
Colburn, Forrest D. 4088
Cole, John P. 5791, 6926
Coleman, Fred 1131, 1453, 4051, 4853, 5203-04
Colfin, B. 6248
Coll, Alberto R. 4089-90
Collins, George W. 270
Collins, Joseph J. 271
Collins, Robert F. 3657
Collins, Susan M. 3347
Colon, Jeffrey M. 3444
Colson, C. W. 7783
Colton, Timothy J. 138, 559, 1646, 2398, 2698, 4854, 5083, 5205-09, 6570, 6664
Comes, F. J. 4539-40
Commander, Simon 2569
Condee, Nancy 561-63, 5630
Confino, Michael 7646
Connor, Walter D. 1432, 5210, 5864, 8193
Conquest, Robert 1143, 1294, 4855, 5631, 6249, 6861
Conroy, Mary Schaeffer 1454
Cook, Edward C. 417, 443, 445
Cook, Linda J. 5792, 5865, 5894-95
Cooper, Ann 1261
Cooper, Julian 1522, 1536-38, 5758, 6665, 8356
Cooper, Leo 4756, 6571
Cooper, Mary H. 3413
Cooper, N. 5632
Cooper, William H. 2570
Copeland, Emily A. 8194
Copetas, A. Craig 898, 2571, 3414
Coppieters, Bruno 6019
Copson, Raymond D. 4541
Corbo, Vittorio 2268
Corcoran, Dan 899
Corcoran, Edward 6572
Corddry, Charles W. 4542
Corelli, R. 4857
Coriceli, Fabrizio 2268
Corneo, Giacomo G. 5896
Cornia, Giovanni Andrea 8126
Cornwell, R. 2699
Correa, Hector 1539
Correll, John T. 3763, 7997
Corrin, Chris 8523
Cortese, A. 3130
Corwin, J. 5484
Cossa, Ralph A. 4153
Costa, Alexandra 2700, 5211-12

Cotler, Irvin 7550
Cotter, Daniel R. 1942
Cotton, James 3764
Coughlin, E. K. 1647
Courter, Jim 6666
Covault, Craig 1296, 1943, 5793-94, 6667, 8357-60
Covington, Stephen R. 5213, 6668, 7998
Cowen, Regina 1857
Cox, David 1800
Cox, Michael 4393
Cox, Tom 4091
Cracraft, James 13, 5214, 8195
Craig, Diane 2985
Crane, Keith 2245
Craumer, Peter R. 5485
Crawford, M. 1540, 8361-62
Crighton, Elizabeth 8196
Critchlow, James 1455, 3131, 3415, 4196, 7443,7486-90, 7784-85
Croan, Melvin 4340
Cromley, Ellen K. 5485
Cronin, Richard P. 4541
Cronin, R. R. 8295
Cross, Sharyl 4092
Crouch, Martin 5084, 5215
Croucher, Murlin 14
Crow, Suzanne 1298, 2399-2400, 3558-60, 3765-68, 4011, 4197-202, 4543, 5216-17, 5897, 6927
Crowe, Gregory D. 8363
Crowley, Joan Frances 15
Crowther, William 7613-14
Crozier, Brian 776, 1299, 1648, 1945-46, 3561, 3658, 3893, 4093, 4203-04, 4544, 4757, 4858-59, 5218-20, 6669
Cruickshank, A. A. 4782
Crummey, Robert O. 139
Csaba, Laszlo 2269
Csapo, L. 8127
Cullen, Robert B. 1300, 3348, 3562, 5221, 7118, 7369, 7551, 8197
Cunningham, Ann-Marie 1541, 5486
Curcio, Frances R. 2966
Curran, Michael W. 46
Currie, Kenneth 6573
Cuthbertson, Ian M. 1802-03
Cutler, Blayne 900
Cutshaw, Charles Q. 6670
Cviic, Christopher 2270
Cynkin, Thomas M. 2401
Czaputowicz, Jacek 1649
Daalder, Ivo H. 1947
Dagne, Theodore S. 17, 2271
D'Agostino, Anthony 5587, 7786
Dahl, Henry 8364
Dahl, Robert A. 1650, 4860
Dahm, Helmut 1133, 7787
Dahrendorf, Ralf 1651-52, 2272
Dalby, Simon 7999
Dale, Patrick 1134

Daley, C. 229
Daley, T. 272
Dalgard, Per 511
Dallin, Alexander 140-42, 4545, 5222-23, 5588, 8046
Dallmeyer, D. 3416
Daly, Conor 564
Damrosch, Lori F. 8198
D'Anastasio, M. 2402, 3894, 4546
Daniel, J. 836
Daniel, W. 7788
Daniels, John D. 828
Daniels, Robert V. 18-19, 1301, 1948, 4547, 4861, 5085-86, 5224-28, 5633
Danilenko, Gennady 5984
Danilenko, Ignat 6671
Danilin, V. I. 5795
Daniloff, Nicholas 722, 5229, 8365
Daniloff, Ruth 7370
Danilov, Sergei 1949
Danilov, Viktor P. 418, 5634
Dannreuther, Roland 4205
Dansokho, Amath 1135
Danton de Rouffignac, Peter 829
Darialova, Natalia 1457
Darrach, B. 777, 4548
Darski, Jozef 1302, 7119, 7371
Darst, Robert G., Jr. 3132
Dasgupta, Gautam 624
Dashkov, V. 1458
Daskal, Steven E. 6672
David, Leonard 8366-69
David, Stephen R. 4299, 4341
Davidson, R. B. 8295
Davies, R. W. 20, 5589
Davies, Richard T. 7789-91, 8199
Davis, Christopher M. 5487, 8000
Davis, Jacquelyn K. 8072
Davis, L. 3133
Davis, Robert B. 1459-60
Davis, R. W. 5635
Davis, Shannon G. 4778
Davison, Kenneth L., Jr. 273
Dawisha, Karen 21, 2274, 2403, 3563
Day, Richard 2702, 4862, 5636
Daycock, Davis W. 5087
Deacon, Bob 8128
Dean, Jonathan 1950-51, 4394
Dean, Richard N. 1019
Deane, R. N. 901
Deane, Stephen E. 2404
Deats, R. L. 7372
DeBardeleben, Joan T. 3055, 3066, 3134, 5088
Debray, R. 4342
Decter, Jacqueline 6217
Dedkov, Igor 6251
Deeb, Mary-Jane 3659
DeGeorge, Gail 4133
DeGeorge, Richard T. 1136

Feiman, Vladimir 8299
Fein, E. B. 8568
Feinberg, G. 6028
Feinberg, Richard E. 3352-53, 4301
Feith, Douglas J. 1973
Feiveson, Harold A. 1974
Feld, Werner J. 8004
Feldbruge, F. J. M. 5985, 6027
Feldman, Gale 6258
Feldman, Jan 3422, 5642
Feldman, T. B. 791
Feldmesser, Robert A. 4876
Felker, T. L. 912
Felton, John 1975, 7124-25
Fennell, T. 2723
Fenson, Melvin 7555
Feodosi, Archbishop 7806
Feofanov, Iurii 6030
Ferdinand, Peter 3901
Ferguson, James 1806
Ferree, Myra Marx 8570
Ferris, Byron 575
Feshbach, Murray 3056, 4556, 4877, 5491, 7931
Fesler, Pamela 4557
Field, Mark G. 5492-94
Fieldhouse, Richard 1807
Fields, Howard 6407-09
Fierman, William 7807, 8203
Filatotchev, Igor 2724
Filatova, Irina 5643
Filipowicz, Halina 6259
Filippov, E. 1663
Filtzer, Donald A. 5799, 5866
Finder, Joseph 1976
Finder, Susan 3149
Fink, Johann 7126
Finkelstein, David M. 3774
Finn, James 2414, 4878
Fireside, Harvey 2209-10
Firkowska-Mankiewicz, Anna 1462
Fischer, David A. B. 2415, 3150
Fischer, Kristian 1977
Fischer, Mary Ellen 725
Fischer, Michael S. 1308, 3423
Fischer, Stanley 2576, 4558
Fish, M. Steven 1543
Fish, Steven 8205
Fishbein, David Joel 1463
Fisher, William 2416
Fitzgerald, David M. 3775
Fitzgerald, Mary C. 6576, 6680-83, 8005
Fitzpatrick, Catherine A. 5472, 8120
Fitzpatrick, Sheila 5644
Flacks, Richard 1141
Flaherty, Patrick 5247
Flakierski, Henryk 2577
Flatow, Sheryl 576
Flavin, Christopher 3057

Fleishman, Lana C. 6031
Fleron, Frederic J., Jr. 3501, 4764, 5645
Fletcher, G. P. 1464, 6032
Florini, Ann M. 8384
Floroff, O. 424, 2727
Flory, Paul J. 5800
Flowerree, Charles C. 1978
Flynn, Gregory 3502, 6577, 8006
Foell, Earl W. 4018, 4560, 5248
Foley, Theresa M. 1979-80
Fomin, Vladimir 1664
Foner, Eric 2728, 5646
Fonkalsrud, E. W. 5495
Forbes, Malcolm S., Jr. 1665, 5249
Ford, Christopher A. 280
Forest, James 577, 5496, 7714-15, 7808-11
Forsberg, Randall 1981-82
Forsythe, David P. 8206
Fortescue, Stephen 8300-01
Fossedal, Gregory A. 4562, 6411
Foster, F. H. 6033
Fought, Stephen O. 8008-09
Fowkes, Ben 2278
Foye, Stephen 1142, 1309-10, 4563, 6684-97, 6938
France, B. 4546
Francis, Arthur 8302
Francis, D. 2729
Francis, Samuel T. 3662
Franck, Thomas M. 3568-69
Frangulov, Vladimir G. 1262
Frank, Alexander 7533
Frank, Peter 1143, 4879, 8207
Frank, William C. 6578
Frankel, Francine R. 3976
Frankel, Sherman 8385
Frankel, W. G. 8386
Frankland, Mark 1076
Franklin, Daniel 425-26, 4880
Franklin, Lynn C. 6412
Franklin, Simon 7812
Fraser, Hugh 578-79
Fraser, Niall 7376
Freedman, Lawrence 1809, 1983
Freedman, Robert O. 4155-56, 4211-12, 7536
Freeman, John R. 3905
Freeman, P. 8572
Frei, Daniel 1810
Freibergs, Imants 7127
Freidin, Gregory 1144, 1261, 1280, 1311, 4881, 7492-93
Freidzon, Sergei 2578
Frelk, J. 8035
French, Hilary F. 3151-53
French, R. A. 207
Frenkel, William G. 915-16, 6034-36
Freund, William 917
Freymann, J. G. 5563
Friedberg, A. L. 6698
Friedberg, Maurice 503, 580, 5250, 7556, 7932

Friedgut, Theodore H. 1145, 5867, 5901
Friedheim, Jerry W. 1312
Friedman, Edward 3902
Friedman, Sharon M. 6414
Friedrich, Otto 581
Friendly, Alfred, Jr. 3056
Frierman, William 7445
Frolic, Michael 4564
Froman, Michael B. 4399
Fronta, Mlada 7813
Frost, Gerald 147, 4882
Frost, H. E. 6699
Frydman, Roman 2279, 2579
Frye, Alton 3472
Frye, Rick 5777
Frye, Timothy 780-81, 1666
Frye, Todd
Fuchs, Michael 5513
Fukuyama, Francis 3776, 4302-06, 4315, 4345-47, 4765, 4883-84
Fulghum, David A. 1313, 6700
Fuller, Elizabeth 782, 7377-95
Fuller, Graham E. 4213-14, 7494
Funk, Nanette 8526
Furtado, Charles F., Jr. 6866
Furtado, Francis J. 6579
Gabanyi, Anneli Ute 7618
Gabor, Francis A. 1667
Gabrisch, Robert 2580
Gachechiladze, Revaz 7396
Gaddis, John Lewis 27, 4565
Gaddy, Clifford G. 1430, 4813, 5868, 5902
Gaffney, C. 8416
Gagnon, V. P., Jr. 5903
Gaidar, Egor 2730
Galazii, Grigori 3154
Galbraith, John K. 1984, 2417, 2731
Gale, Robert P. 3058, 3155-56
Galeotti, Mark 1465
Galey, Margaret E. 8573
Galichenko, Nicholas 505
Galloway, J. L. 4215, 4885
Gallup, George, Jr. 4886
Galster, Steven R. 281
Galuszka, Philip 282, 427, 879, 918-20, 946, 1146-47, 1466-67, 1668-69, 2686, 2732-33, 3424, 3570, 5251, 5801, 6939, 8387
Galvin, John R., General 1985, 4566
Gambrell, Jamey 582-83, 1314, 1468
Gamer, Robert E. 2280
Gammer, Moshe 5647
Gankovsky, Yuri V. 5252
Gannes, S. 8388
Garafola, Lynn 584
Garbus, Martin 6415
Gardner, Anthony 6037, 6416
Gardner, Colin 585
Garelik, G. 8500

Gareyev, Makhmut 6701-02
Garfinkle, Adam M. 1986-87, 4567
Garrard, Carol 6218
Garrard, John 6218, 7557, 7655
Garrett, Banning N. 3777
Garrett, Stephen A. 3778
Garrison, Sean 6013
Garrity, Patrick J. 8010
Garside, A. 586
Garthoff, Raymond L. 1811, 1988-89, 3571, 4568-69, 6580, 8011-12
Garton Ash, Timothy 2281-83, 2418-21, 7128
Garver, John W. 3903, 3977
Gasiorowski, Mark J. 4167
Gass, William H. 6262
Gasteyger, Curt 8013
Gastor, Kristopher 6940-41
Gati, Charles 2284, 2422-25
Gati, Toby T. 4631
Gaunt, Philip 6417
Gavaghan, Helen 8389
Gawad, Atef A. 4216
Gebhardt, James F. 6703
Geipel, Gary L. 2426, 8390-91
Gelb, Alan H. 832, 2576, 4570
Gellner, Charles R. 1990
Gellner, Ernst 4571, 5648, 6942
Gelman, Harry 3503, 3572, 3779, 3997, 5090
Genaite, Sarah 5253
Geneste, Mark 1991
Genscher, Hans-Dietrich 129
Geoffrey, Oliver D. 921
George, A. L. 4572
George, James L. 1812
Georgeoff, John 2989
Georgopoulos, Zach 1470
Gerber, Jane 7554
Gerbner, George 1315
Gerchikov, V. I. 1670, 5904-05
Geremek, Bronislaw 1671
Germroth, David S. 6943
Gemer, Kristian 7080
Gerol, Ilya 6354
Geron, Leonard 28, 3354
Gershunsky, Boris S. 2990
Gerus, Oleh W. 7716
Gervasi, Tom 7933
Getty, J. Arch 29
Gewen, Barry 4887
Gey, Peter 2581
Geyer, Alan 1992, 4573, 7717
Gfoeller, Mike 4830
Ghaus, Abdul S. 233
Ghausuddin 283
Gibbs, D. 284
Giblin, James F. 4019
Gibson, Andrew E. 4574
Gibson, James L. 1672, 7558-59

Goure, Daniel 8019
Goure, Leon 5277, 6709, 8020
Gow, James 7293
Graben, Erik K. 2003
Grabendorff, Wolf 4102
Graffy, Julian 6355
Graham, Daniel O. 2004
Graham, John L. 3351
Graham, Loren R. 2754, 5804, 8211, 8303-05, 8390-91
Grancelli, Bruno 5869
Grant, Steven A. 32
Grant, Wyn 927
Grassman, Hans-Peter 1553
Graubard, Stephen R. 152-53
Grava, Sigurd 7143
Graves, R. L. 6642
Gray, Alfred M. 8021
Gray, Cheryl W. 832
Gray, Colin S. 2005-06, 8022-23
Gray, Francine du Plessix 8530, 8576
Gray, Kenneth R. 363-64
Gray, L. V. 589
Gray, Malcolm 2755, 5805, 7619
Graziani, Giovanni 4309
Grazin, Igor 1676, 6046-47
Greeley, B. M. 8402
Greely, Brendan M., Jr. 2007
Green, Barbara B. 33
Green, Elizabeth E. 3908
Green, Eric 3061
Green, M. 785
Green, William C. 3577, 6582
Greenbaum, Avraham 7568
Greenberg, J. 5499
Greene, Pat Ryan 7144
Greene, Richard E. 3502
Greenfeld, Liah 7656
Greenfield, Meg 4903, 8403
Greenwald, G. Jonathan 3355, 6710
Greenwald, J. 5806
Gregorovich, Andrew 8024
Gregory, Paul R. 2584-85, 2757-58
Greider, W. 4585, 4904
Greising, D. 878
Gremitskikh, Yuri 6267
Grenier, Paul 1524, 5278
Grenier, Richard 590, 4103
Grey, Robert D. 6426
Griffin, Andrew T. 928, 6048-50
Griffith, William E. 2288, 2432
Griffiths, D. 4022
Griffiths, Franklyn 7937, 8025
Grigorieff, Dimitry 7816
Grigorievs, Alexei 7145
Grigory, Margit N. 77, 200
Grimsted, Patricia K. 5590-91, 5655
Grinevetskiy, V. T. 3164
Grishchenko, Dmitri I. 3428, 7294

Gritsiuk, Grigorii 7620
Gromyko, Anatoly A. 3641
Gromyko, Andrei 728
Grondona, M. 5280
Groopman, Jerome E. 5500
Grootings, Peter 8302
Gros, Daniel 2586-87, 3165
Grosfeld, Irena 5807
Gross, Bertram 8138
Gross, Jan T. 2433-34
Gross, Jo-Ann 7446
Gross, Natalie 4023, 6427, 6711-12
Gross, Peter 6428
Grosscup, Beau 286
Grossman, Gregory 1472, 2588-89, 2759
Grossman, Vasilii S. 6220-21
Grove, Eric J. 2008, 6713
Groves, J. E. 3318
Gruliow, Leo 4905-06, 64299
Gruntman, M. A. 7569
Grushin, B. A. 6430
Gruzdeva, Elena 8578
Gryazin, Igor 7146
Grzybowski, Kazimierz 5988
Gu, Xuewu 3909
Guasch, J. Luis 356
Gubar', O. M. 6431
Gudava, Tengiz 7397
Gudkov, Leon 6954
Gudziak, Boris 7817
Guertner, Gary L. 1815, 2009-10, 7938
Guetta, Bernard 2760, 7818
Gunlicks, Arthur B. 4767
Gunn, Gillian 4104
Gureckas, Algimantas P. 7147
Gurenko, E. N. 1738
Gurewich, David 6268
Gurtov, Mel 154
Gusarov, Vladilen 3665
Gustafson, D. Mauritz 8212
Gustafson, Kerstin 786
Gustafson, Thane 2590-91, 3578, 4483, 5281-82, 6570
Gusterson, Hugh 3579
Gutner, Tamar L. 358, 827
Gutsenko, Konstantin 8026
Gvosdev, Nikolas K. 3580
Gwertzman, Bernard 4768
Gyarmati, Istvan 2435
Ha, Yong-Chool 3785
Haas, Richard N. 3786, 4222
Haberman, C. 6714
Habib, Henry 3666
Hagerty, Randy 4349
Haggerty, Brian C. 4105
Hagler, Marian M. 2761
Haglund, David C. 4106
Hahn, Gordon M. 5283, 5656
Hahn, Jeffrey W. 1151, 1677, 5094, 5284-87

Hajda, Lubomyr 6868, 6955
Haley, P. Edward 1816, 2011
Hall, Barbara Welling 3166
Hall, Derek R. 2592
Hall, Robert 6583
Hallenbeck, Ralph A. 1817
Hallick, Stephen P., Jr. 2762
Halliday, Fred 4223-24, 4405, 4586-87
Halloran, Bernard F. 1818
Halperin, Morton H. 2177
Halverson, Thomas 3167
Hamburg, Roger 1321, 4107-08
Hamilton, George 3430
Hamilton, John Maxwell 2763, 3168
Hamman, Terry 3062
Hammer, Darrell P. 4907, 5095
Hammond, Pamela 591
Hampson, Fen Osler 2012
Handelman, Stephen 1473, 1678
Handler, Joshua 6629
Hanke, Steve H. 2764
Hankiss, Elemer 2289
Hannigan, John 1819
Hansen, Carol R. 8213
Hansen, Carl R. 3356
Hansen, Roger D. 4588
Hanson, Eric O. 7718, 7819
Hanson, Philip 430, 929, 1152-53, 1547, 2593, 2765-72, 3431, 4908, 5960, 6051, 7148-50, 8404
Hanstad, Timothy 375-76
Harasymiw, Bohdan 1154-56, 6956
Haraszti, Miklos 2211
Hardenbergh, Chalmers 2013
Hardison, Londre Felicia 592
Hardt, John P. 1548, 2773, 3432
Hardy, J. E. 6432
Hareven, Gail 7570-71
Hargreaves, John D. 5657
Harle, Vilho 155, 4406
Harmon, Danute S. 7151-52
Harries, Owen 2436, 3702, 4589, 6957
Harris, Chauncy D. 7657-58
Harris, David 1322, 7572
Harris, Joanna 619
Harris, Jonathan 5288-89
Harris, Lillian C. 3876
Harris, P. 1474
Harrison, Frank 1157
Harrison, Selig S. 3713, 3787, 7501
Harsanyi, Doina Pasca 8579
Hart, Gary 4769
Hart, Thomas 3877
Hartgrove, J. Dane 109
Hartung, William 2014
Hartwig, M. 6052
Hasegawa, Tsuyoshi 156, 3998
Haslam, Jonathan 167, 1820
Hassner, Pierre 1679, 4590

Haughey, J. C. 7820
Hauner, Milan 235-36
Haupt, R. 431
Haus, Leah 3357, 3433
Hauser, Thomas 3058
Hauslohner, Peter 5909-10
Hausmaninger, Herbert 5911, 6053-54
Havel, Vaclav 729-32, 787-90, 2290, 2437-38
Havlik, Peter 2291
Havrylyshyn, Oleh 2645
Hawkes, Nigel 157, 3063
Hawkesworth, Celia 6222
Hawkins, Robert 931, 6958
Hawkins, Wiliam R. 2015
Hay, Caroline M. 8307
Hayden, Robert M. 6433
Hayes, M. 1021
Haynes, Viktor 3064
Hayward, Dan 2016
Hayward, Thomas B. 3788-89, 6715
Hazan, Barukh 1080-81, 5096
Hazard, John N. 932, 4909, 6055-59, 6959-60
Hearmsro, Dilip 4225
Heath, John 5764
Hecht, James L. 833
Hecht, Leo 34
Hedlund, Stefan 365, 7080
Hehir, J. B. 4226
Heidt, B. 8580
Heilbronner, Robert 2439, 4910
Heim, David 7821-22
Heisbourg, Francois 7939
Heiss, Klaus P. 2017
Heitlinger, Alena 8531
Hejma, Ondrej 593
Held, Joseph 35, 2292
Heleniak, Timothy 110, 4911
Helle, Horst J. 8581
Heller, Agnes 1158, 2440, 4912-13, 5291, 5592
Heller, Leonid 6269
Heller, M. 5658-59
Hellie, Jean Laves 6270
Hellie, Richard 1323
Hellman, J. S. 3548
Helm, L. 4024
Helmer, O. 4591
Helms, R. G. 303
Hemans, Simon 4914
Hemsley, John 3506
Henderson, Breck W. 2018
Hendrickson, David C. 4407
Henige, David P. 36
Henry, Catherine P. 7823
Henze, Paul B. 3642, 3667, 6961, 7353, 7638, 7659
Herd, M. M. 5502
Hergesheimer, John 4915
Herlemann, Horst 8131
Herlihy, Michael 7824

Herman, Paul F. 4408
Hermingshouse, Patricia 5660
Herr, R. A. 3800
Herrmann, Richard 4227, 8027
Herspring, Dale R. 6584, 6716-19
Hertzberg, Arthur 7573
Hertzberg, Hendrick 5292
Hertzfeld, Jeffrey M. 933-34
Herxheimer, Andrew 5503
Hesli, Vicki L. 6362, 7321
Hess, Andrew C. 4228
Hessman, James D. 6720
Hester, Al 6356
Hetmanek, Allen 7825
Hewett, Ed A. 158, 834, 2594, 2774-85, 3169, 3434
Heymann, Hans, Jr. 2786
Heyns, Terry L. 4409
Hiebert, M. 3790-91
Hiebert, Timothy H. 8028
Hildebrandt, Gregory G. 2595
Hildreth, Steven A. 1821
Hilf, Rudolph 7502-03
Hilkes, Peter 2992
Hill, Kent R. 7719-21, 7826-27
Hill, Malcolm R. 8306-07
Hill, Ronald J. 1159-60, 2596, 4916, 5097, 5293-95,
6434, 6962
Hillmer, Norman G., Jr. 4381
Hilton, Ronald 7153
Hines, Jonathan 935
Hines, Robert 996
Hintzman, Bonnie 37
Hiro, Dilip 4229
Hirsch, Daniel 3142
Hirsch, Jacques 4297
Hirsch, Steve 3507, 4770
Hirst, Paul 1681
Hixson, Walter L. 8132
Hober, Kaj 936
Hochfield, Sylvia 594-95
Hochman, J. 5661
Hochschild, Adam 5593
Hodkova, Iveta 3170
Hoffman, George W. 6963
Hoffmann, David L. 1161
Hoffmann, Eric P. 3171, 3435, 3514
Hoffmann, Stanley 3582, 4424
Hofheinz, Paul 1475, 2787-88, 4917
Hogan, John P. 1324
Hogan, Michael J. 4410
Hohenemser, C. 3172
Holbrooke, R. 4593
Holden, Constance 937, 1476, 2212, 5504-06, 8214, 8405
Holden, Gerald 4420, 6585
Holder, Kate 7940
Holland, Barbara 8532
Holland, Mary 6060-61
Hollander, Paul 2993

Hollis, Rosemary 4161
Holloway, David 1162, 6721-22, 8029, 8406
Holman, Paul 159
Holmes, Kim R. 3878
Holmes, Leslie 1082, 1431
Holoboff, Elaine M. 6586
Holowinsky, Ivan Z. 5507
Holstein, W. J. 287
Holt, R. R. 213
Holtz, J. 6435
Holzman, Franklyn D. 2789, 4593, 6723
Homet, Roland S., Jr. 4411
Hooper, R. W. 8030
Hopkins, Mark 3910-11
Hoppman, P. Terrence 1822
Horelick, Arnold L. 3714, 4412-13, 4594, 7941
Horn, M. 596
Horn, N. 2441
Horn, Robert C. 3715, 3792, 3912-14
Hornaday, A. 3173
Horne, Mari K. 4025
Horner, C. 1682
Horowitz, Irving Louis 5296, 7399
Horton, Andrew 507
Horvat, Janos 6436
Horvath, J. 2790
Horyn, Mikhailo 7269
Hosking, Geoffrey A. 38, 1683, 4771, 5098, 5297,
6355, 7660, 7722
Hossein-zadeh, Esmail 4350
Hostler, Charles Warren 7447
Hough, Jerry F. 1324, 2597, 2791-92, 4310, 4351, 4595-97,
4772, 5298-5301, 8031
House, Francis 7723
Howard, A. E. Dick 1594
Howard, Michael 2020, 4918, 5662, 6964, 8032
Howe, Geoffrey, Sir 3583
Howe, Irving 1163, 2213, 2381, 5302, 5663
Howe, Keith 397-400
Howell, LLewellyn D. 4919
Howells, John 7639
Hsiung, J. C. 3915-16
Hsueh, Chun-tu 3917
Hua Di 3793
Huan, Guocang 3918-19, 4598
Huber, Robert T. 4773, 4920
Huda, Walter 3174
Hudelson, Richard H. 4774
Hudson, George E. 7942, 8033
Hughes, H. Stuart 2192
Hughes, L. 598
Hughes, Michael 6965
Hughes, Thomas P. 8407
Huldt, Bo 237
Hull, Richard W. 3668
Hulse, Andrew 2021
Hummel, Arthur W., Jr. 3920
Hunczak, Taras 7295

Lawrence, W. H. 6089
Lawson, Michael 8432
Lawton, Anna 512, 618, 6460
Layne, Christopher 4625-26
Lax, Eric 3194
Lazarev, B. M. 6090
Lea, J. F. 4949, 5331
Leach, Rodney 4950
Leary, Neil A. 5814
Lebow, Richard N. 2067
Lechtman, V. 1037
Lecomte, Bernard 4784
Ledeen, Michael 4627, 5332
Ledkovsky, Marina 8536-37
Lee, D. 3922
Lee, Gary 1698
Lee, J. 6091
Lee, Rensselaer W., III 1434, 1484
Lee, T. V. 1485
Lee, William T. 2068
Leebaert, Derek 6594
Lefever, Ernest W. 169
Legasov, Valery 3195
Leggett, J. 3594
Legro, Jeffrey W. 5106, 5333, 6639
Legvold, Robert 138, 2069, 3516, 3595, 3803, 4252
Lehne, Stefan 7945
Lei, Xi 2822
Leibler, Isi J. 7586
Leighton, Marian 3804, 8047
Leinwoll, S. 6461-62
Leitenberg, Milton 2070
Leitzel, Jim 4813
Lellouche, Pierre 2071
Lemeshev, Mikhail 3067, 3196
Lemke, Christiane 8593
LeMoyne, James 4114
Lempert, David 1486, 5334
Lempert, Robert J. 1827
Lenczowski, John 4628
Lenorovitz, Jeffrey M. 956-57, 5815-16, 8433-36
Lentini, Peter 5336, 8594
Leonard, Thomas M. 4115
Leonhard, Wolfgang 3515
Leontieff, W. W. 2823
Lepingwell, John W. R. 2072, 6742-43, 8048
Lerner, Lawrence 170
Lerner, Michael 1699, 7183
Leslie, D. F. 303
Lesourne, Jacques 4784
Lessing, Doris M. 242
Letica, Slaven 1600
Levada, Yuri 5337
Levchenko, Stanislav 6744
Leven, Bozena 8595
Leventhal, Paul L. 3197
Levering, Ralph B. 4429
Levi, Barbara Gross 3198

Levin, Alexei E. 8437-40
Levin, B. M. 1487
Levin, Carl 2073
Levin, M. B. 1487
Levin, Nora 7587-88
Levine, Herbert S. 2824, 6094
Levine, Robert A. 1828
Levine, Steven I. 3923-24
Levinson, M. 2825
Levinson, R. B. 8596
Levitsky, Serge L. 6095-96
Levy, David 4785
Lewald, R. 958
Lewarne, Stephen 5768, 6097
Lewenz, Susan M. H. 959, 5513
Lewin, Moshe 5599, 5678, 6993
Lewins, Jeffrey 3101
Lewis, Flora 2476, 4951
Lewis, Jonathan 5600
Lewis, K. N. 1829
Lewis, Kevin 2066
Lewis, Paul G. 2302, 2477
Lewis, Robert 397-400, 7451
Lewis, W. 3199
Lewis, W. H. 6994
Libaridian, Gerald J. 7354
Lieberman, A. 4562
Lieberman, Edward H. 960, 3444
Liebowitz, Ronald D. 840, 3361
Liefert, William M. 443
Lieven, Anatol 7082
Lieven, Dominic 4952, 6995-96
Lifschultz, Lawrence 304
Ligachev, Yegor 737
Light, D. W. 5514
Light, Margo 4317, 5924
Lih, Lars T. 5338-40
Likhachev, Dmitrii S. 513, 4786, 6282
Likhacheva, V. M. 8268
Linam, James 1830
Lind, W. S. 4629
Lindeman, Mark 1831
Linden, Carl A. 4787, 4953
Lindsey, Byron 6219
Lingenfelter, Scott 7713
Linz, Susan J. 2613
Lipponen, Paavo 7940
Lipset, Martin 1597
Lipson, Leon 6098
Lipton, David 2478, 4954
Lischkin, Gennady 8122
Liska, George 2303, 4430, 4630, 8049
Lisson, Paul 5679
Litman, Gary V. 5099
Litman, George L. 961
Little, D. Richard 5107
Little, David 7274
Litvin, Valentin 370, 2826

Malik, Hafeez 3520, 3719, 7668, 7849
Malik, J. Mohan 3980
Malinauskas, Anthony P. 3202
Maliuk, Z. 8226
Malle, Silvana 5872
Mallory, Charles K. 6591
Malmgren, Harald B. 3362
Maltsev, Y. M. 2833
Mal'tseva, L. L. 5927
Mamiosa, I. E. 6112
Mamonova, Tatiana 8538-39, 8598
Mamutov, V. K. 5928
Manaev, Oleg T. 6464-65
Manchin, Robert 2339
Mandel, David 5873, 5929, 8599
Mandel, Ernest 5108
Mandel, H. 621
Mandelbaum, Michael 1346, 1834, 2600, 3610, 4435, 4637-38, 6875
Manevich, E. 2834, 5930
Manezhev, Sergei 2835
Mangan, Bonnie F. 3068
Manion, Christopher 4639
Mann, A. 7186
Mann, Dawn 50, 796, 1176-85, 1347, 5281-82, 5345-47, 6113-14
Mann, Paul 2075-81, 4253, 6754-58
Manning, Robert A. 3805
Manoff, R. K. 6466
Mansfield, Don L. 127
Manson, P. D. 2082
Manthrope, William H. J., Jr. 2083-84, 6759-60
Marantz, Paul 3521, 3602, 4436, 4640
Marcella, Gabriel 4116
March, Sally 851, 3368
Marcus, Howard G. 3679
Marcus, Naomi 622-23, 5931
Marcus, S. J. 3203
Marcy, Sam 1088
Maremont, Mark 5817
Maresca, John J. 2085
Mark, Hans 6761
Markish, Simon 6284
Markish, Yuri 445
Markov, Sergei 1599
Markovits, Inga 6115
Marks, John 4377
Marlatt, Alyse 963
Marlin, John Tepper 1524
Marples, David R. 3069-72, 3204-23, 5515, 5818, 5932-33, 7275, 7306-11
Marranca, Bonnie 624
Marrese, Michael 446, 2836
Marsh, Gerald 2086
Marsh, Rosalind 6285-86, 8600
Marshak, Robert E. 8447
Marshall, Bonnie 8601
Marshall, Eliot 3224, 5516-17

Martin, Kate 8153
Martin, Laurence 8052
Martin, Lawrence 797, 4789, 5109
Martin, Peter 6453, 7850
Marty, Martin E. 7851
Martynov, A. 1489
Martz, L. 4961, 7187
Marzani, C. 4641
Masani, P. R. 7852
Maslov, N. N. 5682
Mason, David S. 2305, 2484, 6467, 8196
Mason, M. S. 8602
Massey, Susannah 1343, 3011-13
Massing, Michael 3680, 4642, 6468
Mastny, Vojtech 171
Mastro, Joseph P. 51
Matejka, Ladislav 515
Mathews, T. 5348
Matiaszek, Petro 6117
Matlock, Jack F. 4643, 6118
Matosich, Andrew J. 5819
Matosich, Bonnie K. 5819
Matsaberidze, Malkhaz 7363
Matthews, Chris 964, 4644
Matthews, Mervyn 5110, 5993, 8145, 8321
Matthiessen, Peter 3225
Matuszewski, Daniel C. 3730
Matzko, John R. 3226
Mawdsley, Evan 1186-87
Mayer, Arno J. 1348
Maynes, Charles W. 4645
Mazarr, Michael J. 1835, 2087
Mazurczak, Dorota 8615
Mazzocco, William 4039, 8053
McAdams, A. James 2485-86
McAllister, Ian 5457
McAuley, Alastair 2837-38, 6876
McAuley, Mary 5111, 5349
McBride, Ken 3603
McCain, John 6762
McCain, Morris 307
McCally, Michael 3227
McCarthy, Daniel J. 965
McCarthy, James P. 8054
McCarthy, P. 3445
McCauley, Martin 52-3, 172, 2487-88
MccGwire, Michael 2088-91, 6596, 6763-64, 8055
McClarnand, Elaine 5683
McClellan, Stephen 1349
McClellan, Woodford 54
McColm, Bruce R. 1350, 1704, 2488, 4117-18
McCombs, Phil 7188
McConnell, J. M. 6765
McCormick, Kip 308
McCormick, Samuel D. 3928
McCuaig, Kerry 8603
McDaniel, Donna 966
McDonald, Hamish 3228, 7000

McDonald, K. 8448
McDougall, Derek 4437
McDowell, E. 6287
McFaul, Michael 1188-89, 1351, 1598-99, 1705
McForan, D. W. J. 1707
McGloin, Michael 954
McGrath, P. 5350
McGuire, Sumiye O. 4001
McHenry, W. K. 8395-96
McIntosh, Jack 112
McIntyre, Robert J. 447-48
McKay, Betsy 1352-53
McKay, Ron 6359
McKinney, Judith Record 2839
McKinnon, Robert T. 2614
McKinnon, Ronald I. 2840
McLaughlin, John 4962, 5351
McLaughlin, Sigrid 5684, 8540, 8604
McLeod, J. David 4438
McLure, Charles E., Jr. 2615
McManus, J. 967
McMichael, Scott R. 1354-55, 6766-67
McMillan, Carl H. 968-69, 3446
McMullen, Ronald K. 7670
McNabb, David 3005
McNair, Brian 6360, 6469-70
McNamara, Robert S. 2037, 4439
McNaughter, Thomas L. 4168
McNeill, John H. 4646
McNeill, Terry 3806
McReynolds, Louise 6471
McWhinney, E. 6119-20
Mead, Walter R. 4963
Meadows, James E. 970
Meaney, Constance S. 3929
Mearsheimer, John J. 2489, 4964, 7312, 8056-57
Mecham, Michael 309, 971, 1356
Medish, Vadim 55
Medvedev, Roy 626-28, 4790, 4965, 7001, 8232
Medvedev, Vadim A. 4966
Medvedev, Zhores A. 371, 738, 3073, 8449
Meehan, John F., III 8058
Meerovich, Aleksandr 5352, 6121
Mehrota, Santosh 3965
Meier, Andrew 798
Meilunas, Egidijus 7189-90
Meisler, S. 629
Meissner, Boris 7002
Melcher, R. A. 2841, 3447
Melikian, Richard G. 7355
Meliunas, Egidijus 8233
Melnick, A. James 7853
Melville, Andrei 173
Melvin, Neil 7512, 7623
Menashe, Louis 630-31, 5685
Mendelson, Sarah E. 310
Mendes, Errol P. 3448
Mendez, Jose A. 3449

Mendl, Wolf 4040-41
Mendras, Marie 4361
Menges, Constantine 4440
Menicucci, Garay 4254
Menon, Rajan 181, 3807-08, 4042-43
Menos, Dennis 1836
Menshikov 3450
Meredith, Mark 3363
Meri, Lennart 7191
Merkl, Peter H. 2306
Merkuriev, S. 3014
Merriam, John C. 232
Merridale, Catherine 5601, 5686
Merritt, Jack 1816
Mesa-Largo, Carmelo 4064
Meshabi, Mohiaddin 4318
Messener, Azary 632
Mestrovic, Marta 6288
Mestrovic, Stjepan 1600
Methvin, Eugene H. 799, 1190, 4648, 5353, 5687
Metlif, I. V. 7854
Metzer, Bernhard H. 3229
Meyendorff, Anna 1436
Meyer, E. C. 8065
Meyer, H. N. 6122
Meyer, Peggy F. 3809
Meyer, Stephen M. 1357, 8059
Meyerson, Adam 4649, 4967-68, 5688
Mezhenkov, Vladimir 174-76
Miall, Hugh 1837
Miasnikov, A. L. 5689
Michel, James H. 4119
Michielson, Peter 2490
Michnik, Adam 2491, 5354
Michta, Andrew A. 56, 2307, 6768
Mickiewicz, Ellen 6361, 6472-75, 7003
Micklewright, John 2246, 2560
Micklin, Philip P. 3074, 3230-35
Midford, Paul 7671
Mieczkowski, Z. 3397
Migranian, Andranik 5355-56
Mihajlov, Mihajlo 6476
Mihalisko, Kathleen 468, 3236, 5934-35, 7192, 7313-20, 7855
Mikaelian, Vardges 7410
Mikheyev, Dimitry 4791
Mikheyev, Vasily V. 3810
Miko, Francis T. 2616, 3522, 4441, 4650
Mikoyan, Sergo A. 4120
Milanovic, Branko 830, 2617
Milenkovitch, Deborah 2492
Miles, F. Mike 57, 8146
Milibank 5874
Miljan, Toivo 1706, 7193-96
Millar, James R. 2842, 8147
Miller, Arthur H. 6362, 7321
Miller, Elisa 3811
Miller, Gerald E. 2092
Miller, J. H. 177

Murziya, A. 8608
Myant, Martin 2309
Myers, David 7950
Naby, Eden 7515
Nadell, Bernhardt 5363
Nadkarni, Vidya 8062
Nagle, Timothy J. 2095
Nagler, Jonathan 6775
Nagorski, Andrew 2496
Nagy, Andras 8235
Nahaylo, Bohdan 6880, 7869
Nail, Jim 977
Naishul, V. A. 4793
Nakarada, Radmila 1712
Nakarmi, L. 3813-15
Nakas, Victor A. 7870
Nakasone, Yasuhiro 7934
Nakayama, Taro 4045
Nanayev, K. 7014
Narkiewicz, Olga A. 741
Nathan, K. S. 3816
Nation, R. Craig 7951
Nations, Richard 3817
Nau, Henry R. 8453
Naumov, Vladislav 311
Navarro, Vicente 5519
Navias, Martin S. 2097
Navrozov, Lev 5364
Naylor, Thomas H. 978, 4980, 6484, 8150
Nazarov, M. 2847
Nazimova, A. 4902
Neale, Walter C. 8236
Nechemias, Carol 8609
Neckerman, Peter 2310
Nee, Victor 2311
Neff, R. 4046
Negroponte, John D. 8312
Neier, Aryeh 6126
Nekrich, Aleksandr M. 5694-95
Nel, Philip R. 3681
Nelan, B. W. 802, 5365
Nellis, John 5769
Nelsen, Harvey W. 4443
Nelson, Barbara 8543
Nelson, Daniel N. 181, 1564, 4255, 4444, 4654
Nelson, Lynn D. 2621, 8237
Nelson, Ronald R. 6776
Nelson, Susan H. 113
Nemec, Linda E. 979
Nemeth, M. 1194, 4047
Nepomnyashchy, Catherine T. 640, 6292
Neporozhniy, P. S. 3240
Nersessian, Vrej Nerses 7356
Neu, Carl R. 3364
Neubecker, R. 980
Neubert, Michael 59
Neuchterlein, Donald E. 4655
Neuhauser, Kimberley C. 1437, 5520

Neuman, Stephanie G. 4319, 4363
Newcity, Michael 981-82, 2848, 6127-31, 7672
Newhouse, John 8238
Newman, P. C. 983, 1363
Newport, Frank 4886
Nezhny, Alexander 7872
Nguyen, Hung P. 3932
Nicandros, Constantine S. 987
Nichol, James P. 1090, 3526, 3606, 5602
Nichols, Mark 5521
Nichols, Thomas M. 7952-53
Nicholson, Martin 1196
Nicolaescu, Madalina 8610
Nigh, Douglas 988-89
Nihal, Singh S. 3966
Nihart, F. B. 6777
Niiseki, Kinya 182
Nikandrov, Nikolai D. 3016
Nikiforov, L. 450, 2849
Nikitin, S. 8454
Nikitina, Elena N. 1713, 3241
Nikonov, Aleksandr A. 451, 8455
Nimmo, William F. 4002
Nimroody, R. 6826
Nincic, Miroslav 4657
Nishihara, Masashi 3720
Nissani, Moti 4445
Nitze, Paul H. 742, 1839-40, 2098-99
Nixon, Richard M. 2100, 4658-59, 4794, 4983
Njoroge, Lawrence M. 4048
Nofelt, Ulf 990-91
Nogee, Joseph L. 183
Nolan, Mary I. 2101, 3818
Noonan, Norma 8611-12
Noorzoy, M. Siddieq 312
Nordlinger, E. A. 8063
Nordquist, Joan 62
Noren, James H. 2850-52
Norgaard, Ole 7203
Norlander, David 5697
Norman, C. 3242-43, 7416
Nosov, Fyodor 1364
Nourzad, Farrokh 1565
Novak, Michael 1365, 4660, 5367, 8151-52
Novak, Robert D. 3772, 4209
Nove, Alec 373, 517, 2622, 2853-54, 5113, 5698
Novikova, E. E. 8613
Nowicka, Wanda 8614
Nugent, Margaret Latus 1603
Nuikin, Andrei 8122
Nunn, Sam 1841, 2103
Nuti, Domenico Mario 2855
Nye, Joseph S., Jr. 1842, 2104, 4424
Oates, Joyce C. 6984
O'Ballance, Edgar 3819
Oberdorfer, Don 4446
Oberg, James E. 6364, 8456-57
Oberman, Jan 1366

Rubin, A. 5491
Rubin, Barnett R. 326-28, 7528
Rubin, Barry 4270-71
Rubin, David M. 6496
Rubin, James P. 2140
Rubin, M. 2890
Rubinfien, Elisabeth 1382
Rubinshtein, Natalya 6312
Rubinstein, Alvin Z. 116, 189, 329-30, 3619, 4320, 4364-65, 6497
Ruble, Blair A. 8157
Ruby, W. 7598
Rudall, Nicholas 663
Rudder, Catherine E. 8634
Rudenko, M. 6498
Rudiachenko, Alexander 537
Rudney, Robert 8047
Rudrakumaran, V. 7221
Rudyk, E. 5944
Ruebner, R. 6158
Ruehle, Michael 2141
Rueschmeyer, Marilyn 8547
Ruhle, Hans 6804
Rule, W. 8635
Rumens, Carol 6313-14
Rumer, Boris Z. 1011, 2891-93, 5772, 7454, 7529
Rumer, Eugene B. 2329, 6606
Rumyantsev, Oleg 6159
Runnion, Norman 6499
Rupert, James 7530
Rupesinghe, Kumar 6884
Rupnick, Jacques 1383, 2517, 7030
Rusakov, Evgeny 2142
Rush, Myron 1097, 5013
Rushing, Francis W. 2968
Russell, Kathryn 8670
Russell, Cosmo 5014
Russell, G. 4693
Russett, Bruce 4694
Ruth, Stephen 1013
Ruthchild, Rochelle G. 8548, 8636
Rutland, Peter 1218, 2626, 5015, 5402-03, 5945
Ruus, Jurij 7222
Ryan, J. Ruthven 8255
Ryan, Michael 5473, 8158-59
Ryavec, Karl M. 4452, 4834
Ryback, Timothy W. 522, 661-62
Rybakov, Anatolii N. 6230
Rybakovskii, L. L. 8256
Rybarczyk, Sebastian 7420
Ryder, John 8670
Rywkin, Michael 72, 1219, 7031, 7455
Rzhanitsyna, Liudmilla 8417, 8578
Rzhevsky, Nicholas 664
Saar, Andrus 1386
Sabau, C. S. 3292
Sabau, M. N. 3292
Sabirov, A. 2143

Sablinsky, Afanasy 685
Sachs, Jeffrey D. 2478, 2894-95
Sacks, Arthur B. 3066
Sacks, Michael Paul 7032, 8160
Sadikov, O. N. 5995
Sadomskaya, Natalie 8257
Sadovsky, Vadim N. 8323
Safran, William 7033
Sagan, Carl 5016
Sagdeev, Roald Z. 8258, 8480-81
Sagers, Matthew J. 117, 1499, 3293, 3463, 5773, 5835-40, 7104
Sahai, Agha 3987
Saikal, Amin 246, 331
Sainer, Arthur 2221
Saito, M. 4053
Saivetz, Carol R. 4172, 4272-73, 4321, 4366
Sakharov, Andrei 747-48, 807, 2222
Sakwa, Richard 1387, 1732, 4797
Salamon, Martin 1553
Saliman, S. Gerald 1014
Salisbury, Harrison E. 1733, 3294
Salitan, Laurie P. 7034-35
Sallnow, John 461, 4798
Samhoun, R. 5404
Samuel, Peter 3842-43
Samuelian, Thomas J. 6160, 7036
Samuylov, Sergei M. 5405
Sancton, T. A. 5714
Sand, G. W. 4067
Sandberg, Adele 7537
Sandberg, Mikael 3081
Sander, G. F. 3295
Sanders, A. J. K. 3844
Sanders, Alan 3296
Sanders, Ivan 665
Sanders, Jonathan 808, 3464
Sanders, Sol W. 3366, 4696
Sandrart, Hans-Henning von 6805
Sands, P. 3297
Sanford, Margery 7537
Sanjian, A. S. 5841, 8259
Sanna, Mark 5017
Sanoff, A. P. 6501
Santore, John 5406-07
Sanz, Timothy 4274
Sapiets, Marite 7223
Sardar, Riffat 332
Saroyan, Mark 7421-23
Sarris, Louis G. 3689
Sartori, Leo 2144
Satter, David 462, 2223, 5018-19
Saunin, A. N. 6431
Savchenko, Alexei 6502
Savigear, Peter 4453
Saville, John 5874
Savimbi, Jonas 4367
Sawatsky, Walter 7894-96

Viechtbauer, Volker 6205
Vikhanskii, O. S. 3046
Vikis-Freibergs, Vaira 7261
Viksnins, George J. 7262
Vikulov, S. 6840
Vinokurova, U. A. 3047
Vinton, Louisa 1416, 2540
Vitebsky, P. 2939
Vlachoutsikos, Charalambos A. 1059, 3490
Vlahos, Linda H. 8070
Vlahos, Michael 5128
Vlasihin, V. A. 6206
Vlassov, Yuri 1511
Voas, Jeanette 1990, 6620
Vogel, H. 4732, 5067
Vogel, Heinrich 8297
Vogt, Robert 5877
Vogt-Downey, Marilyn 4805
Voinovich, Vladimir 6536
Volgyes, Ivan 2299, 2541-43, 6841
Volkogonov, Dimitrii 5608
Volkov, A. 2940
Volos, Vadim 6537
Vol'skii, A. 2941
Volten, Peter 1803, 2356
Von Hagen, Mark 5750-51
Von Hippel, Frank N. 1974, 2175-76, 3128
Von Laue, Theodore H. 89
Vorkunova, Olga 6885
Voronina, Ol'ga 8657-60
Voronitsyn, Sergei 5968
Voznesenskaia, Iulia N. 6236
Voznesenskii, Andrei 6338
Vtorov, A. 4733
Vujacic, Veljko 5068, 7070
Wade, Rex A. 4734
Wadekin, Karl-Eugen 355, 393-94, 483-84
Waever, O. 3626
Wagener, H-J. 2942
Waghelstein, John D. 4146
Wagner, Elizabeth 8661
Wagner, R. H. 8106
Waldrop, M. M. 8507-08
Wales, Janes 2177
Walesa, Lech 757
Walker, Christopher J. 7434
Walker, Martin 90, 206, 1762, 4373, 5454, 6339, 6538-39, 8281
Walker, P. 3048-49
Walker, R. B. J. 2202
Walker, Rachel 4806
Walker, Richard W. 692-94
Walker, William 2178
Wall, James M. 4735, 5069, 7913
Wall, Patrick 3330
Wallace, W. V. 5070
Wallach, A. 695
Wallander, Celeste 4374

Waller, Douglas 1417
Waller, Michael 1107, 2544
Wallerstein, Immanuel 2179
Wallis, Victor 1763
Wallop, Malcolm 2180, 8107
Walsh, John 7604
Walsh, J. Richard 3957, 8124
Walters, Peter 989
Walters, Philip 7914
Walters, Vernon A. 3535, 8282
Wander, W. Thomas 7947
Wanniski, Jude 2943
Ward, Benjamin 3935
Ward, Chris 5601
Ward, Michael D. 4736
Wardak, Ghulam D. 6621
Warner, Edward L., III 8108
Warner, Gale 8329
Warnke, Paul 2181
Wasserman, Harvey 3331
Waters, Elizabeth 8662
Watson, Bruce D. 6622
Watson, Peggy 8663
Watson, R. 4853, 7071-72
Watson, Susan M. 6622
Watters, Kathleen 6540, 7532
Weaver, Kitty 8174
Webb, William T. 7264
Webber, M. 3697
Weber, Steve 1882, 2182, 5455
Webster, Alexander F. C. 7738
Wedgwood-Benn, David 6541
Wedgeworth, R. 1418
Weeks, Albert L. 91, 6842, 8109
Weeks, John F. 3536
Weeks, Stan 1916
Wegren, Stephen K. 486-97, 2944-45
Wehling, Fred 4288
Wehner, Peter 1790
Weickhardt, George G. 498, 2946-47, 3627
Weickhardt, John G. 1582
Weigel, George 1419, 2183, 7739
Weigle, Marcia A. 1764
Weilemann, Peter R. 2357
Weinbaum, Marvin G. 256
Weinberg, Alvin M. 3332
Weinberg, Henry H. 7605
Weinberg, Steven 3333, 6542-43
Weinberger, Caspar W. 758, 2184, 2545, 5071, 6623, 8110
Weiner, Douglas R. 3100
Weiner, Myron 7442
Weiner, Sharon K. 8010
Weinrod, W. Bruce 2185, 4739
Weisburd, S. 8111-12
Weisman, Erik 7740
Weisman, Steven R. 346
Weiss, Avraham 7606
Weiss, L. D. 5580

Woods, Larence T. 3959
Woods, Randall B. 5075
Woodward, James B. 6342
Woolgar, Claudia 703
Woolsey, R. James 2146
Work, C. P. 1067
Worley, Norman 3101
Worobec, Christine 8522
Woronitzin, Sergej 100
Worster, Donald 208
Worthington, Peter 3700
Wotzman, Herbert M. 7608
Wozniuk, Vladimir 3852
Wren, Christopher S. 4807
Wren, Melvin C. 101
Wriggins, W. Howard 3994
Wright, Mike 2724
Wright, Richard 8514-15
Wright, Susan 8114
Wrong, Dennis 4744
Wusten, Herman van der 184
Wuzhuan, Zhang 3633
Wyman, L. 1517
Wynar, Bohdan S. 7281
Wynne, B. 3337
Xianju, Wang 1534
Ximin, Song 3632
Xueref, Carol 863
Yahuda, Michael B. 3960
Yakovlev, A. M. 6211
Yakovlev, Alexander G. 3865, 5076, 5136
Yakovlev, Alexander N. 4745
Yanaev, Gennadi I. 5971
Yang, Zhong 1423
Yanov, Alexander 4808, 5077
Yanowitch, Murray 759, 2967, 5877, 8176
Yaroshevski, Dov B. 8285
Yarrow, George 2938
Yasmann, Viktor 1258, 1518, 5466, 6212, 6550-51, 7266
Yatron, Gus 6849
Yavlinsky, Grigory 1585, 2648
Yazov, Dmitrii 6850, 8115
Yeltsin, Boris 760-61
Yergin, Daniel 4483, 5860
Yermishina, Inna 1583
Yerofeyev, V. 6343
Yetiv, S. A. 352
Yevtushenko, Yevgeny 704, 1619, 5078, 6344
Yin, John 395, 5137
Ying-hsien, Pi 3961
Yosie, Terry F. 3338
Yost, David S. 2187
Young, Cathy 705, 1426, 2951-52, 5467, 6552-55
Young, Deborah 706-08
Young, Marilyn J. 6556
Young, Pamela 709-10
Young, Stephen M. 3866
Young, Stephen W. 102

Yu, Bin 3962
Yulina, Nina S. 8670
Yurieff, Michael 711
Yurke, A. F. 6345
"Z" (Martin Malia) 5754
Zabigailo, V. K. 6213
Zabih, Sepehr 4178
Zabijaka, Val 1068, 3491-92
Zacek, J. S. 5138
Zack, A. M.
Zafran, R. 8516
Zagalsky, Leonid 6557
Zagoria, Donald S. 3867-69
Zaharchenko, T. 3339
Zaichenko, Alexandr 1584
Zaitsev, Valery K. 3870
Zakaria, Fareed 4746
Zakharov, Igor 6558
Zakharov, Mark A. 712
Zakheim, D. S. 2121
Zaliubovskaia, E. V. 8613
Zalygin, Sergei 6217, 6237
Zamascikov, Sergei 653, 6624
Zanga, Louis 1427, 6559
Zaprudnik, Jan 7282, 7351
Zaraev, Mikhail 1070, 1428, 5468, 6560
Zarsky, L. 3871
Zaslavskaya, Tatyana 2200, 2953-54, 3052, 5139-40, 5972, 6561, 8286-90
Zaslavsky, Victor 1777, 2955, 5068, 7070
Zaslow, David 500, 5861
Zassoursky, 713
Zawerucha, Ihor 7918
Zdanys, Jonas 6346
Zdravomyslov, A. G. 1778
Zeeman, Bert 6851
Zeidman, P. F. 1071
Zeimetz, Kathryn A. 396
Zeman, Z. A. B. 2362
Zemtsov, Ilya 103, 762-63, 4747, 5469-70
Zenchew, Vladimir 4292
Zhang, Yunwen 2188
Zheutlin, Peter 2189
Zhi, Rong 3633
Zhong, Yang 6852
Zhuk, Olga 8671
Zhukov, Vladimir 5079
Zhurkin, V. 8116
Zickel, Raymond E. 104
Ziebart, Geoffrey 3872
Ziegler, Charles E. 3102, 3340, 3733, 3873, 7075
Zielinska, Eleonora 8672
Zielonka, Jan 8297
Zilper, Nadia 5755, 6562
Zimbalist, Andrew 4149
Zimbler, Brian L. 1072
Zimkewych, Osyp 7741
Zimmerman, William 3634